INTRODUCTION TO mass communication

MEDIA LITERACY AND CULTURE

FIFTH EDITION

Stanley J. Baran
Bryant University

Boston   Burr Ridge, IL   Dubuque, IA   Madison, WI   New York   San Francisco   St. Louis
Bangkok   Bogotá   Caracas   Kuala Lumpur   Lisbon   London   Madrid   Mexico City
Milan   Montreal   New Delhi   Santiago   Seoul   Singapore   Sydney   Taipei   Toronto

Higher Education

Published by McGraw-Hill, an imprint of The McGraw-Hill Companies, Inc., 1221 Avenue of the Americas, New York, NY 10020. Copyright © 2008. All rights reserved. No part of this publication may be reproduced or distributed in any form or by any means, or stored in a database or retrieval system, without the prior written consent of The McGraw-Hill Companies, Inc., including, but not limited to, in any network or other electronic storage or transmission, or broadcast for distance learning.

This book is printed on acid-free paper.

2 3 4 5 6 7 8 9 0 CCI/CCI 0 9 8 7

ISBN-13: 978-0-07-351191-7
ISBN-10: 0-07-351191-9

Editor in Chief: *Emily G. Barrosse*
Publisher: *Frank Mortimer*
Sponsoring Editor: *Suzanne Earth*
Marketing Manager: *Leslie Oberhuber*
Developmental Editor: *Jennie Katsaros*
Production Editor: *Brett Coker*
Manuscript Editor: *Darlene Bledsoe*
Text Designer: *Preston Thomas*
Cover Illustrator and Art Editor: *Ayelet Arbel*
Manager, Photo Research: *Brian J. Pecko*
Production Supervisor: *Tandra Jorgensen*
Composition: *10/13 New Aster by Techbooks*
Printing: 45# *Publisher's Matte Plus by Courier, Inc.*

Cover: © Digital Vision/Getty Images
Credits: The credits section for this book begins on page C-1 and is considered an extension of the copyright page.

Library of Congress Cataloging-in-Publication Data
Baran, Stanley J.
    Introduction to mass communication: media literacy and culture/Stanley J. Baran. – 5th ed.
    p. cm.
Includes bibliographical references and index.
ISBN-13: 978-0-07-351191-7
MHID: 0-07-351191-9
    1. Mass media. I. Title.

P90.B284 2007
302.23—dc22

2006048242

The Internet addresses listed in the text were accurate at the time of publication. The inclusion of a Web site does not indicate an endorsement by the authors or McGraw-Hill, and McGraw-Hill does not guarantee the accuracy of the information presented at these sites.

www.mhhe.com

In loving memory of my mother,
Margaret Baran, she gave me
life; and in honor of my wife, Susan
Baran, she gave that life meaning.

About the Author

Stanley Baran earned his Ph.D. in communication research at the University of Massachusetts after taking his M.A. in journalism at Pennsylvania State University. He taught for four years at Cleveland State University, eventually moving to the University of Texas. He led the Department of Radio-TV-Film's graduate program for six of his nine years in Austin and won numerous teaching awards there, including the AMOCO Teaching Excellence Award as the best instructor on that 40,000 student campus, the College of Communication's Teaching Excellence Award as that college's outstanding professor, and *Utmost Magazine*'s Student Poll for best instructor. Dr. Baran moved to San Jose State University in 1987 and served nine years as chair of the Department of Television, Radio, Film, and Theatre. At SJSU he was named President's Scholar as the university's outstanding researcher. Now, he teaches at Bryant University, where he is the founding chairman of that school's Communication Department. Among the other experiences that helped shape this book are his service as a judge for the Fulbright Scholar Awards and his many years of professional activity in audience research, writing for radio, and producing for television. Dr. Baran has published 10 books and scores of scholarly articles, and he sits or has sat on the editorial boards of six journals. His work has been translated into half a dozen languages. He is a skilled boater and is currently on sabbatical from the Wakefield, Rhode Island, Civic Band, for which he plays tenor sax. He is married to Susan Baran and has three very cool children, Simmony, Matt, and Jordan.

Brief Contents

Contents

MEDIA, MEDIA INDUSTRIES, AND MEDIA AUDIENCES 62

PART TWO

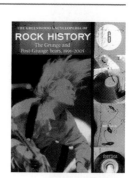

PART THREE

SUPPORTING INDUSTRIES   338

11   Public Relations   338

MASS-MEDIATED CULTURE IN THE INFORMATION AGE   406

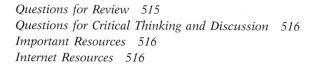

Preface

On September 11, 2001, millions of Americans—in fact, millions of people around the globe—went to bed in shock. The world had changed. The United States no longer seemed invincible. Americans no longer felt safe at home. As everyone, from politicians to pundits to the people next door, said, "Nothing would ever be the same again." Much, in fact, is the same; but not our view of the mass media. The questions we were asking about media in the immediate aftermath of 9/11 and the questions we are raising now are shaped in large part by what happened on that horrific day and by the events it spawned.

At first we were impressed, even moved, by the performance of our mass media. The coverage of the attack and rescue effort in all media was thorough, knowledgeable, courageous, even-handed, and sensitive. But then we started asking, Why were we caught so badly by surprise? Why didn't we know about the anti-American feelings in much of the world? Where were the media? This question was asked again and again as the invasion of Iraq produced none of the weapons of mass destruction that had been the *casus belli*. Had the media been too compliant? Was their lack of aggressive checking a function of economic factors such as concentration and conglomeration? Were the media's failures in the run-up to war the fuel igniting an invigorated media reform movement at home on the political Right as well as the Left?

As our national discussion about media and their roles and responsibilities unfolded, complete with much serious, healthy industry self-examination, Hurricane Katrina destroyed more than the Gulf Coast. It damaged our sense of ourselves as a people. Is this America? Does poverty such as we saw really exist within our borders? Why were the media more focused on runaway brides and missing interns than on the poorest among us? Once again, in the shadow of crisis, the media performed heroically; but once the initial, on-the-spot, reflexive coverage of the storm and its destruction ended, the questions gained new force. Where were the media before the winds and rain struck? Did they not have a higher function in our democracy than making a profit? And where were we—the listeners, readers, and viewers? Did we not have an obligation to demand and expect more from a mass communication system that, by design and tradition, is central to our ability to govern ourselves?

But it did not take a cowardly terrorist attack on civilians, an invasion of a hostile country, or scenes of death and destruction in our own land to start people thinking and talking about the media. These events chased from the cultural forum the relentless criticism of the media's performance in the 2000 and 2004 presidential elections. Dan Rather said that media professionals did not have egg on their faces after his industry's shameful failure of our democracy; they wore the entire omelet. People questioned the media's priorities—news was disappearing from newscasts and newspapers, replaced by promos for upcoming television series and celebrity gossip. Others were complaining that movies were starting to look like extra-long commercials, while television commercials were getting increasingly shorter and all media, even novels, were seemingly drowning in more and more advertising. Critics across the political spectrum were concerned that media companies were merging at an unhealthy-for-democracy rate. Concern about media violence and sexual content remained unabated. Furor followed a television network's proposal to air hard-liquor ads. People who had lost their life savings wanted to know what the media were doing while Enron and WorldCom were stealing from them. To First Amendment advocates, new copyright rules designed to thwart digital piracy were undoing two centuries of fair use copyright protection, with consumers and democracy poorer for it.

The media, like sports and politics, are what we talk about. Argue over. Dissect and analyze.

Those of us who teach media know that these conversations are essential to the functioning of a democratic society. We also know that what moves these conversations from the realm of chatting and griping to that of effective public discourse is media education—the systematic study of media and their operation in our political and economic system, as well as their contribution to the development and maintenance of the culture that binds us together and defines us. We now call this media education *media literacy.*

Regardless of what an individual course is called—Introduction to Mass Communication, Introduction to Mass Media, Media and Society, Media and Culture—media literacy has been a part of university media education for more than four decades. The course has long been designed to fulfill the following goals:

- To increase students' knowledge and understanding of the mass communication process and the mass media industries
- To increase students' awareness of how they interact with those industries and with media content to create meaning
- To help students become more skilled and knowledgeable consumers of media content

These are all aspects of media literacy as it is now understood. This text makes explicit what has been implicit for so long: that media literacy skills can and should be taught directly and that, as we travel through the 21st century, media literacy is an essential survival skill for everyone in our society.

Perspective

This focus on media literacy grows naturally out of a *cultural perspective* on mass communication. This text takes the position that media, audiences, and culture develop and evolve in concert. The current prevailing notion in the discipline of mass communication is that, although not all individuals are directly affected by every media message they encounter, the media nonetheless do have important cultural effects. Today, the media are accepted as powerful forces in the process through which we come to know ourselves and one another. They function both as a forum in which issues are debated and as the storytellers that carry our beliefs across time and space. Through these roles, the media are central to the creation and maintenance of both our dominant culture and our various bounded cultures.

This cultural orientation toward mass communication and the media places much responsibility on media consumers. In the past, people were considered either victims of media influence or impervious to it. The cultural orientation asserts that audience members are as much a part of the mass communication process as are the media technologies and industries. As important agents in the creation and maintenance of their own culture, audience members have an obligation not only to participate in the process of mass communication but also to participate actively, appropriately, and effectively. In other words, they must bring media literacy—the ability to effectively and efficiently comprehend and use mass media—to the mass communication process.

Features of This Text

The features that made this text successful in its earlier editions have been retained in this revision.

- **Emphasis on developing media literacy.** The pedagogical features of this book are designed to support and improve media literacy skills. Chapter 1 lays out the elements of media literacy, and an emphasis on media literacy is woven throughout the text. Chapter 2, "The Evolving Mass Communication Process," is new to this edition. It presents in detail the array of profound changes buffeting the media industries and, by extension, the mass communication process. Naturally, its goal is to explain the expanded need for media literacy as the communication industries with which we interact—and the content they create and dispense—continue to change. Each chapter from Chapter 3 to 15 contains a section, specific to that chapter's medium or issue, on developing media literacy skills. For example, Chapter 4, "Newspapers," offers guidelines for interpreting the relative placement of newspaper stories. Chapter 8, "Television, Cable, and Mobile Video," discusses how to identify staged news events on television. Other media literacy topics include recognizing product placements in movies, identifying video news releases, and interpreting intentional advertiser imprecision.

- **Cultural perspective.** The media—either as forums in which important issues are debated or as storytellers that carry our beliefs and values across people, space, and time—are central to the creation and maintenance of our various cultures. This book advocates the idea that media audiences can take a more active role in the mass communication process and help shape the cultures that, in turn, shape them.

- **Brief historical sections.** Historical sections at the beginning of each chapter on a medium offer relevant background information for students. By providing historical context, these sections help students understand current issues in the media landscape.

- **Focus on convergence.** Each chapter on a medium includes a section called Trends and Convergence. These sections emphasize the influence of new technologies on media and society.

- **Pedagogical boxes included throughout the text.** These boxes give students a deeper understanding of media-related issues and the role of media in society.

  USING MEDIA TO MAKE A DIFFERENCE These boxes highlight interesting examples of how media practitioners and audiences use the mass communication process to further important social, political, or cultural causes. For example, Chapter 6, "Film," highlights the African American films and film industry that grew up in response to the D. W. Griffith film *The Birth of a Nation.*

  CULTURAL FORUM These boxes highlight media-related cultural issues that are currently debated in the mass media. Titles include, for example, "Advertorials Aimed at Young Girls"; "What If There Were No Newspapers?"; and "Rock and Rap: Selling or Selling Out?"

  MEDIA HISTORY REPEATS These boxes demonstrate that the cultural and social debates surrounding the different media tend to be repeated throughout history, regardless of the technology or era in question. For example, the public relations chapter discusses early PR efforts to encourage women to smoke, and the advertising chapter covers advertisers' more recent attempts to attract teenage smokers.

  LIVING MEDIA LITERACY These brief, chapter-ending essays suggest ways in which students can put what they have learned into practice. They are calls to action—personal, social, educational, political. Their goal is to make media literacy a living enterprise, something that has value in how students interact with the culture and media. Several use the stories of "everyday people" who have made a difference. Indicative titles are "Start a Citywide (or Campuswide) Book Conversation," "Help a School Start an Online Newspaper," and "Smoke-Free Movies."

Key Changes to the Fifth Edition

Although the book maintains its commitment to critical thinking throughout its pages, several important changes were made to enhance and update this, the fifth edition.

- A number of important changes have been made to text structure. Chapter 2, "The Evolving Mass Communication Process," is new to this edition. This chapter not only allows for a fuller conversation about the major forces reshaping the mass communication process—convergence, audience fragmentation, concentration and conglomeration, hypercommercialism, and globalization—but it provides in one place a discussion of how these forces are reshaping the structure, economics, content, and expectations of *all* media. Of course, as in past editions, these forces are discussed in the individual media chapters as they reshape the specific media under examination. But these relentless forces are also reshaping the mass communication process itself and, therefore, audience members' media literacy responsibilities. Two more large-scale changes are the direct result of convergence. First, is it "television" if we are watching a program on a PC? On a cell phone? On a portable game console? Is it "television" if we are watching a Hollywood movie, delivered to our home by broadband cable directly to our laptop computer and wirelessly sent to the set in our bedroom? Or is it cable? Or is it Internet? Television, cable, and much, much more have been combined into Chapter 8, "Television, Cable, and Mobile Video." Second, convergence has had a similar impact on radio— is it radio, satellite, Web-streamed, podcast, downloaded? As such, last edition's "Radio and Sound Recording" chapter has been expanded, rewritten, and titled "Radio, Recording, and Popular Music."

- Every chapter has been newly informed by the events of September 11, the war on terrorism, and the conflict in Iraq. Concentration and conglomeration and their contribution to the media's failures in the run-up to the invasion of Iraq are part of Chapter 2. Embedded journalists and the PR of war are discussed in the public relations chapter. Ethical issues—for media professionals and for citizens—raised by the war on terror and the invasion and occupation of Iraq are presented: Does the Patriot Act go too far? Where is popular music's activist voice? Were anonymous sources misused in the outing of a CIA operative? Do you publish photos of war dead? Of civilian casualties?

- Boxes have been updated to cover current topics and issues. The coverage of international news, book censorship, the erosion of the firewall between newspapers' sales and news departments, the Pentagon's massive PR campaign in support of an increasingly unpopular war in Iraq, mandatory cable access for Internet service providers, and changes in the way we think about copyright are a few examples.

- All statistical entries have been updated. These changes include new information on Internet demographics, new media consumption statistics, and new statistics for all media sales and circulation figures.

- Coverage of media ownership has been updated to the extent possible. Although it is challenging to keep up with changes in media ownership, we have made a diligent effort to provide the most recent information on mergers and acquisitions in media conglomerate ownership.

Learning Aids

Several types of learning aids are included in the book to support student learning and to enhance media literacy skills.

- World Wide Web URLs in the margins of every chapter enable students to locate additional resources and encourage students to practice using the Internet.

- Photo essays raise provocative questions, encouraging students to further develop their critical thinking and analytical skills.

- Review Points allow students to make sure they have focused on each chapter's most important material.

- Questions for Review further highlight important content and provide a review of key points.

- Questions for Critical Thinking and Discussion encourage students to investigate their own cultural assumptions and media use and to engage one another in debate on critical issues.

- Margin icons throughout the text direct students to view the *Media World* DVD, which includes Media Tours and Media Talk, the NBC video clips.

- Historical timelines, chapter learning objectives, and chapter-ending lists of key terms guide and focus student learning.

- An exhaustive list of references is provided at the end of the book.

Organization

Introduction to Mass Communication: Media Literacy and Culture is divided into four parts. Part One, "Laying the Groundwork," as its name implies, provides the foundation for the study of mass communication. Its two chapters, "Mass Communication, Culture, and Media Literacy" and "The Evolving Mass Communication Process," define important concepts and establish the basic premises of the cultural perspective on mass communication with its focus on media literacy.

Part Two, "Media, Media Industries, and Media Audiences," includes chapters on the individual mass media technologies and the industries that have grown up around them—"Books" (Chapter 3), "Newspapers" (Chapter 4), "Magazines" (Chapter 5), "Film" (Chapter 6), "Radio, Recording, and Popular Music" (Chapter 7), "Television, Cable, and Mobile Video" (Chapter 8), "Video Games" (Chapter 9), and "The Internet and the World Wide Web" (Chapter 10). All of these chapters open with a short history of the medium and continue with discussions of the medium and its audiences, the scope and nature of the medium, and current trends and convergence in the industry and technology. Each chapter concludes with a section on developing a media literacy skill specifically related to that medium and a call to action in the form of the Living Media Literacy essays. Throughout each chapter there is a focus not just on the industry and technology but also on cultural issues and the interaction of culture, medium, and audience. For example, in Chapter 10, advances in digital technology and computer networking are discussed in terms of our ability to maintain control of our personal data and our privacy. Chapter 3's examination of book censorship asks students to challenge their personal commitment to free expression and to reflect on how that commitment speaks to their belief in democracy. Radio and rock 'n' roll are connected to a discussion of race relations in America in Chapter 7.

Part Three, "Supporting Industries," carries this same approach into two related areas—public relations (Chapter 11) and advertising (Chapter 12). As in the medium-specific chapters, each of these chapters begins with a brief history, continues with a discussion of audience, the scope of the industry, and current trends and convergence, and concludes with guidelines on developing relevant media literacy skills.

Part Four, "Mass-Mediated Culture in the Information Age," tackles several important areas. Chapter 13, "Theories and Effects of Mass Communication," provides a short history of mass communication theory and compares and evaluates the field's major theories. It then explores the ongoing debate over media effects. The chapter considers such topics as media and violence, media and gender and racial/ethnic stereotyping, and media and the electoral process. Chapter 14, "Media Freedom, Regulation, and Ethics," provides a detailed discussion of the First Amendment, focusing on refinements in interpretation and application made over the years in response to changes in technology and culture. The chapter analyzes such topics and issues as privacy, the use of cameras in the courtroom, and changing definitions of indecency. The chapter concludes with an extended discussion of media ethics and professionalism. Chapter 15, "Global Media," looks at media systems in other parts of the world and concludes with a discussion of local cultural integrity versus cultural imperialism.

New and Updated Supplements

The supplements package includes a full array of tools designed to facilitate both teaching and learning.

- An *Instructor's Resource Guide,* available on the Online Learning Center, provides teaching aids for each chapter, including learning objectives, key terms and concepts, lecture ideas, video suggestions, a guide to using the Media Literacy Worksheets, and a test bank of more than 1,000 test items.

- Questions in a computerized test bank can be edited and new questions can be added.

- The *Introduction to Mass Communication* DVD offers students *Media World* video clips. These brief clips bring to life the concepts discussed in the text. Media Talk clips are from NBC News and *The Today Show.* McGraw-Hill's Media Tours provides an inside look at the operations of a television station, *Vibe* magazine, a radio station, a public relations firm, and the Internet. The videos are also available to instructors in VHS format packaged with an instructor's guide.

- The Online Learning Center (www.mhhe.com/baran5) has been thoroughly updated. The new site includes Media Literacy worksheets, PowerPoint® slides, a Web tutorial, chapter self-quizzes with feedback, hot links to media resources for the student, and more.

- *Media Literacy Worksheets and Journal,* now online (www.mhhe.com/baran5), has been revised to include worksheets for each chapter. Activities direct students to selected Web sites, suggest topics for entries in an ongoing Media Journal, and further explore the media literacy skills highlighted in each chapter. There are more than 75 worksheets in total.

- *PageOut: The Course Web Site Development Center.* All online content for this text is supported by WebCT, eCollege.com, Blackboard, and other course management systems. Additionally, McGraw-Hill's PageOut service is available to get you and your course up and running online in a matter of hours, at no cost. PageOut was designed for instructors just beginning to explore Web options. Even the novice computer user can create a course Web site with a template provided by McGraw-Hill (no programming knowledge necessary). To learn more about PageOut, ask your McGraw-Hill representative for details, or fill out the form at www.mhhe.com/pageout.

Acknowledgments

Any project of this magnitude requires the assistance of many people. For this latest edition my colleagues Kevin Pearce from my own campus, Ed Remitz of the College of San Mateo, Robert Prince of the University of Alaska, Fairbanks, and Bruce Plopper of the University of Arkansas at Little Rock were particularly helpful with their sharp eyes and good suggestions. For the first time in this text's history, Southwestern Adventist University's Bob Mendenhall could find nothing for me to change.

Reviewers are an indispensable part of the creation of a good textbook. In preparing for this fifth edition, I was again impressed with the thoughtful comments made by my colleagues in the field. Although I didn't know them by name, I found myself in long-distance, anonymous debate with several superb thinkers, especially about some of the text's most important concepts. Their collective keen eye and questioning attitude sharpened each chapter to the benefit of both writer and reader. (Any errors or misstatements that remain in the book are of course my sole responsibility.) Now that I know who they are, I would like to thank the reviewers by name.

Jennifer Aubrey
University of Missouri

Michael Boyle
Wichita State University

Tim Coombs
Eastern Illinois University

Denise Danford
Delaware County Community College

Tim Edwards
University of Arkansas at Little Rock

Junhao Hong
State University of New York at Buffalo

Mark Kelly
University of Maine

Alyse Lancaster
University of Miami

Carol S. Lomick
University of Nebraska at Kearney

Susan Dawson-O'Brien
Rose State College

Alicia C. Shepard
University of Texas at Austin

Tamala Sheree Martin
Oklahoma State University

Stephen D. Perry
Illinois State University

Selene Phillips
University of Louisville

I would also like to thank the reviewers of the first four editions. **Fourth Edition Reviewers:** Kristen Barton, Florida State University; Kenton Bird, University of Idaho; Katia G. Campbell, University of Colorado; Paul A. Creasman, Azusa Pacific University; Annette Johnson, Georgia State University; James Kelleher, New York University; Polly McLean, University of Colorado; Anthony A. Olorunnisola, Pennsylvania State University; Michael Porter, University of Missouri; Stephen D. Perry, Illinois State University; Stephen J. Resch, Indiana Wesleyan University; Christopher F.

White, Sam Houston State University. **Third Edition Reviewers:** Jenny L. Nelson, Ohio University; Terri Toles Patkin, Eastern Connecticut State University; Alyse Lancaster, University of Miami; Deborah A. Godwin-Starks, Indiana University-Purdue University Fort Wayne; Kevin R. Slaugher, George Mason University; Enid Sefcovic, Florida Atlantic University; David Whitt, Nebraska Wesleyan University; Roger Desmond, University of Hartford; Carol S. Lomicky, University of Nebraska at Kearney; Jules d'Hemecourt, Louisiana State University; Junhao Hong, State University of New York at Buffalo; Gary J. Wingenbach, Texas A&M University. **Second Edition Reviewers:** Rob Bellamy, Duquesne University; Beth Grobman Burruss, DeAnza College; Stephen R. Curtis, Jr., East Connecticut State University; Lyombe Eko, University of Maine; Junhao Hong, State University of New York at Buffalo; Carol Liebler, Syracuse University; Robert Main, California State University, Chico; Stephen Perry, Illinois State University; Eric Pierson, University of San Diego; Ramona Rush, University of Kentucky; Tony Silvia, University of Rhode Island; and Richard Welch, Kennesaw State University. **First Edition Reviewers:** David Allen, Illinois State University; Sandra Braman, University of Alabama; Tom Grimes, Kansas State University; Kirk Hallahan, Colorado State University; Katharine Heintz-Knowles, University of Washington; Paul Husselbee, Ohio University; Seong Lee, Appalachian State University; Rebecca Ann Lind, University of Illinois at Chicago; Maclyn McClary, Humboldt State University; Guy Meiss, Central Michigan University; Debra Merskin, University of Oregon; Scott R. Olsen, Central Connecticut State University; Ted Pease, Utah State University; Linda Perry, *Florida Today* newspaper; Elizabeth Perse, University of Delaware; Tina Pieraccini, State University of New York–College at Oswego; Michael Porter, University of Missouri; Peter Pringle, University of Tennessee at Chattanooga; Neal Robison, Washington State University; Linda Steiner, Rutgers University; and Don Tomlinson, Texas A&M University.

This edition is the third I have written with the support of my skilled team at McGraw-Hill. My development editor, Jennie Katsaros, remains as polished a professional as she is a lunchtime conversationalist. She intuitively understands the soul of this text and encourages me to write in its spirit. My editor, Phil Butcher, is questioning and imaginative. Confident in me, both let me write *my* book. The text and I are better for it.

Finally, my most important inspiration throughout the writing of this book has been my family. My wife, Susan, is educated in media literacy and a strong disciple of spreading its lessons far and wide—which she does with zest. Her knowledge and assistance in my writing is invaluable; her love in my life is sustaining; her fire—for improved media and for us—is emboldening. My children—Jordan, Matthew, and Simmony—simply by their existence require that I consider and reconsider what kind of world we will leave for them. I've written this text in the hope that it helps make the future for them and their friends better than it might otherwise have been.

S. J. B.

A Visual Preview

Media shapes and reflects culture. As we travel through the twenty-first century, media literacy is an essential survival skill for everyone in our society.

Thought-provoking **boxed features** and **photo essays** support and improve media literacy skills.

Using Media to Make a Difference boxes highlight examples of how practitioners and audiences use the mass communication process to further social, political, or cultural causes.

Living Media Literacy boxes are personal, social, educational, and political calls to action.

Cultural Forum boxes examine media-related issues currently debated in the mass media.

Photo Essays raise provocative questions that encourage students to develop their critical thinking skills.

Media History Repeats boxes demonstrate that the cultural and social debates surrounding the different media tend to be repeated throughout history regardless of the technology or era in question.

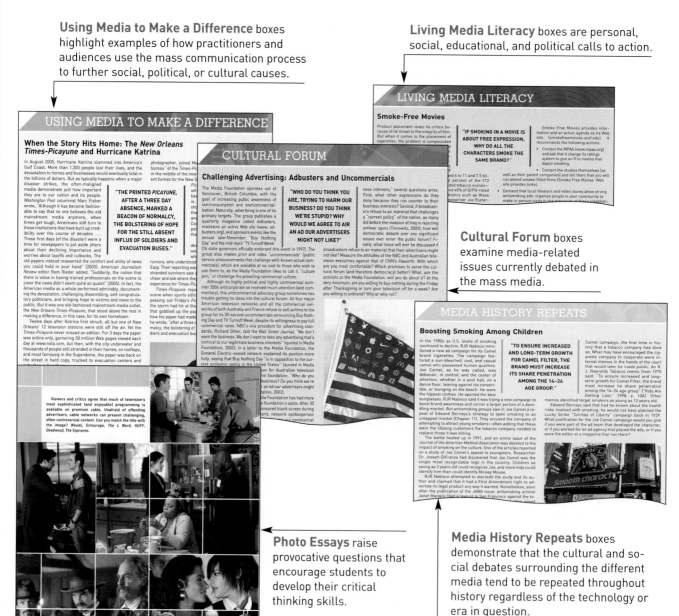

Introduction to Mass Communication offers a rich selection of examples and features that increase students' knowledge and understanding of the **mass communication process** and **mass media industries.**

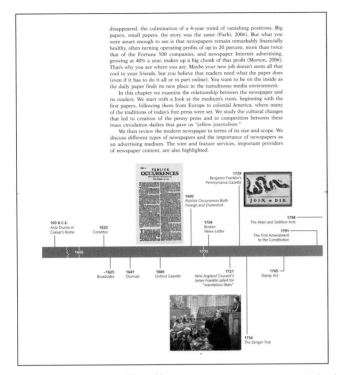

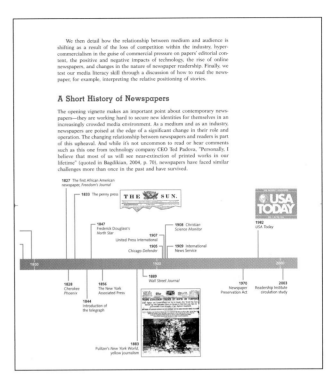

Timelines summarize major events in the development of mass communication.

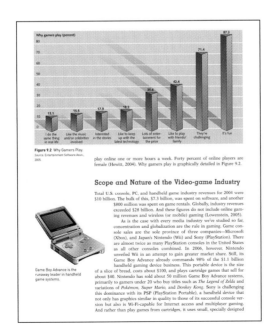

Video Games chapter discusses the interactive, digitally based games at length and the economic, regulatory, and cultural issues surrounding this emerging medium.

Meeting the needs of a fragmented audience—a foreign-language paper, an alternative weekly, the dissident press, and a free commuter paper.

biggest cities. Like the most successful Spanish-language papers, they represent the major dailies' effort to reach a segment of the audience not likely to buy the parent papers' product. Here though, the target is young readers (who are already used to getting free media from the alternative press and the Internet) and the goal is twofold. First, these readers represent a valuable demographic, one especially attractive to local advertisers, the newspaper's bread-and-butter financial base. Second, the big dailies hope these young readers "will develop a daily newspaper-reading habit and will eventually move on to become regular readers of the mother papers" (Morton, 2004, p. 64). Typical of the successful **commuter papers** are the *Boston Globe's Metro*, the *Dallas Morning News' Quick*, the *Washington Post's Express*, and the Tribune Company's *amNewYork*.

THE NEWSPAPER AS AN ADVERTISING MEDIUM

The reason we have the number and variety of newspapers we do is that readers value them. When newspapers prosper financially, it is because advertisers [...] their worth as an ad medium. News[...]

www
National Newspaper Publishers Association

Newspapers chapter provides an in-depth discussion of newspapers and their audiences.

Figure 7.3 The Top 10 Best-selling Albums and Artists of All Time, U.S. Sales Only. Source: Recording Industry Association of America (www.riaa.com).

Best-selling albums

1. *Eagles/Their Greatest Hits* (Eagles)
2. *Thriller* (Michael Jackson)
3. *The Wall* (Pink Floyd)
4. *Led Zeppelin IV* (Led Zeppelin)
5. *Back in Black* (AC/DC)
6. *Greatest Hits Volumes I & II* (Billy Joel)
7. *Come on Over* (Shania Twain)
8. *The Beatles* (The Beatles)
9. *Rumours* (Fleetwood Mac)
10. *Boston* (Boston)

Best-selling artists (units sold in millions)

1. The Beatles — 168.5
2. Elvis Presley — 116.5
3. Led Zeppelin — 107.5
4. Garth Brooks — 105.0
5. Eagles — 89.0
6. Billy Joel — 78.5
7. Pink Floyd — 73.5
8. Barbra Streisand — 70.5
9. Elton John — 69.0
10. AC/DC — 66.0

definition of playable artists. The essay on page 214, "Rock and Rap: Selling or Selling Out" discusses another form of hypercommercialism in the music business.

Trends and Convergence in Radio and Sound Recording

Radio, Recording, and Popular Music chapter discusses trends and convergence in radio and sound recording.

---

discovered in a national survey that when asked to respond to the statement "I am not interested in watching TV programs or movies on my handheld device," 76% said "true" (Siklos, 2006). But, argue the mobile video optimists, one-third of the television audience and 24% of handheld video device users is still a lot of downloads for already-created content. In fact, technology research firm eMarketer's analysis of the market predicts that once a model of free and ad-supported mobile content is settled on, it should produce about $300 million a year by 2010 (Whitney, 2006).

DEVELOPING MEDIA LITERACY SKILLS
Recognizing Staged News

For years studies have shown that a majority of the American public turns to television as the source of most of its news and that viewers rank it as the most believable news source. Television news can be immediate and dramatic, especially when events being covered lend themselves to visual images. But what if they don't? News may be journalism, but television news is also a television *show*, and as such it must attract viewers. Television newspeople have an obligation to truthfully and accurately inform the public, but they also have an obligation to attract a large number of people so their station or network is profitable.

Even the best television journalists cannot inform a public that does not tune in, and the public tunes in to see pictures. Television professionals, driven to get pictures, often walk the fine ethical line of **news staging**—that is, re-creating some event that is believed to or could have happened. Sometimes news staging takes simple forms; for example, a reporter may narrate an account of an event he or she did not witness while video of that event is played. The intended impression is that the reporter is on the scene. What harm is there in this? It's common practice on virtually all U.S. television news shows. But how much of a leap is it from that to ABC's 1994 broadcast of reporter Cokie Roberts, wrapped tightly in winter clothes, seemingly reporting from Capitol Hill on a blustery January night when she was in fact standing in a nearby Washington studio, her presence at the scene staged by computer digital technology?

The broadcasters' defense is, "This is not staging in the sense that the *event* was staged. What does it matter if the reporter was not actually on the spot? What was reported actually did happen." If you accept this view (the event *did* happen, therefore it's not news staging), how would you evaluate Fox News's Geraldo Rivera's reporting from "sacred ground," the scene of a battle in Afghanistan in which U.S. forces suffered heavy losses, even though he was miles from the actual spot? And if you accept digital alteration of news scenes to place network reporters at the scene, how would you evaluate CBS's common practice of digitally inserting its network logo on billboards and buildings that appear behind its reporters and anchors? If this staging is acceptable to you, why not okay the digital enhancement of fires and explosions in the news?

Some media literate viewers may accept the-event-did-happen argument, but another form of news staging exists that is potentially more troublesome—re-creation. In 1992 the producers of *Dateline NBC* re-created the explosion of a GMC truck, justifying the move with the argument that similar explosions "had happened" (Chapter 14). In the mid-1990s a Denver news show ran footage of a pit bull fight it had arranged and defended its action on

Television Cable, and Mobile Video chapter presents examples of staged, simulated news.

Reconceptualizing Life in an Interconnected World

What happens to people in the global village? What becomes of audiences and users as their senses are extended technologically? How free are we to express ourselves? Does greater involvement with others mean a loss of privacy? These are only a few of the questions confronting us as we attempt to find the right balance between the good and the bad that comes from the new communication technologies.

THE INTERNET AND FREEDOM OF EXPRESSION

By its very nature the Internet raises a number of important issues of freedom of expression. There is no central location, no on-and-off button for the Internet, making it difficult for those who want to control it. For free expression advocates, however, this freedom from control is the medium's primary strength. The anonymity of its users provides their expression—even the most radical, profane, and vulgar—great protection, giving voice to those who would otherwise be silenced. This anonymity, say advocates of strengthened Internet control, is a breeding ground for abuse. But opponents of control counter that the Net's affordability and ease of use make it our most democratic medium. Proponents of control argue that this freedom brings with it

Activists at MoveOn.org fought an impeachment, protested a war, tried to run a Super Bowl spot, and rallied millions of people worldwide to their cause.

The Internet and the World Wide Web chapter examines the important issue of the Internet and freedom of expression.

The **Global Media** chapter examines the changing media systems and their impact on world economics, political, and cultural environments.

Discusses the U.S.-based, government-funded television station alternative to Al-Jazeera.

CULTURAL FORUM

Al-Hurra or al-Abda?

The issue of America's ability to provide an effective surrogate service to the Arab world was put squarely into the cultural forum by the February 2004 launch of al-Hurra, a $62 million effort by the Board of International Broadcasting to provide Arabic-language television to all 22 countries in the Middle East. The stated goals of the 24-hour satellite channel are to promote democracy in the region and change for the better the anti-American public opinion that exists there.

Al-Hurra's first moments on the air presented video of windows being opened, symbolizing freedom, and an interview with President George W. Bush in which he praised Iraqi efforts at democracy. The Virginia-based station's daily blend of news, pop culture, and C-SPAN–style broadcasts of the workings of the U.S. government, however, has earned it mixed reviews. Some critics in the United States and the Middle East question whether *al-Hurra*, which translates into "The Free One," might not be more accurately called *al-Abda*, "The Slave," or even "Fox News in Arabic," referring to the cable news channel's decidedly pro-American bent (MacFarquhar, 2004). The debate has several components.

First, many people question whether the United States should be in the business of providing surrogate services at all. Why, they ask, would Middle Eastern viewers want to tune in to a government-financed, clearly pro-American news and culture station when in our era of global telecommunications they can receive objective, high-quality content not only from the BBC World Service but from other American and Western sources such as CNN? These critics point to Radio and TV Marti, both widely ignored by Cuban audiences within easy reach of American commercial broadcasters. A second criti-

> AL-HURRA REFERS TO WESTERN SOLDIERS IN IRAQ AS "COALITION FORCES." ARAB BROADCASTERS CALL THEM "OCCUPATION FORCES."

cism centers on the risk of alienating the very people al-Hurra wants to reach with what, inevitably, will be seen as American propaganda. For example, al-Hurra refers to Western soldiers in Iraq as "coalition forces." Arab broadcasters call them "occupation forces." Arab journalists speak of "Palestinians trying to free themselves from Israeli occupation," and al-Hurra talks of the "historical dispute" between Arabs and Israelis. "The people they have hired look modern, hip, and the beat is fast, but it won't have an impact on the perception of the United States," said Mustafa Hamarneh of the University of Jordan. "I think Americans are mistaken if they assume they can change their image in the region. People became anti-American because they don't like American policies" (MacFarquhar, 2004, p. A3).

The third criticism of al-Hurra is that despite its stated mission of fostering democracy and improving America's image, its real goal is "to provide an antidote to what its founders consider anti-American news coverage on popular Arabic channels such as al-Jazeera" (National Public Radio, 2004, p. 1). Al-Jazeera is popular in the Middle East—45 million daily viewers—precisely because it is seen "on the street" as more objective than both Western news outlets and traditional Arab broadcast operations. The Qatar-based satellite channel's critical coverage, "decidedly untraditional female anchors and producers in Western dress, [and] simultaneously translated interviews with non-Arab sources" have angered just about every Arab government in the Middle East (Klein, 2004, p. 55). It is currently banned in Iraq, Iran, Kuwait, Algeria, and the Sudan. "Before the station began broadcasting in 1996 . . . Arab viewers were largely limited to tame and

To limit cultural intrusion, the South Korean government requires that movie houses in its country screen Korean-made films, such as *The Way Home*, at least 146 days out of the year.

The resistance to U.S. media would not exist among our international friends if they did not worry about the integrity of their own cultures. It is folly, then, to argue that non-native media content will have no effect on local culture—as do many U.S. media content producers. The question today is, How much influence will countries accept in exchange for fuller membership in the global community? In light of instant, inexpensive, and open computer network communication, a parallel question is, Have notions such as national sovereignty and cultural integrity lost their meaning? For example, ESPN is carried on 20 networks in 21 languages to 155 million television households in 183 different countries. *The Simpsons* is drawn in South Korea. The BBC broadcasts daily to a worldwide audience in 40 languages, as does Radio Beijing from China. CNN uses 14 satellites to transmit to a billion viewers in almost 200 countries. Mexican soap operas dominate the television schedules of much of Latin and South America. Three of the four largest U.S. record companies have international ownership. Hollywood's Columbia Pictures is owned by Japanese Sony, and 20th Century Fox is owned by Rupert Murdoch's Australian corporation. As Thomas Middelhoff, former CEO of Bertelsmann, a German company that controls a large portion of the [...] United States [...] "We're not fore[...] port" (as quote[...]

THE CASE F[...]

There are diff[...] nation-specific [...] coming closer [...] tally, as we be[...] the revolution [...] Television Dir[...] There should b[...]

Abaya-clad Saudi Arabian women line up at the women-only counter of a McDonald's in a mall in Dhahran. Although critics of cultural imperialism see this as an intrusion of Western culture into the lives of these people, defenders of the globalization of culture see the expansion of opportunity for both the "sending" and the "receiving" cultures.

disappear, because the world's great diversity will ensure that culture-specific, special-interest fare remains in demand. Modern media technology makes the delivery of this varied content not only possible but profitable. Not only do native-language versions of U.S. television shows like *Jeopardy* exist in virtually every western European country, but other "translations" are taking place. For example, hot on the heels of the success of the Spider-Man movies, Marvel Comics and an Indian company announced the birth of *Spider-Man India*, in which a young Bombay lad, Pavitr Prabhakar, inherits powers from a sacred yogi and accessorizes his Spidey suit with a traditional dhoti while dealing with local problems and challenges (Bal, 2004). As a result of these cultural exchanges, argue proponents of globalization, "a global culture is created, piece by piece, but it grows more variegated and complex along the way. And even as geographically based identities blur and fade, new subcultures, based on shared tastes in music or literature or obscure hobbies, grow up" (Bennett, 2004, p. 62).

Discusses government control over major media and the Internet in China.

The media exist in China to serve the government. Chairman Mao Zedong, founder of the Chinese Communist Party, clarified the role of the media very soon after coming to power in 1949. The media exist to propagandize the policies of the Party and to educate, organize, and mobilize the masses. These are still their primary functions.

Radio came to China via American reporter E. C. Osborn, who established an experimental radio station in China in 1923. Official Chinese broadcasting began 3 years later. Television went on the air in 1958, and from the outset it was owned and controlled by the Party in the form of Central China Television (CCTV), which in turn answers to the Ministry of Radio and Television. Radio, now regulated by China People's Broadcasting Station (CPBS), and television stations and networks develop their own content, but it must conform to the requirements of the Propaganda Bureau of the Chinese Communist Party Central Committee.

Financially, Chinese broadcasting operates under direct government subsidy. But in 1979 the government approved commercial advertising for broadcasting, and it has evolved into an important means of financial support—television billings are at $8 billion a year, for example (Jones, 2002). Coupled with the Chinese government's desire to become a more active participant in the international economy, this commercialization has led to increased diversity in broadcast content. Today, China's 400 million television households (99% penetration) are served by 14 CCTV and hundreds of local and satellite channels. Foreign content is purchased by the state's China TV Programming Agency, which can buy no more than 500 hours a year. Stations can devote no more than 25% of their time to imported content. MTV and the Children's Television Workshop coproduce content with local Chinese broadcasters, and among imported favorites are *The Teletubbies* (*Antenna Babies* in China) and *Little House on the Prairie*. CNN and other

Only 20 American movies a year can be exhibited in China. *Lord of the Rings* made the cut in 2004.

Examines the debate of the trend away from nation-specific cultures.

rollingst

Issue 1
July 13-27, 200

Rolling Stone

JOHNNY DEPP

His Wild
Past &
The Secret
Side of
Capt.
Jack

GONZO
PIRATE

A
GOR

On B
Big Oil
What's N

TO
PET

"I've G
Through
Dark Tur

NAMIB

A Portf
By Sebas
Salg

INSI
IRA

A Visit to
By Matt Ta

Mass Communication, Culture, and Media Literacy

LEARNING OBJECTIVES

Mass communication, mass media, and the culture that shapes us (and that we shape) are inseparable. After studying this chapter you should

- know the definitions of communication, mass communication, mass media, and culture.
- understand the relationships among communication, mass communication, culture, and those who live the culture.
- have a basis for evaluating the impact of technology and economics on those relationships.
- understand the relationship between communication and culture.
- understand the relationship between literacy and power.
- understand media literacy.
- possess the basis for developing good media literacy skills.
- be encouraged to practice media literacy.

The clock radio jars you awake. It's Eminem, the last few bars of "Shake That." The laughing deejay shouts at you that it's 7:41 and you'd better get going. But before you do, he adds, listen to a few words from your friends at Fry's Electronics, home of fast, friendly, courteous service—"We will beat any competitive price!"

In the living room, you find your roommate has left the television on. You stop for a moment and listen: The Supreme Court has

Opposite: What does it mean to "be on the cover of *Rolling Stone*"?

refused to hear an affirmative action appeal, your U.S. representative is under investigation for sexual harassment, and you deserve a break today at McDonald's. As you head toward the bathroom, your bare feet slip on some magazines littering the floor—*Wired, Rolling Stone, Newsweek*. You need to talk to your roommate about picking up!

After showering, you quickly pull on your Levi's, lace up your Nike cross-trainers, and throw on a FUBU pullover. No time for breakfast; you grab a Nature Valley granola bar and the newspaper and head for the bus stop. As the bus rolls up, you can't help but notice the giant ad on its side: *Die Hard IX—Kill Before You're Killed*. Rejecting that as a movie choice for the weekend, you sit down next to a teenager listening to music on his headphones and playing a video game. You bury yourself in the paper, scanning the lead stories and the local news and then checking out *Doonesbury* and *Dilbert*.

Hopping off the bus at the campus stop, you run into Chris from your computer lab. You walk to class together, talking about last night's *Simpsons* episode.

It's not yet 9:00, and already you're awash in media messages.

In this chapter we define communication, interpersonal communication, mass communication, media, and culture and explore the relationships among them and how they define us and our world. We investigate how communication works, how it changes when technology is introduced into the process, and how differing views of communication and mass communication can lead to different interpretations of their power. We also discuss the opportunities mass communication and culture offer us and the responsibilities that come with those opportunities. Always crucial, these issues are of particular importance now, when we find ourselves in a period of remarkable development in new communication technologies. This discussion inevitably leads to an examination of media literacy, its importance and practice.

What Is Mass Communication?

More on McLuhan
www.mcluhan.ca/

"Does a fish know it's wet?" influential cultural and media critic Marshall McLuhan would often ask. The answer, he would say, is "No." The fish's existence is so dominated by water that only when water is absent is the fish aware of its condition.

So it is with people and mass media. The media so fully saturate our everyday lives that we are often unconscious of their presence, not to mention their influence. Media inform us, entertain us, delight us, annoy us. They move our emotions, challenge our intellects, insult our intelligence. Media often reduce us to mere commodities for sale to the highest bidder. Media help define us; they shape our realities.

A fundamental theme of this book is that media do none of this alone. They do it *with* us as well as *to* us through mass communication, and they do it as a central—many critics and scholars say *the* central—cultural force in our society.

COMMUNICATION DEFINED

In its simplest form **communication** is the transmission of a message from a source to a receiver. For nearly 60 years now, this view of communication has been identified with the writing of political scientist Harold Lasswell (1948). He said that a convenient way to describe communication is to answer these questions:

- *Who?*
- Says *what?*
- Through *which* channel?
- To *whom?*
- With *what effect?*

Expressed in terms of the basic elements of the communication process, communication occurs when

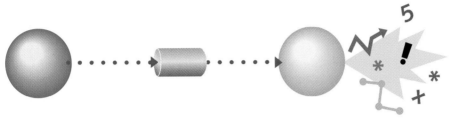

A source sends a message   through a medium   to a receiver   producing some effect

Straightforward enough, but what if the source is a professor who insists on speaking in a technical language far beyond the receiving students' level of skill? Obviously, communication does not occur. Unlike mere message-sending, communication requires the response of others. Therefore, there must be a *sharing* (or correspondence) of meaning for communication to take place.

A second problem with this simple model is that it suggests that the receiver passively accepts the source's message. However, if our imaginary students do not comprehend the professor's words, they respond with "Huh?" or look confused or yawn. This response, or **feedback,** is also a message. The receivers (the students) now become a source, sending their own message to the source (the offending professor), who is now a receiver. Hence, communication is a *reciprocal* and *ongoing process* with all involved parties more or less engaged in creating shared meaning. Communication, then, is better defined as *the process of creating shared meaning.*

Communication researcher Wilbur Schramm, using ideas originally developed by psychologist Charles E. Osgood, developed a graphic way to represent the reciprocal nature of communication (Figure 1.1, p. 6). This depiction of **interpersonal communication**—communication between two or a few people—shows that there is no clearly identifiable source or receiver. Rather, because communication is an ongoing and reciprocal process, all the participants, or "interpreters," are working to create meaning by **encoding** and **decoding** messages. A message is first *encoded,* that is, transformed into an understandable sign and symbol system. Speaking is encoding, as are writing, printing, and filming a television program. Once received, the message is *decoded;* that is, the signs and symbols are interpreted. Decoding occurs through listening, reading, or watching that television show.

The Osgood–Schramm model demonstrates the ongoing and reciprocal nature of the communication process. There is, therefore, no source, no

Figure 1.1 Osgood and Schramm's Model of Communication. *Source:* From *The Process and Effects of Mass Communication* by Wilbur Lang Schramm, 1954. Reprinted by permission of Wilbur Schramm's heirs.

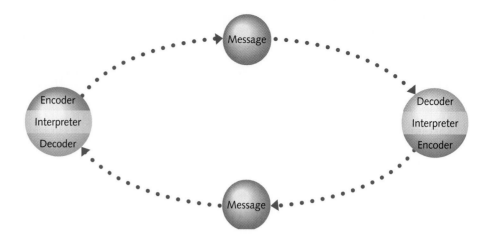

receiver, and no feedback. The reason is that, as communication is happening, both interpreters are simultaneously source and receiver. There is no feedback because all messages are presumed to be in reciprocation of other messages. Even when your friend starts a conversation with you, for example, it can be argued that it was your look of interest and willingness that communicated to her that she should speak. In this example, it is improper to label either you or your friend as the source—Who really initiated this chat?—and, therefore, it is impossible to identify who is providing feedback to whom.

Not every model can show all aspects of a process as complex as communication. Missing from this representation is **noise**—anything that interferes with successful communication. Noise is more than screeching or loud music when you are trying to read. Biases that lead to incorrect decoding, for example, are noise, as is newsprint that bleeds through from page 1 to page 2.

Encoded messages are carried by a **medium,** that is, the means of sending information. Sound waves are the medium that carries our voice to friends across the table; the telephone is the medium that carries our voice to friends across town. When the medium is a technology that carries messages to a large number of people—as newspapers carry the printed word and radio conveys the sound of music and news—we call it a **mass medium** (the plural of medium is **media**). The mass media we use regularly include radio, television, books, magazines, newspapers, movies, sound recordings, and computer networks. Each medium is the basis of a giant industry, but other related and supporting industries also serve them and us—advertising and public relations, for example. In our culture we use the words *media* and *mass media* interchangeably to refer to the communication industries themselves. We say, "The media entertain" or "The mass media are too conservative (or too liberal)."

MASS COMMUNICATION DEFINED

We speak, too, of mass communication. **Mass communication** is the process of creating shared meaning between the mass media and their audiences. Schramm recast his and Osgood's general model of communication to help us visualize the particular aspects of the mass communication process

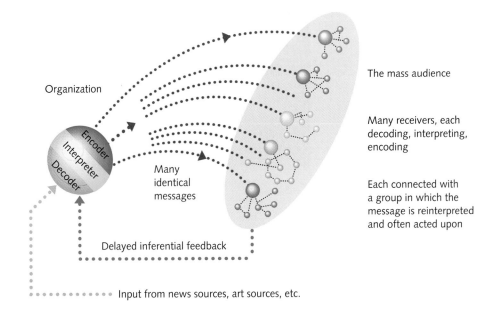

Organization

Encoder
Interpreter
Decoder

Many
identical
messages

The mass audience

Many receivers, each
decoding, interpreting,
encoding

Each connected with
a group in which the
message is reinterpreted
and often acted upon

Delayed inferential feedback

Input from news sources, art sources, etc.

Figure 1.2 Schramm's Model
of Mass Communication.
Source: From *The Process and Effects
of Mass Communication* by Wilbur Lang
Schramm, 1954. Reprinted by
permission of Wilbur Schramm's heirs.

(Figure 1.2). This model and the original Osgood–Schramm model have much in common—interpreters, encoding, decoding, and messages—but it is their differences that are most significant for our understanding of how mass communication differs from other forms of communication. For example, whereas the original model includes "message," the mass communication model offers "many identical messages." In addition, the mass communication model specifies "feedback," whereas the interpersonal communication model does not. When two or a few people communicate face-to-face, the participants can immediately and clearly recognize the feedback residing in the reciprocal messages (our boring professor can see and hear the students' disenchantment as they listen to the lecture). Things are not nearly as simple in mass communication.

In Schramm's mass communication model, feedback is represented by a dotted line labeled delayed **inferential feedback.** This feedback is indirect rather than direct. Television executives, for example, must wait a day, at the very minimum, and sometimes a week or a month, to discover the ratings for new programs. Even then, the ratings measure only how many sets are tuned in, not whether people liked or disliked the programs. As a result, these executives can only infer what they must do to improve programming; hence the term *inferential feedback.* Mass communicators are also subject to additional feedback, usually in the form of criticism in other media, such as a television critic writing a column in a newspaper.

The differences between the individual elements of interpersonal and mass communication change the very nature of the communication process. How those alterations influence the message itself and how the likelihood of successfully sharing meaning varies are shown in Figure 1.3 on page 8. For example, the immediacy and directness of feedback in interpersonal communication free communicators to gamble, to experiment with different approaches. Their knowledge of one another enables them to tailor their messages as narrowly as they wish. As a result, interpersonal communication is often personally relevant and possibly even adventurous and challenging. In contrast, the distance between participants in the mass communication

WWW

TV Critics Assn.
www.tvcritics.org/

	Interpersonal Communication You invite a friend to lunch.		**Mass Communication** Imagine Entertainment produces *24*.	
	Nature	**Consequences**	**Nature**	**Consequences**
Message	Highly flexible and alterable	You can change it in midstream. If feedback is negative, you can offer an alternative. Is feedback still negative? Take a whole new approach.	Identical, mechanically produced, simultaneously sent Inflexible, unalterable The completed *24* episode that is aired.	Once production is completed, *24* cannot be changed. If a plotline or other communicative device isn't working with the audience, nothing can be done.
Interpreter A	One person—in this case, you	You know your mind. You can encode your own message to suit yourself, your values, your likes and dislikes.	A large, hierarchically structured organization—in this case, Imagine Entertainment Productions and the Fox television network	Who really is Interpreter A? Imagine Entertainment's executives? The writers? The director? The actors? The network and its standards and practices people? The sponsors? All must agree, leaving little room for individual vision or experimentation.
Interpreter B	One or a few people, usually in direct contact with you and, to a greater or lesser degree, known to you—in this case, Chris	You can tailor your message specifically to Interpreter B. You can make relatively accurate judgments about B because of information present in the setting. Chris is a vegetarian; you don't suggest a steak house.	A large, heterogeneous audience known to Interpreter A only in the most rudimentary way, little more than basic demographics—in this case, several million viewers of *24*	Communication cannot be tailored to the wants, needs, and tastes of all audience members or even those of all members of some subgroup. Some more or less generally acceptable standard is set.
Feedback	Immediate and direct yes or no response	You know how successful your message is immediately. You can adjust your communication on the spot to maximize its effectiveness.	Delayed and inferential Even overnight ratings too late for this episode of *24* Moreover, ratings limited to telling the number of sets tuned in	Even if the feedback is useful, it is too late to be of value for this episode. In addition, it doesn't suggest how to improve the communication effort.
Result	Flexible, personally relevant, possibly adventurous, challenging, or experimental		Constrained by virtually every aspect of the communication situation A level of communication most likely to meet the greatest number of viewers' needs A belief that experimentation is dangerous A belief that to challenge the audience is to risk failure	

Figure 1.3 Elements of Interpersonal Communication and Mass Communication Compared.

process, imposed by the technology, creates a sort of "communication conservatism." Feedback comes too late to enable corrections or alterations in communication that fails. The sheer number of people in many mass communication audiences makes personalization and specificity difficult. As a result, mass communication tends to be more constrained, less free. This does not mean, however, that it is less potent than interpersonal communication in shaping our understanding of ourselves and our world.

Media theorist James W. Carey (1975) recognized this and offered a **cultural definition of communication** that has had a profound impact on the way communication scientists and others have viewed the relationship between communication and culture. Carey wrote, "Communication is a symbolic process whereby reality is produced, maintained, repaired and transformed" (p. 10).

Carey's definition asserts that communication and reality are linked. Communication is a process embedded in our everyday lives that informs the way we perceive, understand, and construct our view of reality and the world. Communication is the foundation of our culture.

What Is Culture?

Culture is the learned behavior of members of a given social group. Many writers and thinkers have offered interesting expansions of this definition. Here are four examples, all from anthropologists. These definitions highlight not only what culture *is* but also what culture *does:*

> Culture is the learned, socially acquired traditions and lifestyles of the members of a society, including their patterned, repetitive ways of thinking, feeling and acting. (M. Harris, 1983, p. 5)

> Culture lends significance to human experience by selecting from and organizing it. It refers broadly to the forms through which people make sense of their lives, rather than more narrowly to the opera or art of museums. (R. Rosaldo, 1989, p. 26)

> Culture is the medium evolved by humans to survive. Nothing is free from cultural influences. It is the keystone in civilization's arch and is the medium through which all of life's events must flow. We are culture. (E. T. Hall, 1976, p. 14)

> Culture is an historically transmitted pattern of meanings embodied in symbolic forms by means of which [people] communicate, perpetuate, and develop their knowledge about and attitudes toward life. (C. Geertz, as cited in Taylor, 1991, p. 91)

CULTURE AS SOCIALLY CONSTRUCTED SHARED MEANING

Virtually all definitions of culture recognize that culture is *learned*. Recall the opening vignette. Even if this scenario does not exactly match your early mornings, you probably recognize its elements. Moreover, all of us are familiar with most, if not every, cultural reference in it. *The Simpsons, Rolling Stone*, McDonald's, Nike, *Dilbert*—all are points of reference, things that have some meaning for all of us. How did this come to be?

Creation and maintenance of a more or less common culture occurs through communication, including mass communication. When we talk to our friends; when a parent raises a child; when religious leaders instruct their followers; when teachers teach; when grandparents pass on recipes; when politicians campaign; when media professionals produce content that we read, listen to, or watch, meaning is being shared and culture is being constructed and maintained.

FUNCTIONS AND EFFECTS OF CULTURE

Culture serves a purpose. It helps us categorize and classify our experiences; it helps define us, our world, and our place in it. In doing so, culture can have a number of sometimes conflicting effects.

Limiting and Liberating Effects of Culture A culture's learned traditions and values can be seen as patterned, repetitive ways of thinking, feeling, and acting. Culture limits our options and provides useful guidelines for behavior. For example, when conversing, you do not consciously consider, "Now, how far away should I stand? Am I too close?" You simply stand where you stand. After a hearty meal with a friend's family, you do not engage in mental self-debate, "Should I burp? Yes! No! Arghhhh. . . ." Culture provides information that helps us make meaningful distinctions about right and wrong, appropriate and inappropriate, good and bad, attractive and unattractive, and so on. How does it do this?

Obviously, through communication. Through a lifetime of communication we have learned just what our culture expects of us. The two examples given here are positive results of culture's limiting effects. But culture's limiting effects can be negative, such as when we are unwilling or unable to move past patterned, repetitive ways of thinking, feeling, and acting or when we entrust our "learning" to teachers whose interests are selfish, narrow, or otherwise not consistent with our own.

U.S. culture, for example, values thinness and beauty in women. How many women endure weeks of unhealthy diets and succumb to potentially dangerous surgical procedures in search of a body that for most is physically unattainable? How many men (and other women) never get to know, like, or even love those women who cannot meet our culture's standards of thinness and beauty? Why are 81% of all 10-year-old girls "afraid of being fat," and why do 42% of girls in grades 1 to 3 "want to be thinner"? (Kirk, 2003, p. 9)? Why, in 2003 alone, according to the American Society of Plastic Surgeons, did 331,886 *children* 18 years old or younger undergo cosmetic procedures such as nose jobs, ear surgery, cheek implants, and liposuction? And why, in that same year, did another 3,841 girls 18 or younger undergo breast augmentation, up from 978 ten years before (Sherman, 2005)?

Now consider how this situation may have come about. Our mothers did not bounce us on their knees when we were babies, telling us that thin was good and fat was bad. Think back, though, to the stories you were told and the television shows and movies you watched growing up. The heroines (or, more often, the beautiful love interests of the heroes) were invariably tall, beautiful, and thin. The bad guys were usually mean and fat. From Disney's depictions of Snow White, Cinderella, Beauty, Tinker Bell, and Pocahontas to the impossible dimensions of most video-game heroines, the message is embedded in the conscious (and unconscious) mind of every girl and boy: You can't be too thin or too beautiful!

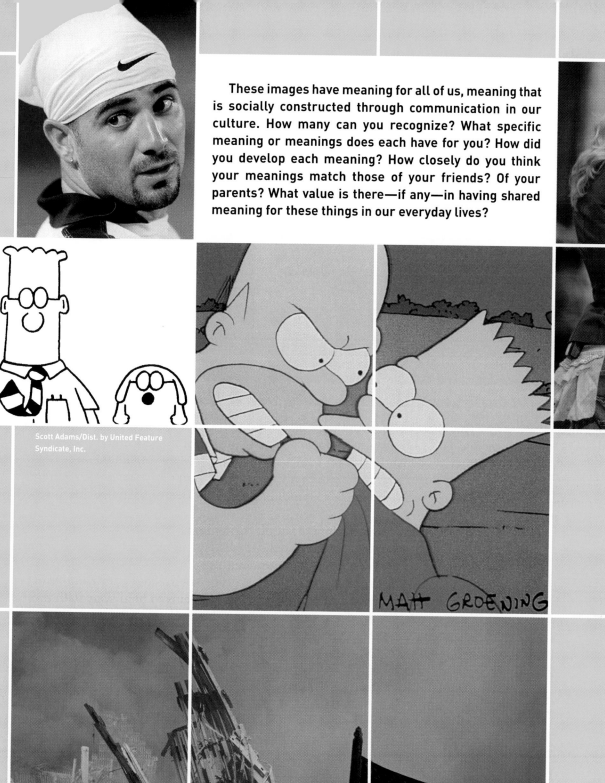

These images have meaning for all of us, meaning that is socially constructed through communication in our culture. How many can you recognize? What specific meaning or meanings does each have for you? How did you develop each meaning? How closely do you think your meanings match those of your friends? Of your parents? What value is there—if any—in having shared meaning for these things in our everyday lives?

Scott Adams/Dist. by United Feature Syndicate, Inc.

MATT GROENING

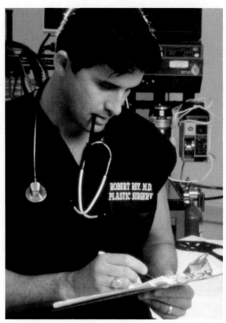

Not only do media set standards of attractiveness, but they remind us that there is little need to feel bad about ourselves if we do not meet them. Television shows like *Nip/Tuck* and *Dr. 90210* tell us that beauty is not something we live but a commodity that can be purchased.

This message and millions of others come to us primarily through the media, and although the people who produce these media images are not necessarily selfish or mean, their motives are undeniably financial. Their contribution to our culture's repetitive ways of thinking, feeling, and acting is most certainly not primary among their concerns when preparing their communication.

Culture need not only limit. That media representations of female beauty often meet with debate and disagreement points up the fact that culture can be liberating as well. This is so because cultural values can be contested.

Especially in a pluralistic, democratic society such as ours, the **dominant culture** (or, **mainstream culture**)—the one that seems to hold sway with the majority of people—is often openly challenged. People do meet, find attractive, like, and even love people who do not fit the standard image of beauty. In addition, media sometimes present images that suggest different ideals of beauty and success. Cooking impresario Rachael Ray; singer-actresses Queen Latifah, Jennifer Lopez, and Raven-Symoné Pearman; and talk show host and influential broadcasting executive Oprah Winfrey all represent alternatives to our culture's idealized standards of beauty, and all have undeniable appeal (and power) on the big and small screens. Liberation from the limitations imposed by culture resides in our ability and willingness to learn and use *new* patterned, repetitive ways of thinking, feeling, and acting; to challenge existing patterns; and to create our own.

Defining, Differentiating, Dividing, and Uniting Effects of Culture Have you ever made the mistake of calling a dolphin, porpoise, or even a whale a fish? Maybe you have heard others do it. This error occurs because when we think of fish, we think "lives in the water" and "swims." Fish are defined by their "aquatic culture." Because water-residing, swimming dolphins and porpoises share that culture, we sometimes forget that they are mammals, not fish.

We, too, are defined by our culture. We are citizens of the United States; we are Americans. If we travel to other countries, we will hear ourselves

Queen Latifah, Rachael Ray, and Jennifer Lopez are prominent women whose presentation in the media suggests different cultural ideals of beauty and success. Each represents an alternative to our culture's idealized standards of beauty. How attractive do you find each woman to be? What is it about each that appeals to you?

labeled "American," and this label will conjure up stereotypes and expectations in the minds of those who use and hear it. The stereotype, whatever it may be, will probably fit us only incompletely, or perhaps hardly at all—perhaps we are dolphins in a sea full of fish. Nevertheless, being American defines us in innumerable important ways, both to others (more obviously) and to ourselves (less obviously).

Within this large, national culture, however, there are many smaller, **bounded cultures** (or, **co-cultures**). For example, we speak comfortably of Italian neighborhoods, fraternity row, the South, and the suburbs. Because of our cultural understanding of these categories, each expression communicates something about our expectations of these places. We think we can predict with a good deal of certainty the types of restaurants and shops we will find in the Italian neighborhood, even the kind of music we will hear escaping from open windows. We can predict the kinds of clothes and cars we will see on fraternity row, the likely behavior of shop clerks in the South, and the political orientation of the suburb's residents. Moreover, the people within these cultures usually identify themselves as members of those bounded cultures. An individual may say, for example, "I am Italian American" or "I'm from the South." These smaller cultures unite groups of people and enable them to see themselves as different from other groups around them. Thus culture also serves to differentiate us from others.

In the United States, we generally consider this a good thing. We pride ourselves on our pluralism and our diversity and on the richness of the cultural heritages represented within our borders. We enjoy moving from one bounded culture to another or from a bounded culture to the dominant national culture and back again.

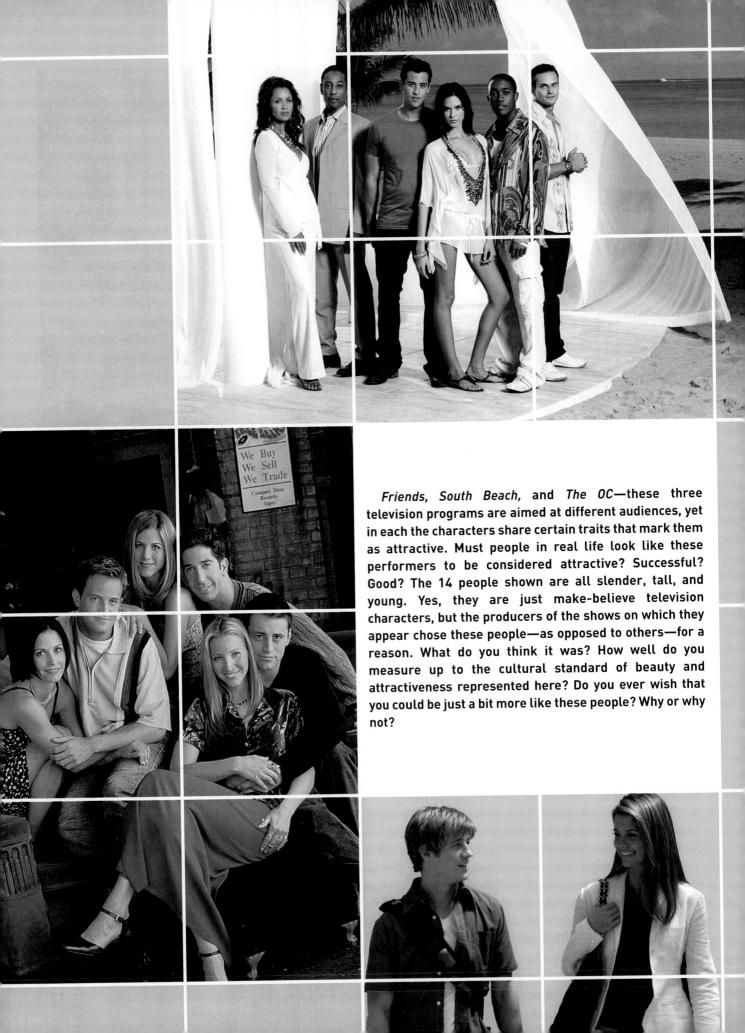

Friends, *South Beach*, and *The OC*—these three television programs are aimed at different audiences, yet in each the characters share certain traits that mark them as attractive. Must people in real life look like these performers to be considered attractive? Successful? Good? The 14 people shown are all slender, tall, and young. Yes, they are just make-believe television characters, but the producers of the shows on which they appear chose these people—as opposed to others—for a reason. What do you think it was? How well do you measure up to the cultural standard of beauty and attractiveness represented here? Do you ever wish that you could be just a bit more like these people? Why or why not?

What is it about Muslim Americans that "communicated disloyalty" to the United States in the wake of the September 11, 2001, terrorist attacks on New York and Washington?

Problems arise, however, when differentiation leads to division. All Americans were traumatized by the horrific events of September 11, 2001, but that tragedy was compounded for Muslim Americans whose patriotism was challenged simply because of membership in their particular bounded culture. The Arab-American Anti-Discrimination Committee reported more than 500 post-9/11 incidents of threats, beatings, arsons, shootings, and at least 6 murders (Levitas, 2002). For these good Americans, regardless of what was in their hearts or minds, their religion, skin color, maybe even their clothing "communicated" disloyalty to the United States to many other Americans. Just as culture is constructed and maintained through communication, it is also communication (or miscommunication) that turns differentiation into division.

Yet, U.S. citizens of all colors, ethnicities, genders and gender preferences, nationalities, places of birth, economic strata, and intelligences often get along; in fact, we *can* communicate, *can* prosper, *can* respect one another's differences. Culture can divide us, but culture also unites us. Our culture represents our collective experience. We converse easily with strangers because we share the same culture. We speak the same language, automatically understand how far apart to stand, appropriately use titles or first or last names, know how much to say, and know how much to leave unsaid. Through communication with people in our culture, we internalize cultural norms and values—those things that bind our many diverse bounded cultures into a functioning, cohesive society.

Defining Culture From this discussion of culture comes the definition of culture on which the remainder of this book is based:

> Culture is the world made meaningful; it is socially constructed and maintained through communication. It limits as well as liberates us; it differentiates as well as unites us. It defines our realities and thereby shapes the ways we think, feel, and act.

Mass Communication and Culture

Because culture can limit and divide or liberate and unite, it offers us infinite opportunities to use communication for good—if we choose to do so. James Carey wrote,

> Because we have looked at each new advance in communication technology as opportunities for politics and economics, we have devoted them, almost exclusively, to government and trade. We have rarely seen them as opportunities to expand [our] powers to learn and exchange ideas and experience. (1975, pp. 20–21)

Who are "we" in this quote? *We* are everyone involved in creating and maintaining the culture that defines us. *We* are the people involved in mass media industries and the people who compose their audiences. Together we allow mass communication not only to occur but also to contribute to the creation and maintenance of culture.

Everyone involved has an obligation to participate responsibly. For people working in the media industries, this means professionally and ethically creating and transmitting content. For audience members, it means behaving as critical and thoughtful consumers of that content. Two ways to understand our opportunities and our responsibilities in the mass communication process are to view the mass media as our cultural storytellers and to conceptualize mass communication as a cultural forum.

There we are, huddled around the tribal campfire, telling and retelling the stories of our people.

Storytellers play an important role in helping us define ourselves. By permission of Jerry Van Amerongen and Creators Syndicate, Inc.

MASS MEDIA AS CULTURAL STORYTELLERS

A culture's values and beliefs reside in the stories it tells. Who are the good guys? Who are the bad guys? How many of your childhood heroines were chubby? How many good guys dressed in black? How many heroines lived happily ever after without marrying Prince Charming? Probably not very many. Our stories help define our realities, shaping the ways we think, feel, and act. Storytellers have a remarkable opportunity to shape culture. They also have a responsibility to do so in as professional and ethical a way as possible.

At the same time, you, the audience for these stories, also have opportunities and responsibilities. You use these stories not only to be entertained but to learn about the world around you, to understand the values, the way things work, and how the pieces fit together. You have a responsibility to question the tellers and their stories, to interpret the stories in ways consistent with larger or more important cultural values and truths, to be thoughtful, to reflect on the stories' meanings and what they say about you and your culture. To do less is to miss an opportunity to construct your own meaning and, thereby, culture.

For example, as journalists tried to tell the story of the destruction wrought by Hurricane Katrina, they had a nearly infinite number of images and words available to craft their narratives. The wire-service photos and accompanying captions featured on this cover of *Extra!* were just two. They had appeared in newspapers around the world and in proximity to each other on Web portal Yahoo! News. The young African American man "walks through chest deep flood water after *looting* a grocery store." The white couple, though, wades "through chest-deep water after *finding* bread and soda from a local grocery store." The plot line is clear—the lazy Black man looted . . . naturally . . . while those hardworking White folks were fortunate enough to have found sustenance! Readers and Web surfers of all races, in an instantaneous (and angry) cultural conversation with newspapers and Yahoo!, rejected their offensive, racially simplistic, stories. The images and captions immediately disappeared from Yahoo! News. Yahoo! and many newspapers apologized (Bacon, 2005).

MASS COMMUNICATION AS CULTURAL FORUM

Imagine a giant courtroom in which we discuss and debate our culture—what it is, and what we want it to be. What do we think about welfare? Single motherhood? Labor unions? Nursing homes? What is the meaning of "successful," "good," "loyal," "moral," "honest," "beautiful," "patriotic"? We have cultural definitions or understandings of all these things and more. Where do they come from? How do they develop, take shape, and mature?

Mass communication has become a primary forum for the debate about our culture. Logically, then, the most powerful voices in the forum have the most power to shape our definitions and understandings. Where should that power reside—with the media industries or with their audiences? If you answer "media industries," you must demand that members of these industries act professionally and ethically. If you answer "audiences," you must insist that individual audience members be thoughtful and critical of the media messages they consume. The forum is only as good, fair, and honest as those who participate in it.

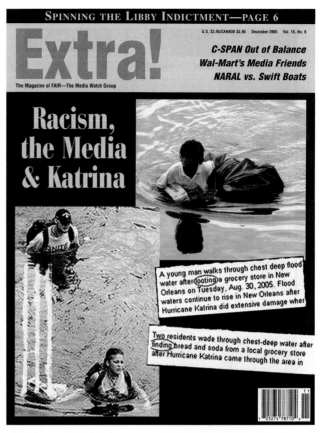

SPINNING THE LIBBY INDICTMENT—PAGE 6

Extra!

The Magazine of FAIR—The Media Watch Group

U.S. $3.95/CANADA $5.95   December 2005   Vol. 18. No. 6

C-SPAN Out of Balance
Wal-Mart's Media Friends
NARAL vs. Swift Boats

Racism, the Media & Katrina

A young man walks through chest deep flood water after looting a grocery store in New Orleans on Tuesday, Aug. 30, 2005. Flood waters continue to rise in New Orleans after Hurricane Katrina did extensive damage wher

Two residents wade through chest-deep water after finding bread and soda from a local grocery store after Hurricane Katrina came through the area in

The events captured in these images sent globally by Yahoo! News were the same—people trying to survive the horrors of Hurricane Katrina. But as the race of the "characters" changed, so too did the stories. People complained. Yahoo! listened.

Scope and Nature of Mass Media

No matter how we choose to view the process of mass communication, it is impossible to deny that an enormous portion of our lives is spent interacting with mass media. On a typical Sunday night, 37 million people in the United States will tune in to a prime-time television show. Television sets are in 98% of our homes, VCRs and DVDs in over 91%. The television set is on for more than 8 hours a day in a typical U.S. household. Two-thirds of U.S. adults will read a newspaper each day; two-thirds will listen to the radio for some part of every day. The worldwide Internet population exceeds 938 million people (Internet World Stats, 2005); 71 million Americans use e-mail every day ("Noted," 2006); and 66% of the entire U.S. population regularly

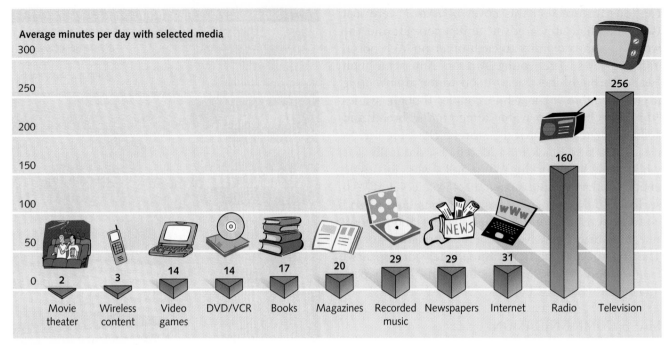

Average minutes per day with selected media

300		
250		256
200		
150	160	
100		
50		
0	2 3 14 14 17 20 29 29 31	

Movie theater · Wireless content · Video games · DVD/VCR · Books · Magazines · Recorded music · Newspapers · Internet · Radio · Television

Figure 1.4 Average Number of Minutes per Day a Typical Adult Spends with Selected Media, 2006. *Source:* Lindsay, 2006.

uses the Internet, the proportion rising to 90% when considering only teens 12 to 17 years old ("Teens," 2005). Americans spent just under $8.8 billion buying 1.4 billion movie tickets in 2005 (Bowles, 2006). In that same year, they spent $10.1 billion on video games (Oser, 2005b). Kids 8 to 18 years old spend more than 8 hours and 33 minutes a day with media content, up by more than 1 hour from only 5 years ago (Rideout, Roberts, & Foehr, 2005). The average American adult spends 9 hours and 35 minutes a day, or 60% of his or her waking time, consuming various forms of media content (Lindsay, 2006). Americans spend more on entertainment media than they do on clothes and health care combined. Figure 1.4 above provides data on a typical U.S. adult's media day.

Despite the pervasiveness of mass media in our lives, many of us are dissatisfied with or critical of the media industries' performance and much of the content provided. For example, a Gallup Poll (Jones, 2004) reported that only 54% of Americans had even a "fair amount of trust and confidence in the media." Only 49% think media news organizations are "highly professional," and only 39% think they are "moral" (Project, 2004). One-third of U.S. adults report being overwhelmed by media and that they are "crowding out other important things in their lives" (Mandese, 2004).

Our ambivalence—we criticize, yet we consume—comes in part from our uncertainties about the relationships among the elements of mass communication. What is the role of technology? What is the role of money? And what is *our* role in the mass communication process?

THE ROLE OF TECHNOLOGY

To some thinkers, it is machines and their development that drive economic and cultural change. This idea is referred to as **technological determinism.** Certainly there can be no doubt that movable type contributed to the Protestant

Reformation and the decline of the Catholic Church's power in Europe or that television changed the way members of American families interact. Those who believe in technological determinism would argue that these changes in the cultural landscape were the inevitable result of new technology.

But others see technology as more neutral and claim that the way people *use* technology is what gives it significance. This perspective accepts technology as one of many factors that shape economic and cultural change; technology's influence is ultimately determined by how much power it is given by the people and cultures that use it.

This disagreement about the power of technology is at the heart of the controversy surrounding the new communication technologies. Are we more or less powerless in the wake of advances such as the Internet, the World Wide Web, and instant global audio and visual communication? If we are at the mercy of technology, the culture that surrounds us will not be of our making, and the best we can hope to do is make our way reasonably well in a world outside our control. But if these technologies are indeed neutral and their power resides in *how* we choose to use them, we can utilize them responsibly and thoughtfully to construct and maintain whatever kind of culture we want. As film director and technophile Steven Spielberg explained, "Technology can be our best friend, and technology can also be the biggest party pooper of our lives. It interrupts our own story, interrupts our ability to have a thought or daydream, to imagine something wonderful because we're too busy bridging the walk from the cafeteria back to the office on the cell phone" (quoted in Kennedy, 2002, p. 109). Or, as Dr. Ian Malcolm (Jeff Goldblum) said in Spielberg's 1997 *The Lost World: Jurassic Park*, "Oooh! Ahhh! That's how it always starts. Then later there's running and screaming."

WWW

More on Spielberg
www.filmmakers.com/artists/spielberg

Technology does have an impact on communication. At the very least it changes the basic elements of communication (see Figure 1.3 on p. 8). What technology does not do is relieve us of our obligation to use mass communication responsibly and wisely.

THE ROLE OF MONEY

Money, too, alters communication. It shifts the balance of power; it tends to make audiences products rather than consumers.

The first newspapers were financially supported by their readers; the money they paid for the paper covered its production and distribution. But in the 1830s a new form of newspaper financing emerged. Publishers began selling their papers for a penny—much less than it cost to produce and distribute them. Because so many more papers were sold at this bargain price, publishers could "sell" advertising space based on their readership. What they were actually selling to advertisers was not space on the page—it was readers. How much they could charge advertisers was directly related to how much product (how many readers) they could produce for them.

This new type of publication changed the nature of mass communication. The goal of the process was no longer for audience and media to create meaning together. Rather, it was to sell those readers to a third participant—advertisers.

Some observers think this was a devastatingly bad development, not only in the history of mass communication but in the history of democracy. It robbed people of their voice, or at least made the voices of the advertisers

CULTURAL FORUM

Audience as Consumer or Audience as Product?

People base their judgments of media performance and content on the way they see themselves fitting into the economics of the media industry. Businesses operate to serve their consumers and make a profit. The consumer comes first, then, but who *is* the consumer in our mass media system? This is a much debated issue among media practitioners and media critics. Consider the following models.

	Producer	Product	Consumer
Basic U.S. Business Model	A manufacturer . . .	produces a product . . .	for consumers who choose to buy or not. The manufacturer must satisfy the consumer. Power resides here.
Basic U.S. Business Model for Cereal: Rice Krispies as Product, Public as Consumer	Kellogg's . . .	produces Rice Krispies . . .	for us, the consumers. If we buy Rice Krispies, Kellogg's makes a profit. Kellogg's must satisfy us. Power resides here.
Basic U.S. Business Model for Television (A): Audience as Product, Advertisers as Consumer	NBC . . .	produces audiences (using its programming) . . .	for advertisers. If they buy NBC's audiences, NBC makes a profit. NBC must satisfy its consumers, the advertisers. Power resides here.
Basic U.S. Business Model for Television (B): Programming as Product, Audience as Consumer	NBC . . .	produces (or distributes) programming . . .	for us, the audience. If we watch NBC's shows, NBC makes a profit. NBC must satisfy us. Power resides here.

The first three models assume that the consumer *buys* the product; that is, the consumer is the one with the money and therefore the one who must be satisfied. The last model makes a different assumption. It sees the audience, even though it does not buy anything, as sufficiently important to NBC's profit-making ability to force NBC to consider its interests above others' (even those of advertisers). Which model do you think best represents the economics of U.S. mass media?

more powerful. Others think it was a huge advance for both mass communication and democracy because it vastly expanded the media, broadening and deepening communication. Models showing these two different ways of viewing mass communication are presented in the box above, "Audience as Consumer or Audience as Product?" Which model makes the most sense to you? Which do you think is the most accurate? ABC newsman Ted Koppel told the *Washington Post*, "[Television] is an industry. It's a business. We exist to make money. We exist to put commercials on the air. The programming that is put on between those commercials is simply the bait we put in the mousetrap" (in "Soundbites," 2005, p. 2). Do you think Koppel is unnecessarily cynical or is he correct in his analysis of television?

The goals of media professionals will be questioned repeatedly throughout this book. For now, keep in mind that ours is a capitalist economic system and that media industries are businesses. Movie producers must sell tickets, book publishers must sell books, and even public broadcasting has bills to pay.

This does not mean, however, that the media are or must be slaves to profit. Our task is to understand the constraints placed on these industries by their economics and then demand that, within those limits, they perform ethically and responsibly. We can do this only by being thoughtful, critical consumers of the media.

Mass Communication, Culture, and Media Literacy

Culture and communication are inseparable, and mass communication, as we've seen, is a particularly powerful, pervasive, and complex form of communication. Our level of skill in the mass communication process is therefore of utmost importance. This skill is not necessarily a simple one to master (it is much more than booting up the computer, turning on the television set, or flipping the pages of your favorite magazine). But it is, indeed, a learnable skill, one that can be practiced. This skill is **media literacy**—the ability to effectively and efficiently comprehend and use any form of mediated communication. But before we can fully understand *media* literacy, we must understand why literacy, in and of itself, is important.

Let's begin by looking at the development of writing and the formation of **literate culture.** An expanding literate population encouraged technological innovation; the printing press transformed the world. Other communication technology advances have also had a significant impact; however, these technologies cannot be separated from how people have used them. Technology can be used in ways beneficial and otherwise. The skilled, beneficial use of media technologies is the goal of media literacy.

ORAL CULTURE

Oral or **preliterate cultures** are those without a written language. Virtually all communication must be face-to-face, and this fact helps to define the culture, its structure, and its operation. Whether they existed thousands of years ago before writing was developed or still function today (for example, among certain Eskimo peoples and African tribes where **griots,** or "talking chiefs," provide oral histories of their people going back hundreds of years), oral cultures are remarkably alike. They share these characteristics:

WWW

More on Storytelling
www.storynet.org

The meaning in language is specific and local. As a result, communities are closely knit, and their members are highly dependent on each other for all aspects of life.

Knowledge must be passed on orally. People must be *shown* and *told* how to do something. Therefore, skilled hunters, farmers, midwives, and the like hold a special status; they are the living embodiments of culture.

Memory is crucial. As repositories of cultural customs and traditions, elders are revered; they are responsible for passing knowledge on to the next generation.

Myth and history are intertwined. Storytellers are highly valued; they are the meaning makers, and, like the elders, they pass on what is important to the culture.

What does the resulting culture look like? People know each other intimately and rely on one another for survival. Roles are clearly defined. Stories teach important cultural lessons and preserve important cultural traditions and values. Control over communication is rarely necessary, but when it is, it is easily achieved through social sanctions.

This Sumerian cuneiform dates from 700 years before the birth of Christ.

THE INVENTION OF WRITING

Writing, the first communication technology, complicated this simple picture. More than 5,000 years ago, alphabets were developed independently in several places around the world. **Ideogrammatic** (picture-based) **alphabets** appeared in Egypt (as hieroglyphics), Sumer (as cuneiform), and urban China.

Ideogrammatic alphabets require a huge number of symbols to convey even the simplest idea. Their complexity meant that only a very select few, an intellectual elite, could read or write. For writing to truly serve as effective and efficient communication, one more advance was required.

The Sumerians were international traders, maintaining trade routes throughout known Europe, Africa, and Asia. The farther the Sumerian traders traveled, the less they could rely on face-to-face communication and the greater their need for a more precise writing form. Sumerian cuneiform slowly expanded, using symbols to represent sounds rather than objects and ideas. Appearing around 1800 B.C., these were the first elements of a **syllable alphabet**—an alphabet employing sequences of vowels and consonants, that is, words.

The syllable alphabet as we know it today slowly developed, aided greatly by ancient Semitic cultures, and eventually flowered in Greece around 800 B.C. Like the Sumerians long before them, the Greeks perfected their easy alphabet of necessity. Having little in the way of natural resources, the Greek city-states depended and thrived on bustling trade routes all around the Aegean and Mediterranean seas. For orders to be placed, deals arranged, manifests compiled, and records kept, writing that was easy to learn, use, and understand was required.

A medium was necessary to carry this new form of communication. The Sumerians had used clay tablets, but the Egyptians, Greeks, and Romans eventually employed **papyrus,** rolls of sliced strips of reed pressed together. Around 100 B.C. the Romans began using **parchment,** a writing material made from prepared animal skins, and in A.D. 105 midlevel Chinese bureaucrat Ts'ai Lun perfected a papermaking process employing a mixture of pressed mulberry tree bark, water, rags, and a sophisticated frame for drying and stretching the resulting sheets of paper. This technology made its way to Europe through various trade routes some 600 years later, and the importance of writing cannot be overemphasized. As explained by historian David Owen, "It made ideas permanent, portable, and endlessly reproducible" (2004, p. 91).

LITERATE CULTURE

But writing required **literacy**—the ability to effectively and efficiently comprehend and use written symbols. And with the coming of literacy the social and cultural rules and structures of preliterate times began to change. People could accumulate a permanent body of knowledge and transmit that knowledge from one generation to another. Among the changes that writing brought were these:

This Egyptian funeral papyrus depicts the weighing of a heart when a person dies.

Meaning and language became more uniform. The words "a bolt of cloth" had to mean the same to a reader in Mesopotamia as they did to one in Sicily. Over time, communities became less closely knit and their members less dependent on one another. The definition of "community" expanded to include people outside the local area.

Communication could occur over long distances and long periods of time. With knowledge being transmitted in writing, power shifted from those who could show others their special talents to those who could write and read about them.

The culture's memory, history, and myth could be recorded on paper. With written histories, elders and storytellers began to lose their status, and new elites developed. Homer (some historians believe he was actually several scribes), for example, compiled in written form several generations of oral stories and histories that we know as the *Iliad* and the *Odyssey.*

What did the resulting culture look like? It was no longer local. Its members could survive not only by hunting or farming together but by commercial, political, or military expansion. Empires replaced communities. There was more compartmentalization of people based on what they did to earn a living—bakers baked, herders herded, merchants sold goods. Yet, at the same time, role and status were less permanently fixed. Slaves who learned to read to serve their masters took on new duties for those masters and rose in status.

Power and influence now resided not in the strongest hunter, wisest elder, or most engaging storyteller but in those who could read and write; that is, power and influence now rested with those who were literate. They could best engage in widespread official communication, and they wrote the histories and passed on cultural values and lessons. With this change from preliterate to literate culture, the first stirrings of a new political philosophy were born. Reading and writing encouraged more open and robust debate, political exchange, and criticism of the powerful; in other words, it fostered democracy.

It is important to remember that in the newly literate cultures, communication was still quite limited. An orator could address at most a few hundred people at a time. Writers could reach only those literate few who held their handwritten scrolls or letters. The printing press would change this, making it possible to duplicate communication, thereby expanding our ability to communicate with one another.

THE GUTENBERG REVOLUTION

Project Gutenberg
www.promo.net/pg/

As it is impossible to overstate the importance of writing, so too is it impossible to overstate the significance of Johannes Gutenberg's development of movable metal type. Historian S. H. Steinberg wrote in *Five Hundred Years of Printing:*

> Neither political, constitutional, ecclesiastical, and economic, nor sociological, philosophical, and literary movements can be fully understood without taking into account the influence the printing press has exerted upon them. (1959, p. 11)

Marshall McLuhan expressed his admiration for Gutenberg's innovation by calling his 1962 book *The Gutenberg Galaxy.* In it he argued that the advent of print is the key to our modern consciousness. Why was Gutenberg's invention so important? Simply, because it allowed *mass* communication.

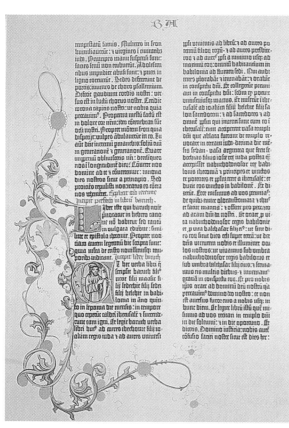

This page from a Gutenberg Bible shows the exquisite care the printer used in creating his works. The artwork in the margins is handpainted, but the text is mechanically printed.

The Printing Press Printing and the printing press existed long before Gutenberg perfected his process in or around 1446. The Chinese were using wooden block presses as early as A.D. 600 and had movable clay type by A.D. 1000. A simple movable metal type was even in use in Korea in the 13th century. Gutenberg's printing press was a significant leap forward, however, for two important reasons.

Gutenberg was a goldsmith and a metallurgist. He hit on the idea of using metal type crafted from lead molds in place of type made from wood or clay. This was an important advance. Not only was movable metal type durable enough to print page after page, but letters could be arranged and rearranged to make any message possible. And Gutenberg was able to produce virtually identical copies.

In addition, Gutenberg's advance over Korean metal mold printing was one of scope and intention. The Korean press was used to produce attractive artwork. Gutenberg saw his invention as a way to produce books—many books—for profit. He was, however, a poor businessman. He stressed quality over quantity, in part because of his reverence for the book he was printing, the Bible. He used the highest-quality paper and ink and turned out far fewer volumes than he otherwise could have.

Other printers, however, quickly saw the true economic potential of Gutenberg's invention. The first Gutenberg Bible appeared in 1456. By the end of that century, 44 years later, printing operations existed in 12 European countries, and the continent was flooded with 20 million volumes of 7,000 titles in 35,000 different editions (Drucker, 1999).

The Impact of Print Although Gutenberg developed his printing press with a limited use in mind, printing Bibles, the cultural effects of mass printing have been profound.

Handwritten or hand-copied materials were expensive to produce, and the cost of an education, in time and money, had made reading an expensive luxury. However, with the spread of printing, written communication was available to a much larger portion of the population, and the need for literacy among the lower and middle classes grew. The ability to read became less of a luxury and more of a necessity; eventually literacy spread, as did education. Soldiers at the front needed to be able to read the emperor's orders. Butchers needed to understand the king's shopping list. So the demand for literacy expanded, and more (and more types of) people learned to read.

Tradespeople, soldiers, clergy, bakers, and musicians all now had business at the printer's shop. They talked. They learned of things, both in conversation and by reading printed material. As more people learned to read, new ideas germinated and spread and cross-pollination of ideas occurred.

More material from various sources was published, and people were freer to read what they wanted when they wanted. Dominant authorities—the Crown and the Church—were now less able to control communication and, therefore, the people. New ideas about the world appeared; new understandings of the existing world flourished.

In addition, duplication permitted standardization and preservation. Myth and superstition began to make way for standard, verifiable bodies of knowledge. History, economics, physics, and chemistry all became part of the culture's intellectual life. Literate cultures were now on the road to modernization.

Printed materials were the first mass-produced product, speeding the development and entrenchment of capitalism. We live today in a world built on these changes. Use of the printing press helped fuel the establishment and growth of a large middle class. No longer were societies composed of rulers and subjects; printing sped the rise of democracy. No longer were power and wealth functions of birth. Power and wealth could now be created by the industrious. No longer was political discourse limited to accepting the dictates of Crown and Church. Printing had given ordinary people a powerful voice.

THE INDUSTRIAL REVOLUTION

More on the Industrial Revolution
www.fordham.edu/halsall/mod/modsbook14.html

By the mid-18th century the printing press had become one of the engines driving the Industrial Revolution. Print was responsible for building and disseminating bodies of knowledge, leading to scientific and technological developments and the refinement of new machines. In addition, industrialization reduced the time necessary to complete work, and this created something heretofore unknown to most working people—leisure time.

Industrialization had another effect as well. As workers left their sunrise-to-sunset jobs in agriculture, the crafts, and trades to work in the newly industrialized factories, not only did they have more leisure time but they had more money to spend on their leisure. Farmers, fishermen, and tile makers had to put their profits back into their jobs. But factory workers took their money home; it was spendable. Combine leisure time and expendable cash with the spread of literacy and the result is a large and growing audience for printed *information* and *entertainment*. By the mid-19th century a mass audience and the means to reach it existed.

Media Literacy

Center for Media Literacy
www.medialit.org/

For more information on this topic, see Media Talk video clip #14, "Debating the Effects of TV Violence," on the *Media World* DVD.

Television influences our culture in innumerable ways. One of its effects, according to many people, is that it has encouraged violence in our society. For example, American television viewers overwhelmingly say there is too much violence on television. Yet, almost without exception, the local television news program that has the largest proportion of violence in its nightly newscast is the ratings leader. "If it bleeds, it leads" has become the motto for much of local television news. It leads because people watch.

So, although many of us are quick to condemn improper media performance or to identify and lament its harmful effects, we rarely question our own role in the mass communication process. We overlook it because we participate in mass communication naturally, almost without conscious effort. We possess high-level interpretive and comprehension skills that make even the most sophisticated television show, movie, or magazine story understandable and enjoyable. We are able, through a lifetime of interaction with the media, to *read media texts*.

Media literacy is a skill we take for granted, but like all skills, it can be improved. And if we consider how important the mass media are in creating and maintaining the culture that helps define us and our lives, it is a skill that *must* be improved.

Hunter College media professor Stuart Ewen emphasized this point in comparing media literacy with traditional literacy. "Historically," he wrote, "links between literacy and democracy are inseparable from the notion of an informed populace, conversant with the issues that touch upon their lives, enabled with tools that allow them to participate actively in public deliberation and social change. . . . Literacy was about crossing the lines that had historically separated men of ideas from ordinary people, about the enfranchisement of those who had been excluded from the compensations of citizenship" (2000, p. 448). To Ewen, and others committed to media literacy, media literacy represents no less than the means to full participation in the culture.

ELEMENTS OF MEDIA LITERACY

Media scholar Art Silverblatt (2001) identifies seven fundamental elements of media literacy. To these we will add an eighth. Media literacy includes these characteristics:

1. *A critical thinking skill enabling audience members to develop independent judgments about media content.* Thinking critically about the content we consume is the very essence of media literacy. Why do we watch what we watch, read what we read, listen to what we listen to? If we cannot answer these questions, we have taken no responsibility for ourselves or our choices. As such, we have taken no responsibility for the outcome of those choices.

2. *An understanding of the process of mass communication.* If we know the components of the mass communication process and how they relate to one another, we can form expectations of how they can serve us. How do the various media industries operate? What are their obligations to us? What are the obligations of the audience? How do different media limit or enhance messages? Which forms of feedback are most effective, and why?

3. *An awareness of the impact of media on the individual and society.* Writing and the printing press helped change the world and the people in it. Mass media do the same. If we ignore the impact of media on our lives, we run the risk of being caught up and carried along by that change rather than controlling or leading it.

4. *Strategies for analyzing and discussing media messages.* To consume media messages thoughtfully, we need a foundation on which to base thought and reflection. If *we* make meaning, we must possess the tools with which to make it (for example, understanding the intent and impact of film and video conventions, such as camera angles and lighting, or the strategy behind the placement of photos on a newspaper page). Otherwise, meaning is made for us; the interpretation of media content will then rest with its creator, not with us.

5. *An understanding of media content as a text that provides insight into our culture and our lives.* How do we know a culture and its people, attitudes, values, concerns, and myths? We know them through communication. For modern cultures like ours, media messages increasingly dominate that communication, shaping our understanding of and insight into our culture.

Media Education Foundation
www.mediaed.org

For more information on this topic, see Media Talk video clip #8, "Author James Steyer Discusses His Book *The Other Parent,*" on the *Media World* DVD.

Media Awareness Network
www.media-awareness.ca/
english/index.cem

The Family Guy is a cartoon about a typical suburban family. It has all the things you would expect from a television situation comedy—an inept dad, a precocious daughter, a slacker son, a solid wife, and zany situations. Yet it also offers an intellectual dog philosopher and a genius, scheming baby. Why do you think the producers have gone to the trouble to populate this show with the usual trappings of a sitcom but then added other, bizarre elements? And what's going on in *V for Vendetta*? Is it another special effects–laden summer action–adventure blockbuster? A classic detective story? A meditation on the justifiable use of violence and terrorism? A commentary on the issues of the day? Or maybe just a cool way to spend a Saturday night, entertained by the same folks who created *The Matrix* and *The Lord of the Rings*?

6. *The ability to enjoy, understand, and appreciate media content.* Media literacy does not mean living the life of a grump, liking nothing in the media, or always being suspicious of harmful effects and cultural degradation. We take high school and college classes to enhance our understanding and appreciation of novels; we can do the same for media texts.

Learning to enjoy, understand, and appreciate media content includes the ability to use **multiple points of access**—to approach media content from a variety of directions and derive from it many levels of meaning. Thus, we control meaning making for our own enjoyment or appreciation. For example, we can enjoy the 2006 fan and critic favorite *V for Vendetta* as an interesting, special effects–laden, action–adventure, summer blockbuster. But as movie-buffs we might see it as a classic detective story (Chief Inspector Finch is always hot on V's tail). Or we might read it as a meditation on the justifiable use of violence and terrorism (V seeks to bring down a totalitarian regime), a cinematic dissertation on revenge (the hero was badly disfigured by government biological experiments and Evey's parents were killed for speaking out against the government), or a commentary on the issues of the day—people's willingness to exchange freedom for security, the use of the mass media to frighten the public into compliance. Or maybe we enjoy it as a cool way to spend a Saturday night, entertained by the same folks who so delighted us with *The Matrix* and *The Lord of the Rings*.

In fact, television programs such as *Desperate Housewives, The Daily Show, The Simpsons, Malcolm in the Middle,* and *The Family Guy* are specifically constructed to take advantage of the media literacy skills of sophisticated viewers while providing entertaining fare for less skilled consumers. The same is true for films such as *Kill Bill, Sin City, Jarhead,* and *Crash,* magazines such as *Mondo 2000,* and the best of jazz, rap, and rock. *Desperate Housewives* and *The Daily Show* are produced as television comedies, designed to make people laugh. But they are also intentionally produced to provide more sophisticated, media literate viewers with opportunities to make personally interesting or relevant meaning. Anyone can laugh while watching these programs, but some people can investigate hypocrisy in suburbia (*Housewives*), or they can examine the failings and foibles of contemporary journalism (*Daily Show*).

7. *Development of effective and responsible production skills.* Traditional literacy assumes that people who can read can also write. Media literacy also makes this assumption. Our definition of literacy (of either type) calls not only for effective and efficient comprehension of content but for its effective and efficient *use.* Therefore, media literate individuals should develop production skills that enable them to create useful media messages. If you have ever tried to make a narrative home video—one that tells a story— you know that producing content is much more difficult than consuming it. Even producing an answering machine message that is not embarrassing is a daunting task for many people.

This element of media literacy may seem relatively unimportant at first glance. After all, if you choose a career in media production, you will get training in school and on the job. If you choose another calling, you may never be in the position of having to produce content. But most professions now employ some form of media to disseminate information: for use in training, to enhance presentations, or to keep in contact with

Media Literacy ClearingHouse
www.medialit.med.sc.edu

Alliance for a Media Literate America
www.amlainfo.org

Media Education
www.mediaeducation.com

clients and customers. The Internet and the World Wide Web, in particular, require effective production skills of their users—at home, school, and work—because online receivers can and do easily become online creators.

8. *An understanding of the ethical and moral obligations of media practitioners.* To make informed judgments about the performance of the media, we also must be aware of the competing pressures on practitioners as they do their jobs. We must understand the media's official and unofficial rules of operation. In other words, we must know, respectively, their legal and ethical obligations. Return, for a moment, to the question of televised violence. It is legal for a station to air graphic violence. But is it ethical? If it is unethical, what power, if any, do we have to demand its removal from our screens? Dilemmas such as this are discussed at length in Chapter 14.

MEDIA LITERACY SKILLS

Consuming media content is simple. Push a button and you have television pictures or music on a radio. Come up with enough cash and you can see a movie or buy a magazine. Media literate consumption, however, requires a number of specific skills:

1. *The ability and willingness to make an effort to understand content, to pay attention, and to filter out noise.* As we saw earlier, anything that interferes with successful communication is called noise, and much of the noise in the mass communication process results from our own consumption behavior. When we watch television, often we are also doing other things, such as eating, reading, or chatting on the phone. We drive while we listen to the radio. Obviously, the quality of our meaning making is related to the effort we give it.

2. *An understanding of and respect for the power of media messages.* The mass media have been around for more than a century and a half. Just about everybody can enjoy them. Their content is either free or relatively inexpensive. Much of the content is banal and a bit silly, so it is easy to dismiss media content as beneath serious consideration or too simple to have any influence.

We also disregard media's power through the **third-person effect**—the common attitude that others are influenced by media messages but that we are not. That is, we are media literate enough to understand the influence of mass communication on the attitudes, behaviors, and values of others but not self-aware or honest enough to see its influence on our lives.

3. *The ability to distinguish emotional from reasoned reactions when responding to content and to act accordingly.* Media content is often

Association for Media Literacy
www.aml.ca

The third-person effect makes it easy to dismiss media's influence on ourselves . . . only those other folks are affected! Media literate people know that not only is this not the case, but even if it were, we all live in a world where people are influenced by mass communication. © David Horsey, Seattle Post-Intelligencer. Used by permission.

designed to touch us at the emotional level. We enjoy losing ourselves in a good song or in a well-crafted movie or television show; this is among our great pleasures. But because we react emotionally to these messages does not mean they don't have serious meanings and implications for our lives. Television pictures, for example, are intentionally shot and broadcast for their emotional impact. Reacting emotionally is appropriate and proper. But then what? What do these pictures tell us about the larger issue at hand? We can use our feelings as a point of departure for meaning making. We can ask, "Why does this content make me feel this way?"

4. *Development of heightened expectations of media content.* We all use media to tune out, waste a little time, and provide background noise. When we decide to watch television, we are more likely to turn on the set and flip channels until we find something passable than we are to read the listings to find a specific program to view. When we are at the video store, we often settle for anything because "It's just a rental." When we expect little from the content before us, we tend to give meaning making little effort and attention.

WWW
Media Alliance
www.media-alliance.org

5. *A knowledge of genre conventions and the ability to recognize when they are being mixed.* The term **genre** refers to the categories of expression within the different media, such as the "evening news," "documentary," "horror movie," or "entertainment magazine." Each genre is characterized by certain distinctive, standardized style elements—the **conventions** of that genre. The conventions of the evening news, for example, include a short, upbeat introductory theme and one or two good-looking people sitting at a space-age desk. When we hear and see these style elements, we expect the evening news. We can tell a documentary film from an entertainment movie by its more serious tone and the number of talking heads. We know by their appearance—the use of color and the amount of text on the cover—which magazines offer serious reading and which provide entertainment.

Knowledge of these conventions is important because they cue or direct our meaning making. For example, we know to accept the details in a documentary film about the sinking of the *Titanic* as more credible than those found in a Hollywood movie about that disaster.

This skill is also important for another reason. Sometimes, in an effort to maximize audiences (and therefore profits) or for creative reasons, media content makers mix genre conventions. Are Oliver Stone's *Nixon* and *JFK* fact or fiction? Is Geraldo Rivera a journalist, a talk show host, or a showman? Is *Bratz* a kid's cartoon or a 30-minute commercial? *Extra!* and *E! News* look increasingly like *Dateline NBC* and the *CBS Evening News.* Reading media texts becomes more difficult as formats are co-opted.

6. *The ability to think critically about media messages, no matter how credible their sources.* It is crucial that media be credible in a democracy in which the people govern because the media are central to the governing process. This is why the news media are sometimes referred to as the fourth branch of government, complementing the executive, judicial, and legislative branches. This does not mean, however, that we should believe everything they report. But it is often difficult to arrive at the proper balance between wanting to believe and accepting what we see and hear unquestioningly, especially when frequently we are willing to suspend disbelief and are encouraged by the media themselves to see their content as real and credible.

Living a Media Literate Life

It is one thing to understand the importance of being a media literate individual, of knowing its fundamental elements and necessary skills. It is quite another to live a media literate life. This is not as difficult as it may seem at first. For one thing, we live lives that are virtually awash in media and their messages, so the opportunities to practice media literacy are always there. But we can (and should) do more. We can live a media literate life *and* make media literacy a living enterprise. We can encourage media literacy and even teach others its value.

The margins of this text are replete with URLs that connect us to educational, professional, scholarly, public interest, governmental, and industry groups that, either directly or indirectly, contribute to our ability to be media literate. This chapter alone offers links to a dozen sites specifically devoted to advancing the cause of media literacy. In addition, every state in the Union maintains standards for teaching media literacy in their schools (Tugend, 2003). Montana and Massachusetts are notable examples. Get a copy of the standards used where you live. Read them and, if need be, challenge them.

Look, too, at the media literacy efforts in other countries. Media literacy is a mandatory part of the school curriculum in Canada, Great Britain, and Australia. The Bertelsmann Foundation has long sponsored media education programs in Germany (and recently in the United States). The British Film Institute and CLEMI in France underwrite similar efforts in their respective countries. The Australian Teachers of Media encourage media education in Australia, New Zealand, and Southeast Asia.

The American media industry, too, is committing itself to the effort. Many contemporary television programs, such as public broadcasting's adolescent reading show *Wishbone*, regularly close with a behind-the-scenes, how-did-we-produce-that-shot feature in an attempt to teach television "readers" the "grammar" of video narrative. The cable network Court TV runs a classroom-style program called *Choices and Consequences* designed to help students read the difference between negative and positive media images. Cable network Odyssey runs a public service campaign featuring "Spokesfrog" Kermit aimed at instructing parents how to pass media literacy skills on to their children. The Discovery Channel offers *Assignment: Media Literacy*, separate kits for elementary, middle, and high school students designed to impart critical viewing skills for all electronic media. The cable industry, in conjunction with the national PTA, sponsors an annual nationwide media literacy event called *Take Charge of Your TV Week*, typically in October. Almost every newspaper of any size

> WE CAN LIVE A MEDIA LITERATE LIFE AND MAKE MEDIA LITERACY A LIVING ENTERPRISE. WE CAN ENCOURAGE MEDIA LITERACY AND EVEN TEACH OTHERS ITS VALUE.

in America now produces a weekly "young person's section" to encourage boys and girls to read the paper and differentiate it from the other news media. Even controversial in-school news/advertising network Channel One (see Chapter 12) offers a media literacy course to schools free of charge.

Again, there is no shortage of ways to improve your media literacy and to advance that of others. This text will help you get started. Each chapter ends with two sections. The first, *Developing Media Literacy Skills*, focuses on improving our personal media literacy. The second, *Living Media Literacy*, offers suggestions for using our media literacy skills in the larger culture—making media literacy a living enterprise.

The PBS young people's reading show Wishbone *always closes with an explanation of how some part of the program was technically produced.*

Consider the *New York Times* motto, "All the News That's Fit to Print," and the title "Eyewitness News." If it is all there, it must all be real, and who is more credible than an eyewitness? But if we examine these media, we would learn that the *Times* in actuality prints all the news that fits (in its pages) and that the news is, at best, a very selective eyewitness.

7. *A knowledge of the internal language of various media and the ability to understand its effects, no matter how complex.* Just as each media genre has its own distinctive style and conventions, each medium also has its own specific internal language. This language is expressed in **production values**—the choice of lighting, editing, special effects, music, camera angle, location on the page, and size and placement of headline. To be able to read a media text, you must understand its language. We learn the grammar of this language automatically from childhood—for example, we know that when the television image goes "all woosie-like," the character is dreaming.

This television show offers all the conventions we'd expect from the news—background digital graphics, an anchor behind his desk, a well-known newsmaker as interviewee. But it also contains conventions we'd expect from a comedy program—a satirist as host and an unruly, loud audience. Why does *The Daily Show* mix the conventions of these two very different genres? Does your knowledge of those conventions add to your enjoyment of this hit cable program?

Let's consider two versions of the same movie scene. In the first, a man is driving a car. Cut to a woman lying tied up on a railroad track. What is the relationship between the man and the woman? Where is he going? With no more information than these two shots, you know automatically that he cares for her and is on his way to save her. Now, here is the second version. The man is driving the car. Fade to black. Fade back up to the woman on the tracks. Now what is the relationship between the man and the woman? Where is he going? It is less clear that these two people even have anything to do with each other. We construct completely different meanings from exactly the same two pictures because the punctuation (the quick cut/fade) differs.

Media texts tend to be more complicated than these two scenes. The better we can handle their grammar, the more we can understand and appreciate texts. The more we understand texts, the more we can be equal partners with media professionals in meaning making.

RESOURCES FOR REVIEW AND DISCUSSION

Review Points

- Communication is the process of creating shared meaning.
- Culture is the world made meaningful. It resides all around us; it is socially constructed and maintained through communication. It limits as well as liberates us; it differentiates as well as unites us. It defines

our realities and shapes the ways we think, feel, and act.

- Mass media are our culture's dominant storytellers and the forum in which we debate cultural meaning.
- Technological determinism argues that technology is the predominant agent of social and cultural change.

But it is not technology that drives culture; it is *how people use* technology.

- With technology, money, too, shapes mass communication. Audiences can be either the consumer or the product in our mass media system.
- As oral, preliterate, cultures gave way to literate cultures, literacy became the avenue to power and control over one's life.
- Media literacy, the ability to effectively and efficiently comprehend and use any form of mediated communication, consists of several components:
  a. critical thinking skills enabling the development of independent judgments about media content
  b. an understanding of the process of mass communication
  c. an awareness of the impact of the media on individuals and society
  d. strategies for analyzing and discussing media messages
  e. an awareness of media content as a "text" providing insight into contemporary culture

  f. a cultivation of enhanced enjoyment, understanding, and appreciation of media content
  g. the development of effective and responsible production skills
  h. the development of an understanding of the ethical and moral obligations of media practitioners
- Media literacy skills include
  a. the ability and willingness to make an effort to understand content, to pay attention, and to filter out noise
  b. an understanding of and respect for the power of media messages
  c. the ability to distinguish emotional from reasoned reactions when responding to content and to act accordingly
  d. the development of heightened expectations of media content
  e. a knowledge of genre conventions and the recognition of their mixing
  f. the ability to think critically about media messages
  g. a knowledge of the internal language of various media and the ability to understand its effects

Key Terms

 Use the text's Online Learning Center at www.mhhe.com/baran5 to further your understanding of the following terminology.

communication, 4
feedback, 5
interpersonal communication, 5
encoding, 5
decoding, 5
noise, 6
medium (pl. media), 6
mass medium, 6
mass communication, 6
inferential feedback, 7

cultural definition of
   communication, 9
culture, 9
dominant culture (mainstream
   culture), 12
bounded culture (co-culture), 13
technological determinism, 18
media literacy, 20
literate culture, 21
oral (preliterate) culture, 21

griots, 21
ideogrammatic alphabet, 21
syllable alphabet, 22
papyrus, 22
parchment, 22
literacy, 23
multiple points of access, 29
third-person effect, 30
genre, 31
conventions, 31
production values, 33

Questions for Review

 Go to the self-quizzes on the Online Learning Center to test your knowledge.

1. What is culture? How does culture define people?
2. What is communication? What is mass communication?
3. What are encoding and decoding? How do they differ when technology enters the communication process?
4. What does it mean to say that communication is a reciprocal process?
5. What is James Carey's cultural definition of communication? How does it differ from other definitions of that process?
6. What do we mean by mass media as cultural storyteller?

7. What do we mean by mass communication as cultural forum?
8. Characterize the communication and organizational styles of preliterate cultures. Where does power reside in these cultures?
9. What social, cultural, and economic factors boosted the development and spread of writing?
10. How did literacy change communication and the organization of preliterate cultures? Characterize the newly literate cultures.
11. How did the printing press make possible mass communication?

12. What was the impact of printing on the culture of western Europe?
13. What was the role of the Industrial Revolution in furthering literacy? The development of the middle class? Democracy?
14. What is media literacy? What are its components?
15. What is meant by multiple points of access? What does it have to do with media literacy?
16. What are some specific media literacy skills?
17. What is the difference between genres and production conventions? What do these have to do with media literacy?

Questions for Critical Thinking and Discussion

1. Do you feel inhibited by your bounded culture? By the dominant culture? How so?
2. Have the events of September 11, 2001, caused you to look at your own culture differently? Amid all the flags and patriotism, are we, as Americans, undergoing a reassessment of the meaning of "American culture"? If so, can you predict the outcome of this reassessment? In addition, what did you know of "Muslim culture" before that fateful day? Where did that knowledge come from? Now that there is more information about that culture available, how different is your understanding of it?
3. Who were your childhood heroes and heroines? Why did you choose them? What cultural lessons did you learn from them?
4. Critique the definition of culture given in this chapter. What would you personally add? Subtract?
5. Consider the changes brought about by the shift from oral to literate cultures. How similar or different do you think the changes will be as we move to a more fully computer literate culture?
6. The Gutenberg printing press had just the opposite effect from what was intended. What optimistic predictions for the cultural impact of the Internet and the World Wide Web do you think will prove as inaccurate as Gutenberg's hopes for his innovation? What optimistic predictions do you think will be realized? Defend your answers.
7. How media literate do you think you are? What about those around you—your parents, for example, or your best friend? What are your weaknesses as a media literate person?
8. Can you take a piece of media content from your own experience and explain how you approach it from multiple points of access?
9. How do you choose which television programs you watch? How thoughtful are your choices? How do you choose videos? Movies? How thoughtful are you in choosing them?

Important Resources

 Go to the Online Learning Center for additional readings.

Internet Resources

More on McLuhan	www.mcluhan.ca/
TV Critics Assn.	www.tvcritics.org/
More on Spielberg	www.filmmakers.com/artists/spielberg
More on Storytelling	www.storynet.org
Project Gutenberg	www.promo.net/pg/
More on the Industrial Revolution	www.fordham.edu/halsall/mod/modsbook14.html
Center for Media Literacy	www.medialit.org
Media Awareness Network	www.media-awareness.ca/english/index.cem
Media Education Foundation	www.mediaed.org
Media Literacy ClearingHouse	www.medialit.med.sc.edu
Alliance for a Media Literate America	www.amlainfo.org
Media Education	www.mediaeducation.com
Association for Media Literacy	www.aml.ca
Media Alliance	www.media-alliance.org

The Evolving Mass Communication Process

LEARNING OBJECTIVES

The mass media system we have today has existed more or less as we know it ever since the 1830s. It is a system that has weathered repeated significant change with the coming of increasingly sophisticated technologies— the penny press newspaper was soon followed by mass market books and mass circulation magazines. As the 1800s became the 1900s, these popular media were joined by motion pictures, radio, and sound recording. A few decades later came television, combining news and entertainment, moving images and sound, all in the home and all, ostensibly, for free. The traditional media found new functions and prospered side by side with television. Then, more recently, came the Internet and World Wide Web. Now, because of the Net's impact, all the media industries are facing profound alterations in how they are structured and do business, the nature of their content, and how they interact with and respond to their audiences. Naturally, as these changes unfold, so too will the very nature of mass communication and our role in that process. After studying this chapter you should

- have a broad overview of current trends in mass media, especially concentration of ownership and conglomeration, globalization, audience fragmentation, hypercommercialization, and convergence.

- recognize how these trends promise to alter the content of the different media, their economics, and their industrial structures.

- be able to make reasoned predictions about the future of the media industries and technologies on which they rely.

- develop a sense of how the mass communication process itself will evolve as the role of the audience in this new media environment is altered.

The offer comes in the mail, addressed to you by name. Even the letter and coupons inside address you personally. You are a trendsetter, an early adopter. Of course you'll want to get the latest, hippest new video technology. You read on, curious and excited. Cable movie channel Starz is offering you its Starz! Ticket video service. For a

For $1.99 you can watch *Lost* on your iPod video player. But do you want to?

mere $12.99 a month you can have "unlimited Starz movie downloads" to your computer or handheld device. Cool, you think. For only about $160 a year you can have the very same movies you already pay for from your Starz cable provider (for somewhere near $85 a month—more than $1,000 a year), and you can watch them on your computer or on a 2-inch-by-3-inch cell phone screen. You wonder how *The Lord of the Rings* trilogy, or the *Star Wars* series, or the *Chronicle of Narnia* will look all shrunk down. But surely there are other pieces of Starz content available to you as a hip, premium Starz! Ticket downloader. You scour the beautifully prepared fliers that came with the offer. Nope, if you can get it on Starz, you can pay extra to get it on Starz! Ticket. Maybe you have to think about this one a bit, even if you are a trendsetter, an early adopter. Maybe Apple's video iPod package would be better. You can get hit ABC television series like *Lost* and *Desperate Housewives* for only $1.99 a download. Still the little screen problem, but the price seems right . . . until a month's worth of viewing shows up on your credit card bill. A lot of $1.99s can add up pretty quickly. You really need to think this through a bit. Anyway, it's 9:00 p.m., *American Idol*'s on. Time to grab a snack and watch the fun.

In this chapter we examine much more than downloadable television shows and video iPods. There is a seismic shift going on in the mass media—and therefore in mass communication—that dwarfs the changes to the media landscape wrought by television's assault in the 1950s and 1960s on the preeminence of radio and the movies. Encouraged by the Internet and digitization, new producers are finding new ways to deliver new content to new audiences. The media industries are in turmoil, and audience members, as they are confronted by a seemingly bewildering array of possibilities, are just now starting to come to terms with the new media future. Will you pay for movie downloads? How much? What will you pay for on-demand television programs? Will you be willing to view the commercials they contain if you could pay a bit less per show? Would you pay more or less for classic programming than for contemporary shows? Would you be willing to watch a movie or television show on a small screen? As *Advertising Age* editor Scott Donaton cautions, "A cell phone isn't a TV" (2006, p. 18).

Is the simultaneous release of *Bubble* on multiple platforms a one-time experiment or a sign of significant change in the way we interact with mass media?

But the future is here, laments NBC Universal CEO Bob Wright, "You can't fight technology. This [digital] technology is real. I don't think we really have a choice here" (in Lieberman, 2005, p. 1). NBC Television's Jeff Zucker offered his response to the upcoming upheaval, "The overall strategy is to make all our content available everywhere" (in Bing, 2006, p. 1). But will this strategy work? And remember, we're talking about *all* media. How will you listen to the radio—satellite radio or terrestrial radio or digital terrestrial radio or streamed Web radio? And what do you think of director Steven Soderbergh's decision to *simultaneously* release his 2006 film *Bubble* to movie houses, DVD, and cable television? On which **platform** (the means of delivering a specific piece of media content) would you most enjoy the film? Can you still call it a film? Would you be willing to pay more or less for the different platforms? These are precisely the kinds of questions that audiences will be answering in the next several years. Media literate audiences will be better equipped to do so.

Industries in Turmoil

Warner Brothers Entertainment's chief operating officer, Alan Horn, told *Variety,* "We are at a crossroads in entertainment today, and it's too soon to know which routes into the future are the decisive paths" (in Bing, 2006, p. 38). This is the reality he and other media executives are facing:

- Movie box office attendance dropped 7% from 2004 to 2005 (Bowles, 2006). In 2002, 1.63 billion tickets were sold; in 2005, that number had dropped 14% to 1.3 billion (Bing, 2006).

- Sales of music CDs dropped nearly 8% from 2004 to 2005 (Bart, 2006). Sales of all album music, including digital downloads, dropped from 785 million units in 2000 to fewer than 602 million in 2005 (Bing, 2006).

- In 2000, the major broadcast networks commanded 63% of all television viewing. In 2005, their share had dropped to 55% (Bing, 2006).

- After years of explosive growth, sales of DVDs have leveled off. For example, between 2003 and 2004, sales rose 15%. From 2004 to 2005, however, the increase was only 2.5% (Snyder, 2006).

- In 2005, video-game sales not only dropped 8% from the previous year's level but failed to show an annual increase for the first time in their existence (Fritz, 2006).

- Between 1998 and 2005, daily newspaper readership fell from 58.6% to 51% of all adults, according to the Newspaper Association of America. For 18- to 24-year-olds, the drop was from 43.5% to 38.4%; for 25- to 34-year-olds, the fall-off was even more precipitous, 45.9% to 36.8% (Kanter, 2006).

- Not only has listenership to commercial radio been flat for the last decade, with small but mounting losses in the number of young people 14 to 21 who tune in, but the industry has come under attack from advertisers who charge that radio overestimates the size of its audience as well as its effectiveness as a marketing medium (Klaassen, 2005a).

To weather the upheaval of restructuring and redefining the modern media industries, CBS reinvented itself in 2006 as an entertainment, rather than a broadcasting, corporation

Announcing a brand-new content-rich broadcasting, narrowcasting, webcasting, publishing, production, syndication, interactive, out-of-home, away-from-home, in-home, world-class entertainment corporation.

The Good News for Media Industries

Indeed, what this turmoil indicates is that the challenge facing the media industries today is how to capture a mass audience now fragmented into millions of niches. What has come about, according to *Variety's* Jonathan Bing, "is an unfamiliar new entertainment landscape, one in which the old rules of media consumption no longer apply" (2006, pp. 1, 38). The "rules" of media consumption may have changed, but media consumption is at an all-time high.

As we saw in Chapter 1, children 8 to 18 years old spend more than 8 hours and 33 minutes a day with media content, up by more than an hour from only 5 years ago. They amass such large amounts of consumption because they are adept at **media multitasking,** simultaneously consuming many different kinds of media (Rideout, Roberts, & Foehr, 2005). The average American adult spends 9 hours and 35 minutes a day, or 60% of his or her waking time, consuming all forms of media content (Lindsay, 2006). The Ball State University Middletown Studies report on media consumption puts the amount of media use even higher—30% of people's waking hours are spent using media "exclusively," and another 39% of their waking time is spent using media in combination with other activities such as making

www

More on Kids' Media Consumption
www.kaisernetwork.org

dinner (Lamb, 2005). Nielsen Media Research (2006) reports that Americans spent record amounts of time in front of the set during the 2004–2005 television season, 8 hours and 11 minutes of television per day, a 2.7% increase from 2003–2004 and the largest amount since television ratings began in 1949. For media industries, these data offer good news—readers, viewers, and listeners are out there in ever-increasing numbers. These data also offer good news for literate media consumers—their consumption choices will shape the media landscape to come and, inevitably, the mass communication process itself.

Together, media industries and media consumers face a number of challenges. Beyond fragmenting audiences and the impact of new technologies (and the **convergence**—the erosion of traditional distinctions among media—they encourage), they must also deal with three other trends that promise to alter the nature of the media industries as well as the relationship between those industries and the people with whom they interact: concentration of media ownership and conglomeration, rapid globalization, and hypercommercialization.

More on American Media Consumption
www.bsu.edu/cmd

Changes

CONCENTRATION OF OWNERSHIP AND CONGLOMERATION

Ownership of media companies is increasingly concentrated in fewer and fewer hands. Through mergers, acquisitions, buyouts, and hostile takeovers, a very small number of large conglomerates is coming to own more and more of the world's media outlets. Media observer Ben Bagdikian reported that in 1997 the number of media corporations with "dominant power in society" was 10. In 2004 columnist William Safire set the number at just 5: Comcast, Fox, Viacom, GE (NBC-Universal), and Time Warner ("Should Comcast," 2004). Elsewhere, the conservative *New York Times* writer warned, "While political paranoids accuse each other of vast conspiracies, the truth is that media mergers have narrowed the range of information and entertainment available to people of all ideologies" (quoted in Plate, 2003, p. B4). Safire was correct; people of all ideologies feel the impact of **concentration of ownership.** FCC Commissioner and Democrat Jonathan Adelstein argued, "The public has a right to be informed by a diversity of viewpoints so they can make up their own minds. Without a diverse, independent media, citizen access to information crumbles, along with political and social participation. For the sake of democracy, we should encourage the widest possible dissemination of free expression" through our media (quoted in Kennedy, 2004, p. 1). Adelstein was echoing Supreme Court Justice Hugo Black's eloquent defense of a vibrant media in his 1945 *Associated Press v. US* decision: "The First Amendment rests on the assumption that the widest possible dissemination of information from diverse and antagonistic sources is essential to the welfare of the public, that a free press is a condition of a free society." Journalist and social critic Bill Moyers calls this concentration of media ownership "the central issue that faces us as a democratic society" (as quoted in Moore, 1999, p. A11).

More on Concentration
www.cjr.org/owners

Maurice Hinchey, U.S. House of Representatives member from New York, explained this threat to our democratic process:

> Changes in media ownership have been swift and staggering. Over the past two decades the number of major US media companies fell by more than one half; most of the survivors are controlled by fewer than ten huge media conglomerates. As media outlets continue to be gobbled up by these giants, the marketplace of ideas shrinks. New and independent voices are stifled. And the companies that remain are under little obligation to provide reliable, quality journalism. Stories that matter deeply to the country's well-being have been replaced by sensationalized murders and celebrity gossip. (2006, p. 15)

We need look no further than the September 11 terrorist attacks for evidence of this misplacing of priorities, according to media critic Todd Gitlin, who wrote, "The machinery of truth-telling has broken down . . . As murderous Islamism oozed out of Afghanistan and Pakistan, and Osama bin Laden fine-tuned his massacre machine, O. J. beckoned . . . and Whitewater . . . and Princess Diana. In 1998 and 1999, when Al Qaeda was gathering force and bombing embassies, the obsession of America's media was . . . . Monica Lewinsky" (2004, p. 58). You can examine the concentration of media holdings of the world's largest media company, Time Warner, in Figure 2.1.

Closely related to concentration is **conglomeration,** the increase in the ownership of media outlets by larger, nonmedia companies. "The threat is clear," wrote media critic Steven Brill:

> The bigger these conglomerates get, the less important their journalism gets and the more vulnerable that journalism becomes to the conglomerate's other interests. . . . These mega-companies, therefore, present a new, sweeping, and unprecedented threat to free expression, independent journalism, and a vibrant, free marketplace of ideas. Their sheer enormity makes it almost routine that they are covering a subject involving one of their own divisions or some competitor to one of their enterprises. And their involvement in so much other than journalism threatens to water down the values that would assure that they deal with those conflicts honorably. (2000, pp. 26–27)

Veteran newsman Bill Moyers adds, "Media owners have businesses to run, and these media-owning corporations have enormous interests of their own that impinge on an ever-widening swath of public policy—hugely important things, ranging from campaign finance reform (who ends up with those millions of dollars spent on advertising?) to broadcast deregulation and antitrust policy, to virtually everything related to the Internet, intellectual property, globalization and free trade, even to minimum wage, affirmative action, and environmental policy . . . In this era, when its broader and broader economic entanglements make media more dependent on state largess, the news business finds itself at war with journalism" (2004, p. 10).

It may matter little that Mike Barz, a correspondent for Disney-owned ABC Television, breathlessly begins his report from the 2005 opening of a new Disneyland in China this way: "Based on all the smiles on all the faces of the children . . . it looks like the magic of Disney is taking hold in China" (in Solomon, 2005). But are you as comfortable with General Electric's ownership of the NBC television and CNBC cable networks? General Electric is a major defense contractor that did $450 million in business in Iraq in 2003

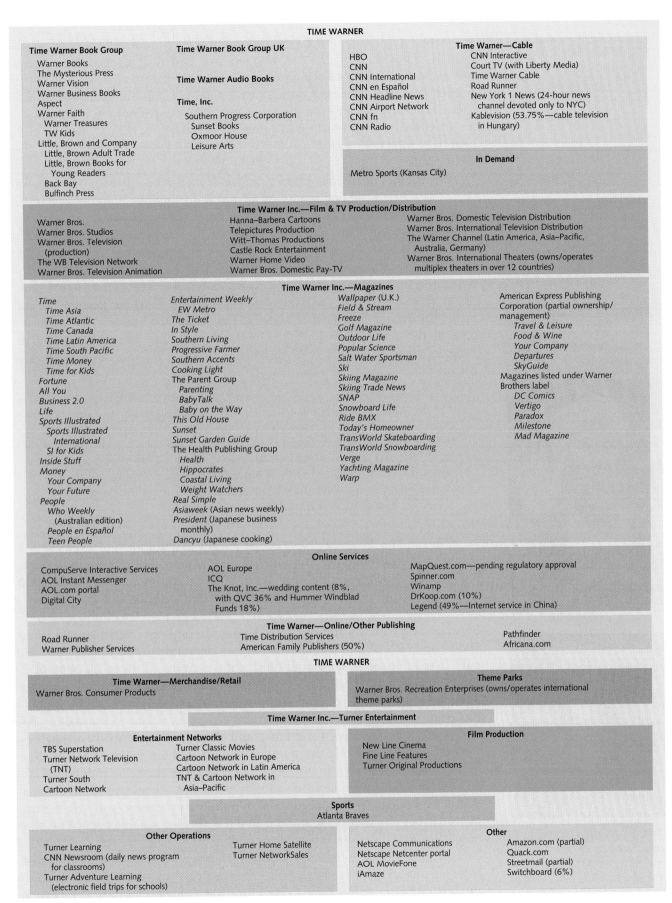

Figure 2.1 Concentration of Ownership: The Example of Time Warner

and had commitments for $3 billion more for the following few years. Additionally, more than one-half of Iraq's power grid is composed of GE technology, and even before the shooting began in 2003, company CEO Jeffrey Immelt told an interviewer on his own CNBC network that war in Iraq was a business opportunity for his company: "We built about a billion-dollar security business [in Iraq] that's going to be growing by 20% a year, so we've been able to play into that" (in Finke, 2004, p. 3). Does this constitute a possible conflict of interest for you?

But conflict of interest is only one presumed problem with conglomeration. The other is the dominance of a bottom-line mentality and its inevitable degradation of media content. *Variety's* Peter Bart explained, "Hence atop every corporation there sits a functionary who is empowered to set a number for every unit of every company. That functionary may in fact have no knowledge whatsoever of the market conditions affecting that entity and no interest in the product it produces. Nonetheless, everyone dances to his tune" (2000, p. 95). Bart was speaking of media in general. As for journalism, former CBS anchor Dan Rather added, "The larger the entities that own and control the news operations, the more distant they become" (quoted in Auletta, 2001, p. 60). New York University law professor Burt Neuborne warned:

> The press has been subsumed into a market psychology, because they are now owned by large conglomerates, of which they are simply a piece. And they (news organizations) are expected to contribute their piece of the profit to the larger pie. You don't have people controlling the press anymore with a fervent sense of responsibility to the First Amendment. Concentrating on who's sleeping with whom, on sensationalism, is concentrating on essentially irrelevant issues. (as quoted in Konner, 1999, p. 6)

Evidence for Professor Neuborne's appraisal abounds. For example, the Project for Excellence in Journalism (2006) found that American newspapers employ 3,500 fewer full-time editorial employees than they did in 2000, a 27% drop; the number of full-time radio news employees dropped 44% between 1994 and 2000; the national television networks have one-third fewer correspondents and one-half the foreign news bureaus they did in the 1980s; and 60% of all local television news operations report budget or staff cuts (although most "commonly hit profit margins of 40 to 50 percent or more") ("Canned News," 2003, p. 9). As for the impact of these cuts on content, the Project for Excellence in Journalism (2004) offered the example of the front pages of the *New York Times, Los Angeles Times,* the ABC, CBS, and NBC nightly news programs, and *Time* and *Newsweek* magazines. Between 1977 and 1997, the number of stories about government in these "elite" media fell from 1 in 3 to 1 in 5. At the same time, the number of stories about celebrities rose from 1 in 50 to 1 in 14. As one major newspaper editor explained, "If you argue about public trust today, you will be dismissed as an obstructionist and a romantic" (Project for Excellence in Journalism, 2006). We have entered an era, according to the critics of concentration and conglomeration, of 24-hour runaway brides, Michael Jackson trials, and celebrity gossip. You can read more about this issue in the box on pages 46–48 titled "Concentration, Conglomeration, and Serving Democracy."

For more information on this topic, see Media Talk video clip #19, "Why Is the United States Viewed So Poorly in the Arab World?" on the *Media World* DVD.

Osama bin Laden and Monica Lewinsky. It's not as if hints of bin Laden's evil weren't there. But who recieved more media attention prior to 9/11? Who should have?

There are, however, less dire observations on concentration and conglomeration. Many telecommunications professionals argue that concentration and conglomeration are not only inevitable but necessary in a telecommunications environment that is increasingly fragmented and internationalized; companies must maximize their number of outlets to reach as much of the divided and far-flung audience as possible. If they do not, they will become financially insecure, and that is an even greater threat to free and effective mediated communication because advertisers and other well-monied forces will have increased influence over them.

Another defense of concentration and conglomeration has to do with **economies of scale;** that is, bigger can in fact sometimes be better because the relative cost of an operation's output declines as the size of that endeavor grows. For example, the cost of collecting the news or producing a television program does not increase significantly when that news report or television program is distributed over 2 outlets, 20 outlets, or 100 outlets. The additional revenues from these other points of distribution can then be plowed back into even better news and programming. In the case of conglomeration, the parallel argument is that revenues from a conglomerate's nonmedia enterprises can be used to support quality work by its media companies.

The potential impact of this **oligopoly**—a concentration of media industries into an ever smaller number of companies—on the mass communication process is enormous. What becomes of shared meaning when the people running communication companies are more committed to the financial demands of their corporate offices than they are to their audiences, who are supposedly their partners in the communication process? What becomes of the process itself when media companies grow more removed from those with whom they communicate? And what becomes of the culture that is dependent on that process when concentration and conglomeration limit the diversity of perspective and information? Or are the critics making too much of the issue? Is Clear Channel (1,200 radio stations) founder Lowry Mays correct when he argues, "We're not in the business of providing news and information. We're simply in the business of selling our customers' products" (quoted in Hightower, 2004a, p. 1)?

GLOBALIZATION

Closely related to the concentration of media ownership is **globalization.** It is primarily large, multinational conglomerates that are doing the lion's share of media acquisitions. The potential impact of globalization on the mass communication process speaks to the issue of diversity of expression. Will distant, anonymous, foreign corporations, each with vast holdings in a variety of nonmedia businesses, use their power to shape news and entertainment content to suit their own ends? Opinion is divided. Some observers feel that this concern is misplaced—the pursuit of profit will force these corporations to respect the values and customs of the nations and cultures in which they operate. Some observers have a less optimistic view, arguing that "respecting" local values and customs is shorthand for pursuing profits at all costs. They point to the recent controversy surrounding the decision of Internet giants Yahoo!, Cisco, Google, and Microsoft to "respect" the local values and customs of the world's second-largest Internet population as well as its fastest growing consumer market—China. Microsoft spokesperson Brooke Richardson explained

More on Media Reform
www.mediareform.net

More on Globalization
www.unescosources.org/

CHAPTER 2   The Evolving Mass Communication Process   **45**

Concentration, Conglomeration, and Serving Democracy

The horrific events of September 11, 2001, put concentration and conglomeration and their effect on news squarely in the public forum. Many observers in and out of the media identified corporate-mandated cost reductions and staff cuts as the primary reason so many Americans were caught off guard. *Philadelphia Inquirer* reporter Thomas Ginsberg explained:

> From the early 1990s until September 11, 2001, the U.S. news media had subtly turned foreign news into a niche subject. By the end of the '90s, with cable TV and the Internet splintering audiences, and media conglomerates demanding news divisions make more money, broadcasters and some publications gradually changed formats to cover more scandal, lifestyle, personalities. There simply were fewer shows and pages where hard news, much less foreign news, could find a home. (2002, p. 50)

"If we had paid more attention to Afghanistan in the '80s we might not have had 9-11," MSNBC reporter Ashleigh Banfield lectured students at Kansas State University (2003, p. 6). "While we can debate whether this failure played a role in our national lack of preparedness, there is no question that we failed our readers," wrote *Manhattan* (Kansas) *Mercury* editor in chief Edward Seaton (quoted in Parks, 2002, pp. 52–53).

The war in Iraq added to the cultural debate. "We failed the American public by being insufficiently critical about elements of the Administration's plan to go to war," said the *New York Times'* John Burns (quoted in Rich, 2004, p. E1). "The credulous press corps, when confronted by an Administration intent on war, sank to new depths of obsequiousness and docility," wrote *The Nation's* Scott Sherman (2004, p. 4). But in this renewed discussion, concentration's critics identified two problems in addition to cost cutting and the reductions in resources.

As in the abandonment of expensive foreign news, the first is also economic—media companies' quest for profits. "Investigative reports share three things: They are risky, they upset the wisdom of the established order, and they are expensive to produce. Do profit-conscious enterprises, whether media companies or widget firms, seek extra costs, extra risk, and the opportunity to be attacked? Not in any business text I've ever read," explained BBC newsman Greg Palast (2003, p. 1). In other words, it was easier, cheaper, and safer to repeat the government's explanations than it was to investigate them. For example, reporter Judith Miller explained her unwillingness to include the views of skeptical intelligence and scientific experts in her numerous government-sourced accounts of Iraq's weapons buildup: "My job isn't to assess the government's information and be an independent intelligence

analyst myself. My job is to tell readers of the *New York Times* what the government thought of Iraq's arsenal" (quoted in Sherman, 2004, pp. 4–5). Rather than "aggressive digging for the dark facts of war," editorialized *Columbia Journalism Review*, the public was left with "passive transmission of the Pentagon line" ("CJR Comment," 2003, p. 7).

The second factor, one critics saw as more corrosive to the relationship between media and democracy, was corporate media shaping the news to serve their own political agendas. Specifically, media companies did not challenge the administration because during the run-up to war and in the year afterward, the government was considering legislation loosening restrictions on media concentration. This "uncritical coverage of the war," this "media conglomerate war cheerleading collusion" occurred, according to Jeffrey Chester, executive editor of AlterNet.org, and Don Hazen, director of the Center for Digital Democracy, as media conglomerates were "heavily lobbying the Bush Administration for giveaways that will net them billions of dollars" (2003, p. 2). Eli Pariser, Campaigns Director for the MoveOn.org Voter Fund, explained that the media, broadcasters specifically, "simply would rather not risk offending powerful people in Washington who decide such critical regulatory matters" as ownership rules (2004, p. 2).

Enter your voice in the cultural forum. Doesn't this seem a bit extreme, media companies shaping news and commentary to fit corporate, rather than journalistic, ends? Placing profit and self-interest over their traditional role of serving the public? Or do you agree with media legal scholar Charles Tillinghast, who wrote, "One need not be a devotee of conspiracy theories to understand that journalists, like other human beings, can judge where their interests lie, and what risks are and are not prudent, given their desire to continue to eat and feed the family" (2000, pp. 145–146)?

But have the media recommitted themselves to the service of democracy? As the press's credulity in the run-up to war became more obvious, especially with the failure to find weapons of mass destruction and an al-Qaeda–Iraq connection, media professionals underwent serious self-examination, as you might have suspected after reading the journalists' comments that opened this Cultural Forum. In addition, the *New York Times* and *Washington Post* offered searing and apologetic critiques of their own prewar reporting. Said *Times* ombudsman Daniel Okrent, "Some of *The Times*'s coverage in the months leading up to the invasion of Iraq was credulous; much of it was inappropriately italicized by lavish front-page display and heavy-breathing-headlines;

> **"THE FIRST AMENDMENT, THE MIRACLE OF OUR SYSTEM, IS NOT JUST A PASSIVE SHIELD OF PROTECTION. IN ORDER TO MAINTAIN OUR TRUE, NATIONALLY DEFINING DIVERSITY, IT OBLIGATES JOURNALISTS TO BE BOLD, WRITERS TO BE FULL-THROATED AND UNINHIBITED, AND THOSE BLUNT INSTRUMENTS OF THE FREE PRESS, CARTOONISTS . . . , NOT TO SELF-CENSOR. WE MUST USE IT OR LOSE IT."**

and several fine articles . . . that provided perspective or challenged information in the faulty stories were played as quietly as a lullaby" (2004, p. 4.2). He later said, a "general rolling-over on the part of the American press allowed the war to happen . . . I think that the press is extremely chastened by it—we all know how bad it was" (In Fact, 2006, p. 8). *Post* media critic Howard Kurtz added that his paper provided "coverage that, despite flashes of groundbreaking reporting, in hindsight looks strikingly one-sided . . . Administration assertions were on the front page. Things that challenged the administration were on A18 on Sunday or A24 on Monday. There was an attitude among editors: Look, we're going to war, why do we even worry about all this contrary stuff?" (2004, p. A1). This reevaluation of their service to democracy at a most crucial time in the nation's history led media critic Todd Gitlin to claim that "never before has American journalism been driven to correct itself so lavishly" (2004, p. 58).

To many in and outside of journalism, that self-correction was short lived. Editorialized industry journal *Broadcasting & Cable,* "After 9/11, we were promised, the news media would toughen up, dig deeper, cover the world for us. What we seem to have gotten was softer coverage and a propensity to pull punches. How odd and dangerous it is that, in these most perilous times, the news business has rarely seemed more frivolous" ("Seriously," 2005, p. 50). The *New Yorker*'s Ken Auletta

uses once-venerable CBS to demonstrate concentration and conglomeration's impact on the coverage of international news: "Today Barry Peterson, a CBS correspondent based primarily in Tokyo, is responsible for covering all of Asia. CBS News usually has nine other correspondents based overseas—five in a hub office in London, three in Tel Aviv, one in Rome. It has no permanent bureau in the Arab or Muslim world, in Africa or South America . . . [I]n the late seventies and early eighties CBS News ran fourteen major foreign bureaus, ten mini foreign bureaus, and **stringers** [freelance reporters] in forty-four countries around the world" (2005c, p. 51).

Again, enter your voice. Media businesses are just that, businesses. They must make a profit. Challenging the powerful carries financial risk. Covering international news, especially in difficult places like Afghanistan and "the Arab or Muslim world," is costly. But what of the argument of the late Senator Paul Wellstone? He wrote, "The media are not just any ordinary industry. They are the lifeblood of American democracy. We depend on the media for the free flow of information that enables citizens to participate in the democratic process. As James Madison wrote in 1822, 'A popular government without popular information, or the means of acquiring it, is but a prologue to a farce or a tragedy, or perhaps both.' That's why freedom of the press is enshrined in our Constitution. No other industry enjoys that kind of protection" (2002, p. 25). In other words, the media

Reports that many TV news programs only feature stories that promote the political views that protect the mega-corporations that own them have been denied & labelled "DISGRACEFUL" and "UNPATRIOTIC" today.

© DAN PIRARO. 8·25·03

BUSH GOOD·BUSH GOOD·

BIZARRO.COM — Dist. By King Features

© Bizarro-Dan Piraro. King Features Syndicate.

WILEY © '04

The DAILY POST NEWS GAZETTE

"SLEEPING SOUNDLY SINCE WATERGATE"®

IF TRUTH IN ADVERTISING WAS STRICTLY ENFORCED...

WILEY@NON-SEQUITUR.COM   DIST. BY UNIVERSAL PRESS SYNDICATE   WWW. ucomics.com

Non-Sequitur © 2004 Wiley Miller. Distributed by Universal Press Syndicate. Reprinted with permission. All rights reserved.

continued

Concentration, Conglomeration, and Serving Democracy *continued*

enjoy special protections because they serve a vital role in the conduct of democracy. Or, especially given the examples here, are these just the complaints of a group of disaffected liberals, opposed to the war in Iraq? But if this is the case, why do prominent conservatives also say that we need to "reclaim the airwaves for our democracy" (Republican Senator John McCain, quoted in Nichols, 2003, p. 5) and that "no other decision [media concentration] made in Washington will more directly affect how you will be informed, persuaded, and entertained" (conservative columnist William Safire, quoted in Franklin, 2003, p. 1)?

Foes of concentration and conglomeration—Left and Right, Democrat and Republican, liberal, moderate, and conservative—subscribe to the philosophy of media and democracy

articulated by Pulitzer Prize–winning editorial cartoonist Doug Marlette:

> One of the great strengths of this nation is our sensitivity to the tyranny of the majority, our sense of justice for all. But the First Amendment, the miracle of our system, is not just a passive shield of protection. In order to maintain our true, nationally defining diversity, it obligates journalists to be bold, writers to be full-throated and uninhibited, and those blunt instruments of the free press, cartoonists like me, not to self-censor. We must use it or lose it. (2003, p. 55)

Where do you stand?

---

her company's position, "Microsoft does business in many countries around the world. While different countries have different standards, Microsoft and other multinational companies have to ensure that our products and services comply with local laws, norms, and industry practices" (in Zeller, 2006, p. 4.4). Google attorney Andrew McLaughlin called it "responding to local conditions" (Bray, 2006, p. A10). But "local conditions" in this case meant censoring searches and keywords and shutting down Web sites on orders from China's Communist leaders. Even more distressing to critics was Yahoo!'s decision to identify one of its customers, dissident Shi Tao, as author of e-mails the Chinese government found subversive. Mr. Shi was arrested and sentenced to 10 years in prison. Would we accept this behavior from any of these companies here in the United States? How much should we accept them elsewhere in the name of "globalization"? Several groups from across the political spectrum called for protests and boycotts against Google and other tech companies that in their view go too far in meeting "local conditions" (Bray, 2006). There is much more on this conflict between localism and globalization in Chapter 15.

Still, defenders of increased globalization point to the need to reach a fragmented and widespread audience—the same factor that fuels concentration—as encouraging this trend. They also cite the growing economic clout of emerging democracies (and the need to reach the people who live in them) and the increasing intertwining of the world's economies as additional reasons globalization is necessary for the economic survival of media businesses.

More on Yahoo! in China
www.booyahoo.blogspot.com

AUDIENCE FRAGMENTATION

More on Improving Media Performance
www.freepress.net

The nature of the other partner in the mass communication process is changing too. The **audience** is becoming more **fragmented,** its segments more narrowly defined. It is becoming less of a mass audience.

Before the advent of television, radio and magazines were national media. Big national radio networks brought news and entertainment to the entire country. Magazines such as *Life, Look,* and the *Saturday Evening Post* once offered limited text and many pictures to a national audience. But television could do these things better. It was radio with pictures; it was magazines with motion. To survive, radio and magazines were forced to find new functions. No longer able to compete on a mass scale, these media targeted smaller audiences that were alike in some important characteristic and therefore more attractive to specific advertisers. So now we have magazines such as *Ski* and *Internet World*, and radio station formats such as Country, Urban, and Lithuanian. This phenomenon is known as **narrowcasting, niche marketing,** or **targeting.**

Technology has wrought the same effect on television. Before the advent of cable television, people could choose from among the three commercial broadcast networks—ABC, CBS, NBC—one noncommercial public broadcasting station, and, in larger markets, maybe an independent station or two. Now, with cable, satellite, and DVD, people have literally thousands of viewing options. The television audience has been fragmented. To attract advertisers, each channel now must find a more specific group of people to make up its viewership. Nickelodeon targets kids, for example; TV Land appeals to baby boomers; Cartoon Network's late-night *Adult Swim* aims at older teens and young adults; and Bravo seeks upper-income older people.

The new digital technologies promise even more audience fragmentation, almost to the point of audiences of one. For example, German magazine *Der Spiegel* and American company IBM have developed a system that permits the printing of individually tailored newspapers for passengers while their train is under way. Bought by credit card, passengers' ticket numbers are used to match passengers to the data profiles the credit card companies have built for them—travel, purchases, hobbies, income, occupation. Then individual newspapers, with very specifically targeted ads, articles, and features, are printed aboard the train and delivered to riders in their seats. On a train carrying 200 people there may well be 200 different versions of the "same" newspaper. Here in the United States, cable companies have the ability to send very specific commercials not only to specific neighborhoods but even to individual sets in individual homes. This technology is sufficiently sophisticated that by analyzing where viewers channel surf, it can determine the age, gender, and interests of those viewers. An airline, for example, might have a "cheap flights to Florida" spot that it wants embedded in a program sent to the home of an older adult, and a "cheap flights to Cancun" spot embedded in the very same show cablecast to a younger person's home (Graves, 2006; Kiley, 2005).

If the nature of the media's audience is changing, then the mass communication process must also change. What will happen as smaller, more specific audiences become better known to their partners in the process of making meaning? What will happen to the national culture that binds us as we become increasingly fragmented into demographically targeted **taste publics**—groups of people bound by little more than an interest in a given form of media content? *Time*'s James Poniewozik offered his vision of our fragmented future: "Through niche media, niche foods, and niche hobbies, we fashion niche lives. We are the America of the iPod ads—stark, black silhouettes tethered by our brilliant white earbuds, rocking out passionately alone. You make your choices, and I make mine. Yours, of course, are wrong. But what do I care?" (2004, p. 84).

Is this our fragmented future, rocking out passionately and alone?

HYPERCOMMERCIALISM

More on Hypercommercialism
www.commercialalert.org/

The costs involved in acquiring numerous or large media outlets, domestic and international, and of reaching an increasingly fragmented audience must be recouped somehow. Selling more advertising on existing and new media and identifying additional ways to combine content and commercials are the two most common strategies. This leads to what media critic Robert McChesney calls **hypercommercialism.** McChesney explained, "Concentrated media control permits the largest media firms to increasingly commercialize their output with less and less fear of consumer reprisal" (1999, pp. 34–35). The rise in the number of commercial minutes in a typical broadcast or cable show is evident to most viewers. *Broadcasting & Cable* reported that in the 10 years from 1993 to 2003, the amount of nonprogram time (commercials and promos) on network evening television increased "an astounding 36%." Viewers now see 17 minutes of commercials per hour, 52 minutes a night, and sit through commercial breaks that average over 3 minutes apiece (McClellan, 2003). Matters have not improved since that report was issued. Television writer Diane Holloway reported in 2005 that commercial breaks in hit shows like *Prison Break* were as long as 5 minutes; *Prison Break* and *CSI* averaged 19 minutes of commercials an hour; and even the 30-minute comedy *Arrested Development* had 11 minutes of ad time in which 24 different products were pitched. She quoted *Boston Legal* creator David E. Kelley, who said he was prepared to leave commercial television altogether. Because of network demands for more time for commercials, he explained, "We're reduced to writing eight-minute acts. It's very difficult storytelling, especially for character scenes. An hour is now 41 minutes, and that's a terrible trim" (Holloway, 2005, p. G9).

The sheer growth in the amount of advertising is one troublesome aspect of hypercommercialism. But for many observers the increased mixing of commercial and noncommercial media content is even more troubling. For example, ABC writes Revlon cosmetics into the story line of its popular soap opera *All My Children.* CBS has Oscar Mayer meats and Lego toys as regulars on *Yes, Dear,* and Nintendo on *King of Queens.* Musical artists, especially rap performers, frequently include brand names in their lyrics in exchange for cash (Kaufman, 2003). So ubiquitous has this **product placement**—the integration, for a fee, of specific branded products into media content—become, that the Writers Guild of America has petitioned the FCC to examine the practice at the same time it has demanded negotiations with television and film producers for additional compensation for writing what are, in effect, commercials (Cohn, 2005). The producers' response is that product placement is not a commercial; rather, it represents a new form of content, **brand entertainment**—when brands are, in fact, part of and essential to the program. Pontiac's Solstice is a "character" in episodes of *The Apprentice,* and the big-hearted workers of *Extreme Makeover—Home Edition* could not wield any tools other than those from Sears. By either name, what was a $98 million business for the television networks in 1999 now generates more than $825 million (Dempsey, 2005). Some radio stations owned by media giant Clear Channel sell naming rights to their news operations. Listeners in Madison, Wisconsin, hear reports from the Amcore Bank News Center. Those in Milwaukee get their news from the PyraMax Bank News Center. At Phoenix's KPHO-TV, Dunkin' Donuts coffee mugs sit on the desks of the morning news set, but the anchors

More on Product Placement
www.Productinvasion.com

The four recurring stars on *American Idol*—Simon Cowell, Paula Abdul, Randy Jackson, and Coke.

don't use them for fear of spoiling the camera shot of the logo (Potter, 2006). Football telecasts on ESPN employ Microsoft's Xbox game system rather than actual video footage to illustrate team play and strategy.

Sometimes hypercommercialism involves direct payments of cash rather than "mere" branding. The *Newark Weekly News* has an annual $100,000 contract to publish only positive stories about the city ("Newark Pays," 2005). Gannett Broadcasting television stations in cities such as Atlanta, Cleveland, and Denver sell entire segments of their morning news and talk shows. For as little as $2,500, sponsors (along with their products or services) can buy not only the exclusive rights to a portion of a show but the assurance that the programs' hosts will conduct interviews with sponsors and demonstrations of their products as part of those segments (Klaassen, 2005b). A poll of 287 journalists in 2000 indicated that 41% censor themselves or otherwise reshape or soften stories rather than produce content that might offend advertisers because they "get signals from their bosses to avoid such stories or ignore them based on how they think their bosses would react" (Kohut, 2000, p. 43). Many radio stations now accept payment from record promoters to play their songs, an activity once illegal and called **payola.** It is now quite acceptable as long as the "sponsorship" is acknowledged on the air.

Again, as with globalization and concentration, where critics see damage to the integrity of the media themselves and disservice to their audiences, defenders of hypercommercialism argue that it is simply the economic reality of today's media world.

EROSION OF DISTINCTIONS AMONG MEDIA: CONVERGENCE

Cable channel Comedy Central produces a six-show lineup exclusively for its Internet channel, *Mother Load*. Movie studios make their titles available not only on DVD but for handheld video-game systems. The Internet's AOL makes thousands of classic television shows (with commercials) available on the Web for free. Fellow Net giants Google, Microsoft, Intel, and Yahoo! sell downloads of classic and current television shows and movies from all the major broadcast and cable channels. Apple sells music videos, cable television

Convergence in action. When you watch CNN on your cell phone, are you watching cable television, surfing wireless Internet, or using the telephone?

WWW

Online Video
www.youtube.com

shows, and movies from studios like Pixar for home computers and its mobile iPod; the price—$1.99. Cable giant Comcast sells computer downloads of current CBS television programs for ninety-nine cents each. Satellite provider DirectTV does the same with shows from broadcasters NBC and Fox and cablecaster FX. ESPN provides sports programming not only to home computers but to Sprint cell phones. Phone company Verizon provides Fox and CBS television programming to its cell phone customers. HBO produces first-run films for its own cable television channel, immediately releasing them on DVD for rental. You can subscribe to *Mountainboarding Magazine* and have it delivered to your home on DVD. There are tens of thousands of U.S. commercial and noncommercial and foreign radio stations delivering their broadcasts over the Web. *Pokémon* is as much a 30-minute TV commercial for licensed merchandise as it is a cartoon.

You can read the *New York Times* or *Time* magazine and hundreds of other newspapers and magazines on your computer screen. Cellular phone maker Life's Good sells a mobile phone that not only allows users to talk to other people but—because it includes a digital camcorder, zoom and rotating lenses, and a digital still camera, complete with flash—allows those same users to "broadcast" their "television programs" and photos. And what do "newspapers, magazines, and books," "radio and recordings," and "television and film" really mean (or more accurately, *really be*) now that people can access printed texts, audio, and moving images virtually anyplace, anytime via **Wi-Fi** (wireless Internet)? This erosion of distinctions among media is called *convergence,* and it is fueled, according to technology attorney Tony Kern, by three elements that have come together "almost simultaneously. First is the digitization of nearly all information, which provides a common means to represent all forms of communication. Second is high-speed connectivity; networks are becoming faster and more pervasive—wired and wireless. And third is a seemingly endless advance in technology in which speed, memory, and power improvements allow a device to do more. That redefines the limits of what is possible" (2005, p. 32). You can examine the likely explosive growth—the endless advance—of the digital platforms that are encouraging convergence in Figure 2.2, and you can make your own predictions of which you might prefer using ideas discussed in the box on p. 54, "The Fraction of Selection."

The traditional lines between media are disappearing. Concentration is one reason. If one company owns newspapers, an online service, television stations, book publishers, a magazine or two, and a film company, it has a strong incentive to get the greatest use from its content, whether news, education, or entertainment, by using as many channels of delivery as possible. The industry calls this **synergy,** and it is the driving force behind several recent mergers and acquisitions in the media and telecommunications industries. In 1997, for example, computer software titan Microsoft paid $1 billion for a 6% interest in cable television operation US West. Microsoft's goal in this and other similar purchases (it already owned part of cable giant Comsat Corporation and, at the time, was negotiating for a one-third stake in TCI Cable) is to make cable and the Internet indistinguishable. Similarly, media giant News Corp. paid well over a billion dollars in 2005 for social networking Web site MySpace.com and video-game maker IGN Entertainment in order to blend its existing broadcast, film, and print media with the

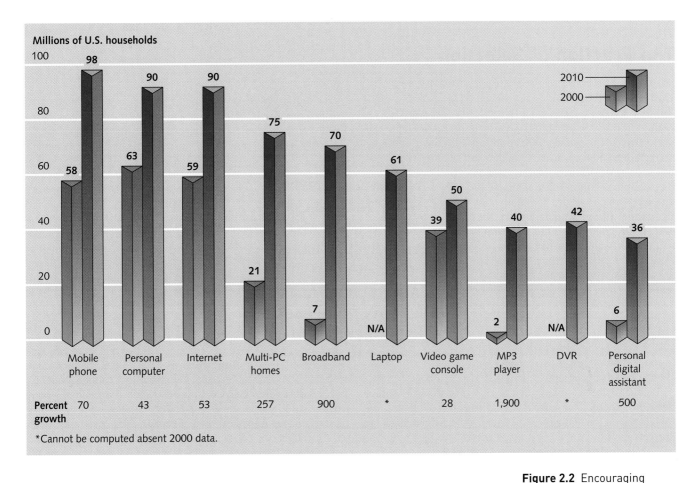

Millions of U.S. households

	Mobile phone	Personal computer	Internet	Multi-PC homes	Broadband	Laptop	Video game console	MP3 player	DVR	Personal digital assistant
2000	58	63	59	21	7	N/A	39	2	N/A	6
2010	98	90	90	75	70	61	50	40	42	36
Percent growth	70	43	53	257	900	*	28	1,900	*	500

*Cannot be computed absent 2000 data.

Figure 2.2 Encouraging Convergence: The Growth of Digital Platforms, 2000–2010.
Source: Adapted from Forrester Research in Atkinson, 2005.

Net and games. In that same year, the New York Times Company sought to converge its newspaper and television operations with the Web when it paid half-a-billion dollars for the popular site About.com.

Another reason for convergence is audience fragmentation. A mass communicator who finds it difficult to reach the whole audience can reach its component parts through various media. A third reason is the audience itself. We are becoming increasingly comfortable receiving information and entertainment from a variety of sources. Will this expansion and blurring of traditional media channels confuse audience members, further tilting the balance of power in the mass communication process toward the media industries? Or will it give audiences more power—power to choose, power to reject, and power to combine information and entertainment in individual ways?

DEVELOPING MEDIA LITERACY SKILLS
Reconsidering the Process of Mass Communication

One essential element of media literacy is *having an understanding of the process of mass communication.* As we saw in Chapter 1, understanding the process—how it functions, how its components relate to one another, how it limits or enhances messages, which forms of feedback are most effective and why—permits us to form expectations of how the media industries and the process itself

WWW

Broadcasting & Cable
www.broadcastingcable.com

Variety
www.variety.com

Editor & Publisher
www.editorandpublisher.com

Advertising Age
www.adage.com

The Fraction of Selection

Media history is repeating itself for today's media industries. They face challenges not unlike those that arose in the 1950s with the coming of television. By 1951, stations were broadcasting from cities all across America and the big television networks had the country wired from coast to coast. Television reshaped the media world of that time in no less a dramatic fashion than the digital technologies promise to reshape the one with which we are familiar today. Back then, movie attendance (and box office) dropped dramatically. Radio listenership—and advertising revenue—were in free fall. Readers and advertisers alike were abandoning newspapers and magazines. Revisit the statistics on page 39. Today's "traditional" media are facing troubling declines. And just as it was in the 1950s, people inside and outside the media industries are struggling to determine which media people will choose for which content.

Pioneer mass communication researcher Wilbur Schramm offered a simple way to address this issue in 1954. His answer to the question "What determines which offerings of mass communication will be selected by a given individual?" was the **fraction of selection** (1954, p. 19):

$$\frac{\text{Expectation of Reward}}{\text{Effort Required}}$$

His argument was that audience members weigh the level of reward they expect from a given medium or piece of content against how much effort—in the broadest sense—they must make to secure that reward. Consider your own media consumption. For example, do you get most of your news from the Internet or from the daily newspaper? What factors might you include in the numerator of Schramm's equation (Expectation of Reward) for news on the Net? Free. Continuously updated. Easily selectable and searchable. Links to related stories at your fingertips. Sound and video accompany the reports. You can read the news before you leave your room in the morning or in class while your professor thinks you're taking notes on your laptop. What factors might you put in the denominator (Effort Required)? You have to log on to your desktop or carry your computer. You have to click on your desired news site.

Now, what factors would you consider for the daily paper? *Expectation of reward:* You like the feel of the paper in your hands; its heft is comforting. You can cut out articles, cartoons, and recipes (but wait, you can print them out from the Web, so that's not much of a reward). *Effort required:* You have to go get it at a newsstand or at the end of your driveway. You have to pay for it. You pay for and sift through a lot of stories and features in which you have no interest. If you want to follow up on a particular story, you have to go somewhere else, more than likely the Web.

Certainly, you can add your own factors to any of these lists, but the odds are that you, like most college students, get most of your news from the Net rather than from the daily paper; and you can see why. Think about Steven Soderbergh's simultaneous release of the 2006 movie *Bubble* in theaters, on DVD, and on cable. Which platform was favored? Would it surprise you to learn that more people chose to see it on its opening weekend on cable than on DVD, and that more people chose to buy the DVD than see the movie at a theater (McBride, 2006)? Can you use the fraction of selection to explain why this might have happened? Which choice would you have made? Can you use the fraction of selection to explain your other media and content choices? For example, do you download tunes or do you buy CDs? Do you read books in hard copy or online? Do you wait for the latest blockbuster movie to "come to cable" or "come to DVD"? Will you *really* watch television shows and movies on a cell phone? Remember, media literacy demands critical thinking skills that enable you to develop your own independent judgments about media and content. The fraction of selection, more than a half century old, just might help.

> AUDIENCE MEMBERS WEIGH THE LEVEL OF REWARD THEY EXPECT FROM A GIVEN MEDIUM OR PIECE OF CONTENT AGAINST HOW MUCH EFFORT—IN THE BROADEST SENSE—THEY MUST MAKE TO SECURE THAT REWARD.

What differences in the newspaper versus Internet fraction of selection might have surfaced for this father and son?

© Zits–Zits Partnership. King Features Syndicate.

can serve us. But throughout this chapter we have seen that the process of mass communication is undergoing fundamental change. Media literate individuals must understand why and how this evolution is occurring. We can do this by reconsidering its elements as described in Figure 1.3 on page 8.

INTERPRETER A—THE CONTENT PRODUCER

Traditionally, the content producer, the source, in the mass communication process is a large, hierarchically structured organization, for example, Pixar Studios, the *Philadelphia Enquirer,* CBS Television. And as we saw, the typical consequence of this organizational structure is scant room for individual vision or experimentation. But in the age of the Internet, with its proliferation of **blogs** (regularly updated online journals that comment on just about everything), social-networking sites such as MySpace.com where users post all variety of free, personal content, and other Web sites, the distinction between content consumer and content provider disappears. Now, Interpreter A can be an independent musician self-releasing her music online, a lone blogger, a solitary online scrapbooker, or two pals who create digital video movies for distribution on Current TV (www.current.tv) where people vote for the best content, which is then redistributed over cable television on the Current TV channel. Already, 30 million people visit blogs each day (Mason, 2006), and the National Academy of Arts and Sciences announced in 2005 a new category of Emmy award to accompany the usual Best Comedy and Best Drama winners: Outstanding Content Distributed via Nontraditional Delivery Platforms.

Current TV
www.current.tv

In the newly evolving mass communication, content providers are just as likely to be individuals who believe in something or who have something to say as they are big media companies in search of audiences and profits. What are the likely consequences of this change? Will the proliferation of content sources help mitigate the effects of concentration and conglomeration in the traditional media industries? Will the cultural forum be less of a lecture and more of a conversation? Will new and different and challenging storytellers find an audience for their narratives? Does journalist William Greider, speaking specifically of the news, overstate when he says, "The centralized institutions of press and broadcasting are being challenged and steadily eroded by widening circles of unlicensed 'news' agents—from talk-radio hosts to Internet bloggers and others—who compete with the official press to be believed. These interlopers speak in a different language and from many different angles of vision. Less authoritative, but more democratic" (2005, p. 31)?

THE MESSAGE

The message in the traditional mass communication process is typically many identical messages, mechanically produced, simultaneously sent, inflexible, and unalterable. Once Fox airs tonight's episode of *24,* it has aired tonight's episode of *24.* The consequence? Audiences either like it or don't like it. The program either succeeds or fails. But we've already seen that different commercial spots can be inserted into programs sent into specific homes and that several hundred people on a train can read several hundred

Director Steven Soderbergh. How will his thinking outside the box office alter movies and the moviegoing experience?

versions of the "same" newspaper. You can buy only four downloaded cuts of an artist's latest CD, add three more from an earlier release, and listen to a completely new, personally created CD. Alternate-ending DVDs permitting viewers to "re-edit" an existing movie at home are old hat by now. But what do you think of director Steven Soderbergh's vision for a digital movie future? He said that in 5 or 10 years, when theaters convert more fully from film to digital projection (Chapter 6), he plans to exhibit multiple, different versions of the same film. "I think it would be very interesting to have a movie out in release," he said, "and then, just a few weeks later say, 'Here's version 2.0, recut, rescored.' The other version is still out there—people can see either or both" (in Jardin, 2005b, p. 257).

What will be the impact on the mass communication process when content producers no longer have to aggregate as large an audience as possible with a single, simultaneously distributed piece of content? When a producer can sell very specific, very idiosyncratic, constantly changing content to very specific, very idiosyncratic, constantly changing consumers, will profitability and popularity no longer be so closely linked? What will happen when the mass communication process, long dependent on **appointment consumption** (audiences consume content at a time predetermined by the producer and distributor; for example, a movie time at a theater, your favorite television show at 9:00 on Tuesdays, news at the top of the hour), evolves more completely to **consumption-on-demand** (the ability to consume any content, anytime, anywhere)?

FEEDBACK AND INTERPRETER B—THE AUDIENCE

In the traditional model of the mass communication process, feedback is inferential and delayed—what is a newspaper's circulation, what were this weekend's box office numbers for that movie, what are that program's ratings? Likewise, the audience is typically seen as large and heterogeneous, known to content producers and distributors in a relatively rudimentary way, little more than basic demographics. But digital media have changed what content creators and distributors know about their audiences (Interpreter B) because they have changed how audiences talk back to those sources (feedback). Silicon Valley marketing consultant Richard Yankowitch explains, "The Internet is the most ubiquitous experimental lab in history, built on two-way, real-time interactions with millions of consumers whose individual consumption patterns can for the first time be infinitesimally measured, monitored, and molded." Adds Google advertising executive Tim Armstrong, "Traditionally, the focus has been on the outbound message. But we think the information coming back in is as important or more important than the messages going out. For years, demographics has been a religion among advertisers because it was the only information they had" (both in Streisand & Newman, 2005, p. 60).

In today's mass communication, every visit to a specific Web address (and every click of a mouse once there), every download of a piece of content, and every product bought online provide feedback to someone. But it isn't just the Internet—every selection of a channel on cable or satellite, every rental or purchase by credit card of a CD, DVD, video game, or movie ticket, and every consumer product scanned at the checkout counter is recorded and stored in order to better identify us to Interpreter A, whoever that might be. But this raises the question, Who is that? It might be content providers who want to serve us more effectively because they know us so much more

Read "The Trades"

Media literacy champion Art Silverblatt identified several goals that media literate people can set for themselves to improve their critical awareness of the media. Three, in particular, suggest one way to make your media literacy a living enterprise:

- Develop an awareness of programming trends as a way of learning about changes in the culture.

- Keep abreast of patterns in ownership and government regulations that affect the media industries.

- Promote discussions about media programming and issues with friends and colleagues (2001, pp. 405–406).

An efficient and possibly fun way to accomplish these goals is to start a media issues discussion group centered on what industry pros call "the trades." Identify three friends with an interest in the mass media and agree to a

Keeping up with "the trades" not only improves your media literacy, but can enhance your career possibilities.

continued

regular schedule of meetings (every few weeks, every month). Each of you takes on the responsibility of reading one of the Big Four media industry trade magazines, that is, the trades: *Broadcasting & Cable*, *Variety*, *Editor & Publisher*, and *Advertising Age*. Because they are very influential and popular periodicals, they are available at almost every campus library and at many municipal libraries as well. *Broadcasting & Cable* not only reports on radio, television, and cable but offers extensive coverage of the Internet and satellite distribution of content. *Variety* covers all media, with a special eye toward the movies and television networks. But it does not ignore the recording, magazine, and book publishing industries. *Editor & Publisher* is the bible of the newspaper industry. The special virtue of *Advertising Age* is that it not only covers the ad industry, but because advertising people need to know where to put their dollars, of necessity it offers

EACH OF YOU TAKES ON THE RESPONSIBILITY OF READING ONE OF THE BIG FOUR MEDIA INDUSTRY TRADE MAGAZINES, THAT IS, THE TRADES: *BROADCASTING & CABLE, VARIETY, EDITOR & PUBLISHER,* AND *ADVERTISING AGE.*

quite realistic views of the state of every medium that relies on advertising for income.

At each session, each individual's task is to report on the most important stories that have appeared in his or her assigned trade since the previous get-together. You can agree to focus on ownership, regulations, and programming, as Silverblatt suggests, or you can let your group interests and conversations suggest different topics. Remember to rotate the titles among yourselves so everyone can become familiar with all four sources. These media chat sessions should improve media literacy and can be fun and informative. There is no better way to predict the future of the media industries—and possibly just as important to you, the career opportunities in them—than by reading the trades.

thoroughly than they once did when relying solely on demographics. Or it could be those who would make less honorable use of the feedback we so willingly provide, for example, identity thieves or insurance companies that would deny us coverage because of our eating and viewing habits.

THE RESULT

How will we use the new communication technologies? What will be our role in the new, emerging mass communication process? The world of content creators and distributors is now more democratic. Audiences, even though they may be fragmented into groups as small as one person or as large as 100 million, are better known to those who produce and distribute content and they can talk back more directly and with more immediacy. Content, the message, is now more flexible, infinitely alterable, unbound by time and space. Clearly, for content producers there is more room for experimentation in content creation and consumption. Clearly, there is less risk, and possibly even great reward, in challenging audiences. The evolving mass communication process promises not only efficiency but great joy, boundless choice, and limitless access to information for all its partners. But as you might remember from Chapter 1, the technologies that help provide these gifts are in fact double-edged swords; they cut both ways, good and bad. Media literate people, because they understand the mass communication process through which they operate, are positioned to best decide how to benefit from their potential and limit their peril.

RESOURCES FOR REVIEW AND DISCUSSION

Review Points

- Encouraged by the Internet and other digital technologies, content producers are finding new ways to deliver content to audiences.
- All of the traditional media have begun to see either flattening or declines in audience, yet overall consumption of media is at all-time highs.
- Five trends are abetting this situation—convergence, audience fragmentation, concentration of ownership and conglomeration, globalization, and hypercommercialism.
- Convergence is fueled by three elements—digitization of nearly all information, high-speed connectivity, and advances in technology's speed, memory, and power.

- As a result of all this change, traditional conceptions of the mass communication process and its elements must be reconsidered:
    a. Content providers can now be lone individuals.
    b. Messages can now be quite varied, idiosyncratic, and freed of the producers' time demands.
    c. Feedback can now be instantaneous and direct, and, as a result, audiences, very small or very large, can be quite well known to content producers and distributors.

Key Terms

 Use the text's Online Learning Center at www.mhhe.com/baran5 to further your understanding of the following terminology.

platform, 39
media multitasking, 40
convergence, 41
concentration of ownership, 41
conglomeration, 42
economies of scale, 45
oligopoly, 45
globalization, 45

stringers, 47
audience fragmentation, 48
narrowcasting, 49
niche marketing, 49
targeting, 49
taste publics, 49
hypercommercialism, 50
product placement, 50

brand entertainment, 50
payola, 51
Wi-Fi, 52
synergy, 52
fraction of selection, 54
blog, 55
appointment consumption, 56
consumption-on-demand, 56

Questions for Review

 Go to the self-quizzes on the Online Learning Center to test your knowledge.

1. What is a platform?
2. Can you describe recent changes in audience size for movies, recorded music, network television, DVD, radio, newspapers, and video games?
3. How would you describe contemporary levels of overall media consumption?
4. What is convergence?
5. What is media multitasking?
6. Differentiate between concentration of media ownership and conglomeration.
7. What is globalization?
8. What is hypercommercialism?
9. What is audience fragmentation?
10. What are economies of scale and oligopoly? How are they related?

11. What are the two major concerns of globalization's critics?
12. What are product placement and branded content?
13. What three elements are fueling today's rampant media convergence?
14. Differentiate between notions of content producers, audiences, messages, and feedback in the traditional view of the mass communication process and more contemporary understandings of these elements of the process.
15. Differentiate between appointment consumption and consumption-on-demand.

Questions for Critical Thinking and Discussion

1. Where NBC executive Bob Wright warns, "You can't fight technology," *Advertising Age*'s Scott Donaton cautions, "A cellphone isn't a TV" (2006, p. 18). What is the concern behind each comment? Is one more correct than the other? With whom would you side in a debate, and why?

2. Many industry insiders attribute the recent falloff in audiences for movies, recorded music, network television, DVD, radio, newspapers, and video games to changes in technology; people are finding new ways to access content. And while this is certainly true to a degree, others say that in this age of concentrated and hypercommercialized media, audiences are simply being turned off. Would you agree with the critics? Why? Can you give examples from your own media consumption?

3. Critics of concentration of media ownership and conglomeration argue that they are a threat to democracy. What is the thrust of their concern? Do you share it? Why or why not?

4. Before reading this chapter, had you noticed in your own media consumption the ascendance of celebrity news over serious coverage? If not, why not? If so, did it raise concern in your mind? Did it alter in any way your choice of news sources?

5. Weigh in on the issue of large, U.S.-based Internet corporations' willingness to sacrifice a bit of the Web's freedom for access to China's large population. How far should a company go to "respond to local conditions"?

6. Do you find product placement and branded content as troublesome as do its critics? Why or why not? Are you sympathetic to those writers who want to be paid extra for inserting "commercials" into their scripts? Why or why not?

7. A close reading of how the mass communication process is evolving has led some observers to argue that it is becoming less "mass" and more akin to interpersonal communication. Revisit Figure 1.3 on page 8. Can you make the argument that the "Result" of the process has the potential to be more "flexible, personally relevant, possibly adventurous, challenging, or experimental"?

Important Resources

 Go to the Online Learning Center for additional readings.

Internet Resources

More on Kids' Media Consumption	www.kaisernetwork.org
More on American Media Consumption	www.su.edu/cmd
More on Concentration	www.cjr.org/owners
More on Media Reform	www.mediareform.net
More on Yahoo! in China	www.booyahoo.blogspot.com
More on Globalization	www.unescosources.org
More on Improving Media Performance	www.freepress.net
More on Hypercommercialism	www.commercialalert.org
More on Product Placement	www.productinvasion.com
Online Video	www.youtube.com
Current TV	www.current.tv
Broadcasting & Cable	www.broadcastingcable.com
Variety	www.variety.com
Editor & Publisher	www.editorandpublisher.com
Advertising Age	www.adage.com

THE GREENWOOD ENCYCLOPEDIA OF

ROCK HISTORY

The Grunge and
Post-Grunge Years, 1991–2005

6

BOB GUL

RHYTH

Books

3

LEARNING OBJECTIVES

Books were the first mass medium and are, in many ways, the most personal. They inform and entertain. They are repositories of our pasts and agents of personal development and social change. Like all media, they mirror the culture. After studying this chapter you should

- be familiar with the history and development of the publishing industry and the book itself as a medium.
- recognize the cultural value of books and the implications of censorship for democracy.
- understand how the organizational and economic nature of the contemporary book industry shapes the content of books.
- be a more media literate consumer of books, especially in recognizing their uniqueness in an increasingly mass-mediated world.

The video began when you hit the play button on the remote control. But the folks who rented the movie before you failed to rewind. So there you were, watching an arresting scene from François Truffaut's 1967 adaptation of Ray Bradbury's (1953/1981) science fiction classic *Fahrenheit 451*.

At first you couldn't make out what was happening. A group of people were wandering about, and each person was talking to him- or herself. You recognized actress Julie Christie, but the other performers and what they were saying were completely unfamiliar. You stayed with the scene. The trees were bare. Snow was falling, covering everything. Puffs of steam floated from people's mouths as they spoke, seemingly to no one. As you watched a bit more, you began to recognize some familiar phrases. These people were reciting passages from famous books! Before you could figure out why they were doing this, the film ended.

So you rewound and watched the entire video, discovering that these people *were* the books they had memorized. In this near-future society, all books had been banned by the authorities, forcing these

Opposite: Have a question about grunge? Read this book.

people—book lovers all—into hiding. They hold the books in their heads because to hold them in their hands is a crime. If discovered with books, people are jailed and the books are set afire—Fahrenheit 451 is the temperature at which book paper burns.

Moved by the film, you go to the library the next day and check out the book itself. Bradbury's main character, Guy Montag, a fireman who until this moment had been an official book burner himself, speaks a line that stays with you, even today. After he watches an old woman burn to death with her forbidden volumes, he implores his ice-cold, drugged, and television-deadened wife to understand what he is only then realizing. He pleads with her to see: "There must be something in books, things we can't imagine, to make a woman stay in a burning house; there must be something there" (1981, pp. 49–50).

In this chapter we examine the history of books, especially in terms of their role in the development of the United States. We discuss the importance that has traditionally been ascribed to books, as well as the scope and nature of the book industry. We address the various factors that shape the contemporary economics and structures of the book industry, examining at some length the impact of convergence, concentration, and hypercommercialism on the book industry and its relationship with its readers. Finally, we discuss the media literacy issues inherent in the wild success of the Harry Potter books.

www

More on Ray Bradbury
www.raybradbury.com

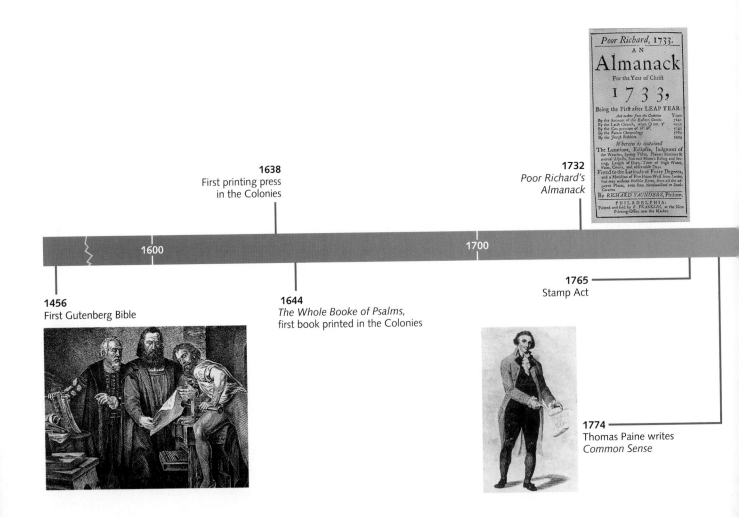

1638
First printing press in the Colonies

1732
Poor Richard's Almanack

1600

1700

1456
First Gutenberg Bible

1644
The Whole Booke of Psalms,
first book printed in the Colonies

1765
Stamp Act

1774
Thomas Paine writes
Common Sense

A Short History of Books

As we saw in Chapter 1, use of Gutenberg's printing press spread rapidly throughout Europe in the last half of the 15th century. But the technological advances and the social, cultural, and economic conditions necessary for books to become a major mass medium were three centuries away. As a result, it was a printing press and a world of books not unlike that in Gutenberg's time that first came to the New World in the 17th century.

BOOKS COME TO COLONIAL NORTH AMERICA

The earliest colonists came to America primarily for two reasons—to escape religious persecution and to find economic opportunities unavailable to them in Europe. Most of the books they carried with them to the New World were religiously oriented. Moreover, they brought very few books at all. Better-educated, wealthier Europeans were secure at home. Those willing to make the dangerous journey tended to be poor, uneducated, and largely illiterate.

There were other reasons early settlers did not find books central to their lives. One was the simple fight for survival. In the brutal and hostile land to which they had come, leisure for reading books was a luxury for which they had little time. People worked from sunrise to sunset just to live. If there

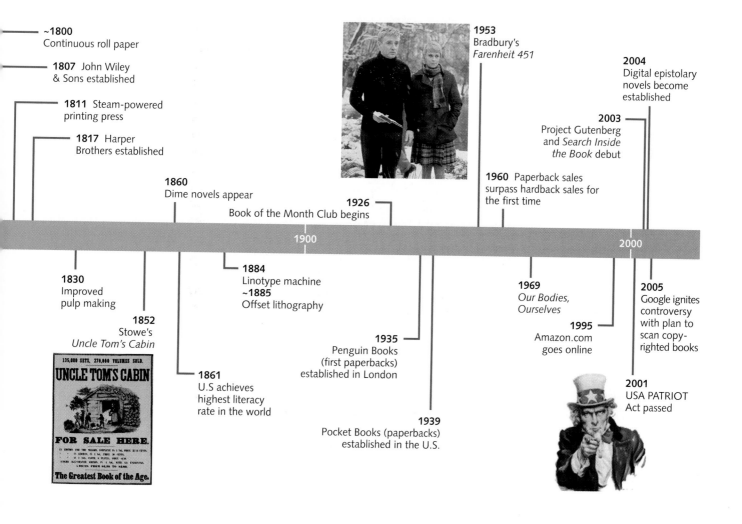

~**1800**
Continuous roll paper

1807 John Wiley
& Sons established

1811 Steam-powered
printing press

1817 Harper
Brothers established

1860
Dime novels appear

1926
Book of the Month Club begins

1953
Bradbury's
Farenheit 451

2004
Digital epistolary
novels become
established

2003
Project Gutenberg
and *Search Inside
the Book* debut

1960 Paperback sales
surpass hardback sales for
the first time

1900

2000

1830
Improved
pulp making

1884
Linotype machine
~**1885**
Offset lithography

1969
*Our Bodies,
Ourselves*

2005
Google ignites
controversy
with plan to
scan copy-
righted books

1852
Stowe's
Uncle Tom's Cabin

1935
Penguin Books
(first paperbacks)
established in London

1995
Amazon.com
goes online

1861
U.S achieves
highest literacy
rate in the world

1939
Pocket Books (paperbacks)
established in the U.S.

2001
USA PATRIOT
Act passed

In the now not-so-distant future of *Fahrenheit 451*, people must memorize the content of books because to own a book is illegal.

More on Ben Franklin
www.english.udel.edu/lemay/franklin

was to be reading, it would have to be at night, and it was folly to waste precious candles on something as unnecessary to survival as reading. In addition, books and reading were regarded as symbols of wealth and status and therefore not priorities for people who considered themselves to be pioneers, servants of the Lord, or anti-English colonists. The final reason the earliest settlers were not active readers was the lack of portability of books. Books were heavy, and few were carried across the ocean. Those volumes that did make it to North America were extremely expensive and not available to most people.

The first printing press arrived on North American shores in 1638, only 18 years after the Plymouth Rock landing. It was operated by a company called Cambridge Press. Printing was limited to religious and government documents. The first book printed in the Colonies appeared in 1644—*The Whole Booke of Psalms*, sometimes referred to as the *Bay Psalm Book*. Among the very few secular titles were those printed by Benjamin Franklin 90 years later. *Poor Richard's Almanack*, which first appeared in 1732, sold 10,000 copies annually. The *Almanack* contained short stories, poetry, weather predictions, and other facts and figures useful to a population more in command of its environment than those first settlers. As the Colonies grew in wealth and sophistication, leisure time increased, as did affluence and education. Franklin also published the first true novel printed in North America, *Pamela*, written by English author Samuel Richardson. Still, by and large, books were religiously oriented or pertained to official government activities such as tax rolls and the pronouncements of various commissions.

The primary reason for this lack of variety was the requirement that all printing be done with the permission of the colonial governors. Because these men were invariably loyal to King George II, secular printing and criticism of the British Crown or even of local authorities was never authorized, and publication of such writing meant jail. Many printers were imprisoned—including Franklin's brother James—for publishing what they believed to be the truth.

The printers went into open revolt against official control in March 1765 after passage of the Stamp Act. Designed by England to recoup money it spent waging the French and Indian War, the Stamp Act mandated that all printing—legal documents, books, magazines, and newspapers—be done on paper stamped with the government's seal. Its additional purpose was to control and limit expression in the increasingly restless Colonies. This affront to their freedom, and the steep cost of the tax—sometimes doubling the price of a publication—was simply too much for the colonists. The printers used their presses to run accounts of antitax protests, demonstrations, riots, sermons, boycotts, and other antiauthority activities, further fueling revolutionary and secessionist sympathies. In November 1765—when the tax was to take effect—the authorities were so cowed by the reaction of the colonists that they were unwilling to enforce it.

Anti-British sentiment reached its climax in the mid-1770s, and books were at its core. Short books, or pamphlets, motivated and coalesced political dissent. In 1774 England's right to govern the Colonies was openly challenged by James Wilson's *Considerations on the Nature and Extent of the Legislative Authority of the British Parliament*, John Adams's *Novanglus Papers*, and Thomas Jefferson's *A Summary View of the Rights of British America*. Most famous of all was Thomas Paine's 47-page *Common Sense*. It sold 120,000 copies in the first 3 months after its release to a total population of 400,000 adults. Between 1776 and 1783 Paine also wrote a series of pamphlets called *The American Crisis*. *Common Sense* and *The American Crisis* made Paine the most widely read colonial author during the American Revolution.

The Early Book Industry After the War of Independence, printing became even more central to political, intellectual, and cultural life in major cities like Boston, New York, and Philadelphia. To survive financially, printers also operated as booksellers, book publishers, and sometimes as postmasters who sold stationery and even groceries. A coffeehouse or tavern often was attached to the print shop. The era was alive with political change, and printer/bookshops became clearinghouses for the collection, exchange, and dissemination of information.

The U.S. newspaper industry grew rapidly from this mix, as we will see in Chapter 4. The book industry, however, was slower to develop. Books were still expensive, often costing the equivalent of a working person's weekly pay, and literacy remained a luxury. However, due in large measure to a movement begun before the Civil War, compulsory education had come to most states by 1900. This swelled the number of readers, which increased demand

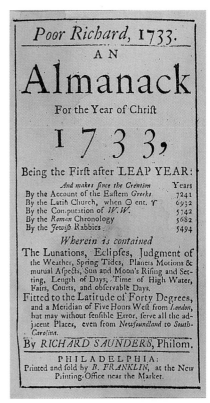

First published in 1732, Benjamin Franklin's *Poor Richard's Almanack* offered readers a wealth of information for the upcoming year.

Campaign for Reader Privacy
www.readerprivacy.com

British-born writer, patriot, and revolutionary leader Thomas Paine wrote *Common Sense* and *The American Crisis* to rally his colonial compatriots in their struggle against the British.

for books. This increased demand, coupled with a number of important technological advances, brought the price of books within reach of most people. In 1861 the United States had the highest literacy rate of any country in the world (58%), and 40 years later at the start of the 20th century, 9 out of every 10 U.S. citizens could read. Today, America's literacy rate stands at 95% (U.S. Adult, 2005).

Improving Printing   The 1800s saw a series of important refinements to the process of printing. Continuous roll paper, which permitted rapid printing of large numbers of identical, standardized pages, was invented in France at the very beginning of the century. Soon after, in 1811, German inventor Friedrich Koenig converted the printing press from muscle to steam power, speeding production of printed material and reducing its cost. In 1830 Americans Thomas Gilpin and James Ames perfected a wood-grinding machine that produced enough pulp to make 24 miles of paper daily, further lowering the cost of printing. The final pieces of this era's rapid production-cost reduction puzzle were fit in the later part of the century. German immigrant Ottmar Mergenthaler introduced his **linotype** machine in the United States in 1884. Employing a typewriter-like keyboard, the linotype enabled printers to set type mechanically rather than manually. Near the same time, **offset lithography** was developed. This advance made possible printing from photographic plates rather than from heavy and relatively fragile metal casts.

The Flowering of the Novel   The combination of technically improved, lower-cost printing (and therefore lower-cost publications) and widespread literacy produced the flowering of the novel in the 1800s. Major U.S. book publishers Harper Brothers and John Wiley & Sons—both in business today—were established in New York in 1817 and 1807, respectively. And books such as Nathaniel Hawthorne's *The Scarlet Letter* (1850), Herman Melville's *Moby Dick* (1851), and Mark Twain's *Huckleberry Finn* (1884) were considered by their readers to be equal to or better than the works of famous European authors such as Jane Austen, the Brontës, and Charles Dickens.

The growing popularity of books was noticed by brothers Irwin and Erastus Beadle. In 1860 they began publishing novels that sold for 10 cents. These **dime novels** were inexpensive, and because they concentrated on frontier and adventure stories, they attracted growing numbers of readers. Within 5 years of their start, Beadle & Company had produced over 4 million volumes of what were also sometimes called **pulp novels** (Tebbel, 1987). Advertising titles like *Malaeska: Indian Wife of the White Hunter* with the slogan "Dollar Books for a Dime!" the Beadles democratized books and turned them into a mass medium.

The Coming of Paperback Books   Dime novels were "paperback books" because they were produced with paper covers. But publisher Allen Lane invented what we now recognize as the paperback in the midst of the Great Depression in London when he founded Penguin Books in 1935. Four years later, publisher Robert de Graff introduced the idea to the United States. His Pocket Books were small, inexpensive (25 cents) reissues of books that had already become successful as hardcovers. They were sold just about everywhere—newsstands, bookstores, train stations, shipping terminals, and drug and department stores. Within weeks of their introduction, de Graff was fielding orders of up to 15,000 copies a day (Tebbel, 1987). Soon, new and existing publishers joined the paperback boom. Traditionalists had some concern about the "cheapening of the book," but that was more than offset by the huge popularity of paperbacks and the willingness of publishers to take chances. For example, in the 1950s and '60s, African American writers such as Richard Wright and Ralph Ellison were published, as were controversial works such as *Catcher in the Rye*. Eventually, paperback books became the norm, surpassing hardcover book sales for the first time in 1960. Today, more than 60% of all books sold in the United States are paperbacks.

Paperbacks are no longer limited to reprints of successful hardbacks. Many books now begin life as paperbacks. The John Jakes books *The Americans* and *The Titans*, for example, were issued initially as paperbacks and later reissued in hardcover. Paperback sales today top 1 million volumes a day, and bookstores generate half their revenue from these sales.

Books and Their Audiences

The book is the least "mass" of our mass media in audience reach and in the magnitude of the industry itself, and this fact shapes the nature of the relationship between medium and audience. Publishing houses, both large and small, produce narrowly or broadly aimed titles for readers, who buy and carry away individual units. This more direct relationship between publishers and readers renders books fundamentally different from other mass media. For example, because books are less dependent than other mass media on attracting the largest possible audience, books are more able and more likely to incubate new, challenging, or unpopular ideas. As the medium least dependent on advertiser support, books can be aimed at extremely small groups of readers, challenging them and their imaginations in ways that many sponsors would find unacceptable in advertising-based mass media. Because books are produced and sold as individual units—as opposed to a single television program simultaneously distributed to millions of viewers or a single edition of a mass circulation newspaper—more "voices" can enter and survive in the industry. This medium can sustain more voices in the cultural forum than can other mass media.

THE CULTURAL VALUE OF THE BOOK

The book industry is bound by many of the same financial and industrial pressures that constrain other media, but books, more than the others, are in a position to transcend those constraints. In *Fahrenheit 451* Montag's boss, Captain Beatty, explains why all books must be burned. "Once," he tells his troubled subordinate, "books appealed to a few people, here, there, everywhere. They could afford to be different. The world was roomy. But then the

The Role of Books in Social Movements

In the 15th and 16th centuries, reformers used one book—the Bible—to create one of history's most important revolutions, the Protestant Reformation. Of course, the reformers did not write this book, but their insistence that it be available to people was a direct challenge to the ruling powers of the time. Englishman John Wycliffe was persecuted and burned at the stake in the mid-1300s for translating the Bible into English. Two hundred years later, another Englishman, William Tyndale, so angered Church leaders with his insistence on printing and distributing English-language Bibles that the Church had him strangled and burned at the stake.

Before printed Bibles became generally available in the 16th and 17th centuries, Bibles and other religious tracts were typically chained to some unmovable piece of the church. Church leaders said this was done because people desperate for the Word of God would steal them, denying others access. If this was true, why were Wycliffe and Tyndale persecuted for trying to *expand* access? Many historians, both secular and religious, now believe that the reason **chained Bibles** existed was to ensure that reading and interpreting their contents could be supervised and controlled. The established elites feared the power of the printed word.

This was also the case during the American Revolution, as we have seen in this chapter, as well as when the country rejected a 200-year evil, slavery. Harriet Beecher Stowe published the realistically painful story of slavery in America in 1852. Her *Uncle Tom's Cabin* had first appeared in two parts in

> **THE REASON CHAINED BIBLES EXISTED WAS TO ENSURE THAT READING AND INTERPRETING THEIR CONTENTS COULD BE SUPERVISED AND CONTROLLED. THE ESTABLISHED ELITES FEARED THE POWER OF THE PRINTED WORD.**

an antislavery magazine, but its greatest impact was as a book hungrily read by a startled public. *Uncle Tom's Cabin* sold 20,000 copies in its first 3 weeks on the market, and 300,000 copies in its first year, eventually reaching sales of 7 million.

It was the tale of a kind, literate slave, Uncle Tom. Tom's reward for his intelligence and his goodness was death at the hands of evil slave owner Simon Legree. A fine work of literature, *Uncle Tom's Cabin* galvanized public feelings against slavery. Abolitionist sentiment

Chained Bibles and other handprinted books in England's Hereford Cathedral.

world got full of eyes and elbows and mouths" (Bradbury, 1981, p. 53). Bradbury's firemen of the future destroy books precisely because they *are* different. It is their difference from other mass media that makes books unique in our culture. Although all media serve the following cultural functions to some degree (for example, people use self-help videos for personal development and popular music is sometimes an agent of social change), books traditionally have been seen as a powerful cultural force for these reasons:

- *Books are agents of social and cultural change.* Free of the need to generate mass circulation for advertisers, offbeat, controversial, even revolutionary ideas can reach the public. For example, Andrew MacDonald's *Turner Diaries* is the ideological and how-to bible of the antigovernment militia movement in the United States. Nonetheless, this radical, revolutionary book is openly published, purchased, and discussed. For a look at the role of other books in social movements, see the box above, "The Role of Books in Social Movements."

135,000 SETS, 270,000 VOLUMES SOLD.

UNCLE TOM'S CABIN

FOR SALE HERE.

AN EDITION FOR THE MILLION, COMPLETE IN 1 Vol., PRICE 37 1-2 CENTS.
" " IN GERMAN, IN 1 Vol., PRICE 50 CENTS.
" " IN 2 Vols. CLOTH, 6 PLATES, PRICE $1.50.
SUPERB ILLUSTRATED EDITION, IN 1 Vol., WITH 153 ENGRAVINGS,
PRICES FROM $2.50 TO $5.00.

The Greatest Book of the Age.

This promotional flier calls Uncle Tom's Cabin *"the greatest book of the age," a fair assessment, given its impact on the times and U.S. history.*

was no longer the domain of the intellectual, social, and religious elite. Everyday people were repulsed by the horrors of slavery. One of Stowe's most ardent readers was Abraham Lincoln, who, as president, abolished slavery.

Books have traditionally been at the center of social change in the United States. Horatio Alger's rags-to-riches stories excited westward migration in the 1800s. Upton Sinclair's *The Jungle* and other muckraking books brought about significant health and labor legislation in the early 1900s. John Steinbeck's *The Grapes of Wrath* took up the cause of migrant farmers in the post-Depression 1930s. Alex Haley's *The Autobiography of Malcolm X* and Ralph Ellison's *Invisible Man* were literary mainstays of the 1960s Civil Rights era, as was Betty Friedan's *The Feminine Mystique* for the women's movement. In the 1970s, the paperback publication of *The Pentagon Papers* hastened the end of the Vietnam War.

The role of books in important social movements will be repeated, as you'll read in Chapter 5's discussion of magazine muckrakers.

- *Books are an important cultural repository.* Want to definitively win an argument? Look it up. We often turn to books for certainty and truth about the world in which we live and the ones about which we want to know. Which countries border Chile? Find the atlas. Nirvana's drummer? Look in Bob Gulla's *Greenwook Encyclopedia of Rock History: The Grunge and Post-Grunge Years, 1991–2005.*

- *Books are our windows on the past.* What was the United States like in the 19th century? Read Alexis de Tocqueville's *Democracy in America.* England in the early 1800s? Read Jane Austen's *Pride and Prejudice.* Written in the times they reflect, these books are more accurate representations than are available in the modern electronic media.

Our Bodies, Ourselves

Books have been central to many of the most important social and political movements in our nation's history. *Our Bodies, Ourselves*, a book for and about women, is credited with beginning the women's health movement. The profits this book generates—some 40 years after its first appearance—continue to support what has become a worldwide undertaking. How did this influential book, with more than 4 million copies sold in 18 different languages, come into being, and how does it continue to be so influential?

The story of *Our Bodies, Ourselves* begins in 1969. That year several women, aged 23 to 39, were attending a workshop on "Women and Their Bodies" at a women's liberation conference in Boston. They began exchanging "doctor stories." They readily came to the conclusion that most women were relatively ignorant about their bodies (and by extension, their sexuality) and that the male-dominated medical profession was not particularly receptive to their needs. So they gave themselves a "summer project." As explained by the women, who began identifying themselves as the Boston Women's Health Book Collective (Norsigian et al., 1999):

> We would research our questions, share what we learned in our group, and then present the information in the fall as a course "by and for women." We envisioned an ongoing process that would involve other women who would go on to teach such a course in other settings. In creating the course, we learned that we were capable of collecting, understanding, and evaluating medical information; that we could open up to one another and find strength and comfort through sharing some of our most private experiences; that what we learned from one another was every bit as important as what we read in medical texts; and that our experience contradicted medical pronouncements. Over time these facts, feelings, and controversies were intertwined in the various editions of *Our Bodies, Ourselves.*

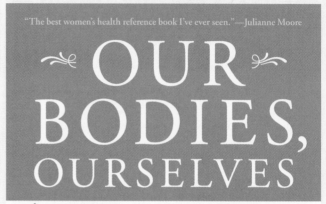

Those various editions offered a woman's perspective on issues such as reproductive health, sexuality, environmental and occupational health, menopause and aging, poverty, racism, hunger, homelessness, and the overmedicalization of "women's lives that turn normal events such as childbearing

More on Our Bodies, Ourselves
www.ourbodiesourselves.org

- *Books are important sources of personal development.* The obvious forms are self-help and personal improvement volumes. But books also speak to us more individually than advertiser-supported media because of their small, focused target markets. For example, *Our Bodies, Ourselves,* introduced by the Boston Women's Health Book Collective in the very earliest days of the modern feminist movement, is still published today. (For more on this influential book, see "Our Bodies, Ourselves" above.) *Dr. Spock's Baby and Child Care* has sold more than 30 million copies. J. D. Salinger's *Catcher in the Rye* was the literary anthem for the baby boomers in their teen years, as is William Gibson's *Neuromancer* for many of today's cyberyouth. It is unlikely that any of these voices would have found their initial articulation in commercially sponsored media.

- *Books are wonderful sources of entertainment, escape, and personal reflection.* Arthur C. Clarke, John Grisham, Judith Krantz, and Stephen

and menopause into disabling conditions requiring medical intervention" (Norsigian et al., 1999).

Profits from *Our Bodies, Ourselves* were used to create the Women's Health Information Center and to fund numerous local, national, and international women's health advocacy groups and movements. Among the achievements of the resulting women's health movement that the Women's Health Information Center lists are women's ability to obtain more and better information about oral contraceptives and other drugs, the eradication of forced sterilization for poor women, improved treatment of breast cancer and increased awareness of nonsurgical treatments for this disease, the growth of women-controlled health centers, and the reinforcement of women's reproductive rights in the form of access to safe and legal abortion.

How does *Our Bodies, Ourselves* continue to make a difference? One of the original Boston Women's Health Book Collective members, Jane Pincus, explains in her introduction to the 1998 edition:

> Unlike most health books on the market, *Our Bodies, Ourselves for the New Century* is unique in many respects: It is based on, and has grown out of, hundreds of women's experiences. It questions the medicalization of women's bodies and lives, and highlights holistic knowledge along with conventional biomedical information. It places women's experiences within the social, political, and economic forces that determine all of our lives, thus going beyond individualistic, narrow, "self-care" and self-help approaches, and views health in the context of the sexist, racist, and financial pressures that affect far too many girls, women, and families

> adversely. It condemns medical corporate misbehavior driven by "bottom-line" management philosophy and the profit motive. Most of all, *Our Bodies, Ourselves* encourages you to value and share your own insights and experiences, and to use its information to question the assumptions underlying the care we all receive so that we can deal effectively with the medical system and organize for better care. . . .

> We have listed and critiqued online health resources for women. The chapters "Body Image" and "Sexuality" deal for the first time with issues of racism. We emphasize overwork, violence, and girls' increasing use of tobacco as major threats to women's health, and we highlight more than ever the importance of good food and exercise. We explore the new issues that arise as more lesbians choose to have children. We include transgender and transsexual issues, and discuss women living with HIV as well as the most recent safer sex advice. We explore more extensively the connections between race, class, and gender-based oppressions as they affect the health of women. We offer tools for negotiating the complex and often unregulated "managed care" system, which affects women's lives much more profoundly than men's, and discuss its advantages and disadvantages. Most important, we advocate for an equitable, single-payer national health care system. (1998, p. 21)

You may disagree with some (or all) of the philosophy and goals of the Boston Women's Health Book Collective, but there is no argument that its book, *Our Bodies, Ourselves*, has made—and continues to make—a difference in the health of women around the world. The latest edition, *Our Bodies, Ourselves: A New Edition for a New Era*, was published in 2005.

> **BOOKS HAVE BEEN CENTRAL TO MANY OF THE MOST IMPORTANT SOCIAL AND POLITICAL MOVEMENTS IN OUR NATION'S HISTORY.**

King all specialize in writing highly entertaining and imaginative novels. The enjoyment found in the works of writers Joyce Carol Oates *(On Boxing, We Were the Mulvaneys)*, John Irving *(The World According to Garp, Hotel New Hampshire, A Prayer for Owen Meany)*, Pat Conroy *(The Prince of Tides, Beach Music)*, and J. K. Rowling (the Harry Potter series) is undeniable.

- *The purchase and reading of a book is a much more individual, personal activity than consuming advertiser-supported (television, radio, newspapers, and magazines) or heavily promoted (popular music and movies) media.* As such, books tend to encourage personal reflection to a greater degree than these other media. We are alone when we read a book; we are part of the tribe, as McLuhan would say, when we engage other media. As such, in the words of author Julius Lester *(Look Out, Whitey! Black Power's Gon' Get Your Mama!; Why Heaven Is Far Away)*:

For more information on this topic, see Media Talk video clip #9, "Publishers of *Wind Done Gone* Ordered to Stop Publication," on the *Media World* DVD.

The mystery and miracle of a book is found in the fact that it is a solitary voice penetrating time and space to go beyond time and space, and to alight for a moment in that place within each of us which is also beyond time and space. . . . Books are the royal road that enable us to enter the realm of the imaginative. Books enable us to experience what it is to be someone else. Through books we experience other modes of being. Through books we recognize who we are and who we might become. . . . Books invite us into realms of the soul by asking us to imagine that we are someone other than who we are. Books require that we temporarily put our egos in a box by the door and take on the spirit of others. . . . This is what a book, any book, offers us the opportunity to do: confess and recognize ourselves. To confess and recognize our fantasies, our joys, and griefs, our aspirations and failures, our hopes and our fears. Deep within the solitary wonder in which we sit alone with a book, we confess and recognize what we would be too ashamed to tell another—and sometimes we are as ashamed of joy and delight and success as we are of embarrassment and failure. (2002, pp. 26–29)

- *Books are mirrors of culture.* Books, along with other mass media, reflect the culture that produces and consumes them.

CENSORSHIP

Because of their influence as cultural repositories and agents of social change, books have often been targeted for censorship. A book is censored when someone in authority limits publication of or access to it. Censorship can and does occur in many situations and in all media (more on this in Chapter 14). But because of the respect our culture traditionally holds for books, book banning takes on a particularly poisonous connotation in the United States.

Reacting to censorship presents a dilemma for book publishers. Publishers have an obligation to their owners and stockholders to make a profit. Yet, if responsible people in positions of authority deem a certain book unsuitable for readers, shouldn't publishers do the right thing for the larger society and comply with demands to cease its publication? This was the argument presented by morals crusader Anthony Comstock in 1873 when he established the New York Society for the Suppression of Vice. It was the argument used on the evening of May 10, 1933, in Berlin when Nazi propaganda chief Joseph Goebbels put a torch to a bonfire that consumed 20,000 books. It was the argument made in 1953 when U.S. Senator Joseph McCarthy demanded the removal of more than 100 books from U.S. diplomatic libraries because of their "procommunist" slant. (Among them was Thomas Paine's *Common Sense*.) It is the argument made today by people like Alabama State Representative Gerald Allen when he explained his 2005 bill to ban from his state's elementary and high schools all books either written by homosexual authors or containing gay characters. Prohibited would be classics such as *The Color Purple* and all works by Tennessee Williams, Truman Capote, and Gore Vidal. "I don't look at it as censorship," he explained. "I look at it as protecting the hearts and souls and minds of our children" (CBS News, 2005, p. 1).

According to the American Library Association Office of Intellectual Freedom and the American Civil Liberties Union, among the library and school books most frequently targeted by modern censors are the *Harry Potter* series, Mark Twain's *The Adventures of Huckleberry Finn*, Harper Lee's *To Kill a*

WWW

American Library Association
www.ala.org

WWW

American Booksellers Foundation for Free Expression
www.abffe.org

WWW

American Civil Liberties Union
www.aclu.org

BANNED BOOKS

- *Harry Potter* (series), by J. K. Rowling
- *Of Mice and Men*, by John Steinbeck
- *The Catcher in the Rye*, by J. D. Salinger
- *The Adventures of Huckleberry Finn*, by Mark Twain
- *The Chocolate War*, by Robert Cormier
- *Bridge to Terabithia*, by Katherine Paterson
- *Scary Stories in the Dark*, by Alvin Schwartz
- *More Scary Stories in the Dark*, by Alvin Schwartz
- *Scary Stories 3: More Tales to Chill Your Bones*, by Alvin Schwartz
- *The Witches*, by Roald Dahl
- *Daddy's Roommate*, by Michael Willhoite
- *A Wrinkle in Time*, by Madeleine L'Engle
- *Forever*, by Judy Blume
- *Blubber*, by Judy Blume
- *Deenie*, by Judy Blume
- *The Giver*, by Lois Lowry
- *Anastasia Krupnik* (series), by Lois Lowry
- *Halloween ABC*, by Eve Merriam
- *A Day No Pigs Would Die*, by Robert Peck
- *Heather Has Two Mommies*, by Leslea Newman
- *It's Perfectly Normal*, by Robbie Harris
- *I Know Why the Caged Bird Sings*, by Maya Angelou
- *Fallen Angels*, by Walter Myers
- *Goosebumps* (series), by R. L. Stine

- *Sex*, by Madonna
- *Go Ask Alice*, by Anonymous
- *The Stupids* (series), by Harry Allard
- *Bumps in the Night*, by Harry Allard
- *My House*, by Nikki Giovanni
- *The New Joy of Gay Sex*, by Charles Silverstein
- *The Goats*, by Brock Cole
- *The Color Purple*, by Alice Walker
- *Kaffir Boy*, by Mark Mathabane
- *Killing Mr. Griffin*, by Lois Duncan
- *We All Fall Down*, by Robert Cormier
- *Final Exit*, by Derek Humphry
- *My Brother Sam Is Dead*, by James Lincoln Collier and Christopher Collier
- *Julie of the Wolves*, by Jean Craighead George
- *The Bluest Eye*, by Toni Morrison
- *Beloved*, by Toni Morrison
- *The Great Gilly Hopkins*, by Katherine Paterson
- *What's Happening to My Body?* by Lynda Madaras
- *To Kill a Mockingbird*, by Harper Lee
- *In the Night Kitchen*, by Maurice Sendak
- *The Outsiders*, by S. E. Hinton
- *Annie on My Mind*, by Nancy Garden
- *The Pigman*, by Paul Zindel
- *Flowers for Algernon*, by Daniel Keyes
- *The Handmaid's Tale*, by Margaret Atwood
- *The Boy Who Lost His Face*, by Louis Sachar

Figure 3.1 Most Frequently Banned Books in the Past 10 Years. Shown here are the 50 books most frequently challenged in U.S. schools and public libraries during the past decade.

Mockingbird, John Steinbeck's *Of Mice and Men*, the *Goosebumps* series, Alice Walker's *The Color Purple*, and children's favorite *In the Night Kitchen* by Maurice Sendak. The 50 most frequently banned books in the United States are shown in Figure 3.1. With how many are you familiar? Which ones have you read? What is it about each of these books that might have brought it to the censors' attention?

Book publishers can confront censorship by recognizing that their obligations to their industry and to themselves demand that they resist censorship. The book publishing industry and the publisher's role in it is fundamental to the operation and maintenance of our democratic society. Rather than accepting the censor's argument that certain voices require silencing for the good of the culture, publishers in a democracy have an

Figure 3.2 Reasons for Banning Books. The American Library Association Office for Intellectual Freedom tallied the reasons that specific books were banned from 1990 to 2000 in America's schools and libraries. Of the 6,364 challenges reported to its offices during that decade, these were the reasons given. The number of reasons exceeds 6,364 because books were often challenged for more than one reason.

Source: American Library Association Office for Intellectual Freedom (www.ala.org/bbooks/bbwdatabase.html).

WWW

Banned Books
www.ala.org/bbooks

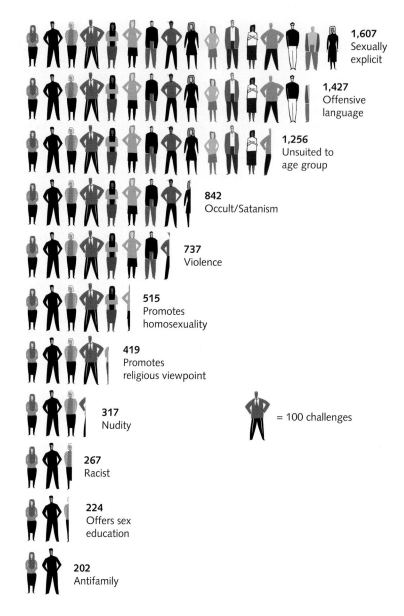

1,607
Sexually explicit

1,427
Offensive language

1,256
Unsuited to age group

842
Occult/Satanism

737
Violence

515
Promotes homosexuality

419
Promotes religious viewpoint

317
Nudity

267
Racist

224
Offers sex education

202
Antifamily

= 100 challenges

obligation to make the stronger argument that free speech be protected and encouraged. The short list of frequently censored titles in the previous paragraph should immediately make it evident why the power of ideas is worth fighting for. You can read why some people feel the need to censor in Figure 3.2, "Reasons for Banning Books," just above, and the box entitled "Freedom to Read" on page 88 examines a controversial government program to monitor reading habits.

Scope and Structure of the Book Industry

More than 195,000 new titles and editions were issued in the United States in 2004, a 14% increase over 2003 and an all-time record (Teague, 2005). Each American spends, on average, just under $100 a year buying and 17 minutes a day reading books (Lindsay, 2006). Total annual national book sales hover just under $30 billion, and the general good health of the industry

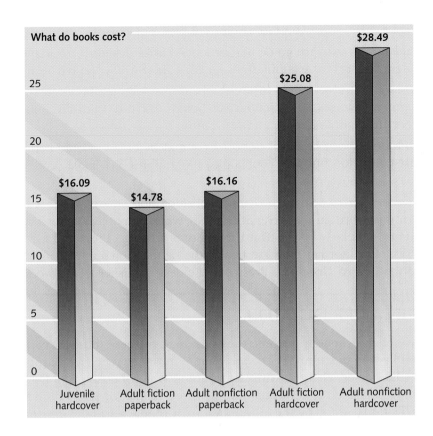

What do books cost?

				$28.49
Juvenile hardcover	Adult fiction paperback	Adult nonfiction paperback	Adult fiction hardcover	Adult nonfiction hardcover
$16.09	$14.78	$16.16	$25.08	$28.49

Figure 3.3 The Average Price of a Book, by Genre, in 2004.
Source: Teague, 2005.

led the Book Industry Study Group to forecast $44 billion in yearly sales by 2008 (BISG, 2004). You can see what books cost in Figure 3.3.

CATEGORIES OF BOOKS

The Association of American Publishers divides books into several sales categories:

- *Book club editions* are books sold and distributed (sometimes even published) by book clubs. There are currently more than 300 book clubs in the United States. These organizations offer trade, professional, and more specialized titles, for example, books for aviation aficionados and expensive republications of classic works. The Book of the Month Club, started in 1926, is the best known; the Literary Guild and the Reader's Digest Book Club are also popular.

- *El-hi* are textbooks produced for elementary and high schools.

- *Higher education* are textbooks produced for colleges and universities.

- *Mail-order books,* such as those advertised on television by Time-Life Books, are delivered by mail and usually are specialized series *(The War Ships)* or elaborately bound special editions of classic novels.

- *Mass market paperbacks* are typically published only as paperbacks and are designed to appeal to a broad readership; many romance novels, diet books, and self-help books are in this category.

- *Professional books* are reference and educational volumes designed specifically for professionals such as doctors, engineers, lawyers, scientists, and managers.

WWW

Association of American Publishers
www.publishers.org

- *Religious books* are volumes such as Bibles, catechisms, and hymnals.

- *Standardized tests* are guide and practice books designed to prepare readers for various examinations such as the SAT or the bar exam.

- *Subscription reference books* are publications such as the *Encyclopaedia Britannica*, atlases, and dictionaries bought directly from the publisher rather than purchased in a retail setting.

- **Trade books** can be hard- or softcover and include not only fiction and most nonfiction but also cookbooks, biographies, art books, coffee-table books, and how-to books.

- *University press books* come from publishing houses associated with and often underwritten by universities. They typically publish serious nonfiction and scholarly books. The University of Chicago Press and the University of California Press are two of the better-known university presses, and the Oxford University Press is the oldest publisher in the world.

FROM IDEA TO PUBLICATION

The ideas that ultimately become the books that fit these different categories reach publishers in a number of ways. Sometimes they reach an **acquisitions editor** (the person charged with determining which books a publisher will publish) unsolicited. This means that ideas are mailed or phoned directly to the acquisitions editor by the author. Many of the larger and better publishers will not accept unsolicited ideas from aspiring writers unless they first secure the services of an agent, an intermediary between publisher and writer. Increasingly, acquisitions editors are determining what books *they* think will do well and seeking out writers who can meet their needs.

At some publishing houses, acquisitions editors have the power to say "Yes" or "No" based on their own judgment of the value and profitability of an idea. At many others, these editors must prepare a case for the projects they want to take on and have them reviewed and approved by a review or proposal committee. These committees typically include not only "book people" but marketing, financial, production, and administrative professionals who judge the merit of the idea from their own perspectives. Once the acquisitions editor says "Yes," or is given permission by the committee to do so, the author and the publisher sign a contract.

Now the book must be written (if it is not already completed). An editor (sometimes the acquiring editor, sometimes not) is assigned to assist the author in producing a quality manuscript. Some combination of the publisher's marketing, promotions, and publicity departments plans the advertising campaign for the book. When available, review copies are sent to appropriate reviewers in other media. Book tours and signings are planned and scheduled. Copy for sales catalogues is written to aid salespeople in their attempts to place the book in bookstores.

All this effort is usually aimed at the first few months of a book's release. The publisher will determine in this time if the book will succeed or fail with readers. If the book appears to be a success, additional printings will be ordered. If the book has generated little interest from buyers, no additional copies are printed. Bookstores will eventually return unsold copies to the publisher to be sold at great discount as **remainders,** often as many as one-third of all copies in the case of hardcover books (Noted, 2005).

WWW

American Booksellers Association
www.ambook.org

Trends and Convergence in Book Publishing

This description of how a book reaches publication might better have been labeled "how a book *traditionally* travels from idea to publication." Because like all the media with which we are familiar, convergence is changing the nature of the book industry. In addition to convergence, contemporary publishing and its relationship with its readers are being reshaped by conglomeration, hypercommercialism and demand for profits, the growth of small presses, restructuring of retailing, and changes in readership.

CONVERGENCE

Convergence is altering almost all aspects of the book industry. Most obviously, the Internet is changing the way books are distributed and sold. But this new technology, in the form of **e-publishing**, the publication of books initially or exclusively online, offers a new way for writers' ideas to be published. Even the physical form of books is changing—many of today's "books" are no longer composed of paper pages snug between two covers. E-publishing can take the form of d-books and print on demand (POD). In its various forms, e-publishing generated $9.6 million in 2004 sales, with the number of books sold doubling to 1.7 million copies from 2002 to 2004 (Italie, 2005b).

WWW
DiskUs Publishing
www.diskuspublishing.com

D-books Manu Herbstein could not find a publisher for his book, *Ama: A Story of the Atlantic Slave Trade*. In fact, several houses had rejected it. But he did find an outlet in the e-publisher E-Reads. In April 2002 his **d-book**, a book downloaded in electronic form from the Internet to a computer or handheld PDA device such as a Palm Pilot, won the prestigious Commonwealth Prize in the category of best first book from the African region. The better-known Stephen King sold 400,000 digital copies (at $2.50 each) of his novella *Riding the Bullet* in 24 hours on Amazon.com's d-book service. King followed this success with the serialized release of *The Plant*. Publishing superstar Michael Crichton of *Jurassic Park* fame also generated significant d-book sales with *Timeline*, an eventual *New York Times* best seller.

WWW
E-Reads
www.ereads.com

Despite the presence of heavyweights like King and Crichton, many book industry observers feel that e-publishing will have its greatest impact with the Herbsteins, rather than the Kings, of the literary world. Because anyone with a computer and a novel to sell can bypass the traditional book publishers, first-time authors or writers of small, niche books now have an outlet for their work. An additional advantage of e-publishing, especially for new or small-market authors, is that d-books can be published almost instantly. Stephen King has made enough money selling his books that he can wait the 1 to 2 years it typically takes for a traditional novel to be produced once it is in the publisher's hands. Rarely can new authors afford this luxury.

Another advantage is financial. Even though many e-publishers require payment of as much as $300 or $400 to carry the work of new or unproven novelists, authors who distribute their work through an established e-publisher

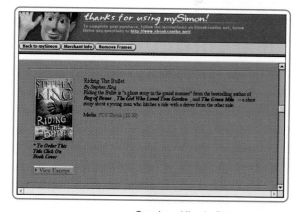

Stephen King's *Riding the Bullet*. CNET Networks, Inc. disclaims any responsibility for products described on their site. All product information, including prices, features, and availability is subject to change without notice. Copyright © 1995–2004 CNET Networks, Inc. All rights reserved. Reprinted by permission.

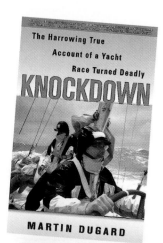
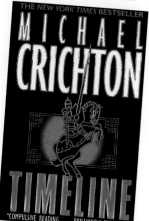

Knockdown is a POD success, and *Timeline* is a successful d-book meant to be read on a computer screen.

usually get royalties of 40% to 70%, compared to the 5% to 10% offered by traditional publishers. Traditional publishers say that the difference is due to the absence of services, such as editorial assistance and marketing, that authors face when using an e-publisher. And while this may have been true in e-publishing's early days, most digital publishers now provide a full range of services—copyediting, publishing, securing or commissioning artwork, jacket design, promotion, and in some cases, even hard-copy distribution to brick-and-mortar bookstores—based on a variable royalty or fee arrangement.

The advantages of d-books and e-publishing for readers are in time and money. Most d-books can be downloaded for as little as $3, with the average cost being around $10. And the electronic bookstore never closes. No matter what time of day or night, readers can download their next book and begin reading immediately.

Print on demand (POD) is another form of e-publishing. Companies such as Xlibris, AuthorHouse, Toby Press, and iUniverse are POD publishers. They store works digitally and, once ordered, a book can be instantly printed, bound, and sent. Alternatively, once ordered, that book can be printed and bound at a bookstore that has the proper technology. The advantage for publisher and reader is financial. POD books require no warehouse for storage, there are no remainders to eat into profits, and the production costs, in both personnel and equipment, are tiny when compared to traditional publishing. These factors not only produce less expensive books for readers but greatly expand the variety of books that can and will be published. And although a large publisher like Oxford University Press produces more than 100,000 POD volumes a year (Carnevale, 2005), smaller POD operations can make a profit on as few as 100 orders. Large commercial publishers have also found a place for POD in their business, using the technology to rush hot, headline-inspired books to readers. For example, Pocket Books produced a POD version of *Knockdown*, Martin Dugard's account of the tragic 1998 Sydney-to-Hobart boat race, getting it into the hands of readers months before the paper version became available.

Industry insiders believe POD is here to stay. After all, it reduces production and distribution costs, and it gets more books to readers faster and cheaper than can the current publishing business model. D-books, however, may not fare as well. The question of their future is a simple one: Will readers read books off computer screens? As best-selling author Jane Smiley (*A Thousand Acres, Horse Heaven, Moo, Ordinary Love & Goodwill*) explained, "Our economy has a way of getting rid of perfectly good and useful items and processes without any of us ever giving permission, just as it is right now trying to get rid of the . . . book. You can't read a novel on the Internet while taking a bath" (1999, p. 10B).

Convergence is reshaping reading in other interesting ways. Several Web sites, www.fictionwise.com, www.gutenberg.net, and www.memoware.com, for example, offer d-books specifically for PDAs and cell phones. Cell phones are the device-of-choice for e-readers preferring novels released in installments (Steuer, 2004). E-mail, too, is being utilized for reading **digital epistolary novels** (or **DENs**), stories that unfold serially through e-mails, instant messaging, and Web sites. Readers not only read the story as it unfolds but also interact with its characters and visit its locations. DEN advocates see this interactivity—expected by the younger Internet generation—as necessary for the success of e-publishing (Baer, 2004). And for readers in search of almost every book ever written or for those who want to search the contents of almost every book ever written (say, for references to the Civil War even though "Civil War" does not appear in the title), there are several developments. Online bookseller Amazon.com has scanned every page of every in-print book into its Search Inside the Book. That means anyone registered (it's free, but readers must provide a credit card number) can eventually search millions (according to Amazon) of books for just about any topic or idea. The pages cannot be downloaded, and there is a limit to how much searching a given reader can do in a specified period of time. Of course, Amazon's goal is to sell more books (you just might want to order one of the books your search has uncovered), but it is developing its own POD service that will provide, instantly, any book searched and requested. Several non-profit organizations are also making searchable and downloadable books available online. Project Gutenberg will offer 1 million noncopyrighted classics; the Million Book Project has set as its goal 1 million government and older titles; and the International Children's Digital Library and the Rosetta Project hope to make downloadable tens of thousands of current and antique children's books from around the world (Wolf, 2003).

Where these efforts at digitizing books have been generally well regarded, the same cannot be said for Google Print. Internet giant Google announced in late 2005 its intention to make available online 15 million books from the New York Public Library and the libraries of the University of Michigan, Stanford University, Harvard University, and Oxford University. The vast majority, 90%, would be out-of-print books not bound by copyright (see Chapter 14). The problem, however, is Google's plan to hold the entire text of all works, in and out of print, on its servers, making only small, fair-use portions of copyrighted works available to Web users. Initially, many publishers agreed to participate if the complete text of their copyrighted works could be stored on *their* servers, but Google refused. A series of lawsuits from the Author's Guild and five major publishers followed (Vise, 2005). Google insists that it will protect the interests of authors and publishers as it strives to "make books and the information within them more discoverable to the world," in the words of the company itself (Neumeister, 2005). But writers and publishers remain unconvinced: "Google may claim that it'll show only a 'snippet,' but what guarantee do we have? Having made copies of the entire work, will they protect it from hackers or even from themselves? The slope is too slippery here" (Weenolsen, 2005, p. 20A).

CONGLOMERATION

More than any other medium, the book industry was dominated by relatively small operations. Publishing houses were traditionally staffed by fewer than 20 people, the large majority by fewer than 10. Today, however, although more than 81,000 businesses call themselves book publishers, only a very small percentage produces four or more titles a year (Teague, 2005). The industry is dominated now by a few giants: Hearst Books, the Penguin Group, Bantam Doubleday Dell, Time Warner Publishing, Farrar, Straus & Giroux, Harcourt General, HarperCollins, and Simon & Schuster. Each of these giants was once, sometimes with another name, an independent book publisher. All are now part of large national or international corporate conglomerates. These major publishers control more than 80% of all U.S. book sales (Schiffrin, 1999). Even e-publishing, heralded by some as the future of book publishing, is dominated by the big companies. Not only do all the major houses and booksellers maintain e-publishing units, but even **POD** sites such as Xlibris (Random House) and iUniverse (Barnes & Noble) are wholly or partly owned by these giants.

Opinion is divided on the benefit of corporate ownership. The positive view is that the rich parent company can infuse the publishing house with necessary capital, enabling it to attract better authors or to take gambles on new writers that would, in the past, have been impossible. Another plus is that the corporate parent's other media holdings can be used to promote and repackage the books for greater profitability.

The negative view is that as publishing houses become just one in the parent company's long list of enterprises, product quality suffers as important editing and production steps are eliminated to maximize profits. Before conglomeration, publishing was often described as a **cottage industry**; that is, publishing houses were small operations, closely identified with their personnel—both their own small staffs and their authors. The cottage imagery, however, extends beyond smallness of size. There was a quaintness and charm associated with publishing houses—their attention to detail, their devotion to tradition, the care they gave to their façades (their reputations). The world of corporate conglomerates has little room for such niceties, as profit dominates all other considerations.

Random House, once an independent book publisher, is now owned by the German conglomerate Bertelsmann, owner of scores of other media outlets such as RCA Records and *McCall's* magazine. A former editor, Andre Schiffrin (1996), wrote of the change from independent to subsidiary, "The drive for profit fits like an iron mask on our cultural output" (p. 29).

DEMAND FOR PROFITS AND HYPERCOMMERCIALISM

The threat from conglomeration is seen in the parent company's overemphasis on the bottom line—that is, profitability at all costs. Unlike in the days when G. P. Putnam's sons and the Schuster family actually ran the houses that carried their names, critics fear that now little pride is taken in the content of books and that risk taking (tackling controversial issues, experimenting with new styles, finding and nurturing unknown authors) is becoming rarer and rarer.

Chairperson of the Writing Seminars at Johns Hopkins University, Mark Miller (1997), wrote, "This is the all important difference between then and now: As book lovers and businessmen, [publishers] did the high-yield trash so as to subsidize the books they loved (although those books might also sell). No longer meant to help some finer things grow, the crap today is not a means but (as it were) the end" (p. 14). Jason Epstein, longtime editor at Random House and founder of Anchor Books, writes that his is an "increasingly distressed industry" mired in "severe structural problems." Among them are the chain-driven bookselling system that favors "brand name" authors and "a bestseller-driven system of high royalty advances." He says that contemporary publishing is "overconcentrated," "undifferentiated," and "fatally rigid" (quoted in Feldman, 2001, p. 35). To Miller, Epstein, and other critics of conglomeration,

WWW
iUniverse
www.iUniverse.com

WWW
Toby Press
www.tobypress.com

WWW
PDA and Cell Phone Books
www.fictionwise.com
gutenberg.org
memoware.com

the industry seems overwhelmed by a blockbuster mentality—lust for the biggest-selling authors and titles possible, sometimes with little consideration for literary merit. Recently, Justin Timberlake of the pop group 'N Sync received a seven-figure advance for his first novel, *Crossover Dribble*. Michael Crichton got $40 million for a two-book deal from HarperCollins; Tom Clancy, $45 million for two books from Penguin Putnam; Mary Higgins Clark, $64 million for five books from Simon & Schuster; and Hillary Rodham Clinton scored an $8 million advance from that same company. Husband Bill collected $12 million. In 2002, Charles Frazier, whose first novel was best-seller *Cold Mountain*, received an $8 million advance for his second book from Random House, based on a one-page outline. "Gossipy, inbred, lunch-dependent, and about two years behind the rest of the nation, corporate publishing is now in the business of sabotaging the very system it's supposed to keep vital," wrote Pat Holt, editor of industry Web site Holt Unlimited. Instead of "selecting good books" and finding a "creative, devoted, and adventurous way to sell them, the big houses continually peddle bland products that are gradually driving readers away" (quoted in "The Crisis," 2003, p. 22). As the resources and energies of publishing houses are committed to a small number of superstar writers and blockbuster books, smaller, more interesting, possibly more serious or important books do not get published. If these books cannot get published, they will not be written. We will be denied their ideas in the cultural forum. We will see, but as we read earlier in this chapter, it is converged technologies like POD and d-books that may well be the vehicle to ensure those ideas access to the forum and us to them.

Publishers attempt to offset the large investments they do make through the sale of **subsidiary rights**, that is, the sale of the book, its contents, and even its characters to filmmakers, paperback publishers, book clubs, foreign publishers, and product producers like T-shirt, poster, coffee cup, and greeting card manufacturers. Frazier's one-page proposal for his second novel, for example, earned his publisher $3 million for the film rights alone from Paramount Pictures. The industry itself estimates that many publishers would go out of business if it were not for the sale of these rights. Writers such as Michael Crichton *(Jurassic Park)*, John Grisham *(The Client)*, and Gay Talese *(Thy Neighbor's Wife)* can command as much as $2.5 million for the film rights to their books. Although this is good for the profitability of the publishers and the superstar authors, critics fear that those books with the greatest subsidiary sales value will receive the most publisher attention.

As greater and greater sums are tied up in blockbusters, and as subsidiary rights therefore grow in importance, the marketing, promotion, and public relations surrounding a book become

"We have a calendar based on the book, stationery based on the book, an audiotape of the book, and a videotape of the movie based on the book, but we don't have the book."

Typical of thousands of small publishing houses, Ten Speed Press offers an array of interesting, odd, or otherwise "small" books that larger publishers may ignore.

FRONTLIST

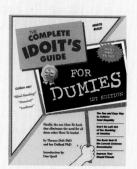

THE COMPLETE IDOIT'S GUIDE FOR DUMIES
The Fun and Easy Way to Achieve Total Stupidity
by Thomas Dolt and Ian Dullard

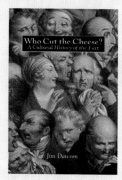

WHO CUT THE CHEESE?
A Cultural History of the Fart
by Jim Dawson

KOKIGAMI
Performance Enhancing Adornments for the Adventurous Man
by Burton Silver and Heather Busch

WWW

Powell's Books
powells.com

Her kidnapping at the hands of a quadruple murderer quickly led to Ashley Smith's instant book *Unlikely Angel.*

crucial. This leads to the additional fear that only the most promotable books will be published—the stores are flooded with Martha Stewart books, celebrity picture books, unauthorized biographies of celebrities, and tell-all autobiographies from the children of famous people.

The importance of promotion and publicity has led to an increase in the release of **instant books**. What better way to unleash millions of dollars of free publicity for a book than to base it on an event currently on the front page and the television screen? Publishers see these opportunities and then initiate the projects. O. J. Simpson's many courtroom trials have been fodder for several instant books, as have the legal travails of Kobe Bryant and other celebrities. The television show *The Apprentice* spawned an instant book, *Trump: How to Get Rich. Unlikely Angel* is the instant product of Atlanta-area widow Ashley Smith's 2005 kidnapping encounter with murderer Brian Nichols. Lost in the wake of instant books, easily promotable authors and titles, and blockbusters, critics argue, are books of merit, books of substance, and books that make a difference.

Several other recent events suggest that the demand for profits is bringing even more hyper-commercialism to the book business. One trend is the "Hollywoodization" of books. Potential synergies between books, television, and movies have spurred big media companies such as Viacom, Time Warner, and News Corp. to invest heavily in publishing, buying up houses big and small. Some movie studios are striking "exclusive" deals with publishers—for example, Walden Media teams with Penguin Young Readers, Focus Films with Random House, and Paramount with Simon & Schuster. In addition, in 2005 ReganBooks (owned by Harper-Collins, which, in turn, is owned by News Corp.) moved its offices from New York to Los Angeles to be in a better position to develop material that has both book and film potential. In that same year, studios Warner Brothers, Columbia, Paramount, DreamWorks, Fox, New Line, Imagine, Tribeca, and Revolution Films set up operations in New York City to find books and "mine magazine articles, theater, and other properties" that can be converted to screen fare (Fleming, 2005, p. 3). Critics fear that only those books with the most synergistic potential will be signed and published. Advocates argue just the opposite—a work that might have had limited profit potential as a "mere" book, and therefore gone unpublished, just might find a home across several mutually promoting platforms. They point to *Sideways*, a small-selling book that became a best-selling book after the movie it inspired became a hit.

Another trend that has created much angst among book traditionalists is the paid product placement. Movies and television have long accepted payments from product manufacturers to feature their brands in their content, but it was not until May 2000 that the first paid-for placement appeared in a fiction novel. Bill Fitzhugh's *Cross Dressing*, published by Avon, contains what are purchased commercials for Seagram liquor. Fay Weldon followed suit in 2001, even titling her book *The Bulgari Connection*, after her sponsor, a jewelry company by the same name. As with other media that accept product placements, critics fear that content will be bent to satisfy sponsors rather than serve the quality of the work itself. For example, on contract with car-maker Ford, Carole Matthews, British writer of "edgy romantic comedy [novels] aimed at young contemporary women," penned a scene in which her heroine is "whizzing around Buckinghamshire in Imogene, my rather snazzy Ford Fiesta complete with six-CD changer, air-conditioning, and thoroughly comfy seats." Said Ms. Matthews, "I've been very pleased with Ford in that they haven't put any constraints on my writing at all." But, asks author and social critic Jim Hightower, how free was she to write something akin to "whizzing around Buckinghamshire, my snazzy Ford Fiesta sputtered and died on me again, just as the six-CD changer went on the fritz and spewed blue smoke in my face" (2004b, p. 3)?

Bookwire
www.bookwire.com

Project Gutenberg
www.promo.net/pg/

GROWTH OF SMALL PRESSES

The overcommercialization of the book industry is mitigated somewhat by the rise in the number of smaller publishing houses. Although these smaller operations are large in number, they account for a very small proportion of books sold. Nonetheless, as recently as 7 years ago there were 20,000 U.S. book publishers. Today there are more than 81,000, the vast majority being small presses. They cannot compete in the blockbuster world. By definition *alternative*, they specialize in specific areas such as the environment, feminism, gay issues, and how-to. They can also publish writing otherwise uninteresting to bigger houses, such as poetry and literary commentary. Relying on specialization and narrowly targeted marketing, books such as Ralph Nader and Clarence Ditlow's *The Lemon Book*, published by Moyer Bell, Claudette McShane's *Warning! Dating May Be Hazardous to Your Health*, published by Mother Courage Press, and *Split Verse*, a book of poems about divorce published by Midmarch Arts, can not only earn healthy sales but also make a difference in their readers' lives. And what may seem surprising, it is the Internet, specifically Amazon, that is boosting the fortunes of these smaller houses. Because it compiles data on customer preferences (books bought, browsed, recommended to others, or wished for), it can make recommendations to potential buyers, and, quite often, those recommendations are from small publishers that the buyer might never have considered (or never have seen at a brick-and-mortar retailer). In other words, Amazon levels the book industry playing field. As Kent Sturgis, president of the Independent Book Publishers Association, explained, "All publishers are basically equal, because just about all publishers' titles are on Amazon and can be delivered to your door in a couple of days" (Gillespie, 2005, p. B2). Amazon even set up a special program in 1998, Advantage, to help smaller publishers with payment and shipping.

RESTRUCTURING OF BOOK RETAILING

There are approximately 20,000 bookstores in the United States, but the number is dwindling as small, independent operations find it increasingly difficult to compete with such chains as Barnes & Noble, Borders, and Books-A-Million. These larger operations are typically located in malls that

WWW

Rosetta Project
www.rosettaproject.org

"Fay Weldon's Object Lesson" by Bruce Handy and Glynis Sweeny. *Time*, 9/17/01.

Copyright © 2001 Glynis Sweeny. Used with permission.

Many major chain bookstores now emulate the comfort and charm of an independent store. Barnes & Noble, the country's second-largest coffee retailer, also offers customers a clean, well-lighted place to peruse their products and sip a latté.

have heavy pedestrian traffic. Barnes & Noble and Borders alone control 2,000 stores and account for 20% of all books sold in this country. Borders claims 30 million walk-in customers a year. Barnes & Noble says it annually serves 400 million customers, and it is the second-largest (after Starbucks) coffee retailer in America. Together the two big chains sell more than $10 billion worth of books and merchandise a year (Learmonth, 2005).

The big booksellers' size enables them to purchase inventory cheaply and then offer discounts to shoppers. Because their location attracts shoppers, they can also profitably stock nonbook merchandise such as audio- and videotapes, CDs, computer games, calendars, magazines, and greeting cards for the drop-in trade. But high-volume, high-traffic operations tend to deal in high-volume books. To book traditionalists, this only encourages the industry's blockbuster mentality. When the largest bookstores in the country order only the biggest sellers, the small books get lost. When floor space is given over to Garfield coffee mugs and pop star calendars, there is even less room for small but potentially interesting books. Although big bookselling chains have their critics, they also have their defenders. At least the big titles, CDs, and cheap prices get people into bookstores, the argument goes. Once folks begin reading, even if it is trashy stuff, they might move on to better material. People who never buy books will never read books.

Although their share of total U.S. retail sales fell from about 33% in the early 1990s to about 15% today, many independent bookstores continue to prosper. Using their size and independence to their advantage, they counter the chains with expert, personalized service provided by a reading-loving staff, coffee and snack bars, cushioned chairs and sofas for slow browsing, and intimate readings by favorite authors. In fact, so successful have these devices been that the big stores now are copying them. Barnes & Noble,

Amazon.com
www.amazon.com

Books.com
www.books.com

CULTURAL FORUM

Freedom to Read

In the immediate aftermath of the terrorist attacks on New York and Washington on September 11, 2001, the U.S. Congress passed the 342-page USA PATRIOT Act, legislation, according to its sponsors, that would give federal authorities increased power to thwart terrorism. Outraged by provisions such as the elimination of probable cause in securing permission to wiretap citizens' phones or intercept their e-mail, civil libertarians from all political leanings quickly found fault with much of the law (Kalet, 2004). But it was one section in particular, 215, that caught the attention of the general public and put reading into the cultural forum.

What so engaged and enraged the public was its attack on our freedom to read. Section 215 allowed the FBI, under secret warrant, to examine our library records. Those receiving the warrant, that is, librarians, were forbidden under threat of prosecution from telling anyone about a search, including the person whose records were examined (Flanders, 2002). The idea of secret police monitoring our reading was as appalling as book burning to much of the public.

Are you so moved? But why? The law only applied to "suspected terrorists." But, say critics, a "suspected terrorist" is whoever the authorities say is a suspected terrorist. Police do not even have to show a judge probable cause for their search. Still, the searches will be rarely used. Slow down, say critics, how will we know how often searches take place when the librarians

> **"THIS ISN'T ABOUT STRIPPING LAW ENFORCEMENT OF THE POWER TO INVESTIGATE TERRORISM. IT'S ABOUT RESTORING CONFIDENCE THAT OUR READING CHOICES AREN'T BEING MONITORED BY THE GOVERNMENT."**

turning over records are forbidden from telling anyone and those whose records are searched are unaware? That is unfortunate, but shouldn't we do all we can to protect ourselves from people who generate suspicion by showing too much interest in Islam, the politics of the Middle East, or pro-Arab versions of the Arab–Israeli conflict? No, said critics, because informed citizens who want to know more about why we are at war with terror and why we are fighting in the Middle East are the very people who would read these books. More important, in a democracy what a person reads, and why a person reads it, is his or her business. Period. Why should it generate suspicion?

Unofficial rejection of Section 215's threat to Americans' freedom to read was widespread. In addition to the seven states and 383 communities (big cities like New York and L.A. and small towns like Northampton, Massachusetts, and Castle Valley, Utah) passing laws making the enforcement of Section 215 a crime in their jurisdictions (Colorado Indy Media, 2005), there was a rebellion of the librarians. Many posted warnings around their reading rooms, alerting patrons that their records are at risk. Some refused to comply. Others shredded patrons' records daily, making them unavailable to any inquisitor. The American Library Association, the American Booksellers Association, and the PEN American Center launched a public relations campaign—the Campaign for Reader privacy—that used the Web (www.readerprivacy.com),

Innovations originally instituted by independent booksellers have redefined "the bookstore."
© Rhymes with Orange-Hilary B. Price. King Features Syndicate.

for example, sponsors a program it calls Discover to promote notable first novels, and Borders does the same with Original Voices. Not only do these efforts emulate services more commonly associated with smaller independents, but they also help blunt some of the criticism suffered by the

Resistance from the political Left and Right, from state and local governments, even from "radical militant" librarians, helped guarantee that readers would not suffer this fate when visiting the library.

printed literature, and "town meetings" to bring the issue to the people and, in turn, encourage them to bring it to their elected officials. "This isn't about stripping law enforcement of the power to investigate terrorism," said Larry Siems of PEN. "It's about restoring confidence that our reading choices aren't being monitored by the government" (quoted in Kalet, 2004, p. 10).

In February 2006, the U.S. Senate joined the House in officially objecting to Section 215. Several congressional Republicans joined Democrats and threatened to filibuster the renewal of the entire PATRIOT Act unless, among other changes, libraries were freed from *secret* searches (searches, however, could continue). The Bush administration and the Justice Department reluctantly agreed. But the rancor remains, especially because the law stipulates that searches can remain secret for up to a full year. An unidentified FBI agent complained by e-mail that it angered him that "radical militant librarians kick us [the FBI] around" (in Ivins, 2006, p. 22). Radical militants or people committed to our freedom to read?

Enter your voice in the cultural forum. Is this much ado about nothing? Do you agree with Stewart Baker, former general counsel to the National Security Agency, who argued, "We as a people are willing to trade a little less privacy for a little more security" (quoted in Streitfeld & Piller, 2002, p. D6), or with Benjamin Franklin, who said, "They that can give up essential liberty to obtain a little temporary safety deserve neither liberty nor safety"?

chains, specifically that they ignore new and smaller-selling books. Still, the big operations cannot or will not emulate some strategies. Specialization is one. Religious, feminist, and animal-lover bookstores exist. The in-store book club for children or poetry fans, for example, is another small-store strategy.

Another alternative to the big mall chain store is buying books online. Amazon.com of Seattle is the best known of the online book sales services. Thorough, fast (it guarantees 2-day delivery), and well stocked (it lists 2.5 million titles and its motto is "Every Book Under the Sun"), Amazon boasts low overhead, and that means better prices for readers. In addition, its Web site offers book buyers large amounts of potentially valuable information. Once online, customers can identify the books that interest them, read synopses, check reviews from multiple sources, and read comments not only from other readers but sometimes from the authors and publishers as well. Of course, they can also order books. Some other popular online bookstores can be found at http://powells.com and www.books.com, and almost all publishers of all sizes now sell their own titles online.

The best-known and most successful of the online booksellers, Amazon.com, offers potential buyers a wealth of information and services.

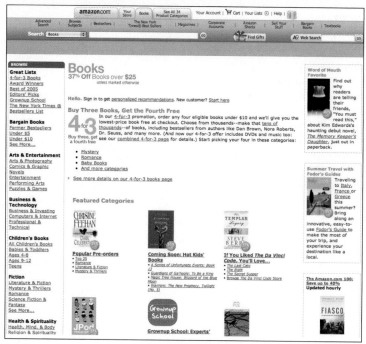

DEVELOPING MEDIA LITERACY SKILLS

The Lessons of Harry Potter

More about Harry
www.mugglenet.com

The excitement surrounding the release in July 2005 of the sixth installment of J. K. Rowling's series on youthful British sorcerer Harry Potter offers several important lessons for the media literate person. Publication of *Harry Potter and the Half-Blood Prince* highlighted several elements of media literacy and called into play a number of media literacy skills. For example, its huge appeal to young people can be used to examine one element of media literacy, understanding content as a text providing insight into our culture and lives. Just why have these books resonated so strongly with young readers? The controversy surrounding the numerous efforts to have the series banned from schools and libraries as antireligious and anti-Christian and its status as the "most challenged" (censored) children's literature in the United States call into play the particular media literacy skill of developing the ability and willingness to effectively and meaningfully understand content (Churnin, 2005).

The publishing industry classifies the Harry Potter books as children's literature. But their phenomenal reception by readers of all ages suggests these works not only have broader appeal but are in themselves something very special. The initial U.S. printing of the 672-page *Half-Blood Prince* was 13.5 million copies—100 times that of a normal best seller and the largest initial print run in publishing history. The book sold 9 million copies in the United States on its first day of release (Italie, 2005a). The six *Harry Potter*s combined have sold more than 300 million copies worldwide, and two-thirds of all American children have read at least one edition. The *Potter* series has been published in over 55 languages (including Greek, Latin, and "Americanized English") in more than 200 countries (Italie, 2003).

With the publication of each installment, talk about the "rebirth of the book" and a "reverse in the decline of reading by young people" heated up. Harry had not only defeated the evil Lord Voldemort (a wizard so evil his name could not be uttered), but he had banished **aliteracy**, wherein people possess the ability to read but are unwilling to do so.

A 1999 survey of U.S. reading habits found that only 45% of readers read anything (books, newspapers, magazines, cereal boxes) for more than 30 minutes a day (Quindlen, 2000). The National Endowment for the Arts issued its report *Reading at Risk* in July 2004. It noted that fewer than half of all Americans over 18 years old read novels, short stories, plays, or poetry. The number of consumers buying books of all kinds is in decline. And "the pace at which the nation is losing readers, especially young readers, is quickening." Moreover, this growing aliteracy holds for all demographic areas (Weber, 2004, p. 1). Aliteracy is as problematic for a robust culture as Lord Voldemort is for the wizard culture for two reasons. First, given the role books play as a major force in the social, political, and intellectual development of the cultures that use them, can any people afford to ignore them? Second, totalitarian governments ban and burn books because they are repositories of ideas, ideas that can be read and considered with limited outside influence or official supervision. What kind of culture develops when, by their own refusal to read books, people figuratively save the dictators the trouble of striking the match?

Harry Potter, the little wizard who launched a million readers.

What has been Harry Potter's impact on reading? In 1963 the Gallup polling organization found that fewer than half of all Americans said they had read a book all the way through in the previous year. But soon after the release of *The Prisoner of Azkaban* in 1999, that number was 84% (Quindlen, 2000). Nobody would claim that Harry alone was responsible, but *Newsweek*'s Anna Quindlen speculated that he had helped "create a new generation of inveterate readers" (p. 64). Fright master Stephen King agreed, writing, "If these millions of readers are awakened to the wonders and rewards of fantasy at 11 or 12 . . . well, when they get to age 16 or so, there's this guy named King" (as quoted in Garchik, 2000, p. D10). Caroline Ward, president of the American Library Association's Services to Children, said, "It's hard to believe that one series of books could almost turn an entire nation back to reading, but that is not an exaggeration," and Diane Roback, children's book editor at *Publishers Weekly*, cited "'the Harry Potter halo effect,' in which children come into stores and libraries asking for books that resemble the Rowling series" (*USA Today*, 2000, p. E4). Neal Coonerty, owner of the independent Bookshop Santa Cruz in California, enthused, "The great thing about these books is they're read by both boys and girls alike, with equal enthusiasm" (as quoted in Beck, 2000, p. 17A).

One element of media literacy is the development of an awareness of the impact of media, and the *Harry Potter* series has amply demonstrated its influence. But its wild success was used by many media critics to castigate

International Children's Digital Library
www.icdlbooks.org

Children's Book Council
www.cbcbooks.org

LIVING MEDIA LITERACY

Start a Citywide (or Campuswide) Book Conversation

You can help fight aliteracy, find new works, and maybe even meet some interesting people by involving yourself in one of the many citywide book-reading clubs that now exist. The movement, begun in 1998 by Nancy Pearl of Seattle's Washington Center for the Book, calls on reading groups in a city to choose one book to be read by everyone in that town. The idea, naturally, is to encourage reading, but also to get people talking about books and the ideas they hold (Angell, 2002).

These readings are organized in Chicago by One Book One Chicago and in New York City by Literary New York. Other towns with established programs are San Francisco, Los Angeles, Palm Beach, Cleveland, Colorado Springs, and Valparaiso, Indiana.

YOU CAN HELP FIGHT ALITERACY, FIND NEW WORKS, AND MAYBE EVEN MEET SOME INTERESTING PEOPLE BY INVOLVING YOURSELF IN ONE OF THE MANY CITYWIDE BOOK-READING CLUBS THAT NOW EXIST.

Check with your local library to see who in your area is running a similar program. If no one is, begin one yourself. The Washington Center for the Book has a how-to Web page. Go to www.spl.org and scroll down to "bookclubs." You can access the Live Literature Network (www.liveliterature.net) to see where there might be a live author's reading near you and tie your selection to that event. Another possibility is to involve one or more area schools in a school-system-wide rather than citywide reading. National Children's Book Week in November is a good time to do it if you choose this path. The Children's Book Council (www.cbcbooks.org) can help. But even more logically, you can start a campuswide or dormwide book-reading club.

both media professionals who underestimate their audiences *and* audience members who encourage that underestimation. In other words, the success (and profitability) of this well-written, thoughtful, high-quality content stood in stark contrast to what critics contend is a steady decline in quality in other media, particularly advertiser-supported media such as radio and television. The argument is simple: Broadcasters, especially the major national television networks, respond to falling viewership not by improving content but by lowering its intelligence and worth. Whereas the Harry Potter books get better (and longer) in response to reader enthusiasm, network television dumbs down, giving its audience *Fear Factor, Survivor,* and other so-called reality programming.

And radio, as you will see in Chapter 6, has responded to 10 years of declining levels of listenership and the loss of interest among its young core audience not with new, imaginative programming but with more homogenization, automation, and the disappearance of local programming and news. The pressures on advertiser-supported media are somewhat different from those on books and film; with the latter two, readers and moviegoers express their desires and tastes directly through the purchase of content (the books themselves and tickets, respectively). But media literate people must ask why their exodus from a particular medium is not more often met with the presentation of better fare. Harry Potter shows that an audience that develops heightened expectations can and will have those expectations met.

RESOURCES FOR REVIEW AND DISCUSSION

Review Points

- Although the first printing press came to the Colonies in 1638, books were not central to early colonial life; but books and pamphlets were at the heart of the colonists' revolt against England in the 1770s.
- Developments in the 18th and 19th centuries, such as improvements in printing, the flowering of the American novel, and the introduction of the paperback, helped make books a mass medium.
- Books have cultural value because they are agents of social and cultural change; important cultural repositories; windows on the past; important sources of personal development; sources of entertainment, escape, and personal reflection; mirrors of culture; and the purchase and reading of a book is a much more individual, personal activity than consuming advertiser-supported or heavily promoted media.
- Censorship threatens these values, as well as democracy itself.

- Convergence is reshaping the book industry as well as the reading experience itself through advances such as e-publishing, POD, d-books, DENs, and several different efforts to digitize most of the world's books.
- Conglomeration affects the publishing industry as it has all media, expressing itself through trends such as demand for profit and hypercommercialization.
- Demand for profit and hypercommercialization manifest themselves in the increased importance placed on subsidiary rights, instant books, "Hollywoodization," and product placement.
- Book retailing is undergoing change. Large chains dominate the business but continue to be challenged by imaginative, high-quality independent booksellers. Much book buying has also gravitated to the Internet.
- The wild success of the *Harry Potter* series holds several lessons for media literate readers.

Key Terms

 Use the text's Online Learning Center at www.mhhe.com/baran5 to further your understanding of the following terminology.

linotype, 68
offset lithography, 68
dime novels, 68
pulp novels, 68
chained Bibles, 70
trade books, 78

acquisitions editor, 78
remainders, 78
e-publishing, 79
d-book, 79
print on demand (POD), 80
digital epistolary novel (DEN), 80

cottage industry, 82
subsidiary rights, 83
instant book, 84
aliteracy, 91

Questions for Review

 Go to the self-quizzes on the Online Learning Center to test your knowledge.

1. What were the major developments in the modernization of the printing press?
2. Why were the early colonists not a book-reading population?
3. What was the Stamp Act? Why did colonial printers object to it?
4. What factors allowed the flowering of the American novel, as well as the expansion of the book industry, in the 1800s?
5. Who developed the paperback in England? In the United States?

6. Name six reasons books are an important cultural resource.
7. What are the major categories of books?
8. What is the impact of conglomeration on the book industry?
9. What are the products of increasing hypercommercialism and demands for profit in the book industry?
10. What are d-books, DENs, and e-publishing?
11. What particular cultural values are served by independent booksellers?
12. What is product placement?

Questions for Critical Thinking and Discussion

1. Do you envision books ever again having the power to move the nation as they did in Revolutionary or anti-slavery times? Why or why not?
2. How familiar are you with the early great American writers such as Hawthorne, Cooper, and Thoreau? What have you learned from these writers?
3. Are you proud of your book-reading habits? Why or why not?
4. Where do you stand in the debate on the overcommercialization of the book? To what lengths should publishers and booksellers go to get people to read?
5. Under what circumstances is censorship permissible? Whom do you trust to make the right decision about what you should and should not read? If you were a librarian, under what circumstances would you pull a book?

Important Resources

 Go to the Online Learning Center for additional readings.

Internet Resources

More on Ray Bradbury	www.raybradbury.com
More on Ben Franklin	www.english.udel.edu/lemay/franklin
More on Our Bodies, Ourselves	www.ourbodiesourselves.org
American Library Association	www.ala.org
American Civil Liberties Union	www.aclu.org
Banned Books	www.ala.org/bbooks
American Booksellers Foundation for Free Expression	www.abffe.org
Association of American Publishers	www.publishers.org
American Booksellers Association	www.ambook.org
E-Reads	www.ereads.com
DiskUs Publishing	www.diskuspublishing.com
Xlibris	www.xlibris.com
1st Books	www.1stbooks.com
AuthorHouse	www.authorhouse.com
Toby Press	www.tobypress.com
PDA and Cell Phone Books	www.fictionwise.com
	www.gutenberg.org
	www.memoware.com
Powell's Books	www.powells.com
Bookwire	www.bookwire.com
Project Gutenberg	www.promo.net/pg/
Rosetta Project	www.rosettaproject.org
Barnes & Noble	www.books.com
Amazon.com	www.amazon.com
More about Harry	www.mugglenet.com
International Children's Digital Library	www.icdlbooks.org

Newspapers

4

LEARNING OBJECTIVES

Newspapers were at the center of our nation's drive for independence and have a long history as the people's medium. The newspaper was also the first mass medium to rely on advertising for financial support, changing the relationship between audience and media from that time on. After studying this chapter you should

- be familiar with the history and development of the newspaper industry and the newspaper itself as a medium.
- understand how the organizational and economic nature of the contemporary newspaper industry shapes the content of newspapers.
- understand the relationship between the newspaper and its readers.
- be familiar with changes in the newspaper industry brought about by emerging technologies and how those alterations may affect the medium's traditional role in our democracy.
- possess improved newspaper-reading media literacy skills, especially in interpreting the relative placement of stories and use of photos.

You've landed a job at your hometown newspaper right out of school. A job in the media! How cool is that?! But how do you explain to your friends that your position isn't quite what they (or even you) think of when you think "working at the daily newspaper"? That image is the tenacious reporter, Woodward and Bernstein unmasking wrong for the good of the people. Okay, so it's not that, but it's not even Jimmy Olsen, cub reporter at the *Daily Planet*, yelled at by editor Perry White, picking up the small stories ignored by Clark Kent as he flies off as Superman to save Lois Lane from the Penguin. Maybe the Penguin's Batman, but still, this isn't what you had foreseen when you were first excited about working in journalism.

"What do you do at the paper?" your friends ask. Your answer—you are in charge of the paper's online classified advertising . . . its *free* online classified advertising. What you know that your pals might not is that the newspaper business is in a period of profound alteration. In 2005 alone, more than 2,100 newspaper jobs across America

Opposite: For many people, the day doesn't begin until they read the paper.

disappeared, the culmination of a 4-year trend of vanishing positions. Big papers, small papers, the story was the same (Farhi, 2006). But what you were smart enough to see is that newspapers remain remarkably financially healthy, often turning operating profits of up to 20 percent, more than twice that of the Fortune 500 companies, and newspaper Internet advertising, growing at 40% a year, makes up a big chunk of that profit (Morton, 2006). That's why you are where you are. Maybe your new job doesn't seem all that cool to your friends, but you believe that readers need what the paper does (even if it has to do it all or in part online). You want to be on the inside as the daily paper finds its new place in the tumultuous media environment.

In this chapter we examine the relationship between the newspaper and its readers. We start with a look at the medium's roots, beginning with the first papers, following them from Europe to colonial America, where many of the traditions of today's free press were set. We study the cultural changes that led to creation of the penny press and to competition between these mass circulation dailies that gave us "yellow journalism."

We then review the modern newspaper in terms of its size and scope. We discuss different types of newspapers and the importance of newspapers as an advertising medium. The wire and feature services, important providers of newspaper content, are also highlighted.

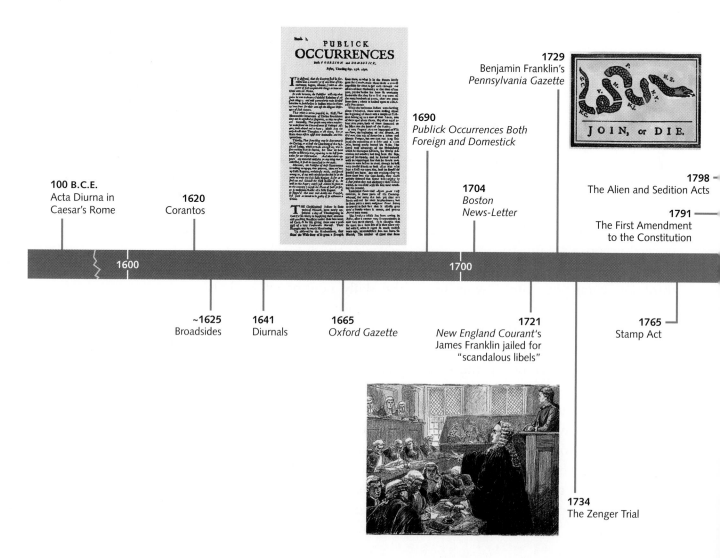

We then detail how the relationship between medium and audience is shifting as a result of the loss of competition within the industry, hyper-commercialism in the guise of commercial pressure on papers' editorial content, the positive and negative impacts of technology, the rise of online newspapers, and changes in the nature of newspaper readership. Finally, we test our media literacy skill through a discussion of how to read the newspaper, for example, interpreting the relative positioning of stories.

A Short History of Newspapers

The opening vignette makes an important point about contemporary newspapers—they are working hard to secure new identities for themselves in an increasingly crowded media environment. As a medium and as an industry, newspapers are poised at the edge of a significant change in their role and operation. The changing relationship between newspapers and readers is part of this upheaval. And while it's not uncommon to read or hear comments such as this one from technology company CEO Ted Padova, "Personally, I believe that most of us will see near-extinction of printed works in our lifetime" (quoted in Bagdikian, 2004, p. 70), newspapers have faced similar challenges more than once in the past and have survived.

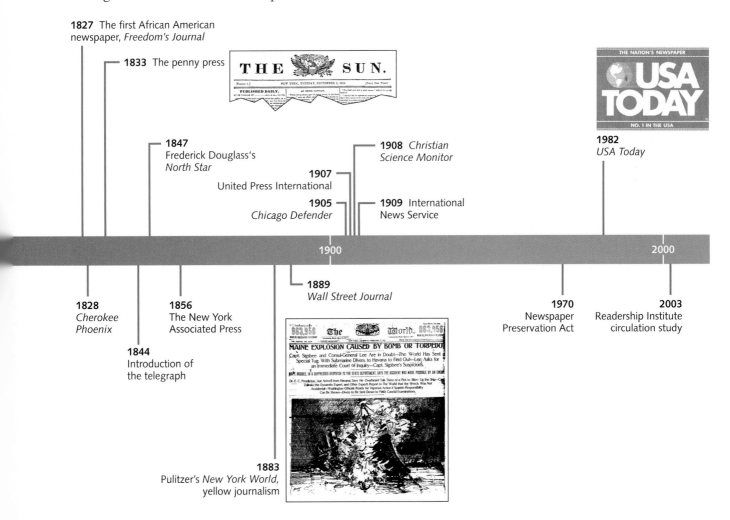

1827 The first African American newspaper, *Freedom's Journal*

1833 The penny press

1847 Frederick Douglass's *North Star*

1908 *Christian Science Monitor*

1907 United Press International

1905 *Chicago Defender*

1909 International News Service

1982 *USA Today*

1900

2000

1889 *Wall Street Journal*

1828 *Cherokee Phoenix*

1856 The New York Associated Press

1844 Introduction of the telegraph

1970 Newspaper Preservation Act

2003 Readership Institute circulation study

1883 Pulitzer's *New York World*, yellow journalism

THE EARLIEST NEWSPAPERS

In Caesar's time Rome had a newspaper. The **Acta Diurna** (actions of the day), written on a tablet, was posted on a wall after each meeting of the Senate. Its circulation was one, and there is no reliable measure of its total readership. However, it does show that people have always wanted to know what was happening and that others have helped them do so.

The newspapers we recognize today have their roots in 17th-century Europe. **Corantos,** one-page news sheets about specific events, were printed in English in Holland in 1620 and imported to England by British booksellers who were eager to satisfy public demand for information about Continental happenings that eventually led to what we now call the Thirty Years' War.

Englishmen Nathaniel Butter, Thomas Archer, and Nicholas Bourne eventually began printing their own occasional news sheets, using the same title for consecutive editions. They stopped publishing in 1641, the same year that regular, daily accounts of local news started appearing in other news sheets. These true forerunners of our daily newspaper were called **diurnals.**

Political power struggles in England at this time boosted the fledgling medium, as partisans on the side of the monarchy and those on the side of Parliament published diurnals to bolster their positions. When the monarchy prevailed, it granted monopoly publication rights to the *Oxford Gazette,* the official voice of the Crown. Founded in 1665 and later renamed the *London Gazette,* this journal used a formula of foreign news, official information, royal proclamations, and local news that became the model for the first colonial newspapers.

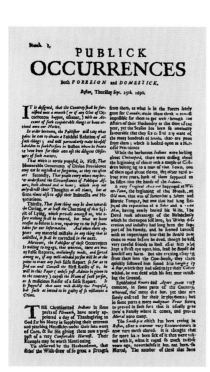

The first daily newspaper to appear in the 13 Colonies, *Publick Occurrences Both Foreign and Domestick,* lasted all of one edition.

Colonial Newspapers   In Chapter 3 we saw how bookseller/print shops became the focal point for the exchange of news and information and how this led to the beginning of the colonial newspaper. It was at these establishments that **broadsides** (sometimes referred to as **broadsheets**), single-sheet announcements or accounts of events imported from England, would be posted. In 1690 Boston bookseller/printer (and coffeehouse owner) Benjamin Harris printed his own broadside, *Publick Occurrences Both Foreign and Domestick.* Intended for continuous publication, the country's first daily lasted only one day. Harris had been critical of local and European dignitaries, and he had also failed to obtain a license.

More successful was Boston Postmaster John Campbell, whose 1704 *Boston News-Letter* survived until the Revolution. The paper featured foreign news, reprints of articles from England, government announcements, and shipping news. It was dull, and it was also expensive. Nonetheless, it established the newspaper in the Colonies.

The *Boston News-Letter* was able to survive in part because of government subsidies. With government support came government control, but the buildup to the Revolution helped establish the medium's independence. In 1721 Boston had three papers. James Franklin's *New-England Courant* was the only one publishing without authority. The *Courant* was popular and controversial, but when it criticized the Massachusetts governor, Franklin was jailed for printing "scandalous libels." When released, he returned to his old ways, earning himself and the *Courant* a publishing ban, which he circumvented by installing his younger brother

Benjamin Franklin published America's first political cartoon—"Join, or Die," a rallying call for the Colonies—in his *Pennsylvania Gazette* in 1754.

Benjamin as nominal publisher. Ben Franklin soon moved to Philadelphia, and without his leadership the *Courant* was out of business in 3 years. Its lasting legacy, however, was in proving that a newspaper with popular support could indeed challenge authority.

In Philadelphia, Benjamin Franklin established a print shop and later, in 1729, took over a failing newspaper, which he revived and renamed the *Pennsylvania Gazette.* By combining the income from his bookshop and printing businesses with that from his popular daily, Franklin could run the *Gazette* with significant independence. Even though he held the contract for Philadelphia's official printing, he was unafraid to criticize those in authority. In addition, he began to develop advertising support, which also helped shield his newspaper from government control by decreasing its dependence on official printing contracts for survival. Ben Franklin demonstrated that financial independence could lead to editorial independence. It was not, however, a guarantee.

In 1734 *New York Weekly Journal* publisher John Peter Zenger was jailed for criticizing that Colony's royal governor. The charge was seditious libel, and the verdict was based not on the truth or falsehood of the printed words but on whether they had been printed. The criticisms had been published, so Zenger was clearly guilty. But his attorney, Andrew Hamilton, argued to the jury, "For the words themselves must be libelous, that is, false, scandalous and seditious, or else we are not guilty." Zenger's peers agreed, and he was freed. The case of Peter Zenger became a symbol of colonial newspaper independence from the Crown, and its power was evident in the refusal by publishers to accept the Stamp Act in 1765 (see Chapter 3). For more on this colonial newspaperman, see the box "Truth as a Defense Against Libel: The Zenger Trial" on page 102.

Newspapers After Independence   After the Revolution, the new government of the United States had to determine for itself just how free a press it was willing to tolerate. When the first Congress convened under the new Constitution in 1790, the nation's founders debated, drafted, and adopted the first 10 amendments to the Constitution, called the **Bill of Rights.** The **First Amendment** reads:

Truth as a Defense Against Libel: The Zenger Trial

Young German immigrant John Peter Zenger started publishing New York's second paper, the *Weekly Journal,* in 1733 with encouragement from several anti-Crown merchants and businesspeople who wanted a voice to counter William Bradford's Crown-supported *Gazette.* Zenger had been an apprentice under Bradford, whose official title was "King's Printer to the Province of New York."

Zenger did his new job well. He was constantly and openly critical of New York's British-born governor, William Cosby. Soon he was arrested and jailed for seditious libel. For the 9 months he was imprisoned, he continued to edit his paper, run on the outside by his wife.

His trial began on August 4, 1735, and at first it did not go well for Zenger. His two original lawyers were disbarred because they argued that the judge, appointed by Cosby, should step down. Zenger's supporters then hired 80-year-old Philadelphia attorney Andrew Hamilton. Hamilton was not only a brilliant lawyer and orator but an astute reader of contemporary political sentiment. He built his defense of the accused printer on growing colonial anger toward Britain. Actually he had little choice. As the law stood, Zenger *was* guilty. British law said that printed words could be libelous, even if true, if they were inflammatory or negative. Truth, Hamilton argued, is a defense against libel. Otherwise, how could anything other than favorable material about government ever be published? Moreover, he added, why should the colonists be bound by a British law they had not themselves approved?

To make his point Hamilton said, "Power may justly be compared to a great river; while kept within its due bounds, it is both beautiful and useful. But when it overflows its banks, it is then too impetuous to be stemmed, it bears down all before it, and

THE JURY RULED ZENGER NOT GUILTY, MAKING IT CLEAR TO THE BRITISH AND THEIR COLONIAL SUPPORTERS THAT THE COLONISTS WOULD NO LONGER ACCEPT THEIR CONTROL OF THE PRESS.

brings destruction and desolation wherever it comes."

The jury ruled Zenger not guilty, making it clear to the British and their colonial supporters that the colonists would no longer accept their control of the press.

Two hundred and seventy-five years later, different people are still fighting for press freedom. The Zenger trial is echoed in Chapter 14 in the travails of Larry Flynt and in Chapter 15 in the account of the battle over Internet freedom in China.

John Peter Zenger, sitting in the dock, is defended by Andrew Hamilton.

Congress shall make no law respecting an establishment of religion, or prohibiting the free exercise thereof; or abridging the freedom of speech, or of the press; or the right of the people peacefully to assemble, and to petition the Government for a redress of grievances.

But a mere 8 years later, fearful of the subversive activities of foreigners sympathetic to France, Congress passed a group of four laws known collectively as the **Alien and Sedition Acts.** The Sedition Act made illegal writing, publishing, or printing "any false scandalous and malicious writing" about the president, Congress, or the federal government. So unpopular were these laws with a people who had just waged a war of independence against similar limits on their freedom of expression that they were not renewed when Congress reconsidered them 2 years later in 1800. We will examine in detail the ongoing commitment to the First Amendment, freedom of the press, and open expression in the United States in Chapter 14.

THE MODERN NEWSPAPER EMERGES

At the turn of the 19th century, New York City provided all the ingredients necessary for a new kind of audience for a new kind of newspaper and a new kind of journalism. The island city was densely populated, a center of culture, commerce, and politics, and especially because of the wave of immigrants that had come to its shores, demographically diverse. Add to this growing literacy among working people, and conditions were ripe for the **penny press,** 1-cent newspapers for everyone. Benjamin Day's September 3, 1833, issue of the *New York Sun* was the first of the penny papers. Day's innovation was to sell his paper so inexpensively that it would attract a large readership, which could then be "sold" to advertisers. Day succeeded because he anticipated a new kind of reader. He filled the *Sun's* pages with police and court reports, crime stories, entertainment news, and human interest stories. Because the paper lived up to its motto, "The Sun shines for all," there was little of the elite political and business information that had characterized earlier papers.

Soon there were penny papers in all the major cities. Among the most important was James Gordon Bennett's *New York Morning Herald.* Although more sensationalistic than the *Sun,* the *Herald* pioneered the correspondent system, placing reporters in Washington, D.C. and other major U.S. cities as well as abroad. Correspondents filed their stories by means of the telegraph, invented in 1844.

Horace Greeley's *New York Tribune* was an important penny paper as well. Its nonsensationalistic, issues-oriented, and humanitarian reporting established the mass newspaper as a powerful medium of social action.

The People's Medium People typically excluded from the social, cultural, and political mainstream quickly saw the value of the mass newspaper. The first African American newspaper was *Freedom's Journal,* published initially in 1827 by John B. Russwurum and the Reverend Samuel Cornish. Forty others soon followed, but it was Frederick Douglass who made best use of the new mass circulation style in his newspaper *The Ram's Horn,* founded expressly to challenge the editorial policies of Benjamin Day's *Sun.* Although this particular effort failed, Douglass had established himself and the minority press as a viable voice for those otherwise silenced. Douglass's *North Star,* founded in 1847 with the masthead slogan "Right is of no Sex—Truth is of no Color—God is the Father of us all, and we are all Brethren," was the most influential African American newspaper before the Civil War.

The most influential African American newspaper after the Civil War, and the first Black paper to be a commercial success (its predecessors typically were subsidized by political and church groups), was the *Chicago Defender.* First published on May 5, 1905, by Robert Sengstacke Abbott, the *Defender* eventually earned a nationwide circulation of more than 230,000. Especially after Abbott declared May 15, 1917,

Volume 1, Number 1 of Benjamin Day's *New York Sun,* the first of the penny papers.

For more information on this topic, see Media Talk video clip #11, "College Newspaper Under Fire for Controversial Advertorial," on the *Media World* DVD.

the start of "the Great Northern Drive," the *Defender's* central editorial goal was to encourage southern Black people to move north.

"I beg of you, my brothers, to leave that benighted land. You are free men. . . . Get out of the South," Abbott editorialized (as quoted in Fitzgerald, 1999, p. 18). The paper would regularly contrast horrific accounts of southern lynchings with northern African American success stories. Within 2 years of the start of the Great Drive, more than 500,000 former slaves and their families moved north. Within 2 more years, another 500,000 followed.

Native Americans found early voice in papers such as the *Cherokee Phoenix*, founded in 1828 in Georgia, and the *Cherokee Rose Bud*, which began operation 20 years later in Oklahoma. The rich tradition of the Native American newspaper is maintained today around the country in publications such as the Oglala Sioux *Lakota Times* and the Shoshone–Bannock *Sho-Ban News*, as well as on the World Wide Web. For example, the *Cherokee Observer* is at http://www.cherokeeobserver.org; the *Navajo Times* is at http://www.navajotimes.com; and *News from Indian Country* can be found at http://www.indiancountrynews.com.

Throughout this early period of the popularization of the newspaper, numerous foreign-language dailies also began operation, primarily in major cities in which immigrants tended to settle. Sloan, Stovall, and Startt (1993) report that in 1880 there were more than 800 foreign-language newspapers publishing in German, Polish, Italian, Spanish, and various Scandinavian languages. As you'll see later in this chapter, the modern foreign language press and its close cousin, the alternative press, are enjoying significant success in today's era of flat or falling readership for more mainstream papers.

The First Wire Services In 1848 six large New York papers, including the *Sun*, the *Herald*, and the *Tribune*, decided to pool efforts and share expenses collecting news from foreign ships docking at the city's harbor. After determining rules of membership and other organizational issues, in 1856 the papers established the first news-gathering (and distribution) organization, the New York Associated Press. Other domestic **wire services** followed—the Associated Press in 1900, the United Press in 1907, and the International News Service in 1909.

This innovation, with its assignment of correspondents to both foreign and domestic bureaus, had a number of important implications. First, it greatly expanded the breadth and scope of coverage a newspaper could offer its readers. This was a boon to dailies wanting to attract as many readers as possible. Greater coverage of distant domestic news helped unite an expanding country while encouraging even more expansion. The United States was a nation of immigrants, and news from people's homelands drew more readers. Second, the nature of reporting began to change. Reporters could now produce stories by rewriting—sometimes a little, sometimes a lot—the actual on-the-spot coverage of others. Finally, newspapers were able to reduce expenses (and increase profits) because they no longer needed to have their own reporters in all locations.

Yellow Journalism In 1883 Hungarian immigrant Joseph Pulitzer bought the troubled *New York World*. Adopting a populist approach to the news, he brought a crusading, activist style of coverage to numerous turn-of-the-century social problems—growing slums, labor tensions, and failing farms, to name a few.

863,956 The World. 863,956

WORLDS CIRCULATED YESTERDAY

"Circulation Books Open to All."

NEW YORK, THURSDAY, FEBRUARY 17,

MAINE EXPLOSION CAUSED BY BOMB OR TORPEDO

Capt. Sigsbee and Consul-General Lee Are in Doubt---The World Has Sent Special Tug, With Submarine Divers, to Havana to Find Out---Lee Asks for an Immediate Court of Inquiry---Capt. Sigsbee's Suspicions.

CAPT. SIGSBEE, IN A SUPPRESSED DESPATCH TO THE STATE DEPARTMENT, SAYS THE ACCIDENT WAS MADE POSSIBLE BY AN ENEMY.

Dr. E. C. Pendleton, Just Arrived from Havana, Says He Overheard Talk There of a Plot to Blow Up the Ship---Capt. Zalinski, the Dynamite Expert, and Other Experts Report to The World that the Wreck Was Not Accidental---Washington Officials Ready for Vigorous Action if Spanish Responsibility Can Be Shown---Divers to Be Sent Down to Make Careful Examinations.

Several of yellow journalism's excesses—dramatic graphics, bold headlines, the reporting of rumor—are evident in this front page from Joseph Pulitzer's *New York World.* Many historians believe that the sinking of the *Maine* was engineered by yellow journalist William Randolph Hearst, publisher of the *New York Morning Journal*, in order to create a war that his papers could cover as a way to build circulation.

WWW

Yellow Journalism
www.humboldt.edu/-jcb10/yellow.html

The audience for his "new journalism" was the "common man," and he succeeded in reaching readers with light, sensationalistic news coverage, extensive use of illustrations, and circulation-building stunts and promotions (for example, an around-the-world balloon flight). Ad revenues and circulation figures exploded.

Soon there were other new journalists. William Randolph Hearst applied Pulitzer's successful formula to his *San Francisco Examiner,* and then in 1895 he took on Pulitzer himself in New York. The competition between Hearst's *Morning Journal* and Pulitzer's *World* was so intense that it debased newspapers and journalism as a whole, which is somewhat ironic in that Pulitzer later founded the prize for excellence in journalism that still bears his name.

Drawing its name from the Yellow Kid, a popular cartoon character of the time, **yellow journalism** was a study in excess—sensational sex, crime, and disaster news; giant headlines; heavy use of illustrations; and reliance on cartoons and color. It was successful at first, and other papers around the country adopted all or part of its style. Although public reaction to the excesses of yellow journalism soon led to its decline, traces of its popular features remain. Large headlines, big front-page pictures, extensive use of photos and illustrations, and cartoons are characteristic even of today's best newspapers.

The years between the era of yellow journalism and the coming of television were a time of remarkable growth in the development of newspapers. From 1910 to the beginning of World War II, daily newspaper subscriptions doubled, and ad revenues tripled. In 1910 there were 2,600 daily papers in the United States, more than at any time before or since. In 1923, the American Society of Newspaper Editors issued the "Canons of Journalism and Statement of Principles" in an effort to restore order and respectability after the yellow era. The opening sentence of the Canons was, "The right of a newspaper to attract and hold readers is restricted by nothing but considerations of public welfare." The wire services internationalized. United Press International started gathering news from Japan in 1909 and was covering South America and Europe by 1921. In response to the competition from radio and magazines for advertising dollars, newspapers began consolidating into **newspaper chains**—papers in different cities across the country owned by a single company. Hearst and Scripps were among the most powerful chains in the 1920s. For all practical purposes, the modern newspaper had now emerged. The next phase of the medium's life, as we'll soon see, begins with the coming of television.

Newspapers and Their Audiences

Nearly 55 million newspapers are sold daily in the United States, and 5 of 10 people report reading a paper every day. The industry that produces those newspapers looks quite different from the one that operated before television became a dominant medium. There are now fewer papers. There are now different types of papers. And more newspapers are part of large chains.

The advent of television coincided with several important social and cultural changes in the United States. Shorter work hours, more leisure, more expendable cash, movement to the suburbs, and women joining the workforce in greater numbers all served to alter the newspaper–reader relationship. Overall, circulation rose from 48 to 62 million between 1945 and 1970, but the amount of time people spent reading their papers decreased. People were reading only 20% of the stories, spending less than 30 minutes a day with the paper, and only 15 minutes was focused primarily on the paper itself. Circulation for big-city papers dropped, and many closed shop. As newspapers struggled to redefine themselves in the expanding television era, the number of chains grew from 60, controlling 42% of the daily circulation in 1945, to 126, controlling 76% of the total number of dailies and 82% of the daily circulation in 1996 (Compaine & Gomery, 2000, p. 8).

Scope and Structure of the Newspaper Industry

Today there are more than 9,800 newspapers operating in the United States. Of these, about 1,500 (15%) are dailies, and the rest are weeklies (77%) and semiweeklies (8%). The dailies have a combined circulation of 56 million, the weeklies more than 70 million. The average weekly has a circulation of just over 9,000. **Pass-along readership**—readers who did not originally

When the Story Hits Home: The *New Orleans Times-Picayune* and Hurricane Katrina

In August 2005, Hurricane Katrina slammed into America's Gulf Coast. More than 1,300 people lost their lives, and the devastation to homes and businesses would eventually total in the billions of dollars. But as typically happens when a major disaster strikes, the often-maligned media demonstrate just how important they are to our nation and its people. *Washington Post* columnist Marc Fisher wrote, "Although it has become fashionable to say that no one believes the old mainstream media anymore, when times get tough, Americans still turn to those institutions that have built up credibility over the course of decades . . . Those first days (of the disaster) were a time for newspapers to put aside jitters about their declining importance and worries about layoffs and cutbacks. The old papers instead reasserted the comfort and utility of news you could hold in your hand" (2005). *American Journalism Review* editor Rem Rieder added, "Suddenly, the notion that there is value in having trained professionals on the scene to cover the news didn't seem quite so quaint" (2005). In fact, the American media as a whole performed admirably, documenting the devastation, challenging dissembling, self-congratulatory politicians, and bringing hope to victims and news to the public. But it was one old-fashioned mainstream media outlet, the *New Orleans Times-Picayune*, that stood above the rest in making a difference, in this case, for its own hometown.

Twelve days after Katrina first struck, all but one of New Orleans' 12 television stations were still off the air. Yet the *Times-Picayune* never missed an edition. For 3 days the paper was online only, garnering 30 million Web pages viewed each day at www.nola.com, but then, with the city underwater and thousands of people still stranded in their homes, on rooftops, and most famously in the Superdome, the paper was back on the street in hard copy, trucked to evacuation centers and suburban subscribers.

Although its published warnings that the levees would not hold were ignored by national media and federal authorities alike, the paper had prepared for the storm. More than 250 staffers and their families had taken refuge in the *Times-Picayune* building on the first day of the hurricane, but by the next day it was clear that this, too, was not safe. Publisher Ashton Phelps ordered the daily's fleet of delivery trucks to assemble at the building's loading dock to transport all to safety. Before long on the ride out of town, sports editor David Meeks approached editor in chief Jim Amoss with a proposal. Rather than abandon their city (and duty), he argued, what if he and a group of volunteers went back into the disaster? Amoss agreed, offering a truck for the return trip, but not much more. Quickly, an odd assortment of journalists, including the editorial page editor, the art critic, the education reporter, a court reporter, the religion writer, and one

> **"THE PRINTED *PICAYUNE*, AFTER A THREE DAY ABSENCE, MARKED A BEACON OF NORMALCY, THE BOLSTERING OF HOPE FOR THE STILL ABSENT INFLUX OF SOLDIERS AND EVACUATION BUSES."**

photographer, joined Meeks in setting up "the New Orleans bureau" of the *Times-Picayune,* a small house on a side street in the middle of the now-dead city. There would be five different homes for the New Orleans bureau in 5 days. Soon, *Times-Picayune* reporters and photographers who had remained in the city and not been in the evacuation began to wander in. Meanwhile, the editorial staff set up shop in Baton Rouge, an hour away, and the production crew settled an hour-and-a-half away, in Houma, home of the *Courier,* a New York Times Company paper that made its facilities available to the *Times-Picayune.*

It was these people, their own homes destroyed, who made the difference. It was local reporters and photographers who knew the police, who could debunk rumors, who understood the racial and class politics of the Big Easy. Their reporting was the truest, the most authentic. When stranded survivors saw a *Times-Picayune* reporter, they would cheer and ask where they could get the paper, a near-universal experience for *Times-Picayune* staffers.

Times-Picayune reporter Brian Thevenot described the scene when sports editor Meeks "turned paper delivery boy, passing out Friday's *Picayune*—the first paper edition since the storm had hit at the beginning of the week—into crowds that gobbled up the papers as if they were food" to explain how his paper had made a difference. "The printed *Picayune,*" he wrote, "after a three day absence, marked a beacon of normalcy, the bolstering of hope for the still absent influx of soldiers and evacuation buses" (2005, p. 30).

Hurricane Katrina devastated New Orleans in August 2005. That year's prestigious Pulitzer Prize for public service journalism went to the New Orleans Times-Picayune, *acknowledging the heroic work of its professionals despite life-changing damage to their own workplace and homes.*

purchase the paper—brings 132 million people a day in touch with a daily and 200 million a week in touch with a weekly. However, overall circulation has remained stagnant despite a growing population. Therefore, to maintain their success and to ensure their future, newspapers have had to diversify.

TYPES OF NEWSPAPERS

We've cited statistics about dailies and weeklies, but these categories actually include many different types of papers. Let's take a closer look at some of them.

For more information on this topic see Media Tours video clip #2, "Newspapers: Inside *The Record*," on the *Media World* DVD.

National Daily Newspapers   We typically think of the newspaper as a local medium, our town's paper. But three national daily newspapers enjoy large circulations and significant social and political impact. The oldest and most respected is the *Wall Street Journal*, founded in 1889 by Charles Dow and Edward Jones. Today, as then, its focus is on the world of business, although its definition of business is broad. The *Journal* has a circulation of 2.1 million and an average household income of its readers of $150,000 makes it a favorite for upscale advertisers.

The *Christian Science Monitor*, begun in 1908, continues to hold to its founding principle as a paper of serious journalism. Begun as a high-minded alternative to Boston's yellow papers by Mary Baker Eddy, founder of the Christian Science religion, it was international in coverage and national in distribution from the start. Today, dwindling subscribership totals less than 70,000.

The newest national daily is *USA Today*. Founded in 1982, it calls itself "The Nation's Newspaper," and despite early derision from industry pros for its lack of depth and apparent dependence on style over substance, "it shed its lightweight 'McPaper' persona in the 1990s, becoming a serious national paper and luring topflight talent from places like the *Washington Post*" (Smolkin, 2004, p. 20). Today, the paper's daily circulation of 2.3 million suggests that readers welcome its mix of short, lively, upbeat stories; full-color graphics; state-by-state news and sports briefs; and liberal use of easy-to-read illustrated graphs and tables.

Large Metropolitan Dailies   To be a daily, a paper must be published at least five times a week. The circulation of big-city dailies has dropped over the past 30 years, with the heavy losses of the evening papers offsetting increases for the morning papers. Dailies continue to lose circulation at a rate of about 2% per year (Kunkel, 2005). Many old, established papers, including the *Philadelphia Bulletin* and the *Washington Star*, have stilled their presses in recent years. When the *Chicago Daily News* closed its doors, it had the sixth-highest circulation in the country. You can see the demographic side of this falloff in Figure 4.1, and you can see the value city dailies still can hold for their communities in the box on page 107, "When the Story Hits Home: The *New Orleans Times-Picayune* and Hurricane Katrina."

As big cities cease to be industrial centers, homes, jobs, and interests have turned away from downtown. Those large metropolitan dailies that are succeeding have used a number of strategies to cut costs and to attract and keep more suburban-oriented readers. Several papers, such as the *Boston Globe*, produce an "all-day newspaper," with multiple editions throughout the day, accommodating everyone's work, commute, or home schedule.

New Orleans Times-Picayune
www.nola.com

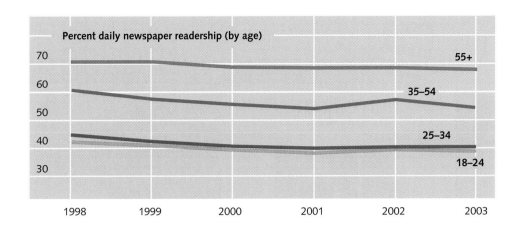

Figure 4.1 Daily Readership, by Age, 1998–2003. *Source:* Newspaper Association of America (Saba, 2004).

Almost all papers publish **zoned editions**—suburban or regional versions of the paper—to attract readers and to combat competition for advertising dollars from the suburban papers. Many big-city dailies have gone as far as to drop the city of their publication from their name. Where is the *Tribune* published? Oakland, California, and Scranton, Pennsylvania, and Warren, Ohio, and Wisconsin Rapids, Wisconsin, each produces a paper called the *Tribune,* but these papers have dropped the city name from their mastheads.

Links to National Newspapers
www.all-links.com/newscentral

The *New York Times* is a special large metropolitan daily. It is a paper local to New York, but the high quality of its reporting and commentary, the reach and depth of both its national and international news, and the solid reputations of its features (such as the weekly *Times Magazine* and the *Book Review*) make it the nation's newspaper of record. Its circulation is 1.1 million a day.

Suburban and Small-Town Dailies   As the United States has become a nation of transient suburb dwellers, so too has the newspaper been suburbanized. Since 1985 the number of suburban dailies has increased by 50%, and one, Long Island's *Newsday,* is the twelfth largest paper in the country, with a circulation of nearly 430,000.

Small-town dailies operate much like their suburban cousins if there is a nearby large metropolitan paper; for example, the *Lawrence Eagle-Tribune* publishes in the shadow of Boston's two big dailies. Its focus is the Merrimack River Valley in Massachusetts, 25 miles northwest of Boston. If the small-town paper has no big-city competition, it can serve as the heart of its community.

Weeklies and Semiweeklies   Many weeklies and semiweeklies have prospered because advertisers have followed them to the suburbs. Community reporting makes them valuable to those people who identify more with their immediate environment than they do with the neighboring big city. Suburban advertisers like the narrowly focused readership and more manageable advertising rates.

The Ethnic Press   The United States is home to more than 35 Spanish-language dailies, and that number continues to grow as publications backed by English-language papers, such as the Tribune Company's *Hoy* (in several cities) and the *Dallas Morning News' Al Día,* compete with and displace more traditional weekly and semiweekly independent Spanish-language

Even though it serves the smallest state in the Union, the *Providence* (RI) *Journal* provides its readers with seven different zoned editions.

papers, such as New Haven's *La Voz Hispana de Connecticut.* This phenomenal growth—Spanish-language dailies had 140,000 readers in 1970; they have nearly 2 million today—is a result of three factors. First, the big dailies have realized, as have all media, that to be successful (and in this case, to reverse long-standing declines in circulation) they must reach an increasingly fragmented audience. Second, at 12.5% of the population, self-described Hispanic or Latino people represent not only a sizable fragment of the overall audience but America's fastest-growing minority group. Third, because the newspaper is the most local of the mass media, and nonnative speakers tend to identify closely with their immediate locales, Spanish-language papers—like most foreign-language papers—command a loyal readership, one attractive to advertisers who, having few other ways to reach this group, boosted their ad spending 565% between 1990 and 2000 (Fitzgerald, 2004a).

African American papers, as they have for a century and a half, remain a vibrant part of this country's **ethnic press.** Like Hispanics and Latinos, African Americans represent about 12% of the total population. But because English is their native language, African Americans typically read mainstream papers. In fact, after Caucasians, they represent the second-largest group of newspaper readers in the country. Still, the 400 dailies, weeklies, and semiweeklies that aim specifically at African Americans attract a combined 15 million readers (Fitzgerald, 2004b). And papers like the *Amsterdam News* in New York, the *Philadelphia New Observer,* and the *Michigan Citizen* in Detroit specialize in urban-based journalism unlike that found in the traditional mainstream dailies.

A robust ethnic press exists beyond Spanish-language and African American papers. For example, New York City is home to foreign-language papers serving nationalities speaking 50 different languages—in the *B*s alone there are Bangladeshi, Bosnian, Bulgarian, Brazilian, and Byelorussian. The *I*s have Indian, Iranian, Irish, Israeli, and Italian.

The Alternative and Dissident Press   Another type of paper, most commonly a weekly and available at no cost, is the **alternative press.** The offspring of the underground press of the 1960s antiwar, antiracism, pro-drug culture, these papers have redefined themselves. The most successful among them—the *Village Voice,* the *L.A. Weekly,* the *Boston Phoenix,* and the *Seattle Weekly*—succeed by attracting upwardly mobile young people and young professionals, not the disaffected counterculture readers who were their original audiences. Their strategy of downplaying politics and emphasizing events listings, local arts advertising, and eccentric personal classified ads has permitted the country's 123 alternative weeklies to attract 7.5 million readers a week and earn ad revenues of $500 million a year (Project, 2004) but has called into question their "alternativeness." The mantle of "alternative" has been picked up by the **dissident press,** weeklies with a very local and very political orientation. Successful examples are Cleveland's *Urban Dialect,* Seattle's *Eat the State!,* the *L.A. Alternative Press,* and the *Philadelphia Independent,* which greeted the 2003 invasion of Iraq with the headline "WAR KILLS PEOPLE."

Commuter Papers   Modeled after a common form of European newspaper, free dailies designed for commuters are becoming commonplace in America's

WWW

National Association of Hispanic Publishers
www.nahp.org

WWW

Alternative Weekly Network
www.awn.org

Meeting the needs of a fragmented audience—a foreign-language paper, an alternative weekly, the dissident press, and a free commuter paper.

biggest cities. Like the most successful Spanish-language papers, they represent the major dailies' effort to reach a segment of the audience not likely to buy the parent papers' product. Here though, the target is young readers (who are already used to getting free media from the alternative press and the Internet) and the goal is twofold. First, these readers represent a valuable demographic, one especially attractive to local advertisers, the newspaper's bread-and-butter financial base. Second, the big dailies hope these young readers "will develop a daily newspaper-reading habit and will eventually move on to become regular readers of the mother papers" (Morton, 2004, p. 64). Typical of the successful **commuter papers** are the *Boston Globe's Metro,* the *Dallas Morning News' Quick,* the *Washington Post's Express,* and the Tribune Company's *amNewYork.*

THE NEWSPAPER AS AN ADVERTISING MEDIUM

The reason we have the number and variety of newspapers we do is that readers value them. When newspapers prosper financially, it is because advertisers recognize their worth as an ad medium. Newspapers account for more than 55% of all advertising spending in the United States. Advertisers annually spend $94.71 for every man, woman, and child, or $253.75 for every household in the country on newspaper advertising, more than on any other medium (Lindsay, 2006). The biggest newspaper advertisers are retail stores (such as Macy's) and telecommunications, auto, computer, and entertainment brands.

Why do so many advertisers choose newspapers? The first reason is their reach. Five out of ten Americans read a paper every day, 85% in a week. Newspapers "deliver the equivalent of the Super Bowl every day," offers Nicholas Cannistraro of the Newspaper National Network (quoted in Case,

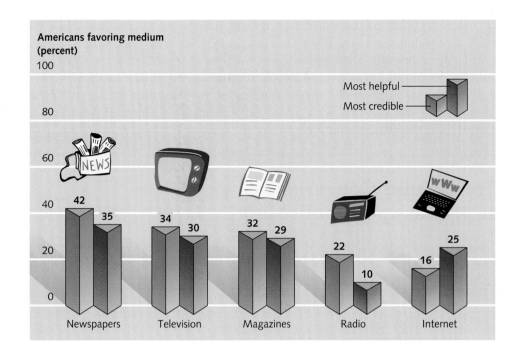

Americans favoring medium (percent)

	Newspapers	Television	Magazines	Radio	Internet
Most helpful	42	34	32	22	16
Most credible	35	30	29	10	25

Figure 4.2 Most Credible and Helpful Advertising. When asked which is the most credible advertising medium and which medium is most helpful in choosing which products to buy, respondents favored newspapers over other media. *Source:* Newspaper National Network 2005 Media Engagement Study (Brown, 2005).

2001, p. SR18). The second is good demographics—newspaper readers tend to be better educated, better off financially, and have more disposable income than the audiences of other media. Third, newspapers are the most trusted, credible ad medium when readers are looking to make a specific product purchase (Brown, 2005). Figure 4.2 demonstrates newspapers' dominance in this regard. Finally, newspapers are local in nature. Supermarkets, local car dealers, department stores, movie theaters, and other local merchants who want to offer a coupon turn automatically to the paper. Approximately 65% of daily newspaper space is given to advertising. Of that space, 60% is devoted to local retail advertising and another 25% to classified, which is overwhelmingly local. This localization is further enhanced by the use of zoned editions, which allow advertisers to place their ads in editions designed for readers' specific locales, that is, closer to the point of sale.

THE WIRE AND FEATURE SERVICES

Much of the 35% of the newspaper that is not advertising space is filled with content provided by outside sources, specifically the wire and feature services. Wire services, as we've already seen, collect news and distribute it to their members. (They draw their name from the way they originally distributed material—by telephone wire. Today material is more likely to come by computer network or satellite.) Unlike the early days of the wire services, today's member is three times more likely to be a broadcast outlet than a newspaper. These radio and television stations receive voice and video, as well as written copy. In all cases, members receive a choice of material, most commonly national and international news, state and regional news, sports, business news, farm and weather reports, and human interest and consumer material.

The feature services, called **feature syndicates,** do not gather and distribute news. Instead, they operate as clearinghouses for the work of columnists, essayists, cartoonists, and other creative individuals. Among the material

Newspaper National Network
www.nnnlp.com

Association of Alternative Newsweeklies
www.aan.org

provided (by wire, by computer, or physically in packages) are opinion pieces such as commentaries by Ellen Goodman or Molly Ivins; horoscope, chess, and bridge columns; editorial cartoons, such as the work of Scott Willis and Ben Sergeant; and comics, the most common and popular form of syndicated material. Among the major syndicates, the best known are the *New York Times* News Service, King Features, Newspaper Enterprise Association (NEA), and the *Washington Post* News Service.

Trends and Convergence in Newspaper Publishing

Loss of competition within the industry, hypercommercialism, convergence, and the evolution of newspaper readership are altering not only the nature of the medium but also its relationship with its audiences.

LOSS OF COMPETITION

The newspaper industry has seen a dramatic decline in competition. This has taken two forms: loss of competing papers and concentration of ownership. In 1923, 502 American cities had two or more competing (having different ownership) dailies. Today, only 20 have separate competing papers. With circulation and advertising revenues leveling out for urban dailies, very few cities can support more than one paper. Congress attempted to reverse this trend with the 1970 Newspaper Preservation Act, which allowed **joint operating agreements (JOAs).** A JOA permits a failing paper to merge most aspects of its business with a successful local competitor as long as their editorial and reporting operations remain separate. The philosophy is that it is better to have two more or less independent papers in one city than to allow one to close. Today, 12 cities have JOAs, including Seattle, Albuquerque, Detroit, and Cincinnati.

The concern is editorial diversity. Cities with only one newspaper have only one newspaper editorial voice. This runs counter to two long-held American beliefs about the relationship between a free press and its readers:

- Truth flows from a multitude of tongues.
- The people are best served by a number of antagonistic voices.

What becomes of political, cultural, and social debate when there are neither multiple nor antagonistic (or at least different) voices? Media critic Robert McChesney (1997) offered this answer: "As ownership concentrated nationally in the form of chains, journalism came to reflect the partisan interests of owners and advertisers, rather than the diverse interests of any given community" (p. 13). The trend toward newspaper concentration is troubling to many observers. The nation's 126 newspaper chains control 82% of daily newspaper circulation, own the 9 biggest circulation papers in the country, and own 1,200 of the nation's 1,500 dailies.

Chains are not new. Hearst owned several big-city papers in the 1880s, but at that time most cities enjoyed significant competition between papers. Now that most communities have only one paper, nonlocal chain or conglomerate control of that voice is more problematic. Among the larger chains are Gannett (100 dailies), McClatchy (32), Advance Publications (29), Hearst (12), New York Times (20), E. W. Scripps (21), and MediaNews Group (53). Additional concern is raised about chain ownership when the chain is also a media conglomerate, owning several different types of media outlets, as well as other nonmedia companies. Will the different media holdings speak with one corporate voice? Will they speak objectively, and will they cover at all the doings of their nonmedia corporations?

Chains do have their supporters. Although some critics see big companies as more committed to profit and shareholder dividends, others see chains such as McClatchy, winner of numerous Pulitzer prizes and other awards, as turning expanded economic and journalistic resources toward better service and journalism. Some critics see outside ownership as uncommitted to local communities and issues, but others see balance and objectivity (especially important in one-paper towns). Ultimately, we must recognize that not all chains operate alike. Some operate their holdings as little more than profit centers; others see profit residing in exemplary service. Some groups require that all their papers toe the corporate line; others grant local autonomy. Gannett, for example, openly boasts of its dedication to local management control.

CONGLOMERATION: HYPERCOMMERCIALISM, EROSION OF THE FIREWALL, AND LOSS OF MISSION

As in other media, conglomeration has led to increased pressure on newspapers to turn a profit. This manifests itself in three distinct but related ways—hypercommercialism, erasure of the distinction between ads and news, and ultimately, loss of the journalistic mission itself.

Many papers, such as *USA Today,* the *Orange County Register,* and Michigan's *Oakland Press* and *Macomb Daily,* sell ad space on their front pages, once the exclusive province of news. Other papers, Rhode Island's *Providence Journal,* for example, take this form of hypercommercialism halfway, affixing removable sticker ads to their front pages. Many papers now permit (and charge for) the placement of pet obituaries alongside those of deceased humans.

A second product of conglomeration, say critics, is that the quest for profits at all costs is eroding the firewall, the once inviolate barrier between newspapers' editorial and advertising missions. Although they find the position of "advertorial editor" at the *Fairbanks* (Alaska) *Daily News-Miner*—whose salary is split equally between the newsroom and advertising department—strikingly inappropriate, their poster child for the erosion of papers' editorial integrity is the experience of the *Los Angeles Times.* In 1996, the *Times* hired former General Mills cereal executive Mark Willes as publisher to ensure that "editorial content conformed to the best commercial interests of the newspaper" (Peterson, 1997, p. C1). The goal, Willes said, was to break down the "Chinese wall between editors and business staffers" with a "Bazooka if necessary" (quoted in Marsh, 1998, p. 47). When it was soon discovered that the *Times* had struck a secret deal with the Staples Center to split the $2 million in ad revenue from a special issue of its Sunday magazine devoted to upbeat stories on the newly opened sports arena, readers and even the paper's employees were enraged. *Times*

Editor & Publisher
www.editorandpublisher.com

American Society of Newspaper Editors
www.asne.org

What If There Were No Newspapers?

There is a national, in fact, a worldwide decline in newspaper circulation (Circulation down, 2004). And, as we've seen throughout this chapter, there are frequent predictions of the death of the newspaper. Remember technology CEO Padova's prognostication: "Personally, I believe that most of us will see near-extinction of printed works in our lifetime" (p. 99). Read ahead to media analyst Wolff's forecast: "If you own a newspaper, you can foresee its almost-certain end" (p. 123). Add to them the views of *Sports Illustrated* president John Squires, who told a roomful of newspaper and magazine circulation executives assembled in Toronto, "Print is dead. Get over it" (in Ahrens, 2005, p. F1).

Declining circulation and constant assertions of foreboding have put the question of the value of the newspaper squarely in the cultural forum. In other words, what if there were no newspapers? If you are not a newspaper reader, your answer might be "So what?" Even if you are a newspaper reader, you might think, "I'll survive, there are plenty of other sources of news and information out there." And in fact, these are the most common responses today (Saba, 2004), but it is not the first time the question has been asked.

In 1949, during a newspaper strike, researcher Bernard Berelson conducted a now-classic study on what it meant to have no newspaper. The people he interviewed said they would lose

> "EVERY AMERICAN CITY AND TOWN HAS VOTERS INVOLVED IN THE PERFORMANCE OF THE SCHOOL SYSTEM IN WHICH THEIR CHILDREN ARE EDUCATED, IN THE TAXES THEY PAY ON THEIR PROPERTY, EVEN THE BEHAVIOR OF THE LOCAL SHERIFF'S DEPARTMENT. THEY VOTE ON THESE ON ELECTION DAY, AND THE ONLY MEDIUM THAT INFORMS THEM ON THESE MATTERS IN ANY DETAIL IS THE PRINTED NEWSPAPER."

- the ability to get information about and interpretation of public affairs.
- tools for daily living (for example, ads, radio and movie listings, and birth, death, and marriage announcements).
- a vehicle for relaxation and escape.
- a source of prestige (newspaper content provided the raw material for conversation).
- social contact (from human interest stories and advice columns).

But what if some modern-day Berelson were to ask you the same question? It's likely you would feel few, if any, of these losses. Why? Functional displacement. **Functional displacement** occurs when the functions of an existing medium are performed better or more efficiently by a newer medium, taking them over. Especially for college-age people, there are indeed other media providing these services better or more efficiently. No doubt your television and Internet use meets all these needs.

So the question remains—what if there were no newspapers? What value does the paper serve that is not or cannot be served by other media? Two powerful voices have been raised to answer this question. The first belongs to long-time journalist-turned-media-critic Ben Bagdikian. He wrote,

> Newspapers have a unique social function that their media competitors do not. They are crucial to American local civic

executives did apologize for the secrecy, but insisted that they would "maintain the policy that businesspeople will share in the selection of the news," a situation, according to media critic Ben Bagdikian, that leaves "a blot on the idea that readers can trust journalists" (both quotes in "*L.A. Times* Takes," 1999, p. A1).

But the *Times* is not alone. Most papers of all sizes face the problem. "The wall is a myth," says former *Times* publisher David Laventhol (in Winokur, 1999, p. D3). "There's definitely more interaction as newspapers have come under more financial pressure," said Steve Proctor, deputy managing editor for sports and features at the *Baltimore Sun*. "It used to be if you had a newspaper in town you were able to make a steady profit. Now, like so many other things in the world, newspapers are more at the whim control of its local schools, police, land use, and most taxes. In other countries these are national functions. Thus, every American city and town has voters involved in the performance of the school system in which their children are educated, in the taxes they pay on their property, even the behavior of the local sheriff's department. They vote on these on election day, and the only medium that informs them on these matters in any detail is the printed newspaper. (2004, p. 70)

The second voice is that of the Readership Institute, a newspaper-industry-funded 12-member team conducting a multiyear, multimillion-dollar study of declining readership and how to stem it. Their early results, after interviewing 37,000 people, echo Bagdikian's argument that newspapers' localization is the function that is least likely to be replaced. In addition to advice on improving the navigability of the newspaper and restructuring the business side of the operation, the Readership Institute advised papers to improve their content in two important ways. The first is to carry more *franchise issues*—issues so central to readers' lives that they depend on the paper's ability to cover them for their own welfare. The Institute specified "schools, kids, family, health, local environment, local economy, and leisure." The second is to run more *chicken-dinner news*—community news, no matter how nondramatic. It specified events such as "news about the smallest of youth sports" (Stepp, 2004, p. 67).

Now enter your voice in the cultural forum. Is the newspaper so vital to the functioning of your local community that you can never see yourself without it? Do, or can, other media serve this function? And what of franchise issues and chicken-dinner news? Can you get these elsewhere? Do you even care? What if there really were no newspapers? How different would your life be? Ask your parents these same questions? How similar are their responses to your own? Why do you think you have differences or similarities?

Chicken-dinner stories like coverage of youth sports can bind readers to their local papers.

life, which in turn, is a unique part of the U.S. political system. No other industrial democracy leaves to each community the

of the opinions of Wall Street analysts. There's a lot more pressure to increase the profit margin of the paper, and so that has led to a lot more interplay between the newsroom and the business side of the paper" (quoted in Vane, 2002, pp. 60–61). American Society of Newspaper Editors president Tim McGuire added, "Editors and staff feel scared. Editors and staff feel powerless. Editors and staff feel isolated. We must decide today whether we are going to take newspapers forward with a genuine sense of values and commitment or if we are going to choose the path of milking our companies of every last dime. If we do that, we will die" (quoted in Strupp, 2002, p. 3).

Newspapers will die, say conglomeration's critics, because they will have abandoned their traditional democratic mission, a failure all the more tragic

For more information on this topic, see Media Talk video clip #10, "Journalism Students Free Wrongly Accused Death Row Inmate," on the *Media World* DVD

because despite falling circulation, newspapers remain remarkably financially healthy. William Falk, editor in chief of newsmagazine *The Week,* wrote that the medium's demise

> will be suicide. Newspapers still make tons of money: The industry's average profit margin is 20 percent—compared with 7 percent for oil companies and 6 percent for the entire Fortune 500. But the mammoth corporations that now run newspapers have responded to the new competitive challenge (of digital technologies) in the stupidest way possible: by cutting quality. They're eliminating foreign bureaus, investigative-reporting teams, and experienced editors, and filling their pages with shallow filler and bland features. Ambitious reporting and edgy writing are disappearing. Once-great newspapers ... are now flat and generic; their authority is leaking away. The corporate guys, who think only of pleasing Wall Street, keep cutting costs and boosting profits—and wringing their hands in puzzlement when circulation keeps going down. Guess what guys? People stop buying newspapers when there's nothing in them that they don't already know. (2005, p. B7)

In a time of record revenues and record profits, papers are laying off staff, closing state and regional bureaus, hiring younger and less experienced reporters, and shrinking their newsholes. Newspaper owners are now so focused on profit margins that the editors who work for them are distracted from finding and running great stories, says Bill Marimow, two-time Pulitzer Prize–winning investigative reporter and former editor of the *Baltimore Sun,* "When editors become focused on accounting rather than journalism, you have a problem for democracy" (in Outing, 2005). Yet, confessed Leo Wolinsky, *L. A. Times'* managing editor, "Money is the first thing we talk about. The readers are always the last thing we talk about" (quoted in Risser, 2000, p. 26).

CONVERGENCE WITH THE INTERNET

Why so much talk about money? You and the new digital technologies are the two answers. *Barron's* online columnist Howard Gold explained, "A crisis of confidence has combined with a technological revolution and structural economic change to create what can only be described as a perfect storm. Print's business model is imploding as younger readers turn toward free tabloids and electronic media to get news" (in Farhi, 2005, p. 52). It is the fear that the newspaper industry will fail to successfully weather the storm—Gold's "crisis of confidence"—that drives owners and their investors to demand higher and higher profits.

The Internet has proven most directly financially damaging in its attack on newspapers' classified advertising business. "Once upon a time, classifieds was the exclusive property of newspapers," said Mort Goldstrom, Newspaper Association of America vice-president of advertising. "That time is over." His association's prediction is that the Net will take away 9%, or "$4 billion in highly profitable classified revenue by 2007" (in Fine, 2005). Losses are most severe in employment and auto sales classifieds (up to 50% in both categories), but even general classified advertising is threatened by commercial and noncommercial sites like www.traderonline.com, www.buysell.com, and www.craigslist.org. The problem of the loss of classified ad income is magnified by the exodus of

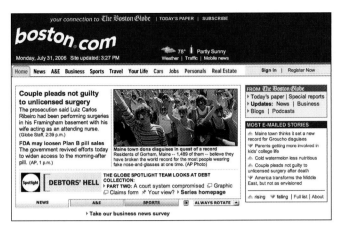

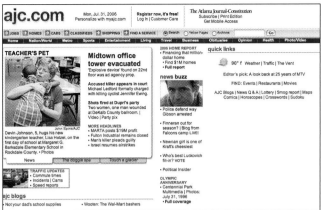

Photo: Shawn Patrick Ouellette/Portland Press Herald.

Two of the more successful online newspapers.

young people, that highly desirable demographic, from print to electronic news sources. Only 19% of 18- to 34-year-olds read the daily paper, compared with the 44% who regularly get their news from the Web (Martinez, 2005). Not only do the Internet and the World Wide Web provide readers with more information and more depth, and with greater speed, than the traditional newspaper, but they empower readers to control and interact with the news, in essence becoming their own editors in chief. As a result, the traditional newspaper is reinventing itself by converging with these very same technologies.

The marriage of newspapers to the Web has not yet proved financially successful for the older medium. There are, however, encouraging signs. And, in fact, the newspaper industry recognizes that it must accept economic losses while it is building online readers' trust, acceptance, and above all regular and frequent use.

The Internet Public Library lists and provides Web links to thousands of online newspapers in the United States, including online papers in every state. These papers have adopted a variety of strategies to become "relevant on the Internet." The *Washington Post,* for example, has joined with *Newsweek* magazine, cable television channel MSNBC, and television network NBC to share content among all the parties' Web sites and to encourage users to link to their respective sites. Others have adopted just the opposite approach, focusing on their strength as local media. The *Boston Globe,* for example, offers readers Boston.com, the *Miami Herald* Miami.com, and the *Kansas City Star* KansasCity.com. Each offers not only what readers might expect to find in these sites' parent newspapers but also significant additional information on how to make the most of the cities they represent. These sites are as much city guides as they are local newspapers.

The local element offers several advantages. Local searchable and archivable classified ads offer greater efficiency than do the big national classified ad Web sites such as Monster.com (jobs) and Cars.com (automobiles). No other medium can offer news on crime, housing, neighborhood politics, zoning, school lunch menus, marriage licenses, and bankruptcies—all searchable by street or zip code. Local newspapers can use their Web sites to develop their own linked secondary sites, thus providing impressive detail on local industry. At the *Detroit Free Press,* for example, Auto.com focuses on car

Online Newspapers
www.ipl.org/div/news/

Online Classifieds
www.traderonline.com
www.buysell.com
www.craigslist.org

manufacturing, while the *San Jose Mercury News*'s SiliconValley.com focuses on the digital industries. Some newspaper Web sites even encourage **community publishing,** that is, they provide their own linked sites, such as New Jersey's *Bergen Record*'s NJCommunity.com, containing pages built by local schools, clubs, and nonprofit groups. Another localizing strategy is for online papers to build and maintain message boards and chat groups on their sites that deal with important issues. One more bow to the power of the Web—and users' demands for interactivity—is that many papers have begun their own blog sites, inviting readers and journalists to talk to one another (Miller, 2005).

Not all papers see their online operations as mere adjuncts to their "real" newspapers. Launching what *Editor & Publisher* called "the second act in the life of the online newspaper" (Robins, 2001, p. 17), in October 2001, the *New York Times* began **digital delivery daily,** delivering the paper, as it looks in print, to home and office computers. Some other papers that can be downloaded in their entirety are the *Akron Beacon Journal*, the *Philadelphia Enquirer*, the *Atlanta Constitution*, the *Boston Globe*, and the *International Herald Tribune*. Any online user who has News-Stand Reader, NewspaperDirect, or other appropriate software on his or her computer can buy a single copy or subscribe to these papers from anyplace in the world. For readers, no more missed deliveries, papers thrown in puddles, and ink-stained fingers. For publishers, newsprint (paper) and delivery costs decline, remote areas can be served, and a paper's "circulation area" can be expanded infinitely.

For now, digital delivery daily papers can be read on home screens, laptops, handheld devices such as Palm Pilots, and cell phones. But that may soon change, as advances in transistor technology make flexible screens a very real possibility. Once perfected, this technology would make reading online newspapers even more convenient, further ensuring the success of digital delivery daily. E Ink Corp. promises to have the technology in readers' hands by 2015, and chief executive Russ Wilcox predicts that not only will papers give it to their subscribers for free to boost circulation, but that it will promote better journalism. "Because space is infinite" on the ever-changing digital newspaper, he wrote, "[t]here will hopefully be more room for thoughtful pieces, longer pieces, the kind that a journalist wishes he or she could do but doesn't have the space" (in Robertson, 2006, p. 57).

But papers face three lingering questions about their online success. The first is whether people will read the paper online. The real question here is whether a newspaper is the news or the paper it's printed on. Clearly, many people, especially young people, will read the news online. Newspapers have experienced journalists and commentators, "brand recognition," and local credibility. The goal is to utilize these assets to make the online paper the destination of choice for news seekers. And while there will always be those who love the feel of a good daily's heft, some news organizations are finding success online. For example, in 1999 only 1 online newspaper, *USA Today*, made the list of the Web's most visited news and information sites. In 2004, 8 of the top 20 news and information sites were affiliated with newspapers: Gannett Newspapers, Knight-Ridder Digital, NYTimes.com, Tribune Newspapers, USAToday.com, Hearst Newspapers, Washingtonpost.com, and Advance Publications ("Newspapers Hold," 2004). NYTimes.com is the

www

More on Newspaper Blogs
www.cyberjournalist.net

world's most heavily trafficked newspaper Web site, drawing 22 million visitors a month (Auletta, 2005a).

The second issue online papers face is how they will earn income from their Web operations. Internet users expect free content, and for years newspapers were happy to provide their product for free, simply to establish their presence on the Net. But, says Rick Edmonds who writes about the online news business, "Content is very expensive to produce . . . and the notion that you're just going to go on forever giving it away is pretty problematic . . . It makes a lot of sense to try something" (in Robertson, 2006). Among those "somethings" are papers that rely on advertising for their online revenue. They continue to provide free access, hoping to attract more readers and, therefore, more advertising revenue. Some papers even offer free online classifieds to draw people to their sites (and their paid advertisers). Other papers, the *Spokesman-Review* in Spokane, Washington, for example, charge for the online edition of the paper, which contains the same material as the print edition plus additional features like reporter blogs and breaking news. Subscribers to the paper version of the *Spokesman-Review* can access the online version for free. Another model is exemplified by the *New York Times*. A truncated version of the paper is still available online for free (the most popular columnists and features are missing), but subscribers to the print edition and those willing to pay for the additional service can access TimesSelect, containing the complete printed *Times*, with its most popular columnists and features intact, and special services such as free, downloadable access to the paper's archives. The *Wall Street Journal* model simply calls for payment for the online version. Subscribers get the print version and more than 1,000 additional articles a day from the Dow Jones Newswire, the paper's owners. Other newspaper sites, however, such as the *Los Angeles Times*, have experimented with paid Web content and then returned to an advertising-based model. Nonetheless, according to the Newspaper Association of America, as 2006 dawned, there were 44 American newspapers charging a fee for some or all of their online content (Robertson, 2006).

This raises the last question faced by online newspapers, How will circulation be measured? In fact, if visitors to a newspaper's Web site are added to its hard-copy readership, newspapers are more popular than ever; that is, they are drawing readers in larger numbers than ever before. Therefore, if the vast majority of electronic papers continue to rely on a free-to-the-user, ad-supported model to boost their "circulation," how do they quantify that readership for advertisers, both print and online? Industry insiders have called for a new metric to more accurately describe a paper's true reach. "Circulation," they say, should be replaced by **market reach,** the total number of readers of the print edition plus those unduplicated Web readers who access the paper only online. For example, the *Des Moines Register* in Iowa reaches 70.1% of its market every week with its print edition. If its unduplicated Web visitors for the month are included, it reaches 74.6%. Other papers do even better. The *Boston Globe* boosts its market reach by 8.7% and the *San Diego Union Tribune* by 8.2% when unique Web users are counted. The daily newspaper industry as a whole increases its market reach from 42.8% to 54.8% (Saba, 2005). The question remains, however, whether these increases in "circulation" can boost the fortunes of the printed papers while supporting their free, ad-based online versions.

Does this front page represent soft news run amok or an effort to give readers what they want? On a day when bloody riots protesting a cartoon of the prophet Muhammad raged across Europe and the Middle East, a controversial election outcome in Haiti resulted in chaos and the shooting of two Haitians by United Nations observers, published reports indicated that the Pentagon had developed plans for an attack on Iran, and e-mails surfaced in which disgraced lobbyist Jack Abramoff bragged of his close ties to the White House, one of the top stories in this respected northern California newspaper, part of the Media News Group chain, was an account of a local couple's victory in a plumbing fixture company's ugliest bathroom promotion. The story was positioned front page, above the fold, with a color photo.

CHANGES IN NEWSPAPER READERSHIP

Newspaper publishers know well that newspaper readership in the United States is least prevalent among younger people. Fewer than 30% of 18- to 29-year-olds read a daily paper. Fewer than 50% of 30- to 44-year-olds do so (in 1972 the proportion was 75%). The number of 25- to 34-year-olds who read the paper has fallen 20% in the past 5 years alone (Moses, 2002). A Media Management Center study predicts that by 2010, only 9% of those in their twenties will read a newspaper every day (Black and White, 2005). Look at Figure 4.3. Note the decline in newspaper readership as people get younger. Note, too, the low interest in overall attention to the news in younger Americans. How do you feel about the fact that 25% of all people aged 18 to 24 from a national sample of your fellow Americans sought no news at all? How do you react to media analyst Michael Wolff's assertion that the flight of young

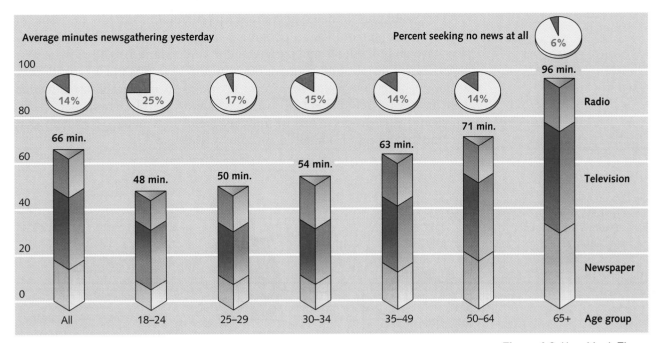

Figure 4.3 How Much Time Did You Spend Newsgathering Yesterday? *Source:* Pew Center for the People and the Press (Moses, 2002).

readers away from the newspaper means that "if you own a newspaper, you can foresee its almost-certain end" (quoted in Alterman, 2002, p. 10)? The problem facing newspapers, then, is how to lure young people (readers of the future) to their pages. Online and free commuter papers might be two solutions, but the fundamental question remains: Should newspapers give these readers what they *should* want or what they *do* want?

Some newspapers confront this problem directly. They add inserts or sections directed toward, and sometimes written by, teens and young people. This is good business. But traditionalists disagree with another youth-targeted strategy—altering other, more serious (presumably more important) parts of the paper to cater to the infrequent and non-newspaper reader. As more newspaper professionals adopt a market-centered approach in their pursuit of what media ethicist Jay Black (2001, p. 21) calls (fairly or unfairly?) the "bifurcating, self-indulgent, highly transient, and significantly younger audiences whose pocketbooks are larger than their attention spans"—using readership studies, focus groups, and other tests of customer satisfaction to design their papers—they increasingly find themselves criticized for "cheapening" both the newspaper as a medium and journalism as an institution.

What happens to journalistic integrity, critics ask, to community service, to the traditional role of newspapers in our democracy, when front pages are given over to reports of starlets' affairs, sports heroes' retirements, and full-color photos of plane wrecks because this is what younger readers want? As topics of interest to the 18- to 35-year-old reluctant reader and nonreader are emphasized, what is ignored? What happens to depth, detail, and precision as stories get shorter and snappier? What kind of culture develops on a diet of **soft news** (sensational stories that do not serve the democratic function of journalism; see Scott & Gobetz, 1992) rather than **hard news** (stories that "help people to make intelligent decisions and/or keep up with important issues of the day"; Wulfemeyer, 1982, p. 483)?

The "softening" of newspapers raises a potential media literacy issue. The media literate person has an obligation to be aware of the impact newspapers have on individuals and society and to understand how the text of newspapers offers insight into contemporary culture. We might ask ourselves: Are we getting what we asked for? What do we as a people and as individuals want from our newspaper? Do we understand the role newspapers play in our democratic process? Are we fully aware of how newspapers help shape our understanding of ourselves and our world?

How far can newspapers go in attracting today's young readers before the papers lose their identity?

© David Horsey, Seattle Post-Intelligencer. Used by permission.

In a 1787 letter, Thomas Jefferson wrote to a colleague, "Were it left to me to decide whether we should have a government without newspapers or newspapers without government, I should not hesitate to prefer the latter." Would he write that about today's newspaper, a newspaper increasingly designed to meet the wants, needs, and interests of younger, occasional newspaper readers or those who do not read at all?

There is another view, however—that there is no problem here at all. Ever since the days of the penny press, newspapers have been dominated by soft news. All we are seeing today is an extension of what has always been. Moreover, nonreaders are simply going elsewhere for the hard news and information that were once the sole province of newspapers. They're going online, to television, and to specifically targeted sources, including magazines and newsletters. The box entitled "What If There Were No Newspapers?" on page 116 frames this debate more fully.

Interpreting Relative Placement of Stories

Newspapers tell readers what is significant and meaningful through their placement of stories in and on their pages. Within a paper's sections (for example, front, leisure, sports, and careers), readers almost invariably read pages in order (that is, page 1, then page 2, and so on). Recognizing this, papers place the stories they think are most important on the earliest pages. Newspaper jargon for this phenomenon has even entered our everyday language. "Front-page news" means the same thing in the living room as in the pressroom.

The placement of stories on a page is also important. English readers read from top to bottom and from left to right. Stories that the newspaper staff deems important tend to be placed above the fold and toward the left of the page. This is an important aspect of the power of newspapers to influence public opinion and of media literacy. As you'll see in Chapter 13, relative story placement is a factor in **agenda setting**—the way newspapers and other media influence not only what we think but what we think about.

Two pages from different newspapers published on the same day in nearby cities are shown here and on the next page. Both chose to report on the Hamas

WWW

Journalism Education Association
www.jea.org

WWW

High School Journalism Institute
www.journalism.indiana.edu/hsji

WWW

The Newseum
www.newseum.org

In February 2006, the militant Islamic group Hamas took control of the Palestinian parliament after open elections there had given it a majority of seats. Its leaders immediately announced that they would no longer honor previous peace agreements with Israel. Two papers, the *Boston Globe* and the *Hartford Courant*, published in two New England capital cities in adjoining states, chose to report the news somewhat differently. The *Globe* put the story on page 1, with a lengthy jump to page 18. The *Courant* ran a somewhat shorter piece on page 4. Would you be surprised to learn that the *Globe's* story was written by one of its own staff reporters and the *Courant* piece was a wire service account from the *Washington Post*? What can you tell about the importance assigned to this story by each of these papers from its respective placement?

takeover of the Palestinian parliament. But notice the different treatments given this story in these newspapers. What judgments can you make about the importance each daily placed on this story? How might *Globe* readers have interpreted this event differently from readers of the *Courant*?

A media literate newspaper reader should be able to make similar judgments about other layout decisions. The use of photos suggests the importance the editors assign to a story, as do the size and wording of headlines, the employment of jumps (continuations to other pages), and placement of a story in a given section. A report of a person's death on the front page, as opposed to the international section or in the obituaries, carries a different meaning, as does an analysis of an issue placed on the front page as opposed to the editorial page.

LIVING MEDIA LITERACY

Help a School Start an Online Newspaper

Newspaper circulation has declined for the past decade and a half; it has not even come close to keeping up with the growth of the American population. But as we have seen in this chapter, many people believe that the newspaper is essential to the operation of our democracy. We have also seen that the greatest decline in paper readership is among young people. What can you do to support newspaper literacy?

Here are some facts that suggest a solution. One of the surest predictors of newspaper readership is parental newspaper readership. That is, "children born into newspaper-reading families tend to keep up the tradition; those born in non-newspaper families tend to become non-readers" (Morton, 2002, p. 64). In addition, industry research makes it clear that if a person doesn't develop the newspaper-reading habit by age 18, she or he never will (Grusin & Edmondson, 2003). We also know that many information-seeking young people ignore the newspaper in favor of "the Internet and personal digital assistants" (Moses, 2002, p. 13). One way, then, to encourage newspaper literacy is to create a situation that involves the technology young people seem to prefer, while offering the newspaper experience that might be absent in their homes. Help a high school start an online newspaper.

Two fine examples are *The Beak* at Greenwich (Connecticut) High School (www.greenwichschools.org/ghs/beak) and *The Arrow* at Flathead High School in Kalispell, Montana (www.netrix.net/fhspub). Both offer just what you would expect from a school newspaper—news, sports, entertainment, and opinion. Many other schools around the country offer online newspapers as part of their curricula as a means of enhancing awareness of technology, media, and information literacies (information seeking, fact checking, referencing, and so on).

> "CHILDREN BORN INTO NEWSPAPER-READING FAMILIES TEND TO KEEP UP THE TRADITION; THOSE BORN IN NON-NEWSPAPER FAMILIES TEND TO BECOME NON-READERS."

There is a wealth of help available to you. Most useful is the National Scholastic Press Association (www.studentpress.org). Founded in 1921 for the express purpose of supporting high school newspapers, this organization offers competitions, critiques of student work, high school newspaper news, First Amendment counsel, and conventions. Of particular value here is its online school newspaper advisory services.

Also of value is the Newspaper Association of America Foundation (www.naa.org/foundation/nie.html), which administers over 700 Newspaper-in-Education programs (www.vermont.today.com/nie/nieinfo.html) designed to encourage use of newspapers in schools. Among its services are discounted newspapers, teacher guides, and other community newspaper education assistance. Finally, the ASNE (www.asne.org/ideas/highschools.htm), whose affiliation includes major papers such as the *Boston Globe,* the *Chicago Tribune,* the *Washington Post,* and the *Seattle Times,* maintains programs offering high school journalism students, teachers, and advisors internships, real-world newspaper experiences, and instruction.

Helping a school lay the groundwork for an online paper encourages readership among youth, promotes civic journalism, and gives students increased knowledge about issues such as First Amendment rights, current events, democratic uses of the media, making news (value) judgments, journalistic ethics, and effective communication. Perhaps more important, it unites the school with its community, teaching students that they, their school, their community, and the larger world are all inevitably linked—further reinforcing the need to develop strong newspaper and information-seeking literacy.

RESOURCES FOR REVIEW AND DISCUSSION

Review Points

- Newspapers have been a part of public life since Roman times, prospering in Europe, and coming to the Colonies in the 1690s.
- The newspaper was at the heart of the American Revolution, and, as such, protection for the press was enshrined in the First Amendment.
- The penny press brought the paper to millions of "regular people," and the newspaper quickly became the people's medium.
- There are several types of newspapers, including national dailies; large metropolitan dailies; suburban and small-town dailies; weeklies and semiweeklies;

- ethnic, alternative, and dissident papers; and free commuter papers.
- Despite falling readership, newspapers remain an attractive advertising medium.
- The number of daily newspapers is in decline, and there are very few cities with competing papers. Chain ownership has become common.
- Conglomeration is fueling hypercommercialism, erosion of the firewall between the business and editorial sides of the newspaper, and the loss of the newspaper's traditional journalistic mission.

- Newspapers have converged with the Internet. Still unanswered are whether people will read the paper online, how to charge for content, and how to measure readership.
- Newspaper readership is changing—it is getting older, as young people abandon the paper for the Net or for no news at all. How newspapers respond will define their future.
- Interpreting the relative placement of stories in the newspaper is an important media literacy skill.

Key Terms

 Use the text's Online Learning Center at www.mhhe.com/baran5 to further your understanding of the following terminology.

Acta Diurna, 100
corantos, 100
diurnals, 100
broadsides (broadsheets), 100
Bill of Rights, 101
First Amendment, 101
Alien and Sedition Acts, 102
penny press, 103
wire services, 104

yellow journalism, 105
newspaper chains, 106
pass-along readership, 106
zoned editions, 109
ethnic press, 111
alternative press, 111
dissident press, 111
commuter papers, 112
feature syndicates, 113

joint operating agreement (JOA), 114
functional displacement, 116
community publishing, 120
digital delivery daily, 120
market reach, 121
soft news, 123
hard news, 124
agenda setting, 125

Questions for Review

 Go to the self-quizzes on the Online Learning Center to test your knowledge.

1. What are Acta Diurna, corantos, diurnals, and broadsheets?
2. What is the significance of *Publick Occurrences Both Foreign and Domestick,* the *Boston News-Letter,* the *New-England Courant,* the *Pennsylvania Gazette,* and the *New York Weekly Journal?*
3. What factors led to development of the penny press? To yellow journalism?
4. What are the similarities and differences between wire services and feature syndicates?
5. When did newspaper chains begin? Can you characterize them as they exist today?

6. What are the different types of newspapers?
7. Why is the newspaper an attractive medium for advertisers?
8. What is a JOA?
9. How has convergence affected newspapers' performance?
10. What is the firewall? Why is it important?
11. How do online papers hope to succeed?
12. What are hard news and soft news?

Questions for Critical Thinking and Discussion

1. What are your favorite syndicated features? Why?
2. Does your town have competing dailies? If yes, how does that competition manifest itself? If not, what do you think you're missing? Does your town have a JOA situation? If yes, can you describe its operation?
3. Where do you stand on the debate over chains? Are they good or bad for the medium?
4. Have you ever used an online newspaper? How would you describe your experience?
5. Compare your local paper, an alternative weekly, and, if available, a dissident weekly. Choose different sections, such as front page, editorials, and classified ads. How are they similar; how are they different? Which one, if any, speaks to you and why?

Important Resources

 Go to the Online Learning Center for additional readings.

Internet Resources

Early Newspaper History	www.bl.uk/collections/britnews.html
History of African American Newspapers	www.iath.virginia.edu/vcdh/afam/reflector/newspaper.html
Yellow Journalism	www.humboldt.edu/~jcb10/yellow.html
Newspaper Association of America	www.naa.org
Links to National Newspapers	www.all-links.com/newscentral
National Association of Hispanic Publishers	www.nahp.org
Alternative Weekly Network	www.awn.org
National Newspaper Publishers Association	www.nnpa.org
Newspaper National Network	www.nnnlp.com
Association of Alternative Newsweeklies	www.aan.org
Editor & Publisher	www.editorandpublisher.com
American Society of Newspaper Editors	www.asne.org
Online Newspapers	www.ipl.org/div/news/
Online Classifieds	www.traderonline.com
	www.buysell.com
	www.craigslist.org
Newspaper Blogs	www.cyberjournalist.net
New Orleans Times-Picayune	www.nola.com
Journalism Education Association	www.jea.org
High School Journalism Institute	www.journalism.indiana.edu/hsji
The Newseum	www.newseum.org

Magazines

LEARNING OBJECTIVES

Magazines were once a truly national mass medium, the television of their time. But changes in the nature of American society and the economics of mass media altered their nature. They are the medium that first made specialization a virtue, and they prosper today by speaking to even more narrowly defined groups of readers. After studying this chapter you should

- be familiar with the history and development of the magazine industry and the magazine itself as a medium.

- recognize how the organizational and economic nature of the contemporary magazine industry shapes the content of magazines.

- understand the relationship between magazines and their readers.

- be familiar with the successes and failures of Web magazines and the reasons for both.

- possess improved magazine-reading media literacy skills, especially when interpreting advertorials and digitally altered images.

I t's November 1994, and you are working at the newspaper. It's an entry-level job, but you're excited about your career prospects. Your paper has been around for most of the century, and its reporters either build good names for themselves in town or move on to bigger markets. You have a lot of responsibility and freedom, but you are admittedly sick and tired of the ongoing battles with management. As it is, you and your colleagues are embroiled in yet another labor dispute.

The arts and features editor, however, impressed by what he's seen from you, offers you an out. It's still early in the history of online publishing, he says, but that's an opportunity, not a problem. Together you can define what an online publication should be. Here's the deal, he tells you. He has $100,000 in start-up money from Apple Computer and wants to be online in a year. Rather than take on the grind of a daily newspaper, he envisions a free biweekly magazine featuring a hip, West Coast mix of cultural criticism, political and social commentary, interviews with authors, and book reviews. You ask, "How will

Opposite: Specialization characterizes today's magazine industry.

the magazine make money?" (though what you really mean is "How will I get paid?"). As bad as management–labor relations are at the paper, at least you earn a living. "Not to worry," he assures you. "Advertisers will line up to get access to the kinds of people who'll read our little online magazine. And I need your answer," he adds, "by tomorrow."

Had you been at the *San Francisco Examiner* with David Talbot (the arts and features editor mentioned above) in 1994, you might have found yourself having to make this decision. Do you stay at a traditional paper-based publication that has many benefits and some drawbacks, or do you gamble on the convergence of magazines and the growing but still new Internet?

Talbot called his online magazine *Salon* and took the *Examiner*'s Gary Kamiya (*Salon*'s executive editor), Andrew Ross (vice president of business and strategic development), Scott Rosenberg (senior technology editor), and Mignon Khargie (design editor) with him to his new venture. And together with *Washington Post*–backed *Slate, Salon* defined (and continues to define) the world of online magazines.

WWW
Salon
www.salon.com

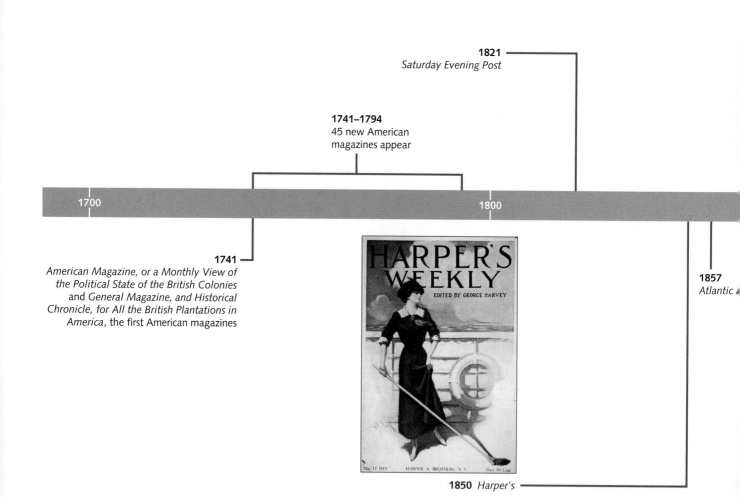

1821
Saturday Evening Post

1741–1794
45 new American
magazines appear

1700   1800

1741
American Magazine, or a Monthly View of the Political State of the British Colonies and *General Magazine, and Historical Chronicle, for All the British Plantations in America*, the first American magazines

1857
Atlantic

1850 *Harper's*

For example, Talbot discovered that users would visit the magazine but disappear until new material was posted. So in early 1997, *Salon* began posting a new issue every weekday. Traffic rose dramatically to 400,000 unique visitors per month (Stein, 1999). As the Net matured, helping usher in the 24-hour-a-day, 7-day-a-week reporting cycle for all news media, the magazine increased its emphasis on breaking news, a smooth transition for an online publication staffed by refugees from a daily newspaper. Today, *Salon* draws 3.5 million demographically upscale visitors a month, but like almost all other online-only content providers, it has not yet begun to earn the kind of profit enjoyed by even moderately successful consumer magazines. Today, *Salon* offers its content, for an annual fee, through its "premium service." Visitors, however, can secure a "free sponsored day pass" that allows them to access most premium services after watching the sponsor's commercial. This strategy has finally helped the old-line (by Internet standards) Web magazine escape the red, earning a quarterly profit for the first time in early 2005. Still, its financial health is sufficiently in doubt that it has been dropped from the NASDAQ stock exchange. So, knowing this, would you make the move from a daily newspaper to Talbot's new venture?

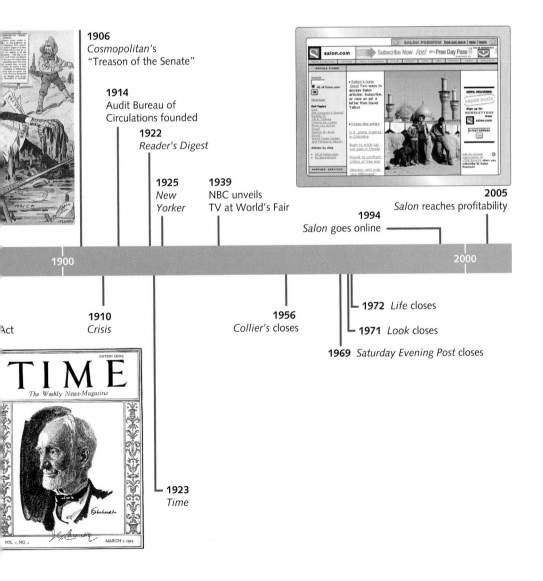

1906
Cosmopolitan's "Treason of the Senate"

1914
Audit Bureau of Circulations founded

1922
Reader's Digest

1925
New Yorker

1939
NBC unveils TV at World's Fair

2005
Salon reaches profitability

1994
Salon goes online

1900

2000

Act

1910
Crisis

1956
Collier's closes

1972 *Life* closes

1971 *Look* closes

1969 *Saturday Evening Post* closes

1923
Time

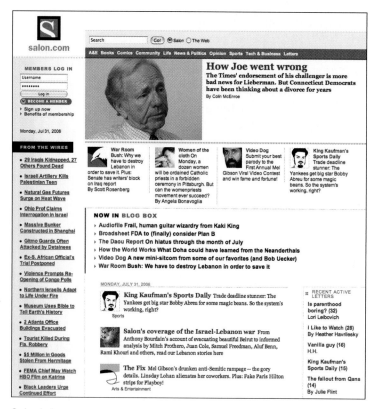

Salon's home page. Reprinted by permission of Salon Media Group, Inc.

In this chapter we examine the dynamics of the contemporary magazine industry—paper and online—and its audiences. We study the medium's beginnings in the Colonies, its pre–Civil War expansion, and its explosive growth between the Civil War and World War I. This was the era of great mass circulation magazines, but it was also the era of powerful writers known as muckrakers.

Influenced by television and by the social and cultural changes that followed World War II, the magazine took on a new, more narrowly focused nature, which provided the industry with a growing readership and increased profits. We detail the various categories of magazines, discuss circulation research, look at the ways the industry protects itself from competition from other media, and how advertisers influence editorial decisions. Finally, we investigate some of the editorial decisions that should be of particular interest to media literate magazine consumers.

Magazine History
www.well.com/user/art/
maghist01.html

A Short History of Magazines

Magazines were a favorite medium of the British elite by the mid-1700s, and two prominent colonial printers hoped to duplicate that success in the New World. In 1741 in Philadelphia, Andrew Bradford published *American Magazine, or a Monthly View of the Political State of the British Colonies*, followed by Benjamin Franklin's *General Magazine, and Historical Chronicle, for All the British Plantations in America*. Composed largely of reprinted British material, these publications were expensive and aimed at the small number of literate colonists. Lacking an organized postal system, distribution was difficult, and neither magazine was successful. *American Magazine* produced three issues; *General Magazine*, six. Yet between 1741 and 1794, 45 new magazines appeared, although no more than 3 were published in the same time period. Entrepreneurial printers hoped to attract educated, cultured, moneyed gentlemen by copying the successful London magazines. Even after the Revolutionary War, U.S. magazines remained clones of their British forerunners.

THE EARLY MAGAZINE INDUSTRY

In 1821 the *Saturday Evening Post* appeared; it was to continue for the next 148 years. Among other successful early magazines were *Harper's* (1850) and *Atlantic Monthly* (1857). Cheaper printing and growing literacy fueled expansion of the magazine as they had the book (see Chapter 3). But an additional factor in the success of the early magazines was the spread of social movements such as abolitionism and labor reform. These issues provided compelling content, and a boom in magazine publishing began. In 1825 there were

100 magazines in operation; by 1850 there were 600. Because magazine articles increasingly focused on matters of importance to U.S. readers, magazines such as the *United States Literary Gazette* and *American Boy* began to look less like London publications and more like a new and unique product. Journalism historians John Tebbel and Mary Ellen Zuckerman (1991) called this "the time of significant beginnings" (p. 13); it was during this time that the magazine developed many of the characteristics we associate with it even today. Magazines and the people who staffed them began to clearly differentiate themselves from other publishing endeavors (such as books and newspapers). The concept of specialist writers took hold, and their numbers rose. In addition, numerous and detailed illustrations began to fill the pages of magazines.

Still, these early magazines were aimed at a literate elite interested in short stories, poetry, social commentary, and essays. The magazine did not become a true national mass medium until after the Civil War.

THE MASS CIRCULATION ERA

The modern era of magazines can be divided into two parts, each characterized by a different relationship between medium and audience.

Mass circulation popular magazines began to prosper in the post–Civil War years. In 1865 there were 700 magazines publishing; by 1870 there were 1,200; by 1885 there were 3,300. Crucial to this expansion was the women's magazine. Suffrage—women's right to vote—was the social movement that occupied its pages, but a good deal of content could also be described as how-to for homemakers. Advertisers, too, were anxious to appear in the new women's magazines, hawking their brand-name products. First appearing at this time are several magazines still familiar today, including *Ladies' Home Journal* and *Good Housekeeping*.

There were several reasons for this phenomenal growth. As with books, widespread literacy was one reason. But the Postal Act of 1879, which permitted mailing magazines at cheap second-class postage rates, and the spread of the railroad, which carried people and publications westward from the East Coast, were two others. A fourth was the reduction in cost. As long as magazines sold for 35 cents—a lot of money for the time—they were read largely by the upper class. However, a circulation war erupted between giants *McClure's*, *Munsey's Magazine*, and the *Saturday Evening Post*. Soon they, as well as *Ladies' Home Journal*, *McCall's*, *Woman's Home Companion*, *Collier's*, and *Cosmopolitan*, were selling for as little as 10 and 15 cents, which brought them within reach of many working people.

This 1870s price war was made possible by the newfound ability of magazines to attract growing amounts of advertising. As we'll see in

This *McClure's* cover captures the spirit of the Roaring Twenties as well as the excitement of the burgeoning magazine industry.

Taking On the Giants: Muckraking in the Magazines

At the start of the 20th century, corruption and greed in business and politics were creating some of the worst abuses this country had ever seen—unsafe food, inhumane child labor practices, unregulated drug manufacture and sale, exploitation of workers, a lack of safety standards in the workplace, blatant discrimination against African Americans, and a disregard for human and civil rights. Industrial giants, the so-called Robber Barons, amassed fortunes through mammoth monopolies controlling mining, manufacturing, banking, railroads, food packing, and insurance.

Why didn't the government step in and stop these abuses? Local politicians and police were in the pay of the industries. The federal government was also hamstrung. At the time, U.S. senators were selected by the legislatures of the individual states. For the right price, an industry could make sure that people favorable to its interests were selected by those legislatures to serve in the Senate. The buying and selling of seats ensured that the Senate would block any attempts to pass legislation designed to break up monopolies or remedy social ills.

> **THE EFFORTS OF THE MUCKRAKERS AND THE MAGAZINES THAT SPREAD THEIR WRITING PRODUCED LEGISLATION AND POLICIES THAT HAVE HELPED DEFINE THE WORLD AS WE KNOW IT.**

Echoing the role of books in social change, magazines, particularly popular mass market magazines, took leadership in challenging these powerful interests and advocating reform. Reaching a nationwide audience, *McClure's, American Magazine,* and *Collier's* shocked and outraged the public with their exposés. Historian Louis Filler (1968) called the crusading magazine articles of writers such as Ida Tarbell, Upton Sinclair, Lincoln Steffens, Jack London, and others "literary rather than yellow" (p. 31). That is, rather than adopting the overexcited, excessive tone of the yellow journalism of the day, these were well written, well researched, and well argued. Articles and series such as Steffens's "The Shame of the Cities," Tarbell's "The History of the Standard Oil Company," Sinclair's novel *The Jungle* (on unclean food and abuse of workers), and Edwin Markham's "The Hoe-Man in the Making" (on unsafe and inhumane child labor practices) galvanized the nation.

One of the greatest successes of magazine journalism was spurred by what we would now consider an unlikely source. However, it produced an amendment to the U.S. Constitution.

The first issue of *Time*.

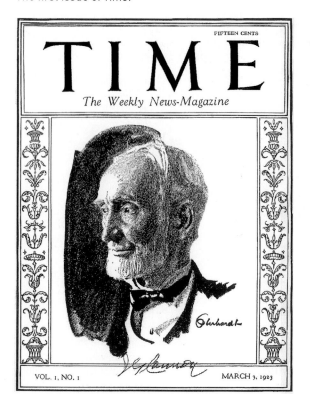

Chapter 12, social and demographic changes in the post–Civil War era—urbanization, industrialization, the spread of roads and railroads, and development of consumer brands and brand names—produced an explosion in the number of advertising agencies. These agencies needed to place their messages somewhere. Magazines were the perfect outlet because they were read by a large, national audience. As a result, circulation—rather than reputation, as had been the case before—became the most important factor in setting advertising rates. Magazines kept cover prices low to ensure the large readerships coveted by advertisers. The fifth reason for the enormous growth in the number of magazines was industrialization, which provided people with leisure and more personal income.

Magazines were truly America's first *national* mass medium, and like books they served as an important force in social change, especially in the **muckraking** era of the first decades of the 20th century (see the box "Taking On the Giants: Muckraking in the Magazines" above). Theodore Roosevelt coined this label as an insult, but the muckrakers wore it proudly, using the pages of

Though President Roosevelt meant the epithet as an insult, the muckrakers wore the title with pride.

A series of articles begun in *Cosmopolitan* in March 1906 changed the way U.S. senators were elected, ensuring passage of reform legislation. "The Treason of the Senate" accused U.S. senators of treason for giving aid and comfort to "the enemies of the nation." Within days of hitting the newsstands, every issue of *Cosmopolitan* had been sold, and President Teddy Roosevelt was compelled to respond to the charges. In a speech delivered on March 17, Roosevelt condemned "the man with the muckrake [who in] magazines makes slanderous and mendacious attack upon men in public life and upon men engaged in public work" (Filler, 1968, p. 252). Thus did the crusading writers and journalists come to be known as "muckrakers." Roosevelt's anguish was no match for the public's anger. In 1913 the 17th Amendment, mandating popular election of senators, was ratified.

The efforts of the muckrakers and the magazines that spread their writing produced legislation and policies that have helped define the world as we know it. They were influential in passage of the Pure Food and Drug Act and the Hepburn Railroad Bill in 1906, the Federal Reserve Bill in 1913, the Clayton Anti-Trust Act in 1914, and numerous child labor laws.

the *Nation, Harper's Weekly,* the *Arena,* and even mass circulation publications such as *McClure's* and *Collier's* to agitate for change. Their targets were the powerful. Their beneficiaries were the poor.

The mass circulation magazine grew with the nation. From the start there were general interest magazines such as the *Saturday Evening Post,* women's magazines such as *Good Housekeeping,* pictorial magazines such as *Life* and *Look,* and digests such as *Reader's Digest,* which was first published in 1922 and offered condensed and tightly edited articles for people on the go in the Roaring Twenties. What these magazines all had in common was the size and breadth of readership. They were mass market, mass circulation publications, both national and affordable. As such, magazines helped unify the nation. They were the television of their time—the dominant advertising medium, the primary source for nationally distributed news, and the preeminent provider of visual, or photo, journalism.

Between 1900 and 1945, the number of families who subscribed to one or more magazines grew from 200,000 to more than 32 million. New and important magazines continued to appear throughout these decades. For example, African American intellectual W. E. B. DuBois founded and edited the *Crisis* in 1910 as the voice of the National Association for the Advancement of Colored People (NAACP). *Time* was first published in 1923. Its brief review of the week's news was immediately popular (it was originally only

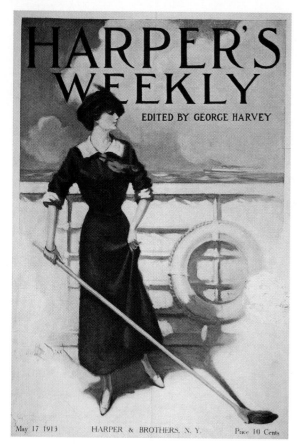

Much respected today, *Harper's* gave early voice to the muckrakers and other serious observers of politics and society.

28 pages long). It made a profit within a year. The *New Yorker*, "the world's best magazine," debuted in 1925.

THE ERA OF SPECIALIZATION

In 1956 *Collier's* declared bankruptcy and became the first mass circulation magazine to cease publication. But its fate, as well as that of other mass circulation magazines, had actually been sealed in the late 1940s and 1950s following the end of World War II. Profound alterations in the nation's culture—and, in particular, the advent of television—changed the relationship between magazines and their audience. No matter how large their circulation, magazines could not match the reach of television. Magazines did not have moving pictures or visual and oral storytelling. Nor could magazines match television's timeliness. Magazines were weekly, whereas television was continuous. Nor could they match television's novelty. In the beginning, *everything* on television was of interest to viewers. As a result, magazines began to lose advertisers to television.

The audience changed as well. As we've seen, World War II changed the nature of American life. The new, mobile, product-consuming public was less interested in the traditional Norman Rockwell world of the *Saturday Evening Post* (closed in 1969) and more in tune with the slick, hip world of narrower interest publications such as *GQ* and *Self,* which spoke to them in and about their new and exciting lives. And because World War II had further urbanized and industrialized America, people—including millions of women who had entered the workforce—had more leisure and more money to spend. They could spend both on a wider array of personal interests *and* on

A wide array of specialized magazines exists for all lifestyles and interests. Here are only 5 of the 17,000 special interest consumer magazines available to U.S. readers.

A change in people's tastes in magazines reflects some of the ways the world changed after World War II. Norman Rockwell's America was replaced by that of *GQ* and *People*.

magazines that catered to those interests. Where there were once *Look* (closed in 1971) and *Life* (closed in 1972), there were now *Flyfishing, Surfing, Ski,* and *Easyrider.* The industry had hit on the secret of success: specialization and a lifestyle orientation. We saw in Chapter 1 that all media have moved in this direction in their efforts to attract an increasingly fragmented audience, but it was the magazine industry that began the trend. In fact, as the editors of the Project for Excellence in Journalism (2004, p. 1) wrote,

> Magazines often are harbingers of change. When large social, economic, or technological shifts begin to reshape the culture, magazines frequently are the first media to move, and the structure of the industry is one reason. Unlike newspapers, most magazines are not so tied to a specific geographic area, but are instead centered on interests or niches. Writers are looking for trends. Publishers can more quickly than in other media add and subtract titles aimed at specific audience segments or interests. Advertisers, in turn, can take their dollars to hot titles of the moment aimed at particular demographics.

Magazines and Their Audiences

Exactly who are the audiences for magazines? Magazine industry research indicates that among people with at least some college, 94% subscribe to at least one magazine. Nearly the same figures apply for households with annual incomes of over $40,000 and for people in professional and managerial careers, regardless of educational attainment. The typical magazine reader is at least a high school graduate, is married, owns his or her own house, is employed full-time, and has an annual household income of just under $40,000. Advertisers find magazine readers an attractive, upscale audience for their pitches.

How people use magazines also makes them an attractive advertising medium. Magazines sell themselves to potential advertisers based not only on the number and demographic desirability of their readers, but on readers' engagement with and affinity for magazine advertising. Ed Kelly, CEO of American Express Publishing, explains *engagement:* "The power of magazines is a personal experience. When I pick up a magazine to read, I choose a certain magazine because it covers topics that interest me, so everything in the issue speaks to me—including the ads." Adds Hearst Magazine's chief marketing officer Michael Clinton, "Unlike a lot of media, consumers pay for magazines. They are spending their good old-fashion dollars to buy the product. That is an engagement in itself in terms of how they are involved with the magazine" (both in "The New Imperative," 2005, p. M24). *Affinity* for magazine advertising is demonstrated by industry research that shows that 61% of all readers have a positive attitude toward magazine advertising; 72% say that ads do not interfere with their magazine reading enjoyment; and 48% say that advertising actually adds to their reading enjoyment ("How Do You," 2005).

Scope and Structure of the Magazine Industry

For more information on this topic, see Media Tours video clip #1, "Magazines: Inside *Vibe* Magazine," on the *Media World* DVD.

In 1950 there were 6,950 magazines in operation. The number now exceeds 22,000, some 17,000 of which are general interest consumer magazines. Of these, 800 produce three-fourths of the industry's gross revenues. Ten new magazine titles are launched every week (Magazine Publishers of America, 2005). Contemporary magazines are typically divided into three broad types:

- *Trade, professional, and business magazines* carry stories, features, and ads aimed at people in specific professions and are either distributed by the professional organizations themselves *(American Medical News)* or by media companies such as Whittle Communications and Time Warner *(Progressive Farmer).*

- *Industrial, company, and sponsored magazines* are produced by companies specifically for their own employees, customers, and stockholders, or by clubs and associations specifically for their members. *Friendly Exchange,* for example, is the magazine of the Fireman's Fund insurance company. *AARP The Magazine* is the magazine for members of the American Association of Retired Persons (AARP).

- *Consumer magazines* are sold by subscription and at newsstands, bookstores, and other retail outlets, including supermarkets, garden shops, and computer stores. *Sunset* and *Wired* fit here, as do *Road & Track, US, TV Guide,* and the *New Yorker* (Figure 5.1).

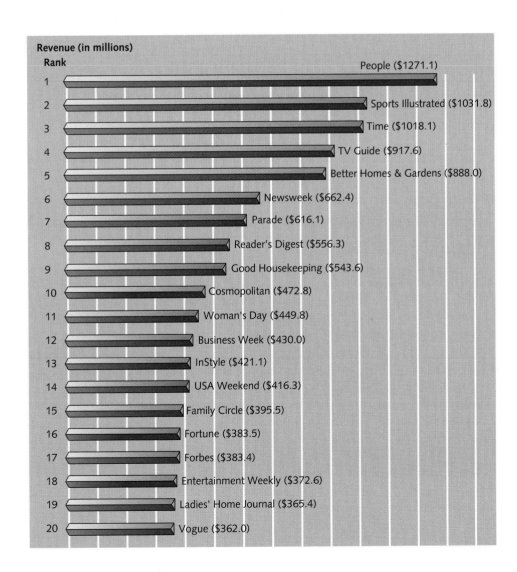

Figure 5.1 The 20 Consumer Magazines with the Highest Advertising and Circulation Revenue, 2004.
Source: Endicott, 2005.

CATEGORIES OF CONSUMER MAGAZINES

The industry typically categorizes consumer magazines in terms of their targeted audiences. Of course, the wants, needs, interests, and wishes of those readers determine the content of each publication. Although these categories are neither exclusive (where do *Chicago Business* and *Sports Illustrated for Women* fit?) nor exhaustive (what do we do with *Hot Rod* and *National Geographic*?), they are at least indicative of the cascade of options. Here is a short list of common consumer magazine categories, along with examples of each type.

Magazine Publishers of America
www.magazine.org

Alternative magazines: *Mother Jones,* the *Utne Reader*
Business/money magazines: *Money, Black Enterprise*
Celebrity and entertainment magazines: *People, Entertainment Weekly*
Children's magazines: *Highlights, Ranger Rick*
Computer magazines: *Internet, PC World*
Ethnic magazines: *Hispanic, Ebony*
Family magazines: *Fatherhood, Parenting*
Fashion magazines: *Bazaar, Elle*
General interest magazines: *Reader's Digest, Life*
Geographical magazines: *Texas Monthly, Bay Area Living*
Gray magazines: *Modern Maturity*
Literary magazines: *Atlantic Monthly, Harper's*
Men's magazines: *GQ, Field & Stream, Playboy*
Newsmagazines: *Time, U.S. News & World Report, Newsweek*
Political opinion magazines: the *Nation, National Review*
Sports magazines: *Sport, Sports Illustrated*
Sunday newspaper magazines: *Parade, USA Weekend*
Women's magazines: *Working Woman, Good Housekeeping, Ms.*
Youth magazines: *Seventeen, Tiger Beat*

Magazine Advertising

Magazine specialization exists and succeeds because the demographically similar readership of these publications is attractive to advertisers. Advertisers want to target ads for their products and services to those most likely to respond to them. This is a lucrative situation for the magazine industry. The top 224 ad-supported magazines in America alone carried over 243,305 pages of advertising in 2005 worth well over $23 billion in revenue (Magazine Publishers of America, 2005). (But for the story of a magazine with no advertising, see the essay on p. 144, "Suzuki Samurai Versus *Consumer Reports.*") Eight and a quarter percent of all advertising expenditures in U.S. media is placed with magazines. How those billions of dollars are spread among different types of advertisers is shown in Figure 5.2.

Magazines are often further specialized through **split runs,** special versions of a given issue in which editorial content and ads vary according to some specific demographic or regional grouping. *Time,* for example, has at least 8 regional editions, more than 50 state editions, and 8 professionally oriented editions.

For more information on this topic, see Media Talk video clip #7, "Media Professionals Discuss State of the Media," on the *Media World* DVD.

Rank	Category
1	Automotive
2	Apparel and Accessories
3	Home Furnishings and Supplies
4	Toiletries and Cosmetics
5	Drugs and Remedies
6	Media
7	Direct Response Companies
8	Retail
9	Financial, Insurance, and Real Estate
10	Food and Food Products

Figure 5.2 Top 10 Magazine Advertiser Categories, 2005.

Source: Publishers Information Bureau, 2005.

TYPES OF CIRCULATION

Magazines price advertising space in their pages based on **circulation,** the total number of issues of a magazine that are sold. These sales can be either subscription or single-copy sales. For the industry as a whole, about 85% of all sales are subscription. Some magazines, *Woman's Day, TV Guide,* and *Penthouse,* for example, rely heavily on single-copy sales, whereas others, such as *Reader's Digest,* earn as much as 60% of their revenues from subscriptions. Subscriptions have the advantage of an assured, ongoing readership, but they are sold below the cover price and have the additional burden of postage included in their cost to the publisher. Single-copy sales are less reliable, but to advertisers they are sometimes a better barometer of a publication's value to its readers. Single-copy readers must consciously choose to pick up an issue, and they pay full price for it.

A third form of circulation, **controlled circulation,** refers to providing a magazine at no cost to readers who meet some specific set of advertiser-attractive criteria. Free airline and hotel magazines fit this category. Although they provide no subscription or single-sales revenue, these magazines are an attractive, relatively low-cost advertising vehicle for companies seeking narrowly defined, captive audiences. These **custom publishing** magazines are discussed in more detail later in this chapter.

MEASURING CIRCULATION

Regardless of how circulation occurs, it is monitored through research. The Audit Bureau of Circulations (ABC) was established in 1914 to provide reliability to a booming magazine industry playing loose with self-announced circulation figures. The ABC provides reliable circulation figures, as well as important population and demographic information. Other research companies, including Simmons Market Research Bureau and Standard Rate and Data Service, also generate valuable data for advertisers and magazines. Circulation data are often augmented by measures of *pass-along readership,* which refers to readers who neither subscribe nor buy single copies but who borrow a magazine or read one in a doctor's office or library.

Audit Bureau of Circulations
www.accessabc.com

Magazine CyberCenter
www.magamall.com

Suzuki Samurai Versus *Consumer Reports*

Very few magazines survive today without accepting advertising. Those that are ad-free insist that freedom from commercial support allows them to make a greater difference in the lives of their readers. *Ms.*, for example, cannot advocate development of strong, individual females if its pages carry ads that suggest beauty is crucial for women's success. But it is *Consumer Reports* that makes this case most strongly—it must be absolutely free of outside influence if its articles about consumer products are to maintain their well-earned reputation for fairness and objectivity. This reputation was put to the test when automobile manufacturer Suzuki went to war with the magazine and its publisher, Consumers Union.

In 1988 *Consumer Reports* tested a number of sports utility vehicles for safety. Several passed the magazine's difficult evaluation, but the Suzuki Samurai did not. The Samurai tipped up severely and repeatedly in a series of avoidance-maneuver tests. *Consumer Reports* rated the Samurai "not acceptable" in its July 1988 issue. Later that same year, the National Highway Transportation and Safety Administration (NHTSA) accepted Consumers Union's petition that it develop minimum stability standards to prevent rollover in all vehicles. Six years later, in 1994, the NHTSA abandoned its plans to develop such a standard, citing the high cost to manufacturers in meeting proposed rules. Instead, argued the NHTSA, an "informed public" would, through its purchases of certain vehicles rather than others, produce the necessary change.

Grudgingly accepting the NHTSA market-based solution, *Consumer Reports* continued its testing as a way to inform the public, despite lawsuits and attacks from Suzuki. Those attacks, and *Consumer Reports'* reputation, were challenged in a 1997 lawsuit.

A 31-year-old Samurai passenger, Katie Rodriguez, was paralyzed from the neck down in a rollover accident on a Missouri highway. She sued Suzuki. Despite testimony from its own expert witnesses that there had been 147 deaths and

> **VERY FEW MAGAZINES SURVIVE TODAY WITHOUT ACCEPTING ADVERTISING. THOSE THAT ARE AD-FREE INSIST THAT FREEDOM FROM COMMERCIAL SUPPORT ALLOWS THEM TO MAKE A GREATER DIFFERENCE IN THE LIVES OF THEIR READERS.**

7,000 injuries resulting from Samurai rollover accidents, the manufacturer made the "unscientific and rigged" *Consumer Reports* research the center of its defense. In its closing arguments, Suzuki lawyers claimed that Rodriguez's suit and other suits against the company (more than 175 to that date) had been the direct result of the magazine's unfair rating in 1988.

But when the jury began its deliberations, one of the first exhibits it asked for was that same 1988 *Consumer Reports* article. When they returned their verdict, jurors awarded Ms. Rodriguez $25 million in compensatory damages and another $11.9 million in punitive damages.

Did the magazine make a difference? Although the NHTSA has yet to develop mandatory antirollover safety standards, *Consumer Reports* believes that the unanimous jury verdict against the Suzuki Samurai shows that it did.

Two other magazines that, like *Consumer Reports*, eschew advertising because they see it as inimical to their larger mission of making a difference with their particular category of reader are *Ms.* and *Adbusters*. *Adbusters*, founded in 1989, boasts a worldwide circulation of 50,000 and won the *Utne Reader* Award for General Excellence three times in its first 6 years of operation. It aims to help stem the erosion of the world's physical and cultural environments by what it views as greed and commercial forces. Its online version, www.adbusters.org, allows users to download spoofs of popular ad campaigns and other anticonsumerism spots for use as banner ads on their own sites. The better-known *Ms.* began life in 1972 as a Warner Communications publication and has gone through several incarnations as both a for-profit and a not-for-profit publication. Today it is published four times a year, carries no advertising, and remains committed to advancing the cause of women and feminism on a global scale. It, too, maintains an online version: www.msmagazine.com.

Source: This box was developed from material available on *Consumer Reports'* Web site (http://www.consumerreports.org).

This traditional model of measurement, however, is under increasing attack. As advertisers demand more precise assessments of accountability and return on their investment (Chapter 12), new metrics beyond circulation are being demanded by professionals inside and outside the industry. "We live in a very short-term measurement world," says advertising sales executive Steve Lanzano. "I need answers now. The time lag hurts [magazines] because everybody wants immediate turnaround. It has been the same measurement system for 25 years. To get the attention of ad agencies, they need

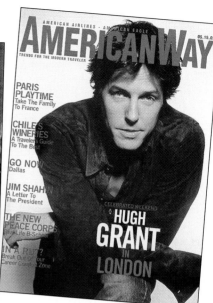

Controlled circulation magazines, like American Airlines' in-flight publications *American Way* and *Nexos*, and Radisson Hotels' *Voyageur*, take advantage of readers' captivity.

to come up with a whole different model" (in Ives, 2006, p. S-2). Speed is only one issue. Others argue that it is one thing for magazine publishers to boast of engagement and affinity (p. 140), but how are they measured? As a result, the advertising and magazine industries are investigating "a whole different model." In 2006, audience assessment firm McPheters & Co. rolled out a new measurement service, Readership.com, designed to provide near real-time information on magazine distribution, readership, and engagement. It tallies not only the number of people a magazine reaches but the effect its ads have on brand awareness, readers' intent to buy, and actual actions taken. If this new model wins enough supporters, measuring "mere" circulation will become a thing of the past.

WWW

Readership.com
www.mcpheters.com

Trends and Convergence in Magazine Publishing

The forces that are reshaping all the mass media have had an impact on magazines as well. Alterations in how the magazine industry does business are primarily designed to help magazines compete with television and the Internet in the race for advertising dollars. Convergence, too, has its impact.

ONLINE MAGAZINES

Another category, **Webzines,** or online magazines, has emerged, made possible by convergence of magazines and the Internet. Many, if not most, magazines, among them *Time* and *Mother Jones*, now produce online editions offering special interactive features not available to their hard-copy readers. In addition, several strictly online magazines have been attempted.

Slate
www.slate.com

Guide to Webzines
www.webreference.com/internet/
magazines

For example, former *New Republic* editor Michael Kinsley moved from Washington, D.C., to Washington State to publish the exclusively online magazine *Slate* for Microsoft (www.slate.com). The Washington Post Company bought *Slate* from Microsoft in 2004 to increase its online presence. And, as we saw in this chapter's opening vignette, *Salon* has become quite popular. Also attracting large numbers of users is the satirical *The Onion* at www.theonion.com.

Online magazines are just beginning to succeed financially. Those produced by existing paper magazine publishers serve primarily as an additional outlet for existing material, a way to extend the reach of the parent publication. Exclusively online magazines, too, are just beginning to produce a profit, but many industry analysts think it will be a long time before they become *very* profitable.

There are several hurdles specific to purely online magazines. First, because Web users have become accustomed to free access to sites, Webzines have yet to find a successful means of charging for subscriptions. *Slate* dropped its plan to do so when faced with a 1997 reader revolt, and, as we saw earlier, *Salon* has instituted a two-tier, both sponsored and subscription, model. Second, as opposed to Webzines produced by paper magazines, purely online magazines must generate original content, an expensive undertaking, yet they compete online for readers and advertisers as equals with Webzines subsidized by paper magazines. In addition, purely online magazines must also compete with all other Web sites on the Internet. They are but one of an infinite number of choices for potential readers. And finally, of the total annual U.S. expenditure on advertising ($183 billion), less than .01% is spent on online magazine advertising. At least for now, there may simply be too little commercial support to sustain this new form of magazine.

Slate's home page

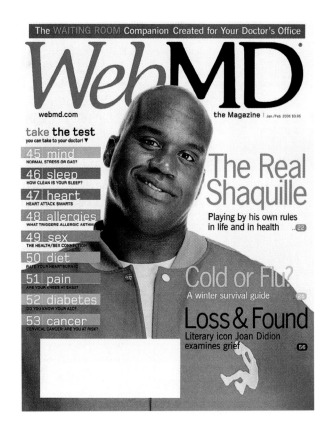

Sea Ray Living and *WebMD the Magazine* are two examples of successful brand magazines.

CUSTOM MAGAZINES

Another trend finds its roots in the magazine industry's response to an increasingly crowded media environment. Custom publishing is the creation of magazines specifically designed for an individual company seeking to reach a very narrowly defined audience, such as favored customers or likely users or buyers. *Web*MD, the medical information Web site, for example, distributes free to 85% of all American doctors' offices a magazine of the same name with a circulation of 1 million—rivaling that of the *New Yorker* and *PC World*, and exceeding that of *BusinessWeek* ("New Highs," 2005). Naturally, such specifically targeted magazines take advantage of readers' engagement with and affinity for magazine advertising.

There are two broad categories of custom publishing. A **brand magazine** is a consumer magazine, complete with a variety of general interest articles and features, published by a retail or other business for readers having demographic characteristics similar to those of consumers with whom it typically does business. These publications carry ad pages not only for the products of its parent business, but for others as well. Benetton publishes *Colors*, computer networker Cisco Systems offers *iQ* (for Internet Quotient), and among others, Dodge, Hallmark, Bloomingdale's, Saks Fifth Avenue, Crunch Fitness, and Sea Ray boats all have successful brand magazines. This new form of magazine recognizes two important contemporary realities of today's media environment: (a) The cost of retaining existing customers is significantly lower than that of recruiting new ones, and (b) marketers must "find ways to stand

WWW

Custom Publishing
www.custompublishingcouncil.com

out from the quantity and clutter of commercial messages and to connect with an increasingly cynical and suspicious public" (Virgin, 2004, p. E1).

Closely related is the **magalogue,** a designer catalogue produced to look like a consumer magazine. Abercrombie & Fitch, J. Crew, Harry Rosen, and Diesel all produce catalogues in which models wear for-sale designer clothes. Magalogues "cut to the chase," says J. Crew's Margot Brunelle; they bring "a fresh point of view, an immediacy and ease of use that quite frankly has been missing from a lot of magazines." Advertising buyer David Verklin agrees, "People have been ripping pages out of magazines and putting them in their purse forever. These magazines are taking it one step further by showing pages of the products and having a point of view" (both in Carr, 2004, p. C1).

Every Fortune 500 company and every major retailer either already engages in custom publishing or plans to do so in the very near future. There were 107,996 different brand magazines and magalogues published in this country in 2005, representing 34.1 billion individual copies. Susan Berman, of custom publisher Underline Communications, explained the success of her $36-billion-a-year industry, "In a world of increasingly commoditized products, marketers must find more creative and effective ways to differentiate their brands and offerings. In our view, being a source of real and relevant information served up in a compelling manner is the ticket to success" (in "New Highs," 2005, p. C1).

The look alone of this magazine's cover makes it clear that it is the German version of what we know in the United States as *Psychology Today.*

MEETING COMPETITION FROM CABLE TELEVISION

As we've seen, the move toward specialization in magazines was forced by the emergence of television as a mass-audience national advertising medium. Interestingly, television once again threatens the preeminence of magazines as a specialized advertising medium. Specifically, the challenge comes from cable television. Advertiser-supported cable channels survive using precisely the same strategy as magazines—they deliver to advertisers a relatively large number of consumers who have some important demographic trait in common. Similar competition, although still insignificant, is also coming from specialized online content providers such as ESPNET SportsZone and The Discovery Channel Online. Magazines are well positioned to fend off these challenges for several reasons.

First is internationalization, which expands a magazine's reach, making it possible for magazines to attract additional ad revenues for content that, essentially, has already been produced. Internationalization can happen in one of several ways. Some magazines, *Time* and *Newsweek,* for example, produce one or more foreign editions in English. Others enter cooperative agreements with overseas companies to produce native-language versions of essentially U.S. magazines. For example, Time Warner and the French company Hachette cooperate to publish a French-language *Fortune.* Often U.S. magazines prepare special content for foreign-language editions. *Cosmopolitan,* for example, produces 50 worldwide editions in 28 languages.

The internationalization of magazines will no doubt increase as conglomeration and globalization continue to have an impact on the magazine industry as they have on other media businesses.

Second is technology. Computers and satellites now allow instant distribution of copy from the editor's desk to printing plants around the world. The result—almost immediate delivery to subscribers and sales outlets—makes production and distribution of even more narrowly targeted split runs more cost-effective. This is an efficiency that cable television has yet to match.

Third is the sale of subscriber lists and a magazine's own direct marketing of products. Advertisers buy space in specialized magazines to reach a specific type of reader. Most magazines are more than happy to sell those readers' names and addresses to those same advertisers, as well as to others who want to contact readers with direct mail pitches. Many magazines use their own subscriber lists for the same purpose, marketing products of interest to their particular readership. Cable television, even the most specialized channels, cannot easily identify individual audience members; therefore, they cannot sell their names.

ADVERTORIALS

Publishers and advertisers increasingly use advertorials as a means of boosting the value of a magazine as an advertising medium. **Advertorials** are ads that appear in magazines and take on the appearance of genuine editorial content. Sometimes they are a page or less, sometimes inserts composed of several pages. They frequently carry the disclaimer "Advertisement," but it is usually in small print. Sometimes the disclaimer is no more than the advertiser's logo in a page corner. The goal is to put commercial content before readers, cloaked in the respectability of editorial content. Advertorial-generated revenue in the magazine industry more than doubled in the 1990s, as did the number of ad pages given over to their use. Advertorials now account for 10% of all magazine advertising income (Kim, Pasadeos, & Barban, 2001). The question for media literate magazine readers is clear: Is an item journalism or is it advertising?

Critics of advertorials argue that this blurring of the distinction between editorial and commercial matter is a breach of faith with readers (see the essay "Advertorials Aimed at Young Girls" on p. 150). Moreover, if the intent is not deception, why is the disclaimer typically small; why use the editorial content format at all? Defenders contend that advertorials are a well-entrenched aspect of contemporary magazines. The industry considers them not only financially necessary in an increasingly competitive media market but proper as well. No one is hurt by advertorials. In fact, they often deliver useful information. Advertisers are free in America to use whatever legal and truthful means are available to sell their products. Magazines always label the paid material as such. And readers aren't idiots, defenders claim. They know an ad when they see one.

ADVERTISER INFLUENCE OVER MAGAZINE CONTENT

Controversial, too, is the influence that some advertisers attempt to exert over content. This influence is always there, at least implicitly. A magazine editor must satisfy advertisers as well as readers. One common way advertisers' interests shape content is in the placement of ads. Airline ads are moved away

Advertorials Aimed at Young Girls

The issue of development of healthy self-esteem and body image for young girls is frequently debated in the cultural forum. We saw in Chapter 1, for example, that even very young people are increasingly dissatisfied with their physical selves. Consider your attitudes on this debate as you evaluate the following situation.

'*Teen* magazine's media kit makes the case for the use of advertorials. Read their presentation, aimed at prospective advertisers, and think about how comfortable you are with the practice.

> 'TEEN's advertorial services are top-notch! Last year we produced 150 advertorial pages...that's more advertorial pages than any other national magazine. 'TEEN has its own advertorial staff: three editors whose only responsibility is the creation and production of advertorial pages. We work with both client and agency from preliminary layouts through the day of the shoot to the final selection of film, copy and color corrections.

Why Advertorials Will Work For You

- TEEN advertorials are designed to look like our editorial pages. Our editors know the looks our readers like and the advertorial pages are presented in this style.

IMAGINE YOURSELF AS A 12-YEAR-OLD. DO YOU THINK YOU COULD TELL THE DIFFERENCE BETWEEN THIS ADVERTISEMENT AND OTHER EDITORIAL CONTENT IN THE MAGAZINE?

- The advertorials can take your campaign one step further by providing additional information that is not provided in your advertisement. Additionally, they dramatically increase the frequency of your advertising message. (as cited in Silverblatt, 2001, p. 172)

Are you at all troubled that this potentially misleading content appears in a magazine aimed at young, relatively unsophisticated media consumers? Why, or why not?

Do you think the first explanation of why advertorials work—advertorials are designed to look like editorial pages—implies an overt effort to deceive readers?

Examine the advertorial's construction. What physical attributes characterize the models? How quickly did you find the "advertisement" disclaimer?

Imagine yourself as a 12-year-old. Do you think you could tell the difference between this advertisement and other editorial content in the magazine? Do you think you would have associated the Sears logo on the second page with the pictures and text on the first? Do you think this is an important issue? Why, or why not?

An article or an ad? Can you tell? Could a 12-year-old reader make the distinction?

from stories about plane crashes. Cigarette ads rarely appear near articles on lung cancer. In fact, it is an accepted industry practice for a magazine to provide advertisers with a heads-up, alerting them that soon-to-be-published content may prove uncomfortable for their businesses. Advertisers can then request a move of their ad, or pull it and wait to run it in the next issue.

Complementary copy—content that reinforces the advertiser's message, or at least does not negate it—is problematic when creating such copy becomes a major influence in a publication's editorial decision making. This happens in a number of ways. Editors sometimes engage in self-censorship, making decisions about how stories are written and which stories appear based on the fear that specific advertisers will be offended. Some magazines, *Architectural Digest,* for example, identify companies by name in their picture caption copy only if they are advertisers. But many critics inside and outside the industry see increased crumbling of the wall between advertising demands and editorial judgment.

This problem is particularly acute today, say critics, because a very competitive media environment puts additional pressure on magazines to bow to advertiser demands. For example, a Sears marketing executive suggested that magazines needed to operate "in much less traditional ways" by allowing advertisers to "become a part of the storyline" in their articles (Atkinson, 2004). Lexus, for example, asks the magazines it advertises in to use its automobiles in photos used to illustrate editorial content. But most troubling are advertisers who institute an **ad-pull policy,** the demand for an advance review of a magazine's content, with the threat of pulled advertising if dissatisfied with that content. The advertising agencies for oil giant BP and financial services company Morgan Stanley recently shocked the magazine industry for demanding just that, in the case of BP, insisting that it be informed "in advance of any news text or visuals magazines plan to publish that directly mention the company, a competitor, or the oil-and-energy industry" (Sanders & Halliday, 2005). Events like this moved *Advertising Age* to editorialize, "Shame on BP. And shame on Morgan Stanley and General Motors and any other advertisers involved in assaults on editorial integrity and independence. By wielding their ad budget as weapons to beat down newsrooms, these companies threaten the bond that media properties have with their audiences, the very thing that gives media their value to advertisers to begin with" ("Shame," 2005).

The question raised by critics is, "How can a magazine function, offering depth, variety, and detail, when BP and Morgan Stanley are joined by dozens of other advertisers, each demanding to preview content, not for its direct comment on matters of importance to their businesses, but for controversy and potential offensiveness? What will be the impact on the ideals of a free press and of free inquiry?"

DEVELOPING MEDIA LITERACY SKILLS
Recognizing the Power of Graphics

Detecting the use of and determining the informational value of advertorials is only one reason media literacy is important when reading magazines. Another necessary media literacy skill is the ability to understand how graphics and other artwork provide the background for interpreting stories. Some recent incidents suggest why.

Teach Teens About Magazines

Cosmo Girl is a magazine aimed at the 12- to 16-year-old girl audience. As such, its June/July 2004 edition featured the pop singer Avril Lavigne. That seems natural. But look a bit closer at the cover. Labeled a "do it yourself issue," this publication includes articles such as *He Only Liked Me for My Chest, Guys Confess: The Real Reason He Didn't Call, Find Your True Love!, Your Best Days for Romance,* and *Get a Beach Ready Body in Two Weeks.* Love, romance, breasts, and bodies. Are these themes of interest to pre- and early teens? Should they be?

Child psychologists, educators, even many parents lament the "adultification" of childhood, and they see our mass media as central to the trend. Criticism aside, *Cosmo Girl*—as well as magazines such as *Seventeen, YM,* and *'Teen*—contribute to, as well as prosper by, promoting topics not significantly different from those found in adult women's magazines. As such, "tweens" must deal with information they may not understand or, worse, may apply incorrectly to their everyday lives (see Chapter 13's discussion of the *early window*). Talking to young people in your area is an effective tool in assuring responsible consumption of magazines and in making media literacy a living enterprise. These three steps can assist you in your efforts:

> LOVE, ROMANCE, BREASTS, AND BODIES. ARE THESE THEMES OF INTEREST TO PRE- AND EARLY TEENS? SHOULD THEY BE?

1. Introduce young people to publications that are specifically designed for them and that place emphasis on art, education, storytelling, community service, current events, and opinion. In addition to offering appropriate content, these magazines are interactive, that is, they encourage participation and editorial submissions from their young readers. Start with *Teen Voices* (www.teenvoices.com) and *Teen Ink* (www.teenink.com).

2. Help young people understand the structure of the magazine industry. Being knowledgeable about why and how the media industries work, as you know from Chapter 1, makes for more critical, literate media users. Three Web sites provide useful magazine information, including industry trends, advertising facts, magazine terminology, and useful links. Try www.magazine.org, www.asme.magazine.org, and www.magazine.org/pib.

3. Ask questions and/or suggest exercises that will prompt young teens to think about magazine issues related to them and their lives:

- Ask them to count the number of ad and editorial pages in their favorite magazines. Have them comment on what this tells them about the true consumer in the magazine–reader interaction.

- Ask them to identify visual tactics such as celebrity endorsements, advertorials, and other selling devices. Ask them to comment on their propriety.

- Ask them to make a list of gender stereotypes found in their favorite magazines. How are boys and girls (and their interests and abilities) portrayed? Ask them to comment on how these images reflect them and their lives. Ask them if they ever feel pressure to behave in a certain way that they might not want.

- Encourage them to introduce their younger siblings to magazines (and other media) that promote literacy, and introduce them to current events in comprehensible and age-appropriate ways. Suggest Time For Kids (www.*timeforkids*.com/TFK/) and *Highlights* (www.highlights.com).

On the magazine cover:

VOTED THE BEST MEN'S MAGAZINE IN BRITAIN–AGAIN

BRITISH GQ

February 2003
US $8.99 CAN $8.95

Peter Mandelson on power dressing

Shaggy on Marvin Gaye

Sigur Rós on ice!

Oh, and the GQ quiz: how healthy are you?

Exclusive!

Kate Winslet

Hollywood's sexiest girl next door*
By Dylan Jones

The $100 million man
Martin Scorsese on Gangs Of New York
By Alex Bilmes

I'm a celebrity, buy me lunch!
Simon Kelner meets Nell McAndrew

The world's favourite band
Coldplay are the new Beatles
By Stuart Maconie

Families at war
Sopranos v Simpsons

Crack Nation
Did the CIA kickstart a drug epidemic?
By Sanjiv Bhattacharya

Kate Winslet photographed for GQ by Jason Bell

Fashion Special

833
Style tips!
The office
GQ lifts the lid on what we wear to work

*(Ding dong)

www.gq.com

This February 2003 British *GQ* cover put the alteration of magazine graphics squarely in the cultural forum when actress Kate Winslet complained that her body had been digitally altered to make her thin. "This is me. Like it or leave it. I'm not a twig and I refuse to be one," she said. "I'm happy with the way I am!"

The notorious June 27, 1994, *Time* O. J. Simpson cover—for which artists altered Simpson's facial tones on an L.A. police department mug shot—is one controversial example of how graphics are used to create meaning. The magazine said it wanted to show the "real" O. J., free of the glamour and hype that usually surround him. Critics claimed that darkening Simpson's face was designed to play to the ugly stereotype of African Americans as criminals. Media literate readers might also ask, "How does changing what was a 'real' photograph make the subject seem more real?"

Two more recent examples of digital fakery raise a different question. In 2003 photos of popular actresses Kate Winslet and Julia Roberts were digitally altered for the covers of *GQ* and *Redbook*, respectively. Both reacted angrily. Ms. Winslet, whose legs were thinned to *GQ*'s standards, complained not only that she was who she was, but that she was quite happy with that. Ms. Roberts, whose head was digitally attached to a photo of her body taken several years before, was indignant not only that she had been misrepresented, but that she was being used to reinforce unrealistic ideals of female beauty. Then there is the photo of Brad Pitt and Angelina Jolie from the May 9, 2005, cover of *Star*. Sources informed the celebrity magazine that the married-to-Jennifer-Aniston Brad Pitt was cavorting on an African island with actress Jolie. Although there was no proof, the magazine's headline screamed, "Brad & Angelina Caught Together! On Vacation." Actually, they weren't caught. The cover shot was a "composite," admitted *Star*'s editors inside (on p. 46); it "represented" the illicit liaison, they explained.

The important media literacy issue here has to do with maintaining the confidence of audience members. As digital altering of images becomes more widespread—and its occurrence better known—will viewers and readers come to question the veracity of even unaltered images and the reports that employ them?

What do you think? Did you see any of these images? Did you know they had been altered? If you did, would that have changed your reading of the stories or events that they represented? Does the fact that major media outlets sometimes alter the images they present to you as news lead you to question their overall performance? Do you believe that media outlets that use altered images have an obligation to inform readers and viewers of their decision to restructure reality? How does it feel to know that "almost all of the images that we see in our daily newspapers and newsmagazines today are digitized" (Huang, 2001, p. 149)?

RESOURCES FOR REVIEW AND DISCUSSION

Review Points

- Magazines, a favorite of 18th-century British elite, made an easy transition to colonial America.
- Mass circulation magazines prospered in the post–Civil War years because of increased literacy, improved transportation, reduced postal costs, and lower cover prices.
- Magazines' large readership and financial health empowered the muckrakers to challenge society's powerful.
- Television changed magazines from mass circulation to specialized media; as a result, they are attractive to advertisers because of their demographic specificity, reader engagement, and reader affinity for the advertising they carry.
- The three broad categories of magazines are trade, professional, and business; industrial, company, and sponsored; and consumer magazines.
- Magazine circulation comes in the form of subscription, single-copy sales, and controlled

circulation. Advertiser demands for better measures of readership and accountability may render circulation an outmoded metric.
- Online magazines, while flourishing in number, have yet to reap significant profits.
- Custom publishing, in the form of brand magazines and magalogues, is one way that magazines stand out in a cluttered media environment.
- Magazines further meet competition from other media, especially cable television, through internationalization, technology-driven improvements in distribution, and the sale of subscriber lists and their own direct marketing efforts.
- Advertorials, complementary copy, ad-pull policies, and the heavy reliance on digitally altered graphics all pose media literacy problems for industry practitioners and readers alike.

Key Terms

 Use the text's Online Learning Center at www.mhhe.com/baran5 to further your understanding of the following terminology.

muckraking, 136
split runs, 142
circulation, 143
controlled circulation, 143

custom publishing, 143
Webzine, 145
brand magazine, 147
magalogue, 148

advertorial, 149
complementary copy, 151
ad-pull policy, 151

Questions for Review

 Go to the self-quizzes on the Online Learning Center to test your knowledge.

1. How would you characterize the content of the first U.S. magazines?
2. Who were Ida Tarbell, Upton Sinclair, Lincoln Steffens, and Jack London? What movement did they represent, and what were some of its accomplishments?
3. What factors fueled the expansion of the magazine industry at the beginning of the 20th century?
4. What factors led to the demise of the mass circulation era and the development of the era of specialization?
5. What are the three broad types of magazines?
6. Why do advertisers favor specialization in magazines?
7. What are engagement and affinity? Why are they important to advertisers?
8. What are the two primary forms of custom publishing?
9. In what different ways do magazines internationalize their publications?
10. Which two media currently challenge the preeminence of magazines as a specialized advertising medium? Why?
11. What is an advertorial? What is its function?
12. What is complementary copy? Why does it trouble critics?
13. What factors limit the success and profitability of online magazines?

Questions for Critical Thinking and Discussion

1. Can you think of any contemporary crusading magazine or muckraking writers? Compared with those of the progressive era, they are certainly less visible. Why is this the case?
2. Are you troubled by trends such as brand and magalogue magazines? Why or why not?
3. Which magazines do you read? Draw a demographic profile of yourself based only on the magazines you regularly read.
4. Which side do you take in the advertorial debate? Why?
5. Are you troubled by the practice of altering photographs? Can you think of times when it might be more appropriate than others?

Important Resources

 Go to the Online Learning Center for additional readings.

Internet Resources

Salon	www.salon.com
Magazine History	www.well.com/user/art/maghist01.html
American Society of Magazine Editors	www.magazine.org/editorial
Magazine Publishers of America	www.magazine.org
Audit Bureau of Circulations	www.accessabc.com
Magazine CyberCenter	www.magamall.com
Guide to Webzines	www.webreference.com/internet/magazines
Slate	www.slate.com
Readership.com	www.mcpheters.com
Custom Publishing	www.custompublishingcouncil.com
How to Start a Magazine	www.laughingbear.com/magazine.html

Film

LEARNING OBJECTIVES

The movies are our dream factories; they are bigger than life. With books, they are the only mass medium not dependent on advertising for their financial support. That means they must satisfy you, because you buy the tickets. This means that the relationship between medium and audience is different from those that exist with other media. After studying this chapter you should

- be familiar with the history and development of the film industry and film itself as a medium.
- have a greater awareness of the cultural value of film and the implications of the blockbuster mentality for film as an important artistic and cultural medium.
- be familiar with the three components of the film industry—production, distribution, and exhibition.
- recognize how the organizational and economic nature of the contemporary film industry shapes the content of films.
- understand the relationship between film and its audiences.
- recognize the promise and peril of the new digital technologies to film as we know it.
- possess improved film-watching media literacy skills, especially in interpreting merchandise tie-ins and product placements.

Paris is cold and damp on this December night, 3 days after Christmas in 1895. But you bundle up and make your way to the Grand Café in the heart of the city. You've read in the morning paper that brothers Auguste and Louis Lumière will be displaying their new invention that somehow makes pictures move. Your curiosity is piqued.

Tables and chairs are set up in the basement room of the café, and a white bedsheet is draped above its stage. The Lumières appear to polite applause. They announce the program: *La Sortie des usines Lumière (Quitting Time at the Factory); Le Repas de bébé,* featuring a Lumière child eating; *L'Arroseur arrosé,* about a practical-joking boy and his victim, the gardener; and finally *L'Arrivée d'un train en gare,* the arrival of a train at a station.

Opposite: Johnny Depp in *Charlie and the Chocolate Factory.*

The lights go out. Somewhere behind you, someone starts the machine. There is some brief flickering on the suspended sheet and then . . . you are completely awestruck. There before you—bigger than life-size—photographs are really moving. You see places you know to be miles away. You spy on the secret world of a prankster boy, remembering your own childhood. But the last film is the most impressive. As the giant locomotive chugs toward the audience, you and most of the others are convinced you are about to be crushed. There is panic. People are ducking under their chairs, screaming. Death is imminent!

The first paying audience in the history of motion pictures has just had a lesson in movie watching.

The Lumière brothers were excellent mechanics, and their father owned a factory that made photographic plates. Their first films were little more than what we would now consider black-and-white home movies. As you can tell from their titles, they were simple stories. There was no editing; the

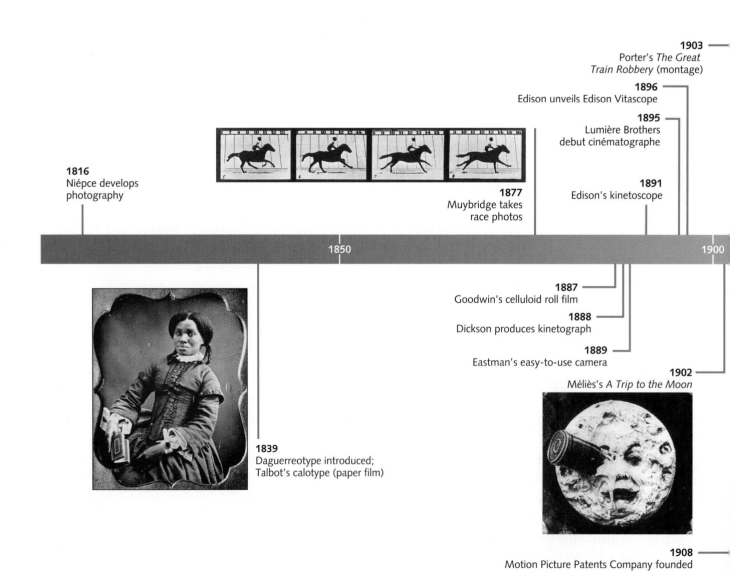

1903
Porter's *The Great Train Robbery* (montage)

1896
Edison unveils Edison Vitascope

1895
Lumière Brothers debut cinématographe

1816
Niépce develops photography

1877
Muybridge takes race photos

1891
Edison's kinetoscope

1850

1900

1887
Goodwin's celluloid roll film

1888
Dickson produces kinetograph

1889
Eastman's easy-to-use camera

1902
Méliès's *A Trip to the Moon*

1839
Daguerreotype introduced; Talbot's calotype (paper film)

1908
Motion Picture Patents Company founded

camera was simply turned on, then turned off. There were no fades, wipes, or flashbacks. No computer graphics, no dialogue, and no music. And yet much of the audience was terrified by the oncoming cinematic locomotive. They were illiterate in the language of film.

We begin our study of the movies with the history of film, from its entrepreneurial beginnings, through introduction of its narrative and visual language, to its establishment as a large, studio-run industry. We detail Hollywood's relationship with its early audiences and changes in the structure and content of films resulting from the introduction of television. We then look at contemporary movie production, distribution, and exhibition systems and how convergence is altering all three, the influence of the major studios, and the economic pressures on them in an increasingly multimedia environment. We examine the special place movies hold for us and how ever-younger audiences and the films that target them may affect our culture. Recognizing the use of product placement in movies is the basis for improving our media literacy skill.

WWW
The Cult Film Site
www.sepnet.com

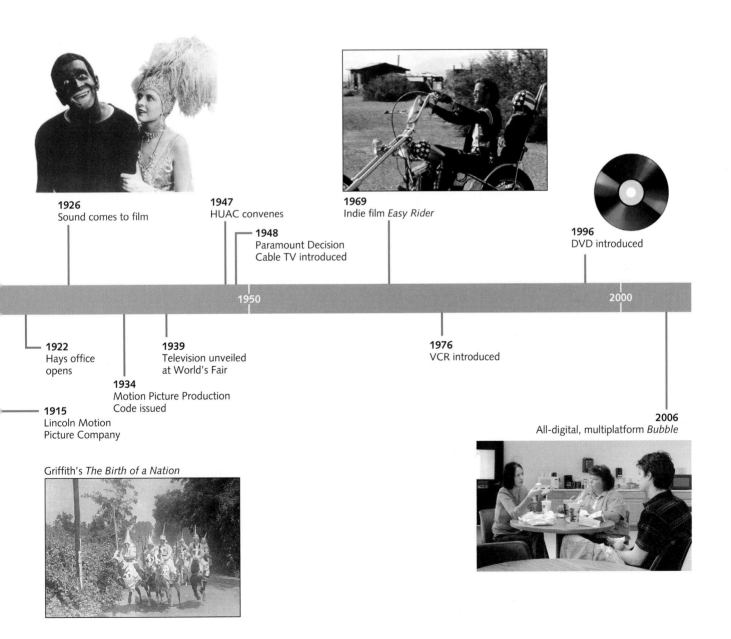

1926
Sound comes to film

1947
HUAC convenes

1948
Paramount Decision
Cable TV introduced

1969
Indie film *Easy Rider*

1996
DVD introduced

1950

2000

1922
Hays office
opens

1939
Television unveiled
at World's Fair

1934
Motion Picture Production
Code issued

1915
Lincoln Motion
Picture Company

Griffith's *The Birth of a Nation*

1976
VCR introduced

2006
All-digital, multiplatform *Bubble*

The Lumières' *L'Arrivée d'un train en gare*. As simple as early films were, their viewers did not have sufficient film literacy to properly interpret, understand, and enjoy them. This scene supposedly sent people screaming and hiding to avoid being crushed by the oncoming train.

A Short History of the Movies

We are no longer illiterate in the grammar of film, nor are movies as simple as the early Lumière offerings. Consider the sophistication necessary for filmmakers to produce a computer-generated movie such as *Finding Nemo* and the skill required for audiences to read *Memento*'s shifts in time, unconventional camera angles, and other twists and turns. How we arrived at this contemporary medium–audience relationship is a wonderful story.

Early newspapers were developed by businesspeople and patriots for a small, politically involved elite that could read, but the early movie industry was built largely by entrepreneurs who wanted to make money entertaining everyone. Unlike television, whose birth and growth were predetermined and guided by the already well-established radio industry (see Chapter 7), there were no precedents, no rules, and no expectations for movies.

Return to the opening vignette. The audience for the first Lumière movies did not "speak film." Think of it as being stranded in a foreign country with no knowledge of the language and cultural conventions. You would have to make your way, with each new experience helping you better understand the next. First you'd learn some simple words and basic customs. Eventually, you'd be able to better understand the language and people. In other words, you'd become increasingly literate in that culture. Beginning with that Paris premiere, people had to become film literate. They had to develop an understanding of cinematic alterations in time and space. They had to learn how images and sound combined to create meaning. But unlike visiting in another culture, there was no existing cinematic culture. Movie creators and their audiences had to grow up together.

Hollywood Online
www.hollywood.com

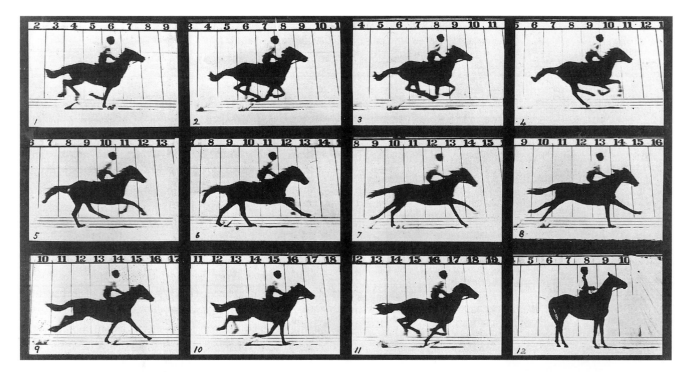

THE EARLY ENTREPRENEURS

In 1873 former California governor Leland Stanford needed help winning a bet he had made with a friend. Convinced that a horse in full gallop had all four feet off the ground, he had to prove it. He turned to well-known photographer Eadweard Muybridge, who worked on the problem for 4 years before finding a solution. In 1877 Muybridge arranged a series of still cameras along a stretch of racetrack. As the horse sprinted by, each camera took its picture. The resulting photographs won Stanford his bet, but more important, they sparked an idea in their photographer. Muybridge was intrigued by the appearance of motion created when photos are viewed sequentially. He began taking pictures of numerous kinds of human and animal action. To display his work, Muybridge invented the **zoopraxiscope,** a machine for projecting slides onto a distant surface.

When people watched the rapidly projected, sequential slides, they saw the pictures as if they were in motion. This perception is the result of a physiological phenomenon known as **persistence of vision,** in which the images our eyes gather are retained in the brain for about 1/24 of a second. Therefore, if photographic frames are moved at 24 frames a second, people perceive them as actually in motion.

Muybridge eventually met the prolific inventor Thomas Edison in 1888. Edison quickly saw the scientific and economic potential of the zoopraxiscope and set his top scientist, William Dickson, to the task of developing a better projector. But Dickson correctly saw the problem as one of developing a better system of *filming*. He understood that shooting numerous still photos, then putting them in sequential order, then redrawing the images they held onto slides was inherently limiting. Dickson combined Hannibal Goodwin's newly invented celluloid roll film with George Eastman's easy-to-use Kodak camera to make a motion picture camera that took 40 photographs a second. He used his **kinetograph** to film all types of theatrical

Muybridge's horse pictures. When these plates were placed sequentially and rotated, they produced the appearance of motion.

Worst Movies Ever
www.ohthehumanity.com

Typical of daguerreotypes, this plate captures a portrait. The method's long exposure time made all but the most stationary subjects impossible to photograph.

performances, some by unknowns and others by famous entertainers such as Annie Oakley and Buffalo Bill Cody. Of course, none of this would have been possible had it not been for photography itself.

The Development of Photography The process of photography was first developed by French inventor Joseph Nicéphore Niépce around 1816. Although there had been much experimentation in the realm of image making at the time, Niépce was the first person to make practical use of a camera and film. He photographed natural objects and produced color prints. Unfortunately, his images would last only a short time.

Niépce's success, however, attracted the attention of countryman Louis Daguerre, who joined with him to perfect the process. Niépce died before the 1839 introduction of the **daguerreotype,** a process of recording images on polished metal plates, usually copper, covered with a thin layer of silver iodide emulsion. When light reflected from an object passed through a lens and struck the emulsion, the emulsion would etch the image on the plate. The plate was then washed with a cleaning solvent, leaving a positive or replica image.

In the same year as Daguerre's first public display of the daguerreotype, British inventor William Henry Fox Talbot introduced a paper film process. This process was more important to the development of photography than the metal film system, but the daguerreotype received widespread attention and acclaim and made the public enthusiastic about photography.

The **calotype** (Talbot's system) used translucent paper, what we now call the negative, from which several prints could be made. In addition, his film was much more sensitive than Daguerre's metal plate, allowing for exposure times of only a few seconds as opposed to the daguerreotype's 30 minutes. Until calotype, virtually all daguerreotype images were still lifes and portraits, a necessity with long exposure times.

The final steps in the development of the photographic process necessary for true motion pictures were taken, as we've just seen, by Goodwin in 1887 and Eastman in 1889 and were adapted to motion pictures by Edison scientist Dickson.

Thomas Edison Edison built the first motion picture studio near his laboratory in New Jersey. He called it Black Maria, the common name at that time for a police paddy wagon. It had an open roof and revolved to follow the sun so the performers being filmed would always be illuminated.

The completed films were not projected. Instead, they were run through a **kinetoscope,** a sort of peep show device. Often they were accompanied by music provided by another Edison invention, the phonograph. Patented in 1891 and commercially available 3 years later, the kinetoscope quickly became a popular feature in penny arcades, vaudeville halls, and big-city Kinetoscope parlors. This marked the beginning of commercial motion picture exhibition.

The Lumière Brothers The Lumière brothers made the next advance. Their initial screenings demonstrated that people would sit in a darkened room

Movie News
www.enn2.com/movies.htm

to watch motion pictures projected on a screen. The brothers from Lyon envisioned great wealth in their ability to increase the number of people who could simultaneously watch a movie. In 1895 they patented their **cinématographe,** a device that both photographed and projected action. Within weeks of their Christmastime showing, long lines of enthusiastic moviegoers were waiting for their makeshift theater to open. Edison recognized the advantage of the cinématographe over his kinetoscope, so he acquired the patent for an advanced projector developed by U.S. inventor Thomas Armat. On April 23, 1896, the Edison Vitascope premiered in New York City, and the American movie business was born.

THE COMING OF NARRATIVE

The Edison and Lumière movies were typically only a few minutes long and showed little more than filmed reproductions of reality—celebrities, weight lifters, jugglers, and babies eating. They were shot in fixed frame (the camera did not move), and there was no editing. For the earliest audiences, this was enough. But soon the novelty wore thin. People wanted more for their money. French filmmaker Georges Méliès began making narrative motion pictures, that is, movies that told a story. At the end of the 1890s he was shooting and exhibiting one-scene, one-shot movies, but soon he began making stories based on sequential shots in different places. He simply took one shot, stopped the camera, moved it, took another shot, and so on. Méliès is often called the "first artist of the cinema" because he brought narrative to the medium in the form of imaginative tales such as *A Trip to the Moon* (1902).

Méliès had been a magician and caricaturist before he became a filmmaker, and his inventive movies showed his dramatic flair. They were

Scene from *A Trip to the Moon*. Narrative came to the movies through the inventive imagination of Georges Méliès.

Scene from *The Great Train Robbery.* Porter's masterpiece introduced audiences to editing, intercutting of scenes, moving cameras . . . and the Western.

extravagant stage plays in which people disappeared and reappeared and other wonders occurred. *A Trip to the Moon* came to America in 1903, and U.S. moviemakers were quick not only to borrow the idea of using film to tell stories but also to improve on it.

Edwin S. Porter, an Edison Company cameraman, saw that film could be an even better storyteller with more artistic use of camera placement and editing. His 12-minute *The Great Train Robbery* (1903) was the first movie to use editing, intercutting of scenes, and a mobile camera to tell a relatively sophisticated tale. It was also the first Western. This new narrative form using **montage**—tying together two separate but related shots in such a way that they took on a new, unified meaning—was an instant hit with audiences. Almost immediately hundreds of **nickelodeons,** some having as many as 100 seats, were opened in converted stores, banks, and halls across the United States. The price of admission was one nickel, hence the name. By 1905 cities such as New York were opening a new nickelodeon every day. From 1907 to 1908, the first year in which there were more narrative than documentary films, the number of nickelodeons in the United States increased tenfold. With so many exhibition halls in so many towns serving such an extremely enthusiastic public, many movies were needed. Literally hundreds and hundreds of new **factory studios,** or production companies, were started.

Because so many movies needed to be made and rushed to the nickelodeons, people working in the industry had to learn and perform virtually all aspects of production. There was precious little time for, or profitability in, the kind of specialization that marks contemporary filmmaking. Writer, actor, cameraman D. W. Griffith perfected his craft in this environment. He was quickly recognized as a brilliant director. He

Movie News
www.movies.go.com

The Ku Klux Klan was the collective hero in D. W. Griffith's *The Birth of a Nation*. This cinematic masterpiece and groundbreaking film employed production techniques never before used; however, its racist theme mars its legacy.

introduced innovations such as scheduled rehearsals before final shooting and production based on close adherence to a shooting script. He lavished attention on otherwise ignored aspects of a film's look—costume and lighting—and used close-ups and other dramatic camera angles to transmit emotion.

All his skill came together in 1915 with the release of *The Birth of a Nation*. Whereas Porter had used montage to tell a story, Griffith used it to create passion, move emotions, and heighten suspense. The most influential silent film ever made, this 3-hour epic was 6 weeks in rehearsal and 9 weeks in shooting, cost $125,000 to produce (making it the most expensive movie made to date), was distributed to theaters complete with an orchestral music score, had a cast of thousands of humans and animals, and had an admission price well above the usual 5 cents—$3. It was the most popular and profitable movie made until unseated in 1939 by *Gone with the Wind*. With other Griffith masterpieces, *Intolerance* (1916) and *Broken Blossoms* (1919), *The Birth of a Nation* set new standards for the American film. They took movies out of the nickelodeons and made them big business. At the same time, however, *The Birth of a Nation* represented the basest aspects of U.S. culture because it included an ugly, racist portrayal of African Americans and a sympathetic treatment of the Ku Klux Klan. The film inspired protests in front of theaters across the country and criticism in some newspapers and magazines, and African Americans fought back with their own films (see the essay on p. 166, "African American Response to D. W. Griffith: The Lincoln and Micheaux Film Companies"). Nevertheless, *The Birth of a Nation* found acceptance by the vast majority of people.

African American Response to D. W. Griffith: The Lincoln and Micheaux Film Companies

The African American community did not sit passively in the wake of D. W. Griffith's 1915 cinematic but hateful wonder, *The Birth of a Nation.* The NAACP fought the film in court and on the picket line, largely unsuccessfully. But other African Americans decided to use film to combat *Birth.* The first was Emmett J. Scott, a quiet, scholarly man. He sought money from the country's Black middle class to produce a short film showing the achievements of African Americans. His intention was to attach his film, *Lincoln's Dream,* as a prologue to screenings of the Griffith film. Together with screenwriter Elaine Sterne, Scott eventually expanded the project into a feature-length movie. He approached Universal Studios with his film but was rejected.

With independent backing from both Black and White investors, the film was released in 1918. Produced by an inexperienced cast and crew working on a production beset by bad weather and technical difficulties, the retitled *The Birth of a Race* filled 12 reels of film and ran more than 3 hours. Its publicity hailed it as "The Greatest and Most Daring of Photoplays . . . The Story of Sin . . . A Master Picture Conceived in the Spirit of Truth and Dedicated to All the Races of the World" (Bogle, 1989, p. 103). It was an artistic and commercial failure. Scott, however, had inspired others.

Even before *The Birth of a Race* was completed, the Lincoln Motion Picture Company was incorporated, in Nebraska in 1916 and in California in 1917, by brothers Noble P. and George Johnson. Their tack differed from Scott's. They understood that their Black films would never be allowed on "White" screens, so they produced movies designed to tell Black-oriented stories to Black audiences. They might not be able to convince White America of Griffith's error, but they could reassure African Americans that their views could find expression. Lincoln's first movie was *The Realization of a Negro's Ambition,* and it told the story of Black American achievements. The Johnson brothers turned U.S. racism to their advantage. Legal segregation in the South and de facto segregation in the North had led to an explosion of Black theaters. These movie houses needed content. Lincoln helped provide it by producing 10 three-reelers between 1916 and 1920.

Two more notable film companies began operation, hoping to challenge Griffith's portrayals at least in Black theaters. Oscar Micheaux founded the Micheaux Film and Book Company in 1918 in Chicago and soon produced *The Homesteader,* an eight-reel film based on the autobiographical novel he'd written 3 years earlier. It was the story of a successful Black homestead rancher in South Dakota. But Micheaux was not content to boost Black self-esteem. He was determined to make "racial photoplays depicting racial life" (as quoted in Sampson, 1977, p. 42). In 1920 he released *Within Our Gates,* a

> **THEY MIGHT NOT BE ABLE TO CONVINCE WHITE AMERICA OF GRIFFITH'S ERROR, BUT THEY COULD REASSURE AFRICAN AMERICANS THAT THEIR VIEWS COULD FIND EXPRESSION.**

drama about the southern lynching of a Black man. Censored and denied a screening in dozens of cities both North and South, Micheaux was undeterred. In 1921 he released the eight-reeler *The Gunsaulus Mystery,* based on a well-known murder case in which a Black man was convicted.

These early film pioneers used their medium to make a difference. They challenged the interpretation of history being circulated by the most popular movie in the world, and they provided encouragement and entertainment to the African American community. Equally important, they began the long tradition of Black filmmaking in the United States. In fact, many industry insiders consider "Black film" an anachronism. They point to the summer of 2005, when *Fantastic Four* director Tim Story joined John Singleton (*2 Fast 2 Furious*), Antoine Fuqua (*King Arthur*), and Keenen Ivory Wayans (*Scary Movie*) as blockbuster film directors who are Black. That same summer saw the release of *Hustle & Flow,* a gritty, hip-hop-inspired film about an African American pimp's dreams of making it in rap, directed and written by Craig Brewer, who is White. Add to this the 2005 Academy Awards for Jamie Foxx (*Ray*) and Morgan Freeman (*Million Dollar Baby*), Will Smith's title role in *Hitch,* Denzel Washington's star turn in *The Manchurian Candidate,* and an audience for Ice Cube's *Are We There Yet?* that was 43% White, 26% African American, and 18% Hispanic, and "Black film" may well now be a meaningless term (Coates, 2005, p. 2.1).

A scene from The Realization of a Negro's Ambition

Many industry insiders saw the 2005 release of *Fantastic Four* as the end of "Black film."

THE BIG STUDIOS

In 1908 Thomas Edison, foreseeing the huge amounts of money that could be made from movies, founded the Motion Picture Patents Company (MPPC), often called simply the Trust. This group of 10 companies under Edison's control, holding the patents to virtually all existing filmmaking and exhibition equipment, ran the production and distribution of film in the United States with an iron fist. Anyone who wanted to make or exhibit a movie needed Trust permission, which typically was not forthcoming. In addition, the MPPC had rules about the look of the movies it would permit: They must be one reel, approximately 12 minutes long, and must adopt a "stage perspective"; that is, the actors must fill the frame as if they were in a stage play.

Many independent film companies sprang up in defiance of the Trust, including Griffith's in 1913. To avoid MPPC scrutiny and reprisal, these companies moved to California. This westward migration had other benefits. Better weather meant longer shooting seasons. Free of MPPC standards, people like Griffith who wanted to explore the potential of films longer than 12 minutes and with imaginative use of the camera were free to do so.

The new studio system, with its more elaborate films and big-name stars, was born, and it controlled the movie industry from California. Thomas H. Ince (maker of the William S. Hart Westerns), Griffith, and comedy genius Mack Sennett formed the Triangle Company. Adolph Zukor's Famous Players in Famous Plays—formed when Zukor was denied MPPC permission to distribute one of his films—joined with several other independents and a distribution company to become Paramount. Other independents joined to create the Fox Film Company (soon called 20th Century Fox) and Universal. Although films were still silent, by the mid-1920s there were more than 20,000 movie theaters in the United States, and more than 350,000 people were making their living in film production. More than 1,240,000 feet of film was shot each year in Hollywood, and annual domestic U.S. box office receipts exceeded $750 million.

The industry prospered not just because of its artistry, drive, and innovation but because it used these to meet the needs of a growing audience. At the beginning of the 20th century, generous immigration rules, combined with political and social unrest abroad, encouraged a flood of European immigrants who congregated in U.S. cities where the jobs were and where people like themselves who spoke their language lived. American farmers, largely illiterate, also swarmed to the cities as years of drought and farm failure left them without home or hope. Jobs in the big mills and factories, although unpleasant, were plentiful. These new city dwellers had money and the need for leisure activities. Movies were a nickel, required no ability to read or to understand English, and offered glamorous stars and wonderful stories from faraway places.

Foreign political unrest proved to be a boon to the infant U.S. movie business in another way as well. In 1914 and 1915, when the California studios were remaking the industry in their own grand image, war raged in Europe. European moviemaking, most significantly the influential French, German, and Russian cinema, came to a halt. European demand for movies, however, did not. American movies, produced in huge numbers for the hungry home audience, were ideal for overseas distribution. Because so few in the domestic audience could read English, few printed titles were used in the then-silent movies. Therefore, little had to be changed to satisfy foreign moviegoers. Film was indeed a universal language, but more important, the American film industry had firmly established itself as the world leader, all within 20 years of the Lumière brothers' first screening.

CHANGE COMES TO HOLLYWOOD

As was the case with newspapers and magazines, the advent of television significantly altered the movie–audience relationship. But the nature of that relationship had been shaped and reshaped in the 3 decades between the coming of sound and the coming of television.

The Talkies   The first sound film was one of three films produced by Warner Brothers. It may have been *Don Juan* (1926), starring John Barrymore, distributed with synchronized music and sound effects. Or perhaps Warner's more famous *The Jazz Singer* (1927), starring Al Jolson, which had several sound and speaking scenes (354 words in all) but was largely silent. Or it may have been the 1928 all-sound *Lights of New York.* Historians disagree because they cannot decide what constitutes a sound film.

There is no confusion, however, about the impact of sound on the movies and their audiences. First, sound made possible new genres—musicals, for example. Second, as actors and actresses now had to really act, performance aesthetics improved. Third, sound made film production a much more complicated and expensive proposition. As a result, many smaller filmmakers closed shop, solidifying the hold of the big studios over the industry. In 1933, 60% of all U.S. films came from Hollywood's eight largest studios. By 1940, they were producing 76% of all U.S. movies and collecting 86% of the total box office. As for the audience, in 1926, the year of *Don Juan*'s release, 50 million people went to the movies each week. In 1929, at the onset of the

Film History
www.filmsite.org/filmh.html

Al Jolson, in blackface, and May McAvoy starred in the 1927 *The Jazz Singer*, one of three claimants to the title of first sound movie.

Great Depression, the number had risen to 80 million. By 1930, when sound was firmly entrenched, the number of weekly moviegoers had risen to 90 million (Mast & Kawin, 1996).

Scandal The popularity of talkies, and of movies in general, inevitably raised questions about their impact on the culture. In 1896, well before sound, *The Kiss* had generated a great moral outcry. Its stars, John C. Rice and May Irwin, were also the leads in the popular Broadway play *The Widow Jones,* which closed with a climactic kiss. The Edison Company asked Rice and Irwin to re-create the kiss for the big screen. Newspapers and politicians were bombarded with complaints from the offended. Kissing in the theater was one thing; in movies it was quite another! The then-newborn industry responded to this and other calls for censorship with various forms of self-regulation and internal codes. But in the early 1920s more Hollywood scandals forced a more direct response.

In 1920 "America's Sweetheart" Mary Pickford obtained a questionable Nevada divorce from her husband and immediately married the movies' other darling, Douglas Fairbanks, himself newly divorced. In 1920 and 1921 comedian Fatty Arbuckle was involved in police problems on two coasts. The first was apparently hushed up after a $100,000 gift was made to a Massachusetts district attorney, but the second involved a murder at a San Francisco hotel party thrown by the actor. Although he was acquitted in his third trial (the first two ended in hung juries), the stain on Arbuckle and the industry remained. Then, in 1922, actor Wallace Reid and director William

Self-Censorship in Hollywood: The Movie Ratings

In 1952 in *Burstyn v. Wilson* the Supreme Court declared that film is "a significant medium for the communication of ideas" designed to "entertain as well as to inform." Movies were finally granted First Amendment protection (undoing the 1915 Supreme Court judgment in *Mutual Film Corp. v. Ohio Industrial Commission*, which had ruled that movies were merely novelty and entertainment, unworthy of protection as expression).

The Supreme Court decision did not affect the industry's own censorship, however. In 1953 director Otto Preminger and United Artists decided to challenge that self-imposed denial of freedom. Preminger and his studio sought the MPPC certificate of approval for *The Moon Is Blue*, a saucy sex comedy starring William Holden and David Niven. Adapted from a popular Broadway play, it was the tale of a woman who flaunted her virginity, and its humor resided in its double entendre and innuendo. Because the film contained words like "virgin" and "mistress," the MPPC denied Preminger and United Artists, forbidding them to release the movie. They released it anyway. Audiences were not overly fond of *The Moon Is Blue*, but the MPPC had not halted its distribution or exhibition, nor did it punish the filmmakers in any effective manner.

In 1955 Preminger and United Artists again battled the MPPC, this time over *The Man with the Golden Arm*, a stark and powerful film starring Frank Sinatra as a drug addict and Eleanor Parker as his crippled wife. The MPPC denied the movie permission to be released because of its portrayal of unsavory morals. Director and studio again defied the industry censors, putting the film in theaters. It was a smash hit, both critically and at the box office. The MPPC was proven powerless, its control of movie content broken for good.

During this time, Hollywood was challenging television with the production of message movies about controversial social problems, including racism, juvenile delinquency, and alcohol abuse. But despite *Burstyn v. Wilson*, the industry still feared government intrusion. Its solution was to develop a different kind of self-regulation, and in 1966 the Motion Picture Association of America's (MPAA) rating system was born.

> DURING THIS TIME, HOLLYWOOD WAS CHALLENGING TELEVISION WITH THE PRODUCTION OF MESSAGE MOVIES ABOUT CONTROVERSIAL SOCIAL PROBLEMS, INCLUDING RACISM, JUVENILE DELINQUENCY, AND ALCOHOL ABUSE.

Desmond Taylor both died in what the newspapers referred to as "a mysterious fashion" in which drugs and sex were thought to have played a part. The cry for government intervention was raised. State legislatures introduced more than 100 separate pieces of legislation to censor or otherwise control movies and their content.

Hollywood responded in 1922 by creating the Motion Picture Producers and Distributors of America (MPPDA) and appointing Will H. Hays—chairman of the Republican party, a Presbyterian church elder, and a former postmaster general—president. The Hays Office, as it became known, undertook a vast effort to improve the image of the movies. Stressing the importance of movies to national life and as an educational medium, Hays promised better movies and founded a committee on public relations that included many civic and religious leaders. Eventually, in 1934, the Motion Picture Production Code (MPPC) was released. The MPPC forbade the use of profanity, limited bedroom scenes to married couples, required that skimpy outfits be replaced by more complete costumes, delineated the length of screen kisses, ruled out scenes that ridiculed public officials or religious leaders, and outlawed a series of words from "God" to "nuts," all enforced by a $25,000 fine (see "Self-Censorship in Hollywood: The Movie Ratings" just above).

New Genres, New Problems By 1932 weekly movie attendance had dropped to 60 million. The Great Depression was having its effect. Yet the industry was able to weather the crisis for two reasons. The first was its creativity. New genres held people's interest. The feature documentaries such as *The*

No longer were moviemakers told what they could and could not do. Instead, audiences were being alerted to what filmmakers were doing. The idea was to give filmmakers as much artistic freedom as they wanted, but to provide moviegoers with some indication of the nature of a film's content. The rating system, which has seen some alteration since its introduction, is familiar today to everyone who goes to a movie or rents a video or DVD:

G   general audiences

PG   parental guidance; for mature audiences

PG–13   parental guidance advised for children under 13 years old

R   restricted; no one under 17 years old admitted unless accompanied by an adult

NC–17   no children under 17; replaces the old X rating

Development of an informational rating system is echoed in the online world (Chapter 10) and in music (Chapter 7).

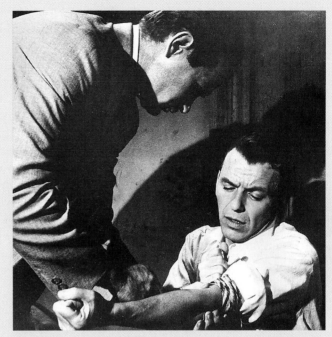

Frank Sinatra shoots heroin into his arm in the 1955 The Man with the Golden Arm.

Plow That Broke the Plains (1936) spoke to audience needs to understand a world in seeming disorder. Musicals such as *42nd Street* (1933) and screwball comedies such as *Bringing Up Baby* (1938) provided easy escapism. Gangster movies such as *Little Caesar* (1930) reflected the grimy reality of Depression city streets and daily newspaper headlines. Horror films such as *Frankenstein* (1931) articulated audience feelings of alienation and powerlessness in a seemingly uncontrollable time. Socially conscious comedies such as *Mr. Deeds Goes to Town* (1936) reminded moviegoers that good could still prevail, and the **double feature** with a **B-movie**—typically a less expensive movie—was a welcome relief to penny-pinching working people.

The movie business also survived the Depression because of its size and power, both residing in a system of operation called **vertical integration.** Using this system, studios produced their own films, distributed them through their own outlets, and exhibited them in their own theaters. In effect, the big studios controlled a movie from shooting to screening, guaranteeing distribution and an audience regardless of quality.

When the 1930s ended, weekly attendance was again over 80 million, and Hollywood was churning out 500 pictures a year. Moviegoing had become a central family and community activity for most people. Yet the end of that decade also brought bad news. In 1938 the Justice Department challenged vertical integration, suing the big five studios—Warner Brothers, MGM, Paramount, RKO, and 20th Century Fox—for restraint of trade; that is, they accused the studios of illegal monopolistic practices. The case would take

WWW
Motion Picture Association of America
www.mpaa.org

WWW
Film Ratings
www.filmratings.com

10 years to decide, but the movie industry, basking in the middle of its golden age, was under attack. Its fate was sealed in 1939 when the Radio Corporation of America (RCA) made the first public broadcast of television from atop the Empire State Building. The impact of these two events was profound, and the medium would have to develop a new relationship with its audience to survive.

 For more information on this topic, see Media Talk video clip #12, "Are Movie Ratings Effective?" on the *Media World* DVD.

Television When World War II began, the government took control of all patents for the newly developing technology of television as well as of the materials necessary for its production. The diffusion of the medium to the public was therefore halted, but its technological improvement was not. In addition, the radio networks and advertising agencies, recognizing that the war would eventually end and that their futures were in television, were preparing for that day. When the war did end, the movie industry found itself competing not with a fledgling medium but with a technologically and economically sophisticated one. The number of homes with television sets grew from 10,000 in 1946 to more than 10 million in 1950 and 54 million in 1960. Meanwhile, by 1955 movie attendance was down to 46 million people a week, fully 25% below even the worst attendance figures for the Depression years.

The Paramount Decision In 1948, 10 years after the case had begun, the Supreme Court issued its Paramount Decision, effectively destroying the studios' hold over moviemaking. Vertical integration was ruled illegal, as was **block booking,** the practice of requiring exhibitors to rent groups of movies, often inferior, to secure a better one. The studios were forced to sell off their exhibition businesses (the theaters). Before the Paramount Decision, the five major studios owned 75% of the first-run movie houses in the United States; after it, they owned none. Not only did they no longer have guaranteed exhibition, but other filmmakers now had access to the theaters, producing even greater competition for the dwindling number of movie patrons.

Red Scare The U.S. response to its postwar position as world leader was fear. So concerned were some members of Congress that communism would steal the people's rights that Congress decided to steal them first. The Hollywood chapter of the virulent anticommunism movement we now call McCarthyism (after the Republican senator from Wisconsin, Joseph McCarthy, its most rabid and public champion) was led by the House Un-American Activities Committee (HUAC) and its chair, J. Parnell Thomas (later imprisoned for padding his congressional payroll). First convened in 1947, HUAC had as its goal to rid Hollywood of communist influence. The fear was that communist, socialist, and leftist propaganda was being inserted secretly in entertainment films by "Reds," "fellow travelers," and "pinkos." Many of the industry's best and brightest talents were called to testify before the committee and were asked, "Are you now or have you ever been a member of the Communist Party?" Those who came to be known as the Hollywood 10, including writers Ring Lardner Jr. and Dalton Trumbo and director Edward Dmytryk, refused to answer the question, accusing the committee, by its mere existence, of being in violation of the Bill of Rights. All were jailed. Rather than defend its First Amendment rights, the film industry abandoned those who were even mildly critical of the "Red Scare," jettisoning

Warren Beatty eats some lead in the climax of the 1967 hit movie *Bonnie and Clyde*.

much of its best talent at a time when it could least afford to do so. In the fight against television, movies became increasingly tame for fear of being too controversial.

The industry was hurt not only by its cowardice but also by its short-sightedness. Hungry for content, the television industry asked Hollywood to sell it old features for broadcast. The studios responded by imposing on themselves the rule that no films could be sold to television and no working film star could appear on "the box." When it could have helped to shape early television viewer tastes and expectations of the new medium, Hollywood was absent. It lifted its ban in 1958.

Fighting Back The industry worked mightily to recapture audiences from television using both technical and content innovations. Some of these innovations remain today and serve the medium and its audiences well. These include more attention to special effects, greater dependence on and improvements in color, and CinemaScope (projecting on a large screen two and one-half times wider than it is tall). Among the forgettable technological innovations were 3-D and smellovision (wafting odors throughout the theater).

Innovation in content included spectaculars with which the small screen could not compete. *The Ten Commandments* (1956), *Ben Hur* (1959), *El Cid* (1960), and *Spartacus* (1960) filled the screen with many thousands of extras and lavish settings. Now that television was catering to the mass audience, movies were free to present challenging fare for more sophisticated audiences. The "message movie" charted social trends, especially alienation of youth (*Blackboard Jungle*, 1955; *Rebel Without a Cause*, 1955) and prejudice (*12 Angry Men*, 1957; *Imitation of Life*, 1959; *To Kill a Mockingbird*, 1962). Changing values toward sex were examined (*Midnight Cowboy*, 1969; *Bob and Carol and Ted and Alice*, 1969), as was the new youth culture's rejection of middle-class values (*The Graduate*, 1967; *Goodbye Columbus*, 1969) and its revulsion/attraction to violence (*Bonnie and Clyde*, 1967). The movies as an industry had changed, but as a medium of social commentary and cultural impact, they may have grown up.

WWW

Hollywood Reporter
www.hollywoodreporter.com

Movies and Their Audiences

We talk of Hollywood as the "dream factory," the makers of "movie magic." We want our lives and loves to be "just like in the movies." The movies are "larger than life," and movie stars are much more glamorous than television stars. The movies, in other words, hold a very special place in our culture. Movies, like books, are a culturally special medium, an important medium. In this sense the movie–audience relationship has more in common with that of books than with that of television. Just as people buy books, they buy movie tickets. Because the audience is in fact the true consumer, power rests with it in film more than it does in television.

For better or worse, today's movie audience is increasingly a young one. The typical moviegoer in the United States is a teenager or young adult. These teens and 20-somethings, although making up less than 20% of the total population, represent more than 30% of the tickets bought. It's no surprise, then, that new screens sprout at malls, where teens and even younger people can be dropped off for a day of safe entertainment. Many movies are aimed at kids—*Hey Arnold! The Movie, Ice Age, Lilo & Stitch,* and *Scooby-Doo;* all the *Toy Story, Rush Hour,* and *American Pie* films; all the movies based on television shows, computer games, and comic books. Look at the top 10 domestic grossing movies of all time in Figure 6.1. With the exception of *Titanic* (1997) and *The Passion of the Christ* (2004), all are fantastic

Figure 6.1 Top 10 All-time Domestic Box Office Hits.

Source: Internet Movie Database (www.imdb.com/boxoffice/alltimegross), 2006.

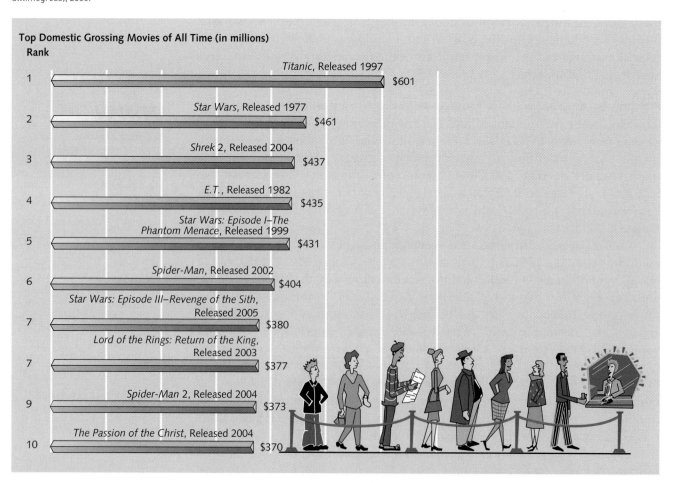

Top Domestic Grossing Movies of All Time (in millions)

Rank

1 — *Titanic,* Released 1997 — $601

2 — *Star Wars,* Released 1977 — $461

3 — *Shrek 2,* Released 2004 — $437

4 — *E.T.,* Released 1982 — $435

5 — *Star Wars: Episode I–The Phantom Menace,* Released 1999 — $431

6 — *Spider-Man,* Released 2002 — $404

7 — *Star Wars: Episode III–Revenge of the Sith,* Released 2005 — $380

7 — *Lord of the Rings: Return of the King,* Released 2003 — $377

9 — *Spider-Man 2,* Released 2004 — $373

10 — *The Passion of the Christ,* Released 2004 — $370

adventure films that appeal to younger audiences. The question asked by serious observers of the relationship between film and culture is whether the medium is increasingly dominated by the wants, tastes, and needs of what amounts to an audience of children. What becomes of film as an important medium, one with something to say, one that challenges people?

What becomes of film as an important medium, say the movies' defenders, is completely dependent on us, the audience. "It's the public," explains popular and distinguished actor John Malkovich. "The public gets the kind of politics, movies, and culture it deserves. The current state of affairs [in American filmmaking] is the result of the lack of [a] fundamental and essential trait, which is curiosity" (as quoted in McKenna, 2000, p. 70).

Movie News
www.movieweb.com

Industry defenders argue that films aimed at young people aren't necessarily movies with nothing to say. *Election* (1999) and *Saved* (2004) are "teen films" offering important insight into American society and youth culture, as well as into the topics they explicitly examine, namely, elections and religion, respectively. In addition, despite Hollywood's infatuation with younger moviegoers, it still produces scores of movies of merit for a wider audience—*Sideways* (2004), *Hotel Rwanda* (2004), *About Schmidt* (2003), *Thirteen* (2003), *The Human Stain* (2003). All five Oscar nominees for best picture in 2005 were adult, important movies that had much to say about us as a people and as a culture: *Brokeback Mountain*, *Capote*, *Crash*, *Good Night, and Good Luck*, and *Munich*. Films whose talent was nominated for best actress and actor were equally grown-up: *Hustle & Flow*, *Transamerica*, *Mrs. Henderson Presents*, *Pride & Prejudice*, *North County*, and *Walk the Line*.

If Hollywood is fixated on kid and teen movies, why does it give us such treasures? True, Michael Eisner, as president of Paramount Pictures and then CEO of Disney, wrote in an internal memo, "We have no obligation to make history. We have no obligation to make art. We have no obligation to make a statement. Our only obligation is to make money" (as quoted in Friend, 2000, p. 214). Nevertheless, the movie industry continues to produce films that indeed make history, art, and a statement while they make money. It does so because we buy tickets to those movies.

Scope and Nature of the Film Industry

Hollywood's record year of 1946 saw the sale of more than 4 billion tickets. Today, about 1.3 billion people a year will see a movie in a U.S. theater. Domestic box office in 2005 was $8.8 billion. Eighteen movies in 2005, including *Wedding Crashers*, *The 40-Year-Old Virgin*, *Hitch*, *King Kong*, and *Charlie and The Chocolate Factory*, exceeded $100 million in U.S.-only box office. Forty-two exceeded that amount worldwide. As impressive as these numbers may seem, they represent a disappointing year for the movie industry, as you can see in the essay on page 176, "Why Don't We Go to the Movies Anymore?"

THREE COMPONENT SYSTEMS

There are three component systems in the movie industry—production, distribution, and exhibition. Each is undergoing significant change in the contemporary digital, converged media environment.

CULTURAL FORUM

Why Don't We Go to the Movies Anymore?

The data tell a troubling tale. The number of movie tickets sold has decreased every year from 2002 to 2005. The amount of money that families spend at the theater also dropped 17% in that span ("Bottom Line," 2006). Then, in 2005, there was a dramatic falloff in box office revenues, down 6.2% from 2004, to $8.8 billion—the biggest 1-year decline in 20 years. The troubling state of the movie business is in the news, but the issue that roils the cultural forum is, "Why are people staying away from the movies?" As you might imagine, there is no shortage of answers.

1. *The recent spate of movies just isn't very good.* Tired sequels (*XXX: State of the Union, Deuce Bigalow: European Gigolo*), undistinguished remakes *(The Longest Yard, Guess Who),* and cheesy TV adaptations *(The Honeymooners, Bewitched)* simply leave moviegoers cold. Sony Pictures' chairwoman Amy Pascal explained, "We can give ourselves every excuse for people not showing up— change in population, the demographic, sequels, this and that—but people just want good movies" (in Holson, 2005, p. A1).

2. Not unrelated, *fewer successful blockbusters* mean that not as many people are making it to the theater in the first place, denying them the opportunity to see trailers for and get excited about other films. Big hits like *King Kong* and *Spider-Man 2* have recently been rare. "If Hollywood builds it, audiences will come," says Brandon Gray of box office–tracking Web site Box Office Mojo, "but Hollywood hasn't been building it lately" (in Germain, 2005b, p. E5). As if to confirm Gray's argument, a 2005 AP-AOL poll revealed that about half of U.S. moviegoers think that movies are getting worse (Germain, 2005a).

3. Bad movies not only hurt box office, but as people go to the movies less frequently, they tend to forget about the movies as an option when looking for entertainment. *Ad Age* critic T. L. Stanley calls this *out of sight, out of mind* (2005, p. 20).

> **PEOPLE'S RELIANCE ON SOPHISTICATED IN-HOME TECHNOLOGIES POSES AN ADDITIONAL THREAT TO THE FILM INDUSTRY BECAUSE IT PRESAGES *A GENERATIONAL SHIFT AWAY FROM MOVIES.* IT IS PRECISELY THOSE YOUNG PEOPLE WHO WILL BE TOMORROW'S SEAT-FILLERS WHO ARE LEAVING THE MOVIE EXPERIENCE WITH THE LEAST REGRET.**

4. This problem is further complicated by people's skepticism about just what they will see should they go to the movies. Stanley calls this *what you see is not what you get.* In other words, desperate studios overhyping every new movie as an event or something special or out of the ordinary eventually turns off inevitably disappointed fans. Michael Lynton, chairman of Sony Pictures, insists that moviegoers aren't as stupid as the studios seem to think, "Audiences have gotten smart to the marketing, they can smell the good ones from the bad ones at a distance" (in Dargis, 2006, p. 2.21).

5. But what faces them when they do arrive at the movies? A very *expensive* outing. The average ticket price has increased 48.6% in the last decade, to $6.21 (Stanley, 2006). Add to this the cost of the overpriced Goobers, popcorn, and soda *plus* the cost of gas to get there *plus* the price of a trustworthy baby-sitter (if necessary), and "catching a flick" becomes quite costly.

6. And what happens when people finally do make it to their seats? Chatty neighbors—that is, *an increasingly loud and rude environment,* especially cell phone users, crying babies, and antsy children at age-inappropriate movies.

7. But surely once the house goes dark, all is well. Well, no. People who have just paid handsomely to be at the movies are then faced with *full-length commercials before the trailers.* From 2004 to 2005, advertisers increased their spending on what they call "pre-show entertainment" 18%, to over $400 million (Stanley, 2005). Audiences notice, and anecdotal evidence suggests they're unhappy. "One thing we sometimes overlook," reminds film critic Richard Roeper, "is the quality of the moviegoing experience. If someone's waiting through 20 minutes of commercials, you've got people behind your seat and talking on cell phones, don't you think a lot of people might say,

Production Production is the making of movies. About 900 feature-length films are produced annually in the United States, a large increase over the early 1980s, when, for example in 1985, 288 features were produced. As we'll see later in this chapter, significant revenues from home video are one reason for the increase, as is growing conglomerate ownership that demands more product for more markets.

'You know what? I've got a great sound system, I've got a 50-inch plasma screen. I'm just going to wait two months until the DVD comes out'?" (in Germain, 2005c).

8. This, in fact, is the industry's greatest fear, *new digital technologies,* especially wired homes (with video-on-demand; high-definition, big-screen TVs; pay-per-view movies), increasingly sophisticated DVDs (that are not only packed with extra features but now released within weeks of the film's big-screen premiere), and home delivery of DVDs. Firms such as Netflix bring a constant flow of new movies to people's homes for a monthly fee. This company alone increased its subscriber base 61% between 2004 and 2005 and will have 20 million subscribers by 2012 (Stanley, 2005).

9. People's reliance on sophisticated in-home technologies poses an additional threat to the film industry because it presages *a generational shift away from movies.* It is precisely those young people who will be tomorrow's seat-fillers who are abandoning the theater experience with the least regret. Even though males between 13 and 25 years old still constitute the largest single moviegoing demographic, their attendance is down 24%, and only one-quarter say there is an "excellent selection" of movies for them (Snyder, 2005). As such, many industry insiders fret that the current downturn in attendance and box office may well solidify into a more permanent cultural alteration in America's moviegoing habits.

Enter your voice. Do you go to the movies as much as you once did? If not, why not? Do any of these reasons that keep people from the movies resonate with you? Which ones? If you remain a regular moviegoer, why? What makes the "moviegoing experience" worth the effort? Many exhibitors are adding "perks," such as video arcades and wine and martini bars (Mohr, 2006). Would moves such as these "improve" the experience for you? Or, like some insiders, do you see the industry's recent box office travails as a temporary thing? "I've been around long enough to see us get down and bounce back," argues Revolution Studios founder Tom Sherak. "We just have to take the storm head on. Keep doing what we're doing, and steer straight for the tidal wave" (in Bowles, 2006). Is Mr. Sherak right, or is he simply whistling past the graveyard?

Do easy-to-get DVDs and outlandish snack prices keep you from going to the movies?

Technology, too, has affected production. Many Hollywood films are shot on videotape. In most cases, this taping is done in conjunction with shooting the movie on film and is used as a form of immediate feedback for directors and cinematographers. However, the success of *The Blair Witch Project* (1999), shot on videotape for $35,000, has moved even more filmmakers to greater use of videotape as a primary shooting format.

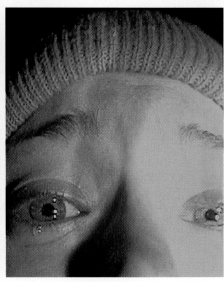

Critics assailed *Titanic* for its weak story line and two-dimensional characters—the real stars of the highest-grossing movie of all time were the special effects. But grand special effects are no guarantee of success. FX-laden *Pluto Nash* was an all-time box office stinker, costing $100 million to make and earning only $14 million in 2002, while *The Blair Witch Project*, devoid of technical legerdemain and made for $35,000, made $220 million in box office worldwide.

Another influence of technology can be seen in the four-top grossing movies of 2005—*Star Wars: Episode III—Revenge of the Sith, Harry Potter and the Goblet of Fire, War of the Worlds,* and *The Chronicles of Narnia.* Digital filmmaking has made grand special effects not only possible but expected. Stunning special effects, of which *Titanic* (1997) is a fine example, can make a good movie an excellent one. The downside of computer-generated special effects is that they can greatly increase production costs. *The Adventures of Pluto Nash,* for example, cost more than $100 million to make; *Titanic,* more than $200 million. The Motion Picture Association of America (MPAA) reported that the *average* cost of producing and marketing a Hollywood feature in 2005 increased by more than 15% from the previous year, to a record high of $103 million, a figure inflated, in large part, by the demands of audience-expected digital legerdemain (Guider, 2004). Many observers see this large increase in production costs as a major reason studios are less willing to take creative chances in a big-budget film.

Distribution Distribution was once as simple as making prints of films and sending them to theaters. Now it means supplying these movies to television networks, cable and satellite networks, and makers of videocassettes and videodiscs. The sheer scope of the distribution business ensures that large companies (most typically the big studios themselves) will dominate. In addition to making copies and guaranteeing their delivery, distributors now finance production and take responsibility for advertising and promotion and for setting and adjusting release dates. The advertising and promotion budget for a Hollywood feature usually equals 50% of the production costs. Sometimes, the ratio of promotion to production costs is even higher. *Pearl Harbor* (2001), for example, cost $140 million to make. Its studio, Disney, spent $70

Brokeback Mountain opened on 5 screens; *The Longest Yard*, on 3,600. Can you guess why?

million in promotion in the United States and another $50 million overseas; in other words, the two sets of costs were nearly equal. Was it worth it? *Pearl Harbor* returned more than $450 million in worldwide box office. So spending $40 million to $50 million to tout a Hollywood movie (the industry average; DiOrio, 2002a) is not uncommon, and the investment is seen as worthwhile, if not necessary. In fact, so important has promotion become to the financial success of a movie that studios such as Universal and MGM include their advertising and marketing people in the **green light process,** that is, the decision to make a picture in the first place. These promotion professionals can say yes or no to a film's production, and they must also declare how much money and effort they will put behind the film if they do vote yes.

Another important factor in a film's promotion and eventual financial success is the distributor's decision to release it to a certain number of screens. One strategy, called the **platform rollout,** is to open a movie on a few screens and hope that critical response, film festival success, and good word-of-mouth reviews from those who do see it will propel it to success. Naturally, the advantage of this approach for the distributor is that it can greatly reduce the cost of promotion. Focus Films, for example, opened 2005's critically acclaimed *Brokeback Mountain* on only 5 screens but had it on nearly 2,100 within weeks. Films that may suffer at the hands of critics or from poor word-of-mouth—for example, *The Longest Yard* (2005, 3,600 screens) and *Date Movie* (2006, 2,900 screens)—typically open in a lot of theaters simultaneously. However, it is not uncommon for a potential hit to open on many screens, as *Spider-Man* did in 2002—on more than 6,000.

Exhibition There are currently about 36,485 movie screens in the United States. More than 80% of theaters have two or more screens and average 340 seats in front of each. In the wake of the Reagan administration policy to deregulate the business, which undid the Paramount Decision in the 1980s, one-half of all screens are now owned by a studio, a trend that is continuing. For example, Sony owns Sony/Loews Theaters, Sony-IMAX Theaters, Magic Johnson Theaters, and Loews-Star Theaters and their 3,000 screens, and Warner Brothers International Theaters has more than 1,000 screens in 12 countries. In 1990 they owned none. Screens not owned by a studio are typically part of larger theater chains, for example, Century Theaters, with 800 screens and plans for 400 more in 11 western American states, and Regal

Entertainment Group (Regal Cinemas, United Artist Theaters, Edwards Theaters) with 6,061 screens in 26 states. Together, the seven largest chains, including studio-owned chains, control more than 80% of U.S. ticket sales.

It is no surprise to any moviegoer that exhibitors make much of their money on concession sales of items that typically have an 80% profit margin, accounting for 25% of a theater's total revenue. This is the reason that matinees and budget nights are attractive promotions for theaters. A low-priced ticket pays dividends in overpriced popcorn and Goobers.

THE STUDIOS

Studios are at the heart of the movie business and increasingly are regaining control of the three component systems of the industry. There are major studios, corporate independents, and independent studios. The majors, who finance their films primarily through the profits of their own business, include Warner Brothers, Columbia, Paramount, 20th Century Fox, Universal, MGM/UA, and Disney. The **corporate independents** (so named because they produce movies that have the look and feel of independent films) include Miramax (Disney), Sony Classics, Warner Independent, Paramount Vantage, Fox Searchlight, and Focus Features (Universal). These companies are in fact specialty or niche divisions of the majors, designed to produce more sophisticated—but less costly—fare to (1) gain prestige for their parent studios and (2) earn significant cable and DVD income after their critically lauded and good word-of-mouth runs in the theaters. Focus Features, for example, was responsible for 2005's *The Constant Gardener* and *Pride & Prejudice,* Warner Independent produced *Good Night, and Good Luck,* and Sony Classics had *Capote.* Two of Hollywood's all-time DVD hits, *Napoleon Dynamite* and *Sideways,* are 2004 offerings from Fox Searchlight.

Together, the majors and their specialty houses account for 80% to 90% of annual U.S. box office revenues, although they produce only about one-half of each year's feature films. The remainder come from independent studios, companies that raise money outside the studio system to produce their films. Lionsgate is one of the few remaining true independents in Hollywood, producing films like the *Saw* and *Hostel* series, as well as *Diary of a Mad Blackwoman* (2005) and *Madea's Family Reunion* (2006). But countless other independents continue to churn out films, often with the hope of winning a distribution deal with one of the Hollywood studios. For example, Wild Bunch/Canal Plus's Oscar-winning documentary *March of the Penguins* (2005) was distributed by Warner Independent; 2005 winner of the Oscar for Best Picture, *Crash,* from Stratus Films, was distributed by Lionsgate; and the 2004–2005 million-dollar box office hit *Million Dollar Baby,* from independent Lakeshore, was distributed by Warner Brothers.

Independent films tend to have smaller budgets. Often this leads to much more imaginative filmmaking

Indie film *Crash* was a critical and box office hit, winning the Oscar for Best Picture in 2005.

The smash success of *Easy Rider* (1969) ushered in the indie film boom.

and more risk taking than the big studios are willing to undertake. The 1969 independent film *Easy Rider*, which cost $370,000 to produce and made over $50 million in theater rentals, began the modern independent film boom. *My Big Fat Greek Wedding* (2002) cost $5 million to make and earned over $300 million in global box office receipts. Some independent films with which you might be familiar are *Eternal Sunshine of the Spotless Mind* (2004), *Fargo* (1997), *Pulp Fiction* (1994), *Crouching Tiger, Hidden Dragon* (2000), *Traffic* (2000), *28 Days Later* (2003), *The Pianist* (2002), *Fahrenheit 9/11* (2004), and *The Quiet American* (2003).

Trends and Convergence in Moviemaking

Stagnant, even declining box office, increased production costs largely brought about by digital special effects wizardry, and the "corporatization" of the independent film are only a few of the trends reshaping the film industry. There are several others, however, including some that many critics see as contributors to Hollywood's box office slide.

CONGLOMERATION AND THE BLOCKBUSTER MENTALITY

Other than MGM, each of the majors is a part of a large conglomerate. Paramount is owned by Viacom, Warner Brothers is part of the huge Time Warner family of holdings, Disney is part of the giant conglomerate formed in the 1996 Disney/Capital Cities/ABC union, and Universal was bought by NBC's parent company, General Electric, in 2004. Much of this conglomeration takes the form of international ownership. Columbia is owned by Japanese Sony and Fox by Australia's News Corp. According to many critics, this combination of conglomeration and foreign ownership forces the industry into a **blockbuster mentality**—filmmaking characterized by reduced risk

Indiewire
www.indiewire.com

taking and more formulaic movies. Business concerns are said to dominate artistic considerations as accountants and financiers make more decisions once made by creative people. As a result, according to *Seattle Weekly* film critic Brian Miller, the movies made in Hollywood today are "all about fiduciary duty and shareholder value. They feel mechanistic because they're made by a self-perpetuating machine, a closed feedback loop of executives worried about their children's tuition payments" ("Hard Lessons," 2003, p. 25). The common outcomes of this blockbuster mentality are several.

Concept Movies   The marketing and publicity departments of big companies love **concept films**—movies that can be described in one line. *Twister* is about a giant, rogue tornado. *The Lost World* is about giant, rogue dinosaurs. *King Kong* (2005) is about a giant ape who comes to New York.

International ownership and international distribution contribute to this phenomenon. High-concept films that depend little on characterization, plot development, and dialogue are easier to sell to foreign exhibitors than are more sophisticated films. *The Matrix* and *XXX* play well everywhere. Big-name stars also have international appeal. That's why they can command huge salaries. The importance of foreign distribution cannot be overstated. Only 2 in 10 U.S. features make a profit on U.S. box office. Much of their eventual profit comes from overseas sales. For example, 2005's *Constantine* disappointed domestically ($76 million) but earned more than $194 million overseas. Likewise, *Kingdom of Heaven* earned $47 million in domestic box office and $163 million in foreign ticket sales. And it's not just domestic disappointments that do well overseas. *Titanic* doubled its $601 million U.S. box office, earning $1.2 billion elsewhere. *Harry Potter and the Chamber of Secrets* tripled its home earnings, $262 million versus $615 million in foreign box office. Overseas box office accounts for 55% of the U.S. movie industry's income.

Ain't It Cool (movie reviews)
www.aint-it-cool.com

Audience Research   Before a movie is released, sometimes even before it is made, its concept, plot, and characters are subjected to market testing. Often multiple endings are produced and tested with sample audiences by companies such as National Research Group and Marketcast. Despite being "voodoo science, a spin of the roulette wheel," says *Chicago Reader* film critic Jonathan Rosenbaum, audience testing is "believed in like a religion at this point. It's considered part of filmmaking" (quoted in Scribner, 2001, p. D3). The question raised by film purists is what has become of the filmmaker's genius? What separates these market-tested films from any other commodity? *Variety* film writer Dade Hayes explains the dilemma facing blockbuster-driven Hollywood, "Testing contributes to the sameness of the movies, and feeds into audience expectations of comfortable patterns and makes them uneasy if a film diverges from that formula . . . [B]ut there cannot be much creative freedom with a $200 million **tentpole**" (an expensive blockbuster around which a studio plans its other releases; 2003, pp. 1, 53).

Sequels, Remakes, and Franchises   Nothing succeeds like success. How many *Mission Impossibles* have there been? *Charlie's Angels? Legally Blondes? Lethal Weapons? American Pies* and *Weddings*? Johnny Depp's *Charlie and the Chocolate Factory* (2005) is a remake of Gene Wilder's 1971 classic *Willie Wonka and the Chocolate Factory. The Stepford Wives* (2004) retells a 1975

We went around the world in 80 days in 2004, 48 years after the original.

story. We went *Around the World in 80 Days* in 1956 and in 2004. *The Longest Yard* (2005) is a replay of the 1974 original. *The Manchurian Candidate* ran in both 1962 and 2004. *The Texas Chainsaw Massacre* (2003), *Ocean's Eleven* (2001), and *Dawn of the Dead* (2004) are other recent remakes. Hollywood, too, is making increasing use of **franchise films,** movies that are produced with the full intention of producing several more sequels. The first James Bond film (1962) has had 21 sequels; *Star Wars* (1977), five. *Harry Potter* (2001) will have as many as there are Potter books, and *The Matrix* put multiple sequels in production at once, as did the *Lord of the Rings* and *Pirates of the Caribbean* franchises.

Television, Comic Book, and Video-Game Remakes Nothing succeeds like success. That, and the fact that teens and preteens still make up the largest proportion of the movie audience, is the reason so many movies are adaptations of television shows, comic books, and video games. In the last few years *Inspector Gadget, Dudley Do-Right, The Flintstones, My Favorite Martian, The Fugitive, The Saint, Mission: Impossible, George of the Jungle, The Dukes of Hazzard, Lost in Space* (and its sequel), *Charlie's Angels, Beavis and Butthead, McHale's Navy, Mr. Magoo, The Brady Bunch, Bewitched,* and *Wayne's World* have moved from small to big screen. *The Addams Family, Dennis the Menace, Richie Rich, Spider-Man, Batman,* and *Superman* have traveled from the comics, through television, to the silver screen. *Tank Girl, Barb Wire, Spawn, X Men, Men in Black, Kull the Conqueror, Steel,* and *The Crow* have moved directly from comics to movies. *Tomb Raider, Resident Evil, Mortal Kombat, Final Fantasy,* and *Grand Theft Auto* went from game box to box office.

Not only lame versions of '60s sitcoms, but also sequels and remakes are keeping people away from the movies.

NON SEQUITUR © 2005 Wiley Miller. Distribution by UNIVERSAL PRESS SYNDICATE. Reprinted with permission. All rights reserved,

Movies from comics and video games are especially attractive to studios because of their built-in merchandise tie-in appeal.

Merchandise Tie-Ins Films are sometimes produced as much for their ability to generate interest for nonfilm products as for their intrinsic value as movies. The Licensing Industry Merchandisers' Association reports that toy and product tie-ins accounted for $2.5 billion in payments to the studios in 2001 (on retail sales of $42 billion; Goldsmith, 2002). *Star Wars: Episode I— The Phantom Menace* alone accounted for more than $1 billion in merchandise sales in the year after its 1999 release (Palmeri, 2001). And as almost all of us know, it is nearly impossible to buy a meal at McDonald's, Burger King, or Taco Bell without being offered a movie tie-in product. Studios often believe it is riskier to make a $7 million film with no merchandising potential than a $100 million movie with greater merchandising appeal.

Product Placement Many movies are serving double duty as commercials. We'll discuss this phenomenon in detail later in the chapter as a media literacy issue.

CONVERGENCE RESHAPES THE MOVIE BUSINESS

So intertwined are today's movie and television industries that it is often meaningless to discuss them separately. As much as 70% of the production done by the studios is for television, Paramount's various *Star Trek* series and Fox's entire television network being two prime examples. But the growing relationship between **theatrical films**—those produced originally for theater exhibition—and television is the result of technological changes in the latter. The convergence of film with satellite, cable, video-on-demand, pay-per-view, digital videodisc (DVD), and videocassette has provided immense distribution and exhibition opportunities for the movies. For example, in 1947 box office receipts accounted for 95% of the studios' revenues. Today they make up less than one-fifth (Surowiecki, 2005). Today's distributors make three times as much from domestic home entertainment (DVD, videotapes, and network and cable television) as they do from rentals to movie houses. Video sales (to individuals and DVD rental stores) are a lucrative business as well. In fact DVD sales of theatrical films earned more ($12 billion) than did domestic box office ($9.5 billion) for the first time in 2003. Today they produce about $20 billion a year (Surowiecki, 2005). The studios also maximize their DVD profits with trailers for their other video and in-theater films and with commercials. Box office failures can turn loss to profit with good DVD sales. *Old School* made $75 million in domestic box office and $83 million in DVD sales. *National Lampoon's Van Wilder* made $21 million in theaters and $32 million in DVD sales. *Jay and Silent Bob Strike Back* made $36 million in DVD sales and only $30 million in box office (Snyder, 2004). Even many box office hits ultimately make more in DVD sales. *Napoleon Dynamite,* made for $400,000 and generating $50 million at the box office, has earned more than $120 million in DVD sales.

The convergence of film with digital technologies is beginning to reshape production, distribution, *and* exhibition. In early 1999, three companies, Kodak, Texas Instruments, and CineComm, began demonstrations of their digital distribution of films to theaters via satellite. Five years later, in 2004, the industry finally agreed on one standard technology. Should this advance take hold, exhibitors will no longer have to physically receive film cans and load

www

Atom Films
www.atomfilms.com

their contents onto projectors. For now, though, even though producers are excited about the promise of saving hundreds of millions of dollars on the production of prints, exhibitors remain wary. Conversion to digital projection costs about $150,000 per screen, and there is little evidence that digital, rather than celluloid, projection sells more tickets. Moreover, because it is the studios that stand to benefit most directly, saving about a billion dollars a year in distribution costs, exhibitors argue that they should pay for the conversion. Naturally, the studios disagree. As a result, today there are only 92 digital projection systems in the United States, fewer than 1% of all screens (Jardin, 2005a).

The surprise 1999 hit *The Blair Witch Project* is the most visible success of the growing **microcinema** movement, through which filmmakers using digital video cameras and desktop digital editing machines are finding audiences, both in theaters and online, for their low-budget (sometimes as little as $10,000) features. But arguably the biggest boost given to digital production of theatrical films (if they can still be called *films*) came in April 2000 when, after a trial run of the equipment, George Lucas announced that he would shoot the live action scenes for the sequel to the *Phantom Menace* using digital video cameras. More recently, director Robert Rodriguez shot the last two *Spy Kids* (2002 and 2003) movies and his dark *Sin City* (2005), all big-budget movies, with digital cameras. Steven Soderbergh used digital cameras for his 2006 low-budget indie *Bubble*. But for every convert to digital production—"If I could go back in time and shoot *Titanic* in 3-D for digital camera, I'd do it. I'll never shoot a movie on film again," said James Cameron—many more remain committed to film—"I was one of the first people to use digital technology to enhance my films, but I'm going to be the last person to use digital technology to shoot my films," insists Steven Spielberg, director of classics *E.T., Jaws, Schindler's List,* and *Saving Private Ryan* (both in Jardin, 2005a, p. 121). The industry's best estimate is that digital shooting will be the standard no sooner than 2015 (Taylor, 2005).

WWW
IFilm
www.ifilm.com

As digitization and convergence are changing exhibition and production, they are also changing distribution. Although slowed by fears of piracy, the online distribution of feature films is starting to take hold. The five major studios joined with IBM in 2002 to launch the movie-on-demand Internet distribution system, Movielink. Two years later, Starz! Ticket began offering subscribers 100 movie downloads a month for $12.95. Much more will be said about Internet distribution of film and video content in Chapter 10.

WWW
Movie Downloads
www.movielink.com
starzticket.com

But a potentially bigger alteration to traditional movie distribution resides in the efforts of studios like IFC Entertainment, directors like Steven Soderbergh, and exhibitors such as billionaire Mark Cuban's Landmark Theaters. All plan for the simultaneous release of movies to theaters, DVD, and cable video-on-demand. Disney has publicly committed to considering this model of distribution as well. Director Soderbergh predicts that once digital production, distribution, and exhibition are firmly in place, "in five or ten years, you're going to see name filmmakers self-distributing" (in Jardin, 2005b, p. 257). These changes will eventually force significant alterations in the economics of Hollywood, argues *Washington Post* media writer Steven Pearlstein. "The studios will be indifferent about how you choose to get a movie—their profit will be the same whether you see it in a theater, rent it, or order it up from Comcast." He sees this as an improvement over the way Hollywood currently operates, forcing studios to become more competitive, efficient, and audience-driven. Studios will no longer be able to rely as heavily on blockbusters and big-name superstars as they do now. Successful studios will be those producing a wide "range of well-done movies for a variety of niche audiences reached through targeted marketing and distribution channels' (2005, p. D1).

DEVELOPING MEDIA LITERACY SKILLS
Recognizing Product Placements

The Gap and Lexus have nearly as much screen time as Tom Cruise in *Minority Report* (2002). The Palm Pilot has a major role in *Little Black Book* (2004). Audi was such a central character in the 2005 *Transporter 2* that it earned top billing on the movie's posters. In a pivotal scene in 2005's *The Island*, a runaway clone (played by Scarlett Johansson) comes upon a Calvin Klein storefront display on a Los Angeles street. The display includes a television playing a Calvin Klein commercial. The commercial stars the actress whose DNA was used to create Scarlett Johansson, leading Scarlett Johansson to the realization that she is the clone of a famous actress. But the commercial is a real (non-movie) commercial for Calvin Klein's Eternity Moment perfume, one that stars the real (non-movie, non-clone) Scarlett Johansson. In other words, "*The Island* took a real Calvin Klein commercial starring Scarlett Johansson and made the commercial a major part of a fictional film in which Scarlett Johansson plays an actress who isn't Scarlett Johansson but stars in the same Calvin Klein commercial" (Sauer, 2006).

The practice of placing brand-name products in movies is not new; Katharine Hepburn throws Gordon's gin into the river in the 1951 *The African Queen*, and Spencer Tracy is splashed with Coca-Cola in the 1950 *Father of the Bride*. But in today's movie industry, product placement has expanded into a business in its own right. About 100 product placement agencies are

In this scene from *The Island*, Scarlett Johansson (the clone) sees Scarlett Johansson (the person from whom she was cloned) in an actual, real-world TV commercial that stars Scarlett Johansson.

LIVING MEDIA LITERACY

Smoke-Free Movies

Product placement vexes its critics because of its threat to the integrity of film. But when it comes to the placement of cigarettes, the problem is compounded by the fact that this frequently placed product kills. Studies from the Center for Tobacco Control Research and Education discovered that movies in theaters delivered 37.4 billion tobacco impressions to Americans between 1999 and 2004, including 2 billion to kids aged 6 to 11 and 7.5 billion to teens 12 to 17. Seventy-eight percent of the 912 movies examined from that span included tobacco scenes—87% of R-rated, 79% of PG-13-rated, and 40% of G/PG-rated films (Smoke Free Movies, 2006). Statistics such as these moved throat cancer survivor and screenwriter Joe Eszterhas (*Basic Instinct, Flashdance*) to apologize for putting so much smoking in his movies. "A cigarette in the hands of a Hollywood star onscreen," he said, "is a gun aimed at a 12- or 14-year-old" ("Verbatim," 2002, p. 16). Once-secret tobacco industry documents indicate that cigarette companies "aggressively pursued product placement in films—even as they told Congress they would not . . . [and] undertook an extensive campaign to hook Hollywood on tobacco by providing free cigarettes to actors" (Smoke Free Movies, 2006).

If you are troubled by this deception (the tobacco companies pledged in 1989 to cease movie product placements), or if you are bothered by the fact that both *Variety* and *Hollywood Reporter* refuse to sell space to Smoke Free Movies for its antismoking ads (P. Goldstein, 2002), or if you dislike the practice of product placement itself, or if you understand that tobacco is "the all-time leading cause of early death" (P. Goldstein, 2002, p. G3), you can act; you can make your own media literacy a living enterprise.

> **"IF SMOKING IN A MOVIE IS ABOUT FREE EXPRESSION, WHY DO ALL THE CHARACTERS SMOKE THE SAME BRAND?"**

Smoke Free Movies provides information and an action agenda on its Web site (smokefreemovies.ucsf.edu). It recommends the following actions:

- Contact the MPAA (www.mpaa.org) and ask that it change its ratings system to give an R to movies that depict smoking.
- Contact the studios themselves (as well as their parent companies) and tell them that you will not attend smoke-filled films (Smoke Free Movies' Web site provides links).
- Demand that local theaters and video stores show strong antismoking ads; organize people in your community to make in-person visits to the managers of these establishments to make these requests.
- Contact the actors themselves and let them know how much they, as people, disappoint you.
- Write letters to the editors of your local papers. When you see a film that glamorizes smoking or pushes a particular brand, tell the world. Make those responsible answer for their actions.

But you love film, respect it as a medium of expression. You don't want to be involved in what looks like censorship. If smoking is integral to the filmmaker's vision, so be it. But why, for example, does Sissy Spacek, descending into madness over the murder of her son in *In the Bedroom* (2001), brood over a strategically placed pack of Marlboros? Why does she order that specific brand, by name, from a shop clerk? Why does a walk-on actor, incidental to the story, request a pack of Marlboros by name? As cancer researcher Stanton Glantz asks, "If smoking in a movie is about free expression, why do all the characters smoke the same brand?" (quoted in McCowan, 2002, p. 2).

---

operating in Hollywood, and there's even an industry association, the Entertainment Resources and Marketing Association (ERMA). The attraction of product placements for sponsors is obvious. For one flat fee paid up front, a product that appears in a movie is in actuality a commercial that lives forever—first on the big screen, then on television and cable, and then on purchased and rented videotapes and discs. The commercial is also likely to have worldwide distribution.

Many people in and outside the movie industry see product placement as inherently deceptive. "Why not identify the ads for what they are?" they ask. From a media literacy standpoint, the issue is the degree to which artistic decisions are being placed second to obligations to sponsors. Film critic Glenn Lovell (1997) wrote, "Scripts are being doctored and camera angles changed to accommodate manufacturers paying for props or promotional

More on Product Placement
www.brandchannel.com

campaigns. It's a classic case of the tail wagging the dog" (p. 7G). David Peoples, the screenwriter for *Blade Runner*, a cinematic testimonial to product placement, calls the practice a "racket . . . a horrifying compromise" (p. 7G). A "hot" Hollywood director who asked critic Lovell not to use his name said, "I've worked with producers who would sell their soul to get a major placement. I say, 'Forget it.' If movie stars want to do commercials, they should do them, and get paid" (p. 7G).

Knowing how media content is funded and how that financial support shapes content is an important aspect of understanding the mass communication process. Therefore, an awareness of the efforts of the movie industry to maximize income from its films is central to good film literacy.

Consider, for example, the following product placements. If you saw these movies, did you recognize the placements?

Madea's Family Reunion	Amstel, Budweiser, Chanel, Chevrolet, Dr. Pepper, Ford Mustang, Heineken, Jansport, Juicy Juice, Land Rover, Lincoln, Mazda, Mercedes, Motorola, Nike, Orion, Pepsi, Philips, Rocawear, Spalding, Viagra, Victoria's Secret, Wonder Bread
The Pink Panther	adidas, Apple, Axe, Chanel, Citroën, Dell, Gretsch, Holiday Inn, Kodak, McDonald's, MSN, Newsweek, Nextel, Nikon, Perrier, Philips, Piaggio, Pilot, Post-its, T.G.I. Friday's, Toyota, USA Today, Viagra, Virgin, Volkswagen, Waldorf-Astoria
Glory Road	adidas, Airstream, Chrysler, Coke, Converse, Dairy Queen, Esso (Exxon), Pontiac, Radio Flyer, Spalding, Sports Illustrated, United Airlines, Western Union

WWW

Product Placement Organization
www.erma.org

Does it trouble you that content is altered, even if sometimes only minimally, to allow for these brand identifications? To what extent would script alterations have to occur to accommodate paid-for messages before you find them intrusive? Do you think it is fair or honest for a moviemaker who promises you film content in exchange for your money to turn you into what amounts to a television viewer by advertising sponsors' products? At least in television, by law, all commercial messages must be identified as such, and the sponsors of those messages must be identified. Do you think such a rule ought to apply to movies?

Literate film consumers may answer these questions differently, especially as individuals hold film in varying degrees of esteem—but they should answer them.

RESOURCES FOR REVIEW AND DISCUSSION

Review Points

- Film's beginnings reside in the efforts of entrepreneurs such as Eadweard Muybridge and inventors like Thomas Edison and William Dickson.
- Photography, an essential precursor to movies, was developed by Hannibal Goodwin, George Eastman, Joseph Nicéphore Niépce, Louis Daguerre, and William Henry Fox Talbot.
- Edison and the Lumière brothers began commercial motion picture exhibition, little more than representations of everyday life. Georges Méliès added narrative; Edwin S. Porter added montage; and D. W. Griffith developed the full-length feature film.
- Movies became big business at the turn of the 20th century, one dominated by big studios, but change soon came in the form of talkies, scandal and control, and new genres to fend off the Depression.

- The three components of the film industry are production, distribution, and exhibition.
- Studios are at the heart of the movie business and are increasingly in control of the three component systems. There are major, corporate independent, and independent studios.
- Conglomeration and concentration affect the movie industry, leading to a blockbuster mentality
- Convergence, too, is reshaping the industry, promising to alter its structure and economics.
- Media literate moviegoers should be aware of the inclusion of product placements in films and their potential influence on the medium.

Key Terms

 Use the text's Online Learning Center at www.mhhe.com/baran5 to further your understanding of the following terminology.

zoopraxiscope, 161
persistence of vision, 161
kinetograph, 161
daguerreotype, 162
calotype, 162
kinetoscope, 162
cinématographe, 163
montage, 164

nickelodeons, 164
factory studios, 164
double feature, 171
B-movie, 171
vertical integration, 171
block booking, 172
green light process, 179
platform rollout, 179

corporate independent studio, 180
blockbuster mentality, 181
concept film, 182
tentpole, 182
franchise film, 183
theatrical film, 184
microcinema, 185

Questions for Review

 Go to the self-quizzes on the Online Learning Center to test your knowledge.

1. What is the significance of these people to film history? Leland Stanford, Eadweard Muybridge, William Dickson, the Lumière brothers, Louis Daguerre, Joseph Niépce, William Henry Fox Talbot, Hannibal Goodwin, George Eastman.
2. What are the kinetograph, kinetoscope, cinématographe, daguerreotype, calotype, and nickelodeon?
3. What were Méliès's, Porter's, and Griffith's contributions to film as a narrative medium?

4. What was the Motion Picture Patents Company, and how did it influence the content and development of the movie industry?
5. What societal, technical, and artistic factors shaped the development of movies before World War II?
6. How did Hollywood scandals and the red scare shape the medium's content?
7. What is vertical integration? How was it ended and reinstated?

8. What are the three component systems of the movie industry?

9. What are major and corporate independent studios? What is an independent?

10. What are concept films? Product tie-ins? Product placement?

11. What is platform rollout? When and why is it used?

12. How are digitization and convergence reshaping exhibition? Distribution? Production?

13. How will distribution change as the industry becomes more fully digital?

Questions for Critical Thinking and Discussion

1. How do you think the entrepreneurial motivation of the early movie pioneers shaped the relationship of the medium with its audience?

2. Hollywood suffered under strict content control and now has shed those restrictions. What restrictions do you think are reasonable for the movies? Why?

3. What do you think of the impact of the blockbuster mentality on movies? Should profit always be the determining factor in producing movie content? Why or why not?

4. Are you a fan of independent movies? When you are watching a movie, how can you tell that it's an independent? If you are an indie fan, do you welcome the microcinema movement? Why or why not?

5. Most industry-watchers see the new distribution model promised by digitization of the three components systems as inevitably changing the economics of Hollywood. Some, though, think it will produce better movies. Do you agree or disagree? Why?

Important Resources

 Go to the Online Learning Center for additional readings.

Internet Resources

The Cult Film Site	www.sepnet.com/
Hollywood Online	www.hollywood.com
Worst Movies Ever	www.ohthehumanity.com
Movie News	www.enn2.com/movies.htm
Movie News	www.movies.go.com
Film History	www.filmsite.org/filmh.html
Film Ratings	www.filmratings.com
Motion Picture Association of America	www.mpaa.org
Hollywood Reporter	www.hollywoodreporter.com
Internet Movie Database	www.imdb.com
Movie News	www.movieweb.com
Indiewire	www.indiewire.com
Ain't It Cool	www.aint-it-cool.com
Atom Films	www.atomfilms.com
IFilm	www.ifilm.com
Movie Downloads	www.movielink.com
	www.starzticket.com
More on Product Placement	www.brandchannel.com
Product Placement Organization	www.erma.org

7

Radio, Recording, and Popular Music

"Can we listen to the radio?"

"We are listening to the radio."

"I mean something other than this."

"You want music?"

"Yes, please, anything but public radio. Too much talk."

"OK. Here."

"What! That's the classical music station!"

"What's wrong with that?"

"Nothing . . . much."

LEARNING OBJECTIVES

Radio was the first electronic mass medium; it was the first national broadcast medium. It produced the networks, program genres, and stars that made television an instant success. But for many years radio and records were young people's media; they gave voice to a generation. As such, they may be our most personally significant mass media. After studying this chapter you should

- be familiar with the history and development of the radio and sound recording industries and radio and sound recording themselves as media.

- recognize the importance of early financing and regulatory decisions regarding radio and how they have shaped the nature of contemporary broadcasting.

- recognize how the organizational and economic natures of the contemporary radio and sound recording industries shape the content of both media.

- understand the relationship between radio, sound recording, popular music, and their listeners.

- be aware of new and emerging radio and recording technologies and their potential impact on music, the industries themselves, and listeners.

- be familiar with the economic and ethical controversies surrounding music file sharing on the Internet.

- possess improved radio-listening media literacy skill, especially in assessing the cultural value of shock jocks.

Opposite: U2's Bono and the Edge at the 2006 Grammy Awards.

"What's that supposed to mean, 'Nothing . . . much?'"

"Nothing . . . much. Let me choose."

"OK. You find a station."

"Fine. Here."

"What's that?!"

"It's the New Hot One. KISS 100. All the hits all the time."

"That's not music."

"You sound like my parents."

"I don't mean the stuff they play isn't music, I mean the deejay is yammering away."

"Hang on. A song is coming up. Anyway, this is funny stuff."

"I don't find jokes about minority wheelchair races funny."

"It's all in fun."

"Fun for whom?"

"What's *your* problem today?"

"Nothing, I just don't find that kind of stuff funny. Here, I'll find something."

"What's that?"

"The jazz station."

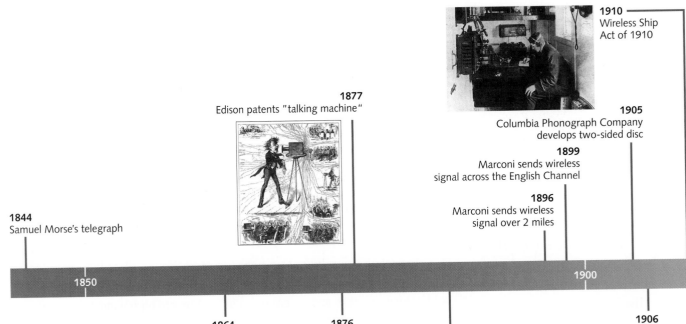

1910
Wireless Ship
Act of 1910

1877
Edison patents "talking machine"

1905
Columbia Phonograph Company
develops two-sided disc

1899
Marconi sends wireless
signal across the English Channel

1896
Marconi sends wireless
signal over 2 miles

1844
Samuel Morse's telegraph

1850

1900

1864
James Clerk Maxwell
mathematically demonstrates
possibility of radio waves

1876
Alexander Graham
Bell's telephone

1906
Fessenden makes first public
broadcast of voice and music
1906
DeForest invents audion tube

1912
Radio Act of 1912

1916
Sarnoff sends Radio
Music Box Memo

1887
Heinrich Hertz sends wireless signals
over short distance in his laboratory;
Berliner develops gramophone

"Give me a break. How about Sports Talk?"

"Nah. How about All News?"

"No way. How about the All Talk station?"

"Why, you need another fix of insulting chatter?"

"How about silence?"

"Yeah, how about it?"

In this chapter we study the technical and social beginnings of both radio and sound recording. We revisit the coming of broadcasting and see how the growth of regulatory, economic, and organizational structures led to the medium's golden age.

The heart of the chapter covers how television changed radio and produced the medium with which we are now familiar. We review the scope and nature of contemporary radio, especially its rebirth as a local, fragmented, specialized, personal, and mobile medium. We examine how these characteristics serve advertisers and listeners. The chapter then explores the relationship between radio, the modern recording industry, popular music, and the way new technologies serve and challenge all three. The popularity of shock jocks inspires our discussion of media literacy.

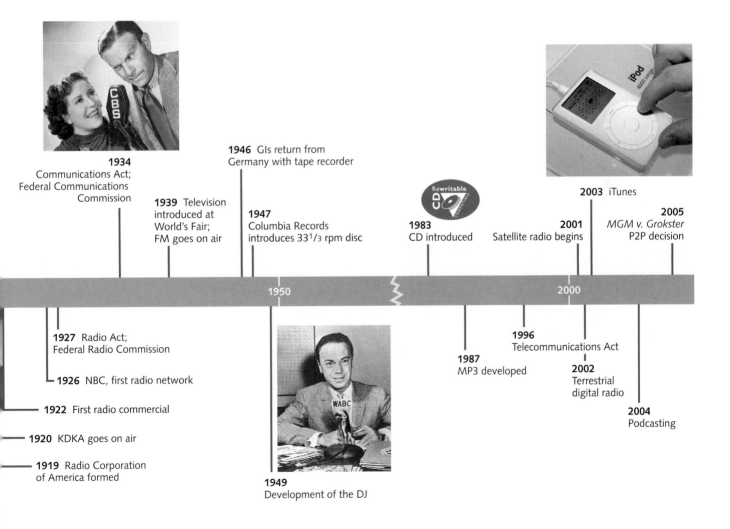

1934 Communications Act; Federal Communications Commission

1939 Television introduced at World's Fair; FM goes on air

1946 GIs return from Germany with tape recorder

1947 Columbia Records introduces 33¹/₃ rpm disc

1983 CD introduced

2001 Satellite radio begins

2003 iTunes

2005 *MGM v. Grokster* P2P decision

1950

2000

1927 Radio Act; Federal Radio Commission

1926 NBC, first radio network

1922 First radio commercial

1920 KDKA goes on air

1919 Radio Corporation of America formed

1949 Development of the DJ

1987 MP3 developed

1996 Telecommunications Act

2002 Terrestrial digital radio

2004 Podcasting

A Short History of Radio and Sound Recording

The particular stations you disagree about may be different, but almost all of us have been through a conversation similar to the one in the opening vignette. Radio, the seemingly ubiquitous medium, matters to us. Because we often listen to it alone, it is personal. Radio is also mobile. It travels with us in the car, and we take it along in our Walkmans. Radio is specific as well. Stations aim their content at very narrowly defined audiences. But these are characteristics of contemporary radio. Radio once occupied a very different place in our culture. Let's see how it all began.

EARLY RADIO

The "Father of Radio," Guglielmo Marconi, son of a wealthy Italian businessman and his Irish wife, had taken to reading scientific reports about the sending of signals through the air without wires. But unlike the early pioneers whom he studied—for example, James Clerk Maxwell and Heinrich Hertz—the young Marconi was interested not in the theory of sending signals through the air but in actually doing it. His improvements over earlier experimental designs allowed him to send and receive telegraph code over distances as great as 2 miles by 1896. His native Italy was not interested in his invention, so he used his mother's contacts in Great Britain to find support and financing there. England, with a global empire and the world's largest navy and merchant fleets, was naturally interested in long-distance wireless communication. With the financial and technical help of the British, Marconi successfully transmitted across the English Channel in 1899 and across the Atlantic in 1901. Wireless was now a reality. Marconi was satisfied with his advance, but other scientists saw the transmission of *voices* by wireless as the next hurdle, a challenge that was soon surmounted.

In 1903 Reginald Fessenden, a Canadian, invented the **liquid barretter,** the first audio device permitting reception of wireless voices. His 1906 Christmas Eve broadcast from Brant Rock, a small New England coastal village, was the first public broadcast of voices and music. His listeners were ships at sea and a few newspaper offices equipped to receive the transmission.

Later that same year American Lee DeForest invented the **audion tube,** a vacuum tube that improved and amplified wireless signals. Now the reliable transmission of clear voices and music was a reality. But DeForest's second important contribution was that he saw radio as a means of *broadcasting*. The early pioneers, Marconi included, had viewed radio as a device for point-to-point communication, for example, from ship to ship or ship to shore. But in the 1907 prospectus for his radio company DeForest wrote, "It will soon be possible to distribute grand opera music from transmitters placed on the stage of the Metropolitan Opera House by a Radio Telephone station on the roof to almost any dwelling in Greater New York and vicinity. . . . The same applies to large cities. Church music, lectures, etc., can be spread abroad by the Radio Telephone" (as

Guglielmo Marconi

quoted in Adams, 1996, pp. 104–106). Soon, countless "broadcasters" went on the air. Some broadcasters were giant corporations, looking to dominate the medium for profit; some were hobbyists and hams, playing with the medium for the sheer joy of it. There were so many "stations" that havoc reigned. Yet the promise of radio was such that the medium continued to mature until World War I, when the U.S. government ordered "the immediate closing of all stations for radio communications, both transmitting and receiving."

EARLY SOUND RECORDING

The late 1800s also saw the beginning of sound recording. In 1877 prolific inventor Thomas Edison patented his "talking machine," a device for replicating sound that used a hand-cranked grooved cylinder and a needle. The mechanical movement caused by the needle passing along the groove of the rotating cylinder and hitting bumps was converted into electrical energy that activated a diaphragm in a loudspeaker and produced sound. The drawback was that only one "recording" could be made of any given sound; the cylinder could not be duplicated. In 1887 that problem was solved by German immigrant Emile Berliner, whose gramophone used a flat, rotating, wax-coated disc that could easily be copied or pressed from a metal master. Two equally important contributions to recording made by Berliner were development of a sophisticated microphone and (through his company, RCA Victor Records) the import from Europe of recordings by famous opera stars. Now people had not only a reasonably priced record

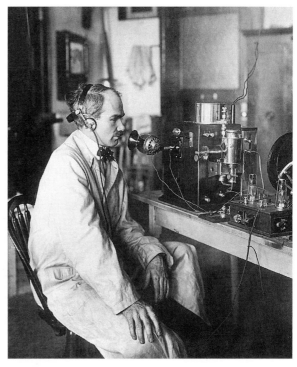

Lee DeForest

In 1887 Emile Berliner developed the flat disc gramophone and a sophisticated microphone, both important to the widespread public acceptance of sound recordings for the home. Nipper, the trademark for his company, RCA Victor, is on the scene even today.

player but records to play on it. The next advance was introduction of the two-sided disc by the Columbia Phonograph Company in 1905. Soon there were hundreds of phonograph or gramophone companies, and the device, by either name, was a standard feature in U.S. homes by 1920. More than 2 million machines and 107 million recordings were sold in 1919 alone. Public acceptance of the new medium was enhanced even more by development of electromagnetic recording in 1924 by Joseph P. Maxwell at Bell Laboratory.

The parallel development and diffusion of radio and sound recording is significant. For the first time in history radio allowed people to hear the words and music of others who were not in their presence. On recordings they could hear words and music that may have been created days, months, or even years before.

THE COMING OF BROADCASTING

The idea of broadcasting—that is, transmitting voices and music at great distances to a large number of people—predated the development of radio. Alexander Graham Bell's telephone company had a subscription music service in major cities in the late 1800s, delivering music to homes and businesses by telephone wires. A front-page story in an 1877 edition of the *New York Daily Graphic* suggested the possibilities of broadcasting to its readers. The public anticipated and, after DeForest's much publicized successes, was eager for music and voices at home. Russian immigrant David Sarnoff, then an employee of American Marconi, recognized this desire and in 1916 sent his superiors what has become famous as the "Radio Music Box Memo." In this memo Sarnoff wrote of

This cover of an 1877 newspaper proved prophetic in its image of speakers' ability to "broadcast" their words.

> a plan of development which would make radio a "household utility" in the same sense as the piano or phonograph. The idea is to bring music into the house by wireless. . . . The receiver can be designed in the form of a simple "Radio Music Box" and arranged for several different wavelengths, which should be changeable with the throwing of a single switch or pressing of a single button. (Sterling & Kitross, 1990, p. 43)

The introduction of broadcasting to a mass audience was delayed in the first 2 decades of the 20th century by patent fights and lawsuits. DeForest and Fessenden were both destroyed financially by the conflict. Yet when World War I ended, an enthusiastic audience awaited what had become a much-improved medium. In a series of developments that would be duplicated for television at the time of World War II, radio was transformed from an exciting technological idea into an entertainment and commercial giant. To aid the war effort, the government took over the patents relating to radio and continued to improve radio for military use. Thus, refinement and development of the technical aspects of radio continued throughout the war. Then, when the war ended in 1919, the patents were returned to their owners—and the bickering was renewed.

Concerned that the medium would be wasted and fearful that a foreign company (British Marconi) would control this vital resource, the government forced the combatants to merge. American Marconi, General Electric, American Telephone & Telegraph, and Westinghouse (in 1921)—each in control of a vital piece of technology—joined to create the Radio Corporation of America (RCA). RCA was a government-sanctioned monopoly, but its creation avoided direct government control of the new medium. Twenty-eight-year-old David Sarnoff, author of the Radio Music Box Memo, was made RCA's commercial manager. The way for the medium's popular growth was paved; its success was guaranteed by a public that, because of the phonograph, was already attuned to music in the home and, thanks to the just-concluded war, was awakening to the need for instant, wide-ranging news and information.

On September 30, 1920, a Westinghouse executive, impressed with press accounts of the number of listeners who were picking up broadcasts from the garage radio station of company engineer Frank Conrad, asked him to move his operation to the Westinghouse factory and expand its power. Conrad did so, and on October 27, 1920, experimental station 8XK in Pittsburgh, Pennsylvania, received a license from the Department of Commerce to broadcast. On November 2 this station, KDKA, made the first commercial radio broadcast, announcing the results of the presidential election that sent Warren G. Harding to the White House. By mid-1922, there were nearly 1 million radios in American homes, up from 50,000 just a year before (Tillinghast, 2000, p. 41).

THE COMING OF REGULATION

As the RCA agreements demonstrated, the government had a keen interest in the development, operation, and diffusion of radio. At first government interest focused on point-to-point communication. In 1910 Congress passed the Wireless Ship Act, requiring that all ships using U.S. ports and carrying more than 50 passengers have a working wireless and operator. Of course, the wireless industry did not object, as the legislation boosted sales. But after the *Titanic* struck an iceberg in the North Atlantic in 1912 and it was learned that hundreds of lives were lost needlessly because many ships in the area had left their radios unattended, Congress passed the Radio Act of 1912, which not only strengthened rules regarding shipboard wireless but also required that wireless operators be licensed by the Secretary of Commerce and Labor.

The Radio Act of 1912 established spheres of authority for both federal and state governments, provided for allocating and revoking licenses and fining violators, and assigned frequencies for station operation. The government was in the business of regulating what was to become broadcasting, a development that angered many operators. They successfully challenged the

The wireless-telegraphy room of the *Titanic*. Despite the heroic efforts of wireless operator Jack Philips, scores of people died needlessly in the sinking of that great ocean liner because the ships in its vicinity did not man their receivers.

1912 act in court, and eventually President Calvin Coolidge ordered the cessation of government regulation of radio despite his belief that chaos would descend on the medium.

He proved prophetic. The industry's years of flouting the 1912 act had led it to the brink of disaster. Radio sales and profits dropped dramatically. Listeners were tired of the chaos. Stations arbitrarily changed frequencies, power, and hours of operation, and there was constant interference between stations, often intentional. Radio industry leaders petitioned Commerce Commissioner Herbert Hoover and, according to historian Erik Barnouw (1966)—who titled his book on radio's early days *A Tower in Babel*—"encouraged firmness" in government efforts to regulate and control the competitors. The government's response was a series of four National Radio Conferences involving industry experts, public officials, and government regulators. These conferences produced the Radio Act of 1927. Order was restored, and the industry prospered. But the broadcasters had made an important concession to secure this saving intervention. The 1927 act authorized them to *use* the channels, which belonged to the public, but not to *own* them. Broadcasters were thus simply the caretakers of the airwaves, a national resource.

The act further stated that when a license was awarded, the standard of evaluation would be the *public interest, convenience, or necessity*. The Federal Radio Commission (FRC) was established to administer the provisions of the act. This **trustee model** of regulation is based on two premises (Bittner, 1994). The first is the philosophy of **spectrum scarcity.** Because broadcast spectrum space is limited and not everyone who wants to broadcast can, those who are granted licenses to serve a local area must accept regulation. The second reason for regulation revolves around the issue of influence. Broadcasting reaches virtually everyone in society. By definition, this ensures its power.

The Communications Act of 1934 replaced the 1927 legislation, substituting the Federal Communications Commission (FCC) for the FRC and cementing its regulatory authority, which continues today.

WWW

Federal Communications Commission
www.fcc.gov

ADVERTISING AND THE NETWORKS

While the regulatory structure of the medium was evolving, so were its financial bases. The formation of RCA had ensured that radio would be a commercial, profit-based system. The industry supported itself through the sale of receivers; that is, it operated radio stations in order to sell radios. The problem was that once everybody had a radio, people would stop buying them. The solution was advertising. On August 22, 1922, New York station WEAF accepted the first radio commercial, a 10-minute spot for Long Island brownstone apartments. The cost of the ad was $50.

The sale of advertising led to establishment of the national radio networks. Groups of stations, or **affiliates,** could deliver larger audiences, realizing greater advertising revenues, which would allow them to hire bigger stars and produce better programming, which would attract larger audiences, which could be sold for even greater fees to advertisers. RCA set up a 24-station network, the National Broadcasting Company (NBC), in 1926. A year later it bought AT&T's stations and launched a second network, NBC Blue (the original NBC was renamed NBC Red). The

Columbia Broadcasting System (CBS) was also founded in 1927, but it struggled until 26-year-old millionaire cigar maker William S. Paley bought it in 1928, making it a worthy competitor to NBC. The fourth network, Mutual, was established in 1934 largely on the strength of its hit Western *The Lone Ranger*. Four midwestern and eastern stations came together to sell advertising on it and other shows; soon Mutual had 60 affiliates. Mutual differed from the other major national networks in that it did not own and operate its own flagship stations (called **O&Os,** for owned and operated). By 1938 the four national networks had affiliated virtually all the large U.S. stations and the majority of smaller operations as well. These corporations grew so powerful that in 1943 the government forced NBC to divest itself of one of its networks. It sold NBC Blue to Life Saver candy maker Edward Noble, who renamed it the American Broadcasting Company (ABC).

The fundamental basis of broadcasting in the United States was set:

- Radio broadcasters were private, commercially owned enterprises, rather than government operations.

- Governmental regulation was based on the public interest.

- Stations were licensed to serve specific localities, but national networks programmed the most lucrative hours with the largest audiences.

- Entertainment and information were the basic broadcast content.

- Advertising formed the basis of financial support for broadcasting.

THE GOLDEN AGE

The networks ushered in radio's golden age. Although the 1929–1939 Great Depression damaged the phonograph industry, with sales dipping to as few as 6 million records in 1932, it helped boost radio. Phonographs and records cost money, but once a family bought a radio, a whole world of entertainment and information was at its disposal, free of charge. The number of homes with radios grew from 12 million in 1930 to 30 million in 1940, and half of them had not one but two receivers. Ad revenues rose from $40 million to $155 million over the same period. Between them, the four national networks broadcast 156 hours of network-originated programming a week. New genres became fixtures during this period: comedy *(The Jack Benny Show, Fibber McGee and Molly)*, audience participation *(Professor Quiz, Truth or Consequences, Kay Kyser's Kollege of Musical Knowledge)*, children's shows *(Little Orphan Annie, The Lone Ranger)*, soap operas *(Oxydol's Ma Perkins, The Guiding Light)*, and drama (Orson Welles's *Mercury Theater of the Air)*. News, too, became a radio staple.

Radio and Sound Recording in World War II   The golden age of radio shone even more brightly after Pearl Harbor was bombed by the Japanese in 1941, propelling the United States into World War II. Radio was used to sell war bonds, and much content was aimed at boosting the nation's morale. The war increased the desire for news, especially from abroad. The war also caused a paper shortage, reducing advertising space in newspapers. No new stations were licensed during the war years, and the 950 existing broadcasters reaped all the broadcast advertising revenues, as well as additional ad revenues that otherwise would have gone to newspapers. Ad revenues were up to $310 million by the end of World War II in 1945.

Sound recording benefited from the war as well. Prior to World War II, recording in the United States was done either directly to master metal disc or on wire recorders, literally magnetic recording on metal wire. But GIs brought a new technology back from occupied Germany, a tape recorder that used an easily handled paper tape on a reel. In 1947, Columbia Records introduced a new 33⅓ rpm (rotations-per-minute) long-playing plastic record perfected by Peter Goldmark. A big advance over the previous standard of 78 rpm, it was more durable than the older shellac discs and played for 23 rather than 3⅓ minutes. Columbia offered the technology free to all other record companies. RCA refused the offer, introducing its own 45 rpm disc in 1948. It played for only 3⅓ minutes and had a huge center hole requiring a special adapter. Still, RCA persisted in its marketing, causing a speed war that was settled in 1950 when the two giants compromised on 33⅓ as the standard for classical music and 45 as the standard for pop. And it was the 45, the single, that sustained the music business until the mid-1960s, when the Beatles not only ushered in the "British invasion" of rock 'n' roll but also transformed popular music into a 33⅓ album-dominant cultural force, shaping today's popular music and helping reinvent radio.

Television Arrives   When the war ended and radio licenses were granted again, the number of stations grew rapidly to 2,000. Annual ad revenues reached $454 million in 1950. Then came television. Network affiliation dropped from 97% in 1945 to 50% by the mid-1950s, as stations "went local" in the face of television's national dominance. National radio advertising income dipped to $35 million in 1960, the year that television found its way into 90% of U.S. homes. If radio were to survive, it would have to find new functions.

George Burns and Gracie Allen were CBS comedy stars during radio's golden age. They were among the many radio performers to move easily and successfully to television.

Radio and Its Audiences

Radio has more than survived; it has prospered by changing the nature of its relationship with its audiences. The easiest way to understand this is to see pretelevision radio as television is today—nationally oriented, broadcasting an array of recognizable entertainment program formats, populated by well-known stars and personalities, and consumed primarily in the home, typically with people sitting around the set. Posttelevision radio is local, fragmented, specialized, personal, and mobile. Whereas pretelevision radio was characterized by the big national networks, today's radio is dominated by formats, a particular sound characteristic of a local station.

Who are the people who make up radio's audience? In an average week, more than 225 million people, 94% of all Americans 12 and over, will listen to the radio. Between the weekday hours of 6:00 and 10:00 a.m., 81% of all 12-year-olds and older will tune in. The majority of Americans, 60%, get their first news of the day from radio, and where the large majority of all listening once occurred in cars, this is no longer the case, as you can see in Figure 7.1.

Radio's audience, though, is not growing. In fact, it is declining. The annual *MTV Networks/Viacom Study of Media, Entertainment, and Leisure Time* released in June 2000 showed a sharp decline from the previous year's level of listening among teens and young adults ("Poll Says," 2000). Radio industry data also indicate a steady decline in listenership. In 1989, 17.5% of the population listened regularly to commercial radio. Today, the proportion is 15.4% (Fonda, 2004). Overall time spent listening to radio decreased 9% between 1993 and 1999, or approximately 2 hours a week (Rathburn, 2000). The primary factors in this loss of audience, according to the industry itself, are the availability of online music, listener dissatisfaction with unimaginative programming ("McRadio" to critics), and hypercommercialization—on average about 12 minutes of commercials an hour for a typical station, a 6% increase between 1998 and 1999 alone (Rathburn, 2000).

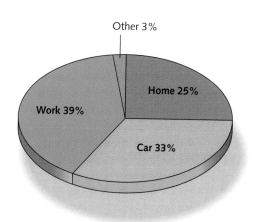

Figure 7.1 Where People Listen to the Radio. *Source:* Project for Excellence in Journalism, 2004.

Scope and Nature of the Radio Industry

There are 13,517 broadcast radio stations operating in the United States today: 4,761 commercial AM stations; 6,205 commercial FM stations; and 2,551 noncommercial FM stations.

There are more than two radios for every person in the United States. The industry as a whole sells about $20 billion a year of ad time (Television Bureau of Advertising, 2006). And despite declining listenership, advertisers annually spend more than $100 for every household in the country to buy air time (Lindsay, 2006).

FM, AM, AND NONCOMMERCIAL RADIO

Although FMs constitute only 57% of all commercial stations (to AMs' 43%), they attract 75% of all radio listeners. This has to do with the technology behind each. The FM (frequency modulation) signal is wider, allowing the

For more information on this topic, view Media Tours video clip #3, "Radio: Inside WKNE-FM," on the *Media World* DVD

broadcast not only of stereo but also of better fidelity to the original sound than the narrower AM (amplitude modulation) signal. As a result, people attracted to music, a radio staple, gravitate toward FM. People favoring news, sports, and information tend to find themselves listening to the AM dial. AM signals travel farther than FM signals, making them perfect for rural parts of the country. But rural areas tend to be less heavily populated, and most AM stations serve fewer listeners. The FCC approved stereo AM in 1985, but relatively few people have AM stereo receivers. There seems to be little demand for news, sports, and information in stereo.

FM came about as a result of the work begun in 1923 by inventor–innovator Edwin Armstrong. By 1935 Armstrong was demonstrating his technology, as well as stereo radio, to his financial benefactor, RCA's David Sarnoff. But RCA rejected this potential competitor to its AM domain to focus on television instead. So Armstrong turned to GE, and together they put the first FM station, W2XMN, on the air in 1939.

Many of today's FM stations are noncommercial—that is, they accept no advertising. When the national frequency allocation plan was established during the deliberations leading to the 1934 Communications Act, commercial radio broadcasters persuaded Congress that they alone could be trusted to develop this valuable medium. They promised to make time available for religious, children's, and other educational programming. No frequencies were set aside for noncommercial radio to fulfill these functions. At the insistence of critics who contended that the commercial broadcasters were not fulfilling their promise, in 1945 the FCC set aside all FM frequencies between 88.1 and 91.9 megahertz for noncommercial radio. Today these noncommercial stations not only provide local service, but many also offer national network quality programming through affiliation with National Public Radio (NPR) and Public Radio International (PRI) or through a number of smaller national networks, such as Pacifica Radio.

National Public Radio
www.npr.org

Public Radio International
www.pri.org

Pacifica Radio
www.pacifica.org

RADIO IS LOCAL

No longer able to compete with television for the national audience in the 1950s, radio began to attract a local audience. Because it costs much more to run a local television station than a local radio station, advertising rates on radio tend to be much lower than on television. Local advertisers can afford radio more easily than they can television, which increases the local flavor of radio. You can see where most listening occurs in Figure 7.1.

RADIO IS FRAGMENTED

Radio stations are widely distributed throughout the United States. Virtually every town—even those with only a few hundred residents—has at least one station. The number of stations licensed in an area is a function of both population and proximity to other towns. Tiny Long Beach, Mississippi, has one FM station. White Bluff, Texas, has one AM station. Chicago has 19 AMs and 30 FMs, and New York City has 17 AM and 28 FM stations. This fragmentation—many stations serving many areas—makes possible contemporary radio's most important characteristic, its ability to specialize.

RADIO IS SPECIALIZED

When radio became a local medium, it could no longer program the expensive, star-filled genres of its golden age. The problem now was how to program a station with interesting content and do so economically. A disc jockey playing records was the best solution. But stations soon learned that a highly specialized, specific audience of particular interest to certain advertisers could be attracted with specific types of music. **Format** radio was born. Of course, choosing a specific format means accepting that many potential listeners will not tune in. But in format radio the size of the audience is secondary to its composition.

Radio ratings service Arbitron annually recognizes about 50 different formats, from the most common, which include Country, Top 40, Album-Oriented Rock, and All Talk, to the somewhat uncommon, for example, Ethnic. Many stations, especially those in rural areas, offer **secondary services** (formats). For example, a country station may broadcast a religious format for 10 hours on Saturday and Sunday.

Format radio offers stations many advantages beyond low-cost operations and specialized audiences that appeal to advertisers. Faced with falling listenership or declining advertising revenues, a station can simply change disc jockeys (DJs) and discs. Neither television nor the print media have this content flexibility. When confronted with competition from a station with a similar format, a station can further narrow its audience by specializing its formula even more. Many midsize and large markets have Album-Oriented Rock (AOR), Hard Rock, Alternative Rock, Classic Rock, Heavy Metal, and Soft Rock stations. There are Country, Contemporary Country, Outlaw Country, Album Country, Spanish Country, and Young Country (YC) stations.

Music format radio requires a disc jockey. Someone has to spin the discs and provide the talk. The modern DJ is the invention of Todd Storz, who bought KOHW in Omaha, Nebraska, in 1949. He turned the radio personality/music formula on its head. Before Storz, radio announcers would talk most of the time and occasionally play music to rest their voices. Storz wanted more music, less talk. He thought radio should sound like a jukebox—the same few songs people wanted to hear played over and over again. His Top 40 format, which demanded strict adherence to a **playlist** (a predetermined sequence of selected records) of popular music for young people, up-tempo pacing, and catchy production gimmicks, became the standard for the posttelevision popular music station. Gordon McClendon of KLIF in Dallas refined the Top 40 format and developed others, such as Beautiful Music, and is therefore often considered, along with Storz, one of the two pioneers of format radio.

RADIO IS PERSONAL

With the advent of television, the relationship of radio and its audience changed. Whereas families had gathered around the radio set to listen together, we now listen to the radio alone. We select personally pleasing formats, and we listen as an adjunct to other personally important activities.

Fans debate whether Todd Storz or Gordon McClendon first invented the DJ. But there is no dispute that Alan Freed, first in Cleveland and then in New York, established the DJ as a star. Freed, here in a 1958 photo, is credited with introducing America's White teenagers to rhythm 'n' blues artists like Chuck Berry and Little Richard and ushering in the age of rock 'n' roll.

RADIO IS MOBILE

The mobility of radio accounts in large part for its personal nature. We can listen anywhere, at any time. We listen at work, while exercising, while sitting in the sun. By 1947 the combined sale of car and alarm clock radios exceeded that of traditional living-room receivers, and in 1951 the annual production of car radios exceeded that of home receivers for the first time. It has continued to do so every year since.

The Business of Radio

The distinctive characteristics of radio serve its listeners, but they also make radio a thriving business.

RADIO AS AN ADVERTISING MEDIUM

Ex-punk-rocker Billy Bragg has seen the future of American radio and rock 'n' roll, and it isn't pretty.

Advertisers enjoy the specialization of radio because it gives them access to homogeneous groups of listeners to whom products can be pitched. Since the entrenchment of specialized formats, there has not been a year in which annual **billings**—dollars earned from the sale of airtime—have declined. Advertisers buy local time (80% of all billings), national spots (for example, Prestone Antifreeze buys time on several thousand stations in winter areas), and network time. The cost of time is based on the ratings, an often controversial reality in radio (see the essay on p. 207, "Problems with Radio Ratings").

Radio is an attractive advertising medium for reasons other than its delivery of a homogeneous audience. Radio ads are inexpensive to produce and therefore can be changed, updated, and specialized to meet specific audience demands. Ads can also be specialized to different times of the day. For example, a hamburger restaurant may have one version of its commercial for the morning audience, in which its breakfast menu is touted, and a different version for the evening audience driving home, dreading the thought of cooking dinner. Radio time is inexpensive to buy, especially when compared with television. An audience loyal to a specific format station is presumably loyal to those who advertise on it. Radio is the listeners' friend; it travels with them and talks to them personally.

DEREGULATION AND OWNERSHIP

The business of radio is being altered by deregulation and changes in ownership rules. To ensure that there were many different perspectives in the cultural forum, the FCC had long limited the number of radio stations one person or company could own to 1 AM and 1 FM locally and 7 AMs and 7 FMs nationally. These numbers were revised upward in the late 1980s, and

Problems with Radio Ratings

Once radio became an advertising-based medium, some way was needed to count listeners so advertising rates could be set. The first rating system, the Crossleys, was begun in 1930 at the behest of the Association of National Advertisers, a group suspicious of broadcasters' own self-serving, exaggerated reports of audience size. Within 10 years, Hooper and Pulse were also offering radio ratings. All used random telephone calls, a method that ignored certain segments of the population (the rich and the poor, for example) and that could not accurately tap mobile use of the medium (such as listening in the car). In 1949 these companies and their methods were replaced by the American Research Bureau, later renamed Arbitron.

> **THE RATINGS—FLAWS AND ALL—ARE ACCEPTED AS THE FINAL WORD, AND BOTH RATINGS SERVICE AND BROADCASTERS PROFIT FROM THEIR USE.**

Arbitron mails diaries to willing listeners in every local market in the country and asks them to note what they listen to every 15 minutes for a period of 1 week. Arbitron reports:

- **Average quarter-hour:** the number of people listening to a station in each 15-minute segment
- **Cume:** the cumulative audience or number of people listening to a station for at least 5 minutes in any 1 day
- **Rating:** the percentage of the total population of a market reached
- **Share:** the percentage of people listening to radio who are tuned in to a particular station

These measures are sophisticated, but the use of diaries incurs some problems. Lying is one; forgetting is another. Uneven diary return rates among different types of audiences is a third. Yet advertisers and radio stations need some standard measure of listenership to set rates. Therefore, the ratings—flaws and all—are accepted as the final word, and both ratings service and broadcasters profit from their use.

As soon as a medium encounters a dip in audience numbers, however, the ratings come under scrutiny and are blamed for the problem. This was the case for radio, and it is the case for television, as you'll see in Chapter 8.

When radio first began losing audience to television, it tried to ignore the problem. The cover from the August 17, 1953, issue of *Broadcasting/Telecasting* vividly demonstrates this technique—the medium is said to be as strong as ever, as central to people's lives as always. But there was no ignoring the continuing and growing loss of listeners. At the September 17 meeting of the NBC Radio Affiliates in Chicago, and after 15 years of using the ratings to make huge profits, new

NBC president David Sarnoff (1953) offered this analysis of the dramatic drop in radio listenership:

> Our industry from the outset has been plagued by rating systems which do not say what they mean and do not mean what they say. They develop figures which give an appearance of precision, even unto decimal points, until you read the fine print.
>
> Unhappily these figures are seized upon by the advertising community as a substitute for analysis and judgment. They are used as the main standard for advertising values in broadcasting, and millions of dollars are spent or withheld each year on the basis of a drop or rise of a few ratings points! . . . Ratings, today, simply do not reflect the real audience. (p. 108)

The problem, in other words, was not the television-fueled exodus of millions of listeners—it was the ratings!

The Iowa radio station that bought space on the cover of the industry's "bible," Broadcasting/ Telecasting, *wanted readers to believe all was well in radio-land in 1953.*

controls were almost totally eliminated by the Telecommunications Act of 1996. Now, thanks to this **deregulation** there are no national ownership limits, and one person or company can own as many as 8 stations in one market, depending on the size of the market. This situation has allowed **duopoly**—one person or company owning and managing multiple radio stations in a single market—to explode. Since the passage of the 1996 act, more than 10,000 radio stations have been sold, and there are now 1,100 fewer station owners, a 30% decline. The vast majority of these sales have been to already large radio groups such as Clear Channel, Cumulus, and Citadel, with 1,207, 268, and 243 stations, respectively. As a result, in 25 of the 50 largest radio markets, three companies claim 80% of all listeners. In 43 different cities, one-third of the radio stations are owned by a single company; in 34 of those 43 cities, one company owns more than 8 stations (Moyers, 2003). Whereas all of Boston's 15 FMs and 14 of Seattle's 17 FMs are owned by four companies, each of the 12 FMs in Toronto, Canada, has a different owner.

This concentration is a source of concern for many radio professionals. Local public affairs shows now make up less than one-half of 1 percent of all commercial broadcast time in this country. Thirty-five percent of all commercial stations have no local news, and 25% have no local public affairs programming at all (FAIR, 2000). The American Federation of Television and Radio Artists has charged that giant group owners such as Clear Channel have "forever transformed and destroyed the radio and recording industries" (quoted in McConnell, 2002, p. 34). Media activist and scholar Robert McChesney agrees: "Radio has been destroyed. A medium that is arguably the least expensive and most accessible of our major media, that is ideally suited for localism, has been converted into a Wal-Mart-like profit machine for a handful of massive chains" (2004, p. 25). Ex-punk- and indie-rocker Billy Bragg commented dramatically on this situation: "I'm worried that we will end up with one record label, one radio station. I went to a place like that once; it was called the Soviet Union" (2004, p. 83). **Low Power FM (LPFM),** 10- to 100-watt nonprofit community radio stations with a reach of only a few miles, are one response to radio concentration. FCC plans to authorize LPFM in 1999 were met with stiff opposition from commercial station owners (already losing listeners) and public broadcasters (afraid of losing listeners to noncommercial competitors). Still, 675 LPFM stations, representing all 50 states, are now on air. Today, the Local Community Radio Act of 2005, co-sponsored by senators from both political parties, and designed to thwart renewed opposition from commercial and public broadcasters, promises to expand the service designed, according to the FCC, to "create opportunities for new voices on the airwaves" and "support programming responsive to local community needs and interests" (in *Free Press,* 2005, p. 1).

Scope and Nature of the Recording Industry

When the DJs and Top 40 formats saved radio in the 1950s, they also changed for all time popular music and, by extension, the recording industry. Disc jockeys were color-deaf in their selection of records. They introduced record

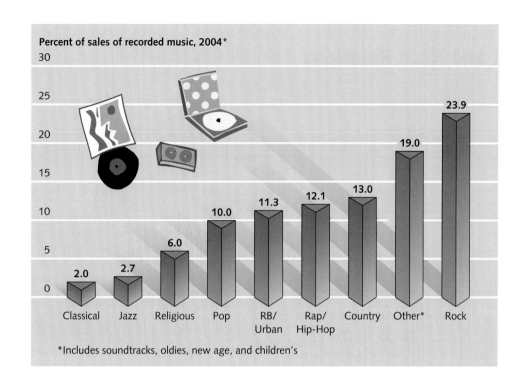

Percent of sales of recorded music, 2004*

Classical 2.0
Jazz 2.7
Religious 6.0
Pop 10.0
RB/Urban 11.3
Rap/Hip-Hop 12.1
Country 13.0
Other* 19.0
Rock 23.9

*Includes soundtracks, oldies, new age, and children's

Figure 7.2 Sales of Recorded Music by Type, 2004. *Source:* Record Industry Association of America (www.riaa.com).

buyers to rhythm 'n' blues in the music of African American artists such as Chuck Berry and Little Richard. Until the mid-1950s the work of these performers had to be **covered**—rerecorded by White artists such as Perry Como—before it was aired. Teens loved the new sound, however, and it became the foundation of their own subculture, as well as the basis for the explosion in recorded music. See the essay on page 210, "Rock 'n' Roll, Radio, and Race Relations" for more on rock's roots.

Today more than 5,000 U.S. companies are annually selling 600 million tapes and discs of recorded music (worth about $12 billion a year) on more than 10,000 labels (Seabrook, 2003). Customers in America annually buy one-third of the world's recorded music. See Figure 7.2 for an idea of what types of music are most popular.

THE MAJOR RECORDING COMPANIES

Four major recording companies control nearly 88% of the recorded music market in the United States. Two (Sony BMG and Universal) control more than 60% of the *world's* $28 billion global music market. Three of the four are foreign-owned:

Billboard Magazine
www.billboard.com

- Sony BMG, controlling 28% of the U.S. music market, is co-owned by two global media conglomerates, Japan's Sony and Germany's Bertlesmann. Its labels include Columbia, Epic, RCA, and Arista.
- New York–based Warner Music Group, controlling 16%, is owned by Edgar Bronfman and several private investors. Its labels include Atlantic, Electra, and Warner Brothers.

Rock 'n' Roll, Radio, and Race Relations

After World War II African Americans in the United States refused to remain invisible. Having fought in segregated units in Europe and proven their willingness to fight and die for freedom abroad, they openly demanded freedom at home. Some Whites began to listen. President Harry Truman, recognizing the absurdity of racial separation in the self-proclaimed "greatest democracy on earth," desegregated the armed forces by executive order in 1948. These early stirrings of equality led to a sense among African Americans that anything was possible, and that feeling seeped into their music. What had been called *cat, sepia,* or *race music* took on a new tone. While this new sound borrowed from traditional Black music—gospel, blues, and sad laments over slavery and racial injustice—it was different, much different. Rock historian Ian Whitcomb called it music about "gettin' loaded, wantin' a bow-legged woman, and rockin' all night long" (1972, p. 212). Music historian Ed Ward said that this bolder, more aggressive music "spoke to a shared experience, not just to Black (usually rural Black) life," and it would become the "truly biracial popular music in this country" (Ward, Stokes, & Tucker, 1986, p. 83).

But before this new music could begin its assault on the cultural walls that divided Americans, it needed a new name (to differentiate itself from older forms of race music and to appear "less Black" to White listeners). Hundreds of small independent record companies sprang up to produce this newly labeled rhythm and blues (R&B), music focusing on Americans' shared experience, and sex and alcohol were part of life for people of all colors. Songs such as Wynonie Harris's "Good Rockin' Tonight," Amos Milburn's "Chicken Shack Boogie," Stick McGhee's "Drinkin' Wine, Spo-De-O-Dee," and Wild Bill Moore's "We're Gonna Rock, We're Gonna Roll" (a song not about dancing) were, for their time, startlingly open in their celebration of sex (not to be confused with love) and drink. With its earthy lyrics and thumping dance beat, R&B very quickly found an audience in the 1950s, one composed largely of urban Blacks (growing in number as African Americans increasingly fled the South) and White teenagers.

The major record companies took notice, and rather than sign already successful R&B artists, they had their White artists cover the Black hits. The Penguins' "Earth Angel" was covered by the reassuringly named Crew Cuts, who also covered the Chords' "Sh-Boom." The McGuire Sisters covered the Spaniels' "Goodnight Sweetheart, Well It's Time to Go." Chuck Berry's "Maybellene" was covered by both the Johnny Long and Ralph Marterie orchestras. Even Bill Haley and the Comets' youth anthem "Shake, Rattle and Roll" was a cover of a Joe Turner tune.

> **R&B AND ROCK 'N' ROLL DID NOT END RACISM. BUT THE MUSIC MADE A DIFFERENCE, ONE THAT WOULD EVENTUALLY MAKE IT POSSIBLE FOR AMERICANS WHO WANTED TO DO SO TO FREE THEMSELVES FROM RACISM'S UGLY HOLD.**

But these covers actually served to introduce even more White teens to the new music, and these kids demanded the original versions. This did not escape the attention of Sam Phillips, who in 1952 founded Sun Records in an effort to bring Black music to White kids ("If I could find a White man who had the Negro sound, I could make a billion dollars," he is reported to have mused ["Why Elvis," 2002]). In 1954 he found that man: Elvis Presley.

The situation also caught the attention of Cleveland DJ Alan Freed, whose nationally distributed radio (and later television) show featured Black R&B tunes, never covers. Freed began calling the music he played rock 'n' roll (to signify that it was Black *and* White youth music), and by 1955, when Freed took his show to New York, the cover business was dead. Black performers were recording and releasing their own music to a national audience, and people of all colors were tuning in.

Now that the kids had a music of their own, and now that a growing number of radio stations were willing to program it, a youth culture began to develop, one that was antagonistic toward their parents' culture. The music was central to this antagonism, not only because it was gritty and nasty but also because it exposed the hypocrisy of adult culture. Nowhere was this more apparent than in Freed's 1953 rock 'n' roll concert at the Cleveland Arena. Although Cleveland was a segregated city, Freed opened the 9,000-seat venue to all the fans of his *Moondog's Rock and Roll Party* radio show. A racially mixed crowd of more than 18,000 teens showed up, forcing the cancellation of the concert. But the kids partied. They sang. They cheered. Not a single one asked for a refund. They had come—Black kids and White kids—to celebrate *their* music, *their* culture.

For young people of the mid-1950s and 1960s, the music of Little Richard, Fats Domino, Ray Charles, and Chuck Berry made a lie of all that their parents, teachers, and government leaders had said about race, the inferiority of African Americans, and Blacks' satisfaction with the status quo. As social critic Robert Pielke wrote,

> A different and conflicting set of fundamental values was introduced into American culture, acquainting white adolescents with the black side of America in the process. But more important than even this was the fact of communication itself: the years of slavery and segregation had made it virtually impossible for the races to communicate honestly face to face. Now, for the first time in American history, whites were authentically hearing what blacks were saying. . . . To be more accurate, it was principally white youth who were doing the listening.

The music of Chuck Berry, Bo Diddley, and Little Richard may have been covered by White performers, but its passion and soul soon attracted young listeners of all races, making a lie of their parents' racial intolerance.

Prejudice, ignorance, superstition, hatred, and fear can only exist in the absence of genuine communication. . . . I don't mean to give the impression that white adolescents, en masse bought into black culture. Hardly. . . . [But] what was really significant was the fact that they were truly listening. It shouldn't seem so strange, then, that it was precisely this generation that found itself uncomfortable with the whole ideology of racism and all its attendant beliefs. Not that racism immediately came to an end with the listening to black music. Far from it. But white youth could no longer feel secure with the attitudes bequeathed to them; they now knew too much. (1986, p. 87)

Ralph Bass, a producer for independent R&B label Chess Records, described the evolution to historian David Szatmary. When he was touring with Chess's R&B groups in the early 1950s, "they didn't let whites into the clubs. Then they got 'white spectator tickets' for the worst corner of the joint.

They had to keep the white kids out, so they'd have white nights sometimes, or they'd put a rope across the middle of the floor. The blacks on one side, the whites on the other, digging how the blacks were dancing and copying them. Then, hell, the rope would come down, and they'd all be dancing together. Salt and pepper all mixed together" (Szatmary, 2000, p. 21).

R&B and rock 'n' roll did not end racism. But the music made a difference, one that would eventually make it possible for Americans who wanted to do so to free themselves of racism's ugly hold. Rock music (and the radio stations that played it) would again nudge the nation toward its better tendencies during the antiwar and civil rights movements of the late 1960s. And it is against this backdrop, a history of popular music making as real a difference as any piece of official legislation, that contemporary critics lament the homogenizing of popular music (see p. 213). Music can and has made a difference. Can and will it ever again? they ask.

The music of The Doors, Busta Rhymes, Nelly, Beastie Boys, Bob Seeger, the Beatles, and B2K is in demand by advertisers for their TV commercials. Among them, who has "sold out" and who has "remained true" to the rebellious spirit of rock and rap? Check your answers by reading the essay entitled "Rock and Rap: Selling or Selling Out?"

- Universal Music Group, controlling 35%, is owned by French conglomerate Vivendi Universal and controls labels such as MCA.
- EMI Records, 9 percent, is owned by England's EMI Group and controls labels such as BMI, Capitol, and Def Jam Records.

Critics voice concern over conglomeration and internationalization in the music business, a concern that centers on the traditional cultural value of music, especially for young people. Multibillion-dollar conglomerates typically are not rebellious in their cultural tastes, nor are they usually willing to take risks on new ideas. These duties have fallen primarily to the independent labels, companies such as Real World Records and IRS. Still, problems with the music industry–audience relationship remain.

WWW
Future of Music Coalition
www.futureofmusic.org

Cultural homogenization is the worrisome outcome of virtually all the world's influential recording being controlled by a few profit-oriented giants. If bands or artists cannot immediately deliver the goods, they aren't signed. So derivative artists and manufactured groups dominate—for example, Britney Spears and Hillary Duff. In fact, when Universal bought Polygram in 1998, it immediately announced that it would drop 250 artists from both companies' lists to focus on teen pop bands such as the Backstreet Boys. Epic Records' Harvey Leeds, senior vice president of artist development, explained, "The days of developing a band are gone. They're manufactured, not developed on the street. Instead of 'There's a new band that's huge in Gainesville, we'd better pay attention,' today they're created in a laboratory" (as quoted in Waller, 2000, p. 1).

The *dominance of profit over artistry* worries many music fans. When a major label must spend millions to sign a bankable group such as R.E.M. ($80 million), Mariah Carey ($80 million), or Whitney Houston ($100 million), it typically pares lesser-known, potentially more innovative artists from its roster. EMI, for example, dropped 400 artists from its various labels in early 2002 in order to come up with the $57 million, five-album deal it thought it needed to keep British pop star Robbie Williams from defecting to another company. Critics fear that the tenuous relationship that "minor" artists have with their conglomerated labels leads to *infringement of artistic freedom.* Said Phyllis Pollack, press agent for rap groups such as NWA and Geto Boys, "It's like we almost have a McCarthyism in the business. But the censorship isn't new; what's new is the fear and the compliance going on to this extent. And I think a lot of artists go along with it because they're afraid of being lost in the corporate shuffle and falling out of favor with their labels" (quoted in Strauss, 2000, p. 5G).

Critics and industry people alike see the ascendance of profits over artistry as a problem for the industry itself, as well as for the music and its listeners. Worldwide record industry sales dropped more than 14% between 2002 and 2003, a loss of more than $3 billion in sales. In the United States alone, more than 100 million fewer units were sold in those 2 years than in the previous 2. The number of music CDs sold fell nearly 8% from 2004 to 2005 (Bart, 2006). Sales of all album music, including digital downloads, dropped from 785 million units in 2000 to fewer than 602 million in 2005 (Bing, 2006). The reason, say many music critics, is not Internet piracy, as asserted by the recording industry, but the industry itself.

WWW
Rock Out Censorship
www.theroc.org

Rock and Rap: Selling or Selling Out?

Rock and rap began as rebellious music, art with attitude. They questioned contemporary thinking about war, culture, race, sex, materialism, adulthood, the police. We've already seen how youngsters' embrace of rock 'n' roll helped confront 1950s racism. In the late 1960s in "For What It's Worth," rockers Buffalo Springfield challenged the Vietnam War and police crackdowns on antiwar protests: "Something's happening here, what it is ain't exactly clear, there's a man with a gun over there, telling me I've got to beware. . . . Young people speaking their mind, getting so much resistance from behind." Crosby, Stills, Nash, and Young, in "Ohio," called President Nixon to task by name for the 1970 shooting of four Kent State University students by the National Guard: "Tin soldiers and Nixon's coming, we're finally on our own, this summer I hear the drumming, four dead in Ohio." In 2003 rapper Jay-Z challenged listeners, taking on racism, the police, and racial profiling in "99 Problems."

Music of protest, the voice of the young generation, or the hip sound track for television commercials? Consolidation in radio and recording has placed the cultural role of popular music squarely in the cultural forum.

For many, the obituary for popular music as the voice of protest has already been written. Here's *New York Times* editor Brent Staples' eulogy: "Independent radio stations that once would have played edgy, political music have been gob-

> BUSTA RHYMES TITLED HIS ODE TO HIS FAVORITE DRINK "PASS THE COURVOISIER." NELLY SUNG SO LONG AND SO PROFITABLY FOR NIKE'S AIR FORCE 1 SNEAKERS THAT THE SHOEMAKER NOW MARKETS NELLY NIKES, 50 CENT RHYMES FOR REEBOK, AND RUN-DMC RAPS ABOUT "MY ADIDAS."

bled up by corporations that control hundreds of stations and have no wish to rock the boat. Corporate ownership has changed what gets played—and who plays it. With a few exceptions, the disc jockeys who once discovered provocative new music have long since been put out to pasture. The new generation operates from play lists dictated by Corporate Central—lists that some DJs describe as 'wallpaper music'" (2003, p. A30).

But the issue that continues to inflame debate in the cultural forum is the use of "our music" to sell "their products," that is, the selling out of rap and rock to advertising. Among the most famous incidents was Nike's use of the Beatles' "Revolution" to sell sneakers. Michael Jackson owned the rights to the Beatles catalogue at the time and when he licensed this classic to the sneaker maker, the surviving ex-Beatles complained loudly. No more Beatles tunes have been sold for commercials; in fact, ex-Beatle Sir Paul McCartney bought the catalogue back from Jackson in part to ensure that their songs would never be used in commercials again. The Doors have steadfastly refused to license their music for commercials, as have Neil Young, the Beastie Boys, Bruce Springsteen, Pearl Jam, James Taylor, R.E.M., and Tom Waits. The latter went as far as to successfully sue Frito-Lay for using a soundalike in a television spot.

But there is money to be made from what is, after all, a commodity, something that is bought and sold—popular

As music critic John Seabrook explains, "The record industry has helped to create these thieving, lazy, and disloyal fans. By marketing superficial, disposable pop stars, labels persuade fans to treat the music as superficial and disposable." He quotes legendary music producer Malcolm McLaren: "The amazing thing about the death of the record industry is that no one cares. If the movie industry died, you'd probably have a few people saying, 'Oh, this is too bad—after all, they gave us Garbo and Marilyn Monroe.' But now the record industry is dying, and no one gives a damn" (2003, p. 52). What kept the red ink from flowing even faster was strong sales in **catalogue albums** (more than 30% of all discs sold), albums more than 3 years old. However, sales of **recent catalogue albums,** that is, those that have been out for 15 months to 3 years, have fallen dramatically over the last 5 years, further damaging the industry's bottom line. "Recent catalogue" cannot become "catalogue" unless a label stays with an artist, allowing him or her to grow, possibly through three or four albums. Look at the music. Sting's "Desert Rose" and the Clash's "London Calling" are used to sell Jaguar automobiles; Microsoft uses the music of Madonna and Budweiser pitchmen/rockers the Rolling Stones to promote Windows. Kid Rock pushes beer, too—Coors. Bob Seeger's "Like a Rock" has been the theme song for Chevy truck commercials since 1991. Bob Dylan, who rose to prominence singing songs of protest and alienation, touts Victoria's Secret lingerie and bank services. Rappers Ms. Jade and Timbaland collected $300,000 for a Hummer H2 product placement in their *Ching Ching* music video. Epic Records actively pursues paid product placements for B2K videos and has told sponsors that it would accept product placements for "most of our pop acts" (Kaufman, 2003). Busta Rhymes titled his ode to his favorite drink "Pass the Courvoisier." Nelly has sung so long and so profitably for Nike's Air Force 1 sneakers that the shoemaker now markets Nelly Nikes; 50 Cent rhymes for Reebok, and Run-DMC raps about "My Adidas."

Enter your voice in the cultural forum. Do you think that this is no big deal; after all, it's only pop music? Why shouldn't entertainers make as much money as they can from their work? Or do you think that by cheapening the music—selling out—music's role in the culture, especially for young people, is altered? We've seen elsewhere in this chapter that some critics argue that transforming music into a superficial, disposable commodity encourages piracy and hurts sales. And how do you respond to Doors drummer John Densmore, who once turned down $15 million from Cadillac to use "Break on Through" in an SUV commercial? "The bottom line is that our songs have a higher purpose, like keeping the integrity of their original meaning for our fans," he said. "Many kids have said to me that 'Light My Fire,' for example, was playing when they first made love or were fighting in Nam or got high—

pivotal moments in their lives" (2003, p. 45). Is this simply nostalgia for a different time, a time when the music mattered? Does music still matter? Can an artist sell products and not sell out?

Rapper or Reebok salesman?

names of the best-selling albums and artists in Figure 7.3. How many recent or current artists and albums do you think will ever join these ranks? Critics of the ascendance of profits over artistry argue that the industry simply lacks the patience to develop careers.

Promotion overshadows the music, say the critics. If groups or artists don't come across well on MTV or are otherwise a challenge to promote (for example, they do not fit an easily recognizable niche), they aren't signed. Again, the solution is to create marketable artists from scratch. Promoting tours is also an issue. If bands or artists do not have corporate sponsorship for their tours, there is no tour. If musicians do not tour, they cannot create an enthusiastic fan base. But if they do not have an enthusiastic fan base, they cannot attract the corporate sponsorship necessary to mount a tour. This makes radio even more important for the introduction of new artists and forms of music, but radio, too, is increasingly driven by profit-maximizing format narrowing and therefore dependent on the major labels'

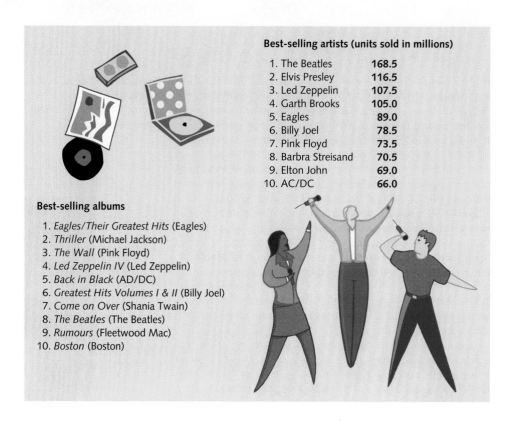

Figure 7.3 The Top 10 Best-selling Albums and Artists of All Time, U.S. Sales Only.

Source: Recording Industry Association of America (www.riaa.com).

Best-selling artists (units sold in millions)

1. The Beatles — 168.5
2. Elvis Presley — 116.5
3. Led Zeppelin — 107.5
4. Garth Brooks — 105.0
5. Eagles — 89.0
6. Billy Joel — 78.5
7. Pink Floyd — 73.5
8. Barbra Streisand — 70.5
9. Elton John — 69.0
10. AC/DC — 66.0

Best-selling albums

1. *Eagles/Their Greatest Hits* (Eagles)
2. *Thriller* (Michael Jackson)
3. *The Wall* (Pink Floyd)
4. *Led Zeppelin IV* (Led Zeppelin)
5. *Back in Black* (AD/DC)
6. *Greatest Hits Volumes I & II* (Billy Joel)
7. *Come on Over* (Shania Twain)
8. *The Beatles* (The Beatles)
9. *Rumours* (Fleetwood Mac)
10. *Boston* (Boston)

definition of playable artists. The essay on page 214, "Rock and Rap: Selling or Selling Out" discusses another form of hypercommercialism in the music business.

Trends and Convergence in Radio and Sound Recording

Emerging and changing technologies have affected the production and distribution aspects of both radio and sound recording.

THE IMPACT OF TELEVISION

We have seen how television fundamentally altered radio's structure and relationship with its audiences. Television, specifically cable channel MTV, changed the recording industry too. MTV's introduction in 1981 helped pull the industry out of its disastrous 1979 slump. However, it altered the radio–record company relationship, and many hits are now introduced on MTV rather than on radio. In addition, the look of concerts has changed. No longer is it sufficient to pack an artist or group into a hall or stadium with a few thousand screaming fans. Now a concert must be an extravagant multimedia event approximating the sophistication of an MTV video. This means that fewer acts take to the road, changing the relationship between musicians and fans.

SATELLITE AND CABLE

The convergence of radio and satellite has aided the rebirth of the radio networks. Music and other forms of radio content can be distributed quite inexpensively to thousands of stations. As a result, one "network" can provide very different services to its very different affiliates. ABC, for example, maintains networks under the names of Disney and ESPN. Westwood One, which bought the NBC Radio network in 1987 and added it to its already large and varied networking and program **syndication** operations, counts among its affiliates 60% of all the commercial stations in the United States. The low cost of producing radio programming, however, makes the establishment of other, even more specialized networks possible. Satellites, too, make access to syndicated content and formats affordable for many stations. Syndicators can deliver news, top 10 shows, and other content to stations on a market-by-market basis. They can also provide entire formats, requiring local stations, if they wish, to do little more than insert commercials into what appears to listeners to be a local broadcast.

Satellite has another application as well. Many listeners now receive "radio" through their cable televisions in the form of satellite-delivered **DMX (Digital Music Express).** Direct satellite home, office, and automobile delivery of audio by **digital audio radio service (DARS),** although still relatively new, has begun to attract listeners, especially when the two providers—XM Satellite Radio, first operational in 2001, and Sirius, debuting in 2002—began programming personalities like Howard Stern, Bob Dylan, and Oprah Winfrey and striking deals with major league baseball, the National Basketball Association, and the National Football League. Home delivery by cable and satellite television has also helped draw subscribers. The larger of the two competitors, XM, has 6 million subscribers listening to 150 channels of music, talk, news, comedy, and sports (Figure 7.4). Sirius, with 3.3 million listeners, offers 120 channels. On both, music channels are commercial-free,

XM Radio
www.xmradio.com

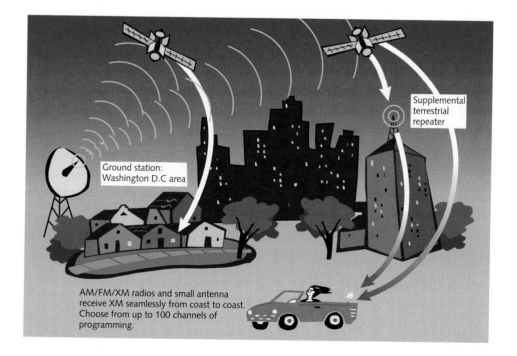

Figure 7.4 The operation of DARS provider XM Satellite Radio.

and listeners appear to enjoy the combination of more variety and no commercials, as only 1.5% a year try, and then drop, the service ("Battle," 2006). But satellite radio's true impact on the radio and recording industries may be something more than simply offering a greater variety of listening options. Because despite the fact that traditional radio station operators continue to dismiss satellite radio for its small audience (even the 45 million listeners anticipated by 2010), those same operators have begun to change the sound of their stations in response to the new technology. They are reducing the number of commercials they air, adding hundreds of new songs and artists to their playlists, and introducing new formats. Many are also beefing up their local news operations. Both radio and popular music should be better for the change (Manly, 2005).

MOBILE PHONES AND THE SOUND OF MONEY

Digital technology, so much a threat to the traditional recording industry business model, has helped the labels' balance sheets in an unlikely manner—the sale of music to mobile phones. Ring-tone downloads, people downloading recorded music to serve as the alerting sound on their phones, is already a global $5 billion business, expected to grow to nearly $7 billion by 2010 (Siklos, 2005). For the record labels, this income is equivalent to "found money," as it is generated from fragments of already existing recordings. Add to this the $875 million the industry earned in 2006 from full-track downloads to mobile phones (an amount expected to increase to $1.4 billion by 2008), and it is clear that mobile music provides a valuable new revenue stream for the recording business (McLean, 2006). Although Europe and Asia provide most of the activity in both types of downloading right now, American consumers are expected to catch up as manufacturers make available more sophisticated services and handsets capable of delivering, storing, and playing music. Two notable examples are Motorola's ROKR phone and Verizon's Vcast Music Service.

TERRESTRIAL DIGITAL RADIO

Since late 2002, 450 radio stations have begun broadcasting **terrestrial** (land-based) **digital radio.** Another 2,000 have committed to the technology. Relying on digital compression technology called **in-band-on-channel (IBOC),** terrestrial digital radio allows broadcasters to transmit not only their usual analog signal, but one or more digital signals using their existing spectrum space. And although IBOC also improves sound fidelity for both AM and FM, most stations using the technology see its greatest value in pay services, for example, subscription data delivery. IBOC proponents optimistically predict that terrestrial digital radio will completely replace analog radio by 2017 (Fleishman, 2005).

WEB RADIO AND PODCASTING

Radio's convergence with digital technologies is nowhere more pronounced and potentially profound than in **Web radio,** the delivery of "radio" directly to individual listeners over the Internet, and in **podcasting,** recording and downloading of audio files stored on servers, or, in the words of *Fortune* technology writer Peter Lewis, "Simultaneously a rebellion against the blandness of commercial radio, a demonstration of time shifting for radio, just as TiVo allows time shifting for television, and a celebration of the Internet's power to let individuals offer their own voices to a global audience" (2005, p. 204).

First, Web radio. Tens of thousands of "radio stations" exist on the Web in one of two forms. *Radio simulcasts* are traditional, over-the-air stations transmitting their signals online. Some simply re-create their original broadcasts, but more often, the simulcast includes additional information, such as song lyrics or artists' biographical information and concert dates. To find one of the more than 20,000 online simulcasts worldwide, simply search the Web using a station's call letters or go to radio-directory.com or www.live365.com.

Bitcasters, Web-only radio stations, can be accessed only online. The thousands of Web-only stations are either fee-based commercial operations such as www.spinner.com offering multiple channels of music, free of commercials and DJ chatter, or they are narrowly targeted bitcasts, such as www.khaha.com, a Los Angeles comedy station, and www.cprxtreme.com, a Christian station Webcasting from Glendale, California. To access Web radio, users must have file compression software such as RealPlayer (available for free at www.real.com) that permits **streaming,** the simultaneous downloading and accessing—playing—of digital audio or video data.

Podcasts, however, because they are posted online, do not require streaming software. They can be downloaded, either on demand or automatically (typically by subscription), to any digital device that has an MP3 player, including PCs, laptops, and iPods. The necessary downloading software is available online for free at www.ipodder.org. You probably already have the required uploading and recording software, the free Audacity MP3 recorder bundled with Windows. It's also available for Macintosh PCs and those that rely on the Linux operating system.

Nearly 10,000 podcasters are now online, and they cover every conceivable topic on which an individual or organization cares to comment. And while podcasting was begun in earnest in 2004 by individual techies, audio bloggers, and DJ-wannabes, within a year they were joined by "professional" podcasters such as record companies, commercial and public radio stations, and big media companies like ESPN, CNN, Bravo, and Disney. Technologists predict that by 2010, as MP3 players become more popular and as broadband Internet access becomes more prevalent, podcasting will be standard Web usage in 12.3 million American homes (Ho, 2005).

DIGITAL TECHNOLOGY

In the 1970s the basis of both the recording and radio industries changed from analog to **digital recording.** That is, sound went from being preserved as waves, whether physically on a disc or tape or through the air, to conversion into 1s and 0s logged in millisecond intervals in a computerized translation process. When replayed at the proper speed, the resulting sound was not only continuous but pristine—no hum, no hiss. The CD, or compact disc, was introduced in 1983 using digital coding on a 4.7-inch disc read by a laser beam. In 1986 *Brothers in Arms* by Dire Straits became the first million-selling CD. In 1988 the sale of CDs surpassed that of vinyl discs for the first time, and today CDs account for 90% of all music sales (Figure 7.5).

WWW

Web Radio
www.radio-directory.com

For more information on this topic, see Media Talk video clip #13, "Radio of the Future May Be on the Internet," on the *Media World* DVD.

WWW

Real Player
www.real.com

WWW

Podcasting
www.ipodder.org

Figure 7.5 Sales of Recorded Music by Format, 2004. *Source:* Adapted from Record Industry Association of America (www.riaa.com).

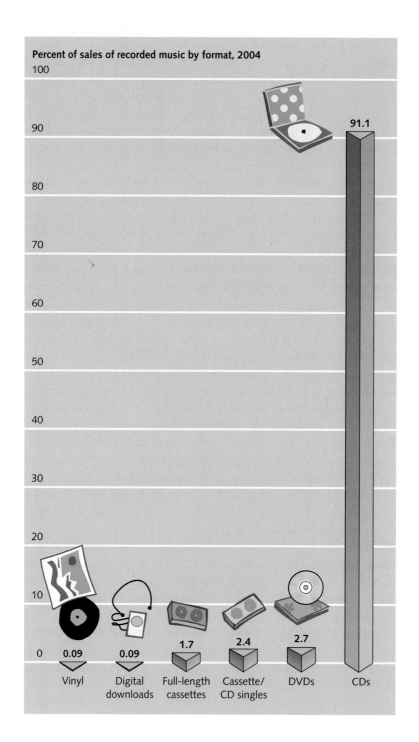

Percent of sales of recorded music by format, 2004

Format	Percent
Vinyl	0.09
Digital downloads	0.09
Full-length cassettes	1.7
Cassette/CD singles	2.4
DVDs	2.7
CDs	91.1

Sirius Radio
www.siriusradio

Convergence with computers and the Internet offers other challenges and opportunities to the radio and recording industries. The way the recording industry operates is likely to be altered by the Internet. Traditionally, a record company signs an artist, produces the artist's music, and promotes the artist and music through a variety of outlets but primarily through the distribution of music to radio stations. Then listeners, learning about the artist and music through radio, go to a record store and buy the music. But this is rapidly changing. Head of Country Music Television, Brian Philips, explains, "The old logic of just get something played a lot on the radio and it will sell seems less and less to be predictably true. . . . The winners these days are

It isn't only unknown indie bands gravitating to the Net to get their music to fans. The Beastie Boys are among the big-name artists going online.

people who can imagine beyond the narrow limitations of the old system" (in Klaassen, 2005c, p. 12). Using the Internet to "imagine beyond the old system" takes a number of forms. One is promotion. Although radio remains the main driver of music sales, labels, big and small, are using direct-to-consumer Net campaigns to boost their artists. Another is distribution. Numerous sites exist at which consumers can buy recorded music. CD Universe (cduniverse.com) and Amazon.com are two of the better known. With the appropriate software, users can sample music before they buy it.

But artists themselves are using the Internet for their own production, promotion, and distribution, bypassing radio and the recording companies altogether. Musicians are using their own sites, social networking sites such as MySpace (www.myspace.com), and sites designed specifically to feature new artists, such as purevolume.com, to connect directly with listeners. Fans can hear (and in some cases, even download) new tunes for free, buy music downloads, CDs, and merchandise, get concert information and tickets, and chat with artists and other fans. You may never have heard of the bands Hawthorne Heights, My Chemical Romance, or Relient K, but using the Internet they have created "a new middle class of popular music: acts that can make a full-time living selling only a modest number of discs, on the order of 50,000 to 500,000 per release" (Howe, 2005a, p. 203). Big-name artists, too, are gravitating to the Web. Public Enemy released *There's a Poison Going On* exclusively online through Atomic Pop (www.atomicpop.com) and the Beastie Boys' 2004 *Call Me, Boroughs* appeared simultaneously online and in stores.

WWW

Online Music Sites
WWW.
purevolume.com
atomicpop.com

The Internet and the Future of the Recording Industry

This direct-to-fans model of production, promotion, and distribution is giving rise to what intellectual property expert Eben Moglen calls the "Pay Artists, Not Owners" movement. Because of the Internet, he writes, "Audiences and

artists don't need the middlemen anymore. Their reason for being is defunct" (2003, p. 32). How this seismic shift in the music industry will eventually play out is still open to question, but the revolution began with the development of **MP3** (for MPEG-1, Audio Layer 3), compression software that shrinks audio files to less than a tenth of their original size. Originally developed in 1987 in Germany by computer scientist Dieter Seitzer at the University of Erlangen in conjunction with the Fraunhofer Institute Integrierte Schaltungen, it began to take off in the early 1990s as more users began to hook up to the Net with increasingly faster **modems.** This **open source software,** or freely downloaded software, permits users to download recorded music, and it is available at sites such as www.MP3.com and www.MP3.box.sk. In addition to "brandless" MP3, users can access commercial versions of the software such as MusicMatch, which offers additional features such as selectable levels of audio quality, the capacity to turn music from home CDs into computer files, and compatibility with other audio streaming technology such as Liquid Audio, a2b, MS Audio, and G2.

The crux of the problem for recording companies is that they sell music "in its physical form," whereas MP3, in either its open source or commercial format, permits music's distribution in a nonphysical form. First conceived of as a means of allowing independent bands and musicians to post their music online where it might attract a following, MP3 became a headache for the recording industry when music from the name artists they controlled began appearing on MP3 sites, making **piracy,** the illegal recording and sale of copyrighted material and high-quality recordings, a relatively simple task. Not only could users listen to their downloaded music from their hard drives, but they could make their own CDs from MP3 files and play those discs wherever and whenever they wished. Matters were made even worse for the recording companies when manufacturers such as Diamond Multimedia introduced portable MP3 players, freeing downloaded music from users' computers. And as software such as Napster became popular, users could easily search for and retrieve individual songs and artists from one another's hard drives.

Rather than embrace MP3, the Recording Industry Association of America (RIAA), representing all of the United States' major labels, responded to the threat with a technological solution. But by the time the industry's "secure" technology was ready for release, it was too late—MP3 had become the technology of choice among digital audio fans. The RIAA went to court in January 2000, and it was victorious. Citing MP3.com's database of more than 80,000 albums, a federal judge in New York ruled that the primary application of MP3 was copying and distributing copyrighted material, not simply storing already purchased music. Soon after, the RIAA and MP3.com (the Net's primary distributor of MP3 files) reached a settlement in which the online company paid $100 million to the record companies in exchange for the right to legally distribute their music. Now, downloading primarily takes two forms—from industry-approved and **P2P** sites.

INDUSTRY-APPROVED DOWNLOADING

Illegal file sharing proved the popularity of downloading music from the Internet. So the five major labels combined to offer three "approved" music download sites—pressplay.com (now napster.com), emusic.com, and music net.com. All three were operative by 2002, and none did well. They offered

downloads by subscription, that is, so many downloads per month for a set fee. In addition, they placed encrypted messages in the tunes that limited how long the song would be playable and where the download could be used and copied. As a result, illegal file sharing continued.

In late 2003 the labels rolled out two nontechnological responses to piracy and declining sales. First, they reduced the price of CDs from an average of $19 to about $10. Second, they started suing some of the country's 67 million individual music-downloaders, a public relations disaster. "Suing your own customers is not a sustainable business model," wrote copyright lawyer Eben Moglen (2003, p. 31). There was a technological response as well, but from a computer company. In April of that year Apple Computers unveiled its iTunes Music Store, featuring the simple sale of albums and individual songs for as little as 99 cents. Apple controlled only 5% of the PC market, yet it sold over a million tunes in its first week of operation. The company immediately announced an upcoming Windows version, and similar services quickly hit the Web; buymusic.com and Listen.com's Rhapsody were two. This activity led Warner Brothers CEO Tom Whalley to enthuse, "This is what the people who are willing to pay for music have been looking for all along" (quoted in Oppelaar, 2003, p. 42). For many observers, CEO Whalley's comments signaled the industry's recognition of the inevitability of the cyber revolution. The distribution and sale of music by Internet would soon be the standard. That future is at hand: In the first half of 2003, more than 600 U.S. brick-and-mortar music stores closed their doors (Kava, 2003). Inexpensive, permanent downloads are now available on the industry's formerly unsuccessful legal sites, as well as outlets like Wal-Mart and Starbucks.

P2P Downloading

Illegal downloading does still occur. Sites such as Gnutella, Freenet, Limewire, Morpheus, BearShare, and eDonkey use P2P technologies, that is, peer-to-peer software that permits direct Internet-based communication or collaboration between two or more personal computers while bypassing centralized servers. P2P allows users to visit a constantly and infinitely changing network of machines through which file sharing can occur. The record companies (and movie studios) challenged P2P by suing the makers of its software. In 2005,

Apple had one answer to piracy: cheap, permanent, go-anywhere downloads.

the Supreme Court, in *MGM v. Grokster,* unanimously supported industry arguments that P2P software, because it "encouraged" copyright infringement, rendered its makers liable for that illegal act. The industry's next challenge, then, is **BitTorrent,** file-sharing software that allows anonymous users to create "swarms" of data as they simultaneously download and upload "bits" of a given piece of content from countless, untraceable servers. BitTorrent now accounts for fully one-third of all data sent across the Net (Thompson, 2005) and one-half of all illegal file-sharing ("File-Sharing," 2004).

No matter what model of music production and distribution eventually results from this technological and financial tumult, serious questions about the Net's impact on **copyright** (protecting content creators' financial interest in

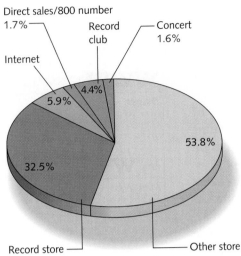

Direct sales/800 number
1.7%
Record club
Concert 1.6%
Internet
4.4%
5.9%
53.8%
32.5%
Record store
Other store

Figure 7.6 Where We Buy Our Music, 2004. *Source:* Record Industry Association of America (www.riaa.org).

their product) will remain. There is more on copyright in Chapter 14. But for now, the 50 million CD burners (copiers) now in use pose an additional threat. As it is, 40% of today's CD buyers already own this technology, and just under 1.25 billion blank CDs are sold in North America every year, 6 billion worldwide. The labels' response to this threat is copy-proof CDs. The first of these were released in early 2002 to negative reaction from buyers and even from some in the recording industry. "I don't think the technology is perfected to a point where it can prevent copying," said Eminem's manager Paul Rosenberg. "The only thing it's going to do is get the fans angry. People who spend money won't be able to play the disc everywhere they want to, and that isn't fair." This sentiment was echoed by a spokeswoman for Philips, the Dutch electronic company that invented the CD. "We are concerned about technology that limits the playability of the CD, because multiple uses of the CD in devices has been the foundation of its success," said Jeannet Harpe (both quoted in Cohen, 2002, pp. 43–44). Philips told the labels that it could not use its familiar CD logo on any copy-protected discs. You can see where we buy our music in Figure 7.6.

DEVELOPING MEDIA LITERACY SKILLS
Listening to Shock Jocks

The proliferation of shock jocks—outrageous, rude, crude radio personalities—offers an example of the importance of media literacy that may not be immediately apparent. Yet it involves four different elements of media literacy: development of an awareness of media's impact, cultivation of an understanding of media content as a text that provides insight into our culture and our lives, awareness of the process of mass communication, and an understanding of the ethical demands under which media professionals operate (Chapter 1). Different media literate radio listeners judge the shock jocks differently, but they all take time to examine their work and their role in the culture.

The literate listener asks this question of shock jocks and the stations that air them: "At what cost to the culture as a whole, and to individuals living in it, should a radio station program an offensive, vulgar personality to attract listeners and, therefore, profit?" Ours is a free society, and freedom of expression is one of our dearest rights. Citing their First Amendment rights, as well as strong listener interest, radio stations have made Howard Stern and other shock jocks like him the fashion of the day. Stern, for example, took poorly rated WXRX in New York to Number 1, and, as Infinity Broadcasting's top attraction, he was syndicated throughout the country where he was free to pray for cancer to kill public officials he did not like, joke constantly about sexual and other bodily functions, make sexist, homophobic, and misogynistic comments, and insult guests and callers. The FCC fined stations carrying Stern more than $1 million, a move called harassment and censorship by his supporters. But when Infinity began pulling Stern from the air in response to the FCC's anti-indecency crusade following the 2004 Janet Jackson/Super Bowl breast-baring incident (Chapter 14), Stern moved his show to satellite radio provider Sirius. He may have fled the AM and FM dials but his 5-year satellite contract worth $500 million suggests he maintains a large and loyal audience.

College Radio

There are few better ways to make media literacy a living enterprise than by becoming a mass communicator yourself—in other words, by engaging in the media. The Internet does indeed make us all potential mass communicators (see Chapter 9), but it does not require us to work within a larger organization, to produce content as part of a group, to meet preexisting audience expectations, or to conform to formal and informal rules and regulations of operation, all those things identified in Chapter 1 as giving mass communication its essential nature. So, if you want to test your own media literacy values in a true mass media setting, check out college radio.

Most colleges and universities have a radio station. In fact, many have two—a student-run noncommercial station and an NPR affiliate. For example, Southampton College in New York has WLIU-AM and WPBX-FM; the University of Massachusetts in Amherst has WMUA-FM and WFCR-FM. Naturally, the student-oriented stations may offer more freedom, whereas an NPR station may offer a more

> **NONCOMMERCIAL COLLEGE RADIO OFFERS REAL MEDIA EXPERIENCE WITH CONTENT VARIETY AND DIVERSITY, THE OPPORTUNITY TO PROGRAM FOR BOUNDED CULTURES, EXTENDED FREEDOM OF SPEECH AND EXPRESSION, AND, VERY OFTEN, MORE INDIVIDUAL CREATIVE CONTROL.**

formal professional experience, but both are committed to programming that prioritizes *public interest* over *what the public is interested in*. In other words, noncommercial college radio offers real media experience with content variety and diversity, the opportunity to program for bounded cultures, extended freedom of speech and expression, and, very often, more individual creative control.

There are numerous sources to which you can turn to help you use college radio to bring your media literacy to life. Metal Index (www.metalindex.com/bands/M/) and the Intercollegiate Broadcast System (www.ibsradio.org) offer information on starting, operating, and improving college radio. In addition, the British Broadcasting Corporation (www.bbc.co.uk/info/), NPR (www.npr.org), and Public Radio International (www.pri.org/PublicSite/home.html) provide information on how to do public service broadcasting. If you are not on a campus that has a station, use any of the online radio station sites identified earlier in this chapter to search for a college station near you. Virtually all college stations welcome volunteers from the community, especially other college students.

Media literate listeners must ask themselves if Stern's "Guess the Jew" contest is just a joke. They must ask themselves if his public prayer for the spread of an FCC commissioner's prostate cancer is just hyperbole. When he teases female guests about the size and shape of their body parts, is this just an example of his provocative interviewing style? When he speaks dismissively about Hispanics and African Americans, is this just a device to tease listeners? Media literate listeners ask if Opie and Anthony's having-sex-in-risky-places contest is simply good fun, even as the Infinity Broadcasting's afternoon shock jocks broadcast, live, a couple's coupling from inside New York's St. Patrick's Cathedral ("N.Y. Shock Jocks," 2002).

If you're Jewish, if one of your parents has cancer, if you're a member of a minority group targeted by Stern, if you're a Catholic (or respect religion), the answer to these questions may not make a difference. But you have a choice, say shock jock defenders: You can switch the station or turn off the radio. This poses a problem for the media literate listener. Literacy demands an understanding of the importance of freedom not only to the operation of our media system but also to the functioning of our democracy. Yet literacy also means that you cannot discount the impact of the shock jocks. Nor can you assume that their expression does not represent a distasteful side of our culture and ourselves.

Media literate consumers also know that Howard Stern, Opie and Anthony, and the other shock jocks exist because people listen to them. They are popular for a reason. Are programs such as Stern's merely a place in

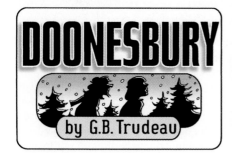

Media literate listeners can, and do, disagree about the value of shock jocks like Howard Stern.

which the culture is contested (Chapter 1)? Are they a safe place for the discussion of the forbidden, for testing cultural limits? In fact, a literate listener can make the argument that Stern and others like him play an important cultural role, as do his fans, who see him as "a hypocracy-buster, a truth-teller, a scatalogical sage" (Cox, 2005).

Do you listen to shock jocks? If you do, how do you justify that listenership? Media literate radio listeners ask and answer these questions.

RESOURCES FOR REVIEW AND DISCUSSION

Review Points

- Guglielmo Marconi's radio allowed long-distance wireless communication; Reginald Fessenden's liquid barretter made possible the transmission of voices; Lee DeForest's audion tube permitted the reliable transmission of voices and music—broadcasting.
- Thomas Edison developed the first sound recording device; Emile Berliner's gramophone improved on it as it permitted multiple copies to be made from a master recording.

- The Radio Acts of 1910, 1912, and 1927 and the Communications Act of 1934 eventually resulted in the FCC and the trustee model of broadcast regulation.
- Advertising and the network structure of broadcasting came to radio in the 1920s, producing the medium's Golden Age, one drawn to a close by the coming of television.
- Radio stations are classified as commercial and noncommercial, AM and FM.

- Radio is local, fragmented, specialized, personal, and mobile.
- Deregulation has allowed concentration of ownership of radio into the hands of a relatively small number of companies.
- Four major recording companies control 88% of the recorded music market in the United States.
- Convergence has come to radio in the form of satellite and cable delivery of radio, terrestrial digital radio, and Web radio and podcasting.

- Digital technology, in the form of Internet creation, promotion, and distribution of music, legal and illegal downloading from the Internet, and mobile phone downloading, promises to reshape the nature of the recording industry.
- Shock jocks pose a vexing problem for media literate listeners—are they signs of our culture's coarseness or a forum for the contesting of culture?

Key Terms

 Use the text's Online Learning Center at www.mhhe.com/baran5 to further your understanding of the following terminology.

liquid barretter, 196
audion tube, 196
trustee model, 200
spectrum scarcity, 200
affiliates, 200
O&O, 201
format, 205
secondary services, 205
playlist, 205
billings, 206
average quarter-hour, 207
cume, 207
rating, 207

share, 207
deregulation, 208
duopoly, 208
Low Power FM (LPFM), 208
cover, 209
catalogue albums, 214
recent catalogue albums, 214
syndication, 217
DMX (Digital Music Express), 217
digital audio radio service (DARS), 217
terrestrial digital radio, 218
in-band-on-channel (IBOC), 218

Web radio, 218
podcast, 218
bitcasters, 219
streaming, 219
digital recording, 219
MP3, 222
modem, 222
open source software, 222
piracy, 222
P2P, 222
BitTorrent, 223
copyright, 224

Questions for Review

 Go to the self-quizzes on the Online Learning Center to test your knowledge.

1. Who were Guglielmo Marconi, Reginald Fessenden, and Lee DeForest?
2. How were the sound recording developments of Thomas Edison and Emile Berliner similar? How were they different?
3. What is the significance of KDKA and WEAF?
4. How do the Radio Acts of 1910, 1912, and 1927 relate to the Communications Act of 1934?
5. What were the five defining characteristics of the American broadcasting system as it entered the golden age of radio?
6. How did World War II and the introduction of television change radio and recorded music?
7. What does it mean to say that radio is local, fragmented, specialized, personal, and mobile?

8. What are the four major recording companies in the United States?
9. What are catalogue albums? Recent catalogue albums?
10. How have cable and satellite affected the radio and recording industries? Computers and digitization?
11. In what two forms is music downloaded to mobile phones?
12. Is the size of radio's audience in ascendance or in decline? Why?
13. What are the two forms of Web radio?
14. What is streaming audio?
15. What is P2P technology?

Questions for Critical Thinking and Discussion

1. Would you have favored a noncommercial basis for our broadcasting system? Why?
2. Are you primarily a commercial AM, commercial FM, or noncommercial FM listener? Which are your favorite formats? Why?
3. What do you think of the argument that control of the recording industry by a few multinational conglomerates inevitably leads to cultural homogenization and the ascendance of profit over music?
4. Have you ever been part of a radio ratings exercise? If yes, how honest were you?
5. How much regulation do you believe is necessary in U.S. broadcasting? If the airwaves belong to the people, how can we best ensure that license holders perform their public service functions?

Important Resources

 Go to the Online Learning Center for additional readings.

Internet Resources

Radio History	www.radiohistory.org
Marconi	www.marconi.com/home/about_us/our%20history
DeForest	www.leedeforest.org
Federal Communications Commission	www.fcc.gov
National Public Radio	www.npr.org
Public Radio International	www.pri.org
Pacifica Radio	www.pacifica.org
Arbitron	www.arbitron.com
Record Industry Association of America	www.riaa.com
***Billboard* magazine**	www.billboard.com
Future of Music Coalition	www.futureofmusic.org
Rock Out Censorship	www.theroc.org
XM Radio	www.xmradio.com
Web Radio	www.radio-directory.com
Real Player	www.real.com
Podcasting	www.ipodder.org
Sirius Radio	www.siriusradio
Online Music Sites	www.purevolume.com
	www.atomicpop.com
MP3	www.MP3.com
eMusic	www.emusic.com
MusicNet	www.musicnet.com
Gnutella	www.gnutella.wego.com
Freenet	www.freenetproject.org

8

Television, Cable, and Mobile Video

LEARNING OBJECTIVES

No one is neutral about television. We either love it or hate it. Many of us do both. The reason is that it is our most ubiquitous and socially and culturally powerful mass medium. Recent and on-the-horizon technological advances promise to make it even more so. After studying this chapter you should

- be familiar with the history and development of the television and cable television industries and television itself as a medium.

- understand in detail how television programs move from concept to broadcast.

- recognize how the organizational and economic nature of the contemporary television and cable industries shapes the content of television.

- understand the relationship between television in all its forms and its viewers.

- be aware of new and emerging video technologies and their potential impact on the television industry and its audience.

- have a clearer concept of the digital and mobile television revolution.

- possess improved television-viewing media literacy skills, especially in recognizing staged news and testing your personal level of control over your viewing.

"Did you watch TV last night?"

"Nope. I was studying, and when I wasn't studying, I was working on my history paper. Why?"

"You missed a great *Family Guy*. Stewie decides to find his roots and . . ."

"Saw it."

"No way. They said it was an 'all new episode.'"

"Saw it."

"Stop being so smug. So, if you didn't watch TV, how'd you see it? Download it to your computer? That still counts as watching TV. A video screen is a video screen."

"Nope. I saw it four months ago on DVD."

"No way."

"Way. Television is changing, my friend, more than you realize."

Opposite: Network and mobile hit *Grey's Anatomy.*

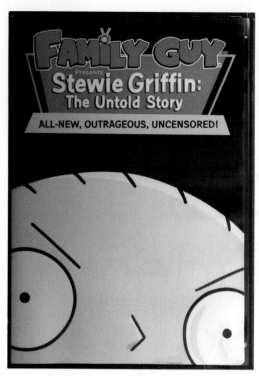

Fox surprised viewers and angered its affiliates when it edited together three episodes of its hit series *Family Guy* to create a DVD movie, releasing it months before the original episodes aired on its prime-time schedule.

This chapter details that change, from early experiments with mechanical scanning to the electronic marvel that sits in our homes to the mobile video screens we may carry in our pockets. We trace the rapid transformation of television into a mature medium after World War II and examine how the medium, the entire television industry in fact, was altered by the emergence and success of cable and satellite television. But significant change is once again remaking what we currently know as television. The "debate" in our opening vignette reflects only a small part of the coming transformation. **Nonlinear TV**—watching television on our own schedules, not on some cable or broadcast programmer's—is here right now. Even more dramatic evolution is in the offing.

The remarkable reach of television—in all its forms—accounts for its attractiveness as an advertising medium. We discuss this reach, and we explore the structure, programming, and economics of the television and cable industries. We consider new technologies and their convergence with television and how they promise to change the interaction between the medium and its audiences. Finally, we discuss media literacy in terms of the practice of recognizing news staging.

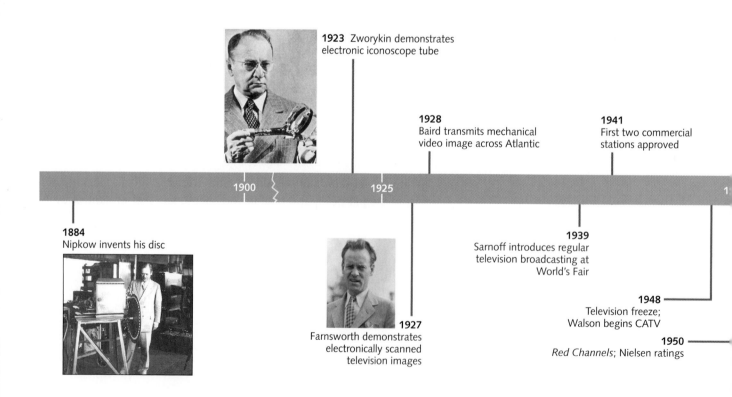

1923 Zworykin demonstrates electronic iconoscope tube

1928 Baird transmits mechanical video image across Atlantic

1941 First two commercial stations approved

1884 Nipkow invents his disc

1927 Farnsworth demonstrates electronically scanned television images

1939 Sarnoff introduces regular television broadcasting at World's Fair

1948 Television freeze; Walson begins CATV

1950 *Red Channels*; Nielsen ratings

A Short History of Television

After the printing press, the most important invention in communication technology to date has been television. Television has changed the way teachers teach, governments govern, and religious leaders preach and the way we organize the furniture in our homes. Television has changed the nature, operation, and relationship to their audiences of books, magazines, movies, and radio. The computer, with its networking abilities, may overtake television as a medium of mass communication, but television defines even its future. Will the promise of the Web be drowned in a sea of commercials? Can online information services deliver faster and better information than television? Even the computer screens we use look like television screens, and we sign up for Internet video, online video conferencing, and the new and improved computer video game. Before we delve deeper into the nature of this powerful medium and its relationship with its audience, let's examine how television developed as it did.

WWW

Television History
www.tvhistory.tv

MECHANICAL AND ELECTRONIC SCANNING

In 1884 Paul Nipkow, a Russian scientist living in Berlin, developed the first workable device for generating electrical signals suitable for the transmission

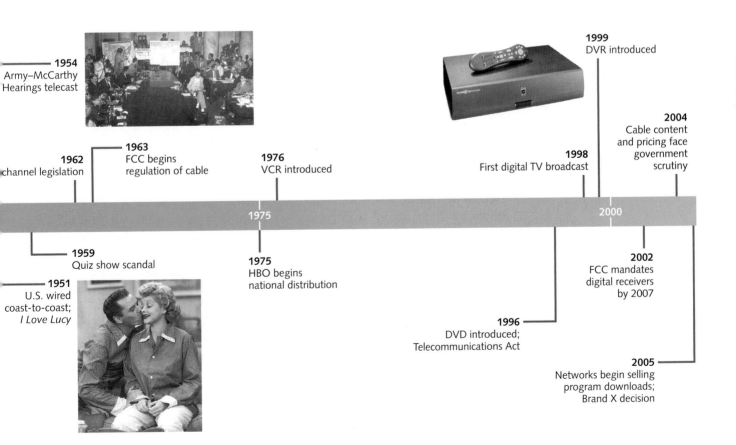

1954
Army–McCarthy
Hearings telecast

1962
channel legislation

1963
FCC begins
regulation of cable

1976
VCR introduced

1999
DVR introduced

1998
First digital TV broadcast

2004
Cable content
and pricing face
government
scrutiny

1975

2000

1959
Quiz show scandal

1951
U.S. wired
coast-to-coast;
I Love Lucy

1975
HBO begins
national distribution

1996
DVD introduced;
Telecommunications Act

2002
FCC mandates
digital receivers
by 2007

2005
Networks begin selling
program downloads;
Brand X decision

A Nipkow disc.

of a scene that people could see. His **Nipkow disc** consisted of a rotating scanning disc spinning in front of a photoelectric cell. It produced 4,000 **pixels** (picture dots) per second, producing a picture composed of 18 parallel lines. Although his mechanical system proved too limiting, Nipkow demonstrated the possibility of using a scanning system to divide a scene into an orderly pattern of transmittable picture elements that could be recomposed as a visual image. British inventor John Logie Baird was able to transmit moving images using a mechanical disc as early as 1925, and in 1928 he successfully sent a television picture from London to Hartsdale, New York.

Electronic scanning came either from another Russian or from a U.S. farm boy; historians disagree. Vladimir Zworykin, an immigrant living near Pittsburgh and working for Westinghouse, demonstrated his **iconoscope tube,** the first practical television camera tube, in 1923. In 1929 David Sarnoff lured him to RCA to head the electronics research lab, and it was there that Zworykin developed the **kinescope,** an improved picture tube. At the same time, young Philo Farnsworth had moved from Idaho to San Francisco to perfect an electronic television system, the design for which he had shown his high school science teacher when he was 15 years old. In 1927, at the age of 20, he made his first public demonstration—film clips of a prize fight, scenes from a Mary Pickford movie, and other graphic images. The "Boy Wonder" and Zworykin's RCA spent the next decade fighting fierce patent battles in court. In 1939 RCA capitulated, agreeing to pay Farnsworth royalties for the use of his patents.

In April of that year, at the World's Fair in New York, RCA made the first true public demonstration of television in the form of regularly scheduled 2-hour NBC broadcasts. These black-and-white telecasts consisted of cooking demonstrations, singers, jugglers, comedians, puppets—just about anything that could fit in a hot, brightly lit studio and demonstrate motion. People could buy television sets at the RCA Pavilion at prices ranging from $200 for the 5-inch screen to $600 for the deluxe 12-inch-screen model. The

Zworykin
www.ieee.org/organizations/
history_center/oral_histories/
transcripts/zworykin21.html

www
Farnsworth
www.invent.org/hall_of_fame/56.html

Philo Farnsworth and Vladimir Zworykin, pioneers in the development of television.

FCC granted construction permits to the first two commercial stations in 1941, but World War II intervened. But as was the case with radio during World War I, technical development and improvement of the new medium continued.

THE 1950s

In 1952, 108 stations were broadcasting to 17 million television homes. By the end of the decade, there were 559 stations, and nearly 90% of U.S. households had televisions. In the 1950s more television sets were sold in the United States (70 million) than there were children born (40.5 million) (Kuralt, 1977). The technical standards were fixed, stations proliferated and flourished, the public tuned in, and advertisers were enthusiastic. The content and character of the medium were set in this decade as well:

- Carried over from the radio networks, television genres included variety shows, situation comedies, dramas (including Westerns and cop shows), soap operas, and quiz shows.
- Two new formats appeared: feature films and talk shows. Talk shows were instrumental in introducing radio personalities to the television audience, which could see its favorites for the first time.
- Television news and documentary remade broadcast journalism as a powerful force in its own right, led by CBS's Edward R. Murrow (*See It Now*, 1951) and NBC's David Brinkley and Chet Huntley. Huntley and Brinkley's 1956 coverage of the major political conventions gave audiences an early glimpse of the power of television to cover news and history in the making.

- AT&T completed its national **coaxial cable** and **microwave relay** network for the distribution of television programming in the summer of 1951. The entire United States was now within the reach of the major television networks, and they came to dominate the medium.

Four other events from the 1950s would permanently shape how television operated: the quiz show scandal, the appearance of *I Love Lucy*, McCarthyism, and the establishment of the ratings system. Another, in 1948, would permanently *reshape* the television industry. That development, as you'll soon see, was cable television.

www

Quiz Show Scandal
www.fiftiesweb.com/quizshow.htm

The Quiz Show Scandal and Changes in Sponsorship   Throughout the 1950s the networks served primarily as time brokers, offering airtime and distribution (their affiliates) and accepting payment for access to both. Except for their own news and sports coverage, the networks relied on outside agencies to provide programs. An advertising agency, for example, would hire a production company to produce a program for its client. That client would then be the show's sponsor—*The Kraft Television Theatre* and *Westinghouse Studio One* are two examples. The agency would then pay a network to air the program over its national collection of stations. This system had enriched the networks during the heyday of radio, and they saw no reason to change.

But in 1959 the quiz show scandal, enveloping independently produced, single-advertiser-sponsored programs, changed the way the networks did business. When it was discovered that popular shows like *The $64,000 Question* had been fixed by advertisers and producers to ensure desired outcomes, the networks, mindful of their reputations, were determined to take control of their schedules. They, themselves, began commissioning or buying the entertainment fare that filled their broadcast days and nights. Now, rather than selling blocks of time to ad agencies and sponsors, the networks paid for the content they aired through **spot commercial sales** (selling individual 60-second spots on a given program to a wide variety of advertisers).

As a result, the content of television was altered. Some critics argue that this change to spot sales put an end to the golden age of television. When sponsors agreed to attach their names to programs, *Alcoa Presents* or the *Texaco Star Theater*, for example, they had an incentive to demand high-quality programming. Spot sales, with network salespeople offering small bits of time to a number of different sponsors, reduced the demand for quality. Because individual sponsors were not identified with a given show, they had no stake in how well it was made—only in how many viewers it attracted. Spot sales also reduced the willingness of the networks to try innovative or different types of content. Familiarity and predictability attracted more viewers and, therefore, more advertisers.

There is a counterargument, however. Once the financial well-being of the networks became dependent on the programming they aired, the networks themselves became more concerned with program quality, lifting television from its dull infancy (remembered now as the golden age only by those small, early audiences committed to serious character-driven televised drama). Different historians and critics offer arguments for both views.

Running from 1947 until 1958, NBC's *Kraft Television Theatre* aired some of the golden age's most respected live anthology dramas. *Top left*, Richard Kiley and Everett Sloane; *lower left*, Ossie Davis; *lower right*, Walter Matthau and Nancy Walker.

***I Love Lucy* and More Changes**   In 1951 CBS asked Lucille Ball to move her hit radio program, *My Favorite Husband*, to television. Lucy was willing but wanted her real-life husband, Desi Arnaz, to play the part of her video spouse. The network refused (some historians say the network objected to the prime-time presentation of an interracial marriage—Desi Arnaz was Cuban—but CBS denies this). But Lucy made additional demands. Television at the time was live—images were typically captured by three large television cameras, with a director in a booth choosing among the three available images. Lucy wanted her program produced in the same manner—in front of a live audience with three simultaneously running cameras—but these cameras would be *film* cameras. Editors could then review the three sets of

I Love Lucy was significant for far more than its comedy. Thanks to Lucille Ball's shrewd business sense, it became the foundation for the huge off-network syndicated television industry.

film and edit them together to give the best combination of action and reaction shots. Lucy also wanted the production to take place in Hollywood, the nation's film capital, instead of New York, the television center at the time. CBS was uncertain about this departure from how television was typically produced and refused these requests as well.

Lucy and Desi borrowed the necessary money and produced *I Love Lucy* on their own, selling the broadcast rights to CBS. In doing so the woman now best remembered as "that zany redhead" transformed the business and look of television:

- Filmed reruns were now possible, something that had been impossible with live television, and this, in turn, created the off-network syndication industry.
- The television industry moved from New York, with its stage drama orientation, to Hollywood, with its entertainment film mind-set. More action, more flash came to the screen.

- Weekly series could now be produced relatively quickly and inexpensively. A 39-week series could be completed in 20 or 24 weeks, saving money on actors, crew, equipment, and facilities. In addition the same stock shots—for example, certain exterior views—could be used in different episodes.

McCarthyism: The Growing Power of Television   The Red Scare that cowed the movie business also touched television, aided by the publication in 1950 of *Red Channels: The Report of Communist Influence in Radio and Television,* the work of three former FBI agents operating a company called American Business Consultants. Its 200 pages detailed the pro-Communist sympathies of 151 broadcast personalities, including Orson Welles and newsman Howard K. Smith. Advertisers were encouraged to avoid buying time from broadcasters who employed these "Red sympathizers." Like the movie studios, the television industry caved in. The networks employed security checkers to look into people's backgrounds, refused to hire suspect talent, and demanded loyalty oaths from performers. In its infancy television had taken the safe path. Many gifted artists were denied not only a paycheck but also the opportunity to shape the medium's content.

Ironically, it was this same Red Scare that allowed television to demonstrate its enormous power as a vehicle of democracy and freedom. Joseph McCarthy, the Republican junior senator from Wisconsin whose tactics gave this era its name, was seen by millions of viewers as his investigation of Reds in the U.S. Army was broadcast by all the networks for 36 days in 1954. Daytime ratings increased 50% (Sterling & Kittross, 1990). At the same time, Edward R. Murrow used his *See It Now* to expose the senator's lies and hypocrisy. As a consequence of the two broadcasts, McCarthy was ruined; he was censured by his Senate colleagues and later died the lonely death of an

McCarthyism
www.mccarthy.cjb.net/

Radio Television News Directors Association
www.rtnda.org

The Army–McCarthy Hearings. Wisconsin's junior Republican senator, Joseph McCarthy (seated at the far right), begins his June 9, 1954, testimony before his fellow senators regarding his claims that the army was rife with Communists, Reds, and "fellow travelers." Network coverage of the senator's erratic behavior helped bring the despot into disrepute.

Can't Find Them or They Aren't There?
Where Have All the Boys and Minorities Gone?

Just as the radio networks questioned the ratings system they had long embraced when television began to erode their audiences, today's television networks are at war with Nielsen, blaming the ratings-taker for precipitous declines in viewers, especially young men and minorities. This echo of an older conflict is a bit different, however, because it involves not only the advent of new technology (cable, video games, the Internet) but the coming of a new way to take the ratings themselves, the personal peoplemeter.

Broadcasters and Nielsen feud often—whenever there are declines in viewership. Things got so bad in 1996 that the networks ran ads in industry magazines criticizing Nielsen and even sued their longtime partner. But Nielsen does try to meet industry needs. When cable began to carve up the audience, television executives said the sample of TV homes was too small. Nielsen tripled the number. When broadcasters complained that Nielsen's intentional bypass of homes with DVR technology led to undercounts of upscale viewers, the ratings company developed technology that allowed measurement of their nontraditional viewing. When advertisers wanted measurement of product placements inside shows in addition to that of traditional commercial spots, Nielsen developed technology to do that. Even the peoplemeter itself was a response to inadequacies in the original measurement technology. The **audimeter** counted only the time the set was turned on and off and the channel to which it was tuned. And the personal peoplemeter itself is a response to inadequacies of the flawed paper-and-pencil diaries (only a third of those distributed are ever completed; people fill them out days after watching; they are inadequate for reflecting channel surfing). So what can the broadcasters be complaining about now? They're losing viewers; that's not Nielsen's fault.

Research from *AdAge* magazine shows, for American adults, a 3-hour-per-week decline in broadcast television viewing between 1997 and 2004 (18 to 15 hours) and a parallel 7-hour increase for cable watching (12 to 19 hours) and 3-hour increase for the Internet (1 to 4 hours; *Advertising Age*, 2004).

What the broadcasters are complaining about is the decline in viewing of two very specific, and very valuable, sets of demographics—young men and minorities, especially Hispanic viewers. It's a measurement problem, claim the broadcasters. It's viewers abandoning your programming, responds Nielsen. Either way, as the Republican senator from Montana, Conrad Burns, argued when calling Senate Communications Subcommittee hearings on the peoplemeter in July 2004, "The public has a right to know that the rating system which defines the public airwaves is accurate and fair to all viewers" ("Breaking," 2004, p. 3).

The broadcasters assert that Nielsen does not attract sufficient numbers of minorities to its sample of viewers, a charge supported by at least one former Nielsen executive (McClellan, 2004). While middle-class White people know what it means to be "a Nielsen family," many minority people, especially Spanish-speaking immigrants, have no idea. They are also wary of all data recording in these times of suspicion toward immigrants.

> "THE PEOPLEMETER HAS ALWAYS BEEN A TIME BOMB WAITING TO EXPLODE FOR YOUNGER DEMOGRAPHICS. I CONSIDER IT INEVITABLE THAT YOUNGER DEMOGRAPHICS WILL BE INCREASINGLY RESISTANT TO CONSTANTLY PUSHING BUTTONS TO PROVE WHAT THEY ARE VIEWING, JUST AS THEY WOULD BE UNWILLING TO MAKE THEIR BEDS OR CALL THEIR PARENTS EVERY HALF-HOUR, OR OTHERWISE ADHERE TO RIGID REQUIREMENTS."

---

alcoholic. Television had given the people eyes and ears—and power—where before they had had little. The Army–McCarthy Hearings and Murrow's challenge to McCarthyism are still regarded as two of television's finest moments.

The Nielsen Ratings   The concept of computing ratings was carried over from radio (see Chapter 7) to television, but the ratings as we know them today are far more sophisticated. The A. C. Nielsen Company began in 1923 as a product-testing company, but soon branched into market research. In 1936 Nielsen started reporting radio ratings and was doing the same for television by 1950.

To produce the ratings, Nielsen selects 15,000 households thought to be representative of the entire U.S. viewing audience. To record data on what people

Young men, according to the networks, are undercounted because they reject the regimen of button pushing and, more important, Nielsen's sample does not include sufficient numbers of "dependent young adults" (18- to 34-year-old men living at home).

Nielsen responds that the problem is not bad measurement, but measurement that is too good (Carter, 2003). Recent precipitous declines in both young men (15%) and minorities (22%) are real, and it is only because measurement has improved so much that they are now showing up. Young men are gravitating toward cable, DVD, the Internet, and video games, and Hispanic people are tuning in to Spanish-language cable offerings such as Univision.

What do you think? Are these steep declines in viewing a product of Nielsen's methods? Do you agree with Cox Broadcasting's CEO, Andy Fisher, who said, "The peoplemeter has always been a time bomb waiting to explode for younger demographics. I consider it inevitable that younger demographics will be increasingly resistant to constantly pushing buttons to prove what they are viewing, just as they would be unwilling to make their beds or call their parents every half-hour, or otherwise adhere to rigid requirements" (quoted in Greppi, 2003)? Or do you side with MTV's chief of research, Betsy Frank, who argues that today's "media actives" (viewers born after 1970) are disenchanted with broadcast television? These young people "are accustomed to having multiple entertainment options: videogames, cable and the Internet, as well as television. And now they are beginning to influence their older cohorts, creating 'the perfect TV storm'" (quoted in Romano, 2003, p. 6).

Are young male viewers undercounted in the ratings, or are they abandoning broadcast television for fare more suited to their tastes, such as MTV's Viva La Bam?

in those TV households are watching, Nielsen employs the **peoplemeter,** a device requiring each member of a television home to press buttons to record his or her individual viewing. (Parents or guardians are responsible for recording children's choices.) The information recorded is sent to Nielsen by telephone lines, and the company can then determine the program watched, who was watching it, and the amount of time each viewer spent with it. But convergence is changing how ratings data will be gathered. Nielsen is rolling out the **personal peoplemeter,** a special remote control with personalized buttons for each viewer in the household. The introduction of the personal peoplemeter has been anything but smooth, as you can see in the essay on page 240, "Can't Find Them or They Aren't There? Where Have All the Boys and Minorities Gone?"

Ratings and shares can be computed using these formulas:

$$\text{Rating} = \frac{\text{Households tuned in to a given program}}{\text{All households with television}}$$

$$\text{Share} = \frac{\text{Households tuned in to a given program}}{\text{All households tuned in to television at that time}}$$

Here's an example. Your talk show is aired in a market that has 1 million television households; 400,000 are tuned in to you. Therefore,

$$\frac{400,000}{1,000,000} = .40, \text{ or a rating of 40.}$$

At the time your show airs, however, there are only 800,000 households using television. Therefore, your share of the available audience is

$$\text{Share} = \frac{400,000}{800,000} = .50, \text{ or a rating of 50.}$$

If you can explain why a specific program's share is always higher than its rating, then you understand the difference between the two.

Figure 8.1 Computing Ratings and Shares.

To draw a more complete picture of the viewing situation and to measure local television viewing, Nielsen conducts diary surveys of viewing patterns four times a year. These **sweeps periods** are in February, May, July, and November. During sweeps, diaries are distributed to thousands of sample households in selected markets. Viewers are asked to write down what they're watching and who is watching it. The diary data are then combined with the peoplemeter data to help stations set their advertising rates for the next 3 months. The company announced in June 2006, however, that it would abandon paper diaries by 2011 and move to completely electronic measurement.

Sweeps, too, may soon be a thing of the past. These quarterly extravaganzas of heavily promoted network programming and titillating local news (High School Binge Drinking? Story and Shocking Video at 6!) are likely to disappear for two reasons. First, the rhythm of broadcast television scheduling is changing because of competition with cable. Cable introduces new shows and big movies throughout the year, rendering such concepts as "The Fall Season" and "Premiere Week" obsolete. Fox already has year-round premieres, and CBS's *Survivor* and NBC's *Fear Factor* both debuted in summer, formerly network television's programming graveyard. With the basic structure of the programming year disrupted, broadcasters can no longer afford to save their best or biggest programming for sweeps weeks. Second, the personal peoplemeter delivers detailed viewing and demographic data every day of the year, making the four-times-a-year, data-intensive ratings periods unnecessary.

A second, more important measure of television's audience is its *share*, which is a direct reflection of a particular show's competitive performance. Share doesn't measure viewers as a percentage of *all* television households (as do the ratings). Instead, the share measures a program audience as a percentage of the *television sets in use* at the time it airs. It tells us what proportion of the *actual* audience a program attracts, indicating how well a particular program is doing on its given night, in its time slot, against its competition (Figure 8.1). For example, *The Tonight Show with Jay Leno* normally gets a rating of around 4—terrible by prime-time standards—but because it's on when fewer homes are tuned in, its share of 15 (15% of the homes with sets in use) is very high.

THE COMING OF CABLE

Mahanoy City, Pennsylvania, appliance salesman John Walson was having trouble selling televisions in 1948. The Pocono Mountains sat between his town and Philadelphia's three new stations. But Walson was also a power-line worker, so he convinced his bosses to let him run a wire from a tower he erected on New Boston Mountain to his store. As more and more people became aware of his system, he began wiring the homes of customers who bought his sets. In June of that year Walson had 727 subscribers for his **community antenna television (CATV)** system (Chin, 1978). Although no one calls it CATV anymore, cable television was born.

The cable Walson used was a twin-lead wire, much like the cord that connects a lamp to an outlet. To attract even more subscribers, he had to offer improved picture quality. He accomplished this by using *coaxial cable* and self-manufactured boosters (or amplifiers). Coaxial cable—copper-clad aluminum wire encased in plastic foam insulation, covered by an aluminum outer conductor, and then sheathed in plastic—had more bandwidth than did twin-lead wire. As a result, it allowed more of the original signal to pass and even permitted Walson to carry a greater number of channels.

As Walson continued to expand his CATV business, Milton Jerrold Shapp, later to become Pennsylvania's governor, noticed thousands of antennas cluttering the roofs of department stores and apartment buildings. Seeing Walson's success, he set up master antennas and connected the sets in these buildings to them, employing a signal booster he had developed. This was the start of **master antenna television (MATV).**

With expanded bandwidth and the new, powerful Jerrold boosters, these systems began experimenting with the **importation of distant signals,** using wires not only to provide improved reception but also to offer a wider variety of programming. They began delivering independent stations from as far away as New York to fill their then-amazing 7 to 10 channels. By 1962, 800 systems were providing cable television to more than 850,000 homes.

The industry today is composed of 8,875 individual cable systems serving 73.2 million homes subscribing to basic cable (67% of all television households). Sixty-seven percent of these cable households, or 46% of all U.S. television homes, receive premium cable. The industry employs nearly 131,000 people and generates revenues of $57.6 billion (NCTA, 2005).

John Walson

Television and Its Audiences

The 1960s saw some refinement in the technical structure of television, which influenced its organization and audience. In 1962 Congress passed **all-channel legislation,** which required that all sets imported into or manufactured in the United States be equipped with both VHF and UHF receivers. This had little immediate impact; U.S. viewers were now hooked on the three national networks and their VHF affiliates. Still, UHF independents and educational stations were able to at least attract some semblance of an audience. The UHF independents would have to wait for the coming of cable to give them clout. Now that the educational stations were attracting more viewers, they began to look less educational in the strictest sense of the word and began programming more entertaining cultural fare (see the essay "The Creation of *Sesame Street*" on p. 244). The Public Broadcasting Act of 1967 united the educational stations into an important network, the Public Broadcasting Service (PBS), which today has over 300 affiliates.

The 1960s also witnessed the immense social and political power of the new medium to force profound alterations in the country's consciousness and behavior. Particularly influential were the Nixon–Kennedy campaign debates of 1960, broadcasts of the aftermath of Kennedy's assassination and funeral in 1963, the

USING MEDIA TO MAKE A DIFFERENCE

The Creation of *Sesame Street*

In 1968 a public affairs program producer for Channel 13 in New York City identified a number of related problems that she believed could be addressed by a well-conceived, well-produced television show.

Joan Ganz Cooney saw that 80% of 3- and 4-year-olds, and 25% of 5-year-olds, in the United States did not attend any form of preschool. Children from financially disadvantaged homes were far less likely to attend preschool at these ages than their better-off peers. Children in these age groups who did go to preschool received little academic instruction; preschool was the equivalent of organized recess. Large numbers of U.S. children, then, entered first grade with no formal schooling, even though education experts had long argued that preschool years were crucial in children's intellectual and academic development. In addition, the disparity in academic preparedness between poor and other children was a national disgrace.

What did these children do instead of going to preschool? Ms. Cooney knew that they watched television. But she also knew that "existing shows for 3- through 5-year-old children . . . did not have education as a primary goal" (Ball & Bogatz, 1970, p. 2). Her idea was to use an interesting, exciting, visually and aurally stimulating television show as an explicitly educational tool "to promote the intellectual and cultural growth of preschoolers, particularly disadvantaged preschoolers" and to "teach children how to think as well as what to think" (Cook et al., 1975, p. 7).

Ms. Cooney established a nonprofit organization, the Children's Television Workshop (CTW), and sought funding for her program. Several federal agencies, primarily the Office of Education, a number of private foundations including Carnegie and Ford, and public broadcasters contributed $13.7 million for CTW's first 4 years.

After much research into producing a quality children's television show and studying the best instructional methods for teaching preschool audiences, CTW unveiled *Sesame Street* during the 1969 television season. It was an instant hit with children and parents. The *New Republic* said, "Judged by the standards of most other programs for preschoolers, it is imaginative, tasteful, and witty" (cited in Ball & Bogatz, 1970, p. 3). *Reader's Digest* said, "The zooming popularity of *Sesame Street* has created a sensation in U.S. television" (p. 3). *Saturday Review* gave its "Television Award" to *Sesame Street* "for the successful illustration of the principle that a major allocation of financial resources, educational research and creative talent can produce a widely viewed and popular series of regular programs for preschool children with an immediate payoff in cognitive learning" (p. 4). Originally scheduled for 1 hour a day during the school week, within months of its debut

> **DID MS. COONEY AND HER SHOW MAKE A DIFFERENCE? SEVERAL NATIONAL STUDIES DEMONSTRATED THAT ACADEMIC PERFORMANCE IN EARLY GRADES WAS DIRECTLY AND STRONGLY CORRELATED WITH REGULAR VIEWING OF *SESAME STREET*.**

Sesame Street was being programmed twice a day on many public television stations, and many ran the entire week's schedule on Saturdays and Sundays. Today, more than 35 years after its debut, *Sesame Street* still airs 26 new episodes a year (Gillies, 2004).

Did Ms. Cooney and her show make a difference? Several national studies demonstrated that academic performance in early grades was directly and strongly correlated with regular viewing of *Sesame Street.* The commercial networks began to introduce educational fare into their Saturday morning schedules. ABC's *Grammar Rock, America Rock* (on U.S. history), and *Multiplication Rock* were critical and educational successes at the time, and a traditional children's favorite, CBS's *Captain Kangaroo,* started airing short films influenced by *Sesame Street* on a wide variety of social and personal skills. *Sesame Street* went international and appears even today in almost every developed nation in the world.

Even *Sesame Street*'s primary failure was a product of its success. Research indicated that *all* children benefited socially and academically from regular viewing. But middle- and upper-class children benefited more than did the disadvantaged children who were a specific target for the show. *Sesame Street* was accused of widening the gap between these children, rather than improving the academic performance of those most in need.

The Sesame Street *gang.*

1969 transmission of Neil Armstrong's walk on the moon, and the use of television at the end of the decade by civil rights and anti–Vietnam War leaders.

The 1960s also gave rise to a descriptive expression often used today when television is discussed. Speaking to the 1961 convention of the National Association of Broadcasters, John F. Kennedy's new FCC chair, Newton Minow, invited broadcasters to

> sit down in front of your television set when your station goes on the air and stay there without a book, magazine, newspaper, profit and loss sheet, or ratings book to distract you, and keep your eyes glued to that set until the station signs off. I can assure you that you will observe a **vast wasteland.**

Whether or not one agrees with Mr. Minow's assessment of television, then or now, there is no doubt that audiences continue to watch:

- There are 110.2 million television households in the United States; 99.9% have color, 79% have more than one set.
- A television is on for an average of 8 hours 11 minutes a day in each U.S. household.
- The average male watches 4 hours 26 minutes a day; the average female 5 hours 7 minutes; the average teen 3 hours 7 minutes; and the average child, 3 hours 16 minutes (all statistics from www.tvb.org).
- Eighty-three percent of adult Americans get most of their news from television. In comparison, newspapers are the source of most news for 42%, radio 19%, and the Internet 15% (Project, 2004; multiple answers were allowed).

There can be no doubt, either, that television is successful as an advertising medium:

- Total 2004 billings for television were $67.8 billion, with approximately 68% generated by broadcast and 32% by cable television.
- The average 30-second prime-time network television spot costs $100,000 (spots on demographically attractive *American Idol* cost $705,000).
- Average ad time on the 2006 Super Bowl Steelers–Seahawks broadcast costs $2.6 million for 30 seconds.
- Eight-two percent of American consumers see television as the most influential ad medium; 67%, the most persuasive; 49%, the most authoritative; and 80%, the most exciting.
- A 30-second local spot can fetch up to $20,000 on a top-rated special in a major market (all statistics from www.tvb.org).

Scope and Nature of the Broadcast Television Industry

Today, as it has been from the beginning, the business of broadcast television is dominated by a few centralized production, distribution, and decision-making organizations. These **networks** link affiliates for the purpose of

For more information on this topic, see Media Tours video clip #4, "Television: Inside WSEE-TV," on the *Media World* DVD.

delivering and selling viewers to advertisers. The large majority of the 1,366 commercial stations in the United States are affiliated with a national broadcasting network: ABC, NBC, and CBS each have over 200 affiliates and Fox has close to that number. Many more stations are affiliated with the CW and My Network TV, often referred to as "weblets." Although cable has introduced us to dozens of new cable networks—ESPN, MTV, Comedy Central, and A&E, to name a few—most programs that come to mind when we think of television were either conceived, approved, funded, produced, or distributed by the broadcast networks.

Local affiliates carry network programs (they **clear time**) in exchange for direct payments for airing a program (called **compensation**) and the right to keep all income from the sale of commercial time in that program to local advertisers. Both compensation and local spot time are negotiated with affiliates on a station-by-station basis, and because the networks have been losing audience, both offerings have been considerably scaled back. In fact, many affiliates receive no compensation at all or are even asked to underwrite the production of some content.

WWW

NBC
www.nbc.com

THE NETWORKS AND PROGRAM CONTENT

Networks control what appears on the vast majority of local television stations, but they also control what appears on non-network television, that is, when affiliates program their own content. In addition, they influence what appears on independent stations and on cable channels. This non-network material not only tends to be network-*type* programming but most often is programming that originally aired on the networks themselves (called **off-network** programs).

Why do network and network-type content dominate television? *Availability* is one factor. There is 65 years' worth of already successful network content available for airing on local stations. A second factor is that the *production and distribution* mechanisms that have long served the broadcast networks are well established and serve the newer outlets just as well as they did NBC, CBS, and ABC. The final reason is us, the audience. The formats we are most comfortable with—our television tastes and expectations—have been and continue to be developed on the networks.

WWW

Episodes of TV Shows
www.epguides.com

WWW

CBS
www.cbs.com

HOW A PROGRAM GETS ON THE AIR

The national broadcast networks look at about 4,000 proposals a year for new television series. Many, if not most, are submitted at the networks' invitation or instigation. Of the 4,000, about 100 will be filmed as **pilots,** or trial programs. Perhaps 20 to 30 will make it onto the air. Only 10 of these will last a full broadcast season. In a particularly good year, at most 3 or 4 will succeed well enough to be called hits. For this reason, the networks prefer to see ideas from producers with established track records and financial and organizational stability—for example, David E. Kelley is the source of *L.A. Law, Picket Fences, Ally McBeal, Boston Public, Chicago Hope, The Practice, The Practice: Fleet Street, The Brotherhood of Poland, N.H., The Girls' Club, Boston Legal, Snoops, The Law Firm,* and *Doogie Howser, M.D.,* and Jerry Bruckheimer produced 10 prime-time series in 2005–2006 alone.

WWW

Children's Television Workshop
www.ctw.org

The way a program typically makes it onto the air differs somewhat for those who have been asked to submit an idea and for producers who bring their concepts to the networks. First, a producer has an *idea;* or a network has an idea and asks a proven producer to propose a show based on it (possibly offering a **put,** a deal that guarantees the producer that the network will order at least a pilot or it has to pay a hefty penalty). The producer must then *shop* the idea to one of the networks; naturally, an invited producer submits the proposal only to the network that asked for it. In either case, if the network is persuaded, it *buys the option* and asks for a written *outline* in which the original idea is refined. If still interested, the network will order a full *script.*

If the network approves that script, it will order the production of a pilot. Pilots are then subjected to rigorous testing by the networks' own and independent audience research organizations. Based on this research, networks will often demand changes, such as writing out characters who tested poorly or beefing up story lines that test audiences particularly liked.

If the network is still interested, that is, if it believes that the show will be a hit, it orders a set number of episodes and schedules the show. In television's early days, an order might be for 26 or 39 episodes. Today, however, because of escalating production costs, the convention is at first to order 6 episodes. If these are successful, a second order of 9 more is placed. Then, if the show is still doing well, a final 9 episodes (referred to as *the back nine*) will be commissioned. Untested program ideas or producers who are not fully established might get initial orders for only 2 or 3 episodes. This is called **short ordering.**

At any point in this process, the network can decline interest. Moreover, the network invests very little of its own money during the developmental stages of a program. Even when a network orders a package of episodes, including those for an established hit that has been on for years, it typically pays producers only half of the show's entire production costs. In other words, producers engage in deficit financing—they *lose* money throughout the development process and continue to lose even more the longer their show stays on the network schedule.

The reason television program producers participate in this expensive enterprise is that they can make vast amounts of money in syndication, the sale of their programs to stations on a market-by-market basis. Even though the networks control the process from idea to scheduling and decide how long a show stays in their lineups, producers continue to own the rights to their programs. Once enough episodes are made (generally about 50, which is the product of 4 years on a network), producers can sell the syndicated package to the highest bidder in each of the 210 U.S. television markets, keeping all the revenues for themselves. This is the legacy of Lucille Ball's business genius. The price of a syndicated program depends on the market size, the level of competition between the stations in the market, and the age and popularity of the program itself. The station buys the right to a specified number of plays, or airings. After that, the rights return to the producer to be sold again and again. A program that has survived at least 4 years on one of the networks has proven its popularity, has attracted a following, and has accumulated enough individual episodes so that local stations can offer weeks of daily scheduling without too many reruns. The program is a moneymaker. Paramount has already earned more than $2 billion from its

Two of syndication's biggest winners, urbane, off-network hits *Frasier* and *Friends*.

syndication of *Frasier,* and Warner Brothers, already collecting more than $4.3 million an episode from its syndication of *Friends,* predicts it will make $3 billion before audiences lose interest (Albiniak, 2004).

Many critics of television argue that it is this deficit financing system that keeps the quality of content lower than it might otherwise be. A producer must attract the interest of a network with an idea that is salable on the network's schedule today, while incurring years of financial loss in hopes of having content that will be of interest to syndication viewers 4, 5, or even 10 years in the future. There is little incentive to gamble with characters or story lines; there is little profit in pushing the aesthetic boundaries of the medium.

Dr. Phil is among the more successful first-run syndicated programs.

It is important to note that there is another form of syndicated programming. **First-run syndication** is programming produced specifically for sale into syndication on a market-by-market basis. It is attractive to producers because they don't have to run the gauntlet of the network programming process and they keep 100% of the income.

Satellites have improved the distribution process for first-run syndicated series, increasing the number and variety of available programs. Game and talk shows, staples of the business in the past, have proliferated and been joined by programs such as *Judge Judy* and *Judge Joe Brown*, court shows distributed daily by satellite to hundreds of stations. They are inexpensive to make, inexpensive to distribute, and easily **stripped** (broadcast at the same time 5 nights a week). They allow an inexhaustible number of episodes with no repeats and are easy to promote ("Watch the case of the peeping landlord. Tune in at 5:30").

In whatever form, the process by which programs come to our screens is changing because the central position of networks in that process has been altered. In 1978 ABC, CBS, and NBC drew 92% of all

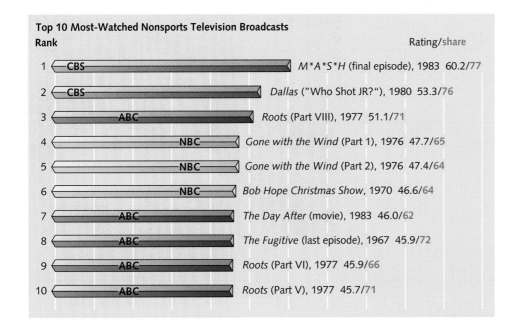

Top 10 Most-Watched Nonsports Television Broadcasts

Rank		Rating/share
1	CBS	*M*A*S*H* (final episode), 1983 60.2/77
2	CBS	*Dallas* ("Who Shot JR?"), 1980 53.3/76
3	ABC	*Roots* (Part VIII), 1977 51.1/71
4	NBC	*Gone with the Wind* (Part 1), 1976 47.7/65
5	NBC	*Gone with the Wind* (Part 2), 1976 47.4/64
6	NBC	*Bob Hope Christmas Show*, 1970 46.6/64
7	ABC	*The Day After* (movie), 1983 46.0/62
8	ABC	*The Fugitive* (last episode), 1967 45.9/72
9	ABC	*Roots* (Part VI), 1977 45.9/66
10	ABC	*Roots* (Part V), 1977 45.7/71

Figure 8.2 Top 10 Most-Watched Nonsports Television Broadcasts. Source: Television Bureau of Advertising (www.tvb.org).

prime-time viewers. In 1988 they collected 70%. In 2002 their share fell "to an historic low: 47%. Not only is it a record low, but it's the first time the four-network share has dropped below 50%, a benchmark broadcasters dreaded to fall beneath" (McClellan, 2002, p. 6). In fact, the much-anticipated *Friends* finale had a rating of just under 30, not even coming close to being one of the most-watched programs (Figure 8.2). New technologies—cable, VCR, DVD, digital video recorders, satellite, the Internet and digitization, and even the remote control—have upset the long-standing relationship between medium and audience. Convergence is also reshaping that relationship.

For more information on this topic, see Media Talk video clip #17, "Future Television," on the *Media World* DVD.

Cable and Satellite Television

John Walson's brainchild reshaped the face of modern television. During cable's infancy, many over-the-air broadcasters saw it as something of a friend. It extended their reach, boosting both audience size and profits. Then, in November 1972, Sterling Manhattan Cable launched a new channel called Home Box Office. Only a handful of homes caught the debut of what we now call HBO, but broadcasters' mild concern over this development turned to outright antagonism toward cable in 1975, when new HBO owner Time Inc. began distributing the movie channel by satellite. Now **premium cable** was eating into the broadcasters' audience by offering high-quality, nationally produced and distributed content. The public enthusiastically embraced cable and that, coupled with the widespread diffusion of **fiber optic** cable (the transmission of signals by light beam over glass, permitting the delivery of hundreds of channels), brought the medium to maturity.

PROGRAMMING

We've already seen that cable's share of the prime-time audience exceeded that of the Big Four broadcast networks for the first time in 2001. Its total

The national distribution by satellite of HBO in 1975 changed cable television, all television in fact, for all time.

WWW

Fox
www.fox.com

Revenues of cable shopping networks such as QVC exceed those of traditional television networks ABC and NBC.

audience share has exceeded that of ABC, CBS, NBC, and Fox every year since. What attracts these viewers is programming, a fact highlighted by the tens of millions of viewers who tuned in to cable network CNN as the drama of the terrorist attacks unfolded on September 11, 2001, and the 45% of all Americans who turned first to cable news, rather than other media, for information on the 2003 war with Iraq ("Getting," 2003). But news is not cable's only programming success. Even home-shopping channels such as QVC (2005 revenues of $4.41 billion, exceeding that of traditional networks ABC and NBC) and HSN ($1.91 billion) have made their mark (Higgins, 2006).

As we've seen, cable operators attract viewers through a combination of basic and premium channels, as well as with some programming of local origin. There are 390 national cable networks and 84 regional cable networks (NCTA, 2005). We all know national networks such as CNN, Lifetime, HBO, and the History Channel. Regional network NorthWest Cable News serves Washington, Oregon, Idaho, Montana, northern California, and parts of Alaska; New England Cable News serves the states that give it its name; and several regional sports-oriented channels serve different parts of the country. The financial support and targeted audiences for these program providers differ, as does their place on a system's **tiers,** groupings of channels made available to subscribers at varying prices.

Basic Cable Programming In recognition of the growing dependence of the public on cable delivery of broadcast service as cable penetration increased, Congress passed the Cable Television Consumer Protection and Competition Act of 1992. This law requires operators to offer a truly basic service composed of the broadcast stations in their area and their access channels. Cable operators also offer another form of basic service, **expanded basic cable,** composed primarily of local broadcast stations and services with broad appeal such as TBS, TNT, the USA Network, and Comedy Central. These networks offer a wide array a wide array of programming not unlike that found on the traditional, over-the-air broadcast networks. The cable networks with the largest number of subscribers appear in Figure 8.3.

Because of concentration, operators are increasingly choosing to carry a specific basic channel because their owners (who have a financial stake in

WWW

*Women in Cable &
Telecommunications*
www.wict.org

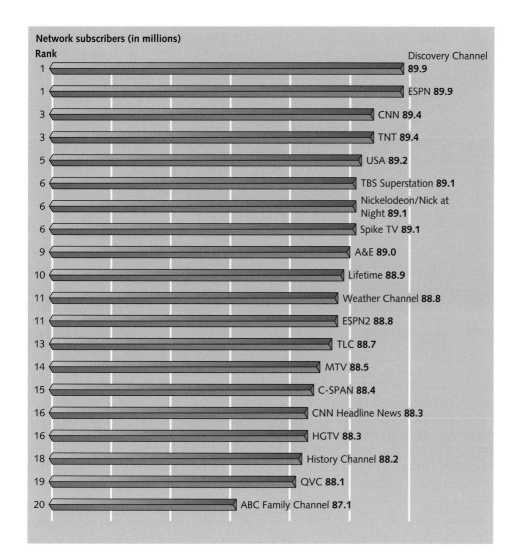

Network subscribers (in millions)

Rank	Network	Subscribers
1	Discovery Channel	89.9
1	ESPN	89.9
3	CNN	89.4
3	TNT	89.4
5	USA	89.2
6	TBS Superstation	89.1
6	Nickelodeon/Nick at Night	89.1
6	Spike TV	89.1
9	A&E	89.0
10	Lifetime	88.9
11	Weather Channel	88.8
11	ESPN2	88.8
13	TLC	88.7
14	MTV	88.5
15	C-SPAN	88.4
16	CNN Headline News	88.3
16	HGTV	88.3
18	History Channel	88.2
19	QVC	88.1
20	ABC Family Channel	87.1

Figure 8.3 Top 20 Cable Networks, 2005. Source: NCTA, 2005.

that channel) insist that they do. **Multiple system operators (MSOs)** are companies that own several cable franchises. Time Warner, Liberty, and Cablevision own Court TV. Comcast has an interest in numerous prime channels. Viacom owns BET. Naturally, these networks are more likely to be carried by systems controlled by the MSOs that own them and less likely to be carried by other systems. This pattern also holds true for MSO-owned premium channels such as HBO and Showtime.

The long-standard concept of different pricing for different packages or tiers of channels is currently under attack by the FCC and some members of Congress. Concerns over viewers' accidental access to unwanted, offensive content (FX's *Nip/Tuck* is a particular target of complaint) and rising cable prices (up 50% since 1996) are leading to calls for **à la carte pricing**—that is, paying for cable on a channel-by-channel basis. The industry argues that à la carte would have precisely the opposite effect desired by its advocates—costs would not be reduced and many favorite, or "safe," channels would disappear. Glenn Britt, Time Warner Cable CEO, explains, "We carry many channels that appeal just to niche groups and minorities. It's by no means clear that those could survive in . . . Cable isn't

Controversial cable programming like *Nip/Tuck* helps fuel the à la carte pricing debate.

about having a few channels that appeal to everybody; it's about having a lot of channels that appeal to everybody. You may not watch C-Span every night, but it's good to know it's there" (in Graves, 2004, p. 88).

Premium Cable   As the FCC lifted restrictions on cable's freedom to import distant signals and to show current movies, HBO grew and was joined by a host of other satellite-delivered pay networks. Today, the most familiar and popular premium cable networks are HBO, Showtime, the Spice Channel, the Sundance Channel, and Cinemax.

In addition to freedom from regulatory constraint, two important programming discoveries ensured the success of the new premium channels. After television's early experiments with over-the-air **subscription TV** failed, many experts believed people simply would not pay for television. So the first crucial discovery was that viewers would indeed pay for packages of contemporary, premium movies. These movie packages could be sold less expensively than could films bought one at a time, and viewers were willing to be billed on a monthly basis for the whole package rather than pay for each viewing.

The second realization boosting the fortunes of the premium networks was the discovery that viewers not only did not mind repeats (as many did with over-the-air television) but welcomed them as a benefit of paying for the provider's slate of films. Premium channel owners were delighted. Replaying content reduced their programming costs and solved the problem of how to fill all those hours of operation.

Premium services come in two forms: movie channels (HBO, Starz!, and Encore, for example) that offer packages of new and old movies along with big sports and other special events—all available for one monthly fee—and pay-per-view channels, through which viewers choose from a menu of offerings (almost always of very new movies and very big sporting events) and pay a fee for the chosen viewing.

Boxing is a premium-cable standard. Even the fighters themselves, here for example Mike Tyson and Lennox Lewis battling in 2002, are "owned" by different cable networks.

People enjoy premium channels in the home for their ability to present unedited and uninterrupted movies and other content not usually found on broadcast channels—for example, adult fare and championship boxing and wrestling. Increasingly, however, that "content not usually found on broadcast channels" consists not of movies and sports but high-quality serial programming—content unencumbered by the need to attract the largest possible audience possessing a specific set of demographics. Premium cable series such as *The Sopranos, Huff, Deadwood, Queer as Folk, The L Word, Weeds,* and *Rome* attract large and loyal followings.

The other dominant multichannel service is direct broadcast satellite (DBS). First available to the public in 1994, it has brought cable's subscriber growth to a near standstill. The early slow diffusion of DBS was the product of efforts by the cable industry to use its financial might (and therefore congressional lobbying power) to thwart the medium. For example, federally mandated limitations on the importation by DBS of local over the-air television stations were finally eliminated in 1999 with the passage of the Satellite Home Viewers Improvement Act, but even now, some restrictions remain. Still, from the viewer's perspective, what is on a DBS-supplied screen differs little from what is on a cable-supplied screen.

DBS in the United States is, for now, dominated by two companies, DirecTV, owned by Rupert Murdoch's News Corporation, and Dish Network (owned by EchoStar, a publicly traded company). DirecTV has 14.5 million subscribers; Dish Network, 11.2 million. And these two companies,

Dave Granlund, Metrowest Daily News.

Rising cable rates are at the heart of the growth of DBS.

Viewers and critics agree that much of television's most sophisticated (and enjoyable) programming is available on premium cable. Unafraid of offending advertisers, cable networks can present challenging, often controversial content. Can you match the title with the image? *Weeds, Entourage, The L Word, HUFF, Deadwood, The Sopranos.*

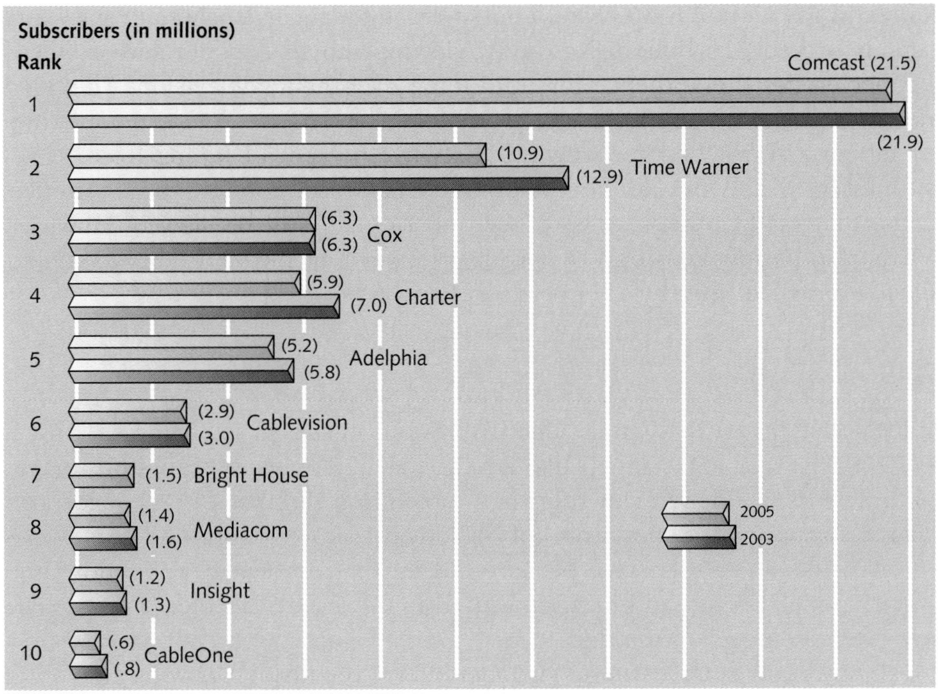

Figure 8.4

Subscribers (in millions)

Rank

Rank	MSO	2005	2003
1	Comcast	(21.5)	(21.9)
2	Time Warner	(10.9)	(12.9)
3	Cox	(6.3)	(6.3)
4	Charter	(5.9)	(7.0)
5	Adelphia	(5.2)	(5.8)
6	Cablevision	(2.9)	(3.0)
7	Bright House	(1.5)	
8	Mediacom	(1.4)	(1.6)
9	Insight	(1.2)	(1.3)
10	CableOne	(.6)	(.8)

Figure 8.4 Top 10 Cable MSOs, 2005. Source: NCTA, 2005.

along with satellite start-up VOOM (owned by cable MSO Cablevision), have recently been taking subscribers away from cable at a furious pace. Now that satellite homes in 70% of the country can receive local stations, it is cable's ever-increasing monthly rates that are at the heart of the switch to DBS. Look at the list of the 10 largest cable MSOs in Figure 8.4 above. Note that all but 2 have suffered declines in subscribers between 2003 and 2005, and if Dish and DirecTV were added to the list, they would be the country's second and third largest MSOs.

WWW

DirecTV
www.directv.com

Trends and Convergence in Television and Cable

The long-standing relationship between television and its audiences is being redefined. Nielsen's chief technology officer, Bob Luff, explains, "Radio is going on the Web, TV is going on cellphones, the Web is going on TV, and everything, it seems, is moving to video-on-demand and quite possibly the iPod and PlayStation Portable. Television and media will change more in the next three to five years than they've changed in the past 50" (in Gertner, 2005, p. 34). This profound change, initially wrought by cable and satellite, has been and is being driven by other new technologies as well—VCR, DVD, DVR, the Internet, digitization, and even the cell phone.

VCR

Introduced commercially in 1976, videocassette recorders (VCRs) are now common in most homes. In some places, Flagstaff, Arizona, for example, they are in more than 97% of homes. There are approximately 30,000 video rental stores in the United States, and annual revenues for videocassette sales and rentals exceed $16 billion. Naturally, viewing rented and purchased videos further erodes the audience for traditional over-the-air television. The good news for the television industry, however, is that VCRs allow **time-shifting,** or taping a show for later viewing. Sixty-five percent of taping from television is from network-affiliated stations. Therefore, content (and commercials) that might otherwise have been missed can still be viewed. However, VCRs also permit **zipping**—that is, fast-forwarding through taped commercials, a practice used by 95% of all VCR owners.

DVD

In March 1996 **DVD** (digital video disc) went on sale in U.S. stores. Using a DVD player that looks much like a VCR machine, viewers can stop images with no loss of fidelity; can subtitle a movie in a number of languages; can search for specific scenes from an on-screen picture menu; and can access information tracks that give background on the movie, its production, and its personnel. Scenes and music not used in the theatrical release of a movie are often included on the disc.

Dish Network
www.dishnetwork.com

Innovations such as these have made DVD the fastest-growing consumer electronic product of all time. Sales of DVD players exceeded those of VCRs for the first time in September 2001. Machines now sit in more than one-third of all U.S. homes, and disc sales exceed $17.3 billion a year ("DVD Sales," 2005). In June 2002, Circuit City, America's second-largest electronic chain, and Borders announced that they were dropping sales of videotapes in favor of exclusive sales of DVDs. We are not likely to see the elimination of the VHS machine any time soon, however, because recordable DVD, while available, is still quite expensive, especially for those who already possess tape machines that can record.

DVR

TiVo
www.tivo.com

In March 1999 Philips Electronics unveiled its version of the **digital video recorder (DVR),** TiVo, and soon after, Replay Networks introduced its ReplayTV. Both contain digital software that puts a significant amount of control over content in viewers' hands. What can viewers do with DVR? They can "rewind" and play back portions of a program while they are watching and recording it without losing any of that show. They can digitally record programs by simply telling the system their titles. By designating their favorite shows, viewers can instruct DVR to automatically record and deliver not only those programs but all similar content over a specified period of time. This application can even be used with the name of a favorite actor. Punch in Adam Sandler, and DVR will automatically record all programming in which he appears. The system accomplishes this through an automatically placed, nightly, toll-free call to the service provider that lasts no more than 3 minutes. If a viewer should use the phone while this call is being placed, DVR hangs up and makes the necessary call later.

Replay TV
www.replay.com

DVR does not deliver programming the way broadcasters, cablecasters, and DBS systems do. Rather, it is employed *in addition to* these content providers. To use either ReplayTV or TiVo, viewers must buy a special receiver, and TiVo requires a monthly service charge. It is too early in the life of this technology to predict its success or failure. Today about 7% of all TV households have DVR, and industry predictions see that proportion rising to 37% by 2010 (Becker, 2005). The devices themselves are expensive. Both systems require access to a telephone jack, often a problem in rooms in which a television typically might sit, such as a den or living room. The two DBS and several cable providers now offer DVR as part of their technology platform, helping overcome somewhat the cost and phone jack problems, and TiVo's point-and-click Internet download technology, in development, may be sufficient incentive for some people who might not otherwise utilize DVR to do so. An additional problem for the technology is that it faces a copyright legal challenge from the broadcast and cable industries, both of which fear its commercial-skipping potential. But, as with DVD, its mere presence is additional evidence that television viewing, as we have long known and practiced it, is changing dramatically.

DIGITAL TELEVISION

Digitization of video signals reduces their size; therefore, more information can be carried over telephone wires (belonging to either a cable or phone company) and stored. The traditional television broadcasters see digitization of television signals as their salvation, because it would allow them to carry multiple forms of content on the spectrum space currently used to carry their one broadcast signal. But digitization for the purpose of transmitting multiple signals conflicts with the use of their spectrum space to transmit high-definition digital television (HDTV). This puts broadcasters in a bind, because viewers want beautiful, clear, wide-screen, high-definition images, but they also want a lot of channels of video and other data. If broadcasters opt to devote their entire spectrum space, as technologically required, to the transmission of high-definition images, they will lose audience share to cable, the Internet, and DBS, all of which offer multiple channels of programming and data. If they opt to use digitization to divide their channels (called **multiplexing**) and in effect become minicable companies themselves, offering over-the-air services such as clearer digital video images (although not of HDTV quality), Internet access, paging services, and constant data flow of information such as stocks and sports scores, they will lose HDTV set owners who want the even-crisper images of DVD.

The digital television revolution is progressing slowly for two primary reasons. First is the lack of availability of digital receivers. Even though many of today's sets are sold as *digital*, this refers to how the set itself constructs the image; they do not have digital tuners. The "vast majority of 'digital television sets' being manufactured, advertised, and sold at retail stores do not allow viewers to access local over-the-air digital stations," according to National Association of Broadcasters' Edward Fritts (2002, p. 2). Viewers wanting to receive digital stations must either incur the additional cost of a set-top digital tuning box or pay much more for a true digital receiving set than they would for a more typical set. This problem should be overcome in a few years, given the FCC's August 2002 ruling that by 2007, all receivers imported into or made in the United States come equipped with digital tuners.

The second problem in the diffusion of digital television is that cable operators, too, must be willing to change over to digital. It does broadcasters who have made the expensive conversion to digital no good if cable operators cannot or will not devote valuable channels to digital signals. Some small steps have been made to resolve this difficulty. Although the over-the-air broadcasters have long lobbied the FCC to pass federal **digital must-carry rules** requiring cable operators to carry all digital, as well as analog, channels, some cable operators are making the move voluntarily. These obstacles notwithstanding, Congress has require all television stations to convert completely to digital transmission by 2009.

TELEVISION AND VIDEO ON THE INTERNET

Television on the Internet was slow to take off because of copyright and piracy concerns, and because few viewers had sufficient **bandwidth,** space on the wires bringing content into people's homes. So for several years the most typical video fare on the Net was a variety of short specialty transmissions such as movie trailers, short independent films, music videos, and news clips. But the development of increasingly sophisticated video compression software and the parallel rise of homes with **broadband** Internet connections (68% of home Internet users; Taylor, 2006) have changed that. Because broadband offers greater information-carrying capacity (that is, it increases bandwidth), television on the Internet is increasingly common, a situation heralded by the 2006 announcements by the three major broadcast networks that they would join providers such as ifilm.com, youtube.com, and atomfilms.com in the download revolution. Each is trying its own model—rent a download for a short time, buy a download without commercials for a higher fee than one with ads, monthly subscriptions for limitless downloads—as the search for the right formula unfolds. The Internet companies, too, have joined in. Apple iTunes (apple.com/itunes) sells complete downloads of programs such as *Lost* and *Desperate Housewives* for $2 each, playable on full-size computers and even on video iPods. Google Video offers new (for example, *CSI*) and old (for example, *The Brady Bunch*) programs ranging in price from free to $4. AOL has In2TV (video.aol.com) offering free downloads of classic shows like *Growing Pains* with commercials, and Yahoo! (video.yahoo.com) provides free downloads of a few contemporary programs, such as *How I Met Your Mother*. Computer hardware manufacturer Intel's chief operating officer, Paul Otellini, proclaimed, "It's clear that the dam has broken. There's an inevitable move to use the Internet as a distribution medium and that's not going to stop" (in Markoff, 2006, p. G5).

Program owners view the Internet as easy money, as it costs very little to transfer programming to new platforms. Syndicators, both off-network and first-run, will be especially well served by the Internet. The broadcast networks, too, welcome the additional revenue stream provided by video downloads. They see the vast majority of viewers content to watch programming when they, the networks, schedule it. "The fact is," according to CBS research executive David Poltrack, "most people try to fit TV viewing into the content of a thing called 'a life'" (in Fritz, 2005, p. 26). Still, more than 94 million Web users each month, better than 50% of the Internet population, report watching video online, averaging about 73 minutes each (Burns, 2005).

INTERACTIVE TELEVISION

The Internet is not the only technology that permits interactivity. Cable and satellite also allow viewers to "talk back" to content providers. But it is **digital cable television,** the delivery of digital images and other information to subscribers, that offers the truest form of interaction. In 2005 there were 25 million digital cable subscribers in the United States (NCTA, 2005). Many digital cable subscribers also use their cable connections to access the Internet. Currently, there are 21 million users with cable modems connecting their computers to the Net via a specified Internet service provider, or ISP (NCTA, 2005). As a result, "must-carry" has taken on new meaning in the Internet age, as Congress and the courts debate cable's power to grant or limit access to its wires to outside service and content providers and those providers' right to demand that access. The essay *"Brand X:* Controlling the Flow of Information" on page 260 explores the landmark—and controversial—June 2005 Supreme Court decision in favor of cable's right to restrict outside providers' access to their lines.

Apple iTunes Video
www.apple.com/itunes

AOL In2TV
www.video.aol.com

Yahoo! Video
www.video.yahoo.com

Cable's digital channels permit multiplexing, carrying two or more different signals over the same channel. This, in turn, is made possible by *digital compression,* which "squeezes" signals to permit multiple signals to be carried over one channel. Digital compression works by removing redundant information from the transmission of the signal. For example, the set behind two actors in a movie scene might not change for several minutes. So why transmit the information that the set is there? Simply transmit the digital data that indicate what has changed in the scene, not what has not.

Cable Positive
www.cablepositive.org

This expanded capacity makes possible *interactive cable,* that is, the ability of subscribers to talk back to the system operator (extra space on the channel is used for this back talk). And *this* permits the following services:

- *Video-on-demand (VOD)*—Viewers can access a virtually unlimited array of pay-per-view movies and other content that can be watched whenever they want; VOD also permits pausing, rewinding, and fast-forwarding as if the content were on videotape.

- *One-click shopping*—Television content, including commercials, can carry hidden graphics and text that can be called up with a remote control; once on screen, a simple click can automatically order the given product.

- *Local information on demand*—Using a remote control, viewers can summon local information to their screens; for example, when watching political debates, viewers might call up information about the candidates' planned visits to their community or the candidates' congressional voting record on issues of local importance.

- *Program interactivity*—Prompted by an on-screen cue, viewers can predict upcoming plays in a football game, choose camera angles in performances and sporting events, play along with game show contestants, or learn more about a favorite sitcom actor's career.

- *Interactive program guides*—Viewers can navigate "smart" program schedules to plan viewing.

CULTURAL FORUM

Brand X: Controlling the Flow of Information

The battle for control of the broadband wires that enter our homes has been raging in government, legal, and technology circles for years, and it hinges on the definition of the services provided by cable companies. The cable industry views itself as an **information service,** a legal designation that allows it, like a broadcast network, to maintain control over what passes over its lines. As an information service, an MSO can limit, grant access, and charge whatever it wishes to whomever it wishes. But many public interest groups and the Internet industries, especially the ISPs, want cable classified as a **telecommunications service,** making it a **common carrier,** like a phone company, required to carry the messages of all comers and with little power to restrict them.

This debate, "an important test of the First Amendment in the age of the Internet," according to the Media Access Project and the Center for Digital Democracy (Schwartzman, 2004, p. 1), was very much unnoticed by the larger public. Inevitably, it was left to the Supreme Court, in its June 2005 *National Cable & Telecommunications Association v. Brand X* decision, to clarify the issue and put it squarely in the cultural forum. In the 6–3 ruling, commonly referred to as the *Brand X* decision (after the small California-based ISP

> **WHAT IS AT STAKE IN THIS DECISION? CRITICS SAY THE VERY FUTURE OF AN OPEN AND FREE INTERNET AND THE PRACTICE OF DEMOCRACY ITSELF ARE THREATENED. "ALLOWING THE 'COZY DUOPOLY' OF THE CABLE AND PHONE COMPANIES TO CONTROL THE FLOW OF INFORMATION INTO OUR HOMES HANDS THEM THE KEY TO LIMITING CHOICE AND COMPETITION IN INTERNET SERVICES."**

that locked horns with the NCTA), the Court ruled that cable was indeed an information service, free to control access to its broadband lines. For advocates of the opposing model, this news was doubly bad, because big phone companies like Verizon and the BOCs immediately announced their intention to seek similar status from the FCC; after all, they argued, they, too, were no longer "just" phone companies; they were providers of a multiple array of information services such as VOD and the Internet.

What is at stake in *Brand X*? The very "future of the Internet as we know it . . . the right of citizens to send and receive any content," and as such, say its critics, the practice of democracy itself (Schwartzman, 2004, p. 1). Allowing the "cozy duopoly," in the words of Consumers Union and the Consumer Federation of America, to control the flow of information into our homes "hands them the key" to limiting choice and competition in Internet services (Hansell, 2005). It not only gives them the power to channel their customers to one or a few ISPs (predictably their own, as most cable systems already do), deny users access to competing, possibly less expensive or more efficient service providers (using a subcontractor to provide Internet telephony, for example, rather than offering

PHONE-OVER-CABLE

Another service offered by many MSOs is phone service over cable wires. Phone-over-cable has spread very slowly. Currently there are only 3 million cable-delivered residential telephone subscribers (NCTA, 2005). There are two reasons. The first is technical—although the technology for quality phone-over-cable exists, the problem is getting manufacturers to agree on compatibility standards. The second reason that phone-over-cable is slow in coming is consumer resistance. Many people, already dissatisfied with the level of service provided by their cable companies, are wary of relying on them for phone service as well.

But phone-over-cable offers an additional benefit to MSOs. If telephone service can be delivered by the same cable that brings television into the home, so too can the Internet. And what's more, if the cable line is broadband capable of handling digitally compressed data, that Internet service can be even faster than the service provided over traditional phone lines. Cable, in other words, can become a one-stop communications provider: television,

www

Cable Television Advertising Bureau
www.onetvworld.org

the more established independent company Vonage), and shut out "disfavored" content providers (as BellSouth did for a time in 2005, blocking the progressive, anti–Iraq war blog Buzzflash), but it could very well "easily stifle the unexpected Next Big Thing from the random startup" (Yang, 2005b, p. 2). After all, with no guarantee of access to users, who will take the necessary risks? The results, according to *Washington Post* technology writer Rob Pegoraro, will be higher Internet connection prices (with little or no competition—why should cable and phone companies charge low rates?); low reliability and poor tech support (again, how happy are you now with your phone and cable companies' track record in these areas?); and limited choice of features (without competition, only the most popular and profitable bundles will be offered). "Broadband Internet access is far too important to be left to the cable guys or the phone company—especially since it will someday eliminate the need for separate phone and TV service," Pegoraro concluded (2005, p. F7). *Brand X* "is both anticonsumer and anticompetition," added House Democrat Edward Markey. Congress must act to "ensure that national broadband policy reflects the open architecture model of the Internet and remains a medium friendly to innovation, entrepreneurial activity, and consumer-centric communications" (in McCullagh, 2005, p. 2). This concern is fueled, in part, by a report from the International Telecommunication Union ranking the United States 16th in the world in high-speed access for its citizens, down from 3rd 5 years ago (Yang, 2005b), falling behind countries that have adopted "a successful policy of encouraging competition through open access to infrastructure." In addition, broadband in these countries costs less than one-half of what it does in the United States for a greater variety of sophisticated services (Yglesias, 2005, p. 21).

The cable and phone companies respond that *Brand X* will correct these problems, as their newfound freedom to control their lines, because it creates additional incentive for them to invest more in their infrastructure, removes economic barriers to innovation. Moreover, opponents may see them as "cozy," but the cable and phone companies are fierce rivals, and it is this competition for customers that will drive greater economies and the growth of services for users.

Enter your voice. How comfortable are you knowing that your cable provider can restrict access to disfavored Web sites or video services refusing to pay a premium price for carriage? Or will the quest for profits drive MSOs (and phone companies) to offer as many services to as many people as possible? But how long can Internet sites expect a "free ride" (in the words of AT&T's chairman, Edward Whitacre) over cable and phone companies' lines? But hasn't **network neutrality**, treating all comers equally, been not only the hallmark of Internet freedom but a driving force behind the Net's development and acceptance? Is tiered access—faster delivery and better service for Net sites willing to pay more for carriage—the answer? But if some sites get faster delivery and better service, by definition, others will get slower delivery and poorer service. This is not network neutrality; or is network neutrality an out-of-date concept? The Internet Non-Discrimination Act, introduced into the U.S. Senate in 2006, would make network neutrality the law of the land. Do you favor such a law, or do you think that the government needs to stay out of Internet issues?

VOD, audio, high-speed Internet access, long-distance and local phone service, multiple phone lines, and fax. This is **bundling.**

How valuable is a bundle-receiving subscriber to a cable/telco combination? Add together the bills you're probably paying right now—basic or premium cable, your Internet service provider, and your phone bill. What does that total? Now speculate on how much pay-per-view and VOD you might buy now that you have broadband and a superfast cable modem. And what would you pay for home delivery of real-time sports or financial data? And the MSO would collect each time you accessed an interactive classified or commercial ad. That's how valuable a bundled subscriber will be.

Bundled services may be profitable for MSOs, but they raise the issue of concentration in a somewhat different form from that we've considered elsewhere. Specifically, what risk for consumers does putting this much power into the hands of one company pose? The chairperson of the U.S. Senate Antitrust Subcommittee, Herb Kohl, Democrat from Wisconsin, sees an ominous future for "average consumers." He said that people "may find almost all of their personal communications and information dominated by a very few, large media companies. Their phone, their movies, their Internet, their cable, their link to the outside world will be priced, processed, and packaged for them by one company that faces virtually no competition" (quoted in Albiniak, 2002, p. 7).

MOBILE VIDEO

The newest way to receive and view television is on a mobile device, either a cell phone or other portable video player. We've already seen in this chapter that Apple iTunes allows downloading of television programs not only to home computers but to portable iPods. DBS provider Dish Network has its version, letting subscribers download movies from their home receiver to their portable PocketDish. As for cell phone video receivers, Verizon's Vcast service (Chapter 7) can download music videos as well as music. Other early entrants into the mobile phone video race are phone companies Sprint, with PCS Vision, and Cingular, offering MobiTV. Fox Mobile Entertainment, the Cartoon Network, ESPN, Court TV, and NBC Mobile are just a few of the content providers striking deals with these services. All are chasing what promises to become a $1.5 billion business by 2009 (Oser, 2006), and the winners will be those who can best answer two questions: What content will people be willing to watch on mobile devices? and How big will the audience actually be?

DBS-provider Dish's Pocket Dish, only one of many mobile video options available to viewers

Cell phone video providers think brief content works best. Fox Mobile, for example, creates **mobisodes**, special 1-minute scenarios of its television hit *24*. VCast provides brief clips of performances from CBS's *Rock Star: INXS*. Spider-Man creator Stan Lee's POW! Mobile distributes 1-minute episodes of comic book action via Cingular's MobiTV system; *The Accuser* and *The Drifter* are his titles.

Portable video device providers such as Apple and Dish seem to think that longer fare will attract more viewers. They are heartened by the success of Sony's PlayStation Portable (PSP) video-game unit, with its 4.3-inch-wide screen. Designed to play specially manufactured video discs as well as games, it has become a successful movie-watching device. In the first 6 months of its availability, fans bought more than 5 million movie and television discs from among the 200 titles available from studios like Disney and Paramount. Content providers are especially excited over another of PSP's capabilities—it can connect to the Web for the downloading, storing, and viewing of even more video (McLean, 2005b). There is more to say about PSP and other mobile game devices in Chapter 9.

"No one would think of putting a newspaper on television. Why would you just put television on a cell phone?" asks CBS Mobile's Cyriac Roeding, expressing some of the doubt surrounding the size of mobile video's potential audience (in "Quote," 2006). Indeed, despite very optimistic predictions of the size of the mobile data business, as high as $16 billion annually by 2009, most of that traffic will be composed of data, rather than video services (Wolf, 2005). CBS's own research indicates that only 7% of the public is interested in purchasing a mobile video unit, and that even among those who already have video-capable mobile devices, only one-third said they'd definitely buy an episode of their favorite television series for as little as $1.95 (Consoli, 2005). An independent research company, RBC Capital Markets, discovered in a national survey that when asked to respond to the statement "I am not interested in watching TV programs or movies on my handheld device," 76% said "true" (Siklos, 2006). But, argue the mobile video optimists, one-third of the television audience and 24% of handheld video device users is still a lot of downloads for already-created content. In fact, technology research firm eMarketer's analysis of the market predicts that once a model of free and ad-supported mobile content is settled on, it should produce about $300 million a year by 2010 (Whitney, 2006).

Recognizing Staged News

For years studies have shown that a majority of the American public turns to television as the source of most of its news and that viewers rank it as the most believable news source. Television news can be immediate and dramatic, especially when events being covered lend themselves to visual images. But what if they don't? News may be journalism, but television news is also a television *show*, and as such it must attract viewers. Television newspeople have an obligation to truthfully and accurately inform the public, but they also have an obligation to attract a large number of people so their station or network is profitable.

Even the best television journalists cannot inform a public that does not tune in, and the public tunes in to see pictures. Television professionals, driven to get pictures, often walk the fine ethical line of **news staging**—that is, re-creating some event that is believed to or could have happened. Sometimes news staging takes simple forms; for example, a reporter may narrate an account of an event he or she did not witness while video of that event is played. The intended impression is that the reporter is on the scene. What harm is there in this? It's common practice on virtually all U.S. television news shows. But how much of a leap is it from that to ABC's 1994 broadcast of reporter Cokie Roberts, wrapped tightly in winter clothes, seemingly reporting from Capitol Hill on a blustery January night when she was in fact standing in a nearby Washington studio, her presence at the scene staged by computer digital technology?

The broadcasters' defense is, "This is not staging in the sense that the *event* was staged. What does it matter if the reporter was not actually on the spot? What was reported actually did happen." If you accept this view (the event *did* happen, therefore it's not news staging), how would you evaluate Fox News's Geraldo Rivera's reporting from "sacred ground," the scene of a battle in Afghanistan in which U.S. forces suffered heavy losses, even though he was miles from the actual spot? And if you accept digital alteration of news scenes to place network reporters at the scene, how would you evaluate CBS's common practice of digitally inserting its network logo on billboards and buildings that appear behind its reporters and anchors? If this staging is acceptable to you, why not okay the digital enhancement of fires and explosions in the news?

Some media literate viewers may accept the-event-did-happen argument, but another form of news staging exists that is potentially more troublesome— re-creation. In 1992 the producers of *Dateline NBC* re-created the explosion of a GMC truck, justifying the move with the argument that similar explosions "had happened" (Chapter 14). In the mid-1990s a Denver news show ran footage of a pit bull fight it had arranged and defended its action on

LIVING MEDIA LITERACY

Turn Off Your TV

The Media Foundation (see Chapter 12) runs an annual campaign called TV Turn Off Week, typically in April. Hundreds of thousands of viewers around the world simply tune out for a week. There is a Web site (adbusters.org/campaigns/tvturnoff), posters, chat rooms, and contact lists, all designed to support communal action. You can involve yourself in the global community of TV-turn-offers by accessing the site and signing on.

But you, as a media literate individual, can test for yourself just how free you are of television's hold. In other words, whether you are a television fan or foe, you can see if you control your viewing or if your viewing controls you. To start, pick a 7-day period (or 5-day if that's how you choose to define a week) and simply stop watching. That means no television at all. No videos. No video games. If you are truly adventurous, enlist one or more friends, family members, or roommates.

Now the hard part. Changing your routine viewing habits for a few days will not do very much for you unless you reflect on its meaning. Ask yourself, and any confederates you may have enlisted, these questions:

1. How easy or difficult was it to break away from television? Why?

> **WHETHER YOU ARE A TELEVISION FAN OR FOE, YOU CAN SEE IF YOU CONTROL YOUR VIEWING OR IF YOUR VIEWING CONTROLS YOU.**

2. What did you learn about your television consumption habits?

3. How did you use the freed-up time? Were you able to find productive activity, or did you spend your time longing for the tube?

4. Describe your interaction with other people during the week. Did your conversations change? That is, were there alterations in duration, depth, subject matter?

5. To which other media did you turn to replace your television viewing? Why those in particular? Did you learn anything about them as "TV substitutes"?

6. If you were unable to complete the week of nonviewing, describe why. How easy or difficult was it to come to the decision to give up? Why?

7. Do you consider it a failure to have resumed watching before the week was up? Why or why not?

8. Once you resume watching, either after the week has passed or when you abandon nonviewing, place yourself on a scale of 1 to 10, with 1 being I-Control-the-TV and 10 being The-TV-Controls-Me. Explain why you rated yourself as you did.

the ground that these things "do happen." *ABC Evening News* simulated surveillance camera recordings of U.S. diplomat Felix Bloch handing over a briefcase to a shady character on the street to accompany a 1989 report on Bloch's arrest on espionage charges. The simulation even had a surveillance

Did Geraldo Rivera engage in permissible or impermissible news staging when he reported from "sacred ground" although he was miles from the actual spot?

camera's dark, grainy look and the time code numbers racing in the corner of the picture. This staging was justified with the claim that it "could have happened."

Where do media professionals draw the line? What happens to the public's trust in its favorite news source as the distinctions between fact and fiction, reality and illusion, what is and what is digital, and reporting and re-creating disappear?

If you see a televised news story labeled as a re-creation or simulation, what leads you to trust the re-creator's or simulator's version? Media literate people develop strategies to analyze content, deciding where *they* draw the line and rejecting staged news that crosses it. The news producer must balance service to the public against ratings and profit, but viewers must balance their desire for interesting, stimulating visuals against confidence that the news is reported rather than manufactured.

Why did ABC feel compelled not only to have Ms. Roberts appear to report from in front of the Capitol Building but also to have it seem, by her dress, that she was quite cold? There are two possible explanations for staging such as this. One is the need to meet television audience demands for visuals. The second explanation is the assumption, widely held by television professionals, that people are incapable of reading, accepting, interpreting, and understanding important issues unless they are presented in a manner that meets viewers' expectations of the news. If this is accurate, media literate viewers must reconsider their expectations of the medium. If this assumption about viewers is incorrect, media literate people must make that clear to those who produce the news, either by choosing news programs that avoid staging or by protesting to those that do.

RESOURCES FOR REVIEW AND DISCUSSION

Review Points

- In 1884 Paul Nipkow developed the first device for transmitting images. John Logie Baird soon used this mechanical scanning technology to send images long distance. Vladimir Zworykin and Philo Farnsworth developed electronic scanning technology in the 1920s, leading to the public demonstration of television in 1939.
- In the 1950s, the quiz show scandal, the business acumen of Lucille Ball, McCarthyism, and the ratings system shaped the nature of broadcast television. Cable, introduced in 1948, would soon effect even more change.
- Cable, designed initially for the importation of distant signals, became a mature medium when it began offering movies and other premium content.
- Cable, dominated by large MSOs, offers programming in tiers that include basic, expanded basic, and

- premium cable. Some favor a new pricing scheme, à la carte.
- Direct broadcast satellite is the primary multichannel competitor to cable.
- A host of technologies influence the television–viewer relationship, including VCR, DVD, and DVR. Digitization and the Internet make possible interactive television, a particular strength of cable. Subscribers may also receive phone service over cable.
- Mobile video—over cell phones or other portable video devices— is beginning to emerge. Questions remain as to what types of content and which pricing models will succeed.
- Staged news raises several questions for media literate people about broadcaster integrity and respect for viewers.

Key Terms

Use the text's Online Learning Center at www.mhhe.com/baran5 to further your understanding of the following terminology.

nonlinear TV, 232
Nipkow disc, 234
pixel, 234
iconoscope tube, 234
kinescope, 234
coaxial cable, 236
microwave relay, 236
spot commercial sales, 236
audimeter, 240
peoplemeter, 241
personal peoplemeter, 241
sweeps periods, 242
community antenna television
   (CATV), 243
master antenna television
   (MATV), 243
importation of distant signals, 243
all-channel legislation, 243

vast wasteland, 245
network, 245
clear time, 246
compensation, 246
off-network, 246
pilot, 246
put, 247
short ordering, 247
first-run syndication, 248
stripping, 248
premium cable, 249
fiber optic, 249
tiers, 250
expanded basic cable, 250
multiple system operator (MSO),
   251
à la carte pricing, 251
subscription television, 252

time-shifting, 256
zipping, 256
DVD, 256
digital video recorder (DVR), 256
multiplexing, 257
digital must-carry rules, 258
bandwidth, 258
broadband, 258
digital cable television, 259
bundling, 260
information service, 260
telecommunications service, 260
common carrier, 260
network neutrality, 261
mobisodes, 262
news staging, 263

Questions for Review

Go to the self-quizzes on the Online Learning Center to test your knowledge.

1. What is the importance of each of the following to the history of television: Paul Nipkow, John Logie Baird, Vladimir Zworykin, Philo Farnsworth, and Newton Minow?
2. How do VCR, DVD, and DVR differ? How are they similar in the services they offer viewers?
3. What was the impact on television of the quiz show scandal, *I Love Lucy*, McCarthyism, and the Nielsen ratings?
4. How are the ratings taken? What are some complaints about the ratings system?
5. What were the contributions of John Walson and Milton Shapp to the development of cable television?
6. How does a program typically make it to the air? How does syndication figure in this process?
7. How have cable, VCR, DVD, DVR, and DBS affected the networks?

8. What are some of the changes in television wrought by cable?
9. What is first-run syndication?
10. Explain the difference between basic cable, expanded basic cable, premium cable, pay-per-view, and à la carte pricing.
11. What are importation of distant signals, premium cable, and fiber optics? How are they related? What do they have to do with cable's maturity as a medium?
12. What is DBS? What factors slowed its diffusion until recently?
13. What are the two forms of mobile video? What questions remain to be answered for the mobile video industry?
14. What are some of the forms that interactive television can take?
15. What is news staging?

Questions for Critical Thinking and Discussion

1. Do you think single-sponsorship of television programs necessarily produces quality fare? Do spot commercial sales necessarily produce mediocre fare? Defend your position.
2. Do you agree with Newton Minow's assessment of television? If so, what can be done to improve the medium's performance?
3. As an independent producer, what kind of program would you develop for the networks? How immune do you think you could be from the pressures that exist in this process?
4. Are you a cable subscriber? Why or why not? At what level? Would you prefer à la carte pricing? Why or why not?
5. Is news staging ever permissible? If not, why not? If yes, under what conditions? Have you ever recognized a report as staged when it was not so identified? Describe what you saw.

Important Resources

 Go to the Online Learning Center for additional readings.

Internet Resources

Television History	www.tvhistory.tv
Zworykin	www.ieee.org/organizations/history_center/oral_histories/transcripts/zworykin21.html
Farnsworth	www.invent.org/hall_of_fame/56.html
Quiz Show Scandal	www.fiftiesweb.com/quizshow.htm
McCarthyism	www.mccarthy.cjb.net/
Radio Television News Directors Association	www.rtnda.org
National Cable & Telecommunications Association	www.nct2.com
National Telecommunications and Information Administration	www.ntia.doc.gov
Cable and Telecommunications Association for Marketing	www.ctam.com
A. C. Nielsen	www.nielsenmedia.com
National Association of Broadcasters	www.nab.org
ABC	www.abc.com
NBC	www.nbc.com
Episodes of TV Shows	www.epguides.com
CBS	www.cbs.com
Fox	www.fox.com
Children's Television Workshop	www.ctw.org
Women in Cable & Telecommunications	www.wict.org
DirecTV	www.directv.com
Dish Network	www.dishnetwork.com
TiVo	www.tivo.com
ReplayTV	www.replay.com
Apple iTunes Video	www.apple.com/itunes
AOL In2TV	www.video.aol.com
Yahoo! Video	www.video.yahoo.com
Cable Positive	www.cablepositive.org
Cable Television Advertising Bureau	www.onetvworld.org

Video Games

LEARNING OBJECTIVES

Video games are accelerating the five trends reshaping mass communication and the mass media industries. They are the product of a highly concentrated industry, they are luring people from the more traditional media (audience fragmentation), they are used as and filled with advertising (hypercommercialization), they know no borders (globalization), and they are played on numerous technologies, from game consoles to personal computers to the Internet to cell phones (convergence). And even though the game industry grosses nearly twice as much as Hollywood does every year, mass communication experts are only now taking this medium seriously. After studying this chapter you should

- be familiar with the history and development of games and the gaming industry.
- understand how the organizational and economic nature of the contemporary gaming industry shapes the content of games.
- understand the relationship between games and their players.
- be familiar with changes in the game industry brought about by emerging technologies.
- be able to use your improved game-playing media literacy skills to understand and apply the industry-standard rating system.

"Why are you playing video games? Don't you have homework or a paper due or something?"

"This is more important. And anyway, what are you, my mother?"

"Nope, I just don't want to have to dig up another roommate, that's all."

"Glad to know you care. And anyway, it may look like I'm playing video games, but I'm really doing research for my global politics class. Check it out. This is a game about genocide in Darfur. Some kids at another school made it and sent it to darfurisdying.com."

"A game about what, where?"

Opposite: Harry Potter, the video game.

"That's the point. It's an MTV thing, a contest to raise awareness of poverty and death in Darfur . . . that's a region in the African country called the Sudan."

"I knew that."

"Anyway, college students can design games and send them in. Anybody can play them, there're about six so far, and vote for their favorite. Then the folks running the competition will use the Net and mtvU, the college cable channel, to promote it. The designers get a great resumé entry and maybe a job offer, and maybe some good gets done. You wanna play, be a little Darfurian kid trying to make it to the water well without being killed by the Sudanese militia?"

"No thanks. If I'm going to play games, I'd like to kill bad guys with a vast array of magnificent weapons and be able to leap tall buildings in a single bound."

In this chapter we examine games played on a variety of electronic, microprocessor-based platforms. But before we get deeper into our discussion of the sophisticated, entertaining, and sometimes (as you can tell from

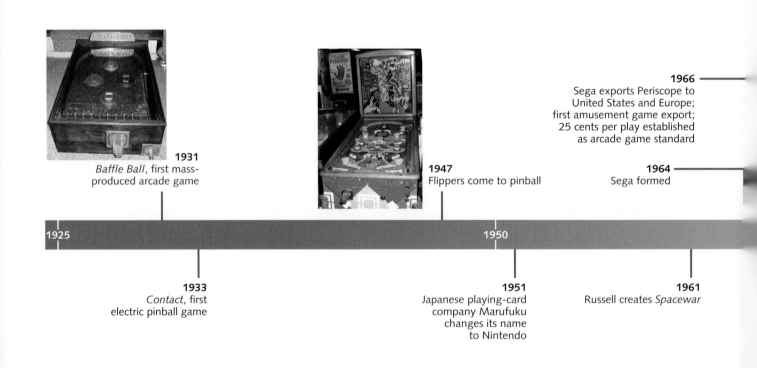

1931
Baffle Ball, first mass-produced arcade game

1947
Flippers come to pinball

1966
Sega exports Periscope to United States and Europe; first amusement game export; 25 cents per play established as arcade game standard

1964
Sega formed

1925

1950

1933
Contact, first electric pinball game

1951
Japanese playing-card company Marufuku changes its name to Nintendo

1961
Russell creates *Spacewar*

our opening vignette) not very playful games that abound today, let's look at their roots in the convergence of pinball machines and military simulators.

A Short History of Computer and Video Games

Carnival man David Gottlieb invented the first mass-produced arcade game, *Baffle Ball*, in 1931. A small wooden cabinet, it had only one moving part, a plunger. Players would launch a ball into the playing field, a slanted surface with metal "pins" surrounding "scoring holes." The object was to get the ball into one of the holes. Gottlieb was soon manufacturing 400 cabinets a day. Just as quickly, he had many imitators. One, Harry Williams, invented *Contact*, the first electric pinball game. Williams was an engineer, and his 1933 gaming innovations were electronic scoring (*Baffle Ball* players had to keep their scores in their heads) and scoring holes, or pockets, that threw the ball back into the playing field (in *Baffle Ball*, when a ball dropped into a hole, it dropped into a hole). The popularity of arcade games exploded, and players' enthusiasm was fueled even more when slot-machine makers entered the field, producing games with cash payouts. With the Depression

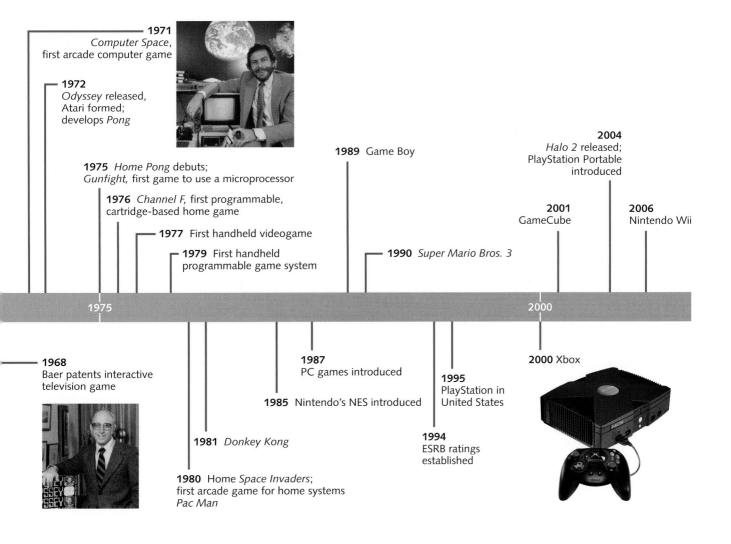

1971
Computer Space,
first arcade computer game

1972
Odyssey released,
Atari formed;
develops *Pong*

1975 *Home Pong* debuts;
Gunfight, first game to use a microprocessor

1976 *Channel F*, first programmable,
cartridge-based home game

1977 First handheld videogame

1979 First handheld
programmable game system

1989 Game Boy

1990 *Super Mario Bros. 3*

2004
Halo 2 released;
PlayStation Portable
introduced

2001
GameCube

2006
Nintendo Wii

1975

2000

1968
Baer patents interactive
television game

1987
PC games introduced

1985 Nintendo's NES introduced

1995
PlayStation in
United States

1994
ESRB ratings
established

2000 Xbox

1981 *Donkey Kong*

1980 Home *Space Invaders*;
first arcade game for home systems
Pac Man

Gottlieb's *Baffle Ball* and
Humpty Dumpty.

in full force in the 1930s, however, civic leaders were not much in favor of this development, and several locales, most notably New York City, banned the games. Pinball was considered gambling.

David Gottlieb had the answer. Games of skill were not gambling. And games that paid off in additional games rather than cash were not gambling. In 1947, he introduced *Humpty Dumpty,* a six-flipper game that rewarded high-scorers with replays. Bans were lifted, pinball returned to the arcades, even more players were attracted to the skills-based electronic games, and the stage was set for what we know today as video and computer games. As Steven Baxter of the *CNN Computer Connection* wrote, "You can't say that video games grew out of pinball, but you can assume that video games wouldn't have happened without it. It's like bicycles and the automobile. One industry leads to the other and then they exist side-by-side. But you had to have bicycles to one day have motor cars." Games writer Steven Kent adds, "New technologies do not simply spring out of thin air. They need to be associated with familiar industries or ideas. People may have jokingly referred to the first automobiles as 'horseless carriages,' but the name also helped define them. The name changed them from nebulous, unexplainable machines to an extension of an already accepted mode of transportation" (both quotes from Kent, 2001, pp. 1–2).

TODAY'S GAMES EMERGE

Throughout the late 1950s and 1960s, computers were hulking giants, filling entire rooms (see Chapter 10). Most displayed their output on paper in the form of teletype. But the very best, most advanced computers, those designed for military research and analysis, were a bit sleeker and had monitors for output display. Only three universities—MIT, University of Utah, and Stanford—and a few dedicated research installations had these machines. At MIT, a group of self-described nerds, the Tech Model Railroad Club (TMRC),

WWW

History of Pinball
www.pinballhistory.com

WWW

Arcade Flyer Archive
www.arcadeflyer.com

began writing programs for fun for a military computer. Club members would leave their work next to the computer so others could build on what had come before. One member, Steve Russell, decided to write the ultimate program, an interactive game. It took him 200 hours over 6 months to produce the first interactive computer game, *Spacewar,* completed in 1961. This version featured toggle switches that controlled the speed and direction of two spaceships and the torpedoes they fired at each other. His final version, completed the next year, had an accurate map of the stars in the background and a sun with a mathematically precise gravitational field that influenced play. Russell and his club-mates even built remote control units with switches for every game function, the first game pad. "We thought about trying to make money off it for two or three days but concluded that there wasn't a way that it could be done," said Russell (quoted in Kent, 2001, p. 20).

This is the universe navigated by *Spacewar* gamers, simple by today's standards, but a dramatic beginning for the medium.

But another college student, Nolan Bushnell, thought differently (DeMaria & Wilson, 2004, p. 16). For 2 years after the completion of Russell's game, the TMRC distributed it to other schools for free. Bushnell, who worked in an arcade to pay for his engineering studies at the University of Utah, played *Spacewar* incessantly. After graduation he dedicated himself to developing a coin-operated version of the game that had consumed so much of his time. He knew that to make money, it would have to attract more than computer enthusiasts, so he designed a futuristic-looking fiberglass cabinet. The result, *Computer Space,* released in 1971, was a dismal failure. It was far too complicated for casual play, doing good business near college campuses but bombing in bowling alleys and beer halls. Yet Bushnell was undeterred. With two friends and investments of $250 each, he quit his engineering job and incorporated Atari in 1972.

Videogame Museum
www.vgmuseum.com

Nolan Bushnell and a few of his toys.

Ralph Baer and *Odyssey*.

Long before this, in 1951, Ralph Baer, an engineer for a military contractor charged with developing "the best TV set in the world," decided a good set should do more than receive a few channels (remember, this was before cable's rise). He suggested building games into the receivers. His bosses were unimpressed. Fifteen years later Baer was working for another defense contractor when he drafted the complete schematics for a video-game console that would sell for about $20. He patented it in 1968 and licensed his device to Magnavox, which, in 1972, marketed the first home video-game system as *Odyssey* and sold it for $100.

Odyssey was a simple game offering two square spots to represent two players (or paddles), a ball, and a center line. It had six plug-in cartridges and transparent, colored screen overlays producing 12 games, all very rudimentary. Its high cost and Magnavox's decision to sell it through its television set dealers—leading to the incorrect perception that it could be played only on Magnavox sets—limited its success. Only 100,000 units were sold. But with *Odyssey* and Atari,

Game Archive
www.gamearchive.com

the stage was set for the introduction of a new art form, and a new industry. The technological foundation was built. The earliest pioneers had seen farther than any others and had made their tentative steps along the path. The world was in flux, as new politics, new music, and new social consciousness began to spread throughout the United States and Europe. The 60s were over. A generation of young people dreamed new dreams and broke down the status quo. It was into that world that first Ralph Baer and then Nolan Bushnell made their humble offerings, and changed the world in ways no one could have foreseen. (DeMaria & Wilson, 2004, p. 17)

The spark that set off the game revolution was *Pong*, Atari's arcade Ping-pong game. Bushnell had seen *Odyssey* at an electronics show and set his people to creating a coin-operated version (Atari later agreed to pay a licensing fee to Magnavox). The two-player game was an overnight hit, selling 100,000 units in its first year—and twice as many knockoffs (Burnham, 2001, p. 61). Players poured quarters into games looking remarkably like *Pong*, including Harry Williams's *Paddle-Ball*, Rally's *For-Play*, and then in an effort to head off what Nolan Bushnell called "the jackals," Atari's own *Pong Doubles*, *Super Pong*, and *Quadrapong* (Sellers, 2001).

The Pong Story
www.pong-story.com

RAPID-FIRE DEVELOPMENTS

What followed, partly as a result of the swift advance of the microchip and computer industries (and a healthy dose of technological genius from a thriving game industry in Japan), was a rapid-fire succession of innovation and development. In 1975 Atari, by marketing *Home Pong* through Sears, made its first steps toward bringing arcade games into the home. Its 1980 release of home *Space Invaders* cemented the trend. Also in 1975,

Midway began importing *Gunfight* from Japanese manufacturer Taito. *Gunfight* was significant for two reasons. Although Sega, with *Periscope,* began importing arcade games into the United States in 1966, *Gunfight* was the first imported video game, and in fact, it was the first game to use a computer microprocessor. In 1976, Fairchild Camera and Instrument introduced *Channel F,* the first programmable, cartridge-based home game. Mattel Toys brought true electronic games to handheld devices in 1977, with titles like *Missile Attack, Auto Race,* and *Football* played on handheld, calculator-sized **LED,** or **light-emitting diode,** and **LCD,** or **liquid crystal display,** screens. In 1979 Milton Bradley released Microvision, the first programmable handheld game system. Two Japanese arcade imports, Namco's *Pac-Man* in 1980 and Nintendo's *Donkey Kong* in 1981, become instant classics, all-time best sellers, and with the introduction of Nintendo's groundbreaking game console NES in 1985, home-version successes.

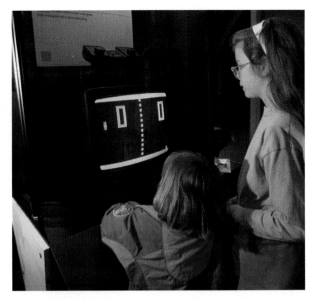

Original *Pong.*

WWW

Sega
www.sega.com

Arcade games, handheld systems, and home game consoles were joined by personal computer games, beginning with the 1987 release of NEC's hybrid PC/console in Japan. Now, with games being played on microprocessor-based consoles, producing them for microprocessor-based PCs was a simple matter. By the early 1990s, CD-ROM-based computer games were common and successful. *Doom* (1993) and *Myst* (1994) were among the first big personal computer game hits. *Doom* hinted at a development soon to come in games because it could be played over **LANs,** or **local area** computer **networks,** typically in a single building; that is, it was an interactive game played by several people over a computer network. It was also the first **first-person perspective** shooting **game;** gamers "carried" the weapon, and all action in the game was seen through their eyes.

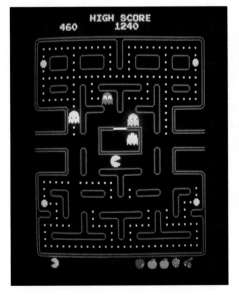
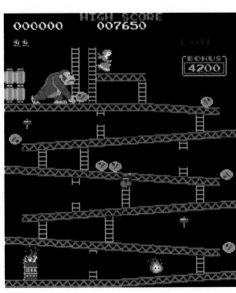

All-time classics *Pac-Man* and *Donkey Kong.*

Two of the first interactive games, *Doom* and *Myst*.

WWW

Game Room Magazine
www.gameroommagazine.com

Games and Their Players

Fifty percent of all Americans play video games (Entertainment Software Association, 2005). But before we look at these people a bit more closely, we need to define exactly what constitutes a video game.

WHAT IS A VIDEO GAME?

As technologies converge, the same game can be played on an increasing number of platforms. *Myst*, for example, was originally a computer game written for Macintosh computers, then IBM PCs, then external CD-ROM drives, then video-game consoles such as PlayStation. Now it can be played online. Versions of *Donkey Kong* can be played in arcades and on consoles, on the Internet, on Macs and PCs, and on handheld players. *Q*bert* can be played on arcade machines and on Nelsonic's wristwatch gameplayers. For our purposes, then, a game is a **video game** when the action of the game takes place interactively on-screen. By this definition, an online text-based game such as a **MUD,** or **multi-user dimension,** which has no moving images, is a video game, but the home version of *Trivial Pursuit*, employing a DVD to offer televised hints to those playing the board game, is not.

That takes care of the technologically based half of the word (*video*), but what is a *game*? For our purposes, a video game is a game when a player has direct involvement in the on-screen action to produce some desired outcome. In a MUD, for example, players use text—words—to create personalities, environments, even worlds in which they interact with others toward some specific end. That's a game. But what about *Mario Teaches Typing*, a cartridge-based learning aid? Even though its goal is teaching, because it has gamelike features (in this case, the famous Super Mario and the manipulation of on-screen action to meet a particular end), it's a game. The essay on page 278 entitled "Using Games for Good" looks at games that function as more than entertainment.

WWW

Links to MUDs
www.mudconnect.com

WWW

Academy of Interactive Arts and Sciences
www.interactive.org

WWW

International Game Developers Association
www.igda.org

WHO IS PLAYING?

What do we know about the 150 million American video-game players? For one thing, they are not necessarily the stereotypical teenage boys gaming away in their parents' basements, as you can see in Figure 9.1.

Regardless of the platform, a game is a video game if the action takes place interactively on-screen.

- Seventy-four percent of heads-of-household play video games.
- The average game player is 30 years old; 19% are over 50.
- Forty-three percent of all gamers are female.
- The average gamer spends 6.8 hours a week playing.

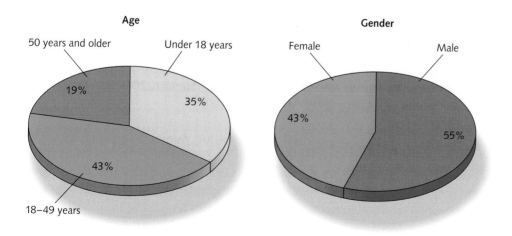

Age

50 years and older

Under 18 years

19%

35%

43%

18–49 years

Gender

Female

Male

43%

55%

Figure 9.1 Game Players' Demographics, 2006. *Source:* Entertainment Software Association, 2005.

USING MEDIA TO MAKE A DIFFERENCE

Using Games for Good

The video-game industry has reached a level of legitimacy and respectability equal to that of other mass media. Now it is being asked the same questions regarding content as they are: What is the impact on kids? What regulations should be imposed? How is the medium used? And just as important, how can we use the medium to make a positive difference?

This last question was recently examined by game industry professionals, social scientists, educators, and parents at the first Serious Games Summit in San Jose, California, in March 2004 (www.gdconf.com/conference/serious games.htm) and three months later at Manhattan's New York Academy of Sciences game conference, "Serious Issues, Serious Games" (www.seriousgames.org). The goal of both meetings was to "explore games as a tool for social change and as a mechanism for achieving the social missions of our [the game industry's] work." Interactive games, said Carl Goodman of the American Museum of the Moving Image, are "not simply the media equivalent of the hula hoop" (Kaye, 2004, p. 1).

Discussion focused on the use of games for policy change, training, and learning. Game developers were encouraged to understand the cognitive learning issues surrounding video games, examine new uses for the technology, and finally, consider the demand for more purposeful content. Educators and policy advocates also targeted issues in education and the use of interactive applications. Participants studied initiatives such as Cisco Systems' *Peter Packet Game and Challenge* (www.netaid.org/youth/peter_packet/game.pt), designed to confront poverty, and the work of nonprofit Global Kids Inc. (www.globalkidsinc.org/), which has teamed with organizations such as Lego, Microsoft, and PBS in an effort to encourage

> **"I REALLY LIKE VIDEOGAMES, AND I WANTED TO DO SOMETHING SPECIAL, SOMETHING MORE THAN GOING ON A DISNEY CRUISE AND STUFF LIKE THAT."**

kids to create their own educational video games. Persuasive Games (persuasivegames.com/) is yet another example of a provider building electronic games designed for "persuasion, instruction, and activism," as is P.O.V. Interactive, which uses interactive games in coordination with PBS documentaries to explore environmental and other issues.

There have been many similar serious games efforts since that inaugural summit. The Darfur Is Dying game-development contest in this chapter's opening vignette is only one example. The National Academy of Sciences is funding game development by the Federation of American Scientists, designed to build enthusiasm for science as a discipline and a career. The National Institute of Drug Abuse and several Department of Defense branches are also funding serious games, specifically health-related games. The United Nations World Food Programme released *Food Force* (www.food-force.com) in spring 2005, and within 6 months it had been downloaded more than 2 million times (Musgrove, 2005).

One of the most successful games-for-good efforts is Games for Health (www.gamesforhealth.org), a community of game developers, researchers, and health care and medical professionals who maintain an ongoing "best practices" conversation—online and in annual conferences—to share information about the impact existing and original games can have on health care and policy. Japanese game-maker Konami's *Dance Dance Revolution*, for example, is an existing **exergame** that invites people to exercise while they play. Players follow cascading arrows on a video screen, mimicking their movements on a large footpad attached by a cable to a game console. Kraft Foods is so committed to

- Adult gamers have been playing for an average of 12 years.
- Eighty percent of all parents play games with their children; 36% introduced their kids to games; 23% were introduced to playing by their children.
- Fifty-two percent of gamers spend less time with television as a result of games; 47% go to the movies less often. (Hewitt, 2004; Entertainment Software Assn., 2005; Woodbury, 2006)

Gamers.com
www.gamers.com

The most frequently employed platforms for gaming are game consoles, computers, and the Internet. Game consoles, the offspring of *Odyssey* and NES, account for most gaming, about two-thirds. Players using dedicated game consoles are primarily male (75%) and under 18 years old (46%). Mac and PC game players, who buy about one-third of all games, also tend to be male and young, but to a lesser degree—61% male, 36% under 18. In addition, 43% of all gamers

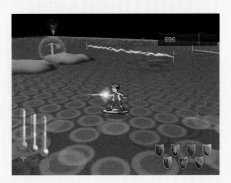

Revolution's health benefits that it sends players a free Kraft Game pad that lets them free-form dance, compete with one another, and count calories expended, all to a variety of music. Sony and Nike teamed up to produce another beneficial exergame, the *EyeToy Kinetic* for PlayStation 2, that encourages users to kickbox, practice yoga, or engage in a number of other physical activities in a variety of simulated environments. Other existing games—just about anything played on a handheld console—are frequently used to reduce children's anxiety before anesthesia, dialysis, or chemotherapy. Research has shown that time on a portable game relaxes preoperative children even more than do their parents (Ault, 2005).

New games, too, are developed specifically to meet people's health needs. Nintendo, which had already developed *GlucoBoy*, an original game to help children manage their diabetes, has created a GameCube-based technology, *Dr. Mario*, to aid patients in managing their own diabetic needs. A much smaller company, BreakAway, has developed *Free Dive*, a fantasy underwater world created to distract pediatric patients from pain or anxiety. Players navigate by joystick as they search for sunken treasure. Although not necessary to the enjoyment of the game, if children wear the accompanying virtual reality helmet while they play, they can dive through a 3-D seascape, accompanied by music and the sound of breathing through a scuba respirator. The U.S. Office of Naval Research has created a virtual reality game to help soldiers returning from Iraq and Afghanistan deal with post-traumatic stress disorder. A therapist controls the game to re-create traumatic events, helping the player/patient slowly revisit the scene of the trauma.

But arguably, the story of 9-year-old Ben Duskin of San Francisco best demonstrates not only the effectiveness of serious games but what can be accomplished when the desire to make a difference is there. When Ben, a fourth-grade student and a leukemia patient, was approached by the

Ben's Game

Make-A-Wish Foundation (www.makewish.org/ben) about his personal wish, he told them he wanted to create a video game that would help other children battle their cancer. "I really like videogames," he said, "and I wanted to do something special, something more than going on a Disney cruise and stuff like that" (in Elias, 2004, p. E2). LucasArts (creators of *Indiana Jones and the Last Crusade, Loom,* and *The Secret of Monkey Island*) was enlisted to fulfill Ben's wish. The game, the product of 6 months' work, is called *Ben's Game*. Playable in nine languages, it was unveiled at a ceremony at the University of California, San Francisco Pediatric Treatment Center. Its "central character, modeled after Ben, zooms around the screen on a skateboard, zapping mutated cells and collecting seven shields to protect against common side effects of chemotherapy, which include nausea, hair loss, and fevers." To ensure that *Ben's Game* makes a difference for as many families as possible, it can be downloaded free of charge through the Make-A-Wish Web site. It has already made a difference in Ben's life. "I feel really good in my heart that lots of people are playing it," he said (Elias, 2004, p. E2).

Wii, Xbox, and PlayStation.

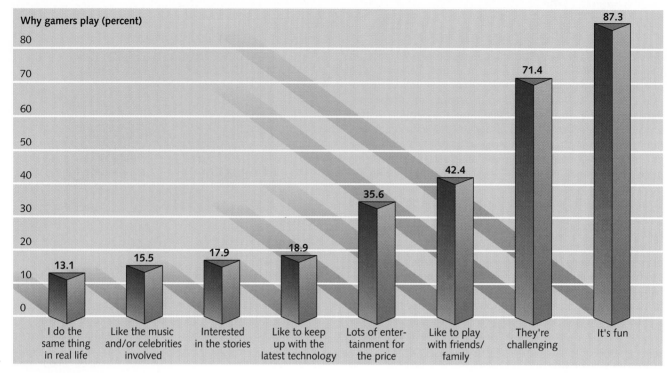

Why gamers play (percent)

Reason	Percent
I do the same thing in real life	13.1
Like the music and/or celebrities involved	15.5
Interested in the stories	17.9
Like to keep up with the latest technology	18.9
Lots of entertainment for the price	35.6
Like to play with friends/family	42.4
They're challenging	71.4
It's fun	87.3

Figure 9.2 Why Gamers Play.

Source: Entertainment Software Assn., 2005.

play online one or more hours a week. Forty percent of online players are female (Hewitt, 2004). Why gamers play is graphically detailed in Figure 9.2.

Scope and Nature of the Video-game Industry

Total U.S. console, PC, and handheld game industry revenues for 2004 were $10 billion. The bulk of this, $7.3 billion, was spent on software, and another $800 million was spent on game rentals. Globally, industry revenues exceeded $28 billion. And these figures do not include online gaming revenues and wireless (or mobile) gaming (Lowenstein, 2005).

As is the case with every media industry we've studied so far, concentration and globalization are the rule in gaming. Game console sales are the sole province of three companies—Microsoft (Xbox), and Japan's Nintendo (Wii) and Sony (PlayStation). There are almost twice as many PlayStation consoles in the United States as all other consoles combined. In 2006, however, Nintendo unveiled Wii in an attempt to gain greater market share. Still, its Game Boy Advance already commands 98% of the $1.1 billion handheld gaming device business. This portable device is the size

Game Boy Advance is the runaway leader in handheld game systems.

of a slice of bread, costs about $100, and plays cartridge games that sell for about $40. Nintendo has sold about 50 million Game Boy Advance systems, primarily to gamers under 20 who buy titles such as *The Legend of Zelda* and variations of *Pokémon, Super Mario,* and *Donkey Kong.* Sony is challenging this dominance with its PSP (PlayStation Portable), a handheld device that not only has graphics similar in quality to those of its successful console version but also is Wi-Fi-capable for Internet access and multiplayer gaming. And rather than play games from cartridges, it uses small, specially designed

CDs, becoming a music and movie player as well. Its target is the over-20 audience. Nintendo hopes to maintain dominance over handheld gaming with DS, a portable that also offers multimedia functions and instant messaging. With the ongoing interaction between the recording and gaming industries—Activision's *Tony Hawk: Underground* won the first MTV prize for Best Video Game Soundtrack in 2004—the development of sophisticated multimedia-capable hardware cannot be underestimated.

Their success in hardware provides Microsoft, Nintendo, and Sony with more than sales revenue. **Third-party publishers,** companies that create games for existing systems, naturally want their best games on the most popular systems. And just as naturally, better games attract more buyers to the systems that support them. Console makers do produce their own titles. Nintendo has the *Pokémon, Super Mario,* and *Pikmin* series. Sony publishes the *Gran Turismo* line, and Microsoft offers titles such as *XNS Sports* and *Halo.* But the hugely popular *Madden NFL,* which sells more than 5 million copies a year, and the *MVP Baseball* series come from EA Sports. *Metal Gear* is from Konami, *Tony Hawk* from Activision, *Roller Coaster Tycoon* from Infogrames, and *Shellshock* from Eidos. Concentration exists in the game software business just as it does on the hardware side. Atari owns several game makers, including Infogrames, and EA controls nearly 50% of all video-game sales.

Third-party publishers produce their most popular titles for all systems. For example, Activision's *Spider-Man 2* is available for the three consoles and Mac and PC. But Codemaster's *MTV Music Generator 3* is available only for PlayStation and Xbox. There is simply too little profit in writing the game for GameCube.

A serious problem faced by third-party game creators is that, as in the more traditional media, especially film, production and marketing costs are skyrocketing. Not only has the production technology itself become more sophisticated and therefore expensive, but games, like movie stars, build followings. Given that, the creative forces behind them can demand more recognition and compensation. In 2001, the average game cost $5 million to produce and $2 million to promote. In 2004, the costs were $15 million and $5 million, respectively. A blockbuster, like *Enter the Matrix* from Atari, cost

WWW

Nintendo
www.nintendo.com

WWW

Xbox
www.xbox.com

WWW

PlayStation
www.playstation.com

Two very popular titles from third-party publishers, *Madden NFL* and *Shellshock: Nam '67.*

As with every medium that has come before, video games have been accused of fostering an addiction. Foxtrot © 2004 Bill Amend. Reprinted with permission of Universal Press Syndicate. All rights reserved.

$50 million just to produce (Fritz & Graser, 2004). Again, as with film, industry insiders and fans are expressing concern over the industry's reliance on sequels of franchises and licensed content, including movie- and television-based games. For example, there are more than 65 Mario games available, and game-maker money is increasingly diverted to paying for licenses for properties such as James Bond 007, *Spider-Man, Lord of the Rings,* and *Catwoman.* According to *Variety,* designers "are growing antsy, eagerly looking for a way to create more innovative games and original titles" (Fritz & Graser, 2004, p. 1). Entertainment Software Association president Lowenstein told his colleagues, "Seventy percent of all male gamers want the game industry to rely less on licensed content and more on original content" (2004, p. 4). But players' and designers' wants are in conflict with three important realities of the contemporary game industry—production, promotion, and distribution costs are soaring; 50% of all games introduced to the market fail (Schiesel, 2004); and every one of the top 10 best-selling games in 2003 was either a sequel to a franchise or a licensed title (Fritz & Graser, 2004). "The issue is that the cost of game development has gone up significantly," said Warner Brothers' video-game unit head Jason Hall. "And the industry wants to mitigate that risk" (quoted in Fritz & Graser, 2004, p. 69).

Trends and Convergence in the Video Game Industry

Like every media industry we've studied, the game industry is experiencing significant change, most of it driven by convergence and hypercommercialism.

CONVERGENCE EVERYWHERE

Cable television giants Comcast and Cox have each launched fee-based game services for their broadband customers; both DBS providers also offer interactive game services. Most Internet service providers (see Chapter 10) provide some form of online interactive game playing. AOL Game, for example, offers 80 games from designers such as EA Sports, TryMedia, and Funkitron. The service is free for AOL subscribers, and its goal is to keep existing broadband

Sony's PSP, Nintendo's DS, and the Rogue. These handheld gamers are also wireless laptops, and in the case of the Rogue, a desktop computer.

users while attracting new ones. The game site of another ISP, Yahoo!, is the single most visited game site on the Web, with 10 million unique visitors a month (Kushner, 2004). Many game makers, too, offer online interactive gaming. EA's Pogo.com has 8.6 million subscribers competing in board, puzzle, word, casino, sports, and card games, some for free and some for a fee.

We've already seen that the new generation of handheld game devices is Internet capable. And in an obvious bow to convergence, the newly released Xbox 360 console is specifically designed to perform a wide range of game and nongame functions, including playing DVDs, burning music CDs, and providing Internet access with music and video streaming capability, all in wide-screen HDTV and digital multichannel sound. It also has built-in access to Xbox Live, a subscription Web-based multiplayer game site.

Home computer users, able to interact with other gamers for decades now via MUDs, have flocked by the millions to **massively multiplayer online role-playing games** (**MMORPG**) such as *Ultima Online, Sims Online, EverQuest,* and *Second Life.* (Aficionados have begun to drop the far-too-long MMORPG name in favor of the sleeker **virtual worlds games.**)

APL Technology and players' comfort with it are two reasons for this wave of convergence—games can be played on cable television, on a dedicated console, on a handheld gamer, online through an ISP, online from a game developer's Web site, online through a game console, online through a PDA or cell phone, and online through a home or office personal computer.

Technology As smaller, faster, more powerful microprocessors were developed and found their way into game consoles, the distinction between games and personal computers began to disappear. A game console with high-speed microprocessors attached to a television set is, for all intents and purposes, a computer and monitor. SL-Interphase, an Arizona high-tech company, has even produced a mobile, wireless handheld game device, the Rogue, that runs on a Pentium 4 processor. When not out and about playing games, a user can plug the Rogue into a dock where it functions as a typical desktop computer (Slagle, 2004).

Comfort with Technology As the distinction between the technologies on which games are played has diminished, players' willingness to play games on different platforms has grown. Demographics help account for this trend. Speaking at the 10th E^3, the game industry's annual trade show, Entertainment Software Association president Douglas Lowenstein explained, "Looking ahead, a child born in 1995, E^3s inaugural year, will be 19 years old in 2014. And according

Online Game Site
www.pogo.com

Online Game Site
www.games.msn.com

Online Game Site
www.games.yahoo.com/games/front

to Census Bureau data, by the year 2020, there will be 174 million Americans between the ages of 5 and 44. That's 174 million Americans who will have grown up with PlayStations, Xboxes, and GameCubes from their early childhood and teenage years. . . . What this means is that the average gamer will be both older and, given their lifetime familiarity with playing interactive games, more sophisticated and discriminating about the games they play" (2005, p. 4).

Evidence of people's comfort with playing games across a variety of technologies resides in the cell phone you most probably already use. There are more than 200 million cell phone subscribers in the United States today (Boyd, 2006), and many have enthusiastically embraced mobile phone gaming. And while many cell phone games can be downloaded and played for free, 64% of all downloaded mobile phone games generated income for the third-party game publisher and/or service provider (Cuneo, 2005). Cell phone gaming already accounts for more than 27% of the revenue generated by the mobile wireless entertainment industry, more than $290 million, and promises to generate $1.1 billion by 2009 (McLean, 2005a). The most sophisticated of today's phones not only support 3-D games, but allow multiplayer, real-time gaming. For example, up to four players can battle each other in *Ghost Recon* over Verizon's Vcast system. Despite these sophisticated technological capabilities, much, if not most, of today's mobile gaming takes the form of **casual games**—classic games such as card games (poker, cribbage, solitaire), table games (checkers, pool), matching games, and word and trivia games. These games can be played in spurts and are easily accommodated by the cell phone's small screen. To be sure, however, casual games are a hit among Internet players as well, with more than 100 million online casual game players regularly visiting sites such as gametap.com, realarcade.com, pogo.com, and games.aol.com (Gnatek, 2006).

HYPERCOMMERCIALISM

Hypercommercialism has come to all media. Advertisers' desire to find new outlets for their messages and avoid the advertising clutter in traditional media has combined with gamers' attractive, segmented demographics to make video games particularly appealing vehicles for many types of commercial and other persuasive campaigns. Advertisers have come to think of games as much like magazines. There are very specific titles that attract very specific audiences. Examine Figure 9.3 for a moment. What an advertiser

Figure 9.3 What Games Are Players Buying, 2004? *Source:* The NPD Group and the Entertainment Software Assn., 2005.

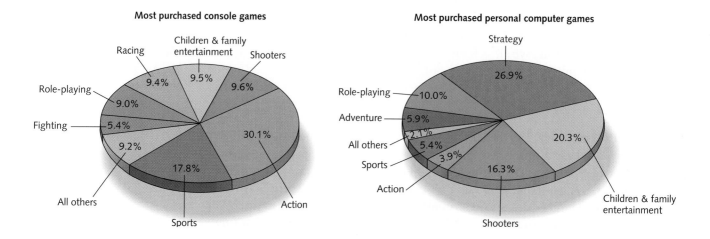

sees is that the most common types of console games sold are action and sports; the most common personal computer games are strategy and family. Video-game industry data also indicate that the average age of a console player is 28, and that 43% of online video gamers are female, the majority of whom are over 35 (Oser, 2004). Clearly, different game platforms attract different types of people.

And even more clearly, different titles attract different demographics—*Mortal Kombat* and *Grand Theft Auto* draw different players than do *Spider-Man* and MSN Games' *Outsmart Florence Henderson*. One reason advertisers are attracted to online games is that they are **sticky.** Players tend to stay (stick) with a game site longer than with other Web sites. Visitors to EA's Pogo.com, for example, spend 25 million hours a month playing games on the site (Kushner, 2004). Regardless of the platform, the average gamer spends 2 to 4 hours playing a single game in a single sitting (Stanley, 2004). Sponsors use games to reach their targets in three ways—product placement, advergaming, and advocacy gaming.

Product Placement   Advertisers like product placement for several reasons. First, a product used in a game is there forever—every time the game is played, the advertiser's brand not only appears but is used. Second, especially for younger players, a product's association with a game renders it "cool." Finally, placements in games seem to be remarkably effective. Ad industry research shows that "30% of in-game ads are recalled in the short-term, which is impressive. Even more amazing is the fact that 15% are recalled after five months—unheard of in advertising" (Leeper, 2004, p. 2).

But why, beyond the cash they earn, do game designers want product placements in their creations, a practice begun in the 1980s when Sega put Marlboro banners in its arcade racing games? First, brand names add a bit of realism to the game's virtual world, presumably enhancing the player's enjoyment. Second, advertisers and game makers frequently engage in cross-promotion. For example, Sprite billboards highlight Activision's *Street Hoops* and the soda maker pushes the game on its cans and in its ads. Champs Sports, featured everywhere in EA's *Arena Football*, encourages shoppers in its 600 stores to play the game on specially designed kiosks in order to win Champs merchandise.

So mutually beneficial has game product placement become that placements, which can cost up to $100,000 in a popular game (Lienert, 2004), are frequently bartered for free; that is, the game maker and the brand advertiser exchange no money. The brand image is provided to the designer (for realism) and the sponsor gets placement (for exposure). Industry estimates are that 2005's $75 million in game ad placement will reach $800 million by 2010 (Stanley, 2006). Read

Crazy Taxi and *Arena Football* are replete with brands and logos.

more about another, somewhat more controversial game-content issue in the essay on page 286 entitled "The Portrayal of Women in Video Games."

The Portrayal of Women in Video Games

The release of new game industry demographic statistics, and not coincidentally the movie *Catwoman*, recently put the issue of the portrayal of women in video games into the cultural forum. Although the gender gap among players is rapidly closing as PC-based games like *Sims* and *Roller Coaster Tycoon* draw just as many girls as boys (Hewitt, 2004; Vargas, 2004), games continue to be considered a "boy thing."

One reason is that game developers "have a blind spot to females." They continue to operate under the assumption that boys are more interested in technology and are more technologically literate than girls (Chmielewski, 2003), an unfounded assumption given the fact that not only are gamers increasingly of both genders, but there are more females than males online (Chapter 10).

This situation has led groups such as the Media Awareness Network (www.media-awareness.ca) to raise concerns not only about the exclusion of and disregard for girls as players, but about the degradation of women through gender stereotyping. When "girl games" first became popular, their success was based on appearance and fashion content. *Barbie's Fashion Designer* and *Cosmopolitan Virtual Makeover*, for example, both emphasized the importance of clothing, hair, makeup, and body type. And when girls began gravitating to "boy games" like *Grand Theft Auto 3*, *Lara Croft: Tomb Raider*, *BMX XXX*, and *Extreme Beach Volleyball*, what they found was women portrayed as prostitutes, victims, and sex objects; violence directed at women; an absence of strong female characters; and wildly misproportioned body types, specifically unnaturally small waists and large breasts.

The simultaneous 2004 release of the movie *Catwoman* and its synergistic sister, *Catwoman* from EA Games, added fuel to the debate. Film star Halle Berry, like her *Lara Croft* counterpart Angelina Jolie, is considered by many young girls to have the ideal female body type. And while these actresses' Hollywood figures may be unattainable by—and certainly are un-

> **IN 2003, 11,326 GIRLS UNDER THE AGE OF 18 HAD BREAST IMPLANTS. THIS WAS TRIPLE THE NUMBER FROM 2002.**

representative of—most women, the video-game versions of their characters are even more unrealistic. The questions in the cultural forum, then, are these: What do these representations do to the way young girls perceive their own bodies? Are girl players participating in their own degradation and subjugation? Is the industry encouraging girls to forgo self-respect in exchange for acceptance? Critics of games' portrayals of women point to statistics such as the following:

1. In 2003, 11,326 girls under the age of 18 had breast implants. This was triple the number from 2002 (Pollitt, 2004).

2. According to the National Institute of Mental Health (www.nimh.nih.gov/), 5% to 10% of girls and women suffer from an eating disorder; 40% of first-, second-, and third-grade girls want to be thinner than they are; 80% of 10-year-old girls are worried about being "fat"; one-third of 8- to 10-year-old girls say they are dissatisfied with their size; and among 9- to 15-year-olds, 50% have taken laxatives or diet pills to lose weight.

Now enter your voice in the cultural forum. Is there a connection between the way women are portrayed in games (in all media) and these data? Are concerns about female role models in games an overreaction, or do you agree with critics who see hypocrisy in an industry that presents young girls with unhealthy, unattainable body images while at the same time creating a product that encourages them to sit in front of a game for hours on end, minimizing their involvement in outdoor activity and exercise? Game covers typically identify violent or sexual content when listing a mature (M) rating; should inappropriate gender stereotyping earn a game an M? As you play, consider these questions. Then, after studying Chapter 13's discussion of media and stereotyping, ask them of yourself again.

The idealized body types of the movies Catwoman *and* Lara Croft *are exaggerated even more in their video game reincarnations.*

Advergaming Product placement in games has proven so successful that, in many instances, brands have become the games themselves in **advergames.** Advergaming typically occurs in two ways, on CD-ROM and online; and online advergaming typically takes the form of brand-specific sites and game sites unaffiliated with a single sponsor but offering brand-based games. The auto industry, for example, makes good use of CD-ROM advergames. Chrysler distributes free games and has even set up gaming kiosks in some dealerships. Its Jeep game encourages players to take a Jeep anywhere, do anything. Crashes are okay . . . a click does the necessary bodywork. "These games are the perfect form of advertising," enthused one player. "You really get to know the product. You can pick a car, accessorize it, tune it, and drive it in the game under realistic conditions. It's better than any brochure, magazine ad, or TV commercial" (quoted in Lienert, 2004, p. 2).

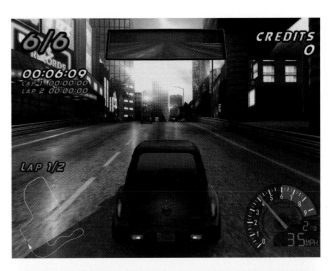

Chrysler (on CD-ROM) and John Deere (online) are only two of the countless companies adding advergaming to their commercial mix.

Brand-specific game Web sites are sometimes downloadable from the Net, sometimes played while connected. Either way, their goal is to produce an enjoyable experience for players while introducing them to the product and product information. The John Deere game site (www.boldgames.com/johndeere.html), for example, encourages players to manage their own successful farm, deciding what crops to plant, which animals to raise, how many employees to hire and structures to build, and, of course, what John Deere equipment to buy for the different scenarios and levels of difficulty. At NabiscoWorld.com, children can play an Oreo dunking game, join a Chips Ahoy party, and play a racing game in a Triscuit 4×4.

Unaffiliated game sites that offer brand-specific games, however, have raised the question of fairness. Critics argue that embedding brand characters and logos in non-brand-specific games masks the true intent of those games Neopets.com, for example, calls itself "the greatest Virtual Pet Site on the Internet." It explains to its primarily preteen players, "With your help, we have built a community of over 70 million virtual pet owners across the world! Neopets has many things to offer including over 160 games, trading, auctions, greetings, messaging, and a tree with a giant brain. Best of all, it's completely FREE!" The games, however, include the *Lucky Charms Super Search Game,* the *Nestlé IceCream Frozen Flights* game, the *Pepperidge Farms Goldfish Sandwich Snacks* game, *McDonald's: Meal Hunt* game, and visits to the Disney or General Mills theaters where points are awarded for watching commercials. "We're not trying to be subliminal or deceive the user," argues Neopet CEO Doug Dohring. "We label all the immersive [game] ad campaigns as paid advertisements" (quoted in Fonda, 2004, p. 53). Critics respond that little kids (39% of Neopet's players are 12 and under) don't know the difference between an ad campaign and a game, even if it is so identified.

Games Under Attack: Addiction and Violence

Perhaps you remember public worries about Internet addiction, online gambling, instant messaging promoting shabby writing skills, and predators using the Web to lure innocents to their doom. You'll see in Chapter 10 that concern, much of it reasonable, also remains about the Net's effect on important matters such as democracy, privacy, and copyright. This is what happens every time a new communication technology is introduced—people express concern about its impact on individuals (almost always children) and society. Here, for example, are a few comments that greeted the coming of some of your favorite media (all from Baran & Davis, 2006, pp. 50–51):

Sound movies

And if the speech recorded in the dialogue of talking pictures is vulgar or ugly, its potential for lowering the speech standard of the country is almost incalculable. The fact that it is likely to be heard by the less discriminating portion of the public operates to increase its evil effects. (From *Commonweal*, April 10, 1929, p. 653)

Radio

Is radio to become a chief arm of education? Will the classroom be abolished, and the child of the future stuffed with facts as he sits at home or even as he walks about the streets with his portable receiving set in his pocket? (From *Century*, June 1924, p. 149)

Television

Seeing constant brutality, viciousness, and unsocial acts results in hardness, intense selfishness, even mercilessness, proportionate to the amount of exposure and its play on the native temperament of the child. (From *New Republic*, November 1, 1954, p. 12)

Because media history does indeed repeat itself, games, too, have faced their "effects questions." Most of this worry centers on addiction and the impact of violent games.

Concern over addiction revolves around how much time young people spend with games to the exclusion of other, presumably more beneficial, endeavors. Games are considered particularly addicting because of their interactivity (kids like "talking" to other kids; involvement breeds commitment),

sense of belonging (developing affinity with other gamers keeps children playing longer), built-in ever-increasing challenges (grabbing children's attention more firmly, keeping them at it longer), and mobility (young people can play them all the time, anywhere and everywhere). Some critics also suggest that dopamine, the same neuron chemical that exists in the brains of drug addicts, is released into players' brains when they play (Tobin, 2004).

And while most of this might appear reasonable, especially because kids do seem to play quite a lot, there is much industry and independent scientific research to suggest that addiction is not the problem many initially thought it to be. For example, a nationwide Kaiser Family Foundation study revealed that although more than 8 in 10 young people have a game console at home, and about half have a game device in their bedroom, these 8- to 18-year-olds play, on average, only 49 minutes a day (out of 8 hours and 33 minutes of daily media use). Even the heaviest players, 8- to 10-year-olds, average just over 1.5 hours a day (Rideout, Roberts, & Foehr, 2005). Industry research paints a picture of gamers as active, involved individuals, clearly beyond addiction to video games. According to the Entertainment Software Association (2005), gamers devote more than triple the amount of time to exercising, volunteering in the community, religious activities, creative endeavors, and reading than they do to gaming, and 93% of gamers read books or daily newspapers on a regular basis. As accurate as this information might be, the last figure, 93% reading a book or a daily paper, should suggest that these data represent all players—who average 30 years old—not just kids. Still, there seems to be little evidence of an epidemic of video-game addiction.

Games and violence, however, present a somewhat different situation. The brutal killings described on page 290 quite naturally raise people's concern over violent video games, and they have led to countless state and local community attempts to pass limits on games featuring violence or sexual content (Hamilton, 2005). And while there is indeed some important research indicating a causal link between violent video games and subsequent player aggression (Anderson et al., 2003, pp. 90–92), much of the public's concern is the result of what they see in the news (Columbine and Jonesboro, for example) and what *they know*, in fact, to be in many games. In *Grand Theft Auto: San*

Advocacy Gaming   Companies or organizations wanting to get their noncommercial messages out are also turning to games, primarily on the Web. Our opening vignette featured an online **advocacy game** as did our discussion of games-for-good. Both 2004 presidential candidates were "supported" by many advocacy games, and the ill-fated insurgent primary campaign of Democratic hopeful Howard Dean, conducted largely online, had the *Howard Dean for Iowa Game* near its center (www.deanforamericagame.com). Its

Andreas, for example, gamers control a character named CJ, bent on revenge for his mother's murder and intent on resurrecting the powerful street gang he once led. He robs people, often pummeling them to death with his feet and fists. He steals cars and runs down anyone unfortunate enough to get in his way. When his spirits need a little boost, he "hires a prostitute and (has) sex with her in his car. While the game does not show the sex on screen, the rocking of the car, the sound of the woman groaning, and the vibration of the PlayStation2 game pad leave little to the imagination" (Hamilton, 2005, p. 60).

The industry responds that fewer than 15% of all games sold contain sex and violence, 87% of players under 18 years old get parental permission before they buy or rent a game, and 92% report that their parents are present when they play (Entertainment Software Association, 2005). If kids are playing violent games (especially those rated for play by more mature people), that's parents' fault, not the games'.

You'll see in Chapter 13 that the media-effects link is much more complicated than the debate over games so far might indicate. True, not every violent game turns every player into a killer. Just as true, research indicates a causal relationship for some children, and parents can do only so much; for instance, they cannot control children other than their own who may, indeed, lack parental supervision. Entertainment Software Association president, Douglas Lowenstein, has offered an apparently reasonable approach to the issue:

> You don't have to be a cynical politician or a cultural extremist to raise questions about videogame content. There are many thoughtful, rational people who share the concerns. And we ignore them at our own peril—they are the Moms and Dads who buy games and increasingly play them. Disrespecting their concerns is dangerous. We can use things like

WHILE THERE IS INDEED SOME IMPORTANT RESEARCH INDICATING A CAUSAL LINK BETWEEN VIOLENT VIDEO GAMES AND SUBSEQUENT PLAYER AGGRESSION, MUCH OF THE PUBLIC'S CONCERN IS THE RESULT OF WHAT THEY SEE IN THE NEWS AND WHAT *THEY KNOW,* IN FACT, TO BE IN MANY GAMES.

the American Constitution's guarantee of free speech as a shield to legitimize virtually any content. Indeed, the very essence of art is that it has no boundaries. . . . But I submit to you it is one thing to say a product is protected speech, which it is, or that it is rated and parents need to accept responsibility for what their kids play, which they do. But it is quite another thing to say we have no larger responsibility for shaping the quality and values of the culture we live in. (2005)

What do you think of Mr. Lowenstein's comments? Clearly, he sees that games, like all media content, serve a cultural storytelling function, one that argues for responsibility on the part of the storyteller. Revisit these comments after you have read Chapter 13's discussion of media effects.

A representative scene from Grand Theft Auto.

creator, Dr. Ian Bogost, told the *New York Times,* "I didn't get into games because I wanted to reach a demographic, I did it because I think games can communicate political concepts and processes better than other forums" (quoted in Erard, 2004, p. G1).

Supporters of political advocacy games see three significant strengths. First, the games are relatively inexpensive. A good political game can be created in about 3 weeks for about $20,000, well under the cost of television time.

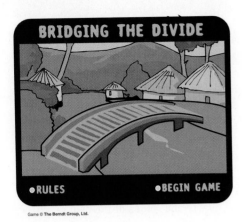
Game © The Berndt Group, Ltd.

Not all advocacy game sites are political. This one advocates international debt relief.

Neopets
www.neopets.com

Links to Political Advocacy Sites
www.watercoolergames.com

Game Rating System
www.esrb.org

Second, like other advergames, they are sticky and the message is reinforced with each play (broadcast ads are fleeting). Finally, they are interactive, making them a powerful means of communicating with potential voters, especially younger ones. More traditional forms of advocacy messaging, such as radio and television ads and campaign fliers, passively engage voters with their campaign rhetoric. But games encourage potential voters to interact with the message.

Not all advocacy games are about politics, however. There are games advocating the overhaul of the popular music industry (emogame.com), the return of independent radio (www .radiotakeover.com), improved HIV awareness (www.supershagland .com), and international debt relief (www.berndtgroup.net/portfolio/ projects/crs/index_042601.html).

DEVELOPING MEDIA LITERACY SKILLS
Using the ESRB Ratings

The link between games and antisocial behavior has been at issue ever since there have been games, finding particular urgency after dramatic events like those in Jonesboro and at Columbine High. In 1998, 13-year-old Mitchell Johnson and 11-year-old Andrew Golden of Jonesboro, Arkansas, heavy players of the shooting game *GoldenEye 007*, set off fire alarms at their middle school and shot at students and teachers as they fled the building. In 1999, *Doom* fans 18-year-old Eric Harris and 17-year-old Dylan Klebold killed 12 students and 1 teacher and wounded 23 at Columbine High School in Colorado. In each instance, the teens' "addiction" to games was prominently noted. The Columbine shooters had even created a custom *Doom* to represent the shooting of their classmates.

Congress first investigated the effects of video games in 1993, the same year that *Doom* was released for home computers. In an effort to head off government restrictions, in 1994 the industry established the Entertainment Software Ratings Board (ESRB) rating system. It has six ratings (a seventh, RP for Rating Pending, is the equivalent of "this film has not yet been rated"):

EC	Early Childhood	ages 3 and up
E	Everyone	ages 6 and up
E10+		ages 10 and up
T	Teen	ages 13 and up
M	Mature	ages 17 and up
AO	Adults Only	ages 18 and up

Like the movie rating system, the ESRB system requires that games offer content descriptors somewhere on the front or back of the game package explaining why a particular rating was assigned. Although the Federal Trade Commission has lauded the ESRB ratings as the most comprehensive of the three industries' (games, recordings, movies), media literate gamers (or friends and parents of gamers) should understand the strengths and weaknesses of this system. Depending on your perspective, this self-regulation is either a good thing because it keeps government's intrusive hand out of people's lives and protects game makers' First Amendment rights, or a bad thing because it is

LIVING MEDIA LITERACY

Start a Responsible Gaming Advocacy Group

Three of the most critical issues surrounding video games are *ratings*, *responsibility,* and *recourse*. Twelve-year-old Danielle Shimotakahara of Oregon was well aware of this when she began a petition against violent video games (www.ama-assn.org/ama/pub/article/2714-3108.html). Danielle asks, among other things, that the government recognize the impact of game violence on kids. Her position strongly concurs with those of advocacy groups such as Mothers Against Videogame Addiction and Violence (www.mavav.org), Children Now (www.childrennow.org), and Mothers Against Violence In America (www.mavia.org/about.html).

Danielle made her media literacy a living enterprise. Media literate college students, representing a large portion of the gaming demographic and possessing extensive knowledge of the industry, can also help make younger audiences more media literate about video-game consumption. One way to do this is to click on the "Take Action" icon in the Media Awareness Network site (www.media-awareness.ca/english/parents/video_games/index.cfm). Another, which takes a bit more effort, is to create your own advocacy group (for instance, **G**raduates **A**gainst **M**edia **E**xploitation . . . yes, it's corny; you can do better). Your advocacy group might distribute flyers to music and video stores where games are rented and sold, encouraging management to act responsibly to children and preteens. The flyer might ask salespeople to routinely do the following:

- Inquire about a child's age when he or she is purchasing or renting a strongly rated game.
- Post signs making parents and teens aware of the store's age and content concerns.

> **THREE OF THE MOST CRITICAL ISSUES SURROUNDING VIDEO GAMES ARE RATINGS, RESPONSIBILITY, AND RECOURSE. TWELVE-YEAR-OLD DANIELLE SHIMOTAKAHARA OF OREGON WAS WELL AWARE OF THIS WHEN SHE BEGAN A PETITION AGAINST VIOLENT VIDEO GAMES.**

- Let parents know there are ratings on the games but that they don't necessarily specify *all* the inappropriate material.
- Provide information about the nature of the game that goes beyond the rating and content descriptors.
- Separate violent/sexual games from E-rated games on the shelves, making the distinction more evident for parents.

While you, as a mature, responsible individual, may see playing video games as a simple escape from the pressures of adult life, or perhaps as a means of passing time between classes, there is little excuse, especially as a media literate individual, for not recognizing the potential impact on those who are not prepared for adult life—children.

Call it GAME or something else, but live your media literacy by engaging game retailers about their responsibilities.

self-serving and rarely enforced. The value of the content descriptors, too, is in dispute. All a game maker is required to list is *any one* of the descriptors that has led to a given rating, for example, *strong lyrics*. For some, this is useful information. For others, it masks potential problems. First, according to the ESRB system, if this content is sufficient to give the game an M rating, no other content that might have contributed to that rating, such as *mature sexual themes* and *violence,* need be listed. Second, *strong lyrics* might apply to song lyrics about sex, violence, alcohol, or drug use. Only when the game is played will the player identify the reason for the rating and descriptor.

An additional concern over the rating system is that it is poorly enforced. A National Institute on Media and the Family study showed that 87% of boys and 46% of girls played M-rated games. Their average age was 13.5 years

www

Children's Software Review
www.childrenssoftware.com

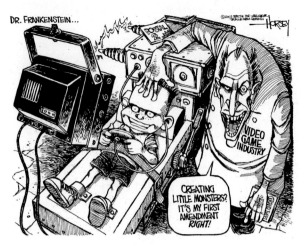

Video games may or may not create little monsters, but the industry does provide a ratings system to help parents identify titles appropriate for their kids.

© David Horsey, Seattle Post-Intelligencer. Used by permission.

old. More than half the parents did not understand the system, and the Federal Trade Commission discovered that 69% of children under 17 who attempted to buy an M-rated game succeeded (Meehan, 2004). One solution, in voluntary use in Canada, is the Retail Council of Canada's "Commitment to Parents" program. Participating game outlets hang posters and distribute brochures explaining the ESRB ratings. Many have installed automatic cash register prompts that alert salespeople when M-rated games are being rented or bought. There is more about what you, as a media literate person, can do about the ESRB ratings in the box on page 291, "Start a Responsible Gaming Advocacy Group," and a fuller explanation of critics' concerns over the influence of games on young people resides in the essay on page 288, "Games Under Attack: Addiction and Violence."

RESOURCES FOR REVIEW AND DISCUSSION

Review Points

- While the pinball games developed by David Gottlieb and Harry Williams are the precursors to video games, Steve Russell, Nolan Bushnell, and Ralph Baer are most responsible for what we now call electronic video games.
- A game is a video game when a player has direct involvement in some on-screen action to produce a desired outcome.
- The demographics of America's 150 million gamers match the demographics of all Americans relatively closely.
- Games are most frequently played on game consoles (home and portable), PCs, and the Internet, but increasingly mobile phones are serving as a popular game platform.

- Game consoles are the sole province of Microsoft (Xbox), Nintendo (Wii), and Sony (PlayStation).
- Third-party publishers design games for the most popular systems.
- Rising costs in the production of games have led to hypercommercialism and a reliance on blockbusters, franchises, and sequels.
- Convergence, driven by more powerful technology and people's comfort with it, has overtaken gaming, as games can be played on a host of platforms.
- Hypercommercialism in games takes the form of product placement and advergaming.
- The ESRB game rating system is much admired but still raises important questions for media literate game players.

Key Terms

 Use the text's Online Learning Center at www.mhhe.com/baran5 to further your understanding of the following terminology.

LED (light-emitting diode), 275
LCD (liquid crystal display), 275
LAN (local area network), 275
first-person perspective game, 275
video game, 276

MUD (multi-user dimension), 276
exergame 278
third-party publishers, 281
massively multiplayer online role-
  playing game (MMORPG), 283

virtual worlds game, 283
casual games, 284
sticky, 285
advergames, 287
advocacy games, 288

Questions for Review

 Go to the self-quizzes on the Online Learning Center to test your knowledge.

1. Why was the development of pinball a necessary precursor to the development of the video game?
2. Who are David Gottlieb and Harry Williams? What were their contributions to the development of pinball?
3. What was the Tech Model Railroad Club, and what is its place in the history of videogaming?
4. Who are Steve Russell, Nolan Bushnell, and Ralph Baer? What were the contributions of each to videogaming?
5. How did *Pong* affect the development of videogaming?
6. What makes a video game a *video game*?
7. What is a MUD?
8. What are the most frequently employed platforms for game playing?
9. What is a third-party publisher?
10. What determines whether a third-party publisher creates a game for a given platform?
11. What is an MMORPG?
12. How does product placement occur in games?
13. What are the different forms of advergaming?
14. What is advocacy gaming?
15. What are the levels of the ESRB rating system?

Questions for Critical Thinking and Discussion

1. If you are a gamer, how well do your reasons for playing match those given in this chapter? If they are different, how and why?
2. What is your favorite game platform? Why? Do you think different types of players gravitate toward different platforms? Why or why not?
3. Have you ever played a role-playing game such as a MUD or an MMORPG? If so, how much do your online personalities match the real-world you? If they are similar, why? If they are dissimilar, why?
4. Does advergaming, especially where children are the players, bother you? Do you find advergaming inherently deceptive for these young players? Why or why not?
5. Have you ever played an advocacy game? What was it? Was it from a group with which you were sympathetic? What would it take to get you to play a game from a site with which you disagree?
6. What do you think of the link between games and antisocial behavior? Remember your answer, and ask yourself this question again after you read Chapter 13.

Important Resources

 Go to the Online Learning Center for additional readings.

Internet Resources

Darfur Is Dying	www.darfurisdying.com
History of Pinball	www.pinballhistory.com
Arcade Flyer Archive	www.arcadeflyer.com
Videogame Museum	www.vgmuseum.com
Game Archive	www.gamearchive.com
The Pong Story	www.pong-story.com
Sega	www.sega.com
Game Room Magazine	www.gameroommagazine.com
Entertainment Software Association	www.theesa.com
Academy of Interactive Arts and Sciences	www.interactive.org
International Game Developers Association	www.igda.org

Gamers.com	www.gamers.com
Nintendo	www.nintendo.com
Xbox	www.xbox.com
PlayStation	www.playstation.com
Links to MUDs	www.mudconnect.com
Online Game Site	www.pogo.com
Online Game Site	www.games.msn.com
Online Game Site	www.games.yahoo.com/games/front
Neopets	www.neopets.com
Links to Political Advocacy Sites	www.watercoolergames.com
Game Rating System	www.esrb.org
Children's Software Review	www.childrenssoftware.com

The Internet and the World Wide Web

LEARNING OBJECTIVES

It is not an overstatement to say that the Internet and World Wide Web have changed the world, not to mention all the other mass media. In addition to being powerful communication media themselves, the Net and the Web sit at the center of virtually all the media convergence we see around us. After studying this chapter you should

- be familiar with the history and development of the Internet and World Wide Web.

- recognize the potential cultural value of the Internet and World Wide Web and the implications of Web censorship and commercialization of the Internet.

- understand how the organizational and economic nature of the contemporary Internet and World Wide Web industries shapes their content.

- recognize alterations in the nature of mass communication made possible by the Internet and World Wide Web.

- develop an awareness of a number of social and cultural questions posed by the Internet, World Wide Web, and related emerging technologies.

- understand the relationship between these new media and their various users and audiences.

- possess improved Internet and World Wide Web media literacy skills, especially in protecting your privacy and reflecting on the Net's double edge of (potentially) good and troublesome change.

William Gibson and Marshall McLuhan have been two of your intellectual heroes ever since you started college. Gibson is the "Godfather of Cyberspace" and author of *Neuromancer* and *Johnny Mnemonic,* and McLuhan is the author of *Understanding Media: The Extensions of Man* and originator of some of your favorite expressions such as "hot and cool media" and "the medium is the message." But now, as you see it, Gibson and McLuhan are in conflict.

Opposite: Web inventor Tim Berners-Lee.

William Gibson

For example, another of McLuhan's famous expressions is "the global village." You understood this to mean that as media "shrink" the world, people will become increasingly involved in one another's lives. As people come to know more about others who were once separated from them by distance, they will form a new, beneficial relationship, a global village.

Then you saw Gibson interviewed on television. His vision of technology's impact on the globe was anything but optimistic. He said, "We're moving toward a world where all the consumers under a certain age will . . . identify more with their consumer status or with the products they consume than they would with an antiquated notion of nationality. We're increasingly interchangeable" (as cited in Trench, 1990).

Maybe you were wrong about McLuhan's ideas. He did his influential writing a long time ago. Where was it you read about the global village? In a magazine interview? You look it up at the library to confirm that you understood him correctly. There it is, just as you thought: "The human tribe can become truly one family and man's consciousness can be freed from the shackles of mechanical culture and enabled to roam the cosmos" ("A Candid Conversation," 1969, p. 158).

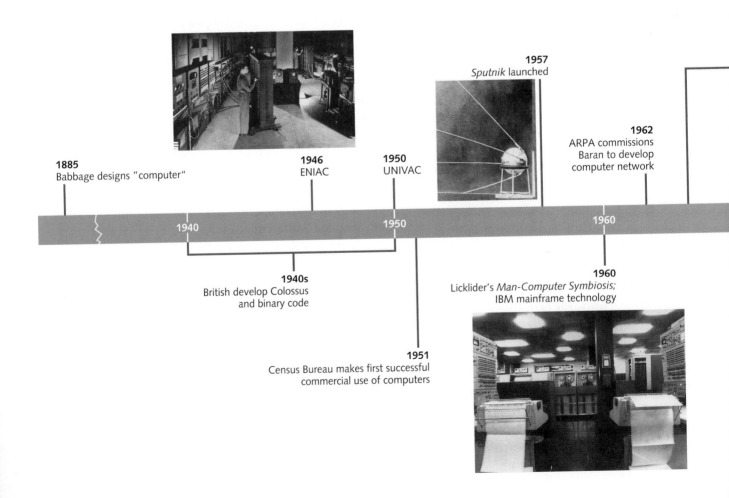

1885
Babbage designs "computer"

1946
ENIAC

1950
UNIVAC

1957
Sputnik launched

1962
ARPA commissions Baran to develop computer network

1940

1950

1960

1940s
British develop Colossus and binary code

1960
Licklider's *Man-Computer Symbiosis;* IBM mainframe technology

1951
Census Bureau makes first successful commercial use of computers

McLuhan's global village is an exciting place, a good place for people enjoying increased contact and increased involvement with one another aided by electronic technology. Gibson's nationless world isn't about involving ourselves in one another's lives and experiences. It's about electronic technology turning us into indistinguishable nonindividuals, rallying around products. We are united by buyable things, identifying not with others who share our common culture but with those who share common goods. McLuhan sees the new communication technologies as expanding our experiences. Gibson sees them more negatively. You respect and enjoy the ideas of both thinkers. How can you reconcile the disagreement you have uncovered?

We begin this chapter with an examination of the Internet, the "new technology" that helped bring Gibson to prominence and gave renewed life to Marshall McLuhan's ideas. We study the history of the Internet, beginning with the development of the computer, and then we look at the Net as it exists today. We examine its formats and its capabilities, especially the popular World Wide Web. The number and nature of today's Internet users are also discussed, and we touch on the ongoing debate over the commercialization of the Internet.

Many of the issues discussed here will be familiar to you. Given the fundamental role that the Internet plays in encouraging and permitting convergence, concentration, audience fragmentation, globalization, and hypercommercialism, you should not be surprised that we've "met" the Internet and the Web before now in discussing the more traditional media.

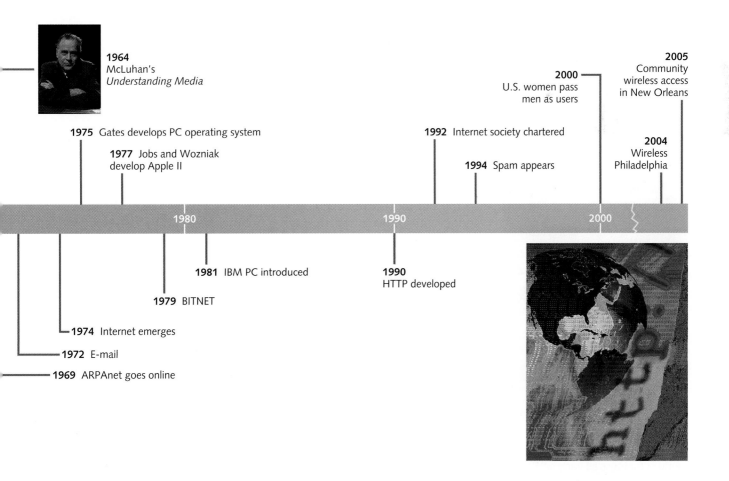

1964
McLuhan's
Understanding Media

1975 Gates develops PC operating system

1977 Jobs and Wozniak
develop Apple II

2000
U.S. women pass
men as users

2005
Community
wireless access
in New Orleans

1992 Internet society chartered

1994 Spam appears

2004
Wireless
Philadelphia

1980

1990

2000

1981 IBM PC introduced

1979 BITNET

1974 Internet emerges

1972 E-mail

1969 ARPAnet goes online

1990
HTTP developed

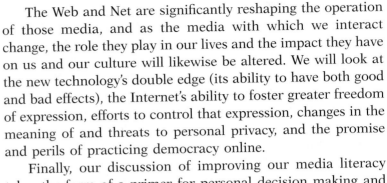

Marshall McLuhan

The Web and Net are significantly reshaping the operation of those media, and as the media with which we interact change, the role they play in our lives and the impact they have on us and our culture will likewise be altered. We will look at the new technology's double edge (its ability to have both good and bad effects), the Internet's ability to foster greater freedom of expression, efforts to control that expression, changes in the meaning of and threats to personal privacy, and the promise and perils of practicing democracy online.

Finally, our discussion of improving our media literacy takes the form of a primer for personal decision making and action in our increasingly media-saturated world. But first, the Internet.

A Short History of the Internet

There are conflicting versions about the origins of the Internet. The more common story is that the Net is a product of the Cold War. In this version, the air force in 1962, wanting to maintain the military's ability to transfer information around the country even if a given area was destroyed in an enemy attack, commissioned leading computer scientists to develop the means to do so. But many researchers and scientists dispute this "myth that [has] gone unchallenged long enough to become widely accepted as fact," that the Internet was initially "built to protect national security in the face of nuclear attack" (Hafner & Lyon, 1996, p. 10).

In the second version, as early as 1956 psychologist Joseph C. R. Licklider, a devotee of Marshall McLuhan's thinking on the power of communication technology, foresaw linked computers creating a country of citizens "informed about, and interested in, and involved in, the process of government" (p. 34). He foresaw "home computer consoles" and television sets connected in a nationwide network. "The political process would essentially be a giant teleconference," he wrote, "and a campaign would be a months-long series of communications among candidates, propagandists, commentators, political action groups, and voters. The key," he added, "is the self-motivating exhilaration that accompanies truly effective interaction with information through a good console and a good network to a good computer" (p. 34).

In what many technologists now consider to be the seminal essay on the potential and promise of computer networks, *Man–Computer Symbiosis*, Licklider, who had by now given up psychology and devoted himself completely to computer science, wrote in 1960, "The hope is that in not too many years, human brains and computing machines will be coupled . . . tightly, and the resulting partnership will think as no human brain has ever thought and process data in a way not approached by the information handling machines we know today" (as quoted in Hafner & Lyon, 1996, p. 35). Scores of computer experts, enthused by Licklider's vision (and many more who saw networked computers as a way to gain access to the powerful but otherwise expensive and unavailable computers just beginning to become available), joined the rush toward the development of what we know today as the **Internet,** a global

Joseph C. R. Licklider envisioned a national system of interconnected home computers as early as 1956.

network of interconnected computers that communicate freely and share and exchange information.

DEVELOPMENT OF THE COMPUTER

The title "Father of the Computer" resides with Englishman Charles Babbage. Lack of money and unavailability of the necessary technology stymied his plan to build an Analytical Engine, a steam-driven computer. But in the mid-1880s, aided by the insights of mathematician Lady Ada Byron Lovelace, Babbage did produce designs for a "computer" that could conduct algebraic computations using stored memory and punch cards for input and output. His work provided inspiration for those who would follow.

Over the next 100 years a number of mechanical and electromechanical computers were attempted, some with success. But Colossus, developed by the British to break the Germans' secret codes during World War II, was the first electronic **digital computer.** It reduced information to a **binary code**—that is, a code made up of the digits 1 and 0. In this form information could be stored and manipulated. The first "full-service" electronic computer, ENIAC (Electronic Numerical Integrator and Calculator), based on the work of Iowa State's John V. Atanasoff, was introduced by scientists John Mauchly and John Presper Eckert of the Moore School of Electrical Engineering at the University of Pennsylvania in 1946. ENIAC hardly resembled the computers we know today: 18 feet tall, 80 feet long, and weighing 60,000 pounds, it was composed of 17,500 vacuum tubes and 500 miles of electrical wire. It could fill an auditorium and ate up 150,000 watts of electricity. Mauchly and Eckert eventually left the university to form their own computer company, later selling it to the Remington Rand Corporation in 1950. At Remington they developed UNIVAC (Universal Automatic Computer), which, when bought for and used by the Census Bureau in 1951, became the first successful commercial computer.

Internet Statistics
www.glreach.com/globalstats

Internet Statistics
www.mit.edu/people/mkgray/net

ENIAC

The Soviet Union's 1-foot-in-diameter, 184-pound *Sputnik* was not only the first human-made satellite to orbit the Earth; it sent shudders throughout the American scientific and military communities.

The commercial computer explosion was ignited by IBM. Using its already well-entrenched organizational system of trained sales and service professionals, IBM helped businesses find their way in the early days of the computer revolution. One of its innovations was to sell rather than rent computers to customers. As a result of IBM's success, by 1960 the computer industry could be described as "IBM and the Seven Dwarfs"—Sperry, Control Data, Honeywell, RCA, NCR, General Electric, and Burroughs (Rosenberg, 1992, p. 60).

MILITARY APPLICATIONS

In 1957 the Soviet Union launched *Sputnik*, Earth's first human-constructed satellite. The once-undisputed supremacy of the United States in science and technology had been usurped, and U.S. scientists and military officials were in shock. The Advanced Research Projects Agency (ARPA) was immediately established to sponsor and coordinate sophisticated defense-related research. In 1962, as part of a larger drive to promote the use of computers in national defense (and giving rise to one of the stories of the Net's origins), ARPA commissioned Paul Baran of the Rand Corporation to produce a plan that would enable the U.S. military to maintain command over its missiles and planes if a nuclear attack knocked out conventional means of communication. The military thought a decentralized communication network was necessary. In that way, no matter where the bombing occurred, other locations would be available to launch a counterattack. Among Baran's plans was one for a "packet switched network." He wrote,

> Packet switching is the breaking down of data into datagrams or packets that are labeled to indicate the origin and the destination of the information and the forwarding of these packets from one computer to another computer until the information arrives at its final destination computer. This (is) crucial to the realization of a computer network. If packets are lost at any given point, the message can be resent by the originator. (As cited in Kristula, 1997, p. 1)

The genius of the system Baran envisioned is twofold: (1) Common communication rules (called **protocols**) and common computer languages would enable any type of computer, running with any operating system, to communicate with another; and (2) destination or delivery instructions embedded in all information sent on the system would enable instantaneous "detours" or "rerouting" if a given computer on the network became unavailable.

Using Honeywell computers at Stanford University, UCLA, the University of California, Santa Barbara, and the University of Utah, the switching network, called ARPAnet, went online in 1969 and became fully operational and reliable within 1 year. Other developments soon followed. In 1972 an engineer named Ray Tomlinson created the first e-mail program (and gave us the ubiquitous @). In 1974 Stanford University's Vinton Cerf and the military's

Internet History
www.isoc.org/internet/history

A 1960s-vintage IBM mainframe computer. The personal computer in your home probably carries more computing power than this giant machine.

Robert Kahn coined the term "the Internet." In 1979 a graduate student at the University of North Carolina, Steve Bellovin, created Usenet and, independent of Bellovin, IBM created BITNET. These two networking software systems enabled virtually anybody with access to a Unix or IBM computer to connect to others on the growing network. By the time the Internet Society was chartered and the World Wide Web was released in 1992, there were more than 1.1 million **hosts**—computers linking individual personal computer users to the Internet. From 1995 to 1999, the number of hosts worldwide octupled. In Asia, the growth rate was double that (Allen, 2001). Today there is an ever-expanding number of hosts, 52 million and growing, serving more than 633.6 million users across the globe, including more than two-thirds of all people 2 years old and older in the United States (Serverwatch, 2004; Kim, 2004).

THE PERSONAL COMPUTER

A crucial part of the story of the Internet is the development and diffusion of personal computers. IBM was fantastically successful at exciting businesses, schools and universities, and other organizations about computers. But IBM's and other companies' **mainframe** and **minicomputers** employed **terminals,** and these stations at which users worked were connected to larger, centralized machines. As a result, the Internet at first was the province of the people who worked in those settings.

When the semiconductor (or integrated circuit, or chip) replaced the vacuum tube as the essential information processor in computers, its tiny size, absence of heat, and low cost made possible the design and production of

www

Definition of Internet Terms
www.whatis.techtarget.com

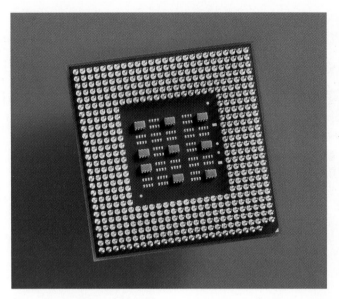
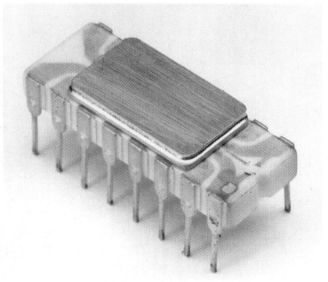

An early computer chip on the right, and today's Pentium 4.

small, affordable **personal** or **microcomputers (PCs).** This, of course, opened the Net to anyone, anywhere.

The leaders of the personal computer revolution were Bill Gates and the duo of Steve Jobs and Stephen Wozniak. As a college freshman in 1975, Gates saw a magazine story about a small, low-powered computer, the MITS Altair 8800, that could be built from a kit and used to play a simple game. Sensing that the future of computing was in these personal computers and that the power of computers would reside not in their size but in the software that ran them, Gates dropped out of Harvard University and, with his friend Paul Allen, founded Microsoft Corporation. They licensed their **operating system**—the software that tells the computer how to work—to MITS. With this advance, people no longer had to know sophisticated operating languages such as FORTRAN and COBOL to use computers. At nearly the same time, in 1977, Jobs and Wozniak, also college dropouts, perfected Apple II, a low-cost, easy-to-use microcomputer designed specifically for personal rather than business use. It was immediately and hugely successful, especially in its development of **multimedia** capabilities—advanced sound and image applications. IBM, stung by its failure to enter the personal computer business, contracted with Microsoft to use the Microsoft operating system in its IBM PC, first introduced in 1981. All of the pieces were now in place for the home computer revolution.

The Internet Today

Online White Pages
www.whitepages.com

The Internet is most appropriately thought of as a "network of networks" that is growing at an incredibly fast rate. These networks consist of LANs (local area networks), connecting two or more computers, usually within the same building, and **WANs (wide area networks),** connecting several LANs in different locations. When people access the Internet from a computer in a university library, they are most likely on a LAN. But when several universities (or businesses or other organizations) link their computer systems, their users are part of a WAN.

The originators of the personal computing revolution—Bill Gates, Steve Jobs, and Stephen Wozniak.

As the popularity of the Internet has grown, so has the number of **ISPs (Internet service providers),** companies that offer Internet connections at monthly rates depending on the kind and amount of access needed. There are 6,000 ISPs operating in the United States, including some of the better known such as America Online, Prodigy, and the wireless provider Ricochet. Through providers, users can avail themselves of numerous services.

USING THE INTERNET

It is only a small overstatement to say that computers are rarely used for computing anymore because the Net has given the computer so much more versatility.

E-mail (Electronic Mail) With an Internet **e-mail** account, users can communicate with anyone else online, any place in the world, with no long-distance fees (just applicable local phone connection charges). Each person online has a unique e-mail address that works just like a telephone number. There are even online "Yellow Pages" and "White Pages" to help users find other people by e-mail. **Instant messaging,** or **IM,** is the real-time version of e-mail, allowing two or more people to communicate instantaneously and in immediate response to one another. IM can also be used for downloading text, audio, and video files and for gaming.

Online Yellow Pages
www.yellowpages.com

Mailing Lists E-mail can be used to join mailing lists, bulletin boards, or discussion groups that cover a huge variety of subjects. The lists are often incorrectly called "listservs," which is the name of the free software program used to run most of them. Users simply subscribe to a group, and then all mail posted (sent) to that group is automatically forwarded to them by the host computer. The lists are typically produced by a single person or central authority such as a university, foundation, or public interest group. A listing of discussion groups can be obtained online from www.lsoft.com/catalist.html.

Usenet Also known as network news, **Usenet** is an internationally distributed bulletin board system. Users enter messages, and within a day or so the messages are delivered to nearly every other Usenet host for everyone to read.

The best way to find a mailing list or discussion group is to access a document called "Publicly Accessible Mailing Lists," which is posted regularly on the Usenet newsgroup site (www.cs.uu.nl/cgi-bin/faqwais).

Voice over Internet Protocol (VoIP) Pronounced "voyp," this is telephone where calls are transferred in digital packets over the Internet rather than on circuit-switched telephone wires. Think of it as "voice e-mail." This transformative technology "means any corporation with a network or any individual with a $30-a-month broadband connection can make calls without paying the phone company" ("Finally," 2004, p. 1). Today, 10% of all phone calls worldwide are VoIP, and as the technology improves—and if providers such as Vonage (www.vonage.com) and Skype (www.skype.com) overcome legal and legislative hurdles being put in their way by frightened traditional phone companies—VoIP "seems destined to spark a market shift as dramatic as the one that followed US telephone deregulation decades ago" (Jardin, 2004, p. 32).

THE WORLD WIDE WEB

Another way of accessing information files is on the Internet via the **World Wide Web** (usually referred to as "the Web"). The Web is not a physical place, or a set of files, or even a network of computers. The heart of the Web lies in the protocols that define its use. The World Wide Web (WWW) uses hypertext transfer protocols (HTTP) to transport files from one place

Tim Berners-Lee
www.w3.org/people/all

to another. Hypertext transfer was developed in the early 1990s by England's Tim Berners-Lee, who was working at Cern, the international particle physics laboratory near Geneva, Switzerland. Berners-Lee gave HTTP to the world for free. "The Web is more a social creation than a technical one," he wrote. "I designed it for a social effect—to help people work together—and not as a technical toy. The ultimate goal of the Web is to support and improve our web-like existence in the world" (Berners-Lee & Fischetti, 1999, p. 128).

The ease of accessing the Web is a function of a number of components: hosts, URLs, browsers, search engines, and home pages.

Hosts (Computers Connected to the Internet) Other than e-mail transactions, most Internet activity consists of users accessing files on remote computers. To reach these files, users must first gain access to the Internet through "wired-to-the-Net" hosts. These hosts are often called servers.

Once users gain access to a host computer on the Internet, they then have to find the exact location of the file they are looking for *on* the host. Each file or directory on the Internet (that is, on the host computer connected to the Internet) is designated by a **URL (uniform resource locator).** A URL is, in effect, a site's official address. But as any user of the Web knows, sites are more commonly recognized by their **domain names.** For example, a dot-COM is a commercial site, a dot-EDU is a school, a dot-ORG is some type of nonprofit. So, Medialit.org is a nonprofit site dedicated to media literacy. In mid-2005 there were more than 353 million hosts connected to the Net (isc.org, 2005), housing nearly 56 million individual domains. More than 335,000 new domains are activated every day. Another 172,000 become inactive and 67,000 change domains, again every day (Whois, 2005).

WWW

Listserv
www.lsoft.com/catalist.html

WWW

Usenet
www.cs.uu.nl/cgi-bin/faqwais

NASA's Pathfinder Web site welcomed millions of daily visitors from around the world during its July 1997 transmissions from the surface of Mars. The *New York Times* announced that, with this event, the World Wide Web had "arrived."

A typical and often visited home page.

WWW

Links to MUDs
www.mudconnect.com

Browsers Software programs loaded onto the user's computer and used to download and view Web files are known as **browsers.** Browsers take separate files (text files, image files, and sound files) and put them all together for viewing. Netscape and Internet Explorer are two of the most popular Web browsers.

Search Engines Finding information on the Web is becoming easier thanks to the growing number of companies creating Web- or Net-search software. These programs are sometimes called **search engines, spiders,** or **Web crawlers.** They all provide on-screen menus that make their navigation as simple as pointing and clicking. Among the better known are Ask Jeeves (ask.com), Netscape (www.netscape.com), and Yahoo! (www.yahoo.com). Arguably the best known but certainly the most frequently used (200 million searches a day) is Google (www.google.com), which produces its search results with technology that uses the "collective intelligence of the Web itself"; that is, search results are presented and ranked based on how frequently a given site is linked to others. "The Web pages that Google says are the best are the pages that the Web as a whole thinks are best" (Surowiecki, 2004, p. 31).

Home Pages Once users reach the intended Web site, they are greeted by a **home page**—the entryway to the site itself. It not only contains the information the site's creators want visitors to know but also provides **hyperlinks** to other material in that site, as well as to material in other sites on other computers linked to the Net anywhere in the world.

The Internet and Its Users

We typically think of people who access a medium as audience members, but the Internet has *users,* not audience members. At any time—or even at the same time—a person may be both *reading* Internet content and *creating* content. E-mail and chat rooms are obvious examples of online users being both audience and creators, but others exist as well. For example, MUDs (Chapter 9) enable entire alternative realities to be simultaneously constructed and engaged, and computer screens that have multiple open windows enable users to "read" one site while creating another, sometimes using the just-read material. With ease we can access the Web, link from site to site and page to page, and even build our own sites. As former NBC and PBS president Lawrence K. Grossman wrote, "Gutenberg made us all readers. Radio and television made us all first-hand observers. Xerox made us all publishers. The Internet makes us all journalists, broadcasters, columnists, commentators, and critics" (1999, p. 17).

It is almost impossible to tell exactly how many users there are on the Internet. People who own computers are not necessarily linked to the Internet, and people need not own computers to use the Net. Some users access the Net through machines at school, a library, or work. Current

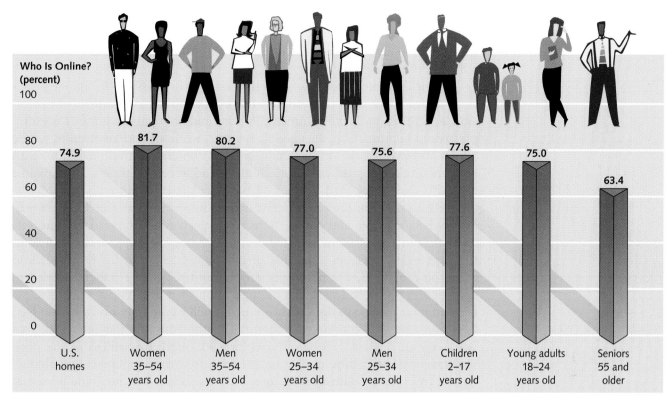

Figure 10.1 U.S. Internet User Profile, 2004. *Source:* Kim, 2004.

best estimates indicate that there are at least 1 billion users worldwide (Cha, 2005). Still, more than three-quarters of all Americans regularly access the Internet from home. The Net's demographics have undergone a dramatic shift in the last few years. In 1996, for example, 62% of U.S. Internet users were men. In 2000, women became the Net's majority gender for the first time (Hamilton, 2000). Today, women in every age group use the Internet more than do men, and not surprisingly, the younger a person, the greater the likelihood he or she has access to the Net (Kim, 2004). Recent Internet demographics are presented in Figure 10.1.

U.S. Census Bureau
www.census.gov

Commercialization of the Internet

Today, 80% of American Internet users report making online purchases. Worldwide online commerce, business-to-business and business-to-consumer, was estimated to be $6.8 trillion in 2004 (with the United States accounting for 47% of that activity). Advertisers spent over $12.9 billion in 2005 to reach the Net's users (Oser, 2005a). This growing number of users and their apparent willingness to go online to buy products have been at the heart of one important debate about the future of the Internet.

Many users fear that the wide-open nature of the Net and the more ordered world of business are a poor fit. Business, they fret, will turn the Internet into an electronic shopping mall and this commercialization of what was once the freest of communication technologies will lead to growing privatization and control. Commerce, they claim, cannot function amid chaos and disorder, but it is just that anarchy that has made the Internet so exciting. Nobody needs permission to get on or off the Internet. Nobody can tell a user what to say.

Online "traditionalists" point to the history of television. In the medium's early stages, there were predictions and promises of a new medium of expression, education, and entertainment. Politics and political discourse, for example, would be transformed as people became aware of and involved in public affairs. The reality, the online traditionalists contend, is that television, with its commercial support, profit orientation, and lowest common denominator mentality, has cheapened politics and political discourse.

Defenders of online commerce argue, however, that the Internet will always be accessible and open. There is no spectrum scarcity to limit access, as there is in broadcasting, so the television analogy is inappropriate. In addition, because very small amounts of money are required for individuals to access and use the Internet, especially in contrast to the budget needed to start and run a broadcast or cable operation or a newspaper or magazine, the commercial orientation of those media will never fully overtake the Net. It is precisely this commercial potential of the Internet, they contend, that will keep the cost of access low and its value high. Regardless of the position taken, there is little doubt that the online world is increasingly characterized by commercialization (Figure 10.2). And there is some indication that that commercialization *is* turning some users off. Recent declines in the average amount of time users spend online and the flight from the Internet by millions of former users (Fitzgerald, 2003) have been attributed, in part, to overcommercialization and the intrusiveness of Internet advertising (see Chapter 12).

Figure 10.2 Worldwide e-commerce Growth. In 2004, worldwide online commerce reached $6.8 trillion. *Source:* Global Reach (www.glreach.com/eng/ed/art/2004.ecommerce.php3).

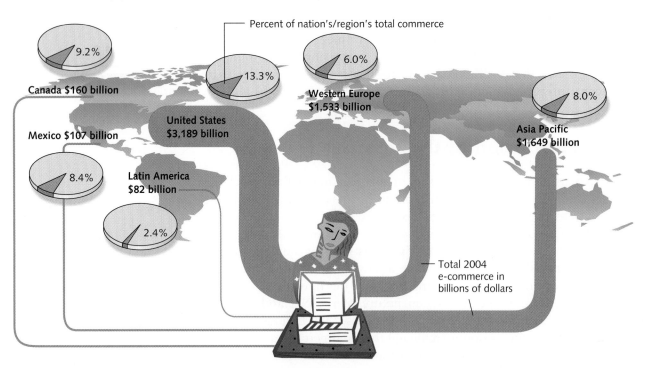

Percent of nation's/region's total commerce

9.2%

Canada $160 billion

13.3%

6.0%

Western Europe $1,533 billion

8.0%

United States $3,189 billion

Mexico $107 billion

Asia Pacific $1,649 billion

8.4%

Latin America $82 billion

2.4%

Total 2004 e-commerce in billions of dollars

Possibly the most annoying form of commercialization of the Internet is **spam,** unsolicited commercial e-mail, and it threatens to alienate even more users. Today, 75% of all e-mail activity is spam, up from 45% in 2003. More than 15 billion pieces of spam are sent every day, and in 2005 alone, 10.3 trillion pieces of junk e-mail passed over the Net. Congress estimates that dealing with spam costs about $10 billion a year in people's time (Hansell, 2006; Drutman, 2005). The Pew Charitable Trust, in presenting the results of its survey on Web use, reported, "Spam is beginning to undermine the integrity of e-mail and degrade life online" (quoted in "Can-Spam," 2004, p. A8).

Legislation to control spam is controversial. Anti-spam advocates call the 2003 Controlling the Assault of Non-Solicited Pornography and Marketing Act (the Can-Spam Act) a fraud. By establishing rules for how unwanted, unsolicited e-mails must be labeled, it legitimizes spam, they say. And in preempting much tougher state laws, it gives the powerful spam industry protection. A preempted California law, for example, would have required senders of unsolicited e-mail to secure a user's permission *before* a commercial e-mail could be sent; in other words, an opt-in requirement.

Less controversial is an FTC ruling that pornographic spam must contain the warning "Sexually-Explicit" to allow ease of filtering. Several e-mail providers—Microsoft, AOL, Yahoo! and Earthlink—have initiated lawsuits against aggressive and large-scale spammers. Technological tools—filters— can help reduce the flow of junk e-mail, as might a newly instituted plan by ISPs AOL and Yahoo! to charge "bulk e-mailers" a fee for delivery of their messages (Hansell, 2006).

Changes in the Mass Communication Process

In Chapter 2 we saw how concentration of ownership, globalization, audience fragmentation, hypercommercialism, and convergence were influencing the nature of the mass communication process. Each redefines the relationship between audiences and media industries. For example, elsewhere in this text we have discussed the impacts of concentration on newspaper readership; of globalization on the type and quality of films available to moviegoers; of audience fragmentation on the variety of channel choices for television viewers; of convergence on the record industry's reinvention; and of hypercommercialism on all media.

The Internet is different from these more traditional media. Rather than changing the relationship between audiences and industries, the Net changes the *definition* of the different components of the process and, as a result, changes their relationship. On the Net a single individual can communicate with as large an audience as can the giant, multinational corporation that produces a network television program. That corporation fits our earlier definition of a mass communication source—a large, hierarchically structured organization—but the Internet user does not. Feedback in mass communication is traditionally described as inferential and delayed, but online feedback can be, and very often is, immediate and direct. It is more similar to feedback in interpersonal communication than to feedback in mass communication.

This Internet-induced redefinition of the elements of the mass communication process is refocusing attention on issues such as freedom of expression, privacy, responsibility, and democracy.

Technology, even one with as much potential as the Internet, is only as good as the uses we make of it.
© Rhymes with Orange-Hilary B. Price. King Features Syndicate.

THE DOUBLE EDGE OF TECHNOLOGY

The solution to the McLuhan–Gibson conflict in the opening vignette is one of perspective. McLuhan was writing and thinking in the relative youth of the electronic media. When *Understanding Media* was published in 1964, television had just become a mass medium, the personal computer wasn't even a dream, and Paul Baran was still envisioning ARPAnet.

Gibson, writing much later in the age of electronic media, was commenting from a more experienced position and after observing real-world evidence. McLuhan was optimistic because he was speculating on what electronic media *could do*. Gibson was pessimistic because he was commenting on what he had seen electronic media *doing*.

Still, neither visionary is completely right or completely wrong. Technology alone, even the powerful electronic media that fascinated both, cannot create new worlds or new ways of seeing them. *We* use technology to do these things. This, as we discussed briefly in Chapter 1, is why technology is a double-edged sword. Its power—for good and for bad—resides in us. The same aviation technology that we use to visit relatives halfway around the world can also be used to destroy the World Trade Center. The same communication technologies used to create a truly global village can be used to dehumanize and standardize the people who live in it.

McLUHAN'S RENAISSANCE

Marshall McLuhan's ideas are in vogue again. The Canadian English professor was at the center of the early intellectual debate over electronic media. His books—especially *The Gutenberg Galaxy* (1962), *Understanding Media: The Extensions of Man* (1964), and *The Medium Is the Massage* (McLuhan & Fiore, 1967)—generated heated comment and earned McLuhan much criticism. His ideas satisfied almost no one. Critics from the humanities castigated him for wasting his time on something as frivolous as television. True culture exists in "real" literature, they argued. McLuhan fared just as badly among mass communication theorists. Social scientists committed to the idea of limited media effects (see Chapter 13) simply disagreed with his view of powerful media technologies, however optimistic. Others who were convinced of media's potential negative influence dismissed him

as blindly in love with technology and overly speculative. Social scientists demanded scientific verification of McLuhan's ideas. Labeled the "High Priest of Popcult," the "Metaphysician of Media," the "Oracle of the Electronic Age," McLuhan may simply have been ahead of his time.

What has returned McLuhan to the forefront of the cultural discussion surrounding the mass media is the Internet. (Remember, some tech historians trace the Net's genesis to a McLuhan acolyte, Joseph C. R. Licklider.) McLuhan's ideas resonate with those who believe the new medium can fulfill his optimistic vision of an involved, connected global village. Those who think the potential of the Internet, like that of television before it, will never fulfill McLuhan's predictions are forced to explain their reasoning in terms of his ideas. McLuhan is back, and, as before, he is controversial. *Wired* magazine, the self-proclaimed "Bible of Cyberspace," has anointed McLuhan its patron saint. But as we saw in the opening vignette, not everyone in the cyberworld trusts the technology as much as he did. Two of his concepts, however—the global village and media as extensions of our bodies—are receiving renewed discussion precisely because of the Net.

The Global Village Many concepts survive McLuhan's 1980 death and serve as his legacy. None is more often quoted than the **global village,** the idea that the new communication technologies will permit people to become

www

Marshall McLuhan
www.mcluhan.ca

The books that put Marshall McLuhan at the center of the debate over electronic communication.

increasingly involved in one another's lives. Skeptics point out that McLuhan, with this notion, reveals his unrealistic, utopian infatuation with technology. But McLuhan himself never said all would be tranquil in the global village. Yes, he did believe electronic media would permit "the human tribe" to become "one family," but he also realized that families fight:

> There is more diversity, less conformity under a single roof in any family than there is with the thousands of families in the same city. The more you create village conditions, the more discontinuity and division and diversity. The global village absolutely insures maximal disagreement on all points. (McLuhan & Stearn, 1967, p. 279)

Involvement does not mean harmony, but it does mean an exchange of ideas. As McLuhan said, the global village is "a world in which people encounter each other in depth all the time" (p. 280).

www

More McLuhan
www.law.pitt.edu/hibbitts/mcl.htm

Media as Extensions of Our Bodies   Central to McLuhan's view of how media and cultures interact is the idea that media do not *bring* the world to us but rather permit us to experience the world with a scope and depth otherwise impossible. Media, then, are extensions of our bodies. Just as clothes are an extension of our skin, permitting us to wander farther from our warm caves into the cold world; just as the automobile is an extension of our feet, enabling us to travel farther than we could ever walk; television extends our vision and hearing, and computers extend our central nervous system. With television we can see and hear around the world, beyond the galaxy, into the future, and into the past. Computers process, sort, categorize, reconfigure, and clarify. McLuhan's message here is not unlike Carey's (1975) ritual view of mass communication. Communication technologies do not deliver or transmit information; they fundamentally alter the relationship between people and their world, encouraging us to construct new meanings for the things we encounter with and through them.

Reconceptualizing Life in an Interconnected World

What happens to people in the global village? What becomes of audiences and users as their senses are extended technologically? How free are we to express ourselves? Does greater involvement with others mean a loss of privacy? These are only a few of the questions confronting us as we attempt to find the right balance between the good and the bad that comes from the new communication technologies.

THE INTERNET AND FREEDOM OF EXPRESSION

By its very nature the Internet raises a number of important issues of freedom of expression. There is no central location, no on-and-off button for the Internet, making it difficult for those who want to control it. For free expression advocates, however, this freedom from control is the medium's primary strength. The anonymity of its users provides their expression—even the most radical, profane, and vulgar—great protection, giving voice to those who would otherwise be silenced. This anonymity, say advocates of strengthened Internet control, is a breeding ground for abuse. But opponents of control counter that the Net's affordability and ease of use make it our most democratic medium. Proponents of control argue that this freedom brings with it

Activists at MoveOn.org fought an impeachment, protested a war, tried to run a Super Bowl spot, and rallied millions of people worldwide to their cause.

MoveOn.org

Frustrated that the nation was spending too much time, money, attention, and emotion on President Bill Clinton's 1998 impeachment, Wes Boyd and Joan Blades, who had become wealthy from their classic flying toaster screen saver, e-mailed 300 of their friends, encouraging them to sign the online petition they had created. Its message was simple—end the impeachment, censure Mr. Clinton, and *move on*. Word spread, and soon, 500,000 other people signed on. Since then, MoveOn.org has grown to more than 2.9 million "members" worldwide (McKelvey, 2004). Critics and admirers alike agree that their model of online advocacy and discourse will be at the heart of most efforts to make a political difference in our increasingly interconnected world. AlterNet (another online advocacy group) political writer Brad deGraf explained why:

> If a paradigm shift from industrial- to information-age and from hierarchies to networks is happening, it will naturally favor those who want that shift to happen. In that sense, it threatens the two-party system in general, Republicans and Democrats alike, because they can't control the game rules as they have in the past, and the "barrier to entry" just went from "establishing a third party" to "self-organizing a movement." (2004, p. 3)

"THAT SUNDAY EVENING, I JOINED 1,500 OF MY NEIGHBORS. SOMEONE HANDED ME A CANDLE AND LIT IT FOR ME; AT SOME POINT A RABBI AND A PASTOR SPOKE TO THE CROWD. BUT OTHERWISE, THERE WAS NO OBVIOUS LEADERSHIP, AND IT DIDN'T SEEM TO MATTER. THERE HAD BEEN NO MEETINGS, NO LEAFLETS, NO CLIPBOARDS, NO PHONE CALLS—WE WERE ALL THERE, ESSENTIALLY, BECAUSE OF AN E-MAIL WE TRUSTED"

MoveOn.org is doing what it can to ensure that this shift does indeed occur, that the Internet itself will be used to make a difference. MoveOn.org provides free online Web tools to assist others in self-organization. Thousands of small groups have taken advantage of this assistance (Boyd, 2003). Also, through its own network advocacy efforts, some very public and some less so, it offers encouragement and an example to others who feel themselves unheard.

Its most famous "example," the January 2004 refusal of CBS to run MoveOn.org's 30-second "Child's Pay" commercial, made the group internationally famous. But it wasn't just the network's resistance to the spot; it was the story behind its creation that caught people's attention. In classic interconnected fashion, MoveOn.org held an online competition, asking "ordinary Americans" to create "Bush in 30 Seconds" video commercials commenting on the policies of the administration of President George W. Bush. Users worldwide could view the submissions as they were entered. The group made online solicitations for the money required to buy airtime from CBS. It easily raised the more-than-$1 million necessary. And when CBS refused to accept the spot, it used the Net and news coverage of the controversy to "air" it globally,

responsibilities that other media—and those who create their content—understand but that are ignored by many online. "The Internet is stuck in the flower-power days of the '60s during which people thought the world would be beautiful if you are just nice," laments Karl Auerbach, formerly of Cisco Systems (in Cha, 2005, p. D2). Internet freedom-of-expression issues, then, fall into two broad categories. The first is the Net's potential to make the First Amendment's freedom-of-the-press guarantee a reality for greater numbers of people. The second is the problem of setting boundaries of control.

FREEDOM OF THE PRESS FOR WHOM?

Veteran *New Yorker* columnist A. J. Liebling, author of that magazine's "Wayward Press" feature and often called the "conscience of journalism," frequently argued that freedom of the press is guaranteed only to those who own one. Theoretically, anyone can own a broadcast outlet or cable television operation. But the number of outlets in any community is limited, and they are unavailable to all but the richest people and corporations. Theoretically, anyone can own a newspaper or magazine, but again the expense involved

For more information on this topic, see Media Talk video clip #21, "The Drudge Report," on the *Media World* DVD.

giving it significantly more exposure than it would have had even if it had run during the Super Bowl, making it, according to *Newsweek*, "the ad that has achieved the most air time with the least dollars expended of any ad in the history of the republic" (MoveOn.org, 2004).

But MoveOn.org had been making a difference long before "Child's Pay." In January 2003 it raised hundreds of thousands of dollars to run television and print ads across America, urging President Bush to forgo invasion and "let the inspections work." A month later it organized a virtual march on Washington in opposition to the impending invasion of Iraq. Forty thousand people registered for the "march," and Congress and the White House were deluged with more than 1 million e-mails and faxes. In 5 days in March 2003, using its five staff people and the networking skills of its members, MoveOn.org organized a candlelight vigil in a last-minute effort to stop an invasion of Iraq. Six thousand individual gatherings totaling more than 1 million people in 130 countries and every state in America assembled at dusk on March 16. Two months later, in May, it urged its members to support the humanitarian efforts of international relief organization Oxfam in Iraq. Nearly 7,000 people responded with more than $500,000, two-thirds of all the money the group had received from all sources. In that same month, it collected contributions of hundreds of thousands of dollars to run anti-media-concentration commercials featuring the glowering image of News Corp's Rupert Murdoch on several major media outlets, including Murdoch's own Fox News. In summer 2004, its online encouragement of *Fahrenheit 9/11* parties helped make Michael Moore's antiwar documentary the most successful nonfiction film of all time in its opening weekend alone, earning more than $22 million.

Has MoveOn.org made a difference with what its campaign director Eli Pariser calls its "postmodern organizing model.

Child's Pay, *MoveOn.org's 30-second critique of record federal deficits created by the administration of George W. Bush, achieved the most exposure for the least dollars spent of any ad in history.*

It's opt-in, it's decentralized, you do it from your home"? One possible answer resides in New York University professor Andrew Boyd's recollection of his participation in the war-eve candlelight vigil: "That Sunday evening, I joined 1,500 of my neighbors. Someone handed me a candle and lit it for me; at some point a rabbi and a pastor spoke to the crowd. But otherwise, there was no obvious leadership, and it didn't seem to matter. There had been no meetings, no leaflets, no clipboards, no phone calls—we were all there, essentially, because of an e-mail we trusted" (2003, p. 14).

makes this an impossibility for most people. Newsletters, like a soap-box speaker on a street corner, are limited in reach, typically of interest to those who already agree with the message, and relatively unsophisticated when compared with the larger commercial media.

The Net, however, turns every user into a potential mass communicator. Equally important, on the Internet every "publisher" is equal. The Web sites of the biggest government agency, the most powerful broadcast network, the newspaper with the highest circulation, the richest ad agencies and public relations firms, the most far-flung religion, and the lone user with an idea or cause sit figuratively side by side. Each is only as powerful as its ideas.

In other words, the Net can give voice to those typically denied expression. Writing for the alternative press news service AlterNet, activist L. A. Kauffman said, "The Internet is an agitator's dream: fast, cheap, far-reaching. And with the planetary reach of the World Wide Web, activist networks are globalizing at nearly the pace of the corporate order they oppose" (as quoted in Cox, 2000, p. 14). After instituting reforms in response to an Internet-led protest of labor practices in its Third World factories in 1998, a company spokesperson for athletic shoe manufacturer Nike said, "You

Officials, in fact much of the world, were caught off guard by antiwar protests that sprang up across the globe in February 2003, action organized by Internet.

WWW

Media Activist Site
www.fair.org

WWW

Blogging
www.blogger.com

make changes because it's the right thing to do. But obviously our actions have clearly been accelerated because of the World Wide Web" (as quoted in Klein, 1999, p. 392).

This acceleration is dramatically demonstrated by **flash mobs** (sometimes called **smart mobs**), "large, geographically dispersed groups connected only by thin threads of communications technology . . . drawn together at a moment's notice like schools of fish to perform some collective action" (Taylor, 2003, p. 53). MoveOn.org is the best-known site for the coordination of flash mobs and, as it has matured, online political action. Using e-mail and instant messaging, MoveOn led the February 15, 2003, worldwide antiwar protest, gathering 400,000 people in New York and 10 million more across the globe to protest the impending war in Iraq. To prove that flash mobs had become "the other superpower," according to the *New York Times,* 1 million people in 6,000 cities in 130 countries flash-mobbed an antiwar candlelight vigil on March 16, 2003, an action called in only 5 days (Boyd, 2003). The essay on page 316, "MoveOn.org," offers a fuller look at online activism.

The Internet also offers expanded expression through Weblogs, or blogs. Before September 11, 2001, blogs were typically personal online diaries. But after that horrible day, possibly because millions of people felt that the mainstream press had left them unprepared and clueless about what was really going on in the world, blogs changed. *Blog* now refers to a "Web journal that comments on the news—often by criticizing the media and usually in rudely clever tones—with links to stories that back up the commentary with evidence" (Seipp, 2002, p. 43). There are more than 23.5 million already on the Internet, and 100,000 new ones go online every day, some constructed by the famous, most by the not-famous (Stepp, 2006; Lyons, 2005). Technology writer and conservative activist Andrew Sullivan argues that "blogging is changing the media world and could foment a revolution in how journalism functions in our culture," not only because individual bloggers have earned their readers' respect, but because their "personal touch is much more in tune with our current sensibilities than (are) the opinionated magazines and newspapers of old. Readers increasingly doubt the authority of the *Washington Post* or *National Review*" (Sullivan, 2002, p. 43).

Sullivan, former editor of the *New Republic,* says this "means the universe of permissible opinions will expand, unconstrained by the prejudices, tastes or interests of the old-media elite" (quoted in Seipp, 2002, p. 43). In other words, because bloggers in effect own their own presses, they have freedom of the press. The power of these "weapons of mass documentation," in comedian Jon Stewart's words, was much on display during the war in and occupation of Iraq. Scores of blogs went online when the invasion began in 2003. One, maintained in English by a young architect student living in Baghdad who called himself Salam Pax, offered dramatic firsthand accounts of the battle. His blog, at www.dear_raed.blogspot.com, gained a worldwide

readership. And it was blog-distributed digital images of soldiers' coffins, taken by a civilian contractor, that were able to circumvent the Pentagon's ban on unofficial photos of the war's victims when the mainstream media, with their vast resources, had been either unwilling or unable.

Blogs are not without their critics. *Advertising Age* media writer Simon Dumenco calls them little more than writers "with a cooler name," referring to membership in the ranks of bloggers of voices from just about every mainstream media outlet and Fortune 500 company (2006, p. 18). A blogger, in other words, is just as likely to be an "insider" as an "outsider." More troubling to blogs' detractors is that bloggers are responsible to no one. Media critic Eric Alterman says that for political blogs, "The very act of weighing evidence, or even presenting any, is suspect. The modus operandi is accuse, accuse, accuse and see what sticks" (2005, p. 10). Additionally, argue critics, corporate bloggers are often little more than fronts set up to attack competitors. "Bloggers are more of a threat than people realize, and they are only going to get more toxic. This is the new reality," explains Peter Blackshaw, chief marketing officer of a company that polices blogs for commercial clients such as Procter & Gamble and Ford. He estimates that 50% to 60% of the online attacks his clients endure come from competitors (in Lyons, 2005, p. 130).

CONTROLLING INTERNET EXPRESSION

Abuses of the Net's freedom such as these are behind the argument for greater control of the Internet. The very same medium that can empower users who wish to challenge those more powerful than themselves can also be used to lie and cheat. The Internet does not distinguish between true and false, biased and objective, trivial and important. Once misinformation has been loosed on the Net, it is almost impossible to catch and correct it.

One victim of Net-bred lies is Alexandra Polier. Conservative "cybergossip" Matt Drudge falsely told the world in February 2004 that the recent college graduate had had an affair with Democratic presidential candidate John Kerry. In 2006, 78-year-old former assistant attorney

Rumors, lies, and innuendo spread far, wide, and fast on the Internet. JUMP START © United Feature Syndicate, Inc.

general and founder of the Freedom Forum's First Amendment Center, John Seigenthaler, fought back Internet lies that he had been directly involved in the assassinations of both John and Bobby Kennedy, a story that began as an Internet joke. In that same year Procter & Gamble was victimized by online stories falsely asserting that one of its cleaners could kill pets. And Starbucks was falsely accused online of refusing to provide coffee to Marines serving in Iraq.

Lies have always been part of human interaction; the Internet only gives them greater reach. There is little that government can do to control this abuse. Legal remedies already exist in the form of libel laws and prosecution for fraud. Users can help by teaching themselves to be more attentive to return addresses and by ignoring messages that are sent anonymously or that have suspicious origins. There is an Internet-based solution as well. Computer security specialists at the U.S. Department of Energy maintain a Web site designed to track and debunk online misinformation (hoax busters.ciac.org).

www

Defeating Internet Hoaxes
www.hoaxbusters.ciac.org

PORNOGRAPHY ON THE WORLD WIDE WEB

Most efforts at controlling the Internet are aimed at indecent or pornographic Web content. We will see in Chapter 14 that indecent and pornographic expression is protected. The particular concern with the Internet, therefore, is shielding children.

The Child Pornography Prevention Act of 1996 forbade online transmission of any image that "appears to be of a minor engaging in sexually explicit conduct." Proponents argued that the impact of child porn on the children involved, as well as on society, warranted this legislation. Opponents argued that child pornography per se was already illegal, regardless of the medium. Therefore they saw this law as an unnecessary and overly broad intrusion into freedom of expression on the Net. In April 2002 the Supreme Court sided with the act's opponents. Its effect would be too damaging to freedom of expression. "Few legitimate movie producers or book publishers, or few other speakers in any capacity, would risk distributing images in or near the uncertain reach of this law," wrote Justice Anthony Kennedy. "The Constitution gives significant protection from over-broad laws that chill speech within the First Amendment's vast and privileged sphere" (in "Justices Scrap," 2002,

p. A3). Kennedy cited the antidrug film *Traffic,* Academy Award–winning *American Beauty,* and Shakespeare's *Romeo and Juliet,* all works containing scenes of minors engaged in sexual activity, as examples of expression that would disappear from the Net.

The primary battleground, then, became protecting children from otherwise legal content. The Net, by virtue of its openness and accessibility, raises particular concerns. Children's viewing of sexually explicit material on cable television can theoretically be controlled by parents. Moreover, viewers must specifically order this content and typically pay an additional fee for it. The purchase of sexually explicit videos, books, and magazines is controlled by laws regulating vendors. But computers sit in homes, schools, and libraries. Children are encouraged to explore their possibilities. A search for the novel *Little Women,* for example, might turn up any number of pornographic sites.

Proponents of stricter control of the Net liken the availability of smut on the Internet to a bookstore or library that allows porn to sit side by side with books that children *should* be reading. In actual, real-world bookstores and libraries, professionals, whether book retailers or librarians, apply their judgment in selecting and locating material, ideally striving for appropriateness and balance. Children are the beneficiaries of their professional judgment. No such selection or evaluation is applied to the Internet. Opponents of control accept the bookstore/library analogy but argue that, as troubling as the online proximity of all types of content may be, it is a true example of the freedom guaranteed by the First Amendment.

The solution seems to be in technology. Filtering software, such as Net Nanny (www.netnanny.com), can be set to block access to Web sites by title and by the presence of specific words and images (see the essay on page 322, "Rating the Web"). Few free speech advocates are troubled by filters on home computers, but they do see them as problematic when used on more public machines, for example, in schools and libraries. They argue that software that can filter sexual content can also be set to screen out birth control information, religious sites, and discussions of racism. Virtually any content can be blocked. This, they claim, denies other users—adults and mature teenagers, for example—their freedoms.

www

Net Nanny
www.netnanny.com

Congress weighed in on the filtering debate, passing the Children's Internet Protection Act in 2000, requiring schools and libraries to install filtering software. But First Amendment concerns invalidated this act as well. A federal appeals court ruled in June 2002 that requiring these institutions to install filters changes their nature from places that provide information to places that unconstitutionally restrict it. Nonetheless, in June 2003 a sharply divided Supreme Court upheld the Children's Internet Protection Act, declaring that Congress did indeed have the power to require libraries to install filters.

But then, in June 2004, as if to emphasize the difficulty of reconciling the First Amendment with the Internet, that same Court, again in a sharply divided opinion, rejected the 1998 Child Online Protection Act, which would have fined commercial pornographic Web sites $50,000 a day if people younger than 17 could access their content. Filters, not criminal penalties, said the Court, were the "least restrictive means" of achieving the "compelling government interest" of protecting children from harmful Net material (Greenhouse, 2004).

Rating the Web

Proponents of a Web rating system see technology, in the form of filtering software, as an appropriate solution to the need to protect children. They see it as similar to the content ratings systems used by the recording, game, film, and television industries. Opponents of rating Web content call these filters **censorware,** but given that individual users can control the level of filtering they deem appropriate for their own households, there is less industry and user resistance to this screening method than there was to that used for television.

Rating proponents envision two forms of filtering—existing rating schemes and specific interest group ratings. As examples of the latter, the National Organization for Women can develop its own ratings scheme, the Catholic Diocese of St. Louis its own, and the Moral Majority its own. Software already exists for setting individual labeling and filtering codes.

Among preexisting filtering software, the three most utilized are the Internet Content Rating Association (ICRA), SafeSurf, and Net Nanny.

ICRA is a nonprofit organization that asks Web sites about the presence of a large number of very-well-defined categories of content (for example, passionate kissing, killing of animals, promoting tobacco use) and the context in which they are presented (for example, appears in a context intended to be artistic and is suitable for young children). A site is then given a PICS (Platform for Internet Content Selection) rating, an industry-standard evaluation scheme that can trigger a filter. Users can set their own levels of restriction and freedom.

SafeSurf is a commercial company that monitors a self-rating system that labels sites by suitable age ranges, as well as by the amount of such content as nudity and drug use. It has rated more than a million sites, and it, too, uses PICS rating.

> **THE USE OF RATINGS, LABELS, AND FILTERS IS GENERALLY ACCEPTED AS A FACT OF LIFE BY BOTH USERS AND THE INTERNET INDUSTRY.**

Net Nanny can be set to screen out individual Web sites, newsgroups, chat rooms, even entire search engines. It can be customized for individual users of the same machine (so that what is filtered for the kids can be there for mom and dad), and it maintains an account of Web and Net use.

The use of ratings, labels, and filters is generally accepted as a fact of life by both users and the Internet industry. Internet Explorer, Netscape Communicator, Yahoo!, Excite, Lycos, Infoseek, and virtually all the well-known browsers and search engines provide some form of built-in, easy-to-use filter. What has happened here in the online world echoes events in the film industry in 1968 and in television programming in 1996.

SafeSurf.Com Screen capture used by permission.

COPYRIGHT (INTELLECTUAL PROPERTY OWNERSHIP)

Another freedom-of-expression issue that takes on a special nature on the Internet is copyright. Copyright protection is designed to ensure that those who create content are financially compensated for their work (see Chapter 14). The assumption is that more "authors" will create more content if assured of monetary compensation from those who use it. When the content is tangible (books, movies, videotapes, magazines, CDs), authorship and use are relatively easy to identify. But in the cyberworld, things become a bit more complex. John Perry Barlow (1996), a cofounder of the Electronic Frontier Foundation, explains the situation:

> The riddle is this: If our property can be infinitely reproduced and instantaneously distributed all over the planet without cost, without our knowledge,

Electronic Frontier Foundation
www.eff.org

without its even leaving our possession, how can we protect it? How are we going to get paid for the work we do with our minds? And, if we can't get paid, what will assure the continued creation and distribution of such work? (p. 148)

Technically, copyright rules apply to the Internet as they do to other media. Material on the Net, even on electronic bulletin boards, belongs to the author, so its use, other than fair use, requires permission and possibly payment. But because material on the Internet is not tangible, it is easily, freely, and privately copied. This renders it difficult, if not impossible, to police those who do copy.

Another confounding issue is that new and existing material is often combined with other existing material to create even "newer" content. This makes it difficult to assign authorship. If a user borrows some text from one source, combines it with images from a second, surrounds both with a background graphic from a third, and adds music sampled from many others, where does authorship reside?

To deal with these thorny issues, in 1998 the U.S. Congress passed the Digital Millennium Copyright Act. Its primary goal was to bring U.S. copyright law into compliance with that of the World Intellectual Property Organization (WIPO), headquartered in Geneva, Switzerland. The act does the following:

- Makes it a crime to circumvent antipiracy measures built into commercial software
- Outlaws the manufacture, sale, or distribution of code-breaking devices used to illegally copy software
- Permits breaking of copyright protection devices to conduct encryption research and to test computer security systems
- Provides copyright exemptions for nonprofit libraries, archives, and educational institutions under certain circumstances
- Limits the copyright infringement liability of Internet service providers for simply transmitting information over the Internet, but ISPs are required to remove material from users' Web sites that appears to constitute copyright infringement
- Requires Webcasters (Chapter 7) to pay licensing fees to record companies
- States explicitly that **fair use**—instances in which copyrighted material may be used without permission or payment, such as taking brief quotes from a book (see Chapter 14)—applies to the Internet

What the debate over Internet copyright represents—like concern about controlling content that children can access, commercialization of the Net, and efforts to limit troublesome or challenging expression—is a clash of fundamental values that has taken on added nuance with the coming of computer networks. Copyright on the Internet is discussed more fully in Chapter 14.

PRIVACY

The issue of privacy in mass communication has traditionally been concerned with individuals' rights to protect their privacy from invasive, intrusive

Privacy Site
www.privacy.net

media (see Chapter 14). For example, should newspapers publish the names of rape victims and juvenile offenders? When does a person become a public figure and forfeit some degree of privacy? In the global village, however, the issue takes on a new character. Whereas Supreme Court Justice Louis Brandeis could once argue that privacy is "the right to be left alone," today privacy is just as likely to mean "the right to maintain control over our own data." Privacy in the global village has two facets. The first is protecting the privacy of communication we wish to keep private. The second is the use (and misuse) of private, personal information willingly given online.

Protecting Privacy in Communication   The 1986 Electronic Communication Privacy Act guarantees the privacy of our e-mail. It is a criminal offense to either "intentionally [access] without authorization a facility through which an electronic communication service is provided; or intentionally [exceed] an authorization to access that facility." In addition, the law "prohibits an electronic communications service provider from knowingly divulging the contents of any stored electronic communication." The goal of this legislation is to protect private citizens from official abuse; it gives e-mail "conversations" the same protection that phone conversations enjoy. If a government agency wants to listen in, it must secure permission, just as it must get a court order for a telephone wiretap.

If a person or company feels that more direct protection of communication is necessary, encryption is one solution, but it is controversial. **Encryption** is the electronic coding or masking of information that can be deciphered only by a recipient with the decrypting key. According to the FBI and many other government officials, however, this total privacy is an invitation for terrorists, drug lords, and mobsters to use the Net to threaten national security. As such, in early January 2000 the Clinton administration proposed "relaxed" rules—relaxed from initial plans to allow the government to hold the key to *all* encryption technologies. The new rules require makers of encryption software to turn over a copy of their code to a designated third party. The government may access it only with a court order.

"Authorized" interception of messages is another problem for privacy. Courts have consistently upheld employers' rights to intercept and read their employees' e-mail. Employers must be able to guarantee that their computer systems are not abused by the people who work for them. Thoughtful companies solve the problem by issuing clear and fair guidelines on the use of computer networks. Therefore, when they do make unannounced checks of employees' electronic communication, the employee understands that these checks do occur, why they occur, and under what circumstances they can lead to problems.

Protecting Privacy of Personal Information   Every online act leaves a "digital trail," making possible easy "**dataveillance**—the massive collection and distillation of consumer data. . . . Information gathering has become so convenient and cost-effective that personal privacy has replaced censorship as our primary civil liberties concern" (Shenk, 1997, p. 146). Ironically, we participate in this intrusion into our privacy. Because of computer

Privacy Protection
www.accessreports.com

PHILADELPHIA DAILY NEWS Philadelphia USA

storage, networking, and cross-referencing power, the information we give to one entity is easily and cheaply given to countless, unknown others.

One form of dataveillance is distributing and sharing personal, private information among organizations other than the one for whom it was originally intended. Information from every credit card transaction (online or at a store), credit application, phone call, supermarket or other purchase made without cash (for example, with a check, debit card, or "club" card), newspaper and magazine subscription, and cable television subscribership is digitally recorded, stored, and most likely sold to others. The increased computerization of medical files, banking information, job applications, and school records produces even more salable data. Eventually, anyone who wants to know something about a person can simply buy the necessary information—without that person's permission or even knowledge. These data can then be used to further invade people's privacy. Employers can withhold jobs for reasons unknown to applicants. Insurance companies can selectively deny coverage to people based on data about their grocery choices. According to the FTC, the single most frequent consumer complaint in 2003 was identity theft, accounting for 42% of all complaints reported to law enforcement agencies ("Top," 2004).

Recognizing the scope of data collection and the potential problems that it raises, Congress passed the 1974 Federal Privacy Act, restricting governments' ability to collect and distribute information about citizens. The act, however, expressly exempted businesses and other nongovernmental organizations from control. This stands in stark contrast to the situation across the Atlantic. In European Union countries it is illegal for an organization of any kind to sell the name and other personal information of a customer or client without permission. Both the FTC and Congress have recently attempted to address this inconsistency—if we have legislation to bring our copyright laws into compliance with those of other nations, why shouldn't we do the same with our privacy laws? In early 2002 the Senate Commerce, Science, and

Community Internet
www.freepress.net/communityinternet

Fight ID Theft
www.consumer.gov/idtheft

Transportation Committee passed an online privacy protection bill, requiring companies to get consumers' permission *before* they sold or otherwise disseminated their personal data (called **opt-in**), rather than providing that security only if consumers specifically request to **opt-out.** But around that same time, the FTC asked Congress to support new rules creating a national opt-out "do not call" registry. Congress approved the FTC plan in 2003, and 50 million Americans availed themselves of the do-not-call registry by dialing a toll-free phone number or through the Internet in its first 3 months (Mayer, 2003).

But privacy advocates remain concerned. The successful (opt-out) do-not-call registry killed any legislative momentum there might have been for a European-style opt-in system, and a new technology, **radio frequency identification chip (RFIC)** poses additional privacy problems. RFIC, already used by many retailers, most notably Wal-Mart, is a grain-of-sand-sized microchip and antenna embedded in consumer products that transmits a radio signal. The advantage to retailers is greater inventory control and lower labor costs. The retailer has an absolute, up-to-the-minute accounting of how many boxes of widgets are on the shelf, and consumers simply walk out the door with their boxes while the RFIC sends a signal charging the correct amount to the proper credit card . . . no checkout personnel needed. The fear of privacy advocates should be clear. That signal keeps on sending. Now marketers, the government, and others will know where you and your box of widgets are at all times, how quickly you go through your box of widgets, and where you are when you run out of widgets. How soon until the phone starts ringing with offers of widgets on sale? What if a burglar could use a RFIC reader from outside your house to preview its contents? What happens when these data are networked with all your other personal information? What if you buy a case of beer rather than a box of widgets? Will your employer know? What if your tastes run to sugared snacks? Should your insurance company know? A 2004 survey by *Wired* magazine indicated that while 20% of its readers liked RFIC, two-thirds disliked it and one-third considered it a violation of their privacy (McHugh, 2004).

A second form of dataveillance is the electronic tracking of the choices we make when we are on the Web, called our **click stream.** Despite the anonymity online users think they enjoy, every click of a key can be, and often is, recorded and stored. This happens whether or not the user actually enters information, for example, a credit card number to make a purchase or a Social Security number to verify identity. This tracking is made possible by **cookies,** an identifying code added to a computer's hard drive by a visited Web site. Normally, only the site that has sent the cookie can read it—the next time you visit that site it "remembers" you. But some sites bring "third-party" cookies to your computer. Maintained by big Internet advertising networks like DoubleClick and Engage, these cookies can be read by any of the thousands of Web sites also belonging to that network, whether you've visited them or not, and without your knowledge. As a result, this software is more commonly referred to as **spyware,** identfying code placed on a computer by a Web site without permission or notification. Spyware not only facilitates tracking by sites and/or people unknown (those "third parties"), but opens a computer to unwanted pop-up ads and other commercial messages.

Anti-Spyware Coalition
www.antispywarecoalition.org

At any given time, a regular Web user will have dozens of cookies on his or her hard drive, but most commercial browsers come equipped with the capacity to block or erase them. The Anti-Spyware Coalition (www.antispy-warecoalition.org) offers information and assistance on how to deal with cookies and spyware. In addition, users can purchase cookie-scrubbing software. Commercial firms such as Anonymizer sell programs that not only block and erase spyware but allow users to surf the Web in anonymity. Industry research indicates that 40% of Internet users regularly disable or erase the cookies on their hard drives ("The Cookies," 2006).

The Internet industry, too, engages in self-regulation. One form, for example, offered by the Electronic Frontier Foundation and CommerceNet, a group of Internet businesses, is TRUSTe. Web sites, if they agree to certain restrictions on their collection and use of user information, will earn the TRUSTe "seal of approval," making them more attractive to privacy-conscious users.

WWW
TRUSTe
www.truste.org

WWW
Surf Anonymously
www.anonymizer.com

VIRTUAL DEMOCRACY

The Internet is characterized by freedom and self-governance, which are also the hallmarks of true democracy. It is no surprise, then, that computer technology is often trumpeted as the newest and best tool for increased democratic involvement and participation. We have already seen Internet political action in the form of flash mobs and online activist groups. As for blogs, "When they write the account of the 2004 campaign, it will include at least one word that has never appeared in any presidential history: blog. Whether or not it elects the next president, the blog may be the first innovation from the Internet to make a real difference in election politics," according to Stanford's Lawrence Lessig (quoted in Packer, 2004, p. 30). "Outsider" Howard Dean made the Net in general and blogs in particular central to his almost-successful 2004 primary campaign to become the Democratic Party's presidential nominee. But even more mainline politicians have come to rely on the Net to interact with constituents and voters. Virtually every politician of any standing—president, vice president, Senate majority leader, Speaker of the House—maintains at least an e-mail address if not a full Web page. Internet voting, too, has become a limited reality, with some localities experimenting with online voting for local candidates and in selected primary contests.

This enthusiasm for a technological solution to what many see as increased disenchantment with politics and the political process mirrors that which followed the introduction of radio and television. A September 3, 1924, *New Republic* article, for example, argued that the high level of public interest in the broadcast of the 1924 political party conventions brought "dismay" to "the most hardened political cynic" (as cited in Davis, 1976, p. 351). The November 1950 *Good Housekeeping* claimed that television would bring greater honesty to politics because "television is a revealing medium, and it is impossible for a man or a woman appearing before those cameras to conceal his or her true self" (p. 359). In 1940 NBC founder and chairman David Sarnoff predicted that television would enrich democracy because it was "destined to provide greater knowledge to larger numbers of people, truer perception of the meaning of current events, more accurate appraisals of men in public life, and a broader understanding of the needs and aspirations of our fellow human beings" (as cited in Shenk, 1997, p. 60).

The power of the Net in electoral politics was much in evidence in the 2004 primaries in the candidacy of Democratic "outsider" Howard Dean.

Some critics argue that the Internet will be no more of an asset to democracy than have been radio and television because the same economic and commercial forces that have shaped the content and operation of those more traditional media will constrain just as rigidly the new. Communication scientist Everette Dennis (1992) condensed the critics' concern into two overarching questions: (1) Will computer networks be readily accessible to all people—even if it means depending on institutions such as schools, churches, and community organizations—or only to some? and (2) Once the technology is in place and people have access to it, are they going to know how to use it?

The Technology Gap An important principle of democracy is "one person, one vote." But if democracy is increasingly practiced online, those lacking the necessary technology and skill will be denied their vote. This is the **technology gap**—the widening disparity between the communication technology haves and have-nots. Even with its rapid diffusion, only three-quarters of the people in the United States use the Internet. This "democratization" of the Net still favors those who have the money to buy the hardware and software needed to access the Net as well as to pay for that connection. This leaves out many U.S. citizens—those on the wrong side of the **digital divide.**

The digital divide describes the lack of technological access among people of color, the poor, the disabled, and those in rural communities. And it is controversial. When asked in 2001 about his plans to bridge the divide, then-FCC chair Michael Powell told reporters that the expression itself is "dangerous in the sense that it suggests that the minute a new and innovative technology is introduced in the market, there is a divide among every part of society, and that is just an unreal understanding of an American capitalistic system. . . . I'm not meaning to be completely flip about this—I think it's an important social issue—but it shouldn't be used to justify the notion of, essentially, the socialization of deployment of the infrastructure. . . . You know, I think there's a Mercedes divide. I'd like to have one; I can't afford one" (in Jackson, 2001, p. 9). Critics pointed out that as the Internet becomes increasingly essential for full membership in America's economic and cultural life, those on the wrong side of the divide will be further disenfranchised. And, in the event that the Net becomes even more essential to the practice of democracy than it already may be, say, through widespread online voting, those on the wrong side of the divide will be denied their basic democratic rights.

How real is the digital divide? Only 25% of U.S. homes with incomes under $15,000 are online, compared with 79% of homes with incomes over $75,000. Although more than 60% of all instructional classrooms in American schools are wired for the Internet, that percentage drops to 39% for schools in areas where poverty levels are highest (Malveaux, 2000). And according to the Census Bureau, there exists a large disparity in Internet usage between minorities and others. Internet use among African Americans and Hispanics is well below the national average: only 39% of African Americans and 31.6% of Hispanics are online (Barmann, 2002).

The Information Gap Another important principle of democracy is that self-governing people govern best with full access to information. This is the rea-

NTIA
www.ntia.doc.gov

son our culture is so suspicious of censorship. The technology gap feeds a second impediment to virtual democracy, the **information gap.** Those without the requisite technology will have diminished access to the information it makes available. In other words, they will suffer from a form of technologically imposed censorship.

Critics of the information gap point to troubling examples of other media failures to deliver important information to all citizens. Cable television subscribership is lowest among urban working-class and poor people. Many newspapers, uninterested in these same people because they do not possess the demographic profile coveted by advertisers, do not promote their papers in the neighborhoods in which they live and, in some large cities, do not even deliver there. For this same reason, there are precious few consumer magazines aimed at less well-off people. If the computer technology gap creates an even wider information gap than already exists between these audiences and other citizens, democracy will surely suffer. The essay entitled "Is Broadband Fast Food or Power" on page 330 offers more on the digital divide.

Information, Knowledge, and Understanding   Some critics of the idea of online democracy are troubled by the amount of information available to contemporary citizens and the speed with which it comes. Add to this the difficulty of assessing the veracity of much online information, and they argue that the cyberworld may not be the best place to practice democracy.

For example, advocates of cyberdemocracy see the Internet as a way to let citizens have more direct access to politicians. Elected officials should hear what the people have to say. But does democracy necessarily benefit when its leaders respond directly, maybe even impulsively, to public sentiment? Until there is no more technology gap, certain voices—the poor, the uneducated, the elderly—will have less access to their leaders than those who are connected. Moreover, claim critics of cyberdemocracy, ours is a representative, deliberative democracy. It was intentionally designed to enable public representatives to talk to one another, to debate ideas and issues, to forge solutions that benefit not just their own but others' constituents as well. They claim that the political alienation felt by many citizens today is the product of politicians listening *too much* to the loudest voices (that is, special interests) and being *too responsive* to the polls. People often criticize politicians for "flip-flopping" or "having no personal conviction." How can the situation improve if elected officials respond daily to the voices in the electronic town hall?

Critics also argue that cyberdemocracy, by its very virtual nature, is antidemocratic. Before the coming of VCR, cable, and satellite television, a president could ask for and almost invariably receive airtime from the three major television networks to talk to the people. Today, however, these technologies have fragmented us into countless smaller audiences. Should a president address the nation today, only a small proportion of citizens is likely to tune in. This fragmentation of the audience (Chapter 2) is exacerbated by the Internet. Not only is there now an *additional* medium to further divide the audience, but by simple virtue of the way it functions—chat rooms, bulletin boards, taste-specific Web sites—the Internet solidifies people into smaller, more homogeneous, more narrowly interested groups. This cannot be good for democracy, say some critics.

Is Broadband Fast Food or Power?

Former FCC chair Michael Powell sees no difference between your need for Internet access and his need for a new Mercedes (p. 328). But is Net access, especially high-speed access, a necessity or a luxury? Because cities all over America have pondered this question, it is now very much in the cultural forum.

Law professor Doug Lichtman asks, "Is broadband fast food, or is it power?" (in Hu & Reardon, 2005, p. 2). In other words, should broadband be viewed as a luxury or as a basic public utility, no different from clean water, fire safety, and police protection? Should municipalities offer free or low-cost access for their citizens, especially where commercial providers are either not doing so or are doing so at such high cost that many people are shut out? By mid-September 2005, more than 300 towns, big and small, had decided that high-speed, low-cost, ubiquitous community Wi-Fi should be a public utility (Yang, 2005a).

Philadelphia is indicative. Plagued with the highest level of poverty of any major American city, the 135-square-mile City of Brotherly Love announced in 2004 "Wireless Philadelphia," its plan to provide low-cost Wi-Fi broadband to its 1.6 million denizens. The goal is to create "free-market competition for communication services, improve schools, enhance public safety and social services, and encourage entrepreneurs through public–private partnerships" (Karr, 2005, p. 1). Philadelphia's chief information officer Dianah Neff explained that municipal Internet is a necessity because "we all have to compete in a knowledge economy. Current providers focus excessively on the affluent" (in Levy, 2005, p. 14). By no means is this a Left/Right political debate. Businesses, too, support the project, seeing municipal broadband as a way to reduce costs and expand markets.

But not everyone is on board. The big ISPs, especially the phone and cable companies, see community broadband as "un-American," and "impractical," little more than "a lazy public utility" (in Karr, 2005, p. 3). Why, they ask, should local governments get involved in a business that commercial operations were handling just fine? Think of the DMV, they suggest. Marshalling their political power, opponents to community Internet have moved the legislatures of 20 states to consider laws banning towns from building municipal systems. But their lone success came in Pennsylvania, where Democratic governor Edward Rendell, over significant public objection, signed a bill that does not ban these systems outright, but does forbid towns from charging users for Internet access *and* requires them to get written permission from area commercial ISPs before they build a system (Philadelphia was grandfathered). And while they have had little success getting community systems *banned outright*, opponents have had some success in rendering them less competitive. Louisiana offers one example. Hurricane-ravaged New Orleans began providing free wireless Internet service to all individuals and businesses in November 2005. Its system is unique in that it is *city-run* and *free*, rather than *in-partnership-with* a commercial provider and *low-cost* (for example, Philadelphia has low-cost access; San Francisco plans free access, but contracts its management to an outside technology company). But as mandated by Louisiana law, New Orleans (and all other municipal systems in the state) must provide slower speeds and less bandwidth than do commercial wireless Internet providers. Similar legislation has been proposed in many other states.

The federal government has now joined the fray. Republican representative Pete Sessions, a former phone company executive, introduced the Preserving Innovation in Telecom Act in May 2005, a federal ban on municipal Internet access. In response, Republican John McCain and Democrat Frank Lautenberg introduced into the Senate the Community Broadband Act, forbidding states from banning municipal systems.

Enter your voice. Are the telecom companies correct, is broadband simply too important and too complex for towns to get involved? But what do you make of the fact that according to the International Telecommunication Union, the United States ranks 16th in the world in high-speed access, down from 3rd, 5 years ago, falling behind countries such as Japan, Korea, and Sweden that actively encourage municipal systems; or that broadband in those countries costs less than half of what it does in the United States, when and where it is available (Yang, 2005b)? Does the question of universal municipal broadband access take on added significance for you in light of the Supreme Court's 2005 *Brand X* decision (Chapter 8)? Does it bother you that people in countries like South Korea and Japan pay half of what you do for broadband access, or is this the price we pay for free enterprise? After all, as Michael Powell says, some people want Internet access, some people want a Mercedes. Is it the government's place to provide either? Do you consider the rejection of banning legislation in all but one state and the powering-up of systems in more than 300 communities a sign that the cultural forum has already rendered its decision?

> SHOULD MUNICIPALITIES OFFER FREE OR LOW-COST ACCESS FOR THEIR CITIZENS, ESPECIALLY WHERE COMMERCIAL PROVIDERS ARE EITHER NOT DOING SO OR ARE DOING SO AT SUCH HIGH COST THAT MANY PEOPLE ARE SHUT OUT? BY MID-SEPTEMBER 2005, MORE THAN 300 TOWNS, BIG AND SMALL, HAD DECIDED THAT HIGH-SPEED, LOW-COST, UBIQUITOUS COMMUNITY WI-FI SHOULD BE A PUBLIC UTILITY.

The Internet and the Web encourage people to splinter into virtual communities based on a shared interest in some given information. This renders actual communities irrelevant. No longer required to coexist with other people in the day-to-day world, cybercitizens have little need to examine their own biases. They need not question their own assumptions about the world and how it works. There is little benefit to seeking out and attempting to understand the biases and assumptions of others outside the self-chosen virtual community. Recall our earlier discussion of blogs.

For example, writes media critic and scholar Robert McChesney, among the criteria that must be met if democracy is to serve the needs of its people are "a sense of community and a notion that an individual's well-being is determined to no small extent by the community's well-being" and "an effective system of political communication, broadly construed, that informs and engages the citizenry, drawing people meaningfully into the polity" (1997, p. 5). Where McLuhan would have seen the new electronic communication technologies doing just this, many others, often likening the Net and the Web to "talk radio writ large," fear the opposite, that the Internet has already become, in the words of *Time* environmental writer John Skow, "a stunning advance in the shoring up of biases, both benign (one's own views) and noxious (other views)" (1999, p. 61).

DEVELOPING MEDIA LITERACY SKILLS

Making Our Way in an Interconnected World

Questions raised by the Internet and the new communication technologies often lack clear-cut, satisfactory answers. For example, a world at peace with itself, its people sharing the common assumptions of a common culture, is a utopian dream. There are those who see it as attainable, but if the common culture that binds us is that of Mickey Mouse, is the harmony worth the loss of individual, idiosyncratic cultures?

Figure 10.3 offers a primer, a self-study guide, to help media literate individuals examine their own beliefs about the double edge of communication technologies. As we saw in Chapter 1, among the elements of media literacy are the development of an awareness of the impact of the media on individuals and society and an understanding of the process of mass communication. Use the primer's good news/bad news format to answer for yourself the questions that are raised, to build your awareness of media's impact, and to examine the possible influence media have on the process of mass communication.

It is important to remember that culture is neither innate nor inviolate. *We* construct culture—both dominant and bounded. Increasingly, we do so through mass communication. Before we can enter the forum in which those cultures are constructed and maintained, we must understand where we stand and what we believe. We must be able to defend our positions. The hallmarks of a media literate individual are analysis and self-reflection; the primer provides a framework for exactly that.

THE ISSUE	THE GOOD NEWS	THE BAD NEWS	THE QUESTIONS
Technological advances have made communication easier and more democratic.	People can consume some media as wanted and needed rather than allowing media producers to schedule consumption time and content. The consumer, rather than the producer, has more control over meaning making. New technology enables participation by groups previously media-neglected (blind, handicapped, etc.). Users can participate anonymously, which leads to less prejudice (you never know who you might really be communicating with). In some cases, new technology enables communication to be accomplished at a fraction of the cost previously established by older media.	Control of much of the most influential content is in the hands of fewer and fewer people (namely, large multinational corporations). This is not democratic. Content decisions are made to fulfill economic or marketing goals, which define users of communication as simply consumers of content. Source anonymity makes it difficult to document and prosecute illegal acts. Electronic communication could lead to social fragmentation (society divided into the information rich and poor). In the information age, hardware, software, and the education to use them cost money. The difference between the "haves" and the "have-nots" will increase, placing a strain on democracy.	Can a smaller number of powerful people create havoc or revolution online (i.e., shutting down governments, bugging worldwide systems)? Should law enforcement have encryption codes on file to use under court order? Or is this an infringement of privacy and First Amendment rights? Will new technology be available to everyone? Will an information underclass form? Who will pay for information technology as it develops (private corporations, governments, users)? Who will control and regulate the information technology? Is official control necessary to ensure equal access and opportunity? Do advancements in technology result from societal need or market demands? Or is there a "technological push" —technologies logically producing the next innovation? What is the public's role in each situation?
Technological advances have made the *creation* and *distribution* of media content easier.	Content can be duplicated and transmitted easily and without loss of quality. Individuals, *themselves,* can now be producers of media. Easier creation and distribution of content leads to more choice for media consumers. People can seek out and receive content they are interested in while ignoring other content. Information can be transmitted in "real time." A person can communicate to any place, from any place, at any time. This affords freedom of movement and more convenience in terms of space and time. Individuals will have access to other people despite lack of physical proximity. We can finally, truly, be a global village.	Destructive (false, hateful, libelous, etc.) or even illegal communication content is also more easily created and distributed. Piracy is easier and more widespread. Questions of copyright and intellectual property are more complex, more difficult to define, and even more difficult to regulate. Too much choice leads to information overload. There is a big difference between having more information and having more understanding or comprehension. Important decisions are made based on instant information (whether it is accurate or not). There is little time for reflection and analysis. Content is sent and received without context. Reliability of sources becomes questionable. Context and continuity are lost; they are simply replaced by more "instant" content. Who wants to be available *all the time*? This "convenience" will add additional stress to life because "time off" becomes more difficult to find.	How can producers of content (corporations, artists, etc.) receive compensation for their work in a digital world of unlimited production and distribution possibilities? What will happen to security of personal information if content can be so easily copied and transmitted (privacy and security issues)? How much choice do audience members *really* want? From where is the information coming? Who will be the "authorities" creating, providing, and regulating the information (setting the agenda, etc.)? How much connection is too much? What kind of physical damage (headaches, carpal tunnel syndrome, etc.) and psychological damage (cyberaddiction, alienation, etc.) can be done by using communication too much or too often?

Figure 10.3 The New Communication Technology Media Literacy Primer.

THE ISSUE	THE GOOD NEWS	THE BAD NEWS	THE QUESTIONS
New technology allows seamless alteration of sound and pictures.	Production and post-production are less expensive than in older media and allow unlimited possibilities for altering content. Creativity is only limited by one's imagination because technology can create the ways and means.	Images and sounds can be digitally (and invisibly) manipulated, so truth and reality are difficult to ascertain.	How will people be able to tell what is real and what is not? Will the definition of "reality" change?
New technology allows communication to be presented in a nonlinear way.	New communication technologies allow for more user control in the creation of content. Form, function, and time take on new meaning.	When immersed in a sea of data, audience members may not see a beginning, middle, or end. Communication errors are likely.	What will be the storytelling, narrative, and aesthetic conventions of the virtual real world?

LIVING MEDIA LITERACY

POP for Privacy

Charlene Nelson, a politically conservative mother of three, made her media literacy a living enterprise and in the process made history. As a college student you, arguably, have the tools at your disposal—time, computers, classmates, education, sophistication—to do the same. Do you share Mrs. Nelson's commitment to privacy? To media literacy? Do you have her courage?

It all began in 1999 when the U.S. Congress passed the Gramm-Leach-Bliley Act. Few people are aware of the bill and its provision that permits banks, insurance companies, and other financial institutions to trade and sell your personal data without your knowledge or permission, unless you choose to opt out. Remember getting all those mailings from your bank and credit card companies, the ones that typically contained a thick leaflet "written in such indecipherable legalese that you either ignored it or passed out trying to read it" (Hightower, 2002, p. 8)? Those mailings contained the details of their privacy policies that companies were obligated to provide to inform you that you had the right to opt out. If you did not respond, that meant you gave them permission to use your personal data as they saw fit.

The problem in North Dakota was that the state already had its own opt-in law. That is, companies could not sell North Dakotans' personal data without their permission. To make North Dakota's law more closely resemble the Gramm-Leach-Bliley law, the state legislature wanted to repeal its own opt-in rules (something that was not required in the federal legislation).

> **DO YOU SHARE MRS. NELSON'S COMMITMENT TO PRIVACY? TO MEDIA LITERACY? DO YOU HAVE HER COURAGE?**

Mrs. Nelson wrote to her representative expressing her opposition, as did thousands of other people. Nonetheless, the legislature made opt-out the new standard. "I was just stunned when it passed," she said (quoted in Hightower, 2002, p. 8). Determined to protect her privacy in the age of dataveillance, Mrs. Nelson and a dozen friends and neighbors near Fargo started Protect Our Privacy (POP). POP used the Web, e-mail, talk radio, and the phones to marshal support for a citizens' petition to overturn the legislature's "treason." POP was able to get hundreds of volunteers to build a left-right coalition, easily putting a binding referendum, something unheard of in North Dakota, on the June 11, 2002, ballot.

The opposition's media budget was five times larger than POP's; it hired public relations firms and television campaign experts. It attacked Mrs. Nelson in the press as "a right-wing wacko." It said that business would flee the state, already troubled by a weak agricultural economy. On election day, POP prevailed, 73% to 27%. Newspapers as far away as the East Coast editorialized, "True to their heritage, North Dakotans took a pioneering stand on privacy this month, in a vote that curbs the power of banks to sell personal data. The referendum was the first in the nation letting citizens directly challenge a 1999 federal banking law" that requires people to opt out. Mrs. Nelson's "example should encourage all of us" ("Victory," 2002, p. B6).

If you are encouraged by Mrs. Nelson's example, you can e-mail her at r.cnelson@juno.com to discuss with her how to put your media literacy values into action. POP's Web site offers information on how to fight for privacy rights in your state, as well as the story of its historic victory. Visit it at www. protectourprivacy.net.

Review Points

- The idea for the Internet came either from technological optimists like Joseph C. R. Licklider or from the military, hoping to maintain communication networks in time of enemy attack—or from both.
- Paul Baran devised a packet-switching network, the technological basis for the Internet, to be used on powerful computers developed by John V. Atanasoff, John Mauchly, and John Presper Eckert.
- The personal computer was developed by Bill Gates and the team of Steve Jobs and Stephen Wozniak.
- The Internet facilitates e-mail, mailing lists, Usenet, VoIP, and the World Wide Web.
- The Web relies on a system of hosts, browsers, and search engines to bring users to Web sites, characterized by URLs and home pages.
- Although there is conflicting opinion about the benefits of commercializing the Internet, it has indeed become a successful and popular commercial medium.

- Questions about the double edge of Internet technology have given rise to renewed interest in Marshall McLuhan, creator of concepts such as the global village and media as extensions of our bodies.
- The Internet makes freedom of expression a reality for anyone linked to it. But abuse of that freedom has led to calls for greater control. Restrictions on access to pornography, protection of copyright, and threats to identity are primary battlegrounds for opponents and proponents of control.
- The Internet's potential contributions to participatory democracy are also in debate, as problems such as the technology and information gaps and the digital divide have yet to be resolved.
- The Internet and Web, especially with their power to reshape all the mass media, raise multiple issues for media literate users hoping to effectively make their way in an interconnected world.

Key Terms

 Use the text's Online Learning Center at www.mhhe.com/baran5 to further your understanding of the following terminology.

Internet, 300
digital computer, 301
binary code, 301
protocols, 302
hosts, 303
mainframe computer, 303
minicomputer, 303
terminals, 303
personal or microcomputer (PC), 304
operating system, 304
multimedia, 304
WAN, 304
ISP (Internet service provider), 305
e-mail, 306

instant messaging (IM), 306
Usenet, 306
Voice over Internet Protocol (VoIP), 306
World Wide Web, 306
URL (uniform resource locator), 307
domain name, 307
browsers, 308
search engines, 308
spiders, 308
Web crawlers, 308
home page, 308
hyperlink, 308
spam, 311
global village, 313

flash mobs (smart mobs), 318
censorware, 322
fair use, 323
encryption, 324
dataveillance, 324
opt-in/opt-out, 326
radio frequency identification chip (RFIC), 326
click stream, 326
cookies, 326
spyware, 326
technology gap, 328
digital divide, 328
information gap, 329

Questions for Review

 Go to the self-quizzes on the Online Learning Center to test your knowledge.

1. What is the importance of each of these people to the development of the computer: Charles Babbage, John Atanasoff, John Mauchly, and John Presper Eckert?
2. What were the contributions of Joseph C. R. Licklider, Paul Baran, Bill Gates, Steve Jobs, and Steve Wozniak to the development and popularization of the Internet?
3. What are digital computers, microcomputers, and mainframe computers?
4. What are the services or capabilities offered by the Internet?
5. What factors have led to the popularity of the World Wide Web?
6. What are the differing positions on the commercialization of the Internet?
7. What are the differing positions on Internet copyright?
8. Both proponents and opponents of greater control over Internet content see advances in technology as one solution to their disagreement. What are they? How do they work?
9. Why is there renewed interest in Marshall McLuhan? What does he mean by the global village and media as extensions of our bodies?
10. What are the two primary privacy issues for online communication?
11. What is a blog? How might blogs alter journalism?
12. What are some of the arguments supporting the idea that the Internet will be a boost to participatory democracy? What are some of the counterarguments?
13. What are the technology and information gaps? What do they have to do with virtual or cyberdemocracy? What is the digital divide?

Questions for Critical Thinking and Discussion

1. Do you believe commercialization of the Internet is a worthy price to pay for its continued success and diffusion? Explain.
2. What controls should be placed on blogs, if any? Do you see them as a way of distributing power in the culture between traditional media outlets and ordinary individuals? Why or why not?
3. Do you ever make personal information available online? If so, how confident are you of its security? Do you take steps to protect your privacy?
4. Do you believe the new communication technologies will improve or damage participatory democracy? Why? Can you relate a personal experience of how the Net increased or limited your involvement in the political process?
5. Do you agree with Michael Powell that no one has a "right" to Internet access? Why or why not?

Important Resources

 Go to the Online Learning Center for additional readings.

Internet Resources

Internet Statistics	www.glreach.com/globalstats/
Internet Statistics	www.mit.edu/people/mkgray/net
Internet History	www.isoc.org/internet/history
Definition of Internet Terms	whatis.techtarget.com
Online White Pages	www.whitepages.com
Online Yellow Pages	www.yellowpages.com
Tim Berners-Lee	www.w3.org/people/all
Listserv	www.lsoft.com/catalist.html

Usenet	www.cs.uu.nl/cgi-bin/faqwais
Links to MUDs	www.mudconnect.com
U.S. Census Bureau	www.census.gov
Marshall McLuhan	www.mcluhan.ca
More McLuhan	www.law.pitt.edu/hibbitts/mcl.htm
Media Activist Site	www.fair.org
Blogging	www.blogger.com
Internet Hoax Deflator	hoaxbusters.ciac.org
Net Nanny	www.netnanny.com
Electronic Frontier Foundation	www.eff.org
Privacy Site	www.privacy.net
Privacy Protection	www.accessreports.com
Community Internet	www.freepress.net/communityinternet
Fight ID Theft	www.consumer.gov/idtheft
Anti-Spyware Coalition	www.antispywarecoalition.org
TRUSTe	www.truste.org
Surf Anonymously	www.anonymizer.com
NTIA	www.ntia.doc.gov

Public Relations

LEARNING OBJECTIVES

It is no small irony that PR has such poor PR. We criticize the flacks who try to spin the truth because PR is most obvious when used to reclaim the reputation of someone or some organization in need of such help. But public relations is essential for maintaining relationships between organizations and their publics. In fact, much PR is used for good. After studying this chapter you should

- be familiar with the history and development of the public relations industry.

- be aware of the controversies surrounding unethical public relations practices.

- recognize how the organizational and economic nature of the contemporary public relations industry shapes the messages with which publics interact.

- be familiar with different types of public relations and the different publics each is designed to serve.

- understand the relationship between public relations and its various publics.

- possess improved media literacy skills when consuming public relations messages, especially video news releases.

You want to run; you have to run! You've been training for 2 months, and next week's 5K through the hills outside campus seems like a reasonable test of your newfound athletic prowess. When your race packet arrives in the mail, it contains your number, 1071; pre- and postrace instructions, a map of the route, and a lot of other material you hadn't expected—a pamphlet on breast cancer self-examinations, for one thing, and a fact sheet explaining that you are part of something a little bigger than a simple road race behind your school. You knew you were running in a Race for the Cure 5K, underwritten by a local radio station and the newspaper, but until you read the mailing, you had no idea that you would be running for a cure for breast cancer; that something called the Susan G. Komen Breast Cancer Foundation was behind this and 100 other 5Ks in the United States

Opposite: The toppling of Saddam's statue . . . authentic news or pseudo-event?

and other countries; and that 1.3 million people like you would be racing for the cure. You're curious, so you check out the foundation's Web site (www.komen.org). The site itself is sponsored by Lee Jeans' National Denim Day. That's nice. A big company like that donating time, money—and even a day—to such a good cause. You link to the site devoted specifically to the race and *its* sponsors. That group reads like a veritable Who's Who of corporate America—the employment firm Adecco, RE/MAX Realtors, Johnson & Johnson, Kellogg, Ford, New Balance Shoes, Yoplait Yogurt, American Airlines. That's pretty cool, you think, these folks getting involved, doing good, especially at a time when Enron, WorldCom, and other big companies seem to be doing their best to shake your confidence in the corporate world, the very world you hope to enter when you graduate.

In this chapter we investigate the public relations industry and its relationship with mass media and their audiences. We first define public relations. Then we study its history and development as the profession matured from its beginnings in hucksterism to a full-fledged, communication-based industry. We see how the needs and interests of the profession's various

WWW

Public Relations Society of America
www.prsa.org

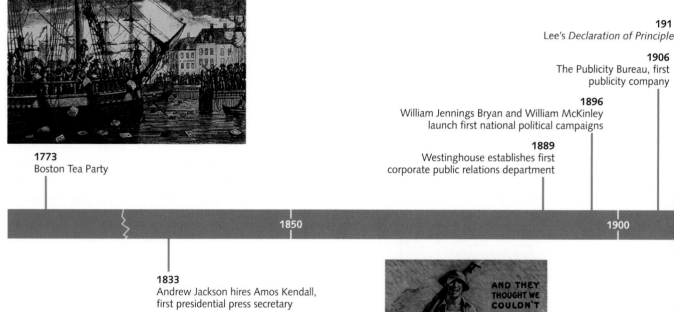

1773
Boston Tea Party

1833
Andrew Jackson hires Amos Kendall,
first presidential press secretary

1850

1889
Westinghouse establishes first
corporate public relations department

1896
William Jennings Bryan and William McKinley
launch first national political campaigns

1906
The Publicity Bureau, first
publicity company

191
Lee's *Declaration of Principle*

1900

1915
Cadillac's Penalty
of Leadership

1917
President Wilson
establishes
Committee on
Public Information

VICTORY LIBERTY LOAN

AND THEY
THOUGHT WE
COULDN'T
FIGHT

publics became part of the public relations process. We also define exactly who those publics are. The scope and nature of the industry are detailed. Types of public relations activities and the organization of a typical public relations operation are described. We study trends such as globalization and specialization, as well as the impact of new communication technologies on the industry. Finally, we discuss trust in public relations. As our media literacy skill, we learn how to recognize video news releases.

Defining Public Relations

The Komen Foundation, like Mothers Against Drunk Driving, Save Venice, Handgun Control Incorporated, the National Environmental Trust, and countless other nonprofit organizations, is an interest group that uses a variety of public relations tools and strategies to serve a variety of publics. It wants to use public relations to do good. The companies that sponsor its activities also want to do good—do good for their communities *and* for

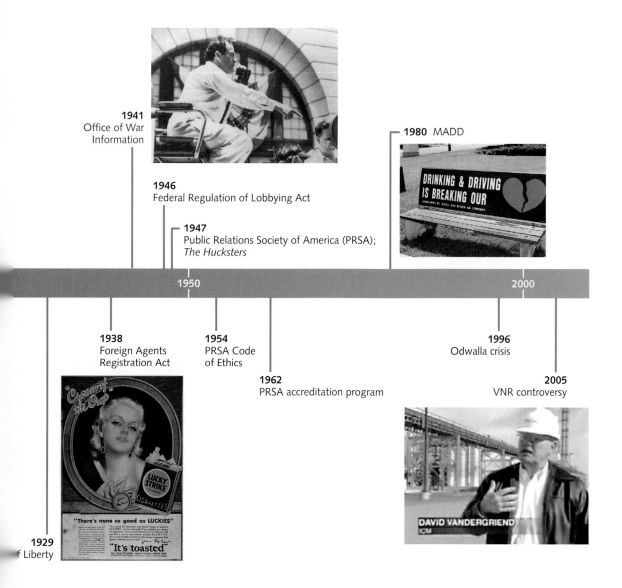

1941 Office of War Information

1946 Federal Regulation of Lobbying Act

1947 Public Relations Society of America (PRSA); *The Hucksters*

1980 MADD

1950

2000

1938 Foreign Agents Registration Act

1954 PRSA Code of Ethics

1962 PRSA accreditation program

1996 Odwalla crisis

2005 VNR controversy

1929 f Liberty

Kellogg and American Airlines are two of the corporations whose support of Race for the Cure helps others while helping us better understand them as companies.

themselves. Even the most cynical person must applaud their efforts on behalf of finding a cure for breast cancer.

But for many people, efforts such as these serve to demonstrate one of the ironies of public relations, both as an activity and as an industry: Public relations has terrible public relations. We dismiss information as "just PR." Public relations professionals are frequently equated with snake oil salespeople, hucksters, and other willful deceivers. They are referred to both inside and outside the media industries as **flacks.** Yet virtually every organization and institution—big and small, public and private, for-profit and volunteer—uses public relations as a regular part of its operation. Many have their own public relations departments. The term "public relations" carries such a negative connotation that most independent companies and company departments now go by the name "public affairs," "corporate affairs," or "public communications."

The problem rests, in part, on confusion over what public relations actually is. There is no universally accepted definition of public relations because it can be and is many things—publicity, research, public affairs, media relations, promotion, merchandising, and more. Much of the contact media consumers have with public relations occurs when the industry defends people and companies who have somehow run afoul of the public. The Saudi Arabian government hired two American PR firms, Patton Boggs and Akin, Gump, Strauss, Hauer, and Feld, to burnish its image after it was learned that the majority of the September 11 terrorists were Saudi citizens and that it had financially supported groups close to Osama bin Laden and al-Qaeda. Starbucks similarly sought PR help after reports that one of its store managers forced rescue crews to pay for bottled water as they worked to save lives on that horrible day. Ford and Firestone waged a PR war against each other in mid-2000 when Firestone's tires were implicated in rollovers of Ford's Explorer SUVs, Exxon used a vast PR army to minimize its responsibility for the environmentally disastrous 1989 oil spill from its tanker *Exxon Valdez,* and politicians and partisan groups habitually use public relations to shape the news. The Iraqi National Congress, a group of dissidents who provided much of the intelligence and

Odwalla's prompt, honest public relations campaign to communicate with its public may have saved additional lives. It did save the 16-year-old company and the jobs of its employees.

support for the decision to invade Iraq, was the creation of and heavily promoted by the Rendon Group, a PR company on contract with the CIA (Bamford, 2005).

Yet when seven people died from cyanide poisoning after taking tainted Tylenol capsules in 1982, a skilled and honest public relations campaign by Johnson & Johnson (makers of Tylenol) and its public relations firm, Burson-Marsteller, saved the brand and restored trust in the product. In late 1996, when Odwalla fresh apple juice was linked to the death of a young child, that company's instant, direct, and honest campaign to identify and eliminate the source of the contamination and rebuild public confidence saved the company and thousands of jobs. The public relations campaign by Mothers Against Drunk Driving (MADD) led directly to passage of tougher standards in virtually every state to remove drunk drivers from the road and to provide stiffer sentences for those convicted of driving under the influence. Dramatic reductions in the number of alcohol-related traffic accidents resulted from this effort (see the essay on page 344, "The MADD Campaign").

"P.R. has a P.R. problem," says Syracuse University public relations professor Brenda Wrigley. "We have to get our own house in order. . . . We are advocates and there's no shame in that as long as it's grounded in ethics and values." Public Relations Society of America president Judy Phair adds, "For public relations to be effective, it has to be built on public trust" (both in O'Brien, 2005, p. 3.1). Accepting, therefore, that public relations should be honest and ethical, our definition of public relations includes two additional elements that individually appear in almost all definitions of PR, *communication* and *management:*

MADD
www.madd.org

The MADD Campaign

After Candy Lightner's child was killed in a drunk-driving accident in 1980, she sought out others like herself, mothers who had lost children to the volatile mix of cars and alcohol. She hoped they could provide one another with emotional support and campaign to ensure that other parents would never know their grief. Thus, Mothers Against Drunk Driving (MADD) was born.

There are now more than 400 chapters of MADD in the United States and a number of foreign groups as well. Individuals and businesses contribute over $40 million a year to MADD's efforts, which include a variety of educational, public relations, and victims' assistance programs. MADD's primary public information campaign, Project Red Ribbon, which runs throughout the Thanksgiving to New Year's holiday season, annually distributes more than 30 million red ribbons. People tie them to the rearview mirrors, door handles, and radio antennae of their cars. This reminder encourages people not to drive if under the influence of drugs or alcohol, to call a cab if necessary, or even to take away a friend's car keys if he or she is drunk. The ribbon also serves as a sign of solidarity against the terrors of drunk driving. MADD has enlisted in Project Red Ribbon such major corporations as Welch's, 7-Eleven Stores, and the national trucking company Consolidated Freightways Motorfreight.

Among MADD's publics are teenagers. With its parallel organization, Students Against Drunk Driving (SADD), MADD targets this high-risk group through various educational campaigns and in the media aimed at teen audiences. The organization also conducts public information campaigns aimed at adult drivers and repeat drunk drivers, often in conjunction with state and other authorities. It also assists legislators in their efforts to pass drunk-driving legislation. Two more of MADD's publics are public servants such as police and paramedics who must deal with the effects of drunk driving, and the families and friends who have lost loved ones in alcohol- or drug-related driving accidents.

Has MADD made a difference? Since 1988, numerous prime-time television programs have featured episodes about the dangers of drunk driving. MADD's professional staff has served as script advisors to these programs. MADD was instrumental in passage of the federal Drunk Driving Prevention Act of 1988, offering states financial incentives to set up programs that would reduce alcohol- and drug-related automobile fatalities. This legislation also made 21 the national minimum legal drinking age. MADD successfully campaigned for the Victim's Crime Act of 1984, making compensation from drunk drivers to victims and their families federal law.

There are two even more dramatic examples of how successful Lightner's group has been. According to the National Commission Against Drunk Driving (2002), there have been significant reductions in the number of alcohol- and drug-related auto fatalities in every year since MADD was founded. But MADD's cultural impact shows most strongly in the way people treat drunk drivers. It is no longer cool to talk about how smashed we got at the party, or how we can't believe we made it home. Almost every evening out with a group of friends includes a designated driver. Drunk drivers are considered nearly as despicable as child molesters. Many in public relations, traffic safety, and law enforcement credit MADD's public relations efforts with this change.

> MADD'S CULTURAL IMPACT SHOWS MOST STRONGLY IN THE WAY PEOPLE TREAT DRUNK DRIVERS. IT IS NO LONGER COOL TO TALK ABOUT HOW SMASHED WE GOT AT THE PARTY, OR HOW WE CAN'T BELIEVE WE MADE IT HOME. ALMOST EVERY EVENING OUT WITH A GROUP OF FRIENDS INCLUDES A DESIGNATED DRIVER. DRUNK DRIVERS ARE CONSIDERED NEARLY AS DESPICABLE AS CHILD MOLESTERS.

MADD reaches its various publics in a variety of ways.

Public relations, at its best, not only tells an organization's "story" to its publics [communication], but also helps shape the organization and the way it performs [management]. Through research, measurement and evaluation, public relations professionals determine the concerns and expectations of the organization's publics and explain them to management. A responsible and effective public relations program is based on the understanding and support of its publics. (PRSA, 2006)

A Short History of Public Relations

The history of this complex field can be divided into four stages: early public relations, the propaganda–publicity stage, early two-way communication, and advanced two-way communication. These stages have combined to shape the character of this industry.

WWW

SADD
www.sadd.org

EARLY PUBLIC RELATIONS

Archaeologists in Iraq have uncovered a tablet dating from 1800 B.C.E. that today we would call a public information bulletin. It provided farmers with information on sowing, irrigating, and harvesting their crops. Julius Caesar fed the people of the Roman Empire constant reports of his achievements to maintain morale and to solidify his reputation and position of power. Genghis Khan would send "advance men" to tell stories of his might, hoping to frighten his enemies into surrendering.

Public relations campaigns abounded in colonial America and helped to create the Colonies. Merchants, farmers, and others who saw their own advantage in a growing colonial population used overstatement, half-truths, and lies to entice settlers to the New World. *A Brief and True Report of the New Found Land of Virginia,* by John White, was published in 1588 to lure European settlers. The Boston Tea Party was a well-planned media event organized to attract public attention for a vital cause. Today we'd call it a **pseudo-event,** an event staged specifically to attract public attention. Benjamin Franklin organized a sophisticated campaign to thwart the Stamp Act, the Crown's attempt to limit colonial press freedom (Chapter 3), using his publications and the oratory skills of criers. *The Federalist Papers* of John Jay, James Madison, and Alexander Hamilton were originally a series of 85 letters published between 1787 and 1789, which were designed to sway public

The December 16, 1773, Boston Tea Party was one of the first successful pseudo-events in the new land. Had cameras been around at the time, it would also have been a fine photo op.

opinion in the newly independent United States toward support and passage of the new Constitution, an early effort at issue management. In all these examples, people or organizations were using communication to inform, to build an image, and to influence public opinion.

THE PROPAGANDA–PUBLICITY STAGE

Mass circulation newspapers and the first successful consumer magazines appeared in the 1830s, expanding the ability of people and organizations to communicate with the public. In 1833, for example, Andrew Jackson hired former newspaperman Amos Kendall as his publicist and the country's first presidential press secretary in an effort to combat the aristocrats who saw Jackson as too common to be president.

Abolitionists sought an end to slavery. Industrialists needed to attract workers, entice customers, and enthuse investors. P. T. Barnum, convinced that "a sucker is born every minute," worked to lure them into his shows. All used the newspaper and the magazine to serve their causes.

Politicians recognized that the expanding press meant that a new way of campaigning was necessary. In 1896 presidential contenders William Jennings Bryan and William McKinley both established campaign headquarters in Chicago from which they issued news releases, position papers, and pamphlets. The modern national political campaign was born.

It was during this era that public relations began to acquire its deceitful, huckster image. PR was associated more with propaganda than with useful information. A disregard for the public and the willingness of public relations experts to serve the powerful fueled this view, but public relations began to establish itself as a profession during this time. The burgeoning press was its outlet, but westward expansion and rapid urbanization and industrialization in the United States were its driving forces. As the railroad expanded to unite the new nation, cities exploded with new people and new life. Markets, once small and local, became large and national.

www
Public Relations History
www.prmuseum.com

As the political and financial stakes grew, business and government became increasingly corrupt and selfish—"The public be damned" was William Vanderbilt's official comment when asked in 1882 about the effects of changing the schedule of his New York Central Railroad. The muckrakers' revelations badly tarnished the images of industry and politics. Massive and lengthy coal strikes led to violence and more antibusiness feeling. In the heyday of the journalistic exposé and the Progressive movement (Chapter 5), government and business both required some good public relations.

In 1889 Westinghouse Electric established the first corporate public relations department, hiring a former newspaper writer to engage the press and ensure that company positions were always clear and in the public eye. Advertising agencies, including N. W. Ayer & Sons and Lord and Thomas, began to offer public relations services to their clients. The first publicity company, The Publicity Bureau opened in Boston in 1906 and later expanded to New York, Chicago, Washington, St. Louis, and Topeka to help the railroad industry challenge federal regulations that it opposed.

The railroads also had other problems, and they turned to *New York World* reporter Ivy Lee for help. Beset by accidents and strikes, the Pennsylvania Railroad usually responded by suppressing information. Lee recognized, however, that this was dangerous and counterproductive in a time

The
PENALTY OF
LEADERSHIP

IN every field of human endeavor, he that is first must perpetually live in the white light of publicity. ¶Whether the leadership be vested in a man or in a manufactured product, emulation and envy are ever at work. ¶In art, in literature, in music, in industry, the reward and the punishment are always the same. ¶The reward is widespread recognition; the punishment, fierce denial and detraction. ¶When a man's work becomes a standard for the whole world, it also becomes a target for the shafts of the envious few. ¶If his work be merely mediocre, he will be left severely alone—if he achieve a masterpiece, it will set a million tongues a-wagging. ¶Jealousy does not protrude its forked tongue at the artist who produces a commonplace painting. ¶Whatsoever you write, or paint, or play, or sing, or build, no one will strive to surpass, or to slander you, unless your work be stamped with the seal of genius. ¶Long, long after a great work or a good work has been done, those who are disappointed or envious continue to cry out that it can not be done. ¶Spiteful little voices in the domain of art were raised against our own Whistler as a mountebank, long after the big world had acclaimed him its greatest artistic genius. ¶Multitudes flocked to Bayreuth to worship at the musical shrine of Wagner, while the little group of those whom he had dethroned and displaced argued angrily that he was no musician at all. ¶The little world continued to protest that Fulton could never build a steamboat, while the big world flocked to the river banks to see his boat steam by. ¶The leader is assailed because he is a leader, and the effort to equal him is merely added proof of that leadership. ¶Failing to equal or to excel, the follower seeks to depreciate and to destroy—but only confirms once more the superiority of that which he strives to supplant. ¶There is nothing new in this. ¶It is as old as the world and as old as the human passions—envy, fear, greed, ambition, and the desire to surpass. ¶And it all avails nothing. ¶If the leader truly leads, he remains—the leader. ¶Master-poet, master-painter, master-workman, each in his turn is assailed, and each holds his laurels through the ages. ¶That which is good or great makes itself known, no matter how loud the clamor of denial. ¶That which deserves to live- lives.

Cadillac Motor Car Co. Detroit, Mich.

Copyright 1914, Cadillac Motor Car Co.

1915 Penalty of Leadership Cadillac image ad. This campaign was an early but quite successful example of image advertising—using paid ads to build goodwill for a product.

when the public was already suspicious of big business, including the railroads. Lee escorted reporters to the scene of trouble, established press centers, distributed press releases, and assisted reporters in obtaining additional information and photographs.

When a Colorado coal mine strike erupted in violence in 1913, the press attacked the mine's principal stockholder, New York's John D. Rockefeller, blaming him for the shooting deaths of several miners and their wives and children. Lee handled press relations and convinced Rockefeller to visit the scene to talk (and be photographed) with the strikers. The strike ended, and Rockefeller was soon being praised for his sensitive intervention. Eventually Lee issued his *Declaration of Principles,* arguing that public relations practitioners should be providers of information, not purveyors of publicity.

Not all public relations at this time was damage control. Henry Ford began using staged events such as auto races to build interest in his cars, started *Ford Times* (an in-house employee publication), and made heavy use of image advertising.

Public relations in this stage was typically one-way, from organization to public. Still, by the outbreak of World War I, most of the elements of today's large-scale, multifunction public relations agency were in place.

EARLY TWO-WAY COMMUNICATION

Because the U.S. public was not particularly enthusiastic about the nation's entry into World War I, President Woodrow Wilson recognized the need for public relations in support of the war effort (Zinn, 1995, pp. 355–357). In 1917 he placed former newspaperman George Creel at the head of the newly formed Committee on Public Information (CPI). Creel assembled opinion leaders from around the country to advise the government on its public relations efforts and to help shape public opinion. The committee sold Liberty Bonds and helped increase membership in the Red Cross. It engaged in public relations on a scale never before seen, using movies, public speakers, articles in newspapers and magazines, and posters.

About this time public relations pioneer Edward Bernays began emphasizing the value of assessing the public's feelings toward an organization. He would then use this knowledge as the basis for the development of the public relations effort. Together with Creel's committee, Bernays's work was the beginning of two-way communication in public relations—that is, public relations talking to people and, in return, listening to them when they talked back. Public relations professionals began representing their various publics to their clients, just as they represented their clients to those publics.

There were other advances in public relations during this stage. During the 1930s, President Franklin D. Roosevelt, guided by advisor Louis McHenry Howe, embarked on a sophisticated public relations campaign to win support for his then-radical New Deal policies. Central to Roosevelt's effort was

www

Canadian Public Relations Society
www.cprs.ca

World War I brought government into large-scale public relations. Even today, the CPI's posters—like this one encouraging citizens to support the war effort through war bonds—are recognized.

AND THEY THOUGHT WE COULDN'T *FIGHT*

VICTORY LIBERTY LOAN

the new medium of radio. The Great Depression that plagued the country throughout this decade once again turned public opinion against business and industry. To counter people's distrust, many more corporations established in-house public relations departments; General Motors opened its PR operation in 1931. Public relations professionals turned increasingly to the newly emerging polling industry, founded by George Gallup and Elmo Roper, to better gauge public opinion as they constructed public relations campaigns and to gather feedback on the effectiveness of those campaigns. Gallup and Roper successfully applied newly refined social science research methods—advances in sampling, questionnaire design, and interviewing—to meet the business needs of clients and their publics.

Better known for hits such as *Mr. Smith Goes to Washington* and *It's a Wonderful Life*, director Frank Capra brought his moviemaking talents to the government's efforts to explain U.S. involvement in World War II and to overcome U.S. isolationism. His *Why We Fight* documentary series still stands as a classic of the form.

The growth of the industry was great enough and its reputation sufficiently fragile that the National Association of Accredited Publicity Directors was founded in 1936. The American Council on Public Relations was established 3 years later. They merged in 1947, creating the Public Relations Society of America (PRSA), the principal professional group for today's public relations professionals.

World War II saw the government undertake another massive campaign to bolster support for the war effort, this time through the Office of War Information (OWI). Employing techniques that had proven successful during World War I, the OWI had the additional advantage of public opinion polling, fully established and powerful radio networks and their stars, and a Hollywood eager to help. Singer Kate Smith's war bond radio telethon raised millions, and director Frank Capra produced the *Why We Fight* film series for the OWI.

During this era both public relations and Ivy Lee suffered a serious blow to their reputations. Lee was the American public relations spokesman for Germany and its leader, Adolf Hitler. In 1934 Lee was required to testify before Congress to defend himself against the charge that he was a Nazi sympathizer. He was successful, but the damage had been done. As a result of Lee's ties with Germany, Congress passed the Foreign Agents Registration Act in 1938, requiring anyone who engages in political activities in the United States on behalf of a foreign power to register as an agent of that power with the Justice Department.

ADVANCED TWO-WAY COMMUNICATION

Post–World War II U.S. society was confronted by profound social change and expansion of the consumer culture. It became increasingly important for organizations to know what their clients were thinking, what they liked and disliked, and what concerned and satisfied them. As a result, public relations

Criticism of public relations found its way into popular culture through a number of popular films and books. This scene is from the movie *The Hucksters.*

turned even more decidedly toward integrated two-way communication, employing research, advertising, and promotion.

As the public relations industry became more visible, it opened itself to closer scrutiny. Best-selling novels such as *The Hucksters* and *The Man in the Gray Flannel Suit* (and the hit movies made from them) painted a disturbingly negative picture of the industry and those who worked in it. Vance Packard's best-selling book *The Hidden Persuaders,* dealing with both public relations and advertising, further eroded PR esteem. As a result of public distrust of the profession, Congress passed the Federal Regulation of Lobbying Act in 1946, requiring, among other things, that those who deal with federal employees on behalf of private clients disclose those relationships. And as the industry's conduct and ethics came under increasing attack, the PRSA responded with a code of ethics in 1954 and an accreditation program in 1962. Both, with modification and improvement, stand today.

The modern era of public relations is characterized by other events as well. More people buying more products meant that greater numbers of people were coming into contact with a growing number of businesses. As consumer markets grew in size, the basis for competition changed. Texaco, for example, used advertising to sell its gasoline. But because its products were not all that different from those of other oil companies, it also sold its gasoline using its good name and reputation. Increasingly, then, advertising agencies began to add public relations divisions. This change served to blur the distinction between advertising and PR.

Women, who had proved their capabilities in all professional settings during World War II, became prominent in the industry. Anne Williams Wheaton was associate press secretary to President Eisenhower; Leone Baxter was president of the powerful public relations firm Whitaker and Baxter. Companies and their executives and politicians increasingly turned to television to burnish their images and shape public opinion. Nonprofit, charitable, and social activist groups also mastered the art of public relations. The latter used public relations especially effectively to challenge the PR power of targeted businesses. Environmentalist, civil rights, and women's rights groups and safety and consumer advocate organizations were successful in moving the public toward their positions and, in many cases, toward action.

SHAPING THE CHARACTER OF PUBLIC RELATIONS

Throughout these four stages in the development of public relations, several factors combined to shape the identity of public relations, influence the way the industry does its job, and clarify the necessity for PR in the business and political world.

Advances in technology. Advances in industrial technology made possible mass production, distribution, and marketing of goods. Advances in communication technology (and their proliferation) made it possible to communicate more efficiently and effectively with ever-larger and more specific audiences.

Growth of the middle class. A growing middle class, better educated and more aware of the world around it, required information about people and organizations.

Growth of organizations. As business, organized labor, and government grew bigger after World War II, the public saw them as more powerful and more remote. As a result, people were naturally curious and suspicious about these forces that seemed to be influencing all aspects of their lives.

Better research tools. The development of sophisticated research methodologies and statistical techniques allowed the industry to know its audiences better and to better judge the effectiveness of public relations campaigns.

Professionalization. Numerous national and international public relations organizations helped professionalize the industry and clean up its reputation.

Public Relations and Its Audiences

Virtually all of us consume public relations messages on a daily basis. Increasingly, the video clips we see on the local evening news are provided by a public relations firm or the PR department of some company or organization. The content of many of the stories we read in our daily newspaper or hear on local radio news comes directly from PR-provided press releases. As one media relations firm explained in a promotional piece sent to prospective clients, "The media are separated into two categories. One is content and the other is advertising. They're both for sale. Advertising can be purchased directly from the publication or through an ad agency, and the content space you purchase from PR firms" (quoted in Jackson & Hart, 2002, p. 24). In addition, the charity food drive we support, the poster encouraging us toward safer sex, the corporation-sponsored art exhibit we attend, and the 5K race we run are all someone's public relations effort. Public relations professionals

WWW
Council of Public Relations Firms
www.prfirms.org

interact with seven categories of publics, and a **public** is any group of people with a stake in an organization, issue, or idea:

Employees. An organization's employees are its lifeblood, its family. Good public relations begins at home with company newsletters, social events, and internal and external recognition of superior performance.

Stockholders. Stockholders own the organization (it it is a public corporation). They are "family" as well, and their goodwill is necessary for the business to operate. Annual reports and stockholder meetings provide a sense of belonging as well as information.

Communities. An organization has neighbors where it operates. Courtesy, as well as good business sense, requires that an organization's neighbors be treated with friendship and support. Information meetings, company-sponsored safety and food drives, and open houses strengthen ties between organizations and their neighbors.

Media. Very little communication with an organization's various publics can occur without the trust and goodwill of professionals in the mass media. Press packets, briefings, and facilitating access to organization newsmakers build that trust and goodwill.

Government. Government is "the voice of the people" and, as such, deserves the attention of any organization that deals with the public. From a practical perspective, governments have the power to tax, regulate, and zone. Organizations must earn and maintain the goodwill and trust of the government. Providing information and access through reports, position papers, and meetings with personnel keeps government informed and builds its trust in an organization. The government is also the target of many PR efforts, as organizations and their lobbyists seek favorable legislation and other action.

Investment community. Corporations are under the constant scrutiny of those who invest their own money, invest the money of others, or make recommendations on investment. The value of a business and its ability to grow are functions of the investment community's respect for and trust in it. As a result, all PR efforts that build an organization's good image speak to that community.

Customers. Consumers pay the bills for companies through their purchase of products or services. Their goodwill is invaluable. That makes good PR, in all its forms, invaluable.

Scope and Structure of the Public Relations Industry

Today some 200,000 people identify themselves as working in public relations, and virtually every major U.S. company has a public relations department, some housing as many as 400 employees. There are over 4,000 public relations firms in the United States, the largest employing as many as 2,000 people. Most, however, have fewer, some as few as 4 employees. American PR firms had $3.7 billion in revenue in 2005, an amount that is expected to grow

WWW
PR Statistics and Commentary
www.odwyerpr.com

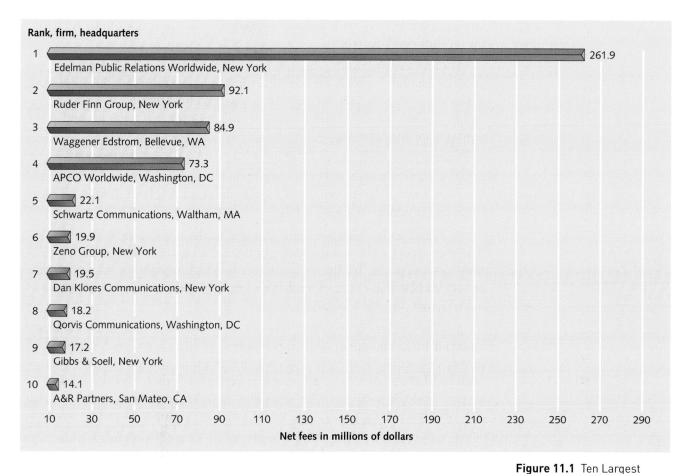

Rank, firm, headquarters

Rank	Firm, headquarters	Net fees
1	Edelman Public Relations Worldwide, New York	261.9
2	Ruder Finn Group, New York	92.1
3	Waggener Edstrom, Bellevue, WA	84.9
4	APCO Worldwide, Washington, DC	73.3
5	Schwartz Communications, Waltham, MA	22.1
6	Zeno Group, New York	19.9
7	Dan Klores Communications, New York	19.5
8	Qorvis Communications, Washington, DC	18.2
9	Gibbs & Soell, New York	17.2
10	A&R Partners, San Mateo, CA	14.1

Net fees in millions of dollars

Figure 11.1 Ten Largest Independent PR Firms in the United States, 2005.
Source: O'Dwyer's Public Relations News at www.odwyerpr.com.

at an annual rate of 9%, to $5.3 billion by 2009 ("Do We," 2006). Figure 11.1 shows the 10 largest independent public relations firms in the United States.

There are full-service public relations firms and those that provide only special services. Media specialists for company CEOs, newspaper clipping services, and makers of video news releases are special service providers. Public relations firms bill for their services in a number of ways. They may charge an hourly rate for services rendered, or they may be on call, charging clients a monthly fee to act as their public relations counsel. Hill and Knowlton, for example, charges a minimum fee of $5,000 a month. Third are **fixed-fee arrangements,** wherein the firm performs a specific set of services for a client for a specific and prearranged fee. Finally, many firms bill for **collateral materials,** adding a surcharge as high as 17.65% for handling printing, research, and photographs. For example, if it costs $3,000 to have a poster printed, the firm charges the client $3,529.50 ($3,000 + [$3,000 × .1765] = $3,000 + $529.50).

PUBLIC RELATIONS ACTIVITIES

Regardless of the way public relations firms bill their clients, they earn their fees by offering all or some of these 14 interrelated services:

1. *Community relations.* This type of public affairs work focuses on the communities in which the organization exists. If a city wants to build a new airport, for example, those whose land will be taken or devalued

For more information on this topic, see Media Talk clip #6, "Advertising and Public Relations: Inside Ogllvy," on the *Media Tours* DVD.

must be satisfied. If they are not, widespread community opposition to the project may develop.

2. *Counseling.* Public relations professionals routinely offer advice to an organization's management concerning policies, relationships, and communication with its various publics. Management must tell its publics "what we do." Public relations helps in the creation, refinement, and presentation of that message.

3. *Development/fund-raising.* All organizations, commercial and non-profit, survive through the voluntary contributions in time and money of their members, friends, employees, supporters, and others. Public relations helps demonstrate the need for those contributions.

4. *Employee/member relations.* Similar to the development function in that the target public is employees and members, this form of public relations responds specifically to the concerns of an organization's employees or members and its retirees and their families. The goal is maintenance of high morale and motivation.

5. *Financial relations.* Practiced primarily by corporate organizations, financial PR is the enhancement of communication between investor-owned companies and their shareholders, the financial community (for example, banks, annuity groups, and investment firms), and the public. Much corporate strategy, such as expansion into new markets and acquisition of other companies, is dependent upon good financial public relations.

6. *Government affairs.* This type of public affairs work focuses on government agencies. **Lobbying**—directly interacting to influence elected officials or government regulators and agents—is often a central activity.

7. *Industry relations.* Companies must interact not only with their own customers and stockholders but also with other companies in their line of business, both competitors and suppliers. In addition, they must also stand as a single voice in dealing with various state and federal regulators. For example, groups as disparate as the Texas Restaurant Association, the

Annual reports are the most visible product of financial public relations.

The fictitious Acme Fishhook Research Council in this Robotman & Monty cartoon is a good example of an organization that engages in industry relations activities.
MONTY © Jim Meddick/Distributed by Newspaper Enterprise Association.

American Petroleum Institute, and the National Association of Manufacturers all require public relations in dealing with their various publics. The goal is the maintenance and prosperity of the industry as a whole.

8. *Issues management.* Often an organization is as interested in influencing public opinion about some larger issue that will eventually influence its operation as it is in the improvement of its own image. Issues management typically uses a large-scale public relations campaign designed to move or shape opinion on a specific issue. Usually the issue is an important one that generates deep feelings. Death penalty activists, for example, employ a full range of communication techniques to sway people to their side. Exxon Mobil frequently runs advertorials that address environmentalism and public transportation—important issues in and of themselves, but also important to the future of a leading manufacturer of gasoline. For a close look at a controversial issues management campaign, see the box on page 356, "The War in Iraq: The Pentagon Does PR."

For more information on this topic, see Media Talk video clip #18, "Pentagon Planning to Plant Misinformation in Foreign News Sources," on the *Media World* DVD.

9. *Media relations.* As the number of media outlets grows and as advances in technology increase the complexity of dealing with them, public relations clients require help in understanding the various media, in preparing and organizing materials for them, and in placing those materials. In addition, media relations requires that the public relations professional maintain good relationships with professionals in the media, understand their deadlines and other constraints, and earn their trust.

10. *Marketing communication.* This is a combination of activities designed to sell a product, service, or idea. It can include the creation of advertising; generation of publicity and promotion; design of packaging, point-of-sale displays, and trade show presentations; and design and execution of special events. It is important to note that PR professionals often use advertising but that the two are not the same. The difference is one of control. Advertising is controlled communication—advertisers pay for ads to appear in specific media exactly as they want. PR tends to be less controlled. The PR firm cannot control how or when its press release is used by the local paper. It cannot control how the media react to Nike's ongoing insistence that it has rectified reported worker abuses in its overseas shops. Advertising becomes a public relations function when its goal is to build an image or to motivate action, as opposed to the usual function of selling products. The Smokey Bear forest fire prevention campaign is a well-known successful public relations advertising campaign.

CULTURAL FORUM

The War in Iraq: The Pentagon Does PR

What are your most enduring images of the 2003 invasion of Iraq? Most Americans can easily name theirs—President Bush landing on the USS *Abraham Lincoln* to announce Mission Accomplished; the president's surprise Thanksgiving Day visit to the troops, complete with turkey; the heroic Private Jessica Lynch, carried away from her Iraqi captors on a stretcher, aglow in green night-vision light; the toppling of Saddam's statue amid throngs of cheering Iraqis. These famous images from that controversial war, sent around the world in all media, put public relations, especially the issue of public relations in wartime, squarely—and emotionally—into the cultural forum.

When President Woodrow Wilson enlisted the country's best advertising and public relations people into the Committee on Public Information to generate support for America's entry into World War I, he had no doubt that their efforts were necessary. Committee member and "Father of Public Relations" Edward L. Bernays argued that freedom of press and speech should be expanded to include the "engineering of consent," the government's "freedom to persuade. . . . Only by mastering the techniques of communication can leadership be exercised fruitfully in the vast complex that is modern democracy . . . because in a democracy, results do not just happen" (quoted in Sproule, 1997, p. 213).

Before we return to the issue of PR in the Gulf War, enter your voice into the cultural forum. Remember, though, the debate here is not whether you supported that action; it is your evaluation of the public relations effort marshaled in its support. Do you believe the government has the right (or obligation) to engineer your consent, because "in a democracy, results don't just happen"? Do you think it is appropriate for leaders in a democracy to employ public relations to gain people's support of their actions when, in fact, their actions are supposed to be the expression of the people's will? What do you think of the fact that the Pentagon employs more than 7,000 public relations specialists (Seitel, 2004)? Revisit your answers to these questions at the end of this box.

There were many public relations practices employed during the invasion and occupation that fueled discussion in the cultural forum, including embedding reporters and **spin,** called by public relations veteran Fraser Seitel "outright lying to hide what really happened." He added, "The propensity in recent years for presumably respected public figures to lie in an attempt to deceive the public has led to the notion that 'spinning' the facts is synonymous with public relations. It isn't. Spin . . . is antithetical to the proper practice of public relations" (2004, p. 11).

Embedding Reporters The Defense Department relied on respected professional Victoria Clarke to manage the war's public relations. The assistant secretary of defense for public affairs joined the Pentagon from her post as head of the Washington,

> **"ONLY BY MASTERING THE TECHNIQUES OF COMMUNICATION CAN LEADERSHIP BE EXERCISED FRUITFULLY IN THE VAST COMPLEX THAT IS MODERN DEMOCRACY . . . BECAUSE IN A DEMOCRACY, RESULTS DO NOT JUST HAPPEN."**

D.C., office of PR giant Hill and Knowlton. Upon assuming her new duties, she told the *Wall Street Journal* that she would run the war's PR "as if it were a political campaign" (quoted in Schechter, 2003a, p. 1). So where campaigns encourage political reporters to join them on the trail—the boys on the bus—Clarke invited them to join the soldiers at the front, as **embedded journalists.** The rules for embeds were simple—in exchange for up-close-and-personal access to the action, they had to agree not to travel independently of their assigned unit, all interviews had to be "on the record," and stories had to be cleared for transmission by military officials. The result was dramatic, heart-wrenching, exciting, real-time coverage of battle. "Sheer genius," said PR consultant Katie Paine; the embedded reporters "have been spectacular, bringing war into our living rooms like never before. . . . The sagacity of the tactic is that it is based on the basic tenet of public relations: It's all about relationships. The better the relationship any of us has with a journalist, the better the chance of that journalist picking up and reporting our messages" (quoted in Rampton & Stauber, 2003, p. 21). From the Pentagon's point of view, "You couldn't hire actors to do as good a job as the press has done," Clarke's predecessor at the Defense Department, Kenneth Baker, told the *Wall Street Journal* (in Schechter, 2003b, p. 1). Did embedding produce "one magnificent recruitment video" for the Pentagon, coverage akin to salted nuts, "very tasty and almost empty of high-quality nourishment," in the words of media expert Alex Jones? Or did it provide "a far more complete mosaic of the fighting—replete with heroism, tragedy, and human error—than would have been possible without it," in the words of journalist Sherry Ricchiardi (both quotes from Ricchiardi, 2003, pp. 29–30)? It was great PR. The question now in the cultural forum is, Was it good journalism?

Spin As the fog of war lifted, the world learned that some of its most enduring images of the conflict in Iraq were spin; they were not real. The "rescue" of Jessica Lynch was revealed to have been scripted for Pentagon camera crews. Jessica Lynch later told ABC's Diane Sawyer in a televised interview, "They used me as a way to symbolize all this stuff. It hurt in a way that people would make up stories that they had no truth about. It's wrong" (quoted in Scheer, 2003, p. 2).

Washington Post reporter Ceci Connelly equated the toppling of Saddam's statue in Baghdad's Firdos Square to the fall of the Berlin Wall: "Just sort of that pure emotional expression, not choreographed, not stage-managed, the way so many things these days seem to be. Really breathtaking" (in Andersen, 2003, p. 9). Unfortunately, it was choreographed and stage-managed. The army later admitted that "the entire stunt was conceived by the U.S. military and enacted with the help of a fast-thinking Army psychological operation

356   PART 3   Supporting Industries

(PSYOP). . . . It was a Marine colonel who decided to topple the statue, with the PSYOP team making it appear to be a spontaneous Iraqi action" ("When Saddam," 2004).

The beautiful Thanksgiving turkey presented by the president to smiling GIs turned out to be "a decorative turkey," according to military sources when questioned a week after the visit to Baghdad ("Bush's Baghdad," 2003). And the president's dramatic landing on the *Lincoln* also turned out to be spin—not only were the Mission Accomplished banner and the need for a jet landing disputed, but hundreds of soldiers were still to perish after the controversial pseudo-event ("Mission Accomplished," 2003). The question of the impact of all this spin has roiled in the cultural forum throughout the war, periodically gaining intensity as new public relations initiatives have been undertaken. For example, in July 2005, with public support for the war falling to the mid-30-percents, the Pentagon, in an effort to lower people's expectations of a timely and neat resolution, re-branded the "war on terror" as "the global struggle against violent extremism." According to the Pentagon's revamped PR campaign, a "war" has a discrete beginning and end, a winner and loser; a "struggle," especially against something as pernicious as violent extremism, is ongoing. "We need to both dispute the gloomy vision and offer a positive alternative," said National Security Adviser Steven Hadley (in Schmitt & Shanker, 2005, p. A7).

So the question remains, is spin sometimes necessary to generate support for an unpopular government action, especially war? That is, is Bernays correct that the people's consent sometimes needs to be engineered to ready them for war? Or is the decision to go to war so monumental that engineering consent, even with ethical (that is, no-spin) public relations, is out of place in a democracy? Does the use (or misuse) of PR contribute to the public's growing distrust of the media, a phenomenon chronicled in numerous recent studies? The Project for Excellence in Journalism (2004), for example, found steep declines in the number of Americans who think that news organizations are highly professional, moral, get the facts straight, and care about people. Can a public mistrustful of its media effectively govern itself? Do you agree with columnist David Broder's observation that "cynicism is epidemic right now. It saps people's confidence in politics and public officials, and it erodes both the standing and the standards of journalism. If the assumption is that nothing is on the level, nothing is what it seems, then citizenship becomes a game for fools and there is no point in trying to stay informed" (in Cappella & Jamieson, 1997, p. 17)? Is there a bit of Chicken Little's worry that the sky is falling in reporter Gene Lyons's contention that the Pentagon's Iraq war PR efforts have produced a "corrosive cynicism" in the public, one that "says that since all politicians lie and the press can't be trusted, it's all a mystery. That way lies the death of a democracy already on life support" (2004, p. 11)?

Advertising and public relations obviously overlap even for manufacturers of consumer products. Chevrolet must sell cars, but it must communicate with its various publics as well. Exxon sells gasoline. But in the wake of the *Valdez* disaster, it needed serious public relations help. One result of the overlap of advertising and public relations is that advertising agencies increasingly own their own public relations departments or firms or associate closely with a PR company. For example, of the 10 highest-earning public relations firms in the United States, only Edelman PR Worldwide is not a subsidiary of an advertising agency.

Another way that advertising and public relations differ is that advertising people typically do not set policy for an organization. Advertising people *implement* policy after organization leaders set it. In contrast, public relations professionals usually are part of the policy decision process because they are the liaison between the organization and its publics. Effective organizations have come to understand that even in routine decisions the impact on public opinion and subsequent consequences can be of tremendous importance. As a result, public relations has become a management function, and a public relations professional typically sits as a member of a company's highest level of management.

11. *Minority relations/multicultural affairs.* Public affairs activities are directed toward specific racial minorities in this type of work. When Denny's restaurant chain was beset by numerous complaints of racial dis-

The best public relations can serve both the client and the public, as demonstrated by this Ronald McDonald House promotional material.

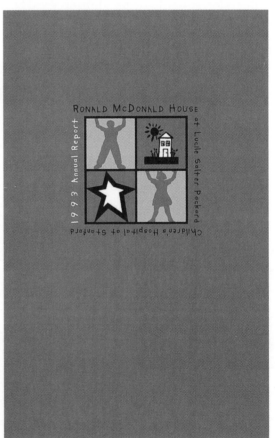

crimination during the 1990s, it undertook an aggressive campaign to speak to those who felt disenfranchised by the events. A secondary goal of its efforts, which were aimed largely at the African American community, was to send a message to its own employees and the larger public that this was the company line, that discrimination was wrong, that everybody was welcome in Denny's.

12. *Public affairs.* The public affairs function includes interacting with officials and leaders of the various power centers with whom a client must deal. Community and government officials and leaders of pressure groups are likely targets of this form of public relations. Public affairs emphasizes social responsibility and building goodwill, such as when a company donates money for a computer lab to the local high school.

13. *Special events and public participation.* As you saw in the opening vignette, public relations can be used to stimulate interest in an organization, person, or product through a well-planned, focused "happening," an activity designed to facilitate interaction between an organization and its publics.

14. *Research.* Organizations often must determine the attitudes and behaviors of their various publics in order to plan and implement the activities necessary to influence or change those attitudes and behaviors.

This is a very successful, long-running advertising campaign. It is also a very successful, long-running public relations campaign.

ORGANIZATION OF A PUBLIC RELATIONS OPERATION

Public relations operations come in all sizes. Regardless of size, however, the typical PR firm or department will have these types of positions (but not necessarily these titles):

Executive. This is the chief executive officer who, sometimes with a staff, sometimes alone, sets policy and serves as the spokesperson for the operation.

Account executives. Each account has its own executive who provides advice to the client, defines problems and situations, assesses the needs and demands of the client's publics, recommends a communication plan or campaign, and gathers the PR firm's resources in support of the client.

Creative specialists. These are the writers, graphic designers, artists, video and audio producers, and photographers—anybody necessary to meet the communication needs of the client.

Media specialists. Media specialists are aware of the requirements, preferences, limitations, and strengths of the various media used to serve the client. They find the right media for clients' messages.

www

PR Watch
prwatch.org

Larger public relations operations may also have these positions as need demands:

Research. The key to two-way public relations communication rests in research—assessing the needs of a client's various publics and the effectiveness of the efforts aimed at them. Polling, one-on-one interviews, and **focus groups,** in which small groups of a targeted public are interviewed, provide the PR operation and its client with feedback.

Government relations. Depending on the client's needs, lobbying or other direct communication with government officials may be necessary.

Financial services. Very specific and sophisticated knowledge of economics, finance, and business or corporate law is required to provide clients with dependable financial public relations.

Trends and Convergence in Public Relations

GLOBALIZATION AND SPECIALIZATION

For more information on this topic, see Media Talk video clip #19, "Why is the United States Viewed So Poorly in the Arab World?" on the *Media World* DVD.

As it has in the media industries themselves, globalization has come to public relations, both in the form of foreign ownership and in the reach of PR firms' operations into foreign countries. For example, 3 of the world's top-10-earning PR firms, despite their U.S. roots, are owned by London-based WPP Group: Hill and Knowlton, Burson-Marsteller, and Ogilvy PR Worldwide. Hill and Knowlton alone has 2,000 employees working in 71 offices in 37 countries around the world. Rowland Company Worldwide is owned by English advertising agency Saatchi & Saatchi. Weber Shandwick, the highest-earning PR firm in the United States, is based in London.

Another trend in public relations is specialization. We've seen the 14 activities of public relations professionals, but specialization can expand that list. This specialization takes two forms. The first is defined by issue. Environmental public relations is attracting ever-larger numbers of people, both environmentalists and industrialists. E. Bruce Harrison Consulting attracts corporate clients in part because of its reputation as a firm with superior **greenwashing** skills. That is, Harrison is particularly adept at countering the public relations efforts aimed at its clients by environmentalists. Health care and pharmaceuticals has also recently emerged as a significant public relations specialty.

CONVERGENCE

Check PR Claims
www.sourcewatch.org

The second impetus driving specialization has to do with the increasing number of media outlets used in public relations campaigns that rely on new and converging technologies. Online information and advertising are a growing part of the total public relations media mix, as are **video news releases** (pre-produced reports about a client or its products distributed free of charge to television stations; see cartoon on p. 361) and videoconferencing. We'll revisit video news releases near the end of this chapter. Television, in the form of the **satellite-delivered media tour,** in which spokespeople can be simultaneously

THIS MODERN WORLD by TOM TOMORROW

IT'S TIME FOR YET ANOTHER LOOK AT *HOW THE NEWS WORKS...STEP ONE:* A CORPORATION WHICH HAS BEEN CAUGHT ENGAGING IN SOME ILLEGAL OR UNETHICAL ACT HIRES A *PUBLIC RELATIONS FIRM...*

PEOPLE ARE *UPSET* BECAUSE WE'VE BEEN DUMPING *TOXIC SLUDGE* INTO THE WATER SUPPLY!

WELL--BY THE TIME *WE'RE* THROUGH, THEY'LL *THANK* YOU FOR IT!

STEP TWO: THE P.R. FIRM PROCEEDS TO MANIPULATE PUBLIC OPINION IN A VARIETY OF DEVIOUS, UNDERHANDED WAYS--SUCH AS ANONYMOUSLY PLANTING OP-ED PIECES IN THE NATION'S *NEWSPAPERS...*

SEPTEMBER 27, 1992

What's So Bad About Toxic Sludge?
by Joe Pundit

...AS WELL AS SENDING OUT SLICKLY-PRODUCED "VIDEO NEWS RELEASES" WHICH MANY CASH-STRAPPED LOCAL NEWS DEPARTMENTS AIR VIRTUALLY *UNEDITED...* GIVING CORPORATE PROPAGANDA THE APPEARANCE OF OBJECTIVE *REPORTING...*

...AND SO YOU SEE, TOXIC SLUDGE IS ACTUALLY QUITE *GOOD* FOR YOU!

STEP THREE: PUBLIC OPINION IS *SWAYED* BY THIS ONSLAUGHT OF MEDIA MANIPULATION MASQUERADED AS *NEWS...*SINCE, AS P.R. FIRMS WELL UNDERSTAND, ANY LIE REPEATED *OFTEN* ENOUGH BECOMES *TRUE...*

I CAN'T IMAGINE *WHY* WE EVER WORRIED ABOUT *TOXIC SLUDGE!*

YES--HOW *SILLY* WE WERE!

This Tom Tomorrow comic satirizes one of the most controversial tools used by public relations firms—the self-promoting video news release. Legal, and sometimes providing useful information, these video clips test the viewer's media literacy skills. © Tom Tomorrow. Reprinted with permission.

interviewed by a worldwide audience connected to the on-screen interviewee via telephone, has further extended the reach of public relations. In addition, desktop publishing has greatly expanded the number and type of available print outlets. All require professionals with quite specific skills.

The public relations industry is responding to the convergence of traditional media with the Internet in other ways as well. One is the development of **integrated marketing communications (IMC).** We saw earlier how advertising and PR often overlap, but in IMC, firms actively combine public relations, marketing, advertising, and promotion functions into a more or less seamless communication campaign that is as at home on the Web as it is on the television screen and magazine page. The goal of this integration is to provide the client and agency with greater control over communication (and its interpretation) in an increasingly fragmented but synergized media environment. For example, a common IMC tactic is to employ **viral marketing,** a strategy that relies on targeting specific Internet users with a given communication and relying on them to spread the word through the communication channels with which they are most comfortable. This is IMC, and it is inexpensive and effective.

The industry has had to respond to the Internet in another way. The Net has provided various publics with a new, powerful way to counter even the best public relations effort (Chapter 10). Tony Juniper of the British environmental group Friends of the Earth calls the Internet "the most potent weapon in the toolbox of resistance." As Peter Verhille of PR giant Entente International explains, "One of the major strengths of pressure groups—in fact the leveling factor in their confrontation with powerful companies—is their ability to exploit the instruments of the telecommunication revolution. Their agile use of global tools such as the Internet reduces the advantages that corporate budgets once provided" (both quotes from Klein, 1999, pp. 395–396). For example, the Internet was central in activists' 1999 efforts to shame Nike into improving conditions for its overseas workers; and in 1995 use of the Net played a prominent part in forcing Shell Oil to find environmentally sensitive ways to dispose of its outdated Atlantic Ocean drilling platforms. Public relations agencies and in-house PR departments have responded in a number of ways. One is IMC. Another is the hiring of in-house Web monitors; a third is the growth of specialty firms such as eWatch, whose function is to alert clients to negative references on the Web and suggest effective countermeasures.

TRUST IN PUBLIC RELATIONS

www

Edward Bernays
www.lib.uwo.ca/business/bernays.html

We began our discussion of public relations with the admission that the profession sometimes bears a negative reputation (see the essay "Boosting Smoking Among Women" on p. 363). Edward Bernays's call for greater sensitivity to the wants and needs of the various publics and Ivy Lee's insistence that public relations be open and honest were the industry's first steps away from its huckster roots. The post–World War II code of ethics and accreditation programs were a second and more important step. Yet Bernays himself was dissatisfied with the profession's progress. The "Father of Public Relations" died in 1995 at the age of 103. He spent the greater part of his last years demanding that the industry, especially the PRSA, police itself. In 1986 Bernays wrote,

> Under present conditions, an unethical person can sign the code of the PRSA, become a member, practice unethically—untouched by any legal sanctions. In law and medicine, such an individual is subject to disbarment from the profession. . . . There are no standards. . . . This sad situation makes it possible for anyone, regardless of education or ethics, to use the term "public relations" to describe his or her function. (p. 11)

The Father of Public Relations, Edward Bernays, used the last years of his long career and life to campaign for improved industry ethics.

Boosting Smoking Among Women

Into the early 1900s, smoking was seen as an unsavory habit, permissible for men, never for women. But with the turn of the century, women too wanted to light up. Advertising campaigns first began targeting female smokers in 1919. The American Tobacco Company slogan "Reach for a Lucky instead of a sweet," along with ads designed to help women understand that they could use cigarettes to keep their figures, was aimed at this new market. The rush to smoke was also fueled by the fight for suffrage; women wanted equality. The right to vote was an important goal, but if men could smoke without a fight, why couldn't women?

As more women began to smoke, antismoking crusades attempted to deter them. The protection of women's morality, not their health, inspired the crusaders. Many cities forbade the use of tobacco by women in public places. Yet the number of women who started smoking continued to grow. George Washington Hill, head of American Tobacco, wanted this lucrative market to continue to expand, and he wanted to own as large a part of it as possible. He turned to public relations and Edward Bernays.

A nephew of Sigmund Freud, Bernays was employed to conduct psychological research aimed at understanding the relationship between women and cigarettes. He learned that women saw cigarettes as symbols of freedom, as the representation of their unfair treatment in a man's world, and

AS THEY MARCHED, THE DEBUTANTES LIT THEIR LUCKY "TORCHES OF FREEDOM" AND SMILINGLY PROCEEDED TO PUFF AND WALK.

Lucky Strike used advertising and an effective public relations campaign to break the taboo on women smokers.

as a sign of their determination to be accepted as equal.

Bernays had several objectives: (1) to let the public know that it was quite all right for women to smoke; (2) to undercut the bans on public smoking by women that existed in many places; and (3) to position Lucky Strike cigarettes as a progressive brand.

In meeting these goals, Bernays perpetrated a publicity stunt that is still heralded as a triumphant coup among public relations practitioners. New York City had a ban on public smoking by females. Because of, rather than despite, this, Bernays arranged for 10 socially prominent young women to enter the 1929 annual Easter Parade down Fifth Avenue as the "Torches of Liberty Contingent." As they marched, the debutantes lit their Lucky "torches of freedom" and smilingly proceeded to puff and walk. For reporters on the scene, this made for much better news and photos than the usual little kids in their spring finery. The blow for female emancipation was front-page news, not only in New York but nationally. The taboo was dead.

Later in his life, Bernays would argue that had he known of the link between cigarette smoking and cancer and other diseases, he would never have taken on American Tobacco as a client. We will see in Chapter 12 whether his strategy—and his later misgivings—are repeated in contemporary efforts to expand the market for cigarettes.

Many people in the profession share Bernays's concern, especially when the industry's own research shows that 85% of the American public thinks that PR practitioners "sometimes take advantage of the media to present misleading information that is favorable to their clients." That same Public Relations Society of America poll revealed that 79% of the general public believes that PR people "are only interested in disseminating information that helps their clients make money" (Burton, 2005). As a result, Burson-Marsteller senior counselor Fraser Seitel is adamant about restoring trust in PR:

The heart of public relations counsel is "to do the right thing." The cardinal rule of public relations is to "never lie." Nonetheless, in one bridling survey of 1,700 public relations executives, it was revealed that 25 percent of those interviewed admitted they had "lied on the job," 39 percent said they had exaggerated the truth, and another 44 percent said they had felt "uncertain" about the ethics of what they did. (2004, p. 132)

Trust, too, is important to Fleishman-Hillard's executive vice president, John Saunders, who called on his colleagues to debate what their industry stands for. He told the 2005 annual meeting of the International Communications Consultancy Organisation,

> This is no longer the golden age of PR. We will need to change to get to where we want to be in the future. . . . We need to devote more energy to ethics. If we are to advise on reputation management, we must be above reproach. . . . We need to impose more rigorous standards on ourselves. (in Marriott, 2005)

In the United States the number of public relations people exceeds the number of journalists (200,000 to 130,000). Estimates from both inside and outside the industry claim that from 50% to 90% of the stories we read in the paper or see on television originate entirely or in part from a public relations operation in the form of either a printed or a video news release. Critics further contend that 40% of what we read and see appears virtually unedited, leading PR professionals to boast that "the best PR is invisible" and "the best PR ends up looking like news" (Stauber & Rampton, 1995, p. 2).

This state of affairs led journalist and former *Mother Jones* editor Mark Dowie to write in his introduction to John Stauber and Sheldon Rampton's *Toxic Sludge Is Good for You: Lies, Damn Lies and the Public Relations Industry,*

> PR has become a communications medium in its own right, an industry designed to alter perception, reshape reality, and manufacture consent. It is run by a fraternity carefully organized so that only insiders can observe their peers at work. . . . It is critical that consumers of media in democratic societies understand the origin of information and the process by which it is mediated, particularly when they are being deceived. (1995, pp. 2–4)

If it is true that the public is being systematically deceived by public relations, the cultural implications could not be more profound. What becomes of the negotiation function of culture, wherein people debate and discuss their values and interests in the cultural forum, if public relations gives some voices advantages not available to others? Dowie suggests the remedy for this potential problem: Consumers must make themselves aware of "the origin of information and the process by which it is mediated" (p. 4). As we've seen throughout this book, we would expect nothing less of a media literate person.

DEVELOPING MEDIA LITERACY SKILLS
Recognizing Video News Releases

The calls from PR professionals for ethics, accountability, and honesty, above and on page 343, were the result of a recent series of public embarrassments for the public relations industry. The Rendon Group's involvement in the selling of the invasion of Iraq and the Pentagon's spin—from Mission Accomplished to Jessica Lynch's rescue—were two. But another that caught the attention of the public and industry alike was the revelation that the federal government was making extensive use of video news releases (VNR) to support a variety of its foreign policy and domestic initiatives. Actors and PR professionals were posing as citizens and, even more troubling, as journalists in favorable stories about progress in the war in Iraq, aviation safety, education, health care, and farming, all paid for with taxpayer money and provided free of charge to news outlets (Barstow & Stein, 2005). In the uproar that followed, VNR themselves became controversial. Congress's own General Accountability Office deemed their use by governmental agencies illegal. The FCC vowed to strengthen its rules on disclosure of the sources of VNR and raised the maximum fine it could level at an offending station. The broadcast industry's Radio–Television News Directors Association clarified and strengthened its rules on VNR identification and disclosure.

But VNR are still used in 90% of all American television newsrooms, primarily because even though many local stations have increased the amount of airtime they devote to news programming, few have the time or resources to produce a sufficient amount of original content to fill it. Moreover, despite the stricter FCC and industry-mandated disclosure rules, a 2006 Center for Media and Democracy study of 69 stations with a total audience of half the country found that while all made use of VNR, not a single station identified them as such (Barstow, 2006). So where the problem for broadcasters is identification and disclosure, the problem for media literate viewers is recognizing VNR. "Discerning real news from pitches has never been harder," according to *Broadcasting & Cable*'s Joe Mandese (2005, p. 24), because VNR typically

- look exactly like genuine news reports, employing the visual and aural conventions we typically associate with television news.
- are narrated by a speaker whose voice, intonation, and delivery match those of a bona fide television news reporter.
- carry the voice-over on a separate audio channel so the station can delete the original narration and have its own anchor or reporter narrate to give the appearance that the report originated locally.
- are accompanied by a script in the event the local station wants its own personnel to do the narration but needs help in writing it.
- come free of titles or other graphics because local stations have their own logos and video character typefaces.

VNR can be used in their entirety or in part, and the companies that produce them consider even a 5-second excerpt aired on a local news show a success. Many stations follow federal rules and industry ethics on disclosure, but often they do so in the "film and video provided by" scroll that flies by at the end of the broadcast, making the matching of source to content difficult. In the end, then, viewers must often depend on their own media literacy skills when confronting VNR.

In instances when a reporter or anchor acknowledges the outside source of a report while it airs, viewers must determine what level of trust they want to give the story. Not all VNR are false or misleading. If we accept that they

According to the Center for Media and Democracy, in January 2006 not a single television news operation receiving this Medialink-produced video on the glowing future of ethanol manufacturing identified it for what it was—a VNR commissioned by Siemens AG, a global engineering corporation that supplies automation systems to two-thirds of the world's ethanol plants.

are created to further a particular individual's or organization's interests, they can provide useful information. In those cases where the source is not identified or is identified apart from the report, media literate people should question not only the report but the value of a news operation that has such limited regard for its viewers.

The question remains, though, of how to identify a VNR when the station fails to do so. This is actually a relatively easy skill to acquire. We are watching a VNR when

- the report is accompanied by visuals that are not from the station's broadcast area.
- no local station personnel appear in the report.
- there is no verbal or visual attribution (for example, "These scenes are from our sister station in Memphis" or a network logo in the corner of the screen).
- the report appears in the part of the newscast typically reserved for soft or feature stories.

LIVING MEDIA LITERACY

Practice Public Relations

We've read in this chapter that despite its sometimes conflicted reputation, public relations often serves quite noble ends. We saw this, for example, in the Race for the Cure campaign from the opening vignette. But media literate individuals can decide for themselves about the value of PR by making it a living enterprise, that is, by actually engaging in the practice of public relations.

There are a number of ways that this can be done. First, every college and university has a public relations office. It might be called Public Information or Relations with Schools or some similar name, but your campus has one. Visit it and talk to the professionals there about what it is they do, how they operate, whom they identify as their primary publics, what different strategies they employ to reach each public, and what you can do to help. You may want to volunteer for a specific period of time, say, 2 weeks on a campaign that interests you—for example, an

> YOU MAY EVEN WANT TO SIGN ON FOR A FORMAL INTERNSHIP WITH THE PUBLIC INFORMATION OFFICE, AS MANY SCHOOLS ENCOURAGE THEIR STUDENTS TO GAIN PREPROFESSIONAL EXPERIENCE RIGHT ON CAMPUS.

effort to get older alums to reconnect with the campus—or a specific event, for example, an open-house weekend for prospective students. You may even want to sign on for a formal internship with that office, as many schools encourage their students to gain preprofessional experience right on campus.

A second way to experience public relations is to contact the Public Relations Student Society of America (www.prssa.org). The PRSSA is a preprofessional PR organization with 8,000 members in chapters on 248 campuses. Its primary goal is to connect student and professional PR practitioners. The PRSSA runs an annual competition—the Bateman Case Study—that allows students to engage in real-world strategic planning and creative execution. If your campus does not have a chapter, you can connect with one that does (you will be welcomed) or begin a chapter at your own school. The PRSSA Web site tells you how.

RESOURCES FOR REVIEW AND DISCUSSION

Review Points

- Public relations tells an organization's "story" to its publics (communication) and helps shape the organization and the way it performs (management).
- The history of public relations can be divided into four stages: early public relations, the propaganda–publicity stage, early two-way communication, and advanced two-way communication.
- The evolution of public relations has been shaped by advances in technology, the growth of the middle class, growth of organizations, better research tools, and professionalization.
- The publics served by the industry include employees, stockholders, communities, media, government, investment communities, and customers.
- Public relations firms provide all or some of these 14 services: community relations, counseling, development and fund-raising, employee/member relations, financial relations, government affairs, industry relations, issues management, media relations, marketing communication, minority relations and multicultural affairs, public affairs, special events and public participation, and research.
- Firms typically are organized around an executive, account executives, creative specialists, and media specialists. Larger firms typically include research, government relations, and financial services professionals.
- Globalization, specialization, and convergence—in the form of video news releases, satellite-delivered media tours, integrated marketing communications, and viral marketing—are reshaping contemporary PR.
- Trust in public relations is essential if the industry is to perform its role for its clients and publics.
- Recognizing video news releases is an increasingly important media literacy skill.

Key Terms

 Use the text's Online Learning Center at www.mhhe.com/baran5 to further your understanding of the following terminology.

flack, 342
pseudo-event, 345
public, 352
fixed-fee arrangement, 353
collateral materials, 353
lobbying, 354

spin, 356
embedded journalists, 356
focus groups, 360
greenwashing, 360
video news release, 360
satellite-delivered media tour, 360

integrated marketing communications (IMC), 361
viral marketing, 361

Questions for Review

 Go to the self-quizzes on the Online Learning Center to test your knowledge.

1. Good definitions of public relations should contain what two elements?
2. What are the four stages in the development of the public relations industry?
3. Who are Ivy Lee, George Creel, and Edward Bernays?
4. What are the CPI and OWI? What is their importance to the development of public relations?
5. Who are George Gallup and Elmo Roper?
6. What is the difference between public relations and advertising?
7. What are some specific divisions of public relations' public affairs activities?
8. Who are public relations' publics? What are their characteristics?
9. What positions typically exist in a public relations operation?
10. How have new communication technologies influenced the public relations industry?
11. What is integrated marketing communications? What is its goal?
12. What is viral marketing? How does it work?

Questions for Critical Thinking and Discussion

1. Are you familiar with any of the companies identified in the opening vignette that are associated with Race for the Cure? What was your opinion of those companies before you read of their support for the fight against breast cancer? What is your opinion now? Does community relations such as this really work, or do most people see it as self-serving? Do you agree or disagree that a company's precrisis reputation can help it weather a crisis should one occur? Why or why not?

2. Have you ever been part of an Internet-fueled movement against the activities of an organization or in support of some good cause? If you were, you were engaged in public relations. Measure your experience against the lessons in this chapter. What kinds of public relations activities did you undertake? Who were your publics? Were you successful? Why or why not?

3. Were you moved at all by the images from the war in Iraq identified in the Cultural Forum box before they were exposed as spin? Were you aware before reading this chapter that they had, in fact, been PR exercises, not authentic, spontaneous events? When you discovered the spin, whom did you fault, the spinners or the media that carried the spin, or both? Do you share PR pro Seitel's conviction that spin is not PR and should never be used? Why or why not?

4. Reread the Dowie quote on page 364. Do you agree with his assessment of the profession? What is your feeling about public relations? When do you think it is useful for the culture? When do you think it is harmful?

5. Would you consider a career in public relations? If not, why not? If yes, what attracts you to this profession? Is there a specific aspect of its operation that interests you more than others? Why?

Important Resources

 Go to the Online Learning Center for additional readings.

Internet Resources

Public Relations Society of America	www.prsa.org
MADD	www.madd.org
SADD	www.sadd.org
Public Relations History	www.prmuseum.com
Canadian Public Relations Society	www.cprs.ca
Public Relations Students Society of America	www.prssa.org
Council of Public Relations Firms	www.prfirms.org
PR Watch	www.prwatch.org
Check PR Claims	www.disinfopedia.org
PR Statistics and Commentary	www.odwyerpr.com
International Communications Consultancy Organisation	www.iccopr.com
Edward Bernays	www.lib.uwo.ca/business/bernays.html

Advertising

12

LEARNING OBJECTIVES

Advertising is everywhere. And as it becomes more ubiquitous, we tend to ignore it. But as we tend to ignore it, advertisers find new ways to make it more ubiquitous. As a result, and as with television, no one is neutral about advertising. We love it or we hate it. Many of us do both. After studying this chapter you should

- be familiar with the history and development of the advertising industry.
- understand contemporary criticisms and defenses of advertising.
- recognize how the organizational and economic nature of the contemporary advertising industry shapes the content of advertising.
- be familiar with different types of advertising and their goals.
- understand the relationship between advertising content and its consumers.
- possess improved media literacy skills when consuming advertising, especially when interpreting intentional imprecision.

Your roommates, both advertising majors, challenge you: "We bet you $10 that you can't go all of tomorrow without seeing an ad." You think, "I'll just stay away from radio and television—no problem, considering I have a CD player in my car and tons of homework to do." That leaves newspapers and magazines, but you can avoid their ads simply by not reading either for 24 hours. Online ads? You'll simply stay unlinked. "What about billboards?" you counter.

"We won't count them," your roomies graciously concede, "but everything else is in."

You shake hands and go to bed planning your strategy. This means no cereal in the morning—the Cheerios box has a McDonald's ad on it. There'll be no bus to school. Not only are the insides packed with ads, but a lot of buses are now covered in vinyl wrap ads that let riders see out the windows but turn buses into gigantic rolling commercials. Can't walk either. There are at least two ad kiosks on the way. It'll cost you more than $10 to take a cab, but this is about winning the bet, not about money. Cab it will be! You sleep well, confident victory will be yours.

Opposite: Advertising is increasingly segmented and fragmented.

The next evening, over pizza, you hand over your $10.

"What was it?" gloats one of your companions. "Sneak a peek at TV?"

"No," you say, and then you begin the list: The cab had an ad for a radio station on its trunk and a three-sided sign on its roof touting the pizza joint you're sitting in, a chiropractor, and American Airlines. Inside, it had an electronic digital display hanging from the ceiling, pushing the lottery. The sidewalk near campus had the message "From here it looks like you could use some new underwear—Bamboo Lingerie" stenciled on it in water-soluble iridescent red paint. The restrooms on campus have Volkswagen ads pasted on their walls. Your ATM receipt carried an ad for a brokerage firm. You encountered a Domino's Pizza ad on the back of the cash register receipt you got at the grocery store; the kiwi you bought there had a sticker on it reminding you to buy Snapple. The shopping basket had a realtor's pitch pasted to the side; even the little rubber bar you used to separate your kiwi and mineral water from the groceries of the shopper in front of you had an ad on each of its four sides.

"Easiest $10 we ever made," smile your roommates.

In this chapter we examine the history of advertising, focusing on its maturation with the coming of industrialization and the Civil War. The development of the advertising agency and the rise of professionalism within its ranks are detailed, as is the impact of magazines, radio, World War II, and television.

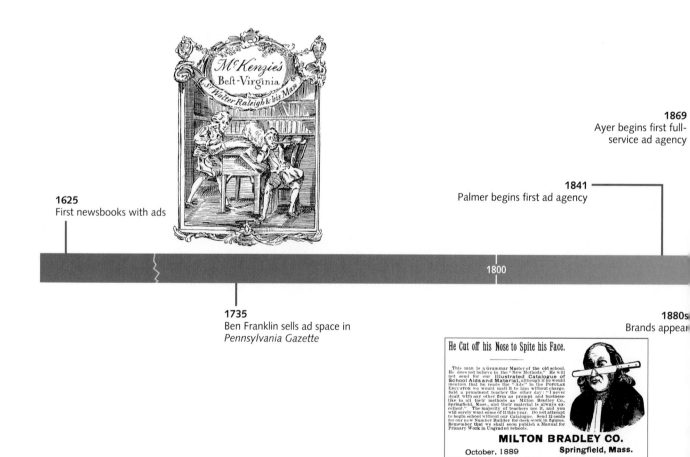

1625
First newsbooks with ads

1735
Ben Franklin sells ad space in *Pennsylvania Gazette*

1800

1841
Palmer begins first ad agency

1869
Ayer begins first full-service ad agency

1880s
Brands appear

We discuss the relationship between consumers and contemporary advertising in terms of how advertising agencies are structured, how various types of advertising are aimed at different audiences, and which trends—converging technologies, audience segmentation, globalization—promise to alter those relationships.

We study the controversies that surround the industry. Critics charge that advertising is intrusive, deceptive, inherently unethical when aimed at children, and corrupting of the culture. We look at industry defenses, too.

Finally, in the media literacy skills section, we discuss advertisers' use of intentional imprecision and how to identify and interpret it.

Even in death, it's difficult to avoid advertising.

A Short History of Advertising

Your roommates had the advantage. They know that U.S. advertisers and marketers spend $500 billion a year—half the world's total—trying to get your attention and influence your decisions (Auletta, 2005b). They also know that you typically encounter 3,500 to 5,000 commercial messages a day—as opposed to 500 to 2,000 a day in the 1970s (Howard, 2005). There are a lot

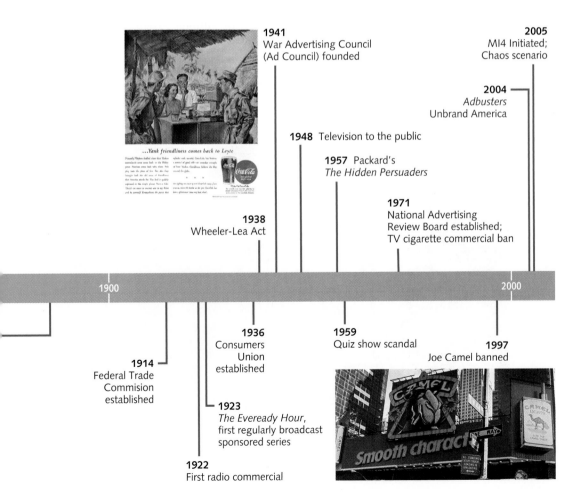

1941
War Advertising Council (Ad Council) founded

2005
MI4 Initiated; Chaos scenario

2004
Adbusters Unbrand America

1948 Television to the public

1957 Packard's *The Hidden Persuaders*

1971
National Advertising Review Board established; TV cigarette commercial ban

1938
Wheeler-Lea Act

1900

2000

1914
Federal Trade Commision established

1936
Consumers Union established

1959
Quiz show scandal

1997
Joe Camel banned

1923
The Eveready Hour, first regularly broadcast sponsored series

1922
First radio commercial

This narrow street in Salzburg, Austria, still exhibits evidence of early European advertising, which often took the form of artistically designed signs announcing the nature of the business below.

of ads and a lot of advertisers, so pitches are showing up in some unusual places. Many public schools sell ad space on their lunch menus. Geico insurance places ads on the turnstiles of Chicago's transit system. CBS touts its new television series with ads stuck to office water coolers. We can relax during December and January and watch some college football, maybe the FedEx Orange Bowl, or the Chick-fil-A Peach Bowl, or the Tostitos Fiesta Bowl. Sony hired graffiti artists in seven major cities, including Philadelphia, Chicago, Atlanta, and New York, to spray-paint commercials for its PlayStation Portable on walls and buildings. The tiny Texas town of Clark changed its name to Dish in a promotional deal with satellite television company Dish Network. A New Jersey company sculpts clients' logos into fresh beach sand so that their ad greets morning beachgoers. Officials in Brooklawn, New Jersey, sell naming rights to school facilities—the gym at the Alice Costello Elementary School is now the ShopRite of Brooklawn Center. Coke is the official drink of Ocean City, Maryland. Nissan is the official truck, Speedo the official bathing suit, and Naya Canadian the official bottled water of Los Angeles County's Department of Beaches and Harbors. MasterCard is the official credit card of South Orange, New Jersey. Sony Ericsson hires actors to pose as tourists, walk up to people, and ask them to photograph them with its new line of phonecams. We see ads on door hangers, on urinal deodorant cakes, in the mail, behind the batter at a baseball game, on basketball

Advertising everywhere— Sony hired graffiti artists in several major American cities to spray-paint commercials for its PlayStation Portable on walls and buildings.

backboards in city parks, on suspended video monitors as we wait in line at the amusement park. We hear ads when we're on hold on the telephone. It wasn't always like this, but advertising itself has been with us for a long time.

EARLY ADVERTISING

Babylonian merchants were hiring barkers to shout out goods and prices at passersby in 3000 B.C.E. The Romans wrote announcements on city walls. This ad was discovered in the ruins of Pompeii:

> The Troop of Gladiators of the Aedil
> Will fight on the 31st of May
> There will be fights with wild animals
> And an Awning to keep off the sun. (Berkman & Gilson, 1987, p. 32)

By the 15th century, ads as we know them now were abundant in Europe. **Siquis**—pinup want ads for all sorts of products and services—were common. Tradespeople promoted themselves with **shopbills,** attractive, artful business cards. Taverners and other merchants were hanging eye-catching signs above their businesses. In 1625 the first **newsbook** containing ads, *The Weekly News*, was printed in England. From the beginning, those who had products and services to offer used advertising.

Advertising came to the Colonies via England. British advertising was already leaning toward exaggeration and hyperbole, but colonial advertising was more straightforward. We saw in Chapter 4 that Ben Franklin was selling advertising space in his *Pennsylvania Gazette*. This 1735 ad is typical:

> A Plantation containing 300 acres of good Land, 30 cleared, 10 or 12 Meadow and in good English Grass, a house and barn & c. [creek] lying in Nantmel Township, upon French-Creek, about 30 miles from Philadelphia. Inquire of Simon Meredith now living on the said place. (Sandage, Fryburger, & Rotzoll, 1989, p. 21)

Advertising, however, was a small business before the Civil War. The United States was primarily an agricultural country at that time, with 90% of the population living in self-sufficiency on farms. Advertising was used by local retailers primarily to encourage area residents to come to their businesses. The local newspaper was the major advertising medium.

INDUSTRIALIZATION AND THE CIVIL WAR

The Industrial Revolution and the Civil War altered the social and cultural landscape and brought about the expansion of advertising. By the 1840s the telegraph made communication over long distances possible. Railroads linked cities and states. Huge numbers of immigrants were welcomed to the

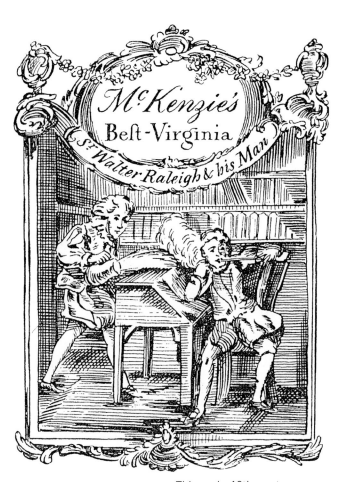

This early-18th-century tobacco label shows that the British had already mastered the use of celebrities in their advertising.

Advertising History
www.scriptorium.lib.duke.edu/hartman

Magazines provided the first national medium for advertisers. Here is an imaginative ad for the famous Milton Bradley game company.

He Cut off his Nose to Spite his Face.

This man is a Grammar Master of the old school. He does not believe in the "New Methods." He will not send for our **Illustrated Catalogue of School Aids and Material,** although if he would mention that he reads the "Ads" in the POPULAR EDUCATOR we would mail it to him without charge. Said a prominent teacher the other day: "I never dealt with any other firm as prompt and business-like in all their methods as Milton Bradley Co., Springfield, Mass., and their material is always excellent." The majority of teachers use it, and you will surely want some of it this year. Do not attempt to begin school without our Catalogue. Send 12 cents for our new Number Builder for desk-work in figures. Remember that we shall soon publish a Manual for Primary Work in Ungraded Schools.

MILTON BRADLEY CO.
October, 1889   **Springfield, Mass.**

United States to provide labor for the expanding factories. Manufacturers wanted access to larger markets for their goods. Advertising copywriter Volney B. Palmer recognized in 1841 that merchants needed to reach consumers beyond their local newspaper readership. He contacted several Philadelphia newspapers and agreed to broker the sale of space between them and interested advertisers. Within 4 years Palmer had expanded his business to Boston, and in 1849, he opened a branch in New York. The advertising agency had been invented.

The Civil War sped industrialization. More factories were needed to produce war material, and roads and railroads were expanded to move that material as well as troops. As farmworkers went to war or to work in the new factories, more farm machinery was needed to compensate for their departure. That meant that more factories were needed to make more machinery, and the cycle repeated.

By the early 1880s the telephone and the electric light had been invented. That decade saw numerous innovations in manufacturing as well as an explosion in the type and availability of products. In the year 1880 alone, there were applications for more than 13,000 U.S. copyrights and patents. Over 70,000 miles of new railroad track were laid in the 1880s, linking cities and towns of all sizes. With more producers chasing the growing purchasing power of more consumers, manufacturers were forced to differentiate their products—to literally and figuratively take the pickle out of the barrel and put it in its own recognizable package. Brands were born: Quaker Oats, Ivory Soap, Royal Baking Powder, and many more. What advertisers now needed was a medium in which to tell people about these brands.

MAGAZINE ADVERTISING

We've seen in Chapter 5 how expansion of the railroads, the rise in literacy, and advantageous postal rates fueled the explosive growth of the popular magazine just before the end of the 19th century. The marriage of magazines and advertising was a natural. Cyrus H. K. Curtis, who founded the *Ladies' Home Journal* in 1883, told a group of manufacturers:

The editor of the Ladies' Home Journal thinks we publish it for the benefit of American women. This is an illusion, but a very proper one for him to have. The real reason, the publisher's [Curtis's] reason, is to give you who manufacture things American women want, a chance to tell them about your product. (Sandage et al., 1989, p. 32)

By the turn of the century magazines were financially supported primarily by their advertisers rather than by their readers, and aspects of advertising we find common today—creativity in look and language, mail-order ads, seasonal ads, and placement of ads in proximity to content of related interest—were already in use.

THE ADVERTISING AGENCY AND PROFESSIONALISM

In the years between the Civil War and World War I, advertising had rapidly become more complex, more creative, and more expensive, and it was conducted on a larger scale. Advertising agencies had to expand their operations to keep up with demand. Where Palmer offered merely to broker the sale of newspaper space, F. Wayland Ayer (whose firm is now the oldest ad agency in the United States) began his "full service" advertising agency in 1869. He named his firm N. W. Ayer and Sons after his father because, at only 20 years old, he felt that clients would not trust him with their business. Ayer (the son) provided clients with ad campaign planning, created and produced ads with his staff of artists and writers, and placed them in the most appropriate media. Some other big agencies still operating today started at this time, including J. Walter Thompson, William Esty, and Lord & Thomas.

During this period, three factors combined to move the advertising industry to establish professional standards and to regulate itself. First was the reaction of the public and the medical profession to the abuses of patent medicine advertisers. These charlatans used fake claims and medical data in their ads to sell tonics that at best were useless, and at worst, deadly. The second was the critical examination of most of the country's important institutions, led by the muckrakers (Chapter 5). The third factor was the establishment in 1914 of the Federal Trade Commission (FTC), which had among its duties monitoring and regulating advertising. A number of leading advertising agencies and publishers mounted a crusade against gross exaggeration, false testimonials, and other misleading forms of advertising. The Audit Bureau of Circulations was established to verify circulation claims. The Advertising Federation of America (now the American Advertising Federation), the American Association of Advertising Agencies, the Association of National Advertisers, and the Outdoor Advertising Association all began operation at this time.

ADVERTISING AND RADIO

The first radio ad, as we've seen in Chapter 7, was broadcast on WEAF in 1922 (the cost was $50 for a 10-minute spot). Radio was important to advertising in three major ways. First, although people both inside and outside government were opposed to commercial support for the new medium, the general public

www

Audit Bureau of Circulations
www.accessabc.com

www

National Advertising Review Council
www.nadreview.org

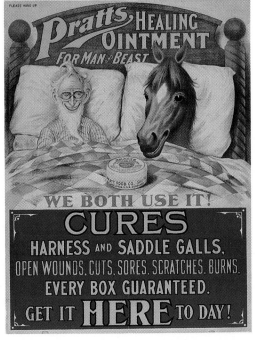

Reaction to the deception and outright lies of patent medicine advertising—such as this 1880 piece for Pratts Healing Ointment—led to important efforts to professionalize the industry.

A Plymouth hard-sell ad from 1931. The hard sell made its debut during the Depression as advertisers worked to attract the little consumer money that was available.

WWW
American Advertising Federation
www.aaf.org

WWW
Ad Council
www.adcouncil.org

had no great opposition to radio ads. In fact, in the prosperous Roaring Twenties, many welcomed them; advertising seemed a natural way to keep radio "free." Second, advertising agencies virtually took over broadcasting, producing the shows in which their commercials appeared. The ad business became show business. The 1923 variety show *The Eveready Hour,* sponsored by a battery maker, was the first regularly broadcast sponsored series. Ad agency Blackett-Sample-Hummert even developed a new genre for its client Procter & Gamble—the radio soap opera. Third, money now poured into the industry. That money was used to expand research and marketing on a national scale, allowing advertisers access to sophisticated nationwide consumer and market information for the first time. The wealth that the advertising industry accrued from radio permitted it to survive during the Depression.

The Depression did have its effect on advertising, however. The stock market crashed in 1929, and by 1933 advertising had lost nearly two-thirds of its revenues. Among the responses were the hard sell—making direct claims about why a consumer *needed* a product—and a tendency away from honesty. At the same time, widespread unemployment and poverty bred a powerful consumer movement. The Consumers Union, which still publishes *Consumer Reports,* was founded in 1936 to protect people from unscrupulous manufacturers and advertisers. And in 1938 Congress passed the Wheeler-Lea Act, granting the FTC extended powers to regulate advertising.

WORLD WAR II

The Second World War, so important in the development of all the mass media, had its impact on advertising as well. Production of consumer products came to a near halt during the war (1941–1945), and traditional advertising was limited. The advertising industry turned its collective skills toward the war effort, and the limited product advertising typically adopted a patriotic theme.

In 1941 several national advertising and media associations joined to develop the War Advertising Council. The council used its expertise to promote numerous government programs. Its best-known campaign, however, was on behalf of the sale of war bonds. The largest campaign to date for a single item, the war bond program helped sell 800 million bonds, totaling $45 billion. When the war ended, the group, now called the Advertising Council, directed its efforts toward a host of public service campaigns on behalf of countless nonprofit organizations (see the essay on p. 380, "Effecting Positive Social Change"). Most of us have read or heard, "This message is brought to you by the Ad Council."

The impact of World War II on the size and structure of the advertising industry was significant. A high excess-profits tax was levied on manufacturers' wartime profits that exceeded prewar levels. The goal was to limit war profiteering and ensure that companies did not benefit too greatly from the death and destruction of war. Rather than pay the heavy tariff, manufacturers reduced their profit levels by putting income back into their businesses. Because the lack of raw materials made expansion or recapitalization difficult, many companies invested in corporate image advertising. They may not have

...*Yank friendliness comes back to Leyte*

Naturally Filipinos thrilled when their Yankee comrades-in-arms came back to the Philippines. Freedom came back with them. Fair play took the place of fear. But also they brought back the old sense of friendliness that America stands for. You find it quickly expressed in the simple phrase *Have a Coke.* There's no easier or warmer way to say *Relax and be yourself.* Everywhere *the pause that*

refreshes with ice-cold Coca-Cola has become a symbol of good will—an everyday example of how Yankee friendliness follows the flag around the globe.

* * *

Our fighting men meet up with Coca-Cola many places overseas, where it's bottled on the spot. Coca-Cola has been a globe-trotter "since way back when".

Coca-Cola
-the global high-sign

"Coke" = Coca-Cola
You naturally hear Coca-Cola called by its friendly abbreviation "Coke". Both mean the quality product of The Coca-Cola Company.

COPYRIGHT 1945, THE COCA-COLA COMPANY

Consumer products go to war. Advertisers and manufacturers joined the war effort. These GIs are enjoying a Coke on Leyte Island in the Pacific in a 1945 *Collier's* ad.

had products to sell to the public, but they knew that the war would end someday and that stored-up goodwill would be important. One result, therefore, was an expansion in the number and size of manufacturers' advertising departments and of advertising agencies. A second result was a public primed by that advertising anticipating the return of consumer goods.

ADVERTISING AND TELEVISION

There was no shortage of consumer products when the war ended. The nation's manufacturing capacity had been greatly expanded to meet the needs of war, and now that manufacturing capability was turned toward the production of consumer products for people who found themselves with more leisure and more money (Chapter 1). People were also having more children and, thanks to the GI Bill, were able to think realistically about owning their own homes. They wanted products to enhance their leisure, please their children, and fill their houses.

USING MEDIA TO MAKE A DIFFERENCE

Effecting Positive Social Change

Advertising can often lead people to do good, and there is no better example of this than the work of the Ad Council. In fact, its mission is "Effecting Positive Social Change." Has it succeeded in making a difference? Who are Smokey the Bear, Rosie the Riveter, McGruff the Crime Dog, the Crash Test Dummies, and the Crying Indian (Chief Iron Eyes Cody)? All are creations of the Ad Council. And with how many of these slogans are you familiar?

- Loose lips sink ships
- Friends don't let friends drive drunk
- Only you can prevent forest fires
- A mind is a terrible thing to waste
- Just say no
- Take a bite out of crime
- I am an American

All are from Ad Council campaigns. Can the ability of the Ad Council to make a difference be quantified? Consider the following:

- Applications for mentors rose from 90,000 a year to 620,000 in the first 9 months after the start of its campaign for Big Brothers/Big Sisters.
- Safety belt use rose from 14% to 79% of drivers since the Ad Council launched its seat belt campaign in 1985.

- Since 1972, the United Negro College Fund campaign—A Mind Is a Terrible Thing to Waste—has raised more than $2 billion and graduated 300,000 minority students.

- The amount of waste Americans recycle has increased 385% since the start of the Environmental Defense campaign in the 1980s (www.adcouncil.org).

> THE AD COUNCIL CURRENTLY HAS MORE THAN 40 DIFFERENT PUBLIC SERVICE CAMPAIGNS ON ITS DOCKET, AND IT IS ABLE TO SECURE ABOUT $1.5 BILLION A YEAR IN DONATED TIME AND SPACE FROM 28,000 DIFFERENT MEDIA OUTLETS.

The Ad Council currently has more than 40 different public service campaigns on its docket, and it is able to secure about $1.5 billion a year in donated time and space from 28,000 different media outlets ("Story," 2001). Its primary focus today is kids' issues, devoting 80% of its resources to its 10-Year Commitment to Children: Helping Parents Help Kids campaign. But the Ad Council does not shy away from controversial issues. In the 1970s it took on sexually transmitted disease with its "VD Is for Everyone" campaign, an effort attacked by many religious groups, and many broadcasters refused to air its "Help Stop AIDS. Use a Condom" spots in 1987.

The Ad Council is able to make a difference because dozens of ad agencies, big and small, donate their time, energy, and creativity. In fact, it is quite common to have several competing for the honor of taking on a particular pro bono campaign in order to put "advertising in the service of righteousness" ("Story," 2001, p. 11).

Advertising was well positioned to put products and people together, not only because agencies had expanded during the war but also because of television. Radio formats, stars, and network structure had moved wholesale to the new medium. Television soon became the primary national advertising medium. Advertisers bought $12 million in television time in 1949; 2 years later they spent $128 million.

Television commercials, by virtue of the fact that consumers could see and hear the product in action, were different from the advertising of all other media. The ability to demonstrate the product—to do the torture test for Timex watches, to smoothly shave sandpaper with Gillette Foamy—led to the **unique selling proposition (USP)**—that is, highlighting the aspect of a product that sets it apart from other brands in the same product category. Once an advertiser discovered a product's USP, it could drive it home in repeated demonstration commercials. Inasmuch as most brands in a given product category are essentially the same—that is, they are **parity products**—advertisers were often forced to create a product's USP. Candy is candy, for example, but M&Ms are unique—they melt in your mouth, not in your hand.

Some observers were troubled by this development. Increasingly, products were being sold not by touting their value or quality but by emphasizing their

www

Television Bureau of Advertising
www.tvb.org

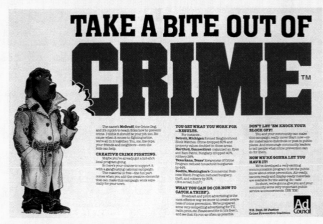

The Ad Council has been using the skill of industry pros to effect positive social change for decades. How many of these campaigns do you recognize?

unique selling propositions. Ads were offering little information about the product, yet people were increasing their spending. This led to growing criticism of advertising and its contribution to the consumer culture (more on this controversy later in the chapter). The immediate impact was the creation of an important vehicle of industry self-regulation. In response to mounting criticism in books such as *The Hidden Persuaders* (Packard, 1957), and concern over increasing scrutiny from the FTC, the industry in 1971 established the National Advertising Review Board (NARB) to monitor potentially deceptive advertising. The NARB, the industry's most important self-regulatory body, investigates consumer complaints as well as complaints made by an advertiser's competitors.

Advertising and Its Audiences

The typical individual living in the United States will spend more than 1 year of his or her life just watching television commercials. It is a rare moment when we are not in the audience of some ad or commercial. This is one of the many reasons advertisers have begun to place their messages in many venues beyond the traditional commercial media (called **ambient advertising**),

WWW

Better Business Bureau's Ad Pledge Program

www.bbb.org/app/appworks.asp

THUNDERING HOOFS OF RACE HORSE TEST TIMEX SHOCK RESISTANCE

Among the earliest demonstration ads, Timex took many a licking but kept on ticking.

hoping to draw our attention. We confront so many ads every day that we overlook them, and they become invisible. As a result, many people become aware of advertising only when it somehow offends them.

CRITICISMS AND DEFENSES OF ADVERTISING

Advertising does sometimes offend, and it is often the focus of criticism. But industry defenders argue the following:

- Advertising supports our economic system; without it new products could not be introduced and developments in others could not be announced. Competitive advertising of new products and businesses powers the engine of our economy, fostering economic growth and creating jobs in many industries.

- People use advertising to gather information before making buying decisions.

- Ad revenues make possible the "free" mass media we use not only for entertainment but for the maintenance of our democracy.

- By showing us the bounty of our capitalistic, free enterprise society, advertising increases national productivity (as people work harder to acquire more of these products) and improves the standard of living (as people actually acquire more of these products).

The first defense is a given. Ours is a capitalistic society whose economy depends on the exchange of goods and services. Complaints, then, have less to do with the existence of advertising than with its conduct and content, and they are not new. At the 1941 founding meeting of the Advertising Council, J. Walter Thompson executive James Webb Young argued that such a public service commitment would go far toward improving the public's attitude toward his industry, one "rooted very deep. It is a sort of repugnance for the manifestations of advertising—or its banality, its bad taste, its moronic appeals, and its clamor" (quoted in "Story of the Ad Council," 2001). The second defense assumes that advertising provides information. But much—critics would say most—advertising is void of useful information about the product. Grant Leach, managing director of the ad agency The Revo Group, declares, "Consumers no longer buy products but rather lifestyles and the stories, experiences, and emotions products convey" (quoted in Williams, 2002, p. 17). The third defense assumes that the only way media can exist is through commercial support, but many nations around the world have built fine media systems without heavy advertiser support (see Chapter 15). To critics of advertising, the fourth defense—that people work hard only to acquire more things and that our standard of living is measured by what material things we have—draws an unflattering picture of human nature.

STATEMENT	% RESPONDING "YES"
1. I resist being exposed to or paying attention to marketing.	54%
2. I avoid buying products that overwhelm me with their marketing.	56%
3. I am interested in products that permit blocking, skipping, or opting out of their marketing.	69%

Figure 12.1 Resistant Consumers, 2005—Americans Turn Away from Traditional Advertising Messages.
Source: Yankelovich Marketing Receptivity Study (in O'Brien, 2006).

SPECIFIC COMPLAINTS

Specific complaints about advertising are that it is often intrusive, deceptive, and, in the case of children's advertising, inherently unethical. Advertising is said to demean or corrupt the culture.

Advertising Is Intrusive Many critics fault advertising for its intrusiveness. Advertising is everywhere, and it interferes with and alters our experience. Giant wall advertisements change the look of cities. Ads beamed by laser light onto night skies destroy evening stargazing. School learning aids provided by candy makers that ask students to "count the Tootsie Rolls" alter education. Many Internet users complain about the commercialization of the new medium and fear advertising will alter its free, open, and freewheeling nature. And as you can see in Figure 12.1, majorities of Americans resist exposure to ads, avoid buying too heavily advertised products, and seek various means of blocking out or otherwise opting out of commercial messages.

Advertising Is Deceptive Many critics say that much advertising is inherently deceptive in that it implicitly and sometimes explicitly promises to improve people's lives through the consumption or purchase of a sponsor's products. Jamieson and Campbell (1997) described this as the "If . . . then" strategy: "A beautiful woman uses a certain brand of lipstick in the ad, and men follow her everywhere. Without making the argument explicit, the ad implies that if you use this product you will be beautiful, and if you are beautiful (or use this product), you will be more attractive to men" (p. 242). They called the opposite strategy "If not . . . then not." When Hallmark says "When you care enough to send the very best," the implication is that when you do not send Hallmark, you simply do not care.

Advertising promises health, long life, sexual success, financial success, companionship, popularity, and acceptance. Industry defenders argue that people understand and accept these as allowable exaggerations, not as deception.

Advertising Exploits Children The average American child sees more than 40,000 television commercials a year, up from 20,000 in the 1970s (Fonda, 2004). Countries like Norway and Sweden, on the other hand, ban television ads aimed at kids altogether, as does the Canadian province of Quebec. Ads and commercialism are increasingly invading the schools—the amount of sponsored educational material used in American schools rose 1,800% in the 1990s alone ("Ad, Subtract," 2001). Companies spend about $14.4 billion a year marketing products to children, and typical kids recognize more than 200 logos by the time they enroll in first grade ("Noted," 2004). Even 61% of

Campaign for a Commercial-free Childhood
www.commercialexploitation.org

Advertising in schools and on educational materials is now common—and quite controversial.

youth marketers polled in a 2004 survey felt that "advertising to children starts too young" (Fonda, 2004, p. 52).

Critics contend that children are simply not intellectually capable of interpreting the intent of these ads, nor are they able before the age of 7 or 8 to rationally judge the worth of the advertising claims (see the essay on p. 385, "Boosting Smoking Among Children"). This makes children's advertising inherently unethical. Television advertising to kids is especially questionable because children consume it in the home—with implicit parental approval, and most often without parental supervision. The question ad critics ask is, "If parents would never allow living salespeople to enter their homes to sell their children products, why do they allow the most sophisticated salespeople of all to do it for 20 minutes every hour every Saturday morning?" Rowan Williams, upon his installation as Archbishop of Canterbury in 2002, spoke not of the ethics of advertising to kids but of the morality. "If a child is a consumer, the child is an economic subject. And what economic subjects do is commit their capital, limit their options by doing so, take risks for profit or gratification." His argument, according to education writer Laura Barton (2002, p. 2), is that "at a time in our lives when the future should be wide open (that is, childhood), we are increasingly encouraged to hem ourselves in, to define ourselves by the trainers [sneakers] we wear and the yogurts we eat. As such, advertising campaigns aimed directly at children amount to a perversion of innocence."

Advertising Demeans and Corrupts Culture   In our culture we value beauty, kindness, prestige, family, love, and success. As human beings we need food, shelter, and the maintenance of the species, in other words, sex. Advertising succeeds by appealing to these values and needs. The basis for this persuasive strategy is the **AIDA approach**—to persuade consumers, advertising must attract *attention*, create *interest*, stimulate *desire,* and promote *action.* According to industry critics, however, problems arise when important aspects of human existence are reduced to the consumption of brand-name consumer products. Freedom is choosing between a Big Gulp and a canned soda at 7-Eleven. Being a good mother is as simple as buying a bottle of Downy Fabric Softener. Success is drinking Chivas Regal. Love is giving your

MEDIA HISTORY REPEATS

Boosting Smoking Among Children

In the 1980s as U.S. levels of smoking continued to decline, RJR Nabisco introduced a new ad campaign for its Camel brand cigarettes. The campaign featured a sun-bleached, cool, and casual camel who possessed human qualities. Joe Camel, as he was called, was debonair, in control, and the center of attention, whether in a pool hall, on a dance floor, leaning against his convertible, or lounging on the beach. He wore the hippest clothes. He sported the best sunglasses. RJR Nabisco said it was trying a new campaign to boost brand awareness and corner a larger portion of a dwindling market. But antismoking groups saw in Joe Camel a repeat of Edward Bernays's strategy to open smoking to an untapped market (Chapter 11). They accused the company of attempting to attract young smokers—often adding that these were the lifelong customers the tobacco company needed to replace those it was killing.

The battle heated up in 1991, and an entire issue of the *Journal of the American Medical Association* was devoted to the impact of smoking on the culture. One of the articles reported on a study of Joe Camel's appeal to youngsters. Researcher Dr. Joseph DiFranza had discovered that Joe Camel was the single most recognizable logo in the country. Children as young as 3 years old could recognize Joe, and more kids could identify him than could identify Mickey Mouse.

RJR Nabisco attempted to discredit the study and its author and claimed that it had a First Amendment right to advertise its legal product any way it wanted. Nonetheless, soon after the publication of the *JAMA* issue, antismoking activist Janet Mangini filed a lawsuit in San Francisco against the tobacco company. Several California counties and cities joined the suit, alleging that the Joe Camel campaign violated state consumer protection laws designed to protect minors from false or misleading tobacco advertising.

Just before it was to go to trial in 1997, the country's second largest tobacco company, while admitting no wrongdoing, agreed to settle out of court with a payment of $10 million. It also agreed to a court order to suspend the Joe

"TO ENSURE INCREASED AND LONG-TERM GROWTH FOR CAMEL FILTER, THE BRAND MUST INCREASE ITS SHARE PENETRATION AMONG THE 14–24 AGE GROUP."

Camel campaign, the first time in history that a tobacco company had done so. What may have encouraged the cigarette company to cooperate were internal memos in the hands of the court that would later be made public. An R. J. Reynolds Tobacco memo from 1975 said: "To ensure increased and long-term growth for Camel Filter, the brand must increase its share penetration among the 14–24 age group" ("Kids Are Getting Lost," 1998, p. 10A). Other memos identified target smokers as young as 12 years old.

Edward Bernays said that had he known about the health risks involved with smoking, he would not have planned the Lucky Strike "Torches of Liberty" campaign back in 1929. What justification for the Joe Camel campaign would you give if you were part of the ad team that developed the character, or if you worked for an ad agency that placed the ads, or if you were the editor at a magazine that ran them?

Joe Camel was ubiquitous . . . and controversial.

husband a shirt without ring-around-the-collar or your fiancée a diamond worth 2 months' salary (see the essay on p. 387, "Challenging Advertising: Adbusters and Uncommercials").

Critics argue that ours has become a **consumer culture**—a culture in which personal worth and identity reside not in ourselves but in the products with which we surround ourselves. The consumer culture is corrupting because it imposes new definitions that serve the advertiser and not the culture on traditionally important aspects of our lives. If love, for example, can be bought rather than being something that has to be nurtured, how important can it be? If success is not something an individual values for the personal

Doonesbury

G. B. TRUDEAU

Large advertisers such as Nike have come under much criticism for their intrusion into virtually all aspects of people's lives. Here Garry Trudeau ponders life on Planet Nike. Doonesbury © 1997 G. B. Trudeau. Reprinted with permission of Universal Press Syndicate. All Rights Reserved.

sense of accomplishment but rather is something chased for the material things associated with it, how does the culture evaluate success? Name the five most successful people you know. How many teachers did you name? How many social workers? How many wealthy or famous people did you name?

Critics further contend that the consumer culture also demeans the individuals who live in it. A common advertising strategy for stimulating desire and suggesting action is to imply that we are inadequate and should not be satisfied with ourselves as we are. We are too fat or too thin, our hair is in need of improvement, our clothes are all wrong, and our spouses don't respect us. Personal improvement is only a purchase away.

The ad-created consumer culture, according to former Wieden + Kennedy and Martin Agency executive Jelly Helm (his clients include Nike, Coke, and Microsoft), has produced an America that is "sick. . . . We work too hard so that we can buy things we don't need, made by factory workers who are paid too little, and produced in ways that threaten the very survival of the earth." It has produced an America that "will be remembered as the greatest wealth-producer ever. It will be a culture remembered for its promise and might and its tremendous achievements in technology and health. It also will be remembered as a culture of hedonism to rival any culture that has ever existed, a culture of materialism and workaholism and individualism, a culture of superficiality and disposability, of poverty and pollution and vanity and violence, a culture denuded of its spiritual wisdom" (Helm, 2002).

Challenging Advertising: Adbusters and Uncommercials

The Media Foundation operates out of Vancouver, British Columbia, with the goal of increasing public awareness of overconsumption and overcommercialization. Naturally, advertising is one of its primary targets. The group publishes a quarterly magazine called *Adbusters*, maintains an active Web site (www. adbusters.org), and sponsors events like the annual late-November "Buy Nothing Day" and the mid-April "TV Turnoff Week" (26 state governors officially endorsed this event in 1997). The group also makes print and video "uncommercials" (public service announcements that challenge well-known actual commercials), which are available at no cost to those who wish to use them to, as the Media Foundation likes to call it, "culture jam," or challenge the prevailing commercial culture.

Although its highly political and highly controversial summer 2004 anticorporate ad received much attention (and commentary), this anticommercial advocacy group sometimes has trouble getting its ideas into the cultural forum. All four major American television networks and all the commercial networks of both Australia and France refuse to sell airtime to the group for its 30-second uncommercials announcing Buy Nothing Day and TV Turnoff Week, despite its willingness to pay full commercial rates. NBC's vice president for advertising standards, Richard Gitter, told the *Wall Street Journal,* "We don't want the business. We don't want to take any advertising that's inimical to our legitimate business interests" (quoted in Media Foundation, 2002). In a letter to the Media Foundation, the General Electric–owned network explained its position more fully, saying that Buy Nothing Day "is in opposition to the current economic policy in the United States" (quoted in Media Foundation, 2002). A spokesperson for Australian television was more to the point, asking the foundation, "Who do you think you are, trying to harm our business? Do you think we're stupid? Why would we agree to air an ad our advertisers might not like?" (quoted in Media Foundation, 2002).

Other times, however, the Media Foundation has had more success. CNN willingly carries the foundation's spots. After 30 seconds of Media Foundation–sponsored blank screen during a 2001 airing of *Wolf Blitzer Reports,* network spokesperson Steven Haworth explained, "We should make our commercial space available to debate issues of the day" (Media Foundation, 2002). In the fall of 1997 the foundation was the subject of an hour-long PBS documentary called *Affluenza.* Its Joe Chemo uncommercials and antismoking posters (parodying Joe Camel) appear in thousands of stores, schools, medical and health offices, and other public places. Many cable access stations run the uncommercials, and they occasionally appear on local commercial stations as well.

Whether or not you believe this effort is effective or even necessary, if you believe in freedom of expression, you have to ask yourself whether it is proper for the commercial television networks to refuse to carry Media Foundation uncommercials. Overcommercialization is a sometimes controversial public issue. If broadcasters feel comfortable refusing to air a side of the debate that they feel is "inimical" to their "legitimate busi-

> **"WHO DO YOU THINK YOU ARE, TRYING TO HARM OUR BUSINESS? DO YOU THINK WE'RE STUPID? WHY WOULD WE AGREE TO AIR AN AD OUR ADVERTISERS MIGHT NOT LIKE?"**

ness interests," several questions arise. First, what other expressions do they deny because they run counter to their business interests? Second, if broadcasters refuse to air material that challenges a "current policy" of the nation, as many did before the invasion of Iraq in rejecting antiwar spots (Tienowitz, 2003), how will democratic debate over any significant issues ever enter the public forum? Finally, what issue *will ever* be discussed if broadcasters refuse to air material that their advertisers might not like? Measure the attitudes of the NBC and Australian television executives against that of CNN's Haworth. With which are you most comfortable? Which promises to serve the cultural forum (and therefore democracy) better? What, ask the activists at the Media Foundation, will you do about it? At the very minimum, are you willing to buy nothing during the Friday after Thanksgiving or turn your television off for a week? Are you willing to unbrand? Why or why not?

The Media Foundation's controversial 2004 culture jam.

Advertising critics fear that our growing consumer culture will produce people who define their self-worth and personal identity by the products they own rather than by who they are, as portrayed in this *Jump Start* cartoon.
JUMP START © United Feature Syndicate, Inc.

American Association of Advertising Agencies
www.aaaa.org

Scope and Nature of the Advertising Industry

The proliferation of the different types of sales pitches described in the opening vignette is the product of an avalanche of advertising. Advertisers are exploring new ways to be seen and heard, to stand out, to be remembered, and to be effective. With so many kinds of commercial messages, the definition of advertising must be very broad. For our purposes, advertising is mediated messages paid for by and identified with a business or institution seeking to increase the likelihood that those who consume those messages will act or think as the advertiser wishes.

In 2006 advertisers spent more than $292 billion to place their messages before the U.S. public and more than $604 billion to reach the world's consumers. These amounts do not include the billions of dollars spent in the planning, production, and distribution of those ads. An overwhelming proportion of all this activity is conducted through and by advertising agencies.

THE ADVERTISING AGENCY

There are approximately 6,000 ad agencies operating in the United States, employing roughly 500,000 people (Figure 12.2). Fewer than 500 agencies annually earn more than $1 million. Many agencies also produce the ads they develop, and virtually all buy time and space in various media for their clients. Production is billed at an agreed-upon price called a **retainer;** placement of advertising in media is compensated through **commissions,** typically 15% of the cost of the time or space. Commissions account for as much as 75% of the income of larger agencies.

Ad agencies are usually divided into departments, the number determined by the size and services of the operation. Smaller agencies might contract with outside companies for the services of these typical ad agency departments:

- *Administration* is the agency's management and accounting operations.
- *Account management* is typically handled by an account executive who serves as liaison between agency and client, keeping communication flowing between the two and heading the team of specialists assigned by the agency to the client.

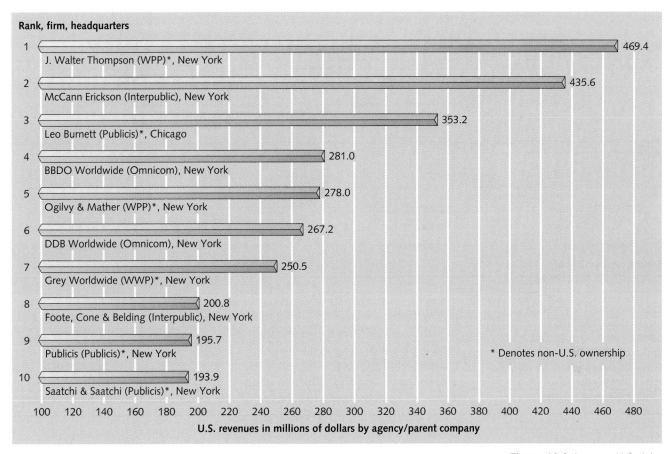

Rank, firm, headquarters

Rank	Firm, headquarters	U.S. revenues (millions)
1	J. Walter Thompson (WPP)*, New York	469.4
2	McCann Erickson (Interpublic), New York	435.6
3	Leo Burnett (Publicis)*, Chicago	353.2
4	BBDO Worldwide (Omnicom), New York	281.0
5	Ogilvy & Mather (WPP)*, New York	278.0
6	DDB Worldwide (Omnicom), New York	267.2
7	Grey Worldwide (WWP)*, New York	250.5
8	Foote, Cone & Belding (Interpublic), New York	200.8
9	Publicis (Publicis)*, New York	195.7
10	Saatchi & Saatchi (Publicis)*, New York	193.9

100 120 140 160 180 200 220 240 260 280 300 320 340 360 380 400 420 440 460 480

U.S. revenues in millions of dollars by agency/parent company

* Denotes non-U.S. ownership

Figure 12.2 Largest U.S. Ad Agencies, 2005. *Source:* Ad Age Special Report (2006, May 1). Top 25 U.S. Agency Brands. *Advertising Age*, p. S-2.

- The *creative department* is where the advertising is developed from idea to ad. It involves copywriting, graphic design, and often the actual production of the piece—for example, radio, television, and Web spots.

- The *media department* makes the decisions about where and when to place ads and then buys the appropriate time or space (Figure 12.3). The effectiveness of a given placement is judged by its **cost per thousand (CPM),** the cost of reaching 1,000 audience members. For example, an ad that costs $20,000 to place in a major newspaper and is read by 1 million people has a CPM of $20.

- *Market research* tests product viability in the market, the best venues for commercial messages, the nature and characteristics of potential buyers, and sometimes the effectiveness of the ads.

- As we saw in Chapter 11, many larger agencies have *public relations departments* as well.

TYPES OF ADVERTISING

The advertising produced and placed by ad agencies can be classified according to the purpose of the advertising and the target market. You may be familiar with the following types of advertising:

WWW

Association of National Advertisers
www.ana.net

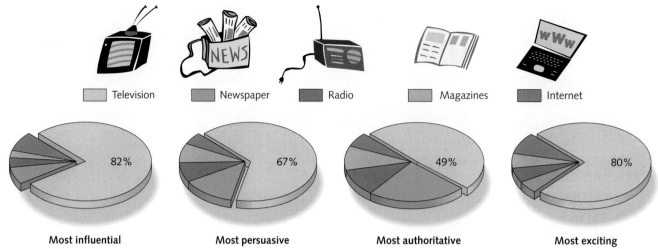

| Television | Newspaper | Radio | Magazines | Internet |

82% — Most influential

67% — Most persuasive

49% — Most authoritative

80% — Most exciting

Figure 12.3 Image of Advertising in Major Media. How do consumers rate the different advertising media in terms of their influence, persuasiveness, authority, and excitement?
Source: Adapted from Media Trends Track 2006, Television Bureau of Advertising Media Comparisons Study. Used by permission.

WWW

Advertising World
www.advertising.utexas.edu/world

Institutional or corporate advertising. Companies do more than just sell products; companies also promote their names and reputations. If a company name inspires confidence, selling its products is easier. Some institutional or corporate advertising promotes only the organization's image, such as "FTD Florists support the U.S. Olympic Team." But some advertising sells the image at the same time it sells the product: "You can be sure if it's Westinghouse."

Trade or professional advertising. Typically found in trade and professional publications, messages aimed at retailers do not necessarily push the product or brand but rather promote product issues of importance to the retailer—volume, marketing support, profit potential, distribution plans, and promotional opportunities.

Retail advertising. A large part of the advertising we see every day focuses on products sold by retailers like Sears and Macy's. Ads are typically local, reaching consumers where they live and shop.

Promotional retail advertising. Typically placed by retailers, promotional advertising focuses not on a product but on a promotion, a special event held by a retailer. "Midnight Madness Sale" and "Back to School Sale" are two promotions that often benefit from heavy advertising, particularly in newspapers.

Industrial advertising. Advertising of products and services directed toward a particular industry is usually found in industry trade publications. For example, *Broadcasting & Cable,* the primary trade magazine for the television industry, runs ads from program syndicators hoping to sell their shows to stations. It also runs ads from transmitter and camera manufacturers.

National consumer advertising. National consumer advertising constitutes the majority of what we see in popular magazines and on television. It is usually product advertising, commissioned by the manufacturer—McDonald's, Honda, Cheerios, Sony, Nike—aimed at potential buyers.

Direct market advertising. Product or service advertising aimed at likely buyers rather than at all consumers is called direct market advertising. These targeted consumers are reached through direct mail, catalogues, and telemarketing. This advertising can be personalized—"Yes, BRUCE

Through this industrial ad appearing in *Broadcasting & Cable* magazine, a programmer hopes to sell its video-on-demand service to cable operators.

FRIEDBERG, you can drive a Lexus for less than you think"—and customized. Computer data from credit card and other purchases, zip codes, telephone numbers, and organizational memberships are a few of the ways consumers are identified. Direct marketing accounts for 47.9% of all U.S. ad spending (Arndorfer, 2005).

Public service advertising. Advertising that does not sell commercial products or services but promotes organizations and themes of importance to the public is public service advertising. The Heart Fund, the United Negro College Fund, and ads for MADD are typical of this form. They are usually carried free of charge by the medium that houses them.

THE REGULATION OF ADVERTISING

The FTC is the primary federal agency for the regulation of advertising. The FCC regulates the commercial practices of the broadcasting industry, and individual states can police deceptive advertising through their own

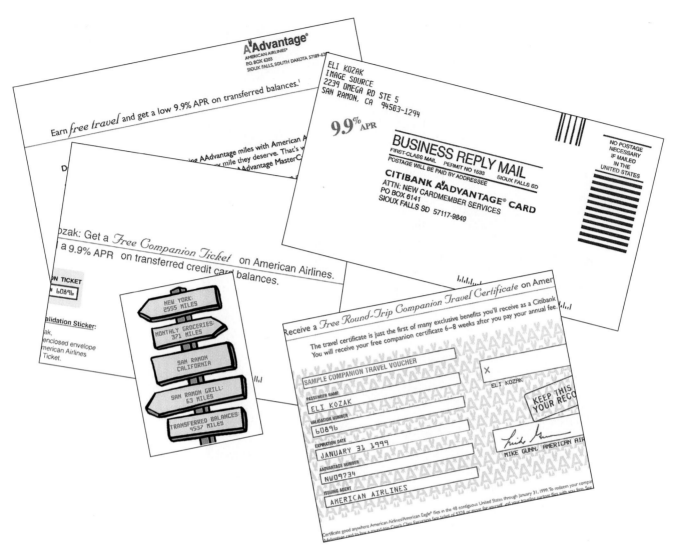

In this direct marketing package, the advertiser has not only personalized the pitch—Dear Eli Kozak—but targeted this consumer's particular interests in restaurants, travel, and other consumer goods and services. American Airlines reserves the right to change the AAdvantage program at any time without notice. American Airlines is not responsible for products or services offered by other participating companies.

regulatory and criminal bureaucracies. In the deregulation movement of 1980, oversight by the FTC changed from regulating unfair and deceptive advertising to regulating and enforcing complaints *against* deceptive advertising.

The FTC has several options for enforcement when it determines that an advertiser is guilty of deceptive practices. It can issue a **cease-and-desist order** demanding that the practice be stopped. It can impose fines. It can order the creation and distribution of **corrective advertising.** That is, a new set of ads must be produced by the offender that corrects the original misleading effort. Offenders can challenge FTC decisions in court, and they are innocent until proven guilty. Meanwhile, the potentially unethical advertising remains in the marketplace.

One of the greatest difficulties for the FTC is finding the line between false or deceptive advertising and **puffery**—that little lie that makes advertising more entertaining than it might otherwise be. "Whiter than white" and "stronger than dirt" are just two examples of puffery. On the assumption that

the public does not read commercials literally—the Jolly Green Giant does not exist; we know that—the courts and the FTC allow a certain amount of exaggeration.

The FTC and courts, however, do recognize that an advertisement can be false in a number of ways. An advertisement is false if it does the following:

- Lies outright. For years Wonder Bread was the bread that "builds strong bodies 12 ways." When the FTC asked Wonder Bread to name them, it could not. Listerine mouthwash was long advertised as "preventing colds and sore throats or lessening their severity." It does neither.

- Does not tell the whole truth. "Each slice of Profile Bread contains half the calories of other breads" was the claim of this brand. True, each slice did have about half the calories. But each slice was half as thick as a normal slice of bread.

- Lies by implication, using words, design, production device, sound, or a combination of these. Television commercials for children's toys now end with the product shown in actual size against a neutral background (a shot called an **island**). This is done because production techniques such as low camera angles and close-ups can make these toys seem larger or better than they actually are.

MEASURING THE EFFECTIVENESS OF ADVERTISING

It might seem reasonable to judge the effectiveness of an ad campaign by a subsequent increase in sales. But many factors other than advertising influence how well a product fares, including changes in the economy, product quality, breadth of distribution, and competitors' pricing and promotion strategies. Department store magnate John Wanamaker is said to have complained in the late 1880s, "I know that fifty-percent of my advertising is wasted. I just don't know which fifty-percent." Today's advertisers feel much the same way, and as you might imagine, they find this a less-than-comforting situation. Agencies, therefore, turn to research to provide greater certainty.

AdAge.com
www.adage.com

A number of techniques may be used before an ad or ad campaign is released. **Copy testing**—measuring the effectiveness of advertising messages by showing them to consumers—is used for all forms of advertising. It is sometimes conducted with focus groups, collections of people brought together to see the advertising and discuss it with agency and client personnel. Sometimes copy testing employs **consumer juries.** These people, considered to be representative of the target market, review a number of approaches or variations of a campaign or ad. **Forced exposure,** used primarily for television advertising, requires advertisers to bring consumers to a theater or other facility (typically with the promise of a gift or other payment), where they see a television program, complete with the new commercials. People are asked their brand preferences before the show, and then after. In this way, the effectiveness of the commercials can be gauged.

Once the campaign or ad is before the public, a number of different tests can be employed to evaluate the effectiveness of the ad. In **recognition tests** people who have seen a given publication are asked, in person or by phone, whether they remember seeing specific ads. In **recall testing** consumers are asked, again in person or by phone, to identify which print or broadcast ads they most easily remember. This recall can be unaided, that is, the researcher offers no hints ("Have you seen any interesting commercials or ads lately?"), or aided, that is, the researcher identifies a specific class of products ("Have you seen any interesting pizza commercials lately?"). In recall testing, the advertisers assume that an easily recalled ad is an effective ad. **Awareness tests** make this same assumption, but they are not aimed at specific ads. Their goal is to measure the cumulative effect of a campaign in terms of "consumer consciousness" of a product. A likely question in an awareness test, usually made by telephone, is "What brands of laundry detergent can you name?"

WWW

Outdoor Advertising Association

www.oaaa.org

What these research techniques lack is the ability to demonstrate the link that is of most interest to the client—did the ad move the consumer to buy the product? Their value lies in helping advertisers understand how people react to specific ads and advertising strategies, aiding advertisers in avoiding costly mistakes, and assisting advertisers in planning and organizing immediate and later campaigns.

Trends and Convergence in Advertising

For more information on this topic, see Media Talk video clip #20, "Your Ad Here: Pizza Hut Places Billboard on Spacecraft," on the *Media World* DVD.

In the summer of 2005, the world's largest advertiser, Procter & Gamble, announced that it would cut $300 million from its television ad expenditures, a 15% drop from its typical annual spending on that medium. Said Jim Stengel, head of global marketing for the company, "I believe today's marketing model is broken. We're applying antiquated thinking and work systems to a new world of possibilities" (in Auletta, 2005b, pp. 35–36). This public rebuke of the "old" marketing model exemplified what most industry professionals already knew—their industry was in need of change in, some even said reinvention of, its *economics, creativity,* and *relationship with consumers.* The advertising business is facing its "chaos scenario," as media writer Bob Garfield called it, "a jarring media universe in which traditional forms of mass entertainment swiftly disappear and advertisers are left in the lurch" (in Klosterman, 2005, p. 63). This new, jarring media universe is forged by the

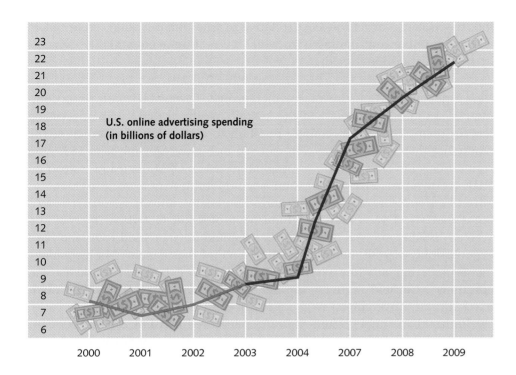

Figure 12.4 U.S. Online Advertising Forecast.
Source: Big Battle, 2005.

interaction of converging technologies and the changes they drive in how, when, and why people consume them (and the ads they contain).

NEW AND CONVERGING TECHNOLOGIES

The production of advertising has inevitably been altered by computers. Computer graphics, morphing (digitally combining and transforming images), and other special effects are now common in national retail television advertising. And the same technology used to change the ads behind the batter in a televised baseball game is now employed to insert product placements into programs where no placement originally existed—a character who was once eating an unbranded cookie can now munch an Oreo.

Computer databases and computerized printing have fueled the rapid growth of direct market advertising, and we saw in Chapter 5 that computerized printing has made possible zoned and other specialized editions of national magazines. But it is **cyberadvertising**—the convergence of print and broadcast advertising with the Web—that is attracting the most industry interest. In 2005 companies spent $12.9 billion on online advertising; industry predictions are that that total will swell to more than $22.3 billion by 2009 (Figure 12.4; Big Battle, 2005).

Web advertising has matured over the last few years, moving well beyond **banners,** static online billboards placed across the top of a Web page, or **skyscrapers,** placed down the side. Users today are likely to confront what the industry refers to as **contextual advertising,** that is, ads that automatically intrude into users' Web sessions whether wanted or not.

Even though these commercial interruptions may turn some Web users off, as we saw in Chapter 10, and even though online advertising appears to be the public's least appreciated commercial form, as suggested in Figure 12.2, the Internet sits firmly at the center of the change buffeting today's ad industry because of its low cost (relative to traditional media), great reach, and, most important, interactivity, which gives it an accountability unparalleled in the traditional media.

New Economics   Consumers are increasingly dissatisfied with hypercommercialism in other media and the lack of relevancy that much advertising has for them. They are becoming resistant to and resentful of much of the marketing they encounter, as you can see in Figure 12.1 on page 383. As a result, many advertisers are now less interested in CPM, focusing instead on **ROI (return on investment),** an accountability-based measurement of advertising success. After all, who cares how many thousands you are reaching if they reject your message? Industry professionals look at Internet and Web advertising and see that it is ideally suited for increased ROI, and have begun asking why all media can't offer some of that benefit. "As technology increasingly enables fine targeting and interaction between marketer and consumer," Garfield argued, "the old measurement and deployment standards are primitive almost to the point of absurdity" (2005, p. 58).

Rather than simple brand exposure, measured by CPM, advertisers have begun to demand accountability. As such, the Web's **performance-based advertising,** for example, provides the ideal. The Web site carrying the ad gets paid only when the consumer takes some specific action, making a purchase or linking to the sponsor's site. This Web-inspired demand for accountability led to a 2005 call for the development of a new measure of the *effectiveness of all advertising*—**engagement.** The Association of National Advertisers, the American Association of Advertising Agencies, and the Advertising Research Foundation joined in a movement, dubbed MI4, to define exactly the psychological and behavioral aspects of engagement and how to measure it (Creamer, 2005). Argues agency executive Rishad Tobaccowalla, "The industry's key currency is basically reach, frequency, exposure, and CPM . . . [T]he currency ought to be about outcomes, engagement, and effectiveness. Because right now all I'm doing is I'm measuring how cheaply or how expensively I'm buying the pig. I'm not figuring out whether the hotdog tastes good" (quoted in Garfield, 2005, p. 57).

New Creativity   "The traditional creative agencies have absolutely lost their way and their relevance," claims Joseph Jaffe, former ad agency executive (in Gross, 2005). Many have, but many others understand that the Internet-fueled fragmentation and democratization of media require a new type of appeal to consumers. If people are increasingly rejecting traditional *mass* media and the commercial messages they carry, the industry must become more creative in its messages and how it gets them to desired consumers. We've already seen many examples—product placement in all media; specially designed and targeted commercials delivered through cable or called up by DVR; online advergames; the sometimes annoying examples of ambient advertising that opened this chapter.

But the Internet has had its impact here as well. Much of advertising's creative community has learned to distinguish between typical, often unappreciated contextual advertising on the Web and imaginative video advertising delivered by the Web, cell phones, mobile video players, MP3 players and iPods, and portable game devices. For example, traditional big-time television advertisers like BMW, Amex, Lincoln-Mercury, Motorola, and Burger

King have moved significant amounts of their advertising dollars to the creation and distribution of short online films, sometimes episodic, to tout their products. And as for ROI, what could be a better measure of accountability than having a user click on an accompanying icon to get more information, receive a call from a salesperson, get a coupon, or even make a purchase? In fact, this on-the-spot, interactive buying is already available from XM Satellite Radio, whose portable receivers permit listeners to simply click a button to buy a tune. The chosen song is bookmarked, and when the player is later connected to the Internet, that piece of music is automatically downloaded and the listener's account is charged the appropriate amount (Klaassen, 2006). TiVo and many interactive cable systems are also moving toward this click-and-buy model tied to engaging content that, according to TiVo's CEO, Tom Rogers, is "halfway between a commercial and a Web site" (in Morrissey, 2005, p. 12).

New Relationship with Consumers   The Internet, as we've seen throughout this text, makes mass communication less of a monologue and more of a conversation. Today's consumers are no longer passive media *receivers*, taking whatever the television networks and movie studios insist they should. Instead, they are empowered media *users*, increasingly free to control and shape the content they receive. "As all media becomes addressable, all media becomes refusable," said Ogilvy & Mather's vice chairman, Steve Hayden. He argues that because the consumer now has the power to accept or reject content, an advertiser has to enter into a transaction with him or her, saying, "'I'll give you this content in exchange for your attention,' which has always been the model of mass advertising. But now, I've got to make that deal on a person-to-person basis" (in Kirsner, 2005).

This new, technology-driven reality, of necessity, has led to a rethinking of the relationship between advertiser and consumer, one in which they act

Burger King is among the many companies moving significant portions of their advertising budgets to the creation and distribution of short online films. Its Web site featuring Subservient Chicken has become a cult favorite, hatching a satellite TV–delivered boxing match between Subservient Chickens representing different chicken sandwiches and even, as seen here, real-world sightings of the big bird.

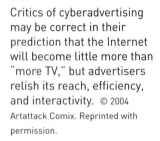

Critics of cyberadvertising may be correct in their prediction that the Internet will become little more than "more TV," but advertisers relish its reach, efficiency, and interactivity. © 2004 Artattack Comix. Reprinted with permission.

like partners, sharing information for mutual benefit. The new model of advertising will, as Mr. Hayden suggests, be a conversation between marketers and **prosumers,** proactive consumers who reject most traditional advertising and use multiple sources—traditional media, the Internet, product-rating magazines, recommendations from friends in the know—to not only research a product but negotiate price and other benefits. Economists call this *expressing disapproval.* Consumers have two choices—*exit*, that is, they simply do not buy the product; or *voice*, that is, they explain exactly why they are dissatisfied and what they'd like instead. Active media users, who are at the same time skilled prosumers, who have access to interactive technologies, ensure that voice will, indeed, replace exit as the measure of advertisers' success.

INCREASED AUDIENCE SEGMENTATION

Advertisers face other challenges as well. As the number of media outlets for advertising grows, and as audiences for traditional media are increasingly fragmented, advertisers have been forced to refine their ability to reach and speak to ever-narrower audience segments. Computer technology facilitates this practice, but segmentation exists apart from the new technologies. The ethnic composition of the United States is changing, and advertising is keeping pace. African Americans constitute just over 12% of the total U.S. population, and Hispanics, now the nation's largest minority, 13%. The Census Bureau reports that middle- and upper-income African Americans and Hispanics are indistinguishable from Whites in terms of such economic indicators as home ownership and consumer purchasing. It also reports that the average household income for African Americans exceeded all previous levels and that that of Hispanic households was growing at a rate five times faster than that of all other citizens. The average rate of growth in household income for African Americans exceeds that of White households (Century, 2001). Asians and Pacific Islanders constitute another fast-growing ethnic segment of the population, and 65% of the Native American population lives in the general community rather than on reservations. Together these groups control billions of dollars of discretionary income and are increasingly targeted by advertisers.

Desempeño y estilo determinan emociones y comportamientos. Una nueva manera de ver y vivir la vida.

NISSAN

SHIFT_inspiración

The growing U.S. Hispanic population is increasingly targeted by advertisers, both in English and Spanish. Here is an example from carmaker Nissan.

PSYCHOGRAPHICS

Demographic segmentation—the practice of appealing to audiences defined by varying personal and social characteristics such as race/ethnicity, gender, and economic level—has long been part of advertisers' strategy. But advertisers are making increased use of **psychographic segmentation**—that is, appealing to consumer groups with similar lifestyles, attitudes, values, and behavior patterns.

Psychographics entered advertising in the 1970s and is receiving growing attention as advertisers work to reach increasingly disparate consumers in increasingly segmented media. **VALS,** a psychographic segmentation strategy that classifies consumers according to values and lifestyles, is indicative of this lifestyle segmentation. Developed by SRI International, a California consulting company, VALS II divides consumers into eight VALS segments. Each segment is characterized by specific values and lifestyles, demographics, and, of greatest importance to advertisers, buying patterns (Television Bureau of Advertising, 2006). The segments, including some of their demographic identifiers, are listed below.

> *Actualizers:* Like using their heads. Resent manipulation. They seek technical and social information to help them act responsibly.
> *Fulfilleds:* Respect and appreciate authority. Are decidedly nonimpulsive. Serious and conservative.
> *Believers:* Very traditional, holding strong home and family values. Ignore flash and style.
> *Achievers:* Want every symbol of success. Seek the very best and work hard to pay for it.
> *Strivers:* Look for ways to simplify their lives. Want directness in commercial appeals.
> *Experiencers:* Self-centered, trendy, and demanding. Look for ways to meet *their* needs.

Makers: Self-sufficient, hardworking. Value is important.
Strugglers: Very cautious, having limited income. Tend to be suspicious.

GLOBALIZATION

As media and national economies have globalized, advertising has adapted. U.S. agencies are increasingly merging with, acquiring, or affiliating with agencies from other parts of the world. Revisit Figure 12.2. You'll see that 6 of the top 10 U.S. agencies are owned by foreign companies. In addition to the globalization of media and economies, a second force driving this trend is the demographic fact that today 80% of the world's population lives in developing countries. The advertising industry is prepared to put its clients in touch with these consumers. As Martin Sorrell, CEO of the WPP Group, the world's largest ad agency, explained, "Look, you've got 1 billion people in India, 1.3 billion in China. By 2014, two-thirds of the world's population will be in Asia" (quoted in Garland, 2002, p. 66). Figure 12.5 shows the world's 10 biggest global advertisers.

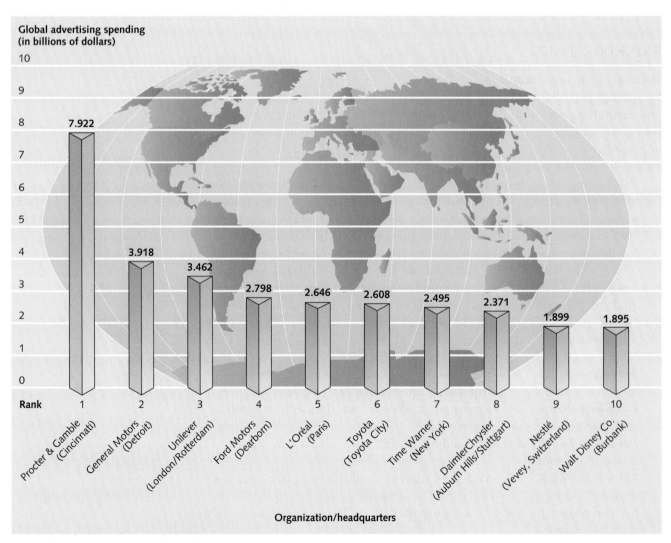

Figure 12.5 World's 10 Biggest Global Advertisers.

Source: Advertising Age, November 14, 2005, p. 30.

Interpreting Intentional Imprecision

Advertisers often use intentional imprecision in words and phrases to say something other than the precise truth, and they do so in all forms of advertising—profit and nonprofit, scrupulously honest and less so. There are three categories of intentional imprecision: unfinished statements, qualifiers, and connotatively loaded words and expressions.

We are all familiar with *unfinished statements,* such as the one for the battery that "lasts twice as long." Others include "You can be sure if it's Westinghouse," "Magnavox gives you more," and "Easy-Off makes oven cleaning easier." A literate advertising consumer should ask, "Twice as long as *what*?" "Of *what* can I be sure?" "Gives me more of *what*?" "Easier than *what*?" Better, more, stronger, whiter, faster—all are comparative adjectives whose true purpose is to create a comparison between two or more things. When the other half of the comparison is not identified, intentional imprecision is being used to create the illusion of comparison.

Qualifiers are words that limit a claim. A product *helps* relieve stress, for instance. It may not relieve stress as well as could rest and better planning and organization. But once the qualifier "helps" appears, an advertiser is free to make just about any claim for the product because all the ad really says is that it helps, not that it does anything in and of itself. It's the consumer's fault for misreading. A product may *fight* grime, but there is no promise that it will win. In the statement "Texaco's coal gasification process could mean you won't have to worry about how it affects the environment," "could" relieves the advertiser of all responsibility. "Could" does not mean "will." Moreover, the fact that you *could stop worrying about the environment* does not mean the product does not harm the environment—only that you could stop worrying about it.

Some qualifiers are more apparent. "Taxes not included," "limited time only," "only at participating locations," "prices may vary," "some assembly required," "additional charges may apply," and "batteries not included" are qualifiers presented after the primary claims have been made. Often these words are spoken quickly at the end of radio and television commercials, or they appear in small print on the screen or at the bottom of a newspaper or magazine ad.

Other qualifiers are part of the product's advertising slogan. Boodles gin is "the ultra-refined British gin that only the world's costliest methods could produce. Boodles. The world's costliest British gin." After intimating that the costliest methods are somehow necessary to make the best gin, this advertiser qualifies its product as the costliest "British" gin. There may be costlier, and possibly better, Irish, U.S., Russian, and Canadian gins. Many sugared children's cereals employ the tactic of displaying the cereal on a table with fruit, milk, and toast. The announcer says or the copy reads, "Coco Yummies are *a part of* this complete breakfast"—so is the tablecloth. But the cereal, in and of itself, adds little to the nutritional completeness of the meal. It is "a part of" it. In December 2003, in order to forestall FTC action, KFC pulled television commercials claiming that its fried chicken was "part of" a healthy diet, a campaign characterized as "desperate and sleazy" by *Advertising Age* (MacArthur, 2003).

BadAds.org

An interesting fact about the Media Foundation and its Adbusters program (see the box "Challenging Advertising: Adbusters and Uncommercials") is that a large proportion of its members are themselves current or former advertising professionals. Some are critical of their profession, or at least its excesses, as are many of us. But some of these disaffected advertising practitioners recognize that advertising cannot be effective if it is not respected. Their membership in the Media Foundation, then, is an expression of their commitment to their profession. They want to preserve its effectiveness. You'll remember from earlier in the chapter that this sentiment played a part in the founding of the Ad Council.

> NO ONE IS NEUTRAL ABOUT ADVERTISING. WE ARE OFTEN DELIGHTED BY ITS SUCCESSES, DISTRESSED BY ITS EXCESSES.

Another activist group interested in improving advertising is BadAds.org (www.badads.org). Its particular targets are intrusive and deceptive advertising. This group attracts parents and teachers more than industry professionals. It maintains archives of what it considers bad ads, a BadAd Blog, links to other advertising activist sites, and discussions of advertising's excesses. It also provides how-to sections. For example, there are instructions on how parents should deal with their children when confronted by the kids' ad-fueled demands for specific brands or products (www.badads.org/teachers.shtml).

BadAds also offers advice on how to write an effective letter of complaint about a piece of advertising (www.badads.org/letter.shtml). Here's what its site suggests:

1. How? Choose your format: mail, fax, or e-mail; complete the company's online feedback form; or leave a message on the company president's voice mail.

2. Where? BadAds provides addresses of what it considers some of the more egregious ad offenders, and it provides links to *Hoovers* and *Big Yellow*, two national business directories.

3. Who? BadAds suggests that complaints *not* be sent to the customer service department. As it explains, "The big cheese (a.k.a. chief executive officer, president, or chairman) has the most power to solve your problem. You can find out his or her name when you get the company address. While you may not hear from the CEO personally, you're more likely to get action than if you send your letter to anyone else."

4. What? Identify what you're complaining about and why you're upset. Offer a means of making it better (stop running the campaign, clean up the language, and so on). Explain what your next step is if you are not satisfied with the response. The Better Business Bureau or FTC or FCC. Spread your dissatisfaction to friends and family. Stop using the brand. But always be polite (and no typos). Thank the company for dealing with your complaint.

No one is neutral about advertising. We are often delighted by its successes, distressed by its excesses. These two organizations provide the means for media literate people to engage advertising and advertisers in a productive way.

Advertising is full of words that are *connotatively loaded*. Best Western Hotels never has to explain what makes them "best." A *best-selling product* may not be the best in its product class, only the one with the best advertising campaign and distribution system. A product that has more of "the pain-relieving medicine doctors prescribe most" merely contains more aspirin. Products that are "cherry-flavored" have no cherries in them. A product that is high in "food energy" is in fact high in calories. Advertisers want consumers to understand the connotations of these words and phrases, not their actual meanings.

Intentional imprecision is puffery. It is not illegal; neither is it sufficiently troubling to the advertising industry to warrant self-regulatory limits. But puffery is neither true nor accurate, and its purpose is to deceive. This means that the responsibility for correctly and accurately reading advertising that is intentionally imprecise rests with the media literate consumer.

Review Points

- Advertising has been a part of commerce for centuries, but it became an industry in its own right with the coming of industrialization and the American Civil War.
- Advertising suffers from a number of criticisms—it is intrusive, it is deceptive, it exploits children, it demeans and corrupts culture.
- Advertising is also considered beneficial—it supports our economic system, it provides information to assist buying decisions, it supports our media system, it improves our standard of living.
- Advertising agencies typically have these departments: administration, account management, creative, media, market research, and public relations.
- There are different types of advertising: institutional or corporate, trade or professional, retail, promotional retail, industrial, national consumer, direct marketing, and public service.
- Regulation of advertising content is the responsibility of the Federal Trade Commission, which recognizes that an ad can be false if it lies outright, does not tell the whole truth, or lies by implication. Puffery, the entertaining "little" lie, is permissible.
- There are several ways to measure an ad's effectiveness—copy testing, consumer juries, forced exposure, recognition tests, recall testing, and awareness tests.
- The interaction of converging technologies and the changes they drive in how, when, and why people consume them (and the ads they contain) is reshaping the economics and creativity of the advertising industry as well as its relationship with consumers.
- Reshaping of the industry has led to calls for better measures of effectiveness, such as engagement, return on investment (ROI), and performance-based advertising.
- Advertisers must also deal with consumers increasingly segmented not only by their media choices but along demographic and psychographic lines.
- As with the media it supports, the advertising industry is increasingly globalized.
- Interpreting advertisers' intentional imprecision—unfinished statements, qualifiers, and connotatively loaded words—test consumers' media literacy skills.

Key Terms

 Use the text's Online Learning Center at www.mhhe.com/baran5 to further your understanding of the following terminology.

siquis, 375
shopbills, 375
newsbook, 375
unique selling proposition (USP), 380
parity products, 380
ambient advertising, 381
AIDA approach, 384
consumer culture, 385
retainer, 388
commissions, 388

cost per thousand (CPM), 389
cease-and-desist order, 392
corrective advertising, 392
puffery, 392
island, 393
copy testing, 394
consumer juries, 394
forced exposure, 394
recognition tests, 394
recall testing, 394
awareness tests, 394

cyberadvertising, 395
banners, 395
skyscrapers, 395
contextual advertising, 395
ROI (return on investment), 396
performance-based advertising, 396
engagement, 396
prosumer, 396
demographic segmentation, 399
psychographic segmentation, 399
VALS, 399

Questions for Review

 Go to the self-quizzes on the Online Learning Center to test your knowledge.

1. Why are we seeing so many ads in so many new and different places?
2. What are siquis, shopbills, and newsbooks?
3. What impact did industrialization and the Civil War have on the advertising industry?

4. What impact did the coming of magazines, radio, and television have on the advertising industry?
5. What is USP? A parity product?
6. Why do some people consider advertising to children unethical? Immoral?

7. What is the AIDA approach? The consumer culture?
8. In what ways can an ad be false?
9. What was the excess-profits tax? How did it benefit advertising agencies?
10. What are the departments in a typical advertising agency? What does each do?
11. What are the different categories of advertising and the goal of each?
12. What is a cease-and-desist order? Corrective advertising? Puffery?
13. What are copy testing, consumer juries, forced exposure, recognition tests, recall testing, and awareness tests? How do they differ?
14. What is ROI? How does it measure engagement? How does it differ from CPM?
15. What is a prosumer? How do prosumers change the relationship between advertisers and their audience?
16. In what two ways do consumers express dissatisfaction? How does this affect contemporary advertising?
17. What are demographic and psychographic segmentation?
18. How can words be used to deceive in advertising?

Questions for Critical Thinking and Discussion

1. If you owned an advertising agency, would you produce advertising aimed at children? Why or why not?
2. If you were an FTC regulator, to what extent would you allow puffery? Where would you draw the line between deception and puffery? Give examples.
3. Do you think U.S. culture is overly materialistic? If you do, what role do you think advertising has had in creating this state of affairs? Do you find it surprising that much of the criticism of our consumer culture comes from people (Jelly Helm [p. 386] and Kalle Lasn, founder of the Media Foundation [see p. 387],

are two examples) who are or were in the advertising industry? Why or why not?
4. Can you identify yourself among the VALS segments? If you can, how accurately does that segment describe your buying habits?
5. What do you think of contemporary television advertising? Are its creativity and technological sophistication adequate substitutes for information about the product?
6. What do you think of the exit-voice dichotomy of consumer behavior? Can you relate it to your own use of advertising? How?

Important Resources

 Go to the Online Learning Center for additional readings.

Internet Resources

Advertising History	scriptorium.lib.duke.edu/hartman
Audit Bureau of Circulations	www.accessabc.com
National Advertising Review Council	www.nadreview.org
American Advertising Federation	www.aaf.org
Ad Council	www.adcouncil.org
Television Bureau of Advertising	www.tvb.org
Better Business Bureau's Ad Pledge Program	www.bbb.org/app/appworks.asp
Campaign for a Commercial-free Childhood	www.commercialexploitation.org
Adbusters	www.adbusters.org
Ad Forum	www.adforum.com
American Association of Advertising Agencies	www.aaaa.org
Association of National Advertisers	www.ana.net
Advertising World	advertising.utexas.edu/world
Federal Trade Commission	www.ftc.gov
AdAge.com	adage.com
Outdoor Advertising Association	www.oaaa.org
Adweek	www.adweek.com
Institute of Practitioners in Advertising	www.ipa.co.uk

13

Theories and Effects of Mass Communication

LEARNING OBJECTIVES

Media have effects. People may disagree about what those effects might be, but media do have effects. Advertisers would not spend billions of dollars a year to place their messages in the media if they did not have effects, nor would our Constitution, in the form of the First Amendment, seek to protect the freedoms of the media if the media did not have important consequences. We attempt to understand and explain these effects through mass communication theory. After studying this chapter you should

■ be familiar with the history and development of mass communication theory.

■ understand what is meant by theory, why it is important, and how it is used.

■ be familiar with some of the most influential traditional and contemporary mass communication theories.

■ be conversant in a number of controversial effects issues, such as violence, media's impact on drug and alcohol consumption, and media's contribution to racial and gender stereotyping.

■ possess improved skill at applying mass communication theory to your own use of media.

"I know this isn't listed on the syllabus. But let's call it a pop quiz." Your instructor has surprised you. "Will this count in our final grade?" you ask. You are seared by the professor's stare.

"Put everything away except a piece of paper and a pen."

You do as instructed.

"Number your paper from 1 to 5. Items 1 through 3 are true–false. One. Most people are just looking out for themselves. Two. You can't be too careful in dealing with people. Three. Most people would

Opposite: The potential of powerful media effects provides a strong argument for increased media literacy.

take advantage of you if they got the chance. Now, number four. How much television do you watch each week?"

Not too tough, you think, you can handle this.

"Finally, number 5. Draw the outline of a dime as close to actual size as possible."

In this chapter we examine mass communication theory. After we define theory and discuss why it is important, we see how the various theories of mass communication that are prevalent today developed. We then study several of the most influential contemporary theories before we discuss the relationship between media literacy and mass communication theory. These theories and their application form the basis of our understanding of how media and culture affect one another, the effects of mass communication.

The Effects Debate

WWW

American Communication Association
www.americancomm.org

Whether the issue is online hate groups, televised violence, the absence of minority characters in prime-time television programming, or a decline in the quality of political discourse, the topic of the effects of mass communication

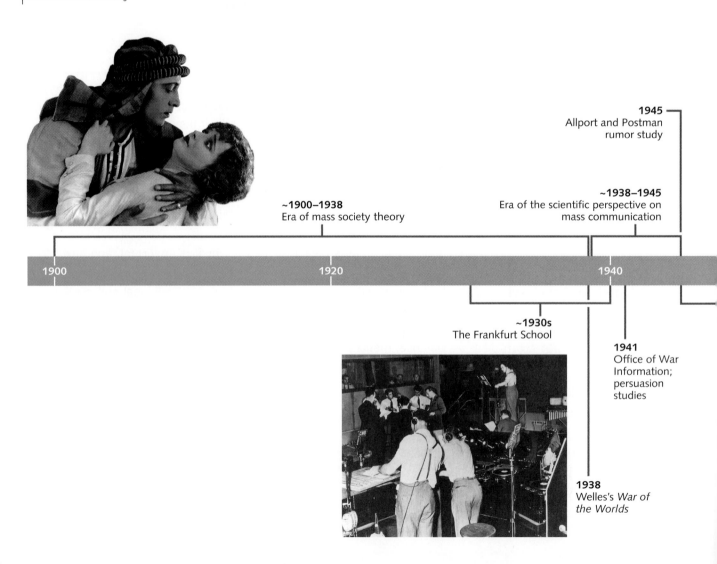

1945
Allport and Postman rumor study

~1938–1945
Era of the scientific perspective on mass communication

~1900–1938
Era of mass society theory

~1930s
The Frankfurt School

1900   1920   1940

1941
Office of War Information; persuasion studies

1938
Welles's *War of the Worlds*

is—and has always been—hotly debated. Later in this chapter we will take detailed looks at such effects issues as media's impact on violence, the use of drugs and alcohol, and stereotyping. But before we can examine specific effects issues, we must understand that there exists fundamental disagreement about the presence, strength, and operation of effects. Many people still hold to the position that media have limited or minimal effects. Here are their arguments, accompanied by their counterarguments.

1. *Media content has limited impact on audiences because it's only make-believe; people know it isn't real.*

The counterarguments: (a) News is not make-believe (at least it's not supposed to be), and we are supposed to take it seriously. (b) Most film and television dramas (for example, *CSI: Crime Scene Investigation* and *House*) are intentionally produced to seem real to viewers, with documentary-like production techniques such as handheld cameras and uneven lighting. (c) Much contemporary television is expressly *real*—reality shows such as *Cops* and *Fear Factor* and talk shows such as *The Jerry Springer Show* purport to present real people. (d) Advertising is supposed to tell the truth. (e) Before they develop the intellectual and critical capacity to know what

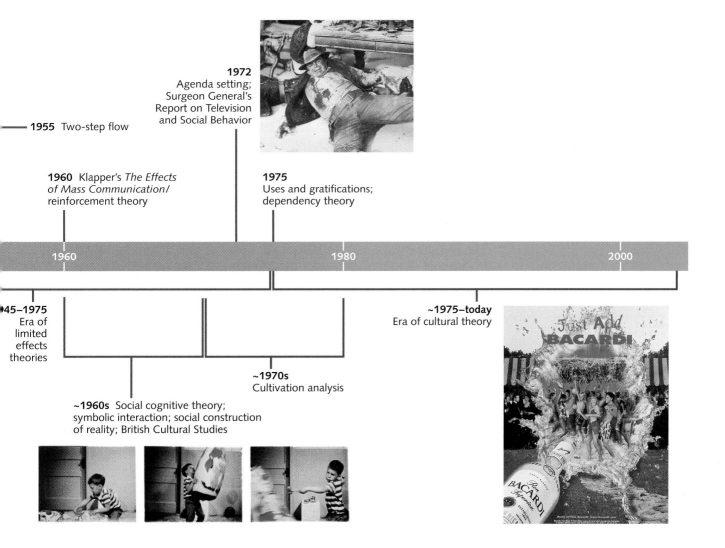

1972
Agenda setting; Surgeon General's Report on Television and Social Behavior

1955 Two-step flow

1960 Klapper's *The Effects of Mass Communication*/ reinforcement theory

1975
Uses and gratifications; dependency theory

1960   1980   2000

~1945–1975
Era of limited effects theories

~1975–today
Era of cultural theory

~1970s
Cultivation analysis

~1960s Social cognitive theory; symbolic interaction; social construction of reality; British Cultural Studies

The mirror that media hold up to culture is like a fun-house mirror—some things appear bigger than they truly are, some things appear smaller, and some disappear altogether.

is not real, children confront the world in all its splendor and vulgarity through television, what television effects researchers call the **early window.** To kids, what they see is real. (f) To enjoy what we consume, we **willingly suspend disbelief;** that is, we willingly accept as real what is put before us.

2. *Media content has limited impact on audiences because it is only play or just entertainment.*

The counterarguments: (a) News is not play or entertainment (at least it's not supposed to be). (b) Even if media content is only play, play is very important to the way we develop our knowledge of ourselves and our world. When we play organized sports, we learn teamwork, cooperation, the value of hard work, obedience to authority, and respect for the rules. Why should play be any less influential if we do it on the Internet or at the movies?

3. *If media have any effects at all, they are not the media's fault; media simply hold a mirror to society and reflect the status quo, showing us and our world as they already are.*

The counterargument: Media hold a very selective mirror. The whole world, in all its vastness and complexity, cannot possibly be represented, so media practitioners must make choices. For example, according to the Parents Television Council, 47% of television's families are headed by married couples. The Census Bureau, however, tells us that in the real world, 72% of all families enjoy the presence of a mom and dad. On television, 14% of the families are headed by a single father. In the real world, 6%

are (Elber, 2002). And when was the last time you saw a car explode in an accident? At best, media hold a fun-house mirror to society and distort what they reflect. Some things are overrepresented, others underrepresented, and still others disappear altogether.

4. *If media have any effect at all, it is only to reinforce preexisting values and beliefs. Family, church, school, and other socializing agents have much more influence.*

The counterarguments: (a) The traditional socializing agents have lost much of their power to influence in our complicated and fast-paced world. (b) Moreover, reinforcing effects are not the same as having no effects. If media can reinforce the good in our culture, media can just as easily reinforce the bad. Is racism eradicated yet? Sexism? Disrespect for others? If our media are doing no more than reinforcing the values and beliefs that already exist, then they are as empty as many critics contend. Former Federal Communications Commission member Nicholas Johnson has long argued of television in particular that the real crime is not what television is doing *to* us but what it could be doing *for* us, but isn't.

5. *If media have any effects at all, they are only on the unimportant things in our lives, such as fads and fashions.*

The counterarguments: (a) Fads and fashions are not unimportant to us. The car we drive, the clothes we wear, and the way we look help define us; they characterize us to others. In fact, it is media that have helped make fads and fashions so central to our self-definition and happiness. Kids don't kill other kids for their $150 basketball shoes because their mothers told them that Air Jordans were cool. (b) If media influence only the unimportant things in our lives, why are billions of dollars spent on media efforts to sway opinion about social issues such as universal health care, nuclear power, and global warming (Chapter 11)?

One reason these arguments about media power and effects continue to rage is that people often come to the issues from completely different perspectives. In their most general form, the debates over media influence have been shaped by three closely related dichotomies.

WWW

International Communication Association
www.icahdq.org

MICRO- VERSUS MACRO-LEVEL EFFECTS

People are concerned about the effects of media. Does television cause violence? Do beer ads cause increased alcohol consumption? Does pornography cause rape? The difficulty here is with the word *cause*. Although there is much scientific evidence that media cause many behaviors, there is also much evidence that they do not.

As long as we debate the effects of media only on individuals, we risk remaining blind to what many believe is media's more powerful influence (both positive and negative) on the way we live. For example, when the shootings at the Littleton, Colorado, Columbine High School in 1999 once again brought public debate on the issue of media effects, USA Network co-president Steve Brenner was forced to defend his industry. "Every American has seen hundreds of films, hundreds of news stories, hundreds of depictions, thousands of cartoons," he said. "Millions don't go out and shoot people" (as quoted in Albiniak, 1999, p. 8).

What are the effects of televised violence? The debate swirls as different people mean different things by "effects." This violent scene is from *Oz*.

Who can argue with this? For most people, media have relatively few *direct* effects at the personal or **micro level.** But we live in a culture in which people *have* shot people or are willing to use violence to settle disputes, at least in part because of the cultural messages embedded in our media fare. The hidden, but much more important, impact of media operates at the cultural or **macro level.** Violence on television contributes to the cultural climate in which real-world violence becomes more acceptable. Sure, perhaps none of us have gone out and shot people. But do you have bars on the windows of your home? Are there parts of town where you would rather not walk alone? Do you vote for the "tough on crime" candidate over the "education" candidate?

The micro-level view is that televised violence has little impact because although some people may be directly affected, most people are not. The macro-level view is that televised violence has a great impact because it influences the cultural climate.

ADMINISTRATIVE VERSUS CRITICAL RESEARCH

Administrative research asks questions about the immediate, observable influence of mass communication. Does a commercial campaign sell more cereal? Does an expanded Living Section increase newspaper circulation? Did *Mortal Kombat* inspire the killings at Columbine High School? For decades the only proofs of media effects that science (and therefore the media industries, regulators, and audiences) would accept were those with direct, observable, immediate effects. Over 60 years ago, however, Paul Lazarsfeld, the "Father of Social Science Research" and possibly the most important mass communication researcher of all time, warned of the danger of this narrow view. He believed **critical research**—asking larger questions about what kind of nation we are building, what kind of people we are becoming—would serve our culture better. Writing long before the influence of television and information access through the World Wide Web, he stated,

Read about Lazarsfeld
www.Columbia.edu/cu/news/01/10/lazarsfeld.html

Today we live in an environment where skyscrapers shoot up and elevateds (commuter trains) disappear overnight; where news comes like shock every few hours; where continually new news programs keep us from ever finding out details of previous news; and where nature is something we drive past in our cars, perceiving a few quickly changing flashes which turn the majesty of a mountain range into the impression of a motion picture. Might it not be that we do not build up experiences the way it was possible decades ago . . . ? (1941, p. 12)

Administrative research concerns itself with direct causes and effects; critical research looks at larger, possibly more significant cultural questions. As the above cartoon shows, Calvin understands the distinction well.

TRANSMISSIONAL VERSUS RITUAL PERSPECTIVE

Last is the debate that led Professor Carey to articulate his cultural definition of communication (Chapter 1). The **transmissional perspective** sees media as senders of information for the purpose of control; that is, media either have effects on our behavior or they do not. The **ritual perspective,** Carey wrote, views media not as a means of transmitting "messages in space" but as central to "the maintenance of society in time." Mass communication is "not the act of imparting information but the representation of shared beliefs" (1975, p. 6). In other words, the ritual perspective is necessary to understand the *cultural* importance of mass communication.

Consider an ad for Skyy malt beverage. What message is being transmitted? Buy Skyy, of course. So people either do or do not buy Skyy. The message either controls or does not control people's alcohol-buying behavior. That is the transmissional perspective. But what is happening culturally in that ad? What reality about alcohol and socializing is shared? Can young people really have fun in social settings without alcohol? What constitutes a good-looking man or woman? What does success look like in the United States? The ritual perspective illuminates these messages—the culturally important content of the ad.

The transmissional message in this liquor ad is obvious— buy Skyy. The ritual message is another thing altogether. What is it?

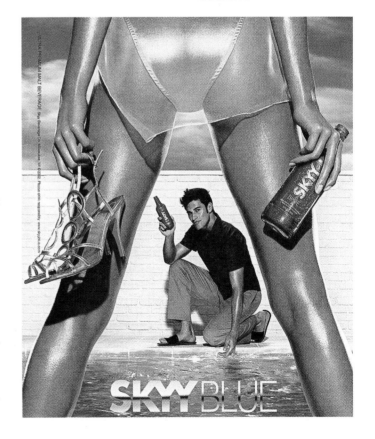

Defining Mass Communication Theory

Whether you accept the limited effects arguments or their counterarguments, all the positions you just read are based in one or more **mass communication theories,** explanations and predictions of social phenomena that attempt to relate mass communication to various aspects of our personal and cultural lives or social systems. Your responses to the five quiz questions that opened the chapter, for example, can be explained (possibly even predicted) by different mass communication theories.

The first four items are a reflection of **cultivation analysis**—the idea that people's ideas of themselves, their world, and their place in it are shaped and maintained primarily through television. People's responses to the three true–false items can be fairly accurately predicted by the amount of viewing they do (question 4). The more people watch, the more likely they are to respond "true" to these unflattering comments about others.

The solution to the dime-drawing task is predicted by **attitude change theory.** Almost everyone draws the dime too small. Because a dime is an inconsequential coin, we perceive it as smaller than it really is, and our perceptions guide our behavior. Even though every one of us has real-world experience with dimes, our attitudes toward that coin shape our behavior regarding it.

To understand mass communication theory, you should recognize these important ideas:

1. As we've just seen, *there is no one mass communication theory.* There is a theory, for example, that describes something as grand as how we give meaning to cultural symbols and how these symbols influence our behavior (symbolic interaction), and there is a theory that explains something as individual as how media influence people in times of change or crisis (dependency theory). Mass communication theorists have produced a number of **middle-range theories** that explain or predict specific, limited aspects of the mass communication process (Merton, 1967).

2. *Mass communication theories are often borrowed from other fields of science.* Attitude change theory (the dime question), for example, comes from psychology. Mass communication theorists adapt these borrowed theories to questions and issues in communication. People's behavior with regard to issues more important than the size of a dime—democracy, ethnicity, government, and gender roles, for example—is influenced by the attitudes and perceptions presented by our mass media.

3. *Mass communication theories are human constructions.* People create them, and therefore their creation is influenced by human biases—the times in which we live, the position we occupy in the mass communication process, and a host of other factors. Broadcast industry researchers, for example, have developed somewhat different theories to explain how violence is learned from television than have university researchers.

4. Because theories are human constructions and the environments in which they are created constantly change, *mass communication theories are dynamic;* they undergo frequent recasting, acceptance, and rejection. For example, theories that were developed before television and computer networks became mass media outlets have to be reexamined and sometimes discarded in the face of these new media.

A Short History of Mass Communication Theory

The dynamic nature of mass communication theory can be seen in its history. All bodies of knowledge pass through various stages of development. Hypotheses are put forth, tested, and proven or rejected. Eventually a uniform theory or **paradigm** results—that is, a theory that summarizes and is consistent with all known facts. However, over time, new facts come to light and our knowledge and understanding increase. This often leads to a **paradigm shift**—a fundamental, even radical, rethinking of what we believe to be true (Kuhn, 1970). Mass communication theory is particularly open to such paradigm shifts due to three factors:

- *Advances in technology or the introduction of new media* fundamentally alter the nature of mass communication. The coming of radio and movies, for example, forced rethinking of theories based on a print-oriented mass communication system.

- *Calls for control or regulation* of these new technologies require, especially in a democracy such as ours, an objective, science-based justification.

- As a country committed to protecting *democracy and cultural pluralism,* we ask how each new technology or medium can foster our pursuit of that goal.

The paradigm shifts that have resulted from these factors have produced four major eras of mass communication theory: the era of mass society theory, the era of the scientific perspective, the era of limited effects theory, and the era of cultural theory. The first three may be considered early eras; the last is the era in which we currently find ourselves.

THE ERA OF MASS SOCIETY THEORY

As we've seen, several important mass media appeared or flourished during the second half of the 19th century and the first decades of the 20th century. Mass circulation newspapers and magazines, movies, talkies, and radio all came to prominence at this time. This was also a time of profound change in the nature of U.S. society. Industrialization and urbanization spread, African Americans and poor southern Whites streamed northward, and immigrants rushed across both coasts in search of opportunity and dignity. People in traditional seats of power—the clergy, politicians, and educators—feared a disruption in the status quo. The country's peaceful rural nature was beginning to slip further into history. In its place was a cauldron of new and different people with new and different habits, all crammed into rapidly expanding cities. Crime grew, as did social and political unrest. Many cultural, political, educational, and religious leaders thought the United States was becoming too pluralistic. They charged that the mass media catered to the low tastes and limited reading and language abilities of these newcomers by featuring simple and sensationalistic content. The media needed to be controlled to protect traditional values.

The successful use of propaganda by totalitarian governments in Europe, especially Germany's National Socialist Party (the Nazis), provided further evidence of the overwhelming power of media. Media needed to be controlled to prevent similar abuses at home.

WWW

American Sociological Association
www.asanet.org

Agnes Ayers swoons in Rudolph Valentino's arms in the 1921 movie *The Sheik*. Mass society theorists saw such common entertainment fare as debasing the culture through its direct and negative effects on helpless audience members.

The resulting paradigm was **mass society theory**—the idea that the media are corrupting influences that undermine the social order and that "average" people are defenseless against their influence. To mass society theorists, "average" people were all those who did not hold their (the theorists') superior tastes and values. The fundamental assumption of this paradigm is sometimes expressed in the **hypodermic needle theory** or the **magic bullet theory.** The symbolism of both is apparent—media are a dangerous drug or a killing force that directly and immediately penetrates a person's system.

Mass society theory is an example of a **grand theory,** one designed to describe and explain all aspects of a given phenomenon. But clearly not all average people were mindlessly influenced by the evil mass media. People made consumption choices. They interpreted media content, often in personally important ways. Media did have effects, often good ones. No single theory could encompass the wide variety of media effects claimed by mass society theorists, and the theory eventually collapsed under its own weight.

Orson Welles directs *War of the Worlds*. The 1938 Halloween eve broadcast of this science fiction classic helped usher in the era of the scientific study of mass communication.

THE ERA OF THE SCIENTIFIC PERSPECTIVE

Paradigm shifts usually happen over a period of time, and this is true of the move away from mass society theory. But media researchers often mark the beginning of the scientific perspective on mass communication as occurring on the eve of Halloween 1938. On that night actor and director Orson Welles broadcast his dramatized version of the H. G. Wells science fiction classic *The War of the Worlds* on the CBS radio network. Produced in what we would now call docudrama style, the realistic radio play in which Earth came under deadly Martian attack frightened thousands. People fled their homes in panic. Proof of mass society theory, argued elite media critics, pointing to a radio play with the power to send people into the hills to hide from aliens.

Research by scientists from Princeton University demonstrated that, in fact, 1 million people had been frightened enough by the broadcast to take some action, but the other 5 million people who heard the show had not, mass society theory notwithstanding. More important, however, these scientists determined that different factors led some people to be influenced and others not (Lowery & DeFleur, 1995).

The researchers had the benefit of advances in survey research, polling, and other social scientific methods developed and championed by Austrian immigrant Paul Lazarsfeld. The researchers were, in fact, his students and colleagues. Lazarsfeld (1941) argued that mere speculation about the impact

Figure 13.1 Model of Two-Step Flow of Media Influence. Media influence passes from the mass media through opinion leaders to opinion followers. Because leaders and followers share common personal and social characteristics, the potential influence of media is limited by their shared assumptions, beliefs, and attitudes.

Source: After Katz & Lazarsfeld, 1955.

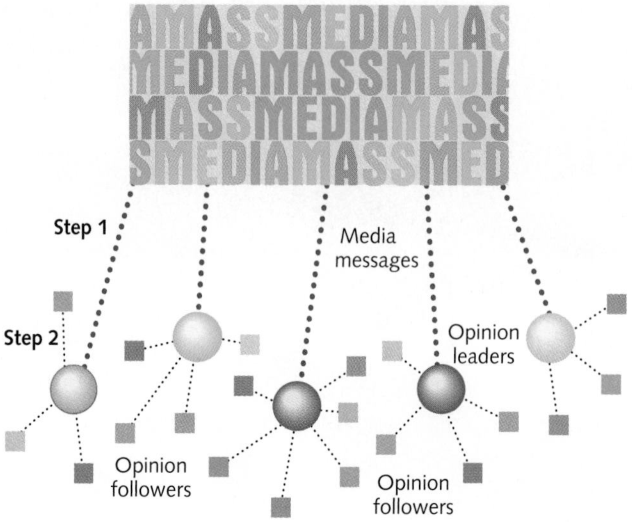

www

Roper Center for Public Opinion Research
www.ropercenter.uconn.edu

of media was insufficient to explain the complex interactions that mass communication comprised. Instead, well-designed, sophisticated studies of media and audiences would produce more valuable knowledge.

Limited Effects Theories   Using Lazarsfeld's work, researchers identified those individual and social characteristics that led audience members to be influenced (or not) by media. What emerged was the view that media influence was limited by *individual differences* (for example, in intelligence and education), *social categories* (such as religious and political affiliation), and *personal relationships* (such as friends and family). The theories that emerged from this era of the first systematic and scientific study of media effects, taken together, are now called **limited effects theories.**

Two-Step Flow Theory   Lazarsfeld's own **two-step flow theory** of mass media and personal influence is a well-known product of this era and an example of a limited effects theory (Katz & Lazarsfeld, 1955). His research on the 1940 presidential election indicated that media influence on people's voting behavior was limited by **opinion leaders**—people who initially consumed media content on topics of particular interest to them, interpreted it in light of their own values and beliefs, and then passed it on to **opinion followers,** people like them who had less frequent contact with media (Figure 13.1).

Two-step flow theory has been rethought since Lazarsfeld's time. For example, television, virtually unavailable in 1940, has given everyone a more or less equal opportunity to consume media content firsthand. There is no doubt that opinion leaders still exist—we often ask friends what they've read or heard about a certain movie, book, or CD—but their centrality to the mass communication process has diminished.

THE ERA OF LIMITED EFFECTS THEORY

During and after World War II, the limited effects paradigm and several theories it supported became entrenched, controlling research and thinking about media until well into the 1960s. And as was the case with virtually all the media and support industries we've studied, the war itself was crucial to the development of mass communication theory during this era.

Memories of World War I were still very much alive, and not all Americans were enthused about entering another seemingly remote world conflict. Those who joined or were drafted into the armed forces apparently knew very little about their comrades-in-arms from different regions of the country and from different backgrounds. German propaganda seemed to prove the view of mass society theorists who claimed that mass media wielded remarkable power. The Office of War Information (OWI), therefore, set out to change public opinion about the wisdom of entering the war, to educate the military about their fellow soldiers and sailors, and to counter Nazi propaganda. Speeches and lectures failed. So, too, did informational pamphlets. The OWI then turned to filmmakers such as Frank Capra (see Chapter 6) and radio personalities such as Kate Smith for their audience appeal and looked to social scientists to measure the effectiveness of these new media campaigns.

The army established the Experimental Section inside its Information and Education Division, staffing it with psychologists who were expert in issues of attitude change. Led by Carl Hovland, these researchers tested the effectiveness of the government's mass communication campaigns. Continuing its work at Yale University after the war, this group produced some of our most influential communication research. Their work led to development of *attitude change theory*, which explains how people's attitudes are formed, shaped, and changed through communication and how those attitudes influence behavior (Hovland, Lumsdaine, & Sheffield, 1949).

Attitude Change Theory   Among the most important attitude change theories are the related ideas of dissonance and selective processes. **Dissonance theory** argues that when confronted by new or conflicting information people experience a kind of mental discomfort, a dissonance. As a result, we consciously and subconsciously work to limit or reduce that discomfort through three interrelated **selective processes**. These processes help us "select" what information we consume, remember, and interpret in personally important and idiosyncratic ways:

- **Selective exposure** (or **selective attention**) is the process by which people expose themselves to or attend to only those messages consistent with their preexisting attitudes and beliefs. How often do you read the work of a newspaper columnist who occupies a different place on the political spectrum from you? You're more likely to read those articles that confirm what you already believe. It's quite common for someone who buys a new car, electronic component, or other expensive item to suddenly start to see more of that product's advertising. You've spent a lot of money; that creates dissonance. The ads confirm the wisdom of your decision, reducing dissonance.

- **Selective retention** assumes that people remember best and longest those messages that are consistent with their preexisting attitudes and beliefs. Television viewers, for example, remember much more detail from the convention broadcasts of the political party to which they are philosophically closer than they do the broadcasts of competing parties.

- **Selective perception** predicts that people will interpret messages in a manner consistent with their preexisting attitudes and beliefs. When your favorite politicians change positions on an issue, they're flexible

Line drawing used in the 1945 Allport and Postman study of rumor. Psychologists Allport and Postman demonstrated the operation of the selective processes. When groups of White Americans were asked to whisper from one to another the subject of this drawing, the razor invariably shifted from the left hand of the White aggressor to that of the African American defender. Can you explain this result in terms of dissonance theory and the selective processes? From "The Basic Psychology of Rumor," by Gordon W. Allport and Leo J. Postman from *Transactions of the New York Academy of Sciences, Series II, VIII:* 61–81.

and heeding the public's will. When those you don't like do so, they're flip-flopping and have no convictions.

The dominant paradigm at the time of the development of dissonance theory was limited effects theory; thus, the selective processes were seen as limiting media impact because content is selectively filtered to produce as little attitude change as possible. Contemporary mass communication theorists accept the power of the selective processes to limit the influence of media content when it is primarily informational. But because so much content is symbolic rather than informational, other theorists see the selective processes as relatively unimportant when it comes to explaining media's contribution to some important cultural effects. You will recognize these differing perspectives on media's power in the distinction made earlier in this chapter between the transmissional and ritual views of mass communication.

Here is an example of the distinction between informational and symbolic content and the way they relate to the selective processes. Few television stations would broadcast lecture programs by people who openly espouse the racist opinion that people of color are genetically more prone to commit crime. If we were to see such a show, however, the selective processes would likely kick in. We would change to another channel (selective exposure). If we did watch, we would interpret the ideas as loony or sick (selective perception); later we would quickly forget the arguments (selective retention).

Fortunately, the media rarely offer such overtly racist messages. The more likely situation in contemporary television is that the production conventions and economic and time demands of television news production lead to the common portrayal of certain people as more likely to be involved in violence and crime. It is easier and cheaper, for example, for stations to cover downtown violent crime—it's handy, it's visual, and it needs no significant research or writing—than to cover nonviolent crime, even though 90% of all felonies

in the United States are nonviolent. As a result of these largely symbolic portrayals of crime, our selective processes do not have an opportunity to reshape the "information" in these news reports. There is little information, only a variety of interesting images.

Cultural theorists (we'll meet them later in this chapter) point to official government statistics as proof of the power of the media to shape attitudes toward race. Crime in the United States is committed by all races in near proportion to their presence in the population, yet African American males are disproportionately represented in the prison population and on death row. Although most illicit drug users are White—78% of all users—African Americans represent 37% of all drug arrests; over 67% of all drug offenders in federal prison are African American. Once arrested, African Americans are treated far more harshly than Whites—33% of convicted White defendants receive prison sentences, but 51% of African Americans are sent to prison. Average sentences for Black convicts are 49% higher than those for White convicts (Glasser, 2006; "Drug War Facts," 2004). If our criminal laws and our justice system are racially neutral, they ask, why do these disparities exist? Does the razor still move to the hand of the young Black man?

Reinforcement Theory The selective processes, however, formed the core of what is arguably the most influential book ever published on the impact of mass communication. In *The Effects of Mass Communication*, written in 1960 by the eminent scientist and eventual head of social research for CBS Broadcasting Joseph Klapper, the core of the limited effects paradigm is articulated firmly and clearly. Klapper's theory is based on social science evidence developed prior to 1960 and is often called **reinforcement theory.** It was very persuasive at a time when the nation's social fabric had yet to feel the full impact of the cultural change brought about by the war. In addition, flush with enthusiasm and optimism for the technology and science that had

Family, school, and church may not have the same socializing power they did in Klapper's time. © Baby Blues-Baby Blues Partnership. King Features Syndicate.

helped the United States defeat the Axis powers, the public could see little but good coming from the media technologies, and they trusted the work of Klapper and other scientists.

In retrospect, the value of reinforcement theory may have passed with its 1960 publication date. With rapid postwar urbanization, industrialization, and the increase of women in the workplace, Klapper's "nexus of mediating factors and influences" (church, family, and school) began to lose its traditional socializing role for many people. During the 1960s, a decade both revered and reviled for the social and cultural changes it fostered, it became increasingly difficult to ignore the impact of media. Most important, however, all the research Klapper had studied in preparation for his book was conducted before 1960, the year in which it is generally accepted that television became a mass medium. Almost none of the science he examined in developing his reinforcement theory considered television.

The Uses and Gratifications Approach Paradigms do not shift easily. Limited effects researchers were unable to ignore obvious media effects such as the impact of advertising, the media's role in sustaining sentiment against the war in Vietnam and in spreading support for civil rights and the feminist movement, and increases in real-world crime that appeared to parallel increases in televised violence. They turned their focus to media consumers to explain how influence is limited. The new body of thought that resulted, called the **uses and gratifications approach,** claimed that media do not do things *to* people; rather, people do things *with* media. In other words, the influence of media is limited to what people allow it to be.

Because the uses and gratifications approach emphasizes *audience members'* motives for making specific consumption choices and the consequences of that intentional media use, it is sometimes seen as being too apologetic for the media industries. In other words, when negative media effects are seen as the product of audience members' media choices and use, the media industries are absolved of responsibility for the content they produce or carry. Media simply give people what they want. This approach is also criticized because it assumes not only that people know why they make the media content choices they do but also that they can clearly articulate those reasons to uses and gratifications researchers. A third criticism is that the approach ignores the fact that much media consumption is unintentional—when we read the newspaper for election news, we can't help but see ads.

DENNIS THE MENACE

"BOY! SHE SURE HAS A LOT OF SKIN, HUH, DAD?"

This Dennis the Menace cartoon demonstrates two criticisms of the uses and gratifications approach. Someone who chooses to read the newspaper may not intentionally select this cartoon but see it nonetheless. In addition, someone who chooses to read this cartoon for its humor will still be confronted with the idealized cultural image of women. Dennis the Menace ® used by permission of Hank Ketcham Enterprises and © by North America Syndicate.

When we go to an action movie, we are presented with various representations of gender and ethnicity that have nothing to do with our choice of that film. A fourth criticism is that the approach ignores media's cultural role in shaping people's media choices and use.

Despite these criticisms, the uses and gratifications approach served an important function in the development of mass communication theory by stressing the reciprocal nature of the mass communication process. That is, scientists began to take seriously the idea that people are important in the process—they choose content, they make meaning, they act on that meaning.

Agenda Setting During the era of limited effects, several important ideas were developed that began to cast some doubt on the assumption that media influence on people and cultures was minimal. These ideas are still respected and examined even today. Among the most influential is **agenda setting,** a theory that argues that media may not tell us what to think, but media certainly tell us what to think *about*. Based on their study of the media's role in the 1968 presidential election, Maxwell McCombs and Donald Shaw wrote in 1972,

> In choosing and displaying news, editors, newsroom staff, and broadcasters play an important part in shaping political reality. Readers learn not only about a given issue, but how much importance to attach to that issue from the amount of information in a news story and its position. . . . The mass media may well determine the important issues—that is, the media may set the "agenda" of the campaign. (p. 176)

The agenda-setting power of the media resides in more than the amount of space or time devoted to a story and its placement in the broadcast or on the page. Also important is the fact that there is great consistency between media sources across all media in the choice and type of coverage they give an issue or event. This consistency and repetition signal to people the importance of the issue or event.

Researchers Shanto Iyengar and Donald Kinder (1987) tested the application of agenda-setting theory to the network evening news shows in a series of experiments. Their conclusions supported McCombs and Shaw. "Americans' views of their society and nation," they wrote, "are powerfully shaped by the stories that appear on the evening news" (p. 112). But Iyengar and Kinder took agenda setting a step or two further. They discovered that the position of a story affected the agenda-setting power of television news. As you might expect, the lead story on the nightly newscast had the greatest agenda-setting effect, in part because first stories tend to have viewers' full attention—they come before interruptions and other distractions can occur. The second reason, said the researchers, is that viewers accept the broadcasters' implicit categorization of the lead story as the most important. Iyengar and Kinder also tested the impact of vivid video presentations, discovering that emotionally presented, powerful images tended to undercut the agenda-setting power of television news because the images focused too much attention on the specific situation or person in the story rather than on the issue.

Dependency Theory In 1975 Melvin DeFleur and Sandra Ball-Rokeach offered a view of potentially powerful mass media, tying that power to audience members' dependence on media content. Their **dependency theory** is composed of several assertions:

- The basis of media's influence resides in the "relationship between the larger social system, the media's role in that system, and audience relationships to the media" (p. 261).
- The degree of our dependence on media and their content is the "key variable in understanding when and why media messages alter audience beliefs, feelings, or behavior" (p. 261).
- In our modern industrial society we are increasingly dependent on media (a) to understand the social world; (b) to act meaningfully and effectively in society; and (c) to find fantasy and escape or diversion.
- Our level of dependency is related to (a) "the number and centrality (importance) of the specific information-delivery functions served by a medium"; and (b) the degree of change and conflict present in society (p. 263).

Limited effects theory has clearly been left behind here. Dependency theory argues that, especially in our complex and changing society, people become increasingly dependent on media and media content to understand what is going on around them, to learn how to behave meaningfully, and for escape. Think of a crisis, a natural disaster, for example. We immediately turn to the mass media. We are dependent on the media to understand what is going on around us, to learn what to do (how to behave), and even sometimes for escape from the reality of the situation. Now think of other, more personal crises—reaching puberty, attending high school, beginning dating, or having a child. Dependency theory can explain or predict our media use and its impact in these situations as well.

Social Cognitive Theory   While mass communication researchers were challenging the limited effects paradigm with ideas such as agenda setting and dependency theory, psychologists were expanding **social cognitive theory**— the idea that people learn through observation—and applying it to mass media, especially television.

Social cognitive theory argues that people model (copy) the behaviors they see and that **modeling** happens in two ways. The first is **imitation,** the direct replication of an observed behavior. For example, a child might see cartoon cat Tom hit cartoon mouse Jerry with a stick and then hit his sister with a stick. The second form of modeling is **identification,** a special form of imitation in which observers do not copy exactly what they have seen but make a more generalized but related response. For example, the child might still be aggressive toward his sister but dump a pail of water on her head rather than hit her with a stick.

The idea of identification was of particular value to mass communication theorists who studied television's impact on behavior. Everyone admits that people can imitate what they see on television. But not all do, and when this imitation does occur in dramatic instances—for example, when someone sets a subway ticket booth and its cashier on fire after watching the movie *Money Train*—it is so outrageous that it is considered an aberration.

Janet Jackson's 2004 Super Bowl "wardrobe malfunction" proved mass society theory is still alive and well. According to many elite critics, it proved the debasement of our culture, led to teen promiscuity, and even explained why America is a target for fundamentalist Muslim terrorism.

Identification, although obviously harder to see and study, is the more likely way that television influences behavior.

Social cognitive theorists demonstrated that imitation and identification are products of three processes:

Observational learning. Observers can acquire (learn) new behaviors simply by seeing those behaviors performed. Many of us who have never fired a handgun can do so because we've seen it done.

Inhibitory effects. Seeing a model, a movie character, for example, punished for a behavior reduces the likelihood that the observer will perform that behavior. In the media we see Good Samaritans sued for trying to help someone, and it reduces our willingness to help in similar situations. That behavior is inhibited by what we've seen.

Disinhibitory effects. Seeing a model rewarded for prohibited or threatening behavior increases the likelihood that the observer will perform that behavior. This is the basis for complaints against the glorification of crime and drugs in movies, for example. Behaviors that people might not otherwise make, those that are inhibited, now become more likely to occur. The behaviors are disinhibited.

The Era of Cultural Theory—A Return to the Idea of Powerful Effects

The obvious and observable impact television has on our culture; the increased sophistication of media industries and media consumers; entrenched social problems such as racial strife; the apparent cheapening of the political process; and the emergence of calls for controls on new technologies such as cable, VCR, satellite, and computer networks are only a few of the many factors that have forced mass communication theorists to rethink media's influence. Clearly, the limited effects idea is inadequate to explain the media impact we see around us every day. But just as clearly, mass society theory tells us very little.

It's important to remember that prominent theories never totally disappear. Joseph McCarthy's efforts to purge Hollywood of communists in the 1950s, for example, were based on mass society notions of evil media and malleable audiences, as were the 1991 attacks on CNN reporter Peter Arnett's broadcasts from Baghdad during the first Persian Gulf War. Unsuspecting viewers would be swayed by this obvious Iraqi propaganda, said the critics (who never explained why they themselves were resistant to it, a perfect example of the third-person effect discussed in Chapter 1). In the 1996 congressional debates and hearings leading up to the Telecommunications Act requirements of a television ratings system and the V-chip, broadcast industry spokespeople consistently raised limited effects and reinforcement theory arguments. Limited effects and uses and gratifications are regularly raised in today's debates over the regulation of video games (Chapter 9).

But the theories that have gained the most support among today's media researchers and theorists are those that accept the potential for powerful media effects, a potential that is *either* enhanced or thwarted by audience members' involvement in the mass communication process. Important to this perspective on audience–media interaction are the **cultural theories.** Stanley Baran and Dennis Davis (2006) wrote that these theories share

> the underlying assumption that our experience of reality is an ongoing, social construction, not something that is only sent, delivered, or otherwise transmitted to a docile public. . . . Audience members don't just passively take in and store bits of information in mental filing cabinets, they actively process this information, reshape it, and store only what serves culturally defined needs. (p. 249)

This book's focus on media literacy is heavily based on cultural theories, which say that meaning and, therefore, effects are negotiated by media and audiences as they interact in the culture. Several theories of mass communication reside under the cultural theories umbrella.

SYMBOLIC INTERACTION

Mass communication theorists borrowed another important theory from the psychologists, **symbolic interaction.** This is the idea that cultural symbols are learned through interaction and then mediate that interaction. In other words, people give things meaning, and that meaning controls their behavior. The flag is a perfect example. We have decided that an array of red, white, and blue cloth, assembled in a particular way, represents not only our nation but its values and beliefs. The flag has meaning because we have given it meaning, and that meaning now governs certain behavior toward the flag. We are not free to remain seated when a color guard carries the flag into a room. We are not free to fold it any way we choose. We are not free to place it on the right side of a stage in a public meeting. This is symbolic interaction.

Communication scholars Don Faules and Dennis Alexander (1978) define communication as "symbolic behavior which results in various degrees of shared meaning and values between participants" (p. 23). In their view, symbolic interaction is an excellent way to explain how mass communication shapes people's behaviors. Accepting that these symbolic meanings are negotiated by participants in the culture, mass communication scholars are left with these questions: What do the media contribute to these negotiations, and how powerful are they?

Symbolic interaction theory is frequently used when the influence of advertising is being studied because advertisers often succeed by encouraging the audience to perceive their products as symbols that have meaning beyond the products' actual function. This is called **product positioning.** For example, what does a Cadillac mean? Success. A Porsche? Virility. General Foods International Coffees? Togetherness and intimacy.

WWW

Critical Theory
www.cla.purdue.edu/academic/enq/theory/

SOCIAL CONSTRUCTION OF REALITY

If we keep in mind James Carey's cultural definition of communication from Chapter 1—communication is a symbolic process whereby reality is produced, maintained, repaired, and transformed—we cannot be surprised that mass communication theorists have been drawn to the ideas of sociologists Peter Berger and Thomas Luckmann. In their 1966 book, *The Social Construction of Reality,* they never mention mass communication, but they offer a compelling theory to explain how cultures use signs and symbols to construct and maintain a uniform reality.

Social construction of reality theory argues that people who share a culture also share "an ongoing correspondence" of meaning. Things generally mean the same to me as they do to you. A stop sign, for example, has just about the same meaning for everyone. Berger and Luckmann call these things that have "objective" meaning **symbols**—we routinely interpret them in the usual way. But there are other things in the environment to which we assign "subjective" meaning. These things they call **signs.** In social construction of reality, then, a car is a symbol of mobility, but a Cadillac or Mercedes Benz is a sign of wealth or success. In either case the meaning is negotiated, but for signs the negotiation is a bit more complex.

Through interaction in and with the culture over time, people bring together what they have learned about these signs and symbols to form **typification schemes**—collections of meanings assigned to some phenomenon or situation. These typification schemes form a natural backdrop for people's interpretation of and behavior in "the major routines of everyday life, not only the typification of others . . . but typifications of all sorts of events and experiences" (Berger & Luckmann, 1966, p. 43). When you enter a classroom, you automatically recall the cultural meaning of its various elements—desks in rows, chalkboard, lectern. You recognize this as a classroom and impose your "classroom typification scheme." You know how to behave: address the person standing at the front of the room with courtesy, raise your hand when you have a question, talk to your neighbors in whispers. These "rules of behavior" were not published on the classroom door. You applied them because they were appropriate to the "reality" of the setting in your culture. In other cultures, behaviors in this setting may be quite different.

Social construction of reality is important to researchers who study the effects of advertising for the same reasons that symbolic interaction has proven valuable. But it is also widely applied when looking at how media, especially news, shape our political realities.

Crime offers one example. What do politicians mean when they say they are "tough on crime"? What is their (and your) reality of crime? It is likely that "crime" signifies (is a sign for) gangs, drugs, and violence. But the statistical (rather than the socially constructed) reality is that there is 10 times more white-collar crime in the United States than there is violent crime. Now think "welfare." What reality is signified? Is it big corporations seeking money and tax breaks from the government? Or is it unwed, unemployed mothers, unwilling to work, looking for a handout? Social construction theorists argue that the "building blocks" for the construction of these "realities" come primarily from the mass media.

CULTIVATION ANALYSIS

Symbolic interaction and social construction of reality provide a strong foundation for *cultivation analysis,* which says that television "cultivates" or constructs a reality of the world that, although possibly inaccurate, becomes accepted simply because we as a culture believe it to be true. We then base our judgments about and our actions in the world on this cultivated reality provided by television.

Although cultivation analysis was developed by media researcher George Gerbner and his colleagues out of concern over the effects of television violence, it has been applied to countless other television-cultivated realities such as beauty, sex roles, religion, the judicial process, and marriage. In all cases the assumptions are the same—television cultivates realities, especially for heavy viewers.

Cultivation analysis is based on five assumptions:

1. *Television is essentially and fundamentally different from other mass media.* Unlike books, newspapers, and magazines, television requires no reading ability. Unlike the movies, television requires no mobility or cash; it is in the home, and it is free. Unlike radio, television combines pictures and sound. It can be consumed from people's very earliest to their last years of life.

2. *Television is the "central cultural arm" of U.S. society.* Gerbner and his colleagues (Gerbner, Gross, Jackson-Beeck, Jeffries-Fox, & Signorielli, 1978) wrote that television, as our culture's primary storyteller, is "the chief creator of synthetic cultural patterns (entertainment and information) for the most heterogeneous mass publics in history, including large groups that have never shared in any common public message systems" (p. 178). The product of this sharing of messages is the **mainstreaming** of reality, moving individual and different people toward a shared, television-created understanding of how things are.

3. *The realities cultivated by television are not necessarily specific attitudes and opinions but rather more basic assumptions about the "facts" of life.* Television does not teach facts and figures; it builds general frames of reference. Return to our earlier discussion of the portrayal of crime on television. Television newscasts never say, "Most crime is violent, most violent crime is committed by people of color, and you should be wary of those people." But by the choices news producers make, television news presents a broad picture of "reality" with little regard for how its "reality" matches that of its audience.

4. *The major cultural function of television is to stabilize social patterns.* That is, the existing power relationships of the culture are reinforced and maintained through television images. Gerbner and his colleagues made this argument:

> The repetitive pattern of television's mass-produced messages and images forms the mainstream of the common symbolic environment that cultivates the most widely shared conceptions of reality. We live in terms of the stories we tell—stories about what things exist, stories about how things work, and stories about what to do—and television tells them all through news, drama, and advertising to almost everybody most of the time. (1978, p. 178)

Because the media industries have a stake in the political, social, and economic structures as they exist, their stories rarely challenge the system that has enriched them.

5. *The observable, measurable, independent contributions of television to the culture are relatively small.* This is not a restatement of limited effects theory. Instead, Gerbner and his colleagues explained its meaning with an "ice-age analogy":

> Just as an average temperature shift of a few degrees can lead to an ice age . . . so too can a relatively small but pervasive influence make a crucial difference. The "size" of an effect is far less critical than the direction of its steady contribution. (Gerbner, Gross, Morgan, & Signorielli, 1980, p. 14)

In other words, even though we cannot always see media effects, they do occur and eventually will change the culture, possibly in profound ways.

CRITICAL CULTURAL THEORY

A major influence on modern mass communication theory comes from European scholarship on media effects. **Critical cultural theory**—the idea that media operate primarily to justify and support the status quo at the expense of ordinary people—is openly political and is rooted in **neo-Marxist theory.** "Old-fashioned" Marxists believed that people were oppressed by those who owned the factories and the land (the means of production). They called the factories and land the *base.* Modern neo-Marxist theorists believe that people are oppressed by those who control the culture, the *superstructure*—in other words, the mass media.

Modern critical cultural theory encompasses a number of different conceptions of the relationship between media and culture. But all share these identifying characteristics:

- *They tend to be macroscopic in scope.* They examine broad, culturewide media effects.

- *They are openly and avowedly political.* Based on neo-Marxism, their orientation is from the political Left.

- *Their goal is at the least to instigate change in government media policies; at the most, to effect wholesale change in media and cultural systems.* Critical cultural theories logically assume that the superstructure, which favors those in power, must be altered.

- *They investigate and explain how elites use media to maintain their positions of privilege and power.* Issues such as media ownership, government–media relations, and corporate media representations of labor and disenfranchised groups are typical topics of study for critical cultural theory because they center on the exercise of power.

The Frankfurt School   The critical cultural perspective actually came to the United States in the 1930s when two prominent media scholars from the University of Frankfurt escaped Hitler's Germany. Theodor Adorno and Max Horkheimer were at the heart of what became known as the **Frankfurt School** of media theory (Arato & Gebhardt, 1978). Their approach, centered in neo-Marxism, valued serious art (literature, symphonic music, and theater) and saw consumption of art as a means to elevate all people toward a better life. Typical media fare—popular music, slapstick radio and movie comedies, the soft news dominant in newspapers—pacified ordinary people while assisting in their repression.

Adorno and Horkheimer's influence on U.S. media theory was minimal during their lifetimes. The limited effects paradigm was about to blossom, neo-Marxism was not well received, and their ideas sounded a bit too much like mass society theory claims of a corrupting and debasing popular media. More recently, though, the Frankfurt School has been "rediscovered," and its influence can be seen in the two final examples of contemporary critical theory, British cultural theory and news production research.

British Cultural Theory   There was significant class tension in England after World War II. During the 1950s and 1960s, working-class people who had fought for their country were unwilling to return to England's traditional notions of nobility and privilege. Many saw the British media—with broadcasting dominated by graduates of the best upper-crust schools, and newspapers and magazines owned by the wealthy—as supporting long-standing class distinctions and divisions. This environment of class conflict produced theorists such as Stuart Hall (1980), who first developed the idea of media as a public forum (Chapter 1) in which various forces fight to shape perceptions of everyday reality. Hall and others in British cultural studies trusted that the media *could* serve all people. However, because of ownership patterns, the commercial orientation of the media, and sympathetic government policies toward media, the forum was dominated by the reigning elite. In other words, the loudest voice in the give-and-take of the cultural forum belonged to those already well entrenched in the power structure.

British cultural theory today provides a home for much feminist research and research on popular culture both in Europe and in the United States.

News Production Research   Another interesting strand of critical cultural theory is **news production research**—the study of how economic and other influences on the way news is produced distort and bias news coverage toward those in power. W. Lance Bennett (1988) identified four common news production conventions used by U.S. media that bolster the position of those in power:

1. *Personalized news.* Most news stories revolve around people. If a newspaper wants to do a report on homelessness, for example, it will typically focus on one person or family as the center of its story. This makes for interesting journalism (and increased ratings or circulation), but it reduces important social and political problems to soap opera levels. The two likely results are that these problems are dismissed by the public as specific to the characters in the story and that the public is not provided with the social and political contexts of the problem that might suggest avenues of public action.

2. *Dramatized news.* News, like other forms of media content, must be attractively packaged. Especially on television, this packaging takes the form of dramatization. Stories must have a hero and a villain, a conflict must be identified, and there has to be a showdown. Again, one problem is that important public issues take on the character of a soap opera or a Western movie. But a larger concern is that political debate is trivialized. Fundamental alterations in tax law or defense spending or any of a number of important issues are reduced to environmental extremists versus greedy corporations or the White House versus Congress. This complaint is often raised about media coverage of campaigns. The issues that should be at the center of the campaign become lost in a sea of stories about the "horse race"—who's ahead; how will a good showing in New Hampshire help Candidate X in her battle to unseat Candidate Y as the front-runner?

3. *Fragmented news.* The daily time and cost demands of U.S. journalism result in newspapers and broadcasts composed of a large number of brief, capsulated stories. There is little room in a given report for perspective and

News production researchers view Judith Miller's prewar reporting on weapons of mass destruction as normalized news at its worst. In defending her controversial journalism, Miller said, "My job isn't to assess the government's information and be an independent intelligence analyst myself. My job is to tell readers of the *New York Times* what the government thought of Iraq's arsenal" (in Sherman, 2004, pp. 4–5). The government said this was a mobile weapons lab, and that's exactly how Miller reported it. Closer inspection showed it to be a weather balloon support vehicle.

For more information on this topic, see Media Talk video clip #19, "Why Is the United States Viewed So Poorly in the Arab World?" on the *Media World* DVD.

context. Another contributor to fragmented news, according to Bennett (1988), is journalists' obsession with objectivity. Putting any given day's story in context—connecting it to other events of the time or the past—would require the reporter to make decisions about which links are most important. Of course, these choices would be subjective, and so they are avoided. Reporters typically get one comment from somebody on one side of the issue and a second comment from the other side, juxtapose them as if they were equally valid, and then move on to tomorrow's assignment.

4. *Normalized news.* The U.S. newswriting convention typically employed when reporting on natural or human-made disasters is to seek out and report the opinions and perspectives of the authorities. When an airplane crashes, for example, the report invariably concludes with these words: "The FAA was quickly on the scene. The cockpit recorder has been retrieved, and the reason for this tragedy will be determined soon." In other words, what happened here is bad, but the authorities will sort it out. Journalists give little independent attention to investigating any of a number of angles that a plane crash or flood might suggest, angles that might produce information different from that of officials.

The cultural effect of news produced according to these conventions is daily reassurance by the media that the system works if those in power are allowed to do their jobs. Any suggestions about opportunities for meaningful social action are suppressed as reporters serve the powerful as "stenographers with amnesia" (Gitlin, 2004, p. 31).

The Effects of Mass Communication— Four Questions

Scientists and scholars use these theories, the earliest and the most recent, to form conclusions about the effects of mass communication. You are of course familiar with the long-standing debate over the effects of television

Ernest Borgnine in Sam Peckinpah's *The Wild Bunch* (1969). In trying to differentiate itself from the television industry, the movie industry turned to graphic violence, fueling the debate over media violence and subsequent real-world aggression.

violence. But there are other media effects questions that occupy thinkers' interest beyond that and the others highlighted here.

DOES MEDIA VIOLENCE LEAD TO AGGRESSION?

No media effects issue has captured public, legislative, and industry attention as has the relationship between media portrayals of violence and subsequent aggressive behavior. Among the reasons for this focus are the facts that violence is a staple of both television and movies and that the United States experienced an upsurge in real violence in the 1960s, just about the time television entrenched itself as the country's dominant mass medium, and that movies turned to increasingly graphic violence to differentiate themselves from and to compete with television.

   The prevailing view during the 1960s was that *some* media violence affected *some* people in *some* ways *some* of the time. Given the dominance of the transmissional perspective of communication and the limited effects paradigm, researchers believed that for "normal" people—that is, those who were not predisposed to violence—*little* media violence affected *few* people in *few* ways *little* of the time. However, increases in youth violence, the assassinations of Robert F. Kennedy and the Reverend Martin Luther King Jr., and the violent eruption of cities during the civil rights, women's rights, and anti–Vietnam War movements led to creation of the Surgeon General's Scientific Advisory Committee on Television and Social Behavior in 1969. After 2 years and $1 million worth of research, the committee (whose members had to be approved by the television networks) produced

www

Surgeon General
www.surgeongeneral.gov

For more information on this topic, see Media Talk video clip #16, "Violence in the Media and Its Effects on Children," on the *Media World* DVD.

findings that led Surgeon General Jesse L. Steinfield to report to the U.S. Senate:

> While the . . . report is carefully phrased and qualified in language acceptable to social scientists, it is clear to me that the causal relationship between televised violence and antisocial behavior is sufficient to warrant appropriate and immediate remedial action. The data on social phenomena such as television and violence and/or aggressive behavior will never be clear enough for all social scientists to agree on the formulation of a succinct statement of causality. But there comes a time when the data are sufficient to justify action. That time has come. (Ninety-Second Congress, 1972, p. 26).

Despite the apparent certainty of this statement, disagreement persists over the existence and extent of the media's contribution to aggressive behavior. Few would argue that media violence *never* leads to aggressive behavior. The disagreement is about what circumstances are needed for such effects to occur, and to whom.

Under What Circumstances? A direct causal relationship between violent content and aggressive behavior—the **stimulation model**—has been scientifically demonstrated in laboratory experiments. So has the **aggressive cues model**—the idea that media portrayals can suggest that certain classes of people, such as women or foreigners, are acceptable targets for real-world aggression, thereby increasing the likelihood that some people will act violently toward people in these groups.

Both the stimulation and aggressive cues models are based on social cognitive theory. Fueled by the research of psychologists such as Albert Bandura,

These scenes from Albert Bandura's media violence research are typical of the laboratory response to portrayals of media violence that social learning researchers were able to elicit from children.

social cognitive theory has made several additional contributions to the violence debate.

Social cognitive theory deflated the notion of **catharsis,** the idea that watching violence in the media reduces people's innate aggressive drive. Social scientists were already skeptical: Viewing people eating does not reduce hunger; viewing people making love does not reduce the drive to reproduce. But social cognitive theory provided a scientific explanation for the research that did show a reduction in aggression after viewing violence. This phenomenon was better explained not by some cathartic power of the media but by inhibitory effects. That is, as we saw in our discussion of social cognitive theory, if media aggression is portrayed as punished or prohibited, it can indeed lead to the reduced likelihood that that behavior will be modeled.

Some people, typically media industry practitioners, to this day defend catharsis theory. But 35 years ago, respected media researcher and theorist Joseph Klapper, who at the time was the head of social research for CBS television, told the U.S. Senate, "I myself am unaware of any, shall we say, hard evidence that seeing violence on television or any other medium acts in a cathartic . . . manner. There have been some studies to that effect; they are grossly, greatly outweighed by studies as to the opposite effect" (Ninety-Second Congress, 1972, p. 60).

Social cognitive theory introduced the concept of **vicarious reinforcement** —the idea that observed reinforcement operates in the same manner as actual reinforcement. This helped direct researchers' attention to the context in which media violence is presented. Theoretically, inhibitory and disinhibitory effects operate because of the presence of vicarious reinforcement. That is, seeing the bad guy punished is sufficient to inhibit subsequent aggression on the part of the viewer. Unfortunately, what researchers discovered is that in contemporary film and television, when the bad guys are punished, they are punished by good guys who out-aggress them. The implication is that even when media portray punishment for aggressive behavior, they may in fact be reinforcing that very same behavior.

Social cognitive theory introduced the concept of **environmental incentives**—the notion that real-world incentives can lead observers to ignore the negative vicarious reinforcement they have learned to associate with a given behavior.

In 1965 Bandura conducted a now-classic experiment in which nursery school children saw a video aggressor, a character named Rocky, punished for his behavior. The children subsequently showed lower levels of aggressive play than did those who had seen Rocky rewarded. This is what social cognitive theory would have predicted. Yet Bandura later offered "sticker-pictures" to the children who had seen Rocky punished if they could perform the same actions they had seen him perform. They all could. Vicarious negative reinforcement may reduce the likelihood that the punished behavior will be performed, but that behavior is still observationally learned. It's just that, at the same time it is observed and learned, observers also learn not to make it. When the real world offers sufficient reward, the originally learned behavior can be demonstrated.

For Whom? The compelling evidence of cognitive learning researchers aside, it's clear that most people do not exhibit aggression after viewing film or video violence. There is also little doubt that those predisposed to violence

For more information on this topic, see Media Talk video clip #14, "Debating the Effects of TV Violence," on the *Media World* DVD.

USING MEDIA TO MAKE A DIFFERENCE

Television and the Designated Driver

Television's ability to serve prosocial ends is obvious in the public service messages we see sprinkled throughout the shows we watch. For example, dozens of national broadcast and cable channels simultaneously ran a 30-second PSA in August 1999 that featured President Clinton urging parents to talk to their kids about violence. And "This is your brain; This is your brain on drugs" is familiar to everyone who can operate a remote control.

But there is a movement among television writers and producers to more aggressively use their medium to produce prosocial effects by embedding important cultural messages in the entertainment fare they create. The one-time ABC series *The Hughleys* is indicative. This 30-minute comedy opened its 1999 season with an episode centering on the show's lead, D. L. Hughley, discovering his children playing with a gun he keeps in the house. Neither pro- nor antigun, this "program-length PSA" was intentionally designed to keep alive the gun debate that began with the horrific string of murderous shootings that blighted 1998 and 1999. *Mad About You* offers another example. Directed to a dealer by the Environmental Media Association, its producers made an electric car part of its series-ending, farewell episode in 1999.

This "prime-time activism" can be traced to Harvard professor Jay Winsten and his 1988 campaign to get Hollywood to push his novel "designated driver" idea. You know what a designated driver is—he or she is the person among a group of friends who is selected to remain alcohol-free during a get-together and then to drive everyone else home. The concept, much less the term, did not even exist until Professor Winsten, through the intervention of CBS executive Frank Stanton, contacted Stanton's friend Grant Tinker, then chairman of NBC, to ask for help. Intrigued by Winsten's plan to develop a new social norm, Tinker put his considerable clout behind the effort, writing letters to the heads of the 13 production companies that did the most business with the networks. If they did not reply quickly enough to suit Tinker, he called them on the phone. Once everyone was in line, Tinker personally escorted Professor Winsten, director of

> **IN THE FOUR NETWORK TELEVISION SEASONS THAT FOLLOWED THESE MEETINGS, DESIGNATED DRIVERS WERE PART OF THE STORY LINES OF 160 DIFFERENT PRIME-TIME SHOWS SEEN BY HUNDREDS OF MILLIONS OF VIEWERS.**

are more likely to be influenced by media aggression. Yet viewers need not necessarily be predisposed for this link to occur, because at any time anyone can become predisposed. For example, experimental research indicates that frustrating people before they view media violence can increase the likelihood of subsequent aggressive behavior.

But the question remains, who, exactly, is affected by mediated violence? If a direct causal link is necessary to establish effects, then it can indeed be argued that some media violence affects some people in some ways some of the time. But if the larger, macro-level ritual view is applied, then we all are affected because we live in a world in which there is more violence than there might be without mass media. We live in a world, according to cultivation analysis, in which we are less trusting of our neighbors and more accepting of violence in our midst. We experience **desensitization.** This need not be the case. As researcher Ellen Wartella (1997) said, "Today, we find wide consensus among experts that, of all the factors contributing to violence in our society, violence on television may be the easiest to control" (p. 4). And in a clear sign of that wide consensus, the American Medical Association, the American Academy of Pediatrics, the American Psychological Association, and the American Academy of Child & Adolescent Psychiatry issued a joint report in summer 2000 offering their combined view that the effects of violent media are "measurable and long lasting" and that "prolonged viewing of media violence can lead to emotional desensitization toward violence in real life" (as quoted in Wronge, 2000, p. 1E).

Harvard's Center for Health Communication, to meetings with all 13 producers.

In the four network television seasons that followed these meetings, designated drivers were part of the story lines of 160 different prime-time shows seen by hundreds of millions of viewers. Professor Winsten was successful in placing his message in entertainment programming, but did his message make a difference? Absolutely. Within 1 year of the introduction of the idea of the designated driver in these television shows, 67% of U.S. adults said they were aware of the concept, and by 1991, 52% of adults under 30 years old said they had served as a designated driver. From 1988, the campaign's first year, to 1997, the number of drunk driver fatalities in the United States dropped by 32% (Cox, 1999). But Professor Winsten acknowledges that embedding public service messages in prime-time television "isn't a magic bullet. It's one component of a larger strategy" (Cox, 1999, p. 22), as can be seen in the work of Mothers Against Drunk Driving, a group of committed women, much like Dr. Winsten, who recognize that mass communication can be used by media literate people to make a real cultural difference (see Chapter 11).

Story lines touting responsible drinking and designated drivers are frequently embedded in many prime-time shows. Do you recognize this type of action from shows such as Dawson's Creek?

DO PORTRAYALS OF DRUGS AND ALCOHOL INCREASE CONSUMPTION?

Concern about media effects reaches beyond the issue of violence. The claims and counterclaims surrounding media portrayals of drugs and alcohol parallel those of the violence debate.

The wealth of scientific evidence linking media portrayals of alcohol consumption, especially in ads, to increases in youthful drinking and alcohol abuse led the U.S. Department of Health and Human Services' National Institute of Alcohol Abuse and Alcoholism to report, "The preponderance of the evidence indicates that alcohol advertising stimulates higher consumption of alcohol by both adults and adolescents" and "There is sufficient evidence to say that alcohol advertising is likely to be a contributing factor to overall consumption and other alcohol-related problems in the long term" (Center for Science in the Public Interest, 2002, p. 2). The National Institute on Media and the Family (2002) reports the following:

Center on Alcohol Marketing and Youth
www.camy.org

National Institute of Media and the Family
www.mediafamily.org

- By the time teenagers reach driving age, they will have seen 75,000 alcohol ads.

- Beer ads are a strong predictor of adolescents' knowledge, preference, and loyalty to beer brands and of their intention to drink.

- Young people report more positive feelings about drinking and their own likelihood to drink after watching alcohol commercials.

What does this magazine ad say about drinking? About attractiveness? About people of color? About having fun? About men? About women? Are you satisfied with these representations of important aspects of your life?

- Fifty-six percent of children in grades 5 through 12 say that alcohol advertising encourages them to drink.
- Ten million people ages 12 to 20 report drinking "in the last month." Seven million are classified as "binge drinkers."
- The average age of first alcohol use is 13.1 years old.

Yet there is a good deal of scientific research—typically from alcohol industry scientists—that discounts the causal link between media portrayals and real-world drinking. Again, researchers who insist on the demonstration of this direct causal relationship will rarely agree on media's influence on behavior. The larger cultural perspective, however, suggests that media portrayals of alcohol, both in ads and in entertainment fare, tell stories of alcohol consumption that predominantly present it as safe, healthy, youthful, sexy, necessary for a good time, effective for dealing with stress, and essential to ceremonies and other rites of passage.

The same scenario exists in the debate over the relationship between media portrayals of nonalcohol drug use and behavior. Relatively little contemporary media content presents the use of illegal drugs in a glorifying manner. In fact, the destructive power of illegal drugs is often the focus of television shows such as *CSI: Miami* and *The Wire* and a central theme in movies such as *Traffic* and *Maria Full of Grace*. Scientific concern has centered therefore on the impact of commercials and other media portrayals of legal over-the-counter drugs. Again, impressive amounts of experimental research suggest a causal link between this content and subsequent abuse of both legal and illegal drugs; however, there also exists research that discounts the causal link between media portrayals and the subsequent abuse of drugs. It cannot be denied, however, that media often present legal drugs as a cure-all for dealing with that pesky mother-in-law, those screaming kids, that abusive boss, and other daily annoyances. You can read more about another important effects issue in the box on page 440, "The Effects of Television Commercials on Childhood Obesity."

WHAT IS MEDIA'S CONTRIBUTION TO GENDER AND RACIAL/ETHNIC STEREOTYPING?

Stereotyping is the application of a standardized image or concept to members of certain groups, usually based on limited information. Because media cannot show all realities of all things, the choices media practitioners make when presenting specific people and groups may well facilitate or encourage stereotyping.

Numerous studies conducted over the last 40 years have demonstrated that women and people of color are consistently underrepresented in all media. An exhaustive analysis of prime-time programming on all the major television networks published in 2002, for example, came to these conclusions:

First, older adults, children, and women are underrepresented on comedies and dramas shown in prime-time network television. Second, white characters, men

These images from *The L Word*, *Queer Eye for the Straight Guy*, *Queer as Folk*, and *Will & Grace* offer samples of contemporary television's portrayals of homosexuals and homosexuality. Researchers believe that repeated and frequent exposure to representations such as these influence people's perceptions of homosexuals and issues relating to homosexuality. For example, despite much heated debate over the issue of gay marriage, a majority of Americans favor civil unions for gay couples ("Civil Unions," 2004). The question, then, as it typically is when discussing media stereotypes, is, Which came first, the culture's perceptions of homosexuals or homosexuals' representation in the media? Clearly, television's presentation of gay people has matured over time—from invisible to realistic and sympathetic. But was television's "evolution" in its representation of homosexuality a *mirror* of culture's already changing attitudes, or did the medium *lead* that change?

CULTURAL FORUM

The Effects of Television Commercials on Childhood Obesity

Two recent scientific reports put the effects of television commercials on childhood obesity, and in an interesting twist, the ethics and legality of advertising to children, squarely into the cultural forum. The first, from the Kaiser Family Foundation, connected several dots:

Dot 1: The number of television commercials an average child sees each year has risen from 20,000 in the 1970s to more than 40,000 today (largely as a result of the proliferation of kids-oriented cable channels), and

Dot 2: The majority of the ads targeted toward children are for food, primarily candy (32%), cereal (31%), and fast food (9%). As such, kids are exposed to one food commercial every 5 minutes, and

Dot 3: As young as 3 years old, a child's amount of television viewing is significantly related to his or her caloric intake and requests that parents buy specific foods seen advertised on television; as a result,

Dot 4: Eleven million American kids are overweight at a time when, according to the American Medical Association, obesity is on track to overtake (in 2005) smoking as the nation's Number One cause of preventable death (McConnell, 2004b; Hellmich, 2004).

Therefore, the report called for the federal government to set nutrition standards for the kinds of food that can and cannot be marketed to children, ban stores from placing candy at kids' eye level, and outlaw manufacturers' payments to schools for selling their junk food. The response from the broadcast industry was immediate—the number of television spots for food has actually declined during the period under study; many sponsors tout healthy alternatives in their commercials; banning food advertising to kids would damage

> **"CHILDREN IN THE UNITED STATES DESERVE THE SAME PROTECTION AGAINST ADVERTISING AS THAT AFFORDED TO ADULTS."**

children's television; the real problem is not television, it's the falling cost of food and lifestyle changes, both in work and leisure, that are less taxing and calorie-burning (McConnell, 2004a).

Although targeting kids is profitable—$8 billion was spent on television marketing to children in 2003, $3 billion on food ads alone (McConnell, 2004b)—several companies did respond to the report. Kids' cable channel Nickelodeon teamed up with several of its advertisers to create new advertising principles calling for the promotion of healthier products on the air and on the shelves. McDonald's announced it would stop "super-sizing" people's orders and offer parents the option of substituting apple slices for fries in kids' Happy Meals. Yet the debate continued. Senator Sam Brownback (R-Kansas) rejected this self-regulation as insufficient. "Stressed-out" two-income couples can't monitor everything their kids see, he said. "I don't think it's fair to say it's just parents' responsibility" (in McConnell, 2004a, p. 21). "The government can't take over the role of parents," countered executive vice president of the Association of National Advertisers Dan Jaffee (in McConnell, 2004b, p. 42).

It was the second report, however, that added the interesting twist to the cultural discussion. A veritable who's who of the most respected children's media effects researchers serving on the American Psychological Association's Task Force on Advertising and Children issued the results of its exhaustive 18-month study "Psychological Issues in the Increasing Commercialization of Childhood" (Kunkel et al., 2004). After lamenting (and documenting) the increasing commercialization of childhood and reviewing "a substantial body of research evidence [that] documents age-related differences in how children understand and are affected by television advertising," these respected researchers connected *their* dots:

Center for Science in the Public Interest
www.cspinet.org

and middle-aged individuals are overrepresented. . . . Third, women tend to be overrepresented in younger adulthood, but underrepresented in later middle-age. Fourth, older adults tend to be portrayed in a more negative fashion than young adults. Latino characters . . . were also underrepresented. . . . [There is] "ghettoization" of black characters in a limited number of shows. Of the black characters in our sample, half were from only seven of the [61] shows [about 11% of the shows studied]. (Harwood & Anderson, 2002, p. 89).

Any of a number of theories, especially cultivation analysis, symbolic interaction, and social construction of reality, can predict the probable outcome of repeated and frequent exposure to these limited and limiting representations. They influence people's perceptions, and people's perceptions influence their behaviors. Examine your own perceptions not only of women

Dot 1: Attempts at the regulation of advertising to children are doomed to failure in the face of industry lobbying and First Amendment concerns, but

Dot 2: Children are psychologically and intellectually incapable of understanding the persuasive intent of television commercials before 8 years of age, and "even at that age, such capability tends to emerge in only rudimentary form"—kids know it's a commercial, but not that its message is biased and warrants some degree of skepticism (p. 9); therefore,

Dot 3: Existing law and public policy are evidence of "a broad societal consensus that children require special treatment and protection from the unbridled efforts of the economic marketplace" (p. 1). Moreover,

Dot 4: There exists "a long-standing principle in communication law that for advertising to be considered fair, it must be readily identifiable as such to its intended audience" (p. 21), and so strong is this principle that

Dot 5: Section 317 of the Communications Act, which governs broadcasting, requires that "all advertising be announced as paid for or furnished as the case may be"; therefore,

Dot 6: "The premise underlying this legal requirement is that it is unfair and deceptive for commercials to bypass the cognitive defenses against persuasion which adults are presumed to have when they understand that a given message consists of advertising content and can identify the source of the message. If it is unfair and deceptive to seek to bypass the defenses that adults are presumed to have when they are aware that advertising is addressed to them, then it must

Sugared cereals, candy, and snack food dominate television advertising to children.

likewise be considered unfair and deceptive to advertise to children in whom these defenses do not yet exist" (p. 21).

This is their interesting twist to the debate. No new regulation is necessary because it is *already* illegal and unethical to advertise to children who do not understand a commercial's intent. "Children in the United States," they conclude, "deserve the same protection against advertising as that afforded to adults" (p. 23).

Enter your voice. Do you agree with the Kaiser Foundation report about the link between food commercials and obesity? Can you find hints in the debate surrounding the report of the three "effects dichotomies" discussed earlier? Should the government intervene on behalf of children? And what of the APA report? Do you come to the same conclusion after connecting their dots, or do you have a different opinion? Why or why not?

and people of color but of the elderly, lawyers, college athletes, and people sophisticated in the use of computers. What images or stereotypes come immediately to mind?

Sure, maybe you were a bit surprised at the data on race and drug use described earlier on page 421; still, you're skeptical. You're a smart, progressive, college-educated individual. Use the following quiz to test yourself on your stereotypes of women, teens, marriage, and family:

1. True or false: Teen pregnancy and out-of-wedlock birthrates continue to climb.

2. What percentage of junior high kids have had sexual intercourse by age 15–45%, 53%, or 17%?

LIVING MEDIA LITERACY

Be a Media Effects Researcher

The debate over media effects means little if it does not produce effects itself. In other words, the experts on all sides of the various effects issues can write and lecture all they want, but until people (and their representatives in the media and government) take up the discussion, nothing will change (if, indeed, you even think it should).

One way, then, for media literate individuals to make the debate over media effects a living enterprise is to take the effects conversation to their friends and family; they can become media effects researchers themselves. This chapter gives you the tools.

First, take the five-question quiz that opens the chapter. Now, add the stereotype questions from page 441. Type them onto a page, followed by a few demographic questions you might want to ask your respondents. Some examples are gender; age; level of education; marital status; number of children; favorite medium; amount of time per day with radio, television, newspapers, magazines, and the Internet; and number of movies attended per month. Choose the ones you are interested in or add any others you think might be important.

Then, select a sample of a reasonable size. If you have a spreadsheet or statistical program on your computer, you can use quite a few respondents, maybe 30 to 50. If you have to do your computations by hand, you may want to talk to 10 or 15 people. Interview those you've chosen and note their responses.

> **THE DEBATE OVER MEDIA EFFECTS MEANS LITTLE IF IT DOES NOT PRODUCE EFFECTS ITSELF.**

What do you do with the data? First, once your respondents have completed your survey, tell them the significance of the first five questions and the correct answers to the stereotype items. Ask them if this information changes what they think about media effects. Does it reinforce their existing belief that media have strong effects? Does it move them, even a little bit, from a limited to a strong effects perspective? Do they remain convinced that media have limited effects? Challenge and debate your respondents. See how strong your convictions are and how well you can articulate the lessons of this chapter.

Analyze your data. Get raw scores; that is, identify the percentage of respondents who answered each item a specific way. What do these results say to you? Then reanalyze your results in terms of respondents' demographics. That is, did men show different patterns than did women? Parents versus nonparents? Heavy versus light television viewers, and so on? What do these data suggest? Then think about the discussions you had with your respondents following the survey. Who seemed most reluctant to accept your effects arguments? Who was most receptive?

Another way to find value in your work is to use it as the basis for an article or essay for your campus or local paper. You may not want to claim your effort as strong science, but your results and the interactions they generated with your respondents should provide the grist for some interesting observations on media and media effects.

3. What percentage of all U.S. families are headed by two parents, that is, a married mother and father—35%, 50%, or 75%?

4. The rate of juvenile crime has risen, stayed about the same, or dropped over the last 20 years?

5. Which of these three states has the highest divorce rate—Mississippi, Oklahoma, or Connecticut? Which set of religious believers has the highest divorce rate—Baptists, nondenominational Christians, or atheists and agnostics?

6. How tall is the average American woman—5'3" or 5'7"? How much does she weigh—110 or 152 pounds?

Are you surprised to learn that teen birthrates and pregnancies are at historic lows and that fewer than 17% of teens experience sexual intercourse by age 15 (Males, 2002)? That 72% of American families are headed by a mother and father (Elber, 2002)? That the juvenile crime rate is at its lowest point in 2 decades (Muwakkil, 2003)? That the divorce rate is lowest in northeastern liberal Connecticut (33%), far lower than the national average of 51% and even further below that of Mississippi (73%) and Oklahoma (79%; Harrop, 2003)? Atheists and agnostics divorce at a rate of 21%, well below that of Baptists (29%) and nondenominational Christians (34%; "Marriage," 2004)? Did you know that the average American woman is 5'3¾" tall and weighs 152 pounds (Irving, 2001)? How did you develop your stereotypes of these people and places? Where did you find the building blocks to construct your realities of their lives?

DO MEDIA HAVE PROSOCIAL EFFECTS?

Virtually every argument that can be made for the harmful or negative effects of media can also be applied to the ability of media to do good. A sizable body of science exists that clearly demonstrates that people, especially children, can and will model the good or prosocial behaviors they see in the media, often to a greater extent than they will the negative behaviors. Research on the impact of media portrayals of cooperation and constructive problem solving (Baran, Chase, & Courtright, 1979) and other "good" behaviors indicates that much more than negative behavior can be socially learned from the media (see the essay on p. 436, "Television and the Designated Driver").

DEVELOPING MEDIA LITERACY SKILLS
Applying Mass Communication Theory

There are many more theories of mass communication and effects issues than we've covered here. Some apply to the operation of media as part of specific social systems. Some examine mass communication at the most micro level; for example, How do viewers process individual television scenes? This chapter has focused on a relatively small number of theories and effects that might prove useful to people trying to develop their media literacy skills. Remember Art Silverblatt's (2001) elements of media literacy in Chapter 1. Among them were understanding the process of mass communication and accepting media content as a "text" providing insight into ourselves and our culture. Among the media literacy skills we identified was an understanding of and respect for the power of media messages. Good mass communication theory speaks to these elements and skills. Good mass communication theorists understand media effects. Media literate people, then, are actually good mass communication theorists. They apply the available conceptions of media use and impact to their own content consumption and the way they live their lives.

RESOURCES FOR REVIEW AND DISCUSSION

Review Points

- In the media effects debate, these arguments for limited media influence have logical counters:
  a. Media content is make-believe; people know it's not real.
  b. Media content is only play or entertainment.
  c. Media simply hold a mirror to society.
  d. If media have any influence, it is only in reinforcing preexisting values and beliefs.

e. Media influence only the unimportant things like fads and fashions.
- Three dichotomies characterize the different sides in the effects debate:
  a. micro- versus macro-level effects
  b. administrative versus critical research
  c. transmissional versus ritual perspective on communication
- In understanding mass communication theory we must recognize that
  a. There is no one mass communication theory.
  b. Theories are often borrowed from other fields of science.

c. Theories are human constructions and they are dynamic.
- Paradigm shifts in mass communication theory are driven by advances in technology or the introduction of new media, calls for their control, and questions about their democratic and pluralistic use.
- The four major eras of mass communication theory are those of mass society theory, the scientific perspective, limited effects theory, and cultural theory, in which there is a return to the idea of powerful media effects.
- Media literate individuals are themselves good mass communication theorists.

Key Terms

 Use the text's Online Learning Center at www.mhhe.com/baran5 to further your understanding of the following terminology.

early window, 410
willing suspension of disbelief, 410
micro-level effects, 412
macro-level effects, 412
administrative research, 412
critical research, 412
transmissional perspective, 413
ritual perspective, 413
mass communication theories, 414
cultivation analysis, 414
attitude change theory, 414
middle-range theories, 414
paradigm, 415
paradigm shift, 415
mass society theory, 416
hypodermic needle theory, 416
magic bullet theory, 416
grand theory, 416
limited effects theory, 418

two-step flow theory, 418
opinion leaders, 418
opinion followers, 418
dissonance theory, 419
selective processes, 419
selective exposure (attention), 419
selective retention, 419
selective perception, 419
reinforcement theory, 421
uses and gratifications approach, 422
agenda setting, 423
dependency theory, 424
social cognitive theory, 425
modeling, 425
imitation, 425
identification, 425
observational learning, 426
inhibitory effects, 426
disinhibitory effects, 426
cultural theory, 427

symbolic interaction, 427
product positioning, 427
social construction of reality, 428
symbols, 428
signs, 428
typification schemes, 428
mainstreaming, 429
critical cultural theory, 430
neo-Marxist theory, 430
Frankfurt School, 430
British cultural theory, 431
news production research, 431
stimulation model, 434
aggressive cues model, 434
catharsis, 435
vicarious reinforcement, 435
environmental incentives, 435
desensitization, 436
stereotyping, 438

Questions for Review

 Go to the self-quizzes on the Online Learning Center to test your knowledge.

1. What are paradigms and paradigm shifts?
2. What are the four eras of mass communication theory?
3. Who are Paul Lazarsfeld, Carl Hovland, Joseph Klapper, and George Gerbner? What is the contribution of each to mass communication theory?

4. How did *The War of the Worlds* radio broadcast influence the development of mass communication theory?
5. What are dissonance theory and the selective processes?

6. What is agenda setting?
7. What is dependency theory?
8. According to uses and gratifications, what is the relationship between media and audience members?
9. What is the distinction between imitation and identification in social cognitive theory?
10. What assumptions about people and media are shared by symbolic interaction and social construction of reality?
11. What are the five assumptions of cultivation analysis?
12. What are the three dichotomies that shape the effects debate?
13. What is the ice-age analogy?
14. What four common news production conventions shape the news to suit the interests of the elite?

15. What are the characteristics of critical cultural studies?
16. What are the early window and willing suspension of disbelief?
17. What is the mirror analogy as it relates to media effects? The fun-house mirror analogy?
18. What are the stimulation and aggressive cues models of media violence? What is catharsis?
19. What are vicarious reinforcement and environmental incentives? How do these ideas figure in the media violence debate?
20. What is meant by desensitization?
21. What is stereotyping? How might media contribute to it?

Questions for Critical Thinking and Discussion

1. Did you draw your dime too small? Whether you did or not, can you explain your behavior in this seemingly simple situation?
2. Some observers today hold to limited effects theories. Do you? If you do, why? If you do not, why not?
3. Do media set the agenda for you? If not, why not? If they do, can you cite examples from your own experience?

4. Can you find examples of magazine or television advertising that use ideas from symbolic interaction or social construction of reality to sell their products? How do they do so?
5. Do you pay attention to alcohol advertising? Do you think it influences your level of alcohol consumption?
6. How did you do on the stereotype quiz on page 441? Why do you think you responded as you did?

Important Resources

 Go to the Online Learning Center for additional readings.

Internet Resources

American Communication Association	www.americancomm.org
International Communication Association	www.icahdq.org
National Communication Association	www.natcom.org
American Sociological Association	www.asanet.org
Roper Center for Public Opinion Research	www.ropercenter.uconn.edu
American Psychological Association	www.apa.org
Critical Theory	www.cla.purdue.edu/academic/enq/theory/
Surgeon General	www.surgeongeneral.gov
Center on Alcohol Marketing and Youth	www.camy.org
National Institute of Media and the Family	www.mediafamily.org
Center for Science in the Public Interest	www.cspinet.org

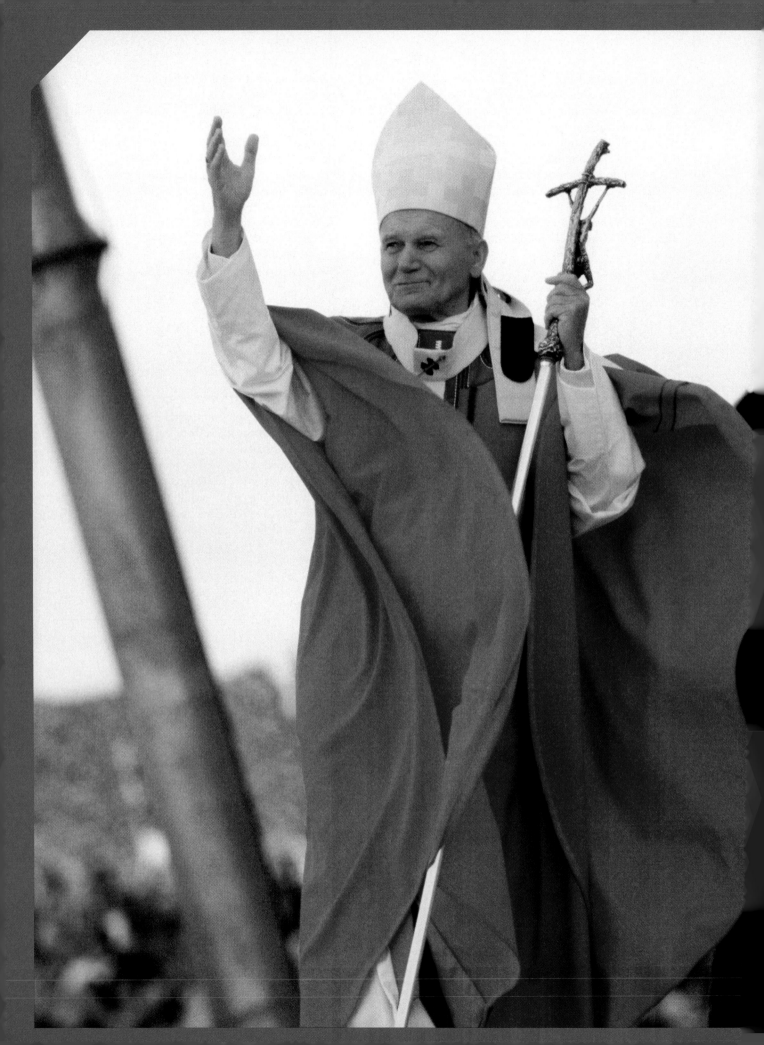

Media Freedom, Regulation, and Ethics

LEARNING OBJECTIVES

Our democracy exists on a foundation of self-governance, and a free and responsible mass media are essential to both democracy and self-governance. But media, because of their power and the often conflicting demands of profit and service under which they operate, are (and should be) open to some control. The level and sources of that control, however, are controversial issues for the media, in the government, and in the public forum. After studying this chapter you should

- be familiar with the history and development of our contemporary understanding of the First Amendment.
- understand the justification for and exercise of media regulation.
- differentiate between a media system that operates under a libertarian philosophy and one that operates under a social responsibility philosophy.
- be conversant in the changes in copyright occasioned by the new digital media and what they mean for content consumers and democracy.
- be able to effectively define and discuss media ethics and how they are applied.
- make personally relevant judgments about media practitioners' conduct in the face of ethical dilemmas.
- understand the operation and pros and cons of self-regulation.
- assess your personal commitment to media reform.

U p until now, everything had been right about the job. Editor of a major college daily newspaper makes a great resumé entry, you are treated like royalty at school events, you get to do something good for your campus, and, if you do your job well, even for the larger world out there. But as the tension around you grows, you start to wonder if it's all worth it.

Opposite: Pope John Paul II, media reform advocate.

First, there were the newly released photos of the torture at Iraq's Abu Ghraib prison. A lawsuit forced the Pentagon to declassify scores of new, disturbing images of detainee abuse at the hands of American soldiers. You wanted to run one. Your staff said "No." You argued First Amendment, your duty as journalists, and the American public's right to know what was being done in its name. Your staffers raised several objections. The images are redundant; readers are tired of Abu Ghraib, said one. They're too political—readers might think the paper is anti-war, offered another. Our brave fighting men and women would be cast in too negative a light by these terrible images, which, protested a third, were merely the actions of a few bad apples.

Then there was the FEMA controversy. Reeling from intense criticism for its failures during Hurricane Katrina and its aftermath, failures that resulted in the needless loss of hundreds of Gulf Coast lives, the Federal Emergency Management Agency issued a "zero access" order on taking pictures of the dead. You wanted to editorialize in opposition to the ban, arguing the public's right to know—how can you fully cover a story whose subject is death if you cannot show images of that subject?—and fairness—the American media have few qualms about running images of death from foreign disasters, so why should they shy away from images of death on our own shores? FEMA has a point, argued your staffers, pictures of the dead would be gruesome, and the failed recovery effort was already becoming too politicized; let's opt for support of the government on this one. Cable channel CNN's successful lawsuit to overturn the government's ban changed no one's mind. So you decide to raise the stakes. You want the paper to not only editorialize in favor of running the disaster photos, but you want to

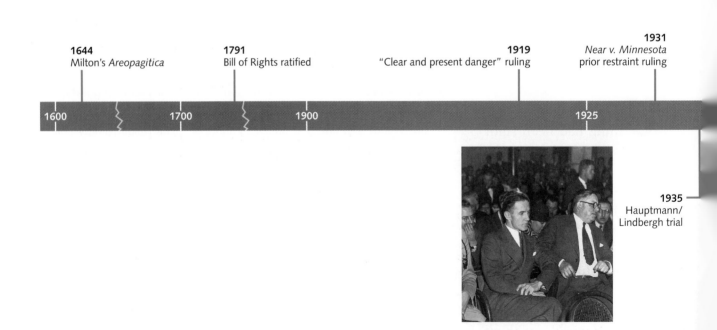

1644
Milton's *Areopagitica*

1791
Bill of Rights ratified

1919
"Clear and present danger" ruling

1931
Near v. Minnesota
prior restraint ruling

1600   1700   1900   1925

1935
Hauptmann/
Lindbergh trial

accompany your opinion piece with an example of an image that FEMA might have banned. This idea is met with even greater resistance. So you try another approach.

Katrina coverage seems to have awaked the American public to the persistence of poverty, especially among people of color, you say. Photos, especially dramatic photos, draw attention to stories readers might otherwise ignore. Everyone's always complaining about apathy on campus, so why not use Katrina to reinvigorate a schoolwide conversation on the nation's obligation to its less fortunate citizens? Is there one? How large should it be? A great photo will further that debate and reemphasize the press's role as the voice of the voiceless. It is precisely the people with the loudest and most powerful voices, in this case FEMA and the administration it represents, who want a quiet and supplicant press.

You sense little change in your listeners' attitude, so you resort to dramatic lessons from journalism class. The press is obligated to serve the people "without fear or favor," you tell your colleagues. As reporters, you tell them, their duty is to "comfort the afflicted and afflict the comfortable." Your friends counsel you to relax. All you're doing is proving them correct: that Katrina, the war—everything—is becoming way too political. "Everything *is* political!" you respond, maybe a little too emphatically. Still, you have little support among your staff members.

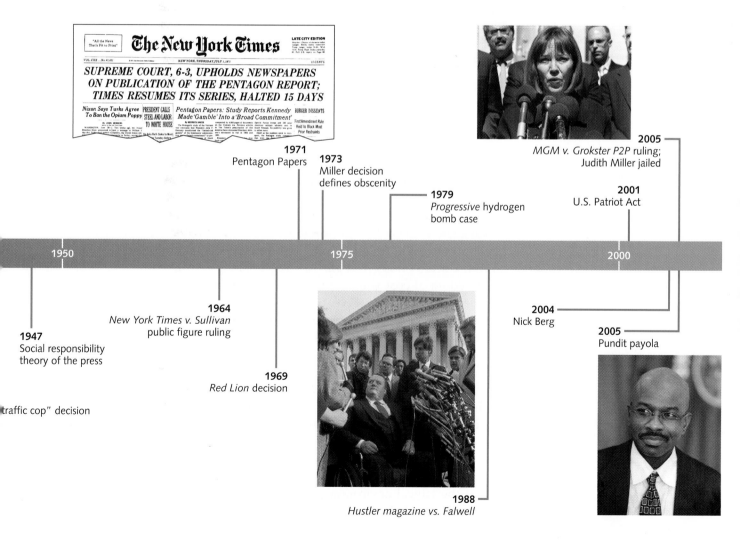

1971
Pentagon Papers

1973
Miller decision
defines obscenity

1979
Progressive hydrogen
bomb case

2005
MGM v. Grokster P2P ruling;
Judith Miller jailed

2001
U.S. Patriot Act

1950　　　　　　　　　　　1975　　　　　　　　　　　2000

1964
New York Times v. Sullivan
public figure ruling

1969
Red Lion decision

1947
Social responsibility
theory of the press

traffic cop" decision

2004
Nick Berg

2005
Pundit payola

1988
Hustler magazine vs. Falwell

The federal government, reeling under intense criticism of its efforts during Hurricane Katrina, issued a ban on photos of dead bodies. CNN successfully sued to have the restriction lifted. Would you have supported CNN's challenge?

Your travails went beyond the issue of the war's toll. You wanted to use your editorial page to support the administration of Rutgers University, which, in the name of free speech, was rejecting calls to shut down the alternative student paper *The Medium* for running an anti-Semitic cartoon. Take a pass, argued your staff; those who would publish a "Knock a Jew in the oven" piece deserve no support (Haynes, 2004).

In each of these situations you decide in favor of more, rather than less, freedom. After all, it's your legal, First Amendment–guaranteed right. You use an Abu Ghraib photo. You get 161 angry phone calls and e-mails. Your anti-FEMA editorial cost your paper nine longtime advertisers. You run the commentary supporting Rutgers. Someone puts a brick through the windshield of your car, and a colleague quits the paper. These events, all recently faced by real college and professional editors, highlight two important lessons offered in this chapter. First, what is legal may not always be what is right. Second, when media practitioners do try to do the right thing, they have to consider the interests, needs, and values of others besides themselves.

In this chapter we look at how the First Amendment has been defined and applied over time. We study how the logic of a free and unfettered press has come into play in the area of broadcast deregulation. We also detail the shift in the underlying philosophy of media freedom from libertarianism to social responsibility theory. This provides the background for our examination of the ethical environment in which media professionals must work as they strive to fulfill their socially responsible obligations.

A Short History of the First Amendment

The U.S. Constitution mentions only one industry by name as deserving special protection—the press. Therefore, our examination of media regulation, self-regulation, and ethics must begin with a discussion of this "First Freedom."

As we saw in Chapter 4, the first Congress of the United States was committed to freedom of the press. The First Amendment to the new Constitution expressly stated that "Congress shall make no law . . . abridging the freedom of speech, or of the press." As a result, government regulation of the media must be not only unobtrusive but also sufficiently justified to meet the limits of the First Amendment. Media industry self-regulation must be sufficiently effective to render official restraint unnecessary, and media practitioners' conduct should be ethical in order to warrant this special protection.

www

First Amendment
www.freedomforum.org

EARLY SENTIMENT FOR A FREE PRESS

Democracy—government by the people—requires a free press. The framers of the Bill of Rights understood this because of their experience with the European monarchies from which they and their forebears had fled. They based their guarantee of this privileged position to the press on **libertarianism,** the philosophy that people cannot govern themselves in a democracy unless they have access to the information they need for that governance. Libertarian philosophy is based on the **self-righting principle,** which was forcefully stated in 1644 by English author and poet John Milton in his book *Areopagitica*. Milton argued from two main points:

- The free flow or trade of ideas serves to ensure that public discourse will allow the truth to emerge.
- Truth will emerge from public discourse because people are inherently rational and good.

But as we also saw in Chapter 4, even the First Amendment and libertarian philosophy did not guarantee freedom of the press. The Alien and Sedition Acts were passed a scant 8 years after the Constitution was ratified. And Milton himself was to become the chief censor of Catholic writing in Oliver Cromwell's English government.

DEFINING AND REFINING THE FIRST AMENDMENT

Clearly, the idea of freedom of the press needed some clarification. One view was (and is) housed in the **absolutist position,** which is expressed succinctly by Supreme Court Justice Hugo Black:

> No law means no law. . . . My view is, without deviation, without exception, without any ifs, buts, or whereases, that freedom of speech means that government shall not do anything to people, either for the views they have or the views they express, or the words they speak or write. (in McMasters, 2005, pl5)

Yet the absolutist position is more complex than this would suggest. Although absolutists accept that the First Amendment provides a central and fundamental wall of protection for the press, several questions about its true meaning remained to be answered over time. Let's look at some of history's answers.

What Does "No Law" Mean?   The First Amendment said that the U.S. Congress could "make no law," but could state legislatures? City councils? Mayors? Courts? Who has the power to proscribe the press? This issue was settled in 1925 in a case involving the right of a state to limit the publication of a socialist newsletter. The Supreme Court, in *Gitlow v. New York*, stated that the First Amendment is "among the fundamental personal rights and 'liberties' protected by the due process clause of the Fourteenth Amendment from impairment by the states" (Gillmor & Barron, 1974, p. 1). Given this, "Congress shall make no law" should be interpreted as "government agencies shall make no law." Today, "no law" includes statutes, laws, administrative regulations, executive and court orders, and ordinances from government, regardless of locale.

What Is "The Press"?   Just what "press" enjoys First Amendment protection? We saw in Chapter 6 that the Supreme Court in its 1952 *Burstyn v. Wilson* decision declared that movies were protected expression. In 1973 Justice William O. Douglas wrote in *CBS v. Democratic National Committee*,

> What kind of First Amendment would best serve our needs as we approach the 21st century may be an open question. But the old fashioned First Amendment that we have is the Court's only guideline; and one hard and fast principle has served us through days of calm and eras of strife, and I would abide by it until a new First Amendment is adopted. That means, as I view it, that TV and radio . . . are all included in the concept of "press" as used in the First Amendment and therefore are entitled to live under the laissez faire regime which the First Amendment sanctions. (Gillmor & Barron, 1974, pp. 7–8)

Advertising, or commercial speech, enjoys First Amendment protection. This was established by the Supreme Court in 1942. Despite the fact that the decision in *Valentine v. Christensen* went against the advertiser, the Court wrote that just because expression was commercial did not necessarily mean that it was unprotected. Some justices argued for a "two-tiered" level of protection, with commercial expression being somewhat less worthy of protection than noncommercial expression. But others argued that this was illogical because almost all media are, in fact, commercial, even when they perform a primarily journalistic function. Newspapers, for example, print the news to make a profit.

In its 1967 *Time, Inc. v. Hill* decision the Supreme Court applied similar logic to argue that the First Amendment grants the same protection to entertainment content as it does to nonentertainment content. Is an entertainingly written news report less worthy of protection than one that is dully written? Rather than allow the government to make these kinds of narrow and ultimately subjective judgments, in the last 6 decades of media development the Supreme Court has consistently preferred expanding its definition of protected expression to limiting it.

What Is "Abridgment"?   Even absolutists accept the idea that limits can be placed on the time, place, and manner of expression—as long as the

Is the man here accused of rape guilty or innocent? If he is guilty, he should want to cover his face to hide his identity. But if he is innocent, wouldn't he be just as likely to want to hide his identity? These so-called perp walks raise the issue of unfair pretrial publicity.

restrictions do not interfere with the substance of the expression. Few, for example, would find it unreasonable to limit the use of a sound truck to broadcast political messages at 4:00 o'clock in the morning. But the Supreme Court did find unconstitutional an ordinance that forbade all use of sound amplification except with the permission of the chief of police in its 1948 decision in *Saia v. New York*. The permissibility of other restrictions, however, is less clear-cut.

Clear and Present Danger   Can freedom of the press be limited if the likely result is damaging? The Supreme Court answered this question in 1919 in *Schenck v. United States*. In this case involving the distribution of a pamphlet urging resistance to the military draft during World War I, Justice Oliver Wendell Holmes wrote that expression could be limited when "the words used are used in such circumstances and are of such a nature as to create a clear and present danger that they will bring about the substantive evils that Congress has a right to prevent." Justice Holmes added, "Free speech would not protect a man in falsely shouting fire in a theater and causing panic." This decision is especially important because it firmly established the legal philosophy that there is no absolute freedom of expression; the level of protection is one of degree.

Balancing of Interests   This less-than-absolutist approach is called the **ad hoc balancing of interests.** That is, in individual First Amendment cases several factors should be weighed in determining how much freedom the press is granted. In his dissent to the Court's 1941 decision in *Bridges v. California,* a case involving a *Los Angeles Times* editorial, Justice Felix Frankfurter wrote that free speech and press is "not so absolute or irrational a conception as to imply paralysis of the means for effective protection of all the freedoms

Media Watchdog
www.tompaine.com

Media intrusion during the 1935 Bruno Hauptmann kidnapping trial led to the banning of radio transmissions and photographers from the courtroom. Hauptmann is seated in the center, hands crossed.

secured by the Bill of Rights. . . . In the cases before us, the claims on behalf of freedom of speech and of the press encounter claims on behalf of liberties no less precious."

Free Press Versus Fair Trial   One example of the clash of competing liberties is the conflict between free press (First Amendment) and fair trial (Sixth Amendment). This debate typically takes two forms: (1) Can pretrial publicity deny citizens judgment by 12 impartial peers, thereby denying them a fair trial? (2) Should cameras be allowed in the courtroom, supporting the public's right to know, or do they so alter the workings of the court that a fair trial is impossible?

Courts have consistently decided in favor of fair trial in conflicts between the First and Sixth Amendments. But it was not until 1961 that a conviction was overturned because of pretrial publicity. In *Irvin v. Dowd* the Court reversed the death sentence conviction of confessed killer Leslie Irvin because his right to a fair trial had been hampered by press coverage that labeled him "Mad Dog Irvin" and reported crimes he had committed as a juvenile, his military court-martial, his identification in a police lineup, his failure to pass a lie detector test, his confession to six killings and numerous robberies, and his willingness to trade a guilty plea for a life sentence. Of 430 potential jurors screened before the trial by attorneys, 370 said they were already convinced Irvin was guilty. Nonetheless, although "tainted" by pretrial publicity, four of the 370 were seated as jurors. The Court determined that Irvin's trial was therefore unfair.

Print reporters have long enjoyed access to trials, but broadcast journalists have been less fortunate. In 1937, after serious intrusion by newspaper photographers during the 1935 trial of Bruno Hauptmann, accused of kidnapping the baby of transatlantic aviation hero Charles Lindbergh, the American Bar

Association (ABA) adopted canon 35 as part of its Code of Judicial Ethics. This rule forbade cameras and radio broadcasting of trials. In 1963 the ABA amended the canon to include a prohibition on television cameras. This, however, did not settle the issue of cameras in the courtroom.

Texas was one of three states that did not subscribe to canon 35. When the conviction for theft, swindling, and embezzlement of Texas financier Billy Sol Estes was overturned by the Supreme Court because of "the insidious influence" (Justice William Douglas's words) of cameras on the conduct of the trial, the debate flared again. Justice Tom Clark wrote for the majority,

> The free press has been a mighty catalyst in awakening public interest in governmental affairs, exposing corruption among public officers and employees and generally informing the citizenry of public events and occurrences, including court proceedings. While maximum freedom must be allowed the press in carrying on this important function in a democratic society its exercise must necessarily be subject to the maintenance of absolute fairness in the judicial process. (*Estes v. State of Texas*, 1965)

Television cameras, then, were out. But Justice Clark continued, "When advances in [broadcast journalism] permit reporting . . . by television without their present hazards to a fair trial we will have another case." Cameras were back in if they posed no hazard to the principle of fair trial.

In 1972 the ABA replaced canon 35 with canon 3A(7), allowing some videotaping of trials for specific purposes but reaffirming its opposition to the broadcast of trial proceedings. But in 1981 the Supreme Court, in *Chandler v. Florida,* determined that television cameras in the courtroom were not inherently damaging to fairness. Today, all 50 states allow cameras in some courts—47 permit them in trial courts—and the U.S. Congress is debating opening up federal courts, including the Supreme Court, to cameras. As for now, photography and broadcast of federal trials is banned by Federal Rule of Criminal Procedure 53. Still, so common has the televising of court proceedings become that Court TV, a cable channel programming nothing but real trials and commentary on them, was launched in 1991.

Libel and Slander **Libel,** the false and malicious publication of material that damages a person's reputation, and **slander,** the oral or spoken defamation of a person's character, are not protected by the First Amendment. The distinction between libel and slander, however, is sufficiently narrow that "published defamation, whether it is in a newspaper, on radio or television, in the movies, or whatever, is regarded since the 1990s as libel. And libel rules apply" (Pember, 1999, p. 134). Therefore, if a report (1) defames a person, (2) identifies that person, and (3) is published or broadcast, it loses its First Amendment protection.

A report accused of being libelous or slanderous, however, is protected if it meets any one of three tests. The first test is *truth.* Even if a report damages someone's reputation, if it is true, it is protected. The second test is *privilege.* Coverage of legislative, court, or other public activities may contain information that is not true or that is damaging to someone's reputation. The press cannot be deterred from covering these important news events for fear that a speaker's or witness's comments will open it to claims of libel or slander. The third test is *fair comment;* that is, the press has the right to express opinions or comment on public issues. For example, theater and film reviews, however severe, are protected, as is commentary on other matters in the public eye.

For public figures, however, a different set of rules applies. Because they are in the public eye, public figures are fair game for fair comment. But does that leave them open to reports that are false and damaging to their reputations? The Supreme Court faced this issue in 1964 in *New York Times v. Sullivan.* In 1960 the Committee to Defend Martin Luther King bought a full-page ad in the *New York Times* asking people to contribute to Dr. King's defense fund. The ad detailed abuse of Dr. King and other civil rights workers at the hands of the Montgomery, Alabama, police. L. B. Sullivan, one of three elected commissioners in that city, sued the *Times* for libel. The ad copy was not true in some of its claims, he said, and because he was in charge of the police, he had been "identified."

The Supreme Court ruled in favor of the newspaper. Even though some of the specific facts in the ad were not true, the *Times* had not acted with **actual malice.** The Court defined the standard of actual malice for reporting on public figures as *knowledge of its falsity or reckless disregard* for whether or not it is true.

Prior Restraint   There is much less confusion about another important aspect of press freedom, **prior restraint.** This is the power of the government to *prevent* the publication or broadcast of expression. U.S. law and tradition make the use of prior restraint relatively rare, but there have been a number of important efforts by government to squelch content before dissemination.

In 1931 the Supreme Court ruled in *Near v. Minnesota* that freedom from prior restraint was a general, not an absolute, principle. Two of the four exceptions it listed were in times of war when national security was involved and when the public order would be endangered by the incitement to violence and overthrow by force of orderly government. These exceptions were to become the basis of two landmark prior restraint decisions. The first, involving the *New York Times,* dealt with national security in times of war; the second, focusing on protecting the public order, involved publishing instructions for building an atomic bomb.

On June 13, 1971, at the height of the Vietnam War, the *New York Times* began publication of what commonly became known as the Pentagon Papers. The papers included detailed discussion and analysis of the conduct of that unpopular war during the administrations of Presidents Kennedy and Johnson. President Nixon's National Security Council (NSC) had stamped them Top Secret. Believing that this was an improper restriction of the public's right to know, NSC staff member Daniel Ellsberg gave copies to the *Times.* After the first three installments had been published, the Justice Department, citing national security, was able to secure a court order stopping further publication. Other newspapers, notably, the *Washington Post* and *Boston Globe,* began running excerpts while the *Times* was silenced until they, too, were enjoined to cease.

On June 30 the Supreme Court ordered the government to halt its restraint of the *Times'*s and other papers' right to publish the Pentagon Papers. Among the stirring attacks on prior restraint written throughout its decision was Justice Hugo Black's:

> In the First Amendment the Founding Fathers gave the free press the protection it must have to fulfill its essential role in our democracy. The press was to

The New York Times

LATE CITY EDITION

VOL. CXX...No. 41,431

NEW YORK, THURSDAY, JULY 1, 1971

15 CENTS

SUPREME COURT, 6-3, UPHOLDS NEWSPAPERS ON PUBLICATION OF THE PENTAGON REPORT; TIMES RESUMES ITS SERIES, HALTED 15 DAYS

The *New York Times* heralds its victory in its First Amendment dispute with the Nixon administration over the publication of the Pentagon Papers.

serve the governed, not the governors. The Government's power to censor the press was abolished so that the press would remain forever free to censure the Government. The press was protected so that it could bare the secrets of government and inform the people. Only a free and unrestrained press can effectively expose deception in government. *(New York Times v. United States)*

Then came the case of the magazine *The Progressive*. In 1979 the magazine announced its intention to publish instructions on how to make a hydrogen bomb. President Jimmy Carter's Justice Department successfully obtained a court order halting publication, even though the article was based on information and material freely obtained from public, nonclassified sources. Before the case could come to court, several newspapers published the same or similar material. The Justice Department immediately abandoned its restraint, and 6 months later *The Progressive* published its original article.

Obscenity and Pornography   Another form of press expression that is not protected is **obscenity.** Two landmark Supreme Court cases established the definition and illegality of obscenity. The first is the 1957 *Roth v. United States* decision. The court determined that sex and obscenity were not synonymous, a significant advance for freedom of expression. It did, however, legally affirm for the first time that obscenity was unprotected expression. The definition or test for obscenity that holds even today was expressed in the 1973 *Miller v. State of California* decision. Chief Justice Warren Burger wrote that the basic guidelines must be

> (a) whether the average person, applying contemporary community standards, would find that the work, taken as a whole, appeals to the prurient interest, (b) whether the work depicts or describes, in a patently offensive way, sexual conduct specifically defined by the applicable state law, and (c) whether the work, taken as a whole, lacks serious literary, artistic, political, or scientific value.

www

Media Watchdog
www.mediachannel.org

The problem for the courts, the media, and the public, of course, is judging content against this standard. For example, what is patently offensive to one person may be quite acceptable to others. What is serious art to one may be serious exploitation to another. And what of an erotic short story written online by an author in New York City but accessed and read by people in Peoria, Illinois? Whose community standards would apply?

An additional definitional problem resides in **pornography,** expression calculated solely to supply sexual excitement. Pornography is protected expression. The distinction between obscenity and pornography may, however, be a legal one. Sexually explicit content is pornography (and protected) until a court rules it illegal; then it is obscene (and unprotected). The difficulty of making such distinctions can be seen in Justice Potter Stewart's famous declaration, "I may not be able to come up with a definition of pornography, but I certainly know it when I see it," and his dissent in *Ginzburg v. United States* (1966), "If the First Amendment means anything, it means that a man cannot be sent to prison merely for distributing publications which offend a judge's sensibilities, mine or any others" (as cited in Gillmor & Barron, 1974, p. 362).

Clearly, the issues of the definition and protection of obscenity and pornography may never be clarified to everyone's satisfaction (see the essay on p. 460, "Larry Flynt and Protection for Expression We Don't Like").

OTHER ISSUES OF FREEDOM AND RESPONSIBILITY

The First Amendment has application to a number of specific issues of media responsibility and freedom.

Indecency   Obscenity and pornography are rarely issues for broadcasters. Their commercial base and wide audience make the airing of such potentially troublesome programming unwise. However, broadcasters frequently do confront the issue of **indecency.** According to the FCC, indecent language or material is that which depicts sexual or excretory activities in a way that is offensive to contemporary community standards.

The commission recently modified, much to broadcasters' dissatisfaction, its way of handling indecency complaints, making it easier for listeners and viewers to challenge questionable content. Stations must now prove they are innocent; in other words, a complaint has validity by virtue of having been made. To broadcasters, this "guilty until proven innocent" approach is an infringement of their First Amendment rights, as it requires them to keep tapes of all their content in the event they are challenged, even in the absence of evidence that a complaint has merit.

The debate over indecency, however, has been confounded by two events. First, the huge surge in complaints (from 111 in 2000 to more than a million in 2004) followed two specific broadcast events: the split-second baring of Janet Jackson's breast at the 2004 Superbowl football game and rocker Bono's spontaneous award show utterance of an expletive later that year. But FCC data revealed that 99.9% of the complaints, most with identical wording, originated with one group, the conservative Christian Parents Television Council (Soundbites, 2005; Rich, 2005). Just how widespread and real, asked broadcasters, was outrage over indecent content? Then, on Veterans Day that same year, when 66 ABC affiliates refused to air the multiple-Oscar-winning

The music of such bands as Slipknot is relegated to the safe harbor of late-night radio, to which children are not usually listening.

Private Ryan, "Steven Spielberg's love letter to American veterans," because it contained men at war swearing, the public, too, aware that the movie had already been broadcast intact twice before, began to question whether the indecency-police had gone too far (Rintels & Charren, 2004, p. 38).

Broadcasters do find some protection when airing potentially offensive material in **safe harbor,** setting aside times of the broadcast day (typically 10:00 p.m. to 6:00 a.m.) when children are not likely to be in the listening or viewing audience.

Deregulation   The difficulty of balancing the public interest and broadcasters' freedom is at the heart of the debate over deregulation and the relaxation of ownership and other rules for radio and television. As we saw in Chapter 8, changes in ownership rules have been controversial, but relaxation of the regulation of broadcasters' public service obligations and other content controls have provided just as much debate.

The courts have consistently supported the FCC's right to evaluate broadcasters' performance in serving the public interest, convenience, and necessity. Naturally, that evaluation must include some judgment of the content broadcasters air. Broadcasters long argued that such "judgment" amounted to unconstitutional infringement of their First Amendment freedom. Many listeners and viewers saw it as a reasonable and quite small price to pay for the use of their (the public's) airwaves.

The Supreme Court resolved the issue in 1943 in *National Broadcasting Co. v. United States.* NBC argued that the commission was no more than a traffic cop, limited to controlling the "flow of traffic." In this view, the regulation of broadcasters' frequency, power, times of operation, and other technical matters was all that was constitutionally allowable. Yet the Court turned what is now known as the **traffic cop analogy** against NBC. Yes, the justices agreed, the commission is a traffic cop. But even traffic cops have the right to control not only the flow of traffic but its composition. For example, drunk

Larry Flynt and Protection for Expression We Don't Like

In the 18th century, newspaper publisher John Peter Zenger's freedom to publish was tested in a famous court case, as we saw in Chapter 4. In the late 20th century, admitted pornographer Larry Flynt has had more than 1 day in court, but his 1988 Supreme Court appearance might be the most important for the First Amendment.

> "IF THE FIRST AMENDMENT WILL PROTECT A SCUMBAG LIKE ME, THEN IT WILL PROTECT ALL OF YOU."

For example, was the attack on Falwell's mother necessary? Where should a media outlet draw the line? Where should the courts? Where should the culture?

Larry Flynt before the Supreme Court.

The November 1983 issue of Flynt's raunchy magazine *Hustler* included a parody of a series of Campari Liqueur ads. The real ads featured celebrities talking about their "first time" trying the drink, clearly a play on the more usual understanding of the expression. The *Hustler* takeoff depicted an intoxicated Jerry Falwell—minister, televangelist, and founder of the Moral Majority—confessing that his "first time" was with his mother in an outhouse. Falwell sued for $45 million, eventually winning $200,000 for intentional infliction of emotional distress. A federal court of appeals upheld the judgment.

Flynt appealed to the Supreme Court. The justices' 1988 unanimous decision supported the man who, in an earlier trial, had worn only an American flag used as a diaper. The case reaffirmed the protection of parody. But *Hustler Magazine v. Falwell,* called by Flynt "the most important First Amendment case in the history of this country," made an even stronger point. As Flynt himself stated, "If the First Amendment will protect a scumbag like me, then it will protect all of you. Because I'm the worst."

Chief Justice Rehnquist made the case for the protection of expression we don't like a bit more delicately:

> At the heart of the First Amendment is the recognition of the fundamental importance of the free flow of ideas. Freedom to speak one's mind is not only an aspect of individual liberty, but essential to the quest for truth and the vitality of the society as a whole. In the world of debate about public affairs, many things done with motives that are less than admirable are nonetheless protected by the First Amendment.

What do you think of this Supreme Court decision? Shouldn't there be limits on what can appear in the media?

drivers can be removed from the road. Potentially dangerous "content," like cars with faulty brakes, can also be restricted. It was precisely this traffic cop function that required the FCC to judge content. The commission was thus free to promulgate rules such as the **Fairness Doctrine,** which required broadcasters to cover issues of public importance and to be fair in that coverage, and **ascertainment,** which required broadcasters to ascertain or actively and affirmatively determine the nature of their audiences' interest, convenience, and necessity (see the essay "The *Red Lion* Decision and the Rights of the Audience" on p. 462).

Broadcast deregulation produced a rush of toy-based children's television shows such as *Pokemon*, which critics contend are inherently unfair to children who cannot recognize them as program-length commercials.

The Fairness Doctrine, ascertainment, and numerous other regulations, such as rules on children's programming and overcommercialization, disappeared with the coming of deregulation during the Reagan administration. License renewal, for example, was once a long and difficult process for stations, which had to generate thousands of pages of documents to demonstrate that they not only knew what their audiences wanted and needed but had met those wants and needs. The burden of proof in their efforts to keep their licenses rested with them. Had they been fair? Had they kept commercial time to acceptable levels? What was their commitment to news and public affairs? Now deregulated, renewal is conducted through a much less onerous process. Broadcasters simply file brief quarterly reports with the commission indicating compliance with technical and other FCC rules. Then, when their licenses are up for renewal (every 8 years), they file a short, postcard-like renewal application.

The deregulation drive began in earnest with President Reagan's FCC chair, Mark Fowler, in the 1980s. Fowler rejected the trustee model of broadcast regulation. He saw many FCC rules as an unconstitutional infringement of broadcasters' rights and believed that "the market" was the audience's best protector. He said that special rules for the control of broadcasting were unnecessary, likening television, for example, to just another home appliance. He called television no more than "a toaster with pictures."

The first FCC chair under President George W. Bush, Michael Powell, was also a strong advocate of deregulation. Of the public interest, he has said that he "has no idea" what it is. "It is an empty vessel," he added, "in which people pour whatever their preconceived views or biases are" (quoted in Hickey, 2002, p. 33). In another press conference he called regulation of telecommunications "the oppressor" (Coen & Hart, 2002, p. 4).

This view of deregulation is not without its critics. Republican and Democratic congressional leaders, liberal and conservative columnists, and numerous public interest groups from across the political spectrum have

WWW

Fairness and Accuracy in Reporting
www.fair.org

The *Red Lion* Decision and the Rights of the Audience

Throughout this book we've seen how media have been used to make a difference, for example, to fight for causes or to alert people to problems. In the specific case of broadcasting, however, it was not decided until the 1960s exactly how much power individuals had in gaining access to broadcasting so they could use it to make a difference. The question was a simple one: Did broadcasters hold their licenses for the purpose of satisfying their own goals, economic and otherwise, or could ordinary citizens expect that they, too, would have access to radio and television?

In November 1964, small AM/FM radio station WGCB in Red Lion, Pennsylvania, aired its weekly installment of "The Christian Crusade." The show's host, Reverend Billy James Hargis, offered his review of a book written by a man named Fred J. Cook. Hargis did not enjoy Cook's book, *Goldwater— Extremist of the Right,* an analysis of the career of conservative politician Barry Goldwater. In his comments on the work, Hargis accused Cook of a number of offenses—lying, being fired from his job as a reporter, being left wing. To Cook this amounted to a personal attack, and under FCC rules he was entitled to time to reply.

The station owner, Red Lion Broadcasting Company, offered to sell time to Cook or, if the writer would plead poverty, to give him free time. Cook refused, claiming the *right* to reply. FCC rules said that reply time must be free in cases of personal attack. The station (and virtually the entire broadcast industry that bankrolled its defense) argued that this free time requirement was an infringement of broadcasters' First Amendment rights. As a result, the stakes were high. The question before the courts was nothing less than an affirmation or denial of the FCC's power to promulgate rules regarding public access to airwaves that the public, in fact, owned.

> ## "IT IS THE RIGHT OF THE VIEWERS AND LISTENERS, NOT THE RIGHT OF THE BROADCASTERS, WHICH IS PARAMOUNT."

In 1966 the United States Court of Appeals for the Seventh Circuit in Chicago District ruled in favor of the station. But the FCC persisted and, in 1967, the United States Court of Appeals for the District of Columbia overturned that decision, siding with Cook and the commission. Red Lion Broadcasting and the Radio Television News Directors Association appealed to the Supreme Court.

On June 9, 1969, the justices delivered what has become known as the *Red Lion* decision. Justice Byron White expressed the Court's support for Mr. Cook and the FCC this way:

> There is nothing in the First Amendment which prevents the Government from requiring a licensee to share his frequency with others and to conduct himself as a proxy or fiduciary with obligations to present those views and voices which are representative of his community and which would otherwise, by necessity, be barred from the airwaves. . . . [T]he people as a whole retain their interest in free speech by radio and their collective right to have the medium function consistently with the ends and purposes of the First Amendment. . . . It is the purpose of the First Amendment to preserve an uninhibited marketplace of ideas in which truth will ultimately prevail, rather than to countenance monopolization of that market, whether it be by the Government itself or a private licensee. *(Red Lion Broadcasting v. United States)*

Justice White's most memorable and meaningful comment on the clash between broadcaster and audience rights remains: *"It is the right of the viewers and listeners, not the right of the broadcasters, which is paramount."*

---

continued to campaign against such fruits of deregulation as concentration, conglomeration, overcommercialization, the abandonment of children, and the lowering of decency standards (Hickey, 2002). As media law attorney Charles Tillinghast argued, "Deregulation of broadcasting means freeing that medium from one of its major obligations to the public—to inform and educate. As ownership of media outlets, including those in broadcasting, becomes more concentrated in the hands of large corporations, unless there is some regulation of content by government (where else can 'public' regulation come from?), broadcasters cannot be trusted to fulfill these obligations" (2000, pp. 150–151).

WWW

Fight for Fair Use
www.digitalconsumer.org

Copyright   The First Amendment protects expression. *Copyright*—identifying and granting ownership of a given piece of expression—is designed to protect the creator's financial interest in that expression. Recognizing that the flow of art, science, and other expression would be enhanced by authors' financial interest in their creation, the framers of the Constitution wrote Article I, Section 8 (8), granting authors exclusive rights to their "writings and discoveries." A long and consistent history of Supreme Court decisions has ensured that this protection would be extended to the content of the mass media that have emerged since that time.

The years 1978 and 1998 saw extensive rewritings of U.S. copyright law. Copyright now remains with creators (in all media) for the span of their lives, plus 70 years. During this time, permission for the use of the material must be obtained from the copyright holder, and if financial compensation (a fee or royalty) is requested, it must be paid. Once the copyright expires, and if the creator does not renew it, the material passes into **public domain,** meaning it can be used without permission.

The exception to copyright is *fair use,* instances in which material can be used without permission or payment. Fair use includes (1) limited non-commercial use, such as photocopying a passage from a novel for classroom use; (2) use of limited portions of a work, such as excerpting a few lines or a paragraph or two from a book for use in a magazine article; (3) use that does not decrease the commercial value of the original, such as videotaping a daytime football game for private, at-home evening viewing; and (4) use in the public interest, such as an author's use of line drawings of scenes from an important piece of film. This latter situation occurred in a dispute over the Zapruder home movie of the 1963 assassination of President Kennedy. A writer used sketches based on the Zapruder film in a book examining the investigation of the Kennedy killing.

Two specific applications of copyright law pertain to recorded music and cable television. Imagine the difficulty cable companies would have in obtaining permission from all the copyright holders of all the material they import and deliver to their subscribers. Yet the cable operators do make money from others' works—they collect material from original sources and sell it to subscribers. The solution to the problem of compensating the creators of the material carried by cable systems was the creation of the Copyright Royalty Tribunal, to which cable companies paid a fee based primarily on the size of their operations. These moneys were then distributed to the appropriate producers, syndicators, and broadcasters. Congress abolished the Copyright Royalty Tribunal in 1993, leaving cable copyright issues in the hands of several different arbitration panels under the auspices of the Library of Congress.

Now imagine the difficulty songwriters would have in collecting royalties from all who use their music—not only film producers and radio and television stations, but bowling alleys, supermarkets, and restaurants. Here the solution is the **music licensing company.** The two biggest are the American Society of Composers, Authors and Publishers (ASCAP) and Broadcast Music Inc. (BMI). Both collect fees based on the users' gross receipts and distribute the money to songwriters and artists.

WWW

Electronic Frontier Foundation
www.eff.org

The Internet and Expanding Copyright   The Internet, as we saw in Chapter 7 with MP3 and in Chapter 10 with file sharing, is forcing a significant rethinking of copyright, one that disturbs many advocates of free expression. They fear that efforts to protect the intellectual property rights of copyright holders are going too far. The expansion of copyright, argues technology writer

Dan Gillmor, gives "the owners of intellectual property vast new authority, simultaneously shredding users' rights" (2000, p. 1C).

For example, in January 2000, a California Superior Court, citing the Digital Millennium Copyright Act (Chapter 10), ruled the posting of DVD decryption software to be illegal. The defendants argued that they did not violate copyright. The court ruled against them because they posted "tools" on the Web that would allow others to violate copyright. Tech writer Gillmor scoffed, "Let's ban cars next. Were you aware that bank robbers use them for getaways?" (2000, p. 6C). In August of that same year, a New York court reaffirmed the ban on posting decryption software, adding that even posting links to sites offering the software was a violation of copyright. And we've already seen the controversy surrounding MP3 and file sharing, neither of which copies anybody's intellectual property, but both of which allow the sharing of copyrighted material.

Copyright exists, say critics of its expansion, to encourage the flow of art, science, and expression, and it grants financial stake to creators, not to enrich those creators but to ensure that there is sufficient incentive to keep the content flowing. "It's always important to remember that copyright is a restriction on free speech, and it's a constitutionally granted restriction on free speech. Therefore, we need to be careful when we play with copyright, because it can have some serious effects on public discourse and creativity," argued copyright expert Siva Vaidhyanathan (as quoted in Anderson, 2000, p. 25). In other words, tightening copyright restrictions can have the effect of inhibiting the flow of art, science, and expression.

Some free-expression champions see the tightening of copyright, or **digital rights management (DRM),** as something other than the justifiable protection of intellectual property. Rather, they argue, it is the drive for more control over and therefore profit from the distribution of content. Technology writer Gillmor argues that new copy-protected digital content and copyright rules combine to "help the entertainment cartel grab absolute control over customers' reading, viewing, and listening" (2002, p. F1). *Wired*'s Jeff Howe (2001, p. 140) writes of technology and copyright-enabled "refrigerators" that will "hold music, movies, books, videogames, and anything else that's digital and salable. Like the perishables stored in that most mundane of household appliances, a media refrigerator's contents will come with expiration dates. They'll need to be refreshed periodically by the shifting of 1s and 0s out of your bank account into [a media company's]. Otherwise, your license to use them will go stale, and the songs, stories, and shows that constitute your daily media diet will wilt like week-old lettuce." And although current copyright law grants you unlimited private use of the media content you legally buy (*and* gives you the right to play it on whatever device you want wherever you want) *and* protects your freedom to copy it for your own private use, "the record companies and Hollywood are scheming to drastically erode your freedom to use legally purchased CDs and videos, and they are doing it behind your back. The only parties represented in the debate are media and technology companies, lawyers, and politicians. Consumers aren't invited. . . . In the new world sought by the media companies," warns *Wall Street Journal* technology columnist Walter Mossberg, you will "not be able to buy a CD or DVD and play it back on your PC. You might not be able to copy to your hard disk, or to a custom-made CD, the few songs you really like from a CD you bought.

You might not be able to tape, or to digitally record, any TV program you like" (2002, p. D7).

The DRM debate escalated with the Supreme Court's 2005 *Grokster* decision (Chapter 7). The entertainment industries were heartened by the ruling that a technology was illegal if it "encouraged" copyright infringement; digital rights activists and technologists were appalled. The Court had disallowed Hollywood's 1984 challenge to videotape (*Sony Corp. v. Universal City Studios,* the so-called *Betamax* decision) because VCR, even if some people used it to violate copyright, had "substantial non-infringing uses." But *Grokster* "relies on a new theory of copyright liability that measures whether manufacturers created their wares with the 'intent' of inducing consumers to infringe. It means that inventors and entrepreneurs will not only bear the costs of bringing new products to market, but also the costs of lawsuits if consumers start using their products for illegal purposes." Who, ask critics, can judge an innovation's intent? Is copyright infringement the *primary* use of P2P networks like Grokster, or is their intent to bring together people making fair use sharing of already purchased material (Gibbs, 2005, p. 50)? What is actually at play here, say *Grokster* critics, is the entertainment industries' dual goal of undoing the Betamax decision and eradicating all fair use of their content (Howe, 2005b). Not to worry, say others, because technology always overruns copyright law. BitTorrent (Chapter 7), for example, will not only make enforcement of *Grokster* impossible but ultimately force the entertainment industries to develop business practices that embrace, rather than resist, emerging technologies.

WWW

Digital Bill of Rights
www.digitalconsumer.org

Social Responsibility Theory

As we saw at the beginning of this chapter, the First Amendment is based on the libertarian philosophy that assumes a fully free press and a rational, good, and informed public. But we have also seen in this and earlier chapters that the media are not necessarily fully free. Government control is sometimes allowed. Corporate control is assumed and accepted. During the 1930s and 1940s, serious doubts were also raised concerning the public's rationality and goodness. As World War II spread across Europe at the end of the 1930s, libertarians were hard pressed to explain how Nazi propaganda could succeed if people could in fact tell right from wrong. As the United States was drawn closer to the European conflict, calls for greater government control of press and speech at home were justified by less-than-optimistic views of the "average American's" ability to handle difficult information. As a result, libertarianism came under attack for being too idealistic.

Time magazine owner and publisher Henry Luce then provided money to establish an independent commission of scholars, politicians, legal experts, and social activists who would study the role of the press in U.S. society and make recommendations on how it should best operate in support of democracy. The Hutchins Commission on Freedom of the Press, named after its chairperson, University of Chicago chancellor Robert Maynard Hutchins, began its work in 1942 and, in 1947, produced its report, "The Social Responsibility Theory of the Press" (see Davis, 1990).

Social responsibility theory is a **normative theory**—that is, it explains how media should *ideally* operate in a given system of social values—and it is the standard against which the public should judge the performance of the U.S. media. Other social and political systems adhere to different normative theories, and these will be detailed in Chapter 15.

Social responsibility theory asserts that media must remain free of government control, but in exchange media must serve the public. The core assumptions of this theory are a cross between libertarian principles of freedom and practical admissions of the need for some form of control on the media (McQuail, 1987):

- Media should accept and fulfill certain obligations to society.
- Media can meet these obligations by setting high standards of professionalism, truth, accuracy, and objectivity.
- Media should be self-regulating within the framework of the law.
- Media should avoid disseminating material that might lead to crime, violence, or civil disorder or that might offend minority groups.
- The media as a whole should be pluralistic, reflect the diversity of the culture in which they operate, and give access to various points of view and rights of reply.
- The public has a right to expect high standards of performance, and official intervention can be justified to ensure the public good.
- Media professionals should be accountable to society as well as to their employers and the market.

In rejecting government control of media, social responsibility theory calls for responsible, ethical industry operation, but it does not free audiences from their responsibility. People must be sufficiently media literate to develop firm yet reasonable expectations and judgments of media performance. But ultimately it is practitioners, through the conduct of their duties, who are charged with operating in a manner that obviates the need for official intrusion.

Media Industry Ethics

A number of formal and informal controls, both external and internal to the industry, are aimed at ensuring that media professionals operate in an ethical manner consistent with social responsibility theory. Among the external formal controls are laws and regulations, codified statements of what can and can't be done and what content is permissible and not permissible, and industry codes of practice. Among the external informal controls are pressure groups, consumers, and advertisers. We have seen how these informal controls operate throughout this text. Our interest here is in examining media's internal controls, or ethics.

DEFINING ETHICS

Thomas Jefferson Center for Free Expression
www.tjcenter.org

Ethics are rules of behavior or moral principles that guide our actions in given situations. The word comes from the Greek *ethos*, which means the customs, traditions, or character that guide a particular group or culture. In our discussion, ethics specifically refer to the application of rational thought by media professionals when they are deciding between two or more competing moral choices.

For example, it is not against the law to publish the name of a rape victim. But is it ethical? It is not illegal to stick a microphone in a crying father's face as he cradles the broken body of his child at an accident scene. But is it ethical?

The application of media ethics almost always involves finding the *most morally defensible* answer to a problem for which there is no single correct or even best answer. Return to the grieving father. The reporter's job is to get the story; the public has a right to know. The man's sorrow is part of that story, but the man has a right to privacy. As a human being he deserves to be treated with respect and to be allowed to maintain his dignity. The reporter has to decide whether to get the interview or leave the grief-stricken man in peace. That decision is guided by the reporter's ethics.

THREE LEVELS OF ETHICS

Because ethics reflect a culture's ideas about right and wrong, they exist at all levels of that culture's operation. **Metaethics** are fundamental cultural values. What is justice? What does it mean to be good? Is fairness possible? We need to examine these questions to know ourselves. But as valuable as they are for self-knowledge, metaethics provide only the broadest foundation for the sorts of ethical decisions people make daily. They define the basic starting points for moral reasoning.

Normative ethics are more or less generalized theories, rules, and principles of ethical or moral behavior. The various media industry codes of ethics or standards of good practice are examples of normative ethics. They serve as real-world frameworks within which people can begin to weigh competing alternatives of behavior. Fairness is a metaethic, but journalists' codes of practice, for example, define what is meant by fairness in the world of reporting, how far a reporter must go to ensure fairness, and how fairness must be applied when being fair to one person means being unfair to another.

Ultimately, media practitioners must apply both the big rules and the general guidelines to very specific situations. This is the use of **applied ethics,** and applying ethics invariably involves balancing conflicting interests.

BALANCING CONFLICTING INTERESTS

In applying ethics, the person making the decisions is called the **moral agent.** For moral agents, sticky ethical issues invariably bring together conflicting interests, for example, those of the editor, readers, and advertisers in this chapter's opening vignette.

Media ethicist Louis Day (2006) identified six sets of individual or group interests that often conflict:

- The interests of the moral agent's *individual conscience;* media professionals must live with their decisions.
- The interests of *the object of the act;* a particular person or group is likely to be affected by media practitioners' actions.

- The interests of *financial supporters;* someone pays the bills that allow the station to broadcast or the newspaper or magazine to publish.
- The interests of *the institution;* media professionals have company loyalty, pride in the organization for which they work.
- The interests of *the profession;* media practitioners work to meet the expectations of their colleagues; they have respect for the profession that sustains them.
- The interests of society; media professionals, like all of us, have a social responsibility. Because of the influence their work can have, they may even have greater responsibilities than do many other professionals.

In mass communication, these conflicting interests play themselves out in a variety of ways. Some of the most common, yet thorniest, require us to examine such basic issues as truth and honesty, privacy, confidentiality, personal conflict of interest, profit and social responsibility, and protection from offensive content.

Truth and Honesty   Can the media ever be completely honest? As soon as a camera is pointed at one thing, it is ignoring another. As soon as a video editor combines two different images, that editor has imposed his or her definition of the truth. Truth and honesty are overriding concerns for media professionals. But what is truth? Take the case of Las Vegas television station KLAS. It wanted to use surveillance footage of a fatal shooting at a casino. The video was dramatic—a full-scale shoot-out in a crowded gambling hall resulting in one death. The images were truthful, but for the evening news they were too "dull, silent" (Rosen, 2002, p. 12). So the station dubbed in casino sounds—slot machines ringing, laughter and chatter, gunfire. These sounds were in the casino when the gunplay occurred, so all the station did was show the truth.

WWW

Electronic Privacy Information Center
www.epic.org

Privacy   Do public figures forfeit their right to privacy? In what circumstances? Are the president's marital problems newsworthy if they do not get in the way of the job? Who is a public figure? When are people's sexual orientations newsworthy? Do you report the names of women who have been raped or the names of juvenile offenders? What about sex offenders? How far do you go to interview grieving parents? When is secret taping permissible?

Our culture values privacy. We have the right to maintain the privacy of our personal information. We use privacy to control the extent and nature of interaction we have with others. Privacy protects us from unwanted government intrusion.

The media, however, by their very nature, are intrusive. Privacy proves to be particularly sensitive because it is almost a metaethic, a fundamental value. Yet the applied ethics of the various media industries allow, in fact sometimes demand, that privacy be denied.

The media have faced a number of very important tests regarding privacy over the last few years. Media pursuit of celebrities is one.

High-profile stories such as the 1999 death of John F. Kennedy Jr. and the 2004 rape investigation of basketball player Kobe Bryant highlight the difficult ethical issues surrounding privacy. JFK Jr., magazine editor and son

To how much privacy was Nick Berg's father entitled in his moment of grief? Was he a "public figure"? Would you have run this photo of the tearful Mr. Berg and his surviving son?

of a martyred president, was a celebrity, a public figure. He therefore loses some right to privacy. But what about his young relatives? They were subjected to a barrage of media attention as they mourned. Kobe Bryant is a celebrity, a public figure. He therefore loses some right to privacy. But what about the woman accusing him of rape? Was it an invasion of her privacy when several publications released her name and photograph after they appeared on the Web? And what of Nick Berg's father? Nick Berg's 2004 beheading by Islamic fundamentalists in Iraq was videotaped and viewed around the world. Did pictures of his father, collapsed in grief at his home, have to follow? Was despondent dad Berg a public figure?

Confidentiality An important tool in contemporary news gathering and reporting is **confidentiality,** the ability of media professionals to keep secret the names of people who provide them with information. Without confidentiality, employees could not report the misdeeds of their employers for fear of being fired; people would not tell what they know of a crime for fear of retribution from the offenders or unwanted police attention. The anonymous informant nicknamed "Deep Throat" would never have felt free to divulge the Nixon White House involvement in the Republican break-in of the Democratic Party's Watergate campaign offices were it not for the promise of confidentiality from *Washington Post* reporters Carl Bernstein and Bob Woodward.

But how far should reporters go in protecting a source's confidentiality? Should reporters go to jail rather than divulge a name? Every state in the Union, except Wyoming, and the District of Columbia have either a **shield law,** legislation that expressly protects reporters' rights to maintain sources' confidentiality in courts of law, or court precedent upholding that right. There is no shield law in federal courts, and most journalists want it that way. Their fear is that once Congress makes one "media law" it may want to make

The *Washington Post*'s Carl Bernstein and Bob Woodward never would have broken the story of the Nixon White House's involvement in the Watergate break-in if it had not been for an anonymous source. The reporters honored their promise of confidentiality for 35 years, until "Deep Throat," then FBI Assistant Director Mark Felt, revealed himself in 2005.

another. For example, media professionals do not want the government to legislate the definition of "reporter" or "journalist."

The ethics of confidentiality are regularly tested by reporters' frequent use of quotes and information from "unnamed sources," "sources who wish to remain anonymous," and "inside sources." Often the guarantee of anonymity is necessary to get the information, but is this fair to those who are commented on by these nameless, faceless newsmakers? Don't these people—even if they are highly placed and powerful themselves—have a right to know their accusers? There is much more to be said about the use and abuse of confidentiality in the essay "Champion or Chump? Judith Miller and the Use of Anonymous Sources" on page 472.

Personal Conflict of Interest   As we've seen, ethical decision making requires a balancing of interests. But what of a media professional's own conflicts of interest? Should media personalities accept speaking fees, free travel, and other gifts from groups and corporations that they may later have to examine? Is it proper for media personalities to fail to disclose the sources and amounts of such gifts?

Armstrong Williams, journalist or PR flack? After it was revealed that he had accepted secret payments from the government to tout Administration programs in his syndicated newspaper column and TV appearances, he was fined.

Syndicated newspaper columnist Maggie Gallagher isn't sure. When the *Washington Post* revealed that she had accepted $41,000 from the federal government to tout its Healthy Marriage Initiative, she said, "Did I violate journalistic ethics by not disclosing it? I don't know. You tell me" (in Notebook, 2005, p. 15). Syndicated columnist and frequent cable news commentator Armstrong Williams offered a somewhat stronger defense for the $240,000 he accepted from the Education Department to support its No Child Left Behind act. Yes, he said, he knew he was on shaky ethical grounds, but he accepted the contract to "regularly comment on N.C.L.B. during the course of his broadcasts" because the law "is something I believe in" (in Alterman, 2005b, p. 10).

Is embedding's trade of increased access in exchange for increased official control ethical? Doonesbury © 2003 G.B. Trudeau. Reprinted with permission of Universal Press Syndicate. All rights reserved.

Obviously, most journalists see this "pundit payola" as ethically bankrupt, not only a violation of journalistic independence, but calling the entire news enterprise into question. Williams's syndication company, Tribune Media Services, fired him. But what of this situation? *Time* columnist Charles Krauthammer is invited to the White House as a consultant to the crafting of President Bush's Second Inaugural Address. Ten days later, interviewed by Fox News, he praises the speech, calling it "revolutionary," but he does not disclose that he was involved in its writing (Dowd, 2005). O.K.? Not O.K.? Would it alter your decision if Krauthammer had informed viewers of his involvement?

Other conflict-of-interest issues bedevil media professionals. The war in Iraq raised the problem of embedding (Chapter 11), reporters accepting military control over their output in exchange for close contact with the troops. The interests in conflict here are objectivity and access—do reporters pay too high a price for their exciting video or touching personal interest stories? Conflicts of interest also arise when media professionals' personal values, if put into action (for example, marching in a pro-choice demonstration), conflict with their obligation to show balance (for example, in reporting on a series of pro-life protests).

Profit and Social Responsibility   The media industries are just that, industries. They exist not only to entertain and inform their audiences but also to make a profit for their owners and shareholders. What happens when serving profit conflicts with serving the public?

The conflict between profit and responsibility was the subject of the Academy Award–nominated 1999 movie *The Insider*. In late 1995, CBS executives killed an exclusive *60 Minutes* interview with Jeffrey Wigand, a former Brown & Williamson tobacco company executive, who told anchor Mike Wallace that cigarette manufacturers manipulated nicotine levels and had lied under oath before Congress. Network officials claimed they only wished to save CBS from a multibillion-dollar lawsuit brought by Brown & Williamson, with whom Wigand had signed a nondisclosure agreement. Many observers at the time—and many moviegoers 4 years later—believed that the company's real fear was that such a lawsuit would reduce the value of the executives' CBS stock.

Champion or Chump? Judith Miller and the Use of Anonymous Sources

The war in Iraq starkly thrust, and then emotionally kept, the already controversial issue of journalists' use of anonymous sources squarely in the cultural forum.

In his 2003 State of the Union address, President George W. Bush told a worried country that British intelligence had confirmed that Iraq was seeking yellow cake uranium from the African nation of Niger for use in the development of nuclear weapons. Soon after, however, former ambassador to Gabon and acting ambassador to Iraq Joseph Wilson wrote an essay in the *New York Times* confirming what many others in Washington and other world capitals already knew: At the request of the CIA, he had gone to Niger 11 months earlier and discovered that the long-made claim was in fact a lie. Upon his return to the United States he informed the State Department, the National Security Council, the CIA, and the office of Vice President Cheney of just that. He accused the president of "misrepresenting the facts on an issue that was a fundamental justification for going to war." A week later "two senior administration officials" phoned six journalists and told them that Wilson's wife, Valerie Plame, was "a CIA operative" (Kurtz, 2003). Only one chose to use the information, syndicated columnist Robert Novak, long associated with conservative causes. But in fact, Plame was more than an operative—she was an NOC (the CIA designation for nonofficial cover), "an agent working under such deep cover that said agent cannot be officially associated with the American intelligence community in any way, shape, or form. . . . The training of these NOC agents, along with the creation of the cover stories known as 'legends' within the agency, requires millions of dollars and delicate work. It is, quite literally, a life and death issue. Little or no protection is given to an exposed NOC by the American government, an arrangement that is understood by all parties involved. A blown NOC can wind up dead very easily" (Pitt, 2004, p. 1). Ambassador Wilson later told the National Press Club that the message was clear, "If you talk, we'll take your family and drag them through the mud" (Kurtz, 2003, p. A4). An unnamed "senior administration official" later confirmed that the leak was "meant purely and simply for revenge" (Alterman, 2003, p. 10).

The damage from the revelation was severe. Plame's CIA mission, now destroyed, was to track the source and movement of weapons of mass destruction (WMD) to terrorists. Not only had her cover been blown, but her front company, Brewster-Jennings, was also exposed, and her network of contacts and agents was ruined, their lives put in jeopardy. It was later revealed that Novak, when he called the CIA for con-

firmation of the Plame leak, was asked by two different agents not to reveal her involvement with the CIA because her work "went much further than her being an analyst" and that an important undercover operation would be compromised (Waas, 2004, p. 1).

> "I DIDN'T WANT TO BE IN JAIL, BUT I KNEW THAT THE PRINCIPLE OF CONFIDENTIALITY WAS SO IMPORTANT THAT I HAD TO, BECAUSE IF PEOPLE CAN'T TRUST US TO COME TO US TO TELL US THE THINGS THAT GOVERNMENT AND POWERFUL CORPORATIONS DON'T WANT US TO KNOW, WE'RE DEAD IN THE WATER. THE PUBLIC WON'T KNOW. THAT'S WHY I WAS SITTING IN JAIL. FOR THE PUBLIC'S RIGHT TO KNOW."

Novak's explanation was straightforward: "I didn't dig it out, it was given to me. They thought it was significant. They gave me the name and I used it" (in Waas, 2004, p. 2), and "I made the judgement it was newsworthy. I think the story has to stand for itself. It's 100 percent accurate" (in Kurtz, 2003, p. A4). It may well have been accurate, but the disclosure of the identity of an American undercover intelligence agent is a felony, and this set off a criminal investigation by the Justice Department, one that eventually led to a grand jury order for Novak and several other reporters to testify and the discovery of the White House leakers' identities—Karl Rove, the president's senior political advisor, and Lewis "Scooter" Libby, the vice president's chief of staff.

Enter the *New York Times*'s Judith Miller, already "with the possible exception of Geraldo Rivera . . . the most-criticized journalist of the war," for her faulty prewar reporting on the search for WMD (Layton, 2003, p. 30). Special Prosecutor Patrick Fitzgerald called Miller and *Time* magazine's Matthew Cooper before the grand jury. He did so reluctantly. "I do not think that a reporter should be subpoenaed anything close to routinely. It should be an extraordinary case," he said. "But if you're dealing with a crime—and what's different here is that the transaction is between a person and a reporter—[the reporter] is the eyewitness to the crime" (in Solomon, 2005, p. A9).

Cooper avoided jail when he agreed to turn over his notes and testify, but Miller, who never wrote about the Plame case but was identified by others as someone who had indeed been given her name, refused. She went to jail for 85 days rather than reveal her source. She agreed to testify after that source, Libby, released her from her promise. "I didn't want to be in jail, but I knew that the principle of confidentiality was so important that I had to, because if people can't trust us to come to us to tell us the things that government and powerful corporations don't want us to know, we're dead in the water. The public won't know. That's why I was sitting in jail. For the public's right to know," she told interviewer Lou Dobbs. CNN's Dobbs saluted her, "The free press in this country is certainly supported and enhanced by your sacrifice" (2005).

But others disagreed. *Editor & Publisher*, the trade journal of the newspaper industry, editorialized that she should "be promptly dismissed for crimes against journalism" (in Kurtz, 2005). War critic Juan Cole called her "a useful idiot" of those in power (2005). As it was, the *Times* "allowed" her to resign. The issue of reporters' privilege, the right to maintain confidentiality, already in the public forum because of the initial Novak story, reerupted. "Journalists are understandably loath to call on a colleague to give up a source who's been promised anonymity, as the credibility of the entire profession can suffer from such a public betrayal," wrote media critic Eric Alterman. "The point is not the principle per se; it is the principle's

pragmatic value in the daily exchange on information between journalist and source. Many such exchanges would not be possible, as the profession is currently practiced, without the guarantee that a source's name not be used" (2004, p. 10).

But other voices in the forum argued that the granting of confidentiality and the protection of anonymity should not be automatic. Former *Times* bureau chief Bill Kovach explained that paper's policy: "If anything the source said was damaging, false, or damaged the credibility of the newspaper, we would identify them . . . Whoever was leaking that information to Novak . . . or Miller was doing it with malice aforethought, trying to set up a deceptive circumstance. That would invalidate your promise of confidentiality. You wouldn't protect a source for telling lies or using you to mislead your audience" (in Huffington, 2005, p. 11). *The Nation*'s Russ Baker (2003, p. 21) argued for a situation-based standard: "Using unnamed sources is a common and necessary technique in journalism. But sources should not be allowed to remain unnamed when the information they are imparting serves to directly advance their own and their employers' objectives. In other words, a reporter needs a very good justification for not naming a source—usually because a source is saying something that could get him or her in big trouble with some powerful entity. But what kind of trouble could befall some unnamed Pentagon source who is leaking material in accord with the objectives of the current Administration? The principle motive for remaining under cover in such circumstances, besides preserving deniability, is to gain greater currency for the leaked material." In other words, confidentiality exists to protect the whistle-blower from the wrath of the powerful; in this

To whom does the public owe the greatest gratitude—Judith Miller, James Risen, or Dana Priest?

continued

situation, Baker argues, confidentiality was misused to secure advantage for those already holding power.

Enter your voice in the debate. Should the promise of confidentiality always be honored? What happens when a reporter discovers he or she has been used? Does this free him or her to reveal the source's identity? Should Miller have been jailed at all? After all, the sources' sole goal was to punish Wilson, a whistle-blower, even if it meant destroying his wife's career and in the process an elaborate, multimillion-dollar CIA covert operation designed to protect America from WMD. And what do you think about ongoing government efforts to punish the *Washington Post*'s Dana Priest, who used anonymous sources in her 2005 revelations that the CIA was maintaining secret overseas prisons, and the *New York Times*'s James Risen, who used leaks "by administration officials deeply concerned with the topic," to bring secret, warrantless government wiretapping to the public's attention in that same year (Learmonth, 2006, p. 8)? Do you see a difference between the Miller situation and these?

These three examples have to do with waging war, the most serious decision any government and its people can make. Should the journalists in question—and their editors—and their readers have demanded better sourcing? What do you think of the standard set by veteran journalist Michael Gross for securing information from unnamed sources? "I have learned," he wrote, "how to offer them, if necessary, anonymity to get that information; how to check it against what I've learned from others until I'm satisfied, attribute it carefully and honestly (if not completely), and how essential it is to come clean with my editor and when necessary, a lawyer, about who my anonymous sources are, what their biases may be, how I've backed up (or failed to back up) what they've told me and why I trust the information" (2003, p. 30).

Concentration and conglomeration raise serious questions about media professionals' willingness to choose responsibility over profit. Media law expert Charles Tillinghast commented,

> One need not be a devotee of conspiracy theories to understand that journalists, like other human beings, can judge where their interests lie, and what risks are and are not prudent, given the desire to continue to eat and feed the family. Nor does one have to be possessed of such theories to understand that wealthy media corporations often share outlooks common to corporations in many different fields, as a result of their status, not of any "agreements." It takes no great brain to understand one does not bite the hand that feeds—or that one incurs great risk by doing so. (2000, pp. 145–146)

Balancing profit and social responsibility is a concern not just for journalists. Practitioners in entertainment, advertising, and public relations often face this dilemma. Does an ad agency accept as a client the manufacturer of sugared children's cereals even though doctors and dentists consider these products unhealthy? Does a public relations firm accept as a client the trade office of a country that forces prison inmates to manufacture products in violation of international rules? Does a production company distribute the 1950s television show *Amos 'n' Andy* knowing that it embodies many offensive stereotypes of African Americans?

Moreover, balancing profit and the public interest does not always involve big companies and millions of dollars. Often, a media practitioner will face an ethical dilemma at a very personal level. What would you do in this situation? The editor at the magazine where you work has ordered you to write an article about the 14-year-old daughter of your city's mayor. The girl's addiction to amphetamines is a closely guarded family secret, but it has been leaked to your publication. You believe that this child is not a public figure. Your boss disagrees, and the boss *is* the boss. By the way, you've just put a down payment on a lovely condo, and you need to make only two more installments to pay off your new car. Do you write the story?

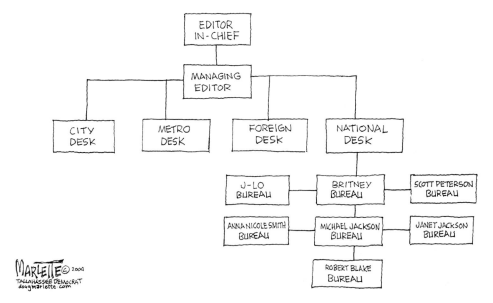

NEWS ORGANIZATION CHART

Offensive Content   Entertainment, news, and advertising professionals must often make decisions about the offensive nature of content. Other than the particular situation of broadcasters discussed earlier in this chapter, this is an ethical rather than a legal issue.

Offensive content is protected. Logically, we do not need the First Amendment to protect sweet and pretty expression. Freedom of speech and freedom of the press exist expressly to allow the dissemination of material that *will* offend. But what is offensive? Clearly, what is offensive to one person may be quite satisfactory to another. Religious leaders on the political Right have attacked the cartoon show *SpongeBob Squarepants* for supposedly promoting homosexuality, and critics from the political Left have attacked the film *Star Wars Episode I: The Phantom Menace* for racist stereotyping. Television stations and networks regularly bleep cusswords that are common on cable television and in the schoolyard but leave untouched images of stabbings, beatings, and shootings. Our culture sanctions the death penalty but is unwilling to view it on television. Where do we draw the line? Do we consider the tastes of the audience? Which members of the audience—the most easily offended? These are ethical, not legal, determinations.

CODES OF ETHICS AND SELF-REGULATION

To aid practitioners in their moral reasoning, all major groups of media professionals have established formal codes or standards of ethical behavior. Among these are the Society of Professional Journalists' *Code of Ethics,* the American Society of Newspaper Editors' *Statement of Principles,* the Radio–Television News Directors Association's *Code of Broadcast News Ethics,* the American Advertising Federation's *Advertising Principles of American Business,* and the Public Relations Society of America's *Code of Professional Standards for the Practice of Public Relations.* These are prescriptive codes that tell media practitioners what they should do.

ACLU
www.aclu.org

To Focus on the Family's James C. Dobson, the friendship between SpongeBob and Patrick is offensive, crossing "a moral line." Others might disagree. Where you draw the line on offensive content is an ethical, not a legal issue.

www

Media Reform
web.takebackthemedia.com

www

Organization of News Ombudsmen
www.newsombudsmen.org

To some, these codes are a necessary part of a true profession; to others, they are little more than unenforceable collections of clichés that restrict constitutional rights and invite lawsuits from outsiders. They offer at least two important benefits to ethical media practitioners: They are an additional source of information to be considered when making moral judgments, and they represent a particular media industry's best expression of its shared wisdom. To others, however, they are meaningless and needlessly restrictive. Ethicists Jay Black and Ralph Barney (1985), for example, argue, "The fact should be evident that the First Amendment has a primary purpose of protecting the distribution of ideas . . . from restriction efforts by legions of 'regulators.' Ethics codes should be considered among those 'regulators'" (p. 28). They continue, "It is indeed not difficult to find examples of codified professional ethics that ultimately become self-serving. That is, they tend to protect the industry, or elements of the industry, at the expense of individuals and other institutions, even of the full society" (p. 29).

In addition to industry professional codes, many media organizations have formulated their own institutional policies for conduct. In the case of the broadcast networks, these are enforced by **Standards and Practices Departments.** Local broadcasters have what are called **policy books.** Newspapers and magazines standardize behavior in two ways: through **operating policies** (which spell out standards for everyday operations) and **editorial policies** (which identify company positions on specific issues). Many media organizations also utilize **ombudsmen,** practitioners internal to the company who serve as "judges" in disputes between the public and the organization. Sometimes they have titles such as public editor, reader advocate, or readers' representative. Some media organizations subscribe to the small number of existing **media councils,** panels of people from both the media and the public who investigate complaints against the media from the public and publish their findings.

These mechanisms of normative ethics are a form of self-regulation, designed in part to forestall more rigorous or intrusive government regulation. In a democracy dependent on mass communication, they serve an important function. We are suspicious of excessive government involvement in media. Self-regulation, however, has certain limitations:

- *Media professionals are reluctant to identify and censure colleagues who transgress.* To do so might appear to be admitting that problems exist; whistle-blowers in the profession are often met with hostility from their peers.

- *The standards for conduct and codes of behavior are abstract and ambiguous.* Many media professionals see this flexibility as a necessary evil; freedom and autonomy are essential. Others believe the lack of rigorous standards renders the codes useless.

UNITED COLORS
OF BENETTON.

This Benetton ad was offensive to many readers. Yet its message—that race should not matter—certainly is not offensive. Why do you think the ad was so controversial and, eventually, pulled from distribution? Would you have pulled it?

- *As opposed to those in other professions, media practitioners are not subject to standards of professional training and licensing.* Again, some practitioners view standards of training and licensing as limiting media freedom and inviting government control. Others argue that licensing has not had these effects on doctors and lawyers.

- *Media practitioners often have limited independent control over their work.* Media professionals are not autonomous, individual professionals. They are part of large, hierarchically structured organizations. Therefore, it is often difficult to punish violations of standards because of the difficulty in fixing responsibility.

Critics of self-regulation argue that these limitations are often accepted willingly by media practitioners because the "true" function of self-regulation is "to cause the least commotion" for those working in the media industries (Black & Whitney, 1983, p. 432). True or not, the decision to perform his or her duties in an ethical manner ultimately rests with the individual media professional. As Black and Barney (1985) explain, an ethical media professional "must rationally overcome the status quo tendencies . . . to become the social catalyst who identifies the topics and expedites the negotiations societies need in order to remain dynamic" (p. 36).

Media Reform

What do these groups and people have in common—Common Cause, the National Rifle Association, the National Organization for Women, Code Pink: Women's Pre-emptive Strike for Peace, the National Association of Black and Hispanic Journalists, the Leadership Conference on Civil Rights, the AFL–CIO, the Consumer Federation of America, the Chicago City Council, the Christian Coalition, the Traditional Values Coalition, the National Association of Broadcasters, the Center for Digital Democracy, Communication Workers of America, MoveOn.org, the Writer's Guild, the Rainbow/PUSH Coalition, Global Exchange, the Parents Television Council, the Catholic Conference, the Screen Actors Guild, the Association of Christian Schools, pop artists Bonnie Raitt, Billy Joel, Pearl Jam, Patti Smith, and Don Henley, media moguls Ted Turner and Barry Diller, Republicans John McCain, Olympia Snowe, Jesse Helms, Kay Bailey Hutchinson, Ted Stevens, and Trent Lott, Democrats John Kerry, John Edwards, Ernest Hollings, Byron Dorgan, and Edward Markey? They all publicly opposed the FCC's 2003 weakening of the country's media ownership rules.

"Take the force of right-wingers upholding community standards who are determined to defend local control of the public airwaves," wrote conservative newspaper columnist William Safire. "Combine that with the force of lefties eager to maintain diversity of opinion in local media; add in independent voters' mistrust of media manipulation; then let all these people have access to their representatives by e-mail and fax, and voilà! Congress awakens to slap down the power grab" (in "Two Cents," 2003, p. 46). The FCC's "drive to loosen the rules," echoed liberal commissioner Michael Copps, "awoke a sleeping giant. American citizens are standing up in never-before-seen numbers to reclaim their airwaves and to call on those who are entrusted to use them to serve the public interest" (in Trigoboff, 2003, p. 36). Those never-before-seen numbers totaled 2 million communications to the Commission just before and soon after its 3-to-2 vote to relax ownership restrictions designed to encourage diversity of opinion in broadcasting. Congress received more comment on the decision that summer than on any other issue besides the invasion of Iraq.

The people had spoken against greater media concentration and for media reform, and they were heard. Over the objections of a Republican-controlled FCC and Republican President George W. Bush, the Republican-controlled House voted 400 to 21 to revoke the FCC's actions. The Republican-controlled Senate followed suit, 55 to 40. And soon the judiciary weighed in. A federal court in Philadelphia issued an emergency stay, prohibiting implementation of the new rules that would have raised the number of television stations one company could own, allow more ownership of multiple stations—as many as three—in one market by one company, allow one company to own both newspapers and television stations in many markets, and expand radio/television cross-ownership.

We have seen throughout this text that culture is created and maintained through communication, and that mass communication is increasingly central to that process. Media literate citizens, then, demand the most robust communication, for it is through our cultural conversations that we create and re-create ourselves, that we know ourselves, the world

Confront and Complain

Media literate people can and should judge the ethical performance of media professionals. Remembering that the application of media ethics almost always involves finding the most morally defensible solution to a problem that has no right or wrong answer, we can evaluate media performance by weighing *our* values against *theirs.* Put the microphone in the grieving father's face? The local station gives priority to the ratings, in other words, the interests of its financial supporters. Its reporter does, too. But you consider the interests of the object of the act and think this unnecessary. The station's decision is not wrong. It simply does not match *your* definition of ethical performance. Judith Miller's uncritical reporting of the government's WMD claims is not wrong. She may well have written her stories with the best interests of society in mind. But you, also considering society's interests, might demand greater objectivity and skepticism. Disagreeing with the judgments made in these two examples, you may choose to find a different local news station and look somewhere other than the *Times* for war reporting.

But what happens when *you* are the object of the act, that is, when the media outlet's ethical decision personally affects you or someone close to you? You can use your media literacy and understanding of the rights and responsibilities of media practitioners to confront those who have made you the object of their act. As businesses that rely in part on their reputations to attract audiences and readers, they will more often than not listen.

This is exactly what happened to Melissa Nathaniel. In late 2001 the athletic 20-something Ms. Nathaniel was the victim of a sexual assault in southern Rhode Island. A state-employed corrections worker, she held off her attacker, a registered sex offender, managing to hold him captive until police arrived.

Much to her surprise, she found herself identified by name in the *Providence Journal*'s account of the crime. Unfazed by the warning, "Don't get into an argument with someone who buys ink by the barrel," she confronted the paper and complained. She was told that the *Journal* had a policy of not printing victims' names in the case of first-degree sexual assault, but inasmuch as her success in fending off her attacker made the charge against him *only* attempted sexual assault, she did not warrant that protection. In other words, had she been raped, the paper would have protected her identity. Because she was not raped, her identity was fair game. Arguing that the paper's policy was not only illogical but a violation of her privacy that robbed her of her right to feel safe in her own home, she later wrote:

During my assault, I experienced intense feelings of fear, vulnerability, and anger. When I discovered that my name and address were in the newspaper,

I relived those feelings. I was terrified that my assailant now knows who I am and where I live. If, and when, he is released from prison, what is going to prevent him from coming to my house and hurting me again? (Nathaniel, 2001, p. B7)

Ms. Nathaniel was faced with an ethical dilemma. She knew that if she were to successfully challenge the paper, she would bring even more notoriety to herself, exactly what she had complained about to the paper. But she chose to put the interests of others—other attack victims—above her own. The paper, to its credit, printed her challenge to it and its policies. Would you have been this brave, this ethical? Would you have confronted and complained? In defense of yourself or someone whom you felt was treated unethically, have you ever engaged in action against a media outlet—for example, writing letters to the editor, addressing a complaint to an ombudsman or media council, canceling a subscription (and telling the publication why), or registering an official complaint with an appropriate self-regulatory or official agency such as the FCC, FTC, or Better Business Bureau?

There are a number of good Web sites that can guide you should you choose to confront a media outlet that you think has not met your ethical standards. San Francisco State University maintains www.journalism.sfsu.edu/www/ethics.html. The Society for Professional Journalists offers advice at www.spj.org/ethics.asp. Two links-oriented ethics sites are Media Ethics Online (www.stlouisspj.org/ethics.htm) and Social Communication and Journalism Resources (www.journalism.uts.edu.au/subjects/jres/ethics.html). Finally, if you are involved in college journalism through a campus publication or broadcast facility and want more on your own ethical operation, go to Ethics On Campus, members.tripod.com/islander/indyethics.html.

> **THE APPLICATION OF MEDIA ETHICS ALMOST ALWAYS INVOLVES FINDING THE MOST MORALLY DEFENSIBLE SOLUTION TO A PROBLEM THAT HAS NO RIGHT OR WRONG ANSWER.**

These people have a family member held as a POW in Iraq. Whose interests should prevail? Theirs? The reporters'? Their stations'? The stations' stockholders'?

Patti Smith, Jesse Jackson Jr., Jesse Helms, and Pearl Jam are committed to media reform. Are you?

around us, and others in it. Because media literate people know that media content is a text that provides insight into our culture and our lives, they insist on more voices, not fewer. The active and growing media reform movement—the sleeping giant—is driven by the desire to make our media more responsive, more integral to how we live our personal, social, and cultural lives. In truth, then, the media reform movement is rooted in media literacy.

If you revisit the diverse cast of activists that opened this section, you'll see that they find wisdom in the words of former FCC commissioner Nicholas Johnson and Pope John Paul II. Johnson said that in our pursuit of a "viable self-governing society . . . whatever your first issue of concern, media [reform] had better be your second, because without change in the media, progress in your primary area is far less likely" (McChesney, 2004, p. 24). Shortly before the death of Pope John Paul II in 2005, the Vatican released the popular religious leader's January 24 letter "to those responsible for communications." "The mass media," wrote the Pontiff, "can and must promote justice and solidarity according to an organic and correct vision of human development by reporting events accurately and truthfully, analyzing situations and problems completely, and providing a forum for different opinions. An authentically ethical approach to using powerful communication media must be situated within the context of a mature exercise of freedom and responsibility, founded upon the supreme criteria of truth and justice" (2005, p. 54).

RESOURCES FOR REVIEW AND DISCUSSION

Review Points

- The First Amendment is based on libertarianism's self-righting principle.
- The absolutist position—no law means no law—is not as straightforward as it may seem. Questions have arisen over the definition of the press, what is abridgement, balancing of interests, the definition of libel and slander, the permissibility of prior restraint, and control of obscenity and pornography.
- Media professionals face other legal issues, such as how to define and handle indecent content, the impact of deregulation, and the limits of copyright.
- Social responsibility theory is the norm against which the operation of the American media system should be judged.
- Ethics, rules of behavior or moral principles that guide our actions, are not regulations, but they are every bit as important in guiding media professionals' behavior.

- There are three levels of ethics—metaethics, normative ethics, and applied ethics.
- Ethics requires the balancing of several interests—the moral agent's individual conscience, the object of the act, financial supporters, the institution itself, the profession, and society.
- Ethics, rather than regulation, influence judgments about matters such as truth and honesty, privacy, confidentiality, personal conflict of interest, the balancing of profit and social responsibility, and the decision to publish or air potentially offensive content.
- There is divergent opinion about the value and true purpose of much industry self regulation.
- The media reform movement generated in response to government plans to further relax industry regulation shows that a media literate public understands the necessity of a free and democratic media system.

Key Terms

 Use the text's Online Learning Center at www.mhhe.com/baran5 to further your understanding of the following terminology.

democracy, 451
libertarianism, 451
self-righting principle, 451
absolutist position, 451
ad hoc balancing of interests, 453
libel, 455
slander, 455
actual malice, 456
prior restraint, 456
obscenity, 457
pornography, 458

indecency, 458
safe harbor, 459
traffic cop analogy, 459
Fairness Doctrine, 460
ascertainment, 460
public domain, 463
music licensing company, 463
digital rights management, 464
normative theory, 465
social responsibility theory, 466
ethics, 466
metaethics, 467

normative ethics, 467
applied ethics, 467
moral agent, 467
confidentiality, 469
shield law, 469
Standards and Practices
   Department, 476
policy book, 476
operating policy, 476
editorial policy, 476
ombudsman, 476
media councils, 476

Questions for Review

 Go to the self-quizzes on the Online Learning Center to test your knowledge.

1. What are the basic tenets of libertarianism? How do they support the First Amendment?
2. What is the absolutist position on the First Amendment?
3. Name important court cases involving the definition of "no law," "the press," "abridgment," clear and present danger, balancing of interests, and prior restraint.

4. What are libel and slander? What are the tests of libel and slander? How do the rules change for public officials?
5. Define obscenity, pornography, and indecency.
6. What is safe harbor?
7. What is the traffic cop analogy? Why is it important in the regulation of broadcasting?

8. What is copyright? What are the exceptions to copyright? What is DRM?
9. What is normative theory?
10. What are the basic assumptions of social responsibility theory?
11. What are ethics? What are the three levels of ethics?
12. What are some of the individual and group interests that often conflict in the application of media ethics?
13. What is confidentiality? Why is confidentiality important to media professionals and to democracy?
14. What are some examples of personal and professional conflict of interest faced by media practitioners?
15. What are the different grounds on which critics object to media codes of conduct?
16. What are some forms of media self-regulation? What are the strengths and limitations of self-regulation?

Questions for Critical Thinking and Discussion

1. Are you a libertarian? That is, do you believe that people are inherently rational and good and that they are best served by a fully free press? Defend your position.
2. What is your position on pornography? It is legally protected expression. Would you limit that protection? When?
3. How much regulation or, if you prefer, deregulation do you think broadcasters should accept?
4. Of all the groups whose interests must be balanced by media professionals, which ones do you think would have the most influence over you?
5. In general, how ethical do you believe media professionals to be? Specifically, print journalists? Television journalists? Advertising professionals? Public relations professionals? Television and film writers? Direct mail marketers?

Important Resources

 Go to the Online Learning Center for additional readings.

Internet Resources

First Amendment	www.freedomforum.org
Media Watchdog	www.mediatransparency.org
Media Watchdog	www.tompaine.com
Journalism Watchdog	www.onlinejournal.com
Center for Democracy and Technology	www.cdt.org
Fairness and Accuracy in Reporting	www.fair.org
Electronic Frontier Foundation	www.eff.org
Digital Bill of Rights	www.digitalconsumer.org
Media Reform	web.takebackthemedia.com
Organization of News Ombudsmen	www.newsombudsmen.org
Media Watchdog	www.consortiumnews.com
Thomas Jefferson Center for Free Expression	www.tjcenter.org
Electronic Privacy Information Center	www.epic.org
ACLU	www.aclu.org
Media Reform	www.freepress.net

Global Media

LEARNING OBJECTIVES

Satellites and the Internet have made mass media truly global. Earth has become a global village. But not all countries use mass media in the same ways. Moreover, many people around the world resent the "Americanization" of their indigenous media systems. After studying this chapter you should

■ be familiar with the development of global media.

■ be familiar with the practice of comparative analysis.

■ be familiar with different media systems from around the world.

■ be aware of the debate surrounding the New World Information Order and other controversies raised by the globalization of media.

■ understand the global nature of the media literacy movement and be familiar with other countries' efforts to improve their citizens' ability to engage the media.

Henri and you have been pen pals since seventh grade. He's visited you here in the United States, and you've been to his house in the small, walled village of Alet, near Carcassonne in southern France. You treat each other like family. Which means you sometimes fight. But unlike siblings living under the same roof, you have to carry on your dispute by e-mail.

Dear Henri,
What's with you guys and your language police? For everyone else it's *e-mail*. For you it's *courrier electronique*. People around the world are getting rich with Internet *start-ups*. You have *jeune-pousses*. My French isn't as good as yours, but doesn't that mean little flower or something?

Opposite: The Mongolian Cow Sour Yogurt Supergirl Contest—China's version of *American Idol*.

Mon ami,

Close, *mais pas de cigare* (but no cigar, my linguistically challenged friend). I admit that we may seem a little foolish to the rest of you, but the Académie Française (what you called the language police) is simply trying to protect our language because it represents the deepest expression of our national identity. The French speak French, our popular culture reflects and is reflected in French, and our history and literature are preserved in French. Maybe as an American speaking another country's language (English from England) you don't understand.

Dear Henri,

You dissin' the USA? Check it out. English is the first language of 400 million people and the second of another 400 million. The world's air traffic control systems all use English for their communication. Three-quarters of all the world's mail is written in English. English is the primary language for the publication of scientific and scholarly reports and for many international organizations such as the European Union and the Association of Southeast Asian Nations. Protecting the culture of a country that reveres Jerry Lewis is one thing, but keeping up with the rest of the planet is another.

www

Radio Free Europe/Radio Liberty
www.rferl.org

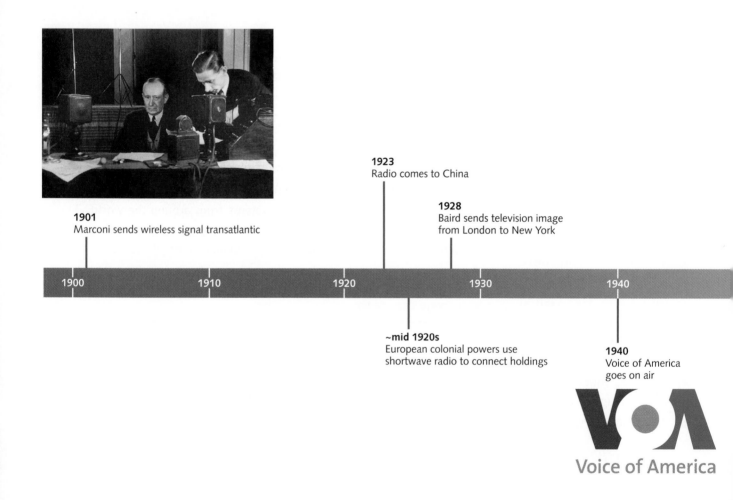

1901
Marconi sends wireless signal transatlantic

1923
Radio comes to China

1928
Baird sends television image
from London to New York

1900   1910   1920   1930   1940

~mid 1920s
European colonial powers use
shortwave radio to connect holdings

1940
Voice of America
goes on air

Voice of America

Mon ami,

Sacre bleu, we do keep up with the rest of the world! In fact, we are the globe's cultural leaders, the avant garde. Surely you've recently seen *Le Fabuleux Destin d'Amélie Poulain* and *Un Long Dimanche de Fiançailles* at your local cinema. I think in America they were called *Amélie* and *The Very Long Engagement*. They were worldwide hits. And *ô mon dieu*, our new television shows! *Les Maîtresses de Maison Désespéré* and *Justice et Order: Intention Criminel*. Because like most of your countrymen you are monolingual, I give you translations. *Law & Order: Criminal Intent*, or something close. The other is easier to translate—*Desperate Housewives*. It's about intrigue (a nice French word, btw) in a small Parisian suburb.

Dear Henri,

You are nuts! *Fou* in French, I think. *Loco* in Spanish. These are American shows!

Mon ami,

Non! They are *Français*. French actors. French writers. French settings. French dialogue. It is you who are *fou!*

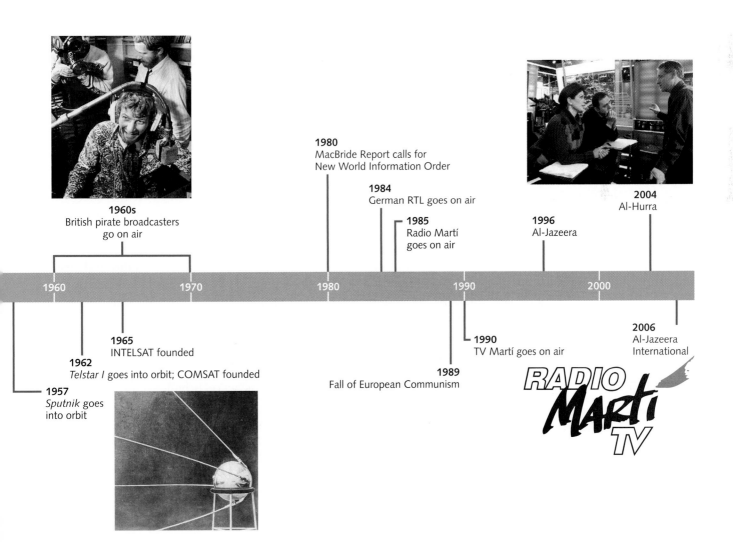

1960s
British pirate broadcasters
go on air

1980
MacBride Report calls for
New World Information Order

1984
German RTL goes on air

1985
Radio Martí
goes on air

1996
Al-Jazeera

2004
Al-Hurra

1957
Sputnik goes
into orbit

1962
Telstar I goes into orbit; COMSAT founded

1965
INTELSAT founded

1989
Fall of European Communism

1990
TV Martí goes on air

2006
Al-Jazeera
International

RADIO
Marti
TV

Neither you nor Henri is *fou;* you are both correct. *Law & Order: Criminal Intent* and *Desperate Housewives* are only two of the many American television shows whose formats have been sold to dozens of other countries for local production. Foreign language *Law & Order* and *Desperate Housewives* clones exist all over the world. *The Apprentice* is another format that has been sold globally. In China it's called *Wise Man Takes All.* China also has a version of *American Idol—The Mongolian Cow Sour Yogurt Supergirl Contest.*

Throughout this text we have seen how globalization is altering the operation of the various mass media industries, as well as the process of mass communication itself. In this chapter, we focus specifically on this globalization and its impact.

In doing so we will look at the beginnings of international media and examine the impact of satellites in creating truly global mass media systems. To study today's global media we will use comparative analyses, looking at the media systems of Britain (the Western concept), Honduras (the development concept), Poland (the revolutionary concept), and China (the authoritarian and communist concepts). Naturally, we will discuss the programming available in other countries. And because global media influence the cultures that use them both positively and negatively, we visit the debate over cultural imperialism. Finally, our media literacy discussion deals with practicing media literacy in our global village.

A Short History of Global Media

In Chapters 7 and 8 we saw that radio and television were, in effect, international in their earliest days. Guglielmo Marconi was the British son of an Italian diplomat, and among his earliest successes was the 1901 transmission of a wireless signal from England to Newfoundland. American inventors, in the persons of Philo Farnsworth and Russian immigrant Vladimir Zworykin, met and eventually overcame the challenge posed by Scotsman John Logie Baird, among whose greatest achievements was the successful transmission of a television picture from London to New York in 1928. But both the Marconi and the Baird transmissions were experimental, designed to attract attention and money to their infant technologies.

However, it was not much later in the development of radio and television that these media did indeed become, if not truly global, at least international. To understand best how this happened, we divide our discussion into two eras, before satellites and after satellites.

INTERNATIONAL MASS MEDIA BEFORE SATELLITES

www
Radio Caroline
www.radiocaroline.co.uk

Almost from the very start, radio signals were broadcast internationally. Beginning in the mid-1920s, the major European colonial powers—the Netherlands, Great Britain, and Germany—were using **shortwave radio** to connect with their various colonies in Africa, Asia, and the Middle East, as well as, in the case of the British, North America (Canada) and the South Pacific (Australia). Shortwave was (and still is) well suited for transmission over very long distances, because its high frequencies easily and efficiently reflect—or **skip**—off the ionosphere, producing **sky waves** that can travel vast distances.

Clandestine Stations It was not only colonial powers that made use of international radio. Antigovernment or antiregime radio also constituted an important segment of international broadcasting. These **clandestine stations** typically emerged "from the darkest shadows of political conflict. They [were] frequently operated by revolutionary groups or intelligence agencies" (Soley & Nichols, 1987, p. vii). In World War II, for example, stations operating from Britain and other Allied nations encouraged German soldiers and sailors to sabotage their vehicles and vessels rather than be killed in battle. Allied stations, such as the Atlantic Station and Soldiers' Radio Calais, also intentionally broadcast misleading reports. Posing as two of the many official stations operated by the German army, they frequently transmitted false reports to confuse the enemy or to force official Nazi radio to counter with rebuttals, thus providing the Allies with exactly the information they sought.

But it was in the Cold War that clandestine broadcasting truly flowered. In the years between the end of World War II and the fall of European communism in 1989, thousands of radio, and sometimes television, pirates took up the cause of either revolutionary (pro-communist) or counterrevolutionary (anti-communist) movements. In addition, other vements tangentially related to this global struggle—especially the growing anticolonial movements in South and Central America and in Africa—made use of clandestine broadcasting.

During the Cold War the unauthorized, clandestine opposition stations typically operated outside the nations or regions to which they broadcast to avoid discovery, capture, and imprisonment or death. Today the relatively few clandestine operations functioning inside the regions to which they transmit can be classified as **indigenous stations,** whereas those operating from outside are **exogenous stations.** FreeNK is an example of an exogenous (or international) station. It broadcasts from South Korea in opposition to the despotic rule of North Korea's Kim Jong Il.

Pirate Broadcasters Another type of broadcast operation transmitting from outside its desired audience's geographic location involved something a bit more benign than war and revolution. These were stations that began broadcasting into Great Britain in the 1960s. Called **pirate broadcasters,** they were illegally operated stations broadcasting to British audiences from offshore or foreign facilities. Among the more notable were Radio Caroline, which reached a daily audience of a million listeners with its signal broadcast from the MV *Frederika* anchored 3½ miles off the Isle of Man, and Radio Veronica, broadcasting from a ship off the coast of the Netherlands.

These pirates, unlike their politically motivated clandestine cousins, were powerful and well subsidized by advertisers and record companies. Moreover, much like the commercial radio stations with which we are now familiar, they broadcast 24 hours a day, every day of the year. These pirates offered listeners an alternative to the controlled and low-key programming of the British Broadcasting Corporation's (BBC) stations. Because the BBC was noncommercial, pirate stations represented the only opportunity for advertisers who wanted to reach British consumers. Record companies intent on introducing Britain's youth to their artists and to rock 'n' roll also saw the pirates as the only way to reach their audience, which the staid BBC all but ignored.

Clandestine Radio
www.clandestineradio.com

RIAS
www.scripps.ohiou.edu/rias/history
.htm

For more information on this topic, see Media Talk video clip #19, "Why Is the United States Viewed So Poorly in the Arab World?" on the *Media World* DVD.

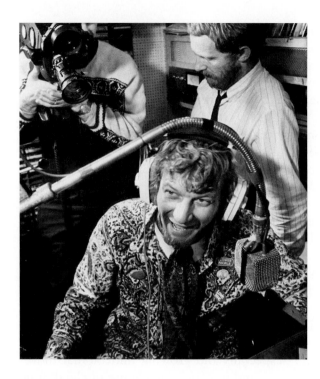

Disc jockey Robby Dale broadcasts from pirate station Radio Caroline aboard the MV *Frederika*, anchored off Great Britain's Isle of Man.

Enterprising broadcasters also made use of foreign locales to bring commercial television to audiences otherwise denied. The top-rated network in Germany today, for example, is RTL. Now broadcasting from the German city of Cologne, it began operations in January 1984 in Luxembourg, transmitting an American-style mix of children's programming, sports, talk shows, and action–adventure programming into Germany to compete with that country's two dominant public broadcasters, ARD and ZDF.

The United States as International Broadcaster World War II brought the United States into the business of international broadcasting. Following the lead of Britain, which had just augmented its colonial broadcast system with an **external service** called the BBC World Service, the United States established in 1940 what would eventually be known as the Voice of America (VOA) to counter enemy propaganda and disseminate information about America. The VOA originally targeted countries in Central and South America friendly to Germany, but as the war became global, it quickly began broadcasting to scores of other nations, attracting, along with Britain's World Service, a large and admiring listenership, first in countries occupied by the Axis powers, and later by those in the Soviet sphere of influence.

It was this Cold War with the Soviets that moved the United States into the forefront of international broadcasting, a position it still holds today. To counter the efforts of the Soviet Union's external service, Radio Moscow, the United States established three additional services. Radio in the American Sector (RIAS), broadcasting in German, served people inside East Berlin and East Germany; Radio Free Europe (RFE) broadcast to all of the other Communist-bloc Eastern European countries in their native languages; and Radio Liberty (RL) was aimed at listeners in the Soviet

The Voice of America logo.
Reprinted by permission of Voice of America.

Union itself. When these services were initiated, people both in the United States and abroad were told that they were funded by contributions from American citizens. However, as a result of the furor that arose when it was revealed in 1971 that they were in fact paid for by the Central Intelligence Agency, they were brought openly under government control and funded and administered by the Board of International Broadcasting, whose members were appointed by the president.

Radio Martí's logo

The communist nations targeted by these services attempted to jam their signals by broadcasting on the same frequencies at higher powers, but they were only minimally successful in keeping their people from listening to these Western broadcasts. It was the success of these **surrogate services**—broadcast operations established by one country to substitute for another's own domestic service—that prompted President Ronald Reagan in 1985 to establish a special division of the VOA, Radio Martí, to broadcast into Communist Cuba. Radio Martí, still in operation, was joined by TV Martí in 1990.

AFRTS
www.afrts.osd.mil

A final United States external service established during World War II and the Cold War, Armed Forces Radio and Television Service (AFRTS), remains active today under its new name, American Forces Radio and Television Service. Maintained by the American military, its stated mission is "to deliver Department of Defense internal information and radio and television programming services which provide 'a touch of home' to Department of Defense personnel and their families serving overseas" (AFRTS, 2005). It employs nine Earth-orbiting satellites and MP3 technology to reach listeners and viewers in 177 countries and aboard U.S. ships with commercial-free fare.

The VOA Today   Today, 100 million listeners a day tune in to VOA broadcasts in 53 languages, and another 20 million people in 23 developing countries listen to its surrogate operations, RFE, RL, Radio Martí, and the recently added Radio Free Asia and Arabic language Radio Sawa (Pein, 2005). Throughout its history, the VOA has frequently vacillated between two roles in response to world events and political pressures at home: (1) disseminating Western propaganda and (2) providing objective information. With the threat of communist world domination now almost nonexistent, it attempts to meet the far less contradictory goals of spreading American culture and disseminating health and social information.

For more information on this topic, see Media Talk video clip #18, "Pentagon Planning to Plant Misinformation in Foreign News Sources," on the *Media World* DVD.

The VOA's commitment to the spread of American culture is evidenced by the establishment in 1992 of a 24-hour top 40–style service, VOA Europe, and in 1998 of a 24-hour, all-news English-language worldwide radio service characterized by a snappy style reminiscent of domestic commercial stations. The VOA's focus on transmitting health and other practical information can be seen in the increased efforts it devotes to programs aimed at Third World nations on AIDS prevention, nutrition, and vaccination. In pursuit of this humanitarian goal, the VOA now frequently strikes agreements with local stations in these countries to broadcast its programs over their AM and FM stations, making them accessible to people who listen outside the shortwave band. You can read more about America's latest surrogate service effort in the essay on page 492, "Al-Hurra or al-Abda?"

Al-Hurra or al-Abda?

The issue of America's ability to provide an effective surrogate service to the Arab world was put squarely into the cultural forum by the February 2004 launch of al-Hurra, a $62 million effort by the Board of International Broadcasting to provide Arabic-language television to all 22 countries in the Middle East. The stated goals of the 24-hour satellite channel are to promote democracy in the region and change for the better the anti-American public opinion that exists there.

Al-Hurra's first moments on the air presented video of windows being opened, symbolizing freedom, and an interview with President George W. Bush in which he praised Iraqi efforts at democracy. The Virginia-based station's daily blend of news, pop culture, and C-SPAN–style broadcasts of the workings of the U.S. government, however, has earned it mixed reviews. Some critics in the United States and the Middle East question whether al-Hurra, which translates into "The Free One," might not be more accurately called al-Abda, "The Slave," or even "Fox News in Arabic," referring to the cable news channel's decidedly pro-American bent (MacFarquhar, 2004). The debate has several components.

First, many people question whether the United States should be in the business of providing surrogate services at all. Why, they ask, would Middle Eastern viewers want to tune in to a government-financed, clearly pro-American news and culture station when in our era of global telecommunications they can receive objective, high-quality content not only from the BBC World Service but from other American and Western sources such as CNN? These critics point to Radio and TV Martí, both widely ignored by Cuban audiences within easy reach of American commercial broadcasters. A second criti-

> **AL-HURRA REFERS TO WESTERN SOLDIERS IN IRAQ AS "COALITION FORCES." ARAB BROADCASTERS CALL THEM "OCCUPATION FORCES."**

cism centers on the risk of alienating the very people al-Hurra wants to reach with what, inevitably, will be seen as American propaganda. For example, al-Hurra refers to Western soldiers in Iraq as "coalition forces." Arab broadcasters call them "occupation forces." Arab journalists speak of "Palestinians trying to free themselves from Israeli occupation," and al-Hurra talks of the "historical dispute" between Arabs and Israelis. "The people they have hired look modern, hip, and the beat is fast, but it won't have an impact on the perception of the United States," said Mustafa Hamarneh of the University of Jordan. "I think Americans are mistaken if they assume they can change their image in the region. People became anti-American because they don't like American policies" (MacFarquhar, 2004, p. A3).

The third criticism of al-Hurra is that despite its stated mission of fostering democracy and improving America's image, its real goal is "to provide an antidote to what its founders consider anti-American news coverage on popular Arabic channels such as al-Jazeera" (National Public Radio, 2004, p. 1). Al-Jazeera is popular in the Middle East—45 million daily viewers—precisely because it is seen "on the street" as more objective than both Western news outlets *and* traditional Arab broadcast operations. The Qatar-based satellite channel's critical coverage, "decidedly untraditional female anchors and producers in Western dress, [and] simultaneously translated interviews with non-Arab sources" have angered just about every Arab government in the Middle East (Klein, 2004, p. 55). It is currently banned in Iraq, Iran, Kuwait, Algeria, and the Sudan. "Before the station began broadcasting in 1996 . . . Arab viewers were largely limited to tame and uninformative state

SATELLITES AND GLOBAL MASS MEDIA

We saw in Chapter 8 how satellites turned cable television from primarily an importer of distant signals into a provider of original programming, setting off a revolution in television. The impact of satellites on international mass communication was no less profound. With the coming of satellites, signals could be distributed not only internationally, that is, between two specific countries, as had previously been the case, but all over the world.

The satellite revolution began in 1957 with the successful launch and orbit of the Soviet Union's *Sputnik*. *Sputnik* had no real function other than to prove (especially to the United States) that the Soviets could indeed produce the world's first artificial satellite. But it fulfilled this function admirably—shaking the confidence of the Western nations and leading the United States to redouble its efforts to conquer space.

that the United States is the "Great Satan." For example, Steven Cook of the Council on Foreign Relations wrote, "After revelations about torture at Abu Ghraib prison, Al-Hurra broadcast Donald Rumsfeld's testimony before the Senate Armed Services Committee to the Arab world. The spectacle of the secretary of defense of the United States answering questions from elected legislators about the conduct of American soldiers transfixed many Arabs. After all, many leaders in the Middle East are unelected and unaccountable, and most Arabs have never seen a senior government official called to account" (2004, p. A19). This transparency would have several other benefits, they argue. It would dispel Arab notions that al-Hurra is little more than American propaganda; it would deepen Arab understanding of how American foreign policy is developed and implemented; and it would provide a standard against which Arabs could judge the operation of their own political systems.

Can al-Hurra's efforts to win Arab hearts and minds succeed?

broadcasting outlets," editorialized the *New York Times*. "Now tens of millions of people across the Arab world see news that their own government would prefer to keep quiet" ("Banning," 2004, p. A20). As such, success for al-Hurra, say critics, will not be found in being "the non-al-Jazeera"; it will come only with a change in U.S. foreign policy.

Al-Hurra's supporters, however, are more optimistic. They believe that its news and talk programs and schedule of shows about technology, exercise, fashion, and movies will show a fuller, more accurate picture of America. They believe that unvarnished coverage of our system at work will dispel the idea

Enter your voice. Is it a mistake to set al-Hurra up as an alternative to al-Jazeera? Isn't one culture's news another culture's propaganda? Can a U.S.-based, government-funded television station ever hope to change Arab hearts and minds, or is there simply too much resentment in the region? Before you answer these questions, read the following comments from Web columnist Muhammad Abdalah Nab; they are typical of the "word on the Arab street." "Only one Apache (helicopter), which American policy makers gave to (Israel) for free to kill unarmed children, women, and elderly Palestinians, makes the mission of this channel not only difficult, but impossible and stupid at the same time" (quoted in MacFarquhar, 2004, p. A3).

The United States placed the second satellite, AT&T's *Telstar I*, in orbit in 1962. In that same year, Congress established the Communications Satellite Corporation (COMSAT) to coordinate ownership and operation of America's communications satellite system. It was clear even at the time, however, that satellites' greatest potential was in their ability to globalize telecommunications. To this end, President John F. Kennedy convened a consortium of Western and nonaligned countries to establish the International Telecommunications Satellite Organization (INTELSAT). Kennedy had two goals in mind: first, to effect the creation and maintenance of a global communication satellite system serving its many member nations; and second, to ensure that its leadership remained with the United States.

U.S. leadership in global satellites was ensured when COMSAT was declared managing agent of INTELSAT's system, begun on April 6, 1965, with the launch of INTELSAT I, better known in the United States as Early Bird.

WWW

Al-Hurra
www.alhurra.com

The 1965 launch of INTELSAT I, better known as Early Bird, made possible the first regularly scheduled transmission of live television between Europe and North America and established the United States' leadership in global satellites.

WWW

Al-Jazeera
www.english.aljazeera.net

WWW

INTELSAT
www.intelsat.com

Within 1 year of that success, 55 nations had joined INTELSAT, and Early Bird allowed the first regularly scheduled transmission of live television between Europe and North America.

INTELSAT's role as a facilitator of global mass communication began slowly but rapidly expanded. Early Bird contained 240 voice/data circuits and one television channel, but by the time the INTELSAT VI generation of satellites was operational in 1989, each had the capacity to handle 120,000 voice/data circuits and three television channels (Stevenson, 1994). However, 1982 is considered the benchmark year for global media; it was then that INTELSAT's system became large and technologically sophisticated enough to begin offering its television customers full-time leases rather than the customary single-show service. Now, satellites not only enabled global distribution of media content, they encouraged it—once a company had paid for its lease, it incurred no additional cost no matter how much additional content it sent.

In 1973 COMSAT gave up control of INTELSAT, and the latter became an independent consortium of member nations, each paying a yearly fee. However, at the 1999 INTELSAT Assembly of Parties, the official meeting of all 143 member governments, the consortium unanimously decided to privatize its service, largely in response to the growing number of

competing systems. Among these are Europe's EUTELSAT and several regional and national systems. Most significant, though, are the numerous private, commercial systems that commenced operation in 1984. Today, companies such as Globalstar (partners with Loral and Qualcomm), Inmarsat (partners with Lockheed Martin and Matra Marconi Space), Hughes Electronics' Spaceway, and Lockheed Martin's Astrolink manage the majority of the globe's nearly 800 working communication satellites. And the capacity of these satellites has grown to the point that, for example, two providers alone, INTELSAT and PanAmSat, were able to transmit more than 35,000 hours of 2006 World Cup Soccer coverage to thousands of cable and other pay television operators on every habitable continent on Earth (Dickson, 2006).

Global Media Today

After *Who Wants to Be a Millionaire?* became the hot new show on American television, native-language versions of the game show were soon being broadcast in 29 other countries, and the producers made plans to extend the franchise into 50 more. The Cartoon Network is satellite- and cablecast in 145 countries in 14 languages. The Discovery Channel has 63 million subscribers in Asia, 35 million in Europe, the Middle East, and Africa, 30 million in India, and 18 million in Latin America. Nickelodeon is the globe's most distributed kids channel, viewable in more than 320 million households worldwide. *Desperate Housewives* (the original, not the locally produced version mentioned in this chapter's opening vignette) wins its time slot in Germany, England, Norway, Sweden, and the Netherlands. *Lost* wins it in Russia. All but 4 of the top 100 worldwide box office leaders in 2005 were American-made movies. Britain's Channel 4 *alone* pays Fox Television $1 million per episode for *The Simpsons,* and the half-hour comedy makes another $600,000 per episode from other foreign broadcasters. U.S. networks collect $1 million an episode from individual countries' broadcasters for *Desperate Housewives, Lost,* and *24. Everybody Hates Chris* sells for $500,000 per half hour (Guider & James, 2005). Martha Stewart's talk show, *Martha,* airs in Iceland, Kenya, Sweden, Portugal, Poland, New Zealand, the Philippines, Indonesia, and Korea. Britain's BBC has a channel on hundreds of American cable systems, and its storied *BBC Television News* can be watched by some 36 million American PBS viewers. Al-Jazeera International, the English-language version of the pan-Arab satellite news network, debuted into more than 40 million households worldwide in May 2006. If you're in the right place, you can join the 366 million households worldwide that watch MTV Latin America, MTV Asia, MTV Australia, MTV Brazil, MTV Japan, MTV Europe, or other MTV international channels (see Table 15.1). TV France International, that country's umbrella distribution organization, has partnership agreements with Fox, Warner Brothers, the Discovery and Sundance channels, and Bravo. Its all-French channel is available to viewers in the United States on satellite provider DirecTV. Close to 200 nations receive CNN by satellite. Radio Beijing broadcasts to a worldwide audience in 40 languages. Hundreds of millions of Internet users spread throughout scores of countries can tune in to thousands of Web radio stations originating from every continent except Antarctica. AT&T, the United States' largest telecommunications and cable

TABLE 15.1 They Want Their MTV. MTV's International Channels, 2004.

MTV Adria	MTV Germany	MTV Poland
MTV Australia	MTV2 Germany	MTV Portugal
MTV Base (Africa)	MTV Holland	MTV Romania
MTV Brazil	MTV India	MTV Russia
MTV Europe	MTV Italy	MTV South East Asia
MTV2 Europe	MTV Japan	MTV Spain
MTV Canada	MTV Korea	MTV Taiwan/Hong Kong
MTV China	MTV Latin America	MTV UK
MTV France	MTV Nordic	MTV Base (UK)

Source: www.mtv.com/mtvinternational.

Desperate Housewives sells for $1 million an episode overseas; *Everybody Hates Chris* earns $500,000 per 30-minute show.

company, and British Telecom, Britain's biggest telecommunications provider, have merged their international operations into a single $10 billion unit. Media know few national borders.

But the global flow of expression and entertainment is not welcomed by everyone. French law requires that 40% of all music broadcast by its radio stations be in French. Iran bans "Western music" altogether from radio and television. Turkey forbids the use of the letters *Q* and *W*, punishable by fine, because they do not belong to the Turkish alphabet. Fearing that Google Print, the Internet giant's plan to digitize millions of books (Chapter 3), will entrench English as the dominant language on the Internet and thus "lead to an imbalance, to the benefit of a mainly Anglo-Saxon view of the world," French intellectuals have called on their government to work through the European Union to halt the effort ("The World," 2005). While *The Simpsons* is widely distributed across the Middle East by Saudi Arabian DBS provider MBC, all references to Duff Beer have been changed to soda, and Moe's Bar does not appear at all. Sri Lanka forbade the import and distribution of foreign movies until 2000, and in the kingdom of Bhutan, near India and Tibet, television itself was illegal until June 1999. To ensure that its people do not access "foreign" or otherwise "counterrevolutionary" Internet content, the Chinese government requires all Internet accounts to be registered with the police. It employs 40,000 "e-police" to enforce its dozens of Net-related laws. Media may know few national borders, but there is growing concern that they at least respect the cultures within them.

One traditional way to understand the workings of the contemporary global media scene is to examine the individual media systems of the different countries around the world. In doing so, we can not only become familiar with how different folks in different places use media but also better evaluate the workings of our own system. Naturally, not every media system resembles that of the United States. As a result, such concepts as audience expectations, economic foundations, and the regulation of mass media differ across nations. The study of different countries' mass media systems is called **comparative analysis** or **comparative studies.**

www

Population Communication International
www.population.org

COMPARATIVE ANALYSES

Different countries' mass media systems reflect the diversity of their levels of development and prosperity, values, and political systems. Often, a country's

You can enjoy *The Simpsons* just about everywhere in the Middle East, but if you do catch it there, you'll never see Homer drink a beer or visit Moe's Bar.

geography also influences the type of media system it embraces. The level of diffusion of different communication technologies in different countries offers a clear example. The United States is prosperous, and its people enjoy considerable mobility and leisure. Americans also tend to live in bigger homes than do their counterparts in most other lands. As a result, the United States has two radios for every citizen and almost one television per person. Australia, a prosperous country, is very large. Many of its people live in quite remote parts of this continent nation. It, too, has more than one radio per person, but only one television for every 2 people. Uganda, a developing African nation, has almost no television, and despite the remote locations in which many of its people live, its lack of prosperity makes even radio ownership a rarity. In the oil-rich desert nation of Oman, on the other hand, even though only 1 in 11 people has a telephone (the hostile terrain makes the stringing and maintenance of phone lines difficult), there is one television (served by a domestic satellite system) for every 2 people (Peterson, 1998; Hilliard & Keith, 1996).

That a country's political system will be reflected in the nature of its media system is only logical. Authoritarian governments need to control the mass media to maintain power. Therefore, they will institute a media system very different from that of a democratic country with a capitalistic, free economy. The overriding philosophy of how media ideally operate in any given system of social values is called a normative theory (Chapter 14). The classic work on normative theory is *The Four Theories of the Press* by Fred Siebert, Theodore Peterson, and Wilbur Schramm, but because so much has changed in the world of mass communication since it was written in 1956, these "four theories" have required "a little sprucing up" (Stevenson, 1994, p. 108), carried out by media scholar William Hachten.

Hachten (1992) offered "five concepts" that guide the world's many media systems—Western, development, revolutionary, authoritarianism, and communism. We'll examine each and provide a look at examples that exemplify them.

The Western Concept: Great Britain   The **Western concept** is an amalgamation of the original libertarian and social responsibility models (Chapter 14). It recognizes two realities: There is no completely free (libertarian) media system on Earth, and even the most commercially driven systems include the expectation not only of public service and responsibility but also of "significant communication-related activities of government" to ensure that media professionals meet those responsibilities (Stevenson, 1994, p. 109).

Great Britain offers a good example of a media system operating under the Western concept. The BBC was originally built on the premise that broadcasting was a public trust (the social responsibility model). Long before television, BBC radio offered several services—one designed to provide news and information, another designed to support high or elite culture such as symphony music and plays, and a third designed to provide popular music and entertainment. To limit government and advertiser control, the BBC was funded by license fees levied on receivers (currently about $215 a year), and its governance was given over to a nonprofit corporation. Many observers point to this goal-oriented, noncommercial structure as the reason that the BBC developed, and still maintains, the most respected news operation in the world.

Eventually, Britain, like all of western Europe, was forced by public demand to institute more American-style broadcasting. It now has local commercial radio stations in addition to the BBC's 9 domestic radio networks: Radio 1 (pop and rock music), Radio 2 (popular music such as folk and other regional music), Radio 3 (live music and arts), Radio 4 (drama and talk), Radio 5 (news and sports), Radio 6 (eclectic contemporary music), Radio 7 (comedy, kids, and drama), Five Live (live sports), and Radio 1xtra (new Black music). In addition to television networks BBC1 (more popular) and BBC2 (more serious), there are commercial Channels 4 and 5 and several regional commercial networks operating under the auspices of the Independent Television Authority (ITA). ITA has regional channels for Ireland, Scotland, Wales, southern England, and so on. But even these must accept limits on the amount of advertising they air and agree to specified amounts of public affairs and documentary news programming in exchange for their licenses to broadcast. This is referred to as their **public service remit.**

Cable was slow to develop in Great Britain for two reasons. First, many people simply did not want their beautiful or historic towns sullied by cable's overhead wires, nor did they want their cobbled streets dug up to accommodate underground cables. The second reason is that virtually all of the country has long had access to Rupert Murdoch's DBS system, SkyTV. Murdoch pioneered the mini-dish receiver, which not only gave viewers multiple channels but also satisfied

WWW
BBC
www.bbc.co.uk

Unlike U.S. media, British media do not enjoy First Amendment protections, but as their notorious tabloids demonstrate, they nonetheless operate with a great deal of freedom.

Britons' traditional aesthetic sensibilities (no big, obtrusive dish, no unsightly wires, and no excavated streets). Today, satellite provider BSkyB has 5.7 million viewers in Great Britain, whereas total cable subscribership is 3.5 million in a country of 24.5 million television households (Westcott, 2002).

In terms of regulation, the media in Great Britain do not enjoy a First Amendment–like guarantee of freedom. Prior restraint does occur, but only when a committee of government officials and representatives of the media industry can agree on the issuance of what is called a **D-notice.** British media are also forbidden to report on court trials in progress, and Parliament can pass other restrictions on the media whenever it wishes—for example, the ban, imposed in 1988 and maintained for several years, on broadcasting the voice of anyone associated with the Irish Republican or other paramilitary movements.

The Development Concept: Honduras The media systems of many Third World or developing African, Asian, Latin and South American, and eastern European nations formerly part of the Soviet bloc best exemplify the **development concept.** Here government and media work in partnership to ensure that media assist in the planned, beneficial development of the country. Content is designed to meet specific cultural and societal needs, for example, teaching new farming techniques, disseminating information on methods of disease control, and improving literacy. This isn't the same as authoritarian control. There is less censorship and other official control of content.

Honduras offers one example. This Central American country has government as well as privately owned commercial radio and television stations. A government-authorized and -controlled private commission, the Honduran Contractors of Television, coordinates much of the commercial outlets' operation. In addition, HONDUTEL, the Honduran equivalent of the FCC, exerts tight regulatory control over all broadcasting. Together these two bodies ensure that Honduran broadcasting meets the nation's developmental needs, as determined by the government.

The Honduran government is forbidden by its constitution from taking over or shutting down media outlets because of the content they distribute. Control, however, comes in other forms. One is the requirement that media professionals hold membership in a government-run "official press organization." Naturally, if the government decides who can and cannot function in media organizations, it can easily control those organizations. Another resides in "the close ties of the owners of the most powerful media to the military and to government leaders. The media, therefore, by and large operate with little freedom despite strong constitutional guarantees" (Hilliard & Keith, 1996, p. 161).

The Revolutionary Concept: Poland No country "officially" embraces the **revolutionary concept** as a normative theory, but this does not mean that a nation's media will never serve the goals of revolution. Stevenson (1994) identified four aims of revolutionary media: ending government monopoly over information, facilitating the organization of opposition to the incumbent powers, destroying the legitimacy of a standing government, and bringing down a standing government. In Yugoslavia, for example, 33 radio and

The Polish workers' and democracy movement, Solidarity, was greatly aided by media, both official outlets from beyond Poland's borders and its own extensive network of clandestine new and old communication technologies.

18 television stations combined in 1998 to form the Association of Independent Electronic Media (ANEM) for the purpose of challenging the regime of President Slobodan Milosevic and asserting Serbian independence. ANEM operated with significant public support despite repressive legislation, threats of jail and huge fines, and even military and police confiscation of members' equipment (Aumente, 1999). Milosevic's ouster in October 2000 is testimony to ANEM's effectiveness. The experience of the Polish democracy movement Solidarity, however, offers a better-known example of the use of media as a tool of revolution.

By the first years of the 1980s, the Polish people had grown dissatisfied with the domination of almost all aspects of their lives by a national Communist Party perceived to be a puppet of the Soviet Union. This frustration was fueled by the ability of just about all Poles to receive radio and television signals from neighboring democratic lands (Poland's location in central Europe made it impossible for the authorities to block what the people saw and heard). In addition, Radio Free Europe, the Voice of America, and the BBC all targeted Poland with their mix of Western news, entertainment, and propaganda. Its people's taste for freedom thus whetted, Solidarity established an extensive network of clandestine revolutionary media. Much of it was composed of technologies traditionally associated with revolution—pamphlets, newsletters, audiotapes and videocassettes—but much of it was also sophisticated radio and television technology used to disrupt official broadcasts and disseminate information. Despite government efforts to shut the system down, which went as far as suspending official broadcasting and mail services in order to deny Solidarity these communication channels, the revolution was a success, making Poland the first of the Eastern-bloc nations to defy the Party apparatus and install a democratically elected government.

The Authoritarianism and Communism Concepts: China   Because only three communist nations remain and because the actual operation of the media in these and other **authoritarian systems** is quite similar, we can discuss authoritarianism and communism as a single concept. Both call for the subjugation of media for the purpose of serving the government. China is not only a good example of a country that operates its media according to the authoritarian/communist concepts; it also demonstrates how difficult it is becoming for authoritarian governments to maintain strict control over media and audiences.

The Chinese media system is based on that of its old ideological partner, the now-dissolved Soviet Union. For a variety of reasons, however, it has developed its own peculiar nature. China has more than a billion people living in more than a million hamlets, villages, and cities. Despite sophisticated life in many big cities, there is nearly universal illiteracy in the countryside. Because good pulpwood is not native to China and importing it from abroad is too expensive, newspapers are printed on costly but poor-quality paper made from bamboo. Daily circulation is 116 million copies, around one paper for every 13 adults. As a result, print is not a major national medium. In fact, face-to-face communication remains a primary means of transmitting news and information among the country's enormous personal communication system. This process is aided by the wide distribution of **wired radio,** centrally located loudspeakers—for example, in a town square—that deliver primarily political and educational broadcasts.

A Chinese reading wall. The newspaper is not a major national mass medium in China—there is only one copy for every 13 people. Most read the newspaper at public postings such as this one.

The media exist in China to serve the government. Chairman Mao Zedong, founder of the Chinese Communist Party, clarified the role of the media very soon after coming to power in 1949. The media exist to propagandize the policies of the Party and to educate, organize, and mobilize the masses. These are still their primary functions.

Radio came to China via American reporter E. C. Osborn, who established an experimental radio station in China in 1923. Official Chinese broadcasting began 3 years later. Television went on the air in 1958, and from the outset it was owned and controlled by the Party in the form of Central China Television (CCTV), which in turn answers to the Ministry of Radio and Television. Radio, now regulated by China People's Broadcasting Station (CPBS), and television stations and networks develop their own content, but it must conform to the requirements of the Propaganda Bureau of the Chinese Communist Party Central Committee.

Financially, Chinese broadcasting operates under direct government subsidy. But in 1979 the government approved commercial advertising for broadcasting, and it has evolved into an important means of financial support—television billings are at $8 billion a year, for example (Jones, 2002). Coupled with the Chinese government's desire to become a more active participant in the international economy, this commercialization has led to increased diversity in broadcast content. Today, China's 400 million television households (99% penetration) are served by 14 CCTV and hundreds of local and satellite channels. Foreign content is purchased by the state's China TV Programming Agency, which can buy no more than 500 hours a year. Stations can devote no more than 25% of their time to imported content. MTV and the Children's Television Workshop coproduce content with local Chinese broadcasters, and among imported favorites are *The Teletubbies* (*Antenna Babies* in China) and *Little House on the Prairie*. CNN and other

Only 20 American movies a year can be exhibited in China. *Lord of the Rings* made the cut in 2004.

MEDIA HISTORY REPEATS

Helping or Hurting Freedom of Expression in China?

John Peter Zenger went to jail for his exercise of free expression, and his name is forever linked to the fight against official intrusion into journalism. Larry Flynt spent millions of dollars on legal fees to protect his magazine's right to publish unpopular expression. He was immortalized in a big-budget Hollywood movie. Americans have been in the vanguard of the fight for freedom of speech and press from colonial to modern times. It is a history of which America is justly proud, and it is in this tradition that a diverse group of U.S. citizens and human rights groups are fighting for freedom of expression in China. They have written letters of protest, called for boycotts, dropped advertising, and besieged congressional leaders. The irony, however, is that they are doing battle not with the Chinese government but with fellow Americans—Internet companies Yahoo!, Cisco, Google, and Microsoft, all of whom have altered the way they normally do business to meet the demands of Chinese Internet censors (Chapter 2).

"This makes you a functionary of the Chinese government," U.S. House of Representatives member Jim Leach scolded the companies at congressional hearings called in early 2006 to investigate their dealings in China ("Yahoo, Google," 2006, p. A7). Reporters Without Borders called their collusion with authorities "a black day for freedom of expression in China," and the negative publicity dropped Google's stock value more than $30 billion, or about 25%. Of Google, *Advertising Age* editorialized, "a great, authentic brand sold its soul" (Drutman, 2006, p. B4; "Google Sells," 2006, p. 11). *New York Times* columnist Nicholas D. Kristof wrote, "Suppose that Anne Frank had maintained an e-mail account while in hiding in 1944, and that the Nazis had asked Yahoo for cooperation in tracking her down. It seems, based on Yahoo's behavior in China, that it might have complied" (2006, p. 4.13). "Your abhorrent activities in China are a disgrace," charged

> **"MILLIONS OF CHINESE BLOGS AND PODCASTS ARE TAKING OFF, AND THEY ARE INFLICTING ON THE COMMUNIST PARTY THE ANCIENT PUNISHMENT OF 'LING CHI,' USUALLY TRANSLATED AS 'DEATH BY A THOUSAND CUTS.'"**

Silicon Valley House member Tom Lantos (in "Google Sells," 2006, p. 11).

The technology firms offered their defense. "Microsoft does business in many countries around the world. While different countries have different standards, Microsoft and other multinational companies have to ensure that our products and services comply with local laws, norms, and industry practices," explained a company spokesperson (in Zeller, 2006, p. 4.4). Google's attorney called it "responding to local conditions" (in Bray, 2006, p. A10).

What was each company's "response to local conditions" that so angered critics? Cisco Systems sells hardware to the Chinese police that facilitates censorship, for example, by blocking users' access to the Internet. Microsoft shuts down blogs at the specific request of Chinese authorities and censors "sensitive words" in its Chinese blog-hosting software, words such as "freedom of speech," "democracy," "human rights," and "liberty." Google, the company whose motto is "Don't be evil," and whose Code of Conduct contains "truths" such as "Focus on the user and all else will follow," "Democracy on the Web works," and "The need for information crosses all borders," licenses Google.cn to the Chinese government. Its searches produce very specific, very limited, and predetermined-by-the-censors results. Search Tiananmen Square, and nice tourist photos appear, not the iconic man-stopping-tank image from the 1989 democracy movement and massacre available at Google.com. History, religion, and political searches are controlled. To its credit, Google has pushed back at the Chinese government a bit. It refused to make available its e-mail and blogging services because it would not accept China's conditions and because of fears of official snooping on users, and it demanded the right to alert users when information from a search was being withheld by official orders.

satellite-delivered services are also available to China's 100 million cable and 150 million satellite television households (Jones, 2002).

Basic government control over major media and the Internet remains, however. For example, only 20 American movies are permitted exhibition in China each year, and in December 1997 the government began enforcing criminal sanctions against those who would use the Net to "split the country," "injure the reputation of state organs," "defame government agencies," "promote feudal superstitions," or otherwise pose a threat to "social stability" ("China Adopts," 1997, pp. C1, C4; Dobson, 1998, p. 20). Internet accounts have to be registered with the police. The state has established a

The actions of Yahoo!, however, have most enraged freedom of expression and democracy advocates. The company provided police with the names of e-mail users who had anonymously posted messages about Tiananmen Square and other taboo topics. They were given prison sentences ranging from 4 to 10 years. "Yahoo sold its soul and is a national disgrace," wrote Kristof, "Nobody should touch Yahoo until it provides financially for the families of the three men it helped lock up" (2006, p. 4.13).

Few observers excuse Yahoo! for its complicity in the jailing of the three democracy advocates, but many see the activities of the four American technology companies as the first step toward fuller freedom of expression in China. There are already 4 million blogs and 100 million Web users in China, and officials there are expanding broadband access throughout the country (Kristof, 2005). Chinese people are communicating across values, interests, and political opinion, as well as across the country's huge geography. Microsoft's global marketing director, Adam Sohn, explains, "Even with filters, we're helping millions of people communicate, share stories, share photographs, and build relationships" (in Mangier & Menn, 2005, p. A12). In addition, as users' Internet sophistication grows, so too will the already frequent use of anonymous proxy servers (servers outside China that provide false or substitute addresses for forbidden sites) and software such as Tor, available from the Electronic Frontier Foundation, that anonymizes Net communication. Tor can be accessed in China by those skilled enough to find and download it.

Information wants to be free, say Internet advocates, and even the best efforts of Chinese censors cannot contain information once the people have access to it and the ability to spread it. Even as harsh a critic of the four companies as the *Times*'s Kristof sees a silver lining in the presence of Yahoo!, Cisco, Google, and Microsoft in China. He wrote, "Millions of Chinese blogs and podcasts are taking off, and they are inflicting on the Communist Party the ancient punishment of 'ling chi,' usually translated as 'death by a thousand cuts'" (2006, p. 4.13).

Your turn. Are these companies helping or hurting the cause of freedom of expression in China? Do you see their work as an extension of the struggles of Peter Zenger and Larry Flynt? Why or why not?

A Google.cn search for Tiananmen Square will produce a tourist photo, not the globally recognized image from the 1989 Chinese democracy movement.

24-hour Internet task force to find and arrest senders of "counter-revolutionary" commentary. Popular bulletin boards are shut down when their chat becomes a bit too free. Web sites such as Human Rights Watch, the *New York Times,* and publications about China that are independent of government control, such as *China News Digest,* are officially blocked, but not very successfully, as skilled Internet users can easily access the Web by routing themselves through distant servers or at one of the country's 150,000 unlicensed Internet cafés (Beech, 2002). The essay "Helping or Hurting Freedom of Expression in China?" on page 504 looks at another Internet freedom issue in China, one that involves the United States.

PROGRAMMING

Regardless of the particular concept guiding media systems in other countries, those systems produce and distribute content, in other words, programming. In most respects, radio and television programming throughout the world looks and sounds much like that found in the United States. There are two main reasons for this situation: (1) The United States is a world leader in international distribution of broadcast fare, and (2) very early in the life of television, American producers flooded the world with their programming at very low prices. Foreign operators of emerging television systems were delighted to have access to this low-cost content, because they typically could not afford to produce their own high-quality domestic material. For American producers, however, this strategy served the dual purpose of building markets for their programming and ensuring that foreign audiences would develop tastes and expectations similar to those in the United States, further encouraging future sales of programs originally produced for American audiences (Barnouw, 1990).

Naturally, programming varies somewhat from one country to another. The commercial television systems of most South American and European countries are far less sensitive about sex and nudity than are their counterparts in the United States. In Brazil, for example, despite a constitutional requirement that broadcasters respect society's social and ethical values, television networks such as SBT, TV Record, and TV Globo compete in what critics call the *guerra da baixaria,* the war of the lowest common denominator. Guests on variety shows wrestle with buxom models dressed only in bikinis and eat sushi off other women's naked bodies. On game shows, male contestants who give wrong answers can be punished by having patches of

Many countries hope their fare will find a worldwide audience, especially an American one. Here are ads for Spanish and Estonian companies that appeared in *Variety.*

leg hair ripped out, while those who answer correctly are rewarded by having a nearly naked model sit in their laps. European commercial operations regularly air shows featuring both male and female nudity, sometimes because it is integral to the plot, sometimes simply for titillation.

Another difference between American programming and that of its global neighbors is how that content is utilized in different places. As telecommunications professors Robert Hilliard and Michael Keith observed, "In systems relying on commercial advertising for their support, the value of programming is based on how many viewers any given presentation attracts. . . . In systems operated by public corporations that rely on sources of funding other than advertising, the purpose of programming is oriented principally to the educational, social, and/or political purpose of the operating entity" (1996, p. 109). And, in general, this is the case. But many nations, even those with commercially supported systems, use a particular genre, the soap opera, for educational and social purposes. You can read more about the power of soap operas to make a difference in the essay on page 508, "Telling Stories, Saving Lives."

The Debate over Cultural Imperialism

There are few physical borders between countries in a globally mediated world. Governments that could once physically prohibit the introduction and distribution of unwanted newspapers, magazines, and books had to work harder at jamming unwanted radio and television broadcasts. But they could do it, until satellite came along. Governments cannot disrupt satellite signals. Only lack of the necessary receiving technology can limit their reach. Now, with the Internet, a new receiving technology is cheap, easy to use, and on the desks of more and more millions of people in every corner of the world. As a result, difficult questions of national sovereignty and cultural diversity are being raised anew.

THE MACBRIDE REPORT AND THE NWIO

The debate reached its height with the 1980 release of the MacBride Report by the United Nations Educational, Scientific, and Cultural Organization (UNESCO). The report was named after the chairman of the commission set up to study the question of how to maintain national and cultural sovereignty in the face of rapid globalization of mass media. At the time, many Third World and communist countries were concerned that international news coverage was dominated by the West, especially the United States, and that Western-produced content was overwhelming the media of developing countries, which lacked sufficient resources to create their own quality fare. The fear was that Western cultural values, especially those of the United States, would overshadow and displace those of other countries. These countries saw this as a form of colonialization, a **cultural imperialism**—the invasion of an indigenous people's culture by powerful foreign countries through mass media.

UNESCO
www.unesco.org

The MacBride Report, endorsed by UNESCO, called for establishment of a New World Information Order (NWIO) characterized by several elements problematic to Western democracies. In arguing that individual nations should be free to control the news and entertainment that entered their lands, it called for monitoring of all such content, monitoring and licensing

USING MEDIA TO MAKE A DIFFERENCE

Telling Stories, Saving Lives

"They may be tawdry and titillating, but they have reach and they can teach," said one participant at the Soap Summit, the annual 10-day meeting of worldwide media industry professionals and public health officials. South African soap opera actor David Dennis said in praise of soaps' ability to make a difference, "The people in the developing world have a more intimate and personalized relationship to television" (both quotes in Guider, 2003, p. 7). He might also have added that soap operas—both radio and television—are inexpensive to produce, a necessity in disadvantaged countries. Do sudsers, as *Variety* calls them, make a difference?

- In India, *Detective Vijay* deals with issues such as wife beating, female empowerment, and education for girls. Targeted toward rural males, it is among that country's top 10 television shows.

- Also in India, the radio soap *Taru*, aimed at the most impoverished states of that large nation, draws a listenership of between 20 to 25 million people. It targets young women with stories encouraging them to take charge of their health, seek out health services, and improve their own lives. Soon after its debut, sales in the broadcast area of contraceptives and home pregnancy tests rose, traffic at regional health clinics spiked, and *Taru* listening clubs proliferated.

- *Soul City* in South Africa tackles AIDS, alcoholism, diarrhea, illiteracy, debt, and depression. Two-thirds of the population watches. Following the airing of one story line in which poor women beat pots and pans to signal an abusive husband that they knew what he was doing, similar noisy protests sprang up around the country. One town even renamed itself Soul City.

> **FOLLOWING THE AIRING OF ONE STORY LINE IN WHICH POOR WOMEN BEAT POTS AND PANS TO SIGNAL AN ABUSIVE HUSBAND THAT THEY KNEW WHAT HE WAS DOING, SIMILAR NOISY PROTESTS SPRANG UP AROUND THE COUNTRY.**

- In China, the daily soap *Ordinary People* has raised such issues as that culture's traditional preference for sons, mistreatment of women, and AIDS. Eight hundred million people tune in every day ("Soaps," 2003).

The force behind these efforts is Population Communications International (PCI), founded in 1985 to "encourage people to make choices that lead to better health and sustainable development." The New York—headquartered group has as its motto *Telling Stories, Saving Lives* and bases its efforts on social cognitive theory (Chapter 13). As such, PCI "produces carefully researched and culturally sensitive radio and television soap operas that combine the power of storytelling with the reach of broadcast media. . . . These serial dramas motivate individuals to adopt new attitudes and behavior by modeling behaviors that promote family health, stable communities, and a sustainable environment. Each series is written, performed, and produced by the creative talent in that country" (PCI, 2004).

PCI's particular mission involves ameliorating soaring population growth, gender inequality in social, health, and educational life, and the spread of AIDS. It uses soap operas because "these long-running dramatic productions are not just fanciful stories. They portray people's own everyday lives. The serials dramatize the everyday problems people struggle with, and model functional strategies and solutions to them. This approach succeeds because it informs, enables, motivates, and guides people for personal and social changes that improve their lives" (PCI, 2004).

How does PCI use media, in this case, soap operas, to make a difference? As explained on its Web site (www.population.org), PCI "trains local creative teams to apply its methodology to their own unique programs. When shaping their stories, creative

of foreign journalists, and requiring that prior government permission be obtained for direct radio, television, and satellite transmissions into foreign countries. Western nations rejected these rules as a direct infringement on the freedom of the press.

Western allies of the United States may have agreed that the restrictions of the NWIO were a threat to the free flow of information, yet virtually every one had in place rules (in the form of quotas) that limited U.S. media content in their own countries. Canada, our closest cultural neighbor, required that specific proportions of all content—print and broadcast—either be produced in Canada or reflect Canadian cultural identity. The French made illegal the printing of certain U.S. words, including "hamburger" and "cartoon"

South Africa's Soul City, *China's* Ordinary People, *and India's* Taru *are three examples of using soap operas to save lives.*

teams include positive characters who are rewarded, negative characters who are punished, and transitional characters whose experiences embody the difficult choices we all face in life. Over the course of the drama, audience members tend to bond with the transitional characters who move to more positive behaviors, whether protecting themselves against HIV/AIDS, pursuing education, or keeping their children in school."

(France maintains an official office to prosecute those who would "debase" its language, the Académie Française). The European Union's Television without Frontiers Directive requires member countries' broadcasters to dedicate a majority of their air time to European-produced programming and to commission at least 10% of all their shows from local, independent producers. South Korean law mandates that movie houses show native films at least 146 days out of each year (Kim, 2002). Canadian law forbids foreign (read American) ownership in its commercial broadcasting channels. In October 2005 UNESCO approved the *Convention on the Protection and Promotion of the Diversity of Cultural Expressions* by a vote of 148 to 2. The two dissenters were the United States and Israel (UNESCO, 2005). The convention

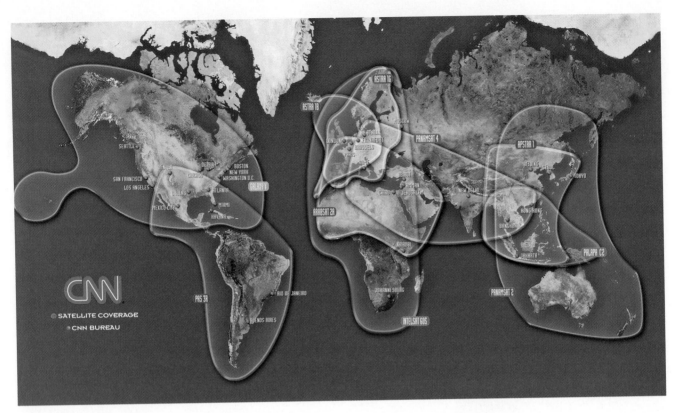

CNN uses 14 satellites to transmit to a billion viewers in almost 200 countries.

permits countries to treat "cultural products" such as movies, books, music, and television shows differently than they do other, more durable commodities. That is, countries can legally establish quotas and subsidies to protect their local media industries. And while the convention's text argued that the defense of every country's cultural heritage is "an ethical imperative, inseparable from respect for human dignity," it was clear from the debate preceding its passage that its true goal was protecting other countries' "culture heritage" from American media ("How They," 2005).

What does it say about American "cultural integrity" when the most popular magazine among college men in the United States is *Maxim*, a direct copy of England's *Maxim*? Can you tell which cover is from which nation?

The resistance to U.S. media would not exist among our international friends if they did not worry about the integrity of their own cultures. It is folly, then, to argue that non-native media content will have no effect on local culture—as do many U.S. media content producers. The question today is, How much influence will countries accept in exchange for fuller membership in the global community? In light of instant, inexpensive, and open computer network communication, a parallel question is, Have notions such as national sovereignty and cultural integrity lost their meaning? For example, ESPN is carried on 20 networks in 21 languages to 155 million television households in 183 different countries. *The Simpsons* is drawn in South Korea. The BBC broadcasts daily to a worldwide audience in 40 languages, as does Radio Beijing from China. CNN uses 14 satellites to transmit to a billion viewers in almost 200 countries. Mexican soap operas dominate the television schedules of much of Latin and South America. Three of the four largest U.S. record companies have international ownership. Hollywood's Columbia Pictures is owned by Japanese Sony, and 20th Century Fox is owned by Rupert Murdoch's Australian corporation. As Thomas Middelhoff, former CEO of Bertelsmann, a German company that controls a large proportion of the U.S. book publishing market and earns more money from the United States than from any other nation, including its homeland, explained, "We're not foreign. We're international. I'm an American with a German passport" (as quoted in McChesney, 1999, p. 104).

THE CASE FOR THE GLOBAL VILLAGE

There are differing opinions about the benefits of this trend away from nation-specific cultures. Global village proponents see the world community coming closer together as a common culture is negotiated and, not incidentally, as we become more economically interconnected. "We are witnessing the revolution of the empowerment of the media consumer," argues Reuters Television Director Enriqué Jara (as cited in Hilliard & Keith, 1996, p. 1). There should be little fear that individual cultures and national identities will

SPIDER-MAN © 2004 Marvel Characters Inc.

Proponents of the global flow of communication find value in the local adoption of varied cultures. In India, Spider-Man's Peter Parker is transformed into Pavitr Prabhakar.

Abaya-clad Saudi Arabian women line up at the women-only counter of a McDonald's in a mall in Dhahran. Although critics of cultural imperialism see this as an intrusion of Western culture into the lives of these people, defenders of the globalization of culture see the expansion of opportunity for both the "sending" and the "receiving" cultures.

disappear, because the world's great diversity will ensure that culture-specific, special-interest fare remains in demand. Modern media technology makes the delivery of this varied content not only possible but profitable. Not only do native-language versions of U.S. television shows like *Jeopardy* exist in virtually every western European country, but other "translations" are taking place. For example, hot on the heels of the success of the Spider-Man movies, Marvel Comics and an Indian company announced the birth of *Spider-Man India*, in which a young Bombay lad, Pavitr Prabhakar, inherits powers from a sacred yogi and accessorizes his Spidey suit with a traditional dhoti while dealing with local problems and challenges (Bal, 2004). As a result of these cultural exchanges, argue proponents of globalization, "a global culture is created, piece by piece, but it grows more variegated and complex along the way. And even as geographically based identities blur and fade, new subcultures, based on shared tastes in music or literature or obscure hobbies, grow up" (Bennett, 2004, p. 62).

THE CASE AGAINST THE GLOBAL VILLAGE

The global village is here, say those with a less optimistic view, and the problem is what it looks like. *Time* media writer James Poniewozik (2001, p. 69) calls it "the new cold war—between the Hollywood/Mickey D's axis and every other world culture." Professor Richard Rosenberg (1992) predicts the erosion of national sovereignty. "The advanced nations of the world, through their multi-national corporations, will greatly expand their control over the international flow of information. As a result, much of the world may become even more heavily dependent on the Western nations and Japan" (p. 331). He also predicts the demise of native cultures. "The ongoing assault on national cultures will continue, fostered by direct satellite broadcasts and worldwide information distribution networks" (p. 332).

Media critic Robert McChesney (1997) fears for worldwide democracy. "The present course," he writes, "is one where much of the world's entertainment and journalism will be provided by a handful of enormous firms, with invariably pro-profit and pro-global market political positions on the central issues of our times. The implications for political democracy, by any standard, are troubling" (p. 23).

He elaborated elsewhere:

> The global commercial-media system is radical in that it will respect no tradition or custom, on balance, if it stands in the way of profits.... The global media system is better understood as one that advances corporate and commercial interests and values and denigrates or ignores that which cannot be incorporated into its mission. There is no discernible difference in the firms' content, whether they are owned by shareholders in Japan or Belgium or have corporate headquarters in New York or Sydney. (1999, pp. 13–14)

There is no simple answer to the debate over protecting the integrity of local cultures. As we've just seen, there is even disagreement over the wisdom of doing so. Media literate people should at least be aware of the debate and its issues.

DEVELOPING MEDIA LITERACY SKILLS

Making Our Way in the Global Village

Questions raised by the new communication technologies often lack clear-cut, satisfactory answers. In fact, as the major controversy addressed in this chapter—the impact of new communication technologies on national sovereignty and culture—demonstrates, different answers flow from different perspectives. For example, a world at peace with itself, its people sharing the common assumptions of a common culture, is a utopian dream. There are those who see it as attainable. But if the common culture that binds us is that of Mickey Mouse, is the harmony worth the loss of individual, idiosyncratic cultures?

There may be no easy—or even correct—solution to the problem of protecting the integrity of local cultures in our increasingly interconnected, mediated world. But at the very least, the simple existence of the problem requires that we remain open to and appreciative of the cultures of all our neighbors in the global village. The new communication technologies will

Support the Media Literacy Movement

One of the ironies of contemporary mass communication is that the United States, no doubt the world's most media-saturated country, lags behind most of the developed world in its commitment to media literacy. We saw in Chapter 1, for example, that not only do many countries have aggressive and active media literacy movements but these movements are supported and funded by those countries' media companies and governments.

But the United States may be catching up. As you saw in Chapter 14, there is growing dissatisfaction from across the political and social spectrum with the operation of the American media, especially on the issues of privacy, concentration, and the pace and products of deregulation. This dissatisfaction, according to media activists John Nichols and Robert McChesney (2002), is producing the basis for a true media literacy movement in the United States. "During the 1990s," they wrote, media literacy "activists began to recognize the need to do more than just critique increasingly monopolized and monotonous media. Local groups formed across the nation to monitor the local news media, keep commercialism out of schools, and banish liquor billboards from working-class and minority neighborhoods. In the past several years, media activism has blossomed at both the local and national levels" (Nichols & McChesney, 2002, p. 26). Media literacy has become a bipartisan issue, they continue, because "no more than leftists do sincere conservatives want their children's brains marinated in advertising; they do not want political campaigns to be centered entirely around expensive, inaccurate, and insulting political advertising; and they do not want America's democratic discourse reduced to poll-tested soundbites and

> **"THEY DO NOT WANT AMERICA'S DEMOCRATIC DISCOURSE REDUCED TO POLL-TESTED SOUNDBITES AND ARGUMENTS ABOUT WHICH TELEVISION ANCHOR IS WEARING THE BIGGEST FLAG PIN."**

arguments about which television anchor is wearing the biggest flag pin" (p. 27).

Live your media literacy by actively promoting a true American media literacy movement. There is a lot of help available from overseas, because if media are globalized, there is no reason that a strong American media literacy movement should not be, too. Examine the organization and efforts of these nations' movements to inform your own living media literacy:

Canada

Canadian Association of Media Education Organizations (CAMEO)
interact.uoregon.edu/MediaLit/CAMEO/index.htm

Ontario Media Literacy
www.angelfire.com/ms/MediaLiteracy/index.html

United Kingdom

The United Kingdom Media Education Web Site
www.mediaed.org.uk

Media and Communication Studies Site
www.aber.ac.uk/media/sections/meded04.php

South Africa

Media Institute of South Africa (MISA)
www.misa.org

Australia

Australian Children's Television Foundation
www.actf.com.au/

put them and us together in ways that were unimaginable in pre-Internet times. Are you ready?

The hallmarks of a media literate individual are surely analysis and self-reflection. Revisit the primer on pages 332–333. Reread its good news and bad news, and answer again the questions it raises. Have any of your answers changed? If they have, which ones, how, and most important, why? Are you a media literate, competent citizen of the global village? What contribution can you and will you make?

Review Points

- For decades, international mass media took the form of shortwave radio broadcasts, especially in the form of clandestine stations, both exogenous and indigenous.
- Other exogenous operations are pirate broadcasters and many countries' external services such as the BBC and VOA.
- Satellites ushered in true global mass communication.
- Different countries rely on different media systems to meet their national needs. The study of these varying models is called comparative analysis.
- There are five main models or concepts—Western, development, revolutionary, authoritarianism, and communism.

- Naturally, different systems make varying use of different programming as their nations' needs demand.
- There is serious debate about the free and not-so-free flow of mass communication across borders. The conflict is between those who want the free flow of information and those who worry about the erosion of local culture.
- Much of this controversy, however, has more to do with protecting countries' media systems from American influence than it does with protecting all countries' cultural integrity.
- Many nations are ahead of the United States in their media literacy efforts. Media literate people should become aware of these activities.

Key Terms

 Use the text's Online Learning Center at www.mhhe.com/baran5 to further your understanding of the following terminology.

shortwave radio, 488
skip, 488
sky waves, 488
clandestine stations, 489
indigenous station, 489
exogenous station, 489
pirate broadcaster, 489

external service, 490
surrogate service, 491
comparative analysis
   (studies), 498
Western concept, 499
public service remit, 499
D-notice, 500

development concept, 500
revolutionary concept, 500
authoritarian system, 502
wired radio, 502
cultural imperialism, 507

Questions for Review

 Go to the self-quizzes on the Online Learning Center to test your knowledge.

1. What are clandestine broadcast stations? Differentiate between indigenous and exogenous stations.
2. What are pirate broadcasters? What differentiates them from traditional clandestine operators?
3. How did World War II and the Cold War shape the efforts of the United States in terms of its external and surrogate services?
4. Describe the goals of the Voice of America, Radio and TV Martí, Armed Forces Radio and Television Services, and Radio Free Europe/Radio Liberty?
5. What are COMSAT and INTELSAT? How are they related?

6. What is comparative analysis?
7. What are the main characteristics of media systems operating under Hachten's Western concept?
8. What are the main characteristics of media systems operating under Hachten's development concept?
9. What are the main characteristics of media systems operating under Hachten's revolutionary concept?
10. What are the main characteristics of media systems operating under Hachten's authoritarianism and communism concepts?
11. In British media, what is the public service remit? What is a D-notice?

12. What is meant by wired radio?
13. What is cultural imperialism? What two telecommunications technologies fuel current concern over its operation?
14. What was the MacBride Report? Why did most Western nations reject it?
15. What is meant by the New World Information Order?

Questions for Critical Thinking and Discussion

1. Britain's external service, the BBC, is available on shortwave radio and American cable and satellite television. Listen to or watch the BBC. How does its content compare to the homegrown radio and television with which you are familiar? Think especially of news. How does its reporting differ from that of cable networks such as CNN and from broadcast networks such as ABC, CBS, and NBC? Why do you think differences exist? Similarities?

2. Do you have experience with another country's media? If so, which one? Can you place that system's operation within one of the concepts listed in this chapter? Describe how that system's content was similar to and different from that with which you are familiar in the United States. Do you favor one system's fare over another's? Why or why not?

3. Do you think countries, especially developing nations, should worry about cultural imperialism? Would you argue that they should use low-cost Western fare to help their developing system get "off the ground," or do you agree with critics that this approach unduly influences their system's ultimate content?

4. Compared with the United States, much of the rest of the world allows more sex and nudity in television programming. What does this tell us about these other countries and their people? About American audiences? Would you favor more sex and nudity on American television? Why or why not?

Important Resources

 Go to the Online Learning Center for additional readings.

Internet Resources

Radio Free Europe/Radio Liberty	www.rferl.org
Radio Caroline	www.radiocaroline.co.uk
Clandestine Radio	www.clandestineradio.com
RIAS	www.scripps.ohiou.edu/rias/history.htm
Voice of America	www.voa.gov
AFRTS	www.afrts.osd.mil
Al-Hurra	www.alhurra.com
Al-Jazeera	english.aljazeera.net
INTELSAT	www.intelsat.com
MTV International	www.mtv.com/mtvinternational
Population Communications International	www.population.org
BBC	www.bbc.co.uk
UNESCO	www.unesco.org

Glossary

à la carte pricing   charging cable subscribers by the channel, not for tiers

absolutist position   regarding the First Amendment, the idea that no law means no law

acquisitions editor   the person in charge of determining which books a publisher will publish

Acta Diurna   written on a tablet, account of the deliberations of the Roman senate; an early "newspaper"

actual malice   the standard for libel in coverage of public figures consisting of "knowledge of its falsity" or "reckless disregard" for whether or not it is true

ad hoc balancing of interests   in individual First Amendment cases, several factors should be weighed in determining how much freedom the press is granted

ad-pull policy   demand by an advertiser for an advance review of a magazine's content, with the threat of pulled advertising if dissatisfied with that content

administrative research   studies of the immediate, practical influence of mass communication

advergames   videogames produced expressly to serve as brand commercials

advertorials   ads in magazines and newspapers that take on the appearance of genuine editorial content

advocacy games   primarily online games supporting an idea rather than a product

affiliate   a broadcasting station that aligns itself with a network

agenda setting   the theory that media may not tell us what to think but do tell us what to think about

aggressive cues model   of media violence; media portrayals can indicate that certain classes of people are acceptable targets for real-world aggression

AIDA approach   the idea that to persuade consumers advertising must attract *attention*, create *interest*, stimulate *desire*, and promote *action*

Alien and Sedition Acts   series of four laws passed by 1798 U.S. Congress making illegal the writing, publishing, or printing of "any false scandalous and malicious writing" about the president, the Congress, or the U.S. government

aliteracy   possessing the ability to read but being unwilling to do so

all-channel legislation   1962 law requiring all television sets imported into or manufactured in the United States to be equipped with both VHF and UHF receivers

alternative press   typically weekly, free papers emphasizing events listings, local arts advertising, and "eccentric" personal classified ads

ambient advertising   advertising content appearing in nontraditional venues

applied ethics   the application of metaethics and normative ethics to very specific situations

appointment consumption   audiences consume content at a time predetermined by the producer and distributor

ascertainment   requires broadcasters to ascertain or actively and affirmatively determine the nature of their audiences' interest, convenience, and necessity; no longer enforced

attitude change theory   theory that explains how people's attitudes are formed, shaped, and changed and how those attitudes influence behavior

audience fragmentation   audiences for specific media content becoming smaller and increasingly homogeneous

audimeter   device for recording when the television set is turned on, the channel to which it is tuned, and the time of day; used in compiling ratings

audion tube   vacuum tube developed by DeForest that became the basic invention for all radio and television

authoritarian/communism system   a national media system characterized by authoritarian control

average quarter hour   how many people are listening to a broadcast station in each 15-minute day part

awareness tests   ad research technique that measures the cumulative effect of a campaign in terms of a product's "consumer consciousness"

B-movie   the second, typically less expensive, movie in a double feature

bandwidth   a communication channel's information-carrying capacity

banners   online advertising messages akin to billboards

basic cable   television channels provided automatically by virtue of subscription to a cable provider

Bill of Rights   the first 10 amendments to the U.S. Constitution

billings   total sale of broadcast airtime

binary code   information transformed into a series of digits 1 and 0 for storage and manipulation in computers

bitcasters   "radio stations" that can be accessed only over the World Wide Web

BitTorrent   file-sharing software that allows users to create "swarms" of data as they simultaneously download and upload "bits" of a given piece of content

block booking   the practice of requiring exhibitors to rent groups of movies (often inferior) to secure a better one

blockbuster mentality filmmaking characterized by reduced risk taking and more formulaic movies; business concerns are said to dominate artistic considerations

blogs regularly updated online journals

bounded cultures (co-cultures) groups with specific but not dominant cultures

brand entertainment when commercials are part of and essential to a piece of media content

brand magazine a consumer magazine published by a retail business for readers having demographic characteristics similar to those consumers with whom it typically does business

British cultural theory theory of elites' domination over culture and its influence on bounded cultures

broadband a channel with broad information-carrying capacity

broadsides (sometimes **broadsheets**) early colonial newspapers imported from England, single-sheet announcements or accounts of events

browsers software programs loaded on personal computers and used to download and view Web files

bundling delivering television, VOD, audio, high-speed Internet access, long-distance and local phone service, multiple phone lines, and fax via cable

cable modem modem connecting a computer to the Internet via a specified Internet service provider

calotype early system of photography using translucent paper from which multiple prints could be made

casual games classic games most often played in spurts and accommodated by small-screen devices

catalogue albums in record retailing, albums more than 3 years old

catharsis theory that watching mediated violence reduces people's inclination to behave aggressively

cease-and-desist order demand made by a regulatory agency that a given illegal practice be stopped

censorware unflattering name given to Web content–filtering software by its opponents

chained Bibles Bibles attached to church furniture or walls by early European church leaders

cinématographe Lumière brothers' device that both photographed and projected action

circulation the number of issues of a magazine or newspaper that are sold

clandestine stations illegal or unlicensed broadcast operations frequently operated by revolutionary groups or intelligence agencies for political purposes

clear time when local affiliates carry a network's program

click stream the series of choices made by a user on the Web

coaxial cable copper-clad aluminum wire encased in plastic foam insulation, covered by an aluminum outer conductor, and then sheathed in plastic

collateral materials printing, research, and photographs that PR firms handle for clients, charging as much as 17.65% for this service

commissions in advertising, placement of advertising in media is compensated, at typically 15% of the cost of the time or space, through commissions

common carrier a telecommunications company required to carry others' messages with no power to restrict them—for example, a phone company

communication the process of creating shared meaning

community antenna television (CATV) outmoded name for early cable television

community publishing Web pages built by local schools, clubs, and nonprofit groups carried on online newspaper Web sites

commuter papers free dailies designed for younger commuters

comparative analysis the study of different countries' mass media systems

comparative studies see **comparative analysis**

compensation network payments to affiliates for clearing content

complementary copy newspaper and magazine content that reinforces the advertiser's message, or at least does not negate it

consumption-on-demand the ability to access any content, anytime, anywhere

concentration of ownership ownership of different and numerous media companies concentrated in fewer and fewer hands

concept films movies that can be described in one line

confidentiality the ability of media professionals to keep secret the names of people who provide them with information

conglomeration the increase in the ownership of media outlets by nonmedia companies

consumer culture a culture in which personal worth and identity reside not in the people themselves but in the products with which they surround themselves

consumer juries ad research technique in which people considered representative of a target market review a number of approaches or variations of a campaign or ad

contextual advertising in online advertising, ads that automatically intrude into users' Web sessions whether wanted or not

controlled circulation a magazine provided at no cost to readers who meet some specific set of advertiser-attractive criteria

conventions in media content, certain distinctive, standardized style elements of individual genres

convergence the erosion of traditional distinctions among media

cookie an identifying code added to a computer's hard drive by a visited Web site

copy testing measuring the effectiveness of advertising messages by showing them to consumers; used for all forms of advertising

copyright identifying and granting ownership of a given piece of expression to protect the creators' financial interest in it

corantos one-page news sheets on specific events, printed in English but published in Holland and imported into England by British booksellers; an early "newspaper"

corporate independent studio specialty or niche division of a major studio designed to produce more sophisticated—but less costly—movies

corrective advertising a new set of ads required by a regulatory body and produced by the offender that correct the original misleading effort

cost per thousand (CPM) in advertising, the cost of reaching 1,000 audience members, computed by the cost of an ad's placement divided by the number of thousands of consumers it reaches

cottage industry an industry characterized by small operations closely identified with their personnel

cover rerecording of one artist's music by another

critical cultural theory idea that media operate primarily to justify and support the status quo at the expense of ordinary people

critical research studies of media's contribution to the larger issues of what kind of nation we are building, what kind of people we are becoming

cruising see **channel surfing**

cultivation analysis idea that television "cultivates" or constructs a reality of the world that, although possibly inaccurate, becomes the accepted reality simply because we as a culture believe it to be the reality

cultural definition of communication communication is a symbolic process whereby reality is produced, maintained, repaired, and transformed; from James Carey

cultural imperialism the invasion of an indigenous people's culture, through mass media, by outside, powerful countries

cultural theory the idea that meaning and therefore effects are negotiated by media and audiences as they interact in the culture

culture the world made meaningful; socially constructed and maintained through communication, it limits as well as liberates us, differentiates as well as unites us, defines our realities and thereby shapes the ways we think, feel, and act

cume the cumulative audience, the number of people who listen to a radio station for at least 5 minutes in any one day

custom publishing publications specifically designed for an individual company seeking to reach a narrowly defined audience

cyberadvertising placement of commercials on various online sites

d-book a book that is downloaded in electronic form from the Internet to a computer or handheld device

D-notice in Great Britain, an officially issued notice of prior restraint

daguerreotype process of recording images on polished metal plates, usually copper, covered with a thin layer of silver iodide emulsion

dataveillance the massive electronic collection and distillation of consumer data

decoding interpreting sign/symbol systems

democracy government by the people

demographic segmentation advertisers' appeal to audiences composed of varying personal and social characteristics such as race, gender, and economic level

dependency theory idea that media's power is a function of audience members' dependency on the media and their content

deregulation relaxation of ownership and other rules for radio and television

desensitization the idea that viewers become more accepting of real-world violence because of its constant presence in television fare

development concept of media systems; government and media work in partnership to ensure that media assist in the planned, beneficial development of the country

digital audio radio service (DARS) direct home or automobile delivery of audio by satellite

digital cable television delivery of digital video images and other information to subscribers' homes

digital computer a computer that processes data reduced to a binary code

digital delivery daily the online distribution of entire versions of printed newspapers

digital divide the lack of technological access among people of color, the poor, the disabled, and those in rural communities

digital epistolary novel (DEN) novel that unfolds serially through e-mails, instant messaging, and Web sites

digital must-carry rules in cable television, rules requiring that cable systems carry the signal of every television station, both analog and digital, within a specified radius

digital recording recording based on conversion of sound into 1s and 0s logged in millisecond intervals in a computerized translation process

digital rights management (DRM) protection of digitally distributed intellectual property

digital video recorder (DVR) video recording device attached to a television, which gives viewers significant control over content

dime novels inexpensive late 19th- and early 20th-century books that concentrated on frontier and adventure stories; sometimes called **pulp novels**

disinhibitory effects in social cognitive theory, seeing a model rewarded for prohibited or threatening behavior increases the likelihood that the observer will perform that behavior

dissident press free, alternative weeklies with a local and political orientation

dissonance theory argues that people, when confronted by new information, experience a kind of mental discomfort, a dissonance; as a result, they consciously and subconsciously work to limit or reduce that discomfort through the selective processes

diurnals daily accounts of local news printed in 1620s England; forerunners of our daily newspaper

DMX (Digital Music Express) home delivery of audio by cable

domain name on the World Wide Web, an identifying name, rather than a site's formal URL, that gives some indication of the nature of a site's content or owner

dominant culture (mainstream culture) the culture that seems to hold sway with the large majority of people; that which is normative

double feature two films on the same bill

duopoly single ownership and management of multiple radio stations in one market

e-mail (electronic mail) function of Internet allowing communication via computer with anyone else online, anyplace in the world, with no long-distance fees

e-publishing the publication and distribution of books initially or exclusively online

early window the idea that media give children a window on the world before they have the critical and intellectual ability to judge what they see

economies of scale concept that relative cost declines as the size of the endeavor grows

editorial policy newspapers' and magazines' positions on certain specific issues

embedded journalists war correspondents who exchange control of their output for access to the front

encoding transforming ideas into an understandable sign/symbol system

encryption electronic coding or masking of information on the Web that can be deciphered only by a recipient with the decrypting key

engagement psychological and behavioral measure of ad effectiveness designed to replace CPM

environmental incentives in social learning theory, the notion that real-world incentives can lead observers to ignore negative vicarious reinforcement

ethics rules of behavior or moral principles that guide actions in given situations

ethnic press papers, often in a foreign language, aimed at minority, immigrant, and non-English readers

exergame video game designed to encourage beneficial physical activity

exogenous stations clandestine broadcast operations functioning from outside the regions to which they transmit

expanded basic cable in cable television, a second, somewhat more expensive level of subscription

external service in international broadcasting, a service designed by one country to counter enemy propaganda and disseminate information about itself

factory studios the first film production companies

fair use in copyright law, instances in which material may be used without permission or payment

Fairness Doctrine requires broadcasters to cover issues of public importance and to be fair in that coverage; abolished in 1987

feature syndicates clearinghouses for the work of columnists, cartoonists, and other creative individuals, providing their work to newspapers and other media outlets

feedback the response to a given communication

fiber optics signals carried by light beams over glass fibers

First Amendment Congress shall make no law respecting an establishment of religion, or prohibiting the free exercise thereof; or abridging the freedom of speech, or of the press; or the right of the people peacefully to assemble, and to petition the Government for a redress of grievances

first-person perspective game video game in which all action is through the eyes of the player

first-run syndication original programming produced specifically for the syndicated television market

fixed-fee arrangement when a PR firm performs a specific set of services for a client for a specific and prearranged fee

flack a derogatory name sometimes applied to public relations professionals

flash mobs (sometimes **smart mobs**) large, geographically dispersed groups connected only by communications technology, quickly drawn together to perform collective action

focus groups small groups of people who are interviewed, typically to provide advertising or public relations professionals with detailed information

forced exposure ad research technique used primarily for television commercials, requiring advertisers to bring consumers to a theater or other facility where they see a television program, complete with the new ads

format a radio station's particular sound or programming content

fraction of selection graphic description of how individuals make media and content choices based on expectation of reward and effort required

franchise films movies produced with full intention of producing several sequels

Frankfurt School media theory, centered in neo-Marxism, that valued serious art, viewing its consumption as a means to elevate all people toward a better life; typical media fare was seen as pacifying ordinary people while repressing them

functional displacement when the functions of an existing medium are performed better or more efficiently by a newer medium

genre a form of media content with a standardized, distinctive style and conventions

global village a McLuhan concept; new communication technologies permit people to become increasingly involved in one another's lives

globalization ownership of media companies by multinational corporations

grand theory   a theory designed to describe and explain all aspects of a given phenomenon

green light process   the process of deciding to make a movie

greenwashing   public relations practice of countering the public relations efforts aimed at clients by environmentalists

griots   the "talking chiefs" in orally based African tribes

hard news   news stories that help readers make intelligent decisions and keep up with important issues

home page   entryway into a Web site, containing information and hyperlinks to other material

hosts   computers linking individual personal computer users to the Internet

hypercommercialism   increasing the amount of advertising and mixing commercial and noncommercial media content

hyperlink   connection, embedded in Internet or Web site, allowing instant access to other material in that site as well as to material in other sites

hypodermic needle theory   idea that media are a dangerous drug that can directly enter a person's system

iconoscope tube   first practical television camera tube, developed in 1923

identification   in social cognitive theory, a special form of imitation by which observers do not exactly copy what they have seen but make a more generalized but related response

ideogrammatic alphabet   a symbol- or picture-based alphabet

imitation   in social cognitive theory, the direct replication of an observed behavior

importation of distant signals   delivery of distant television signals by cable television for the purpose of improving reception

in-band-on-channel (IBOC)   digital radio technology that uses digital compression to "shrink" digital and analog signals, allowing both to occupy the same frequency

indecency   in broadcasting, language or material that depicts sexual or excretory activities in a way offensive to contemporary community standards

indigenous stations   clandestine broadcast operations functioning from inside the regions to which they transmit

inferential feedback   in the mass communication process, feedback is typically indirect rather than direct; that is, it is inferential

information gap   the widening disparity in amounts and types of information available to information haves and have-nots

information service   legal designation allowing a telecommunication service provider to maintain control over what passes over its lines

inhibitory effects   in social cognitive theory, seeing a model punished for a behavior reduces the likelihood that the observer will perform that behavior

instant books   books published very soon after some well-publicized public event

instant messaging (IM)   real-time e-mail, allowing two or more people to communicate instantaneously and in immediate response to one another

integrated marketing communications (IMC)   combining public relations, marketing, advertising, and promotion into a seamless communication campaign

Internet   a global network of interconnected computers that communicate freely and share and exchange information

Internet service provider   see **ISP**

interpersonal communication   communication between two or a few people

island   in children's television commercials, the product is shown simply, in actual size against a neutral background

ISP (Internet service provider)   company that offers Internet connections at monthly rates depending on the kind and amount of access needed

joint operating agreement (JOA)   permits a failing paper to merge most aspects of its business with a successful local competitor, as long as editorial and reporting operations remain separate

kinescope   improved picture tube developed by Zworykin for RCA

kinetograph   William Dickson's early motion picture camera

kinetoscope   peep show devices for the exhibition of kinetographs

LAN (local area network)   network connecting two or more computers, usually within the same building

LCD (liquid crystal display)   display surface in which electric currents of varying voltage are passed through liquid crystal, altering the passage of light through that crystal

LED (light-emitting diode)   light-emitting semiconductor manipulated under a display screen

libel   the false and malicious publication of material that damages a person's reputation (typically applied to print media)

libertarianism   philosophy of the press that asserts that good and rational people can tell right from wrong if presented with full and free access to information; therefore, censorship is unnecessary

limited effects theory   media's influence is limited by people's individual differences, social categories, and personal relationships

linotype   technology that allowed the mechanical rather than manual setting of print type

liquid barretter   first audio device permitting the reception of wireless voices; developed by Fessenden

literacy   the ability to effectively and efficiently comprehend and utilize a given form of communication

literate culture   a culture that employs a written language

lobbying   in public relations, directly interacting with elected officials or government regulators and agents

Low Power FM (LPFM) 10- to 100-watt nonprofit community radio stations with a reach of only a few miles

macro-level effects media's widescale social and cultural impact

magalogue a designer catalogue produced to look like a consumer magazine

magic bullet theory the idea from mass society theory that media are a powerful "killing force" that directly penetrates a person's system

mainframe computer a large central computer to which users are connected by terminals

mainstreaming in cultivation analysis, television's ability to move people toward a common understanding of how things are

market reach total number of readers of the print edition of a newspaper plus unduplicated Web readers

mass communication the process of creating shared meaning between the mass media and their audiences

mass communication theories explanations and predictions of social phenomena relating mass communication to various aspects of our personal and cultural lives or social systems

mass medium (pl. **mass media**) a medium that carries messages to a large number of people

mass society theory the idea that media are corrupting influences; they undermine the social order, and "average" people are defenseless against their influence

massively multiplayer online role-playing game (MMORPG) interactive online game where characters and actions are controlled by other players, not the computer; also called **virtual worlds games**

master antenna television (MATV) connecting multiple sets in a single location or building to a single, master antenna

media councils panels of people from both the media and the public who investigate complaints against the media and publish their findings

media literacy the ability to effectively and efficiently comprehend and utilize mass communication

media multitasking simultaneously consuming many different kinds of media

medium (pl. **media**) vehicle by which messages are conveyed

metaethics examination of a culture's understanding of its fundamental values

microcomputer a very small computer that uses a microprocessor to handle information (also called a **personal computer** or **PC**)

microcinema filmmaking using digital video cameras and desktop digital editing machines

micro-level effects effects of media on individuals

microwave relay audio and video transmitting system in which super-high-frequency signals are sent from land-based point to land-based point

middle-range theories ideas that explain or predict only limited aspects of the mass communication process

minicomputer a relatively large central computer to which users are connected by terminals; not as large as a mainframe computer

mobisodes brief video episodes of television programs created specifically for mobile screens

modeling in social cognitive theory, learning through imitation and identification

modem a device that translates digital computer information into an analog form so it can be transmitted through telephone lines

montage tying together two separate but related shots in such a way that they take on a new, unified meaning

moral agent in an ethical dilemma, the person making the decision

MP3 file compression software that permits streaming of digital audio and video data

muckraking a form of crusading journalism that primarily used magazines to agitate for change

MUD (multi-user dimension) online text-based interactive game

multimedia advanced sound and image capabilities for microcomputers

multiple points of access ability of a literate media consumer to access or approach media content from a variety of personally satisfying directions

multiple system operator (MSO) a company owning several different cable television operations

multiplexing the practice of using one channel to transmit multiple forms of content; in television and cable, through signal compression

music licensing company an organization that collects fees based on recorded music users' gross receipts and distributes the money to songwriters and artists

narrowcasting aiming broadcast programming at smaller, more demographically homogeneous audiences

neo-Marxist theory the theory that people are oppressed by those who control the culture, the superstructure, as opposed to the base

network centralized production, distribution, decision-making organization that links affiliates for the purpose of delivering their viewers to advertisers

network neutrality granting equal carriage over phone and cable lines to all Web sites

news production research the study of how economic and other influences on the way news is produced distort and bias news coverage toward those in power

news staging re-creation on television news of some event that is believed to have happened or which could have happened

newsbook early weekly British publications that carried ads

newspaper chains businesses that own two or more newspapers

niche marketing aiming media content or consumer products at smaller, more demographically homogeneous audiences

nickelodeons the first movie houses; admission was one nickel

Nipkow disc first workable device for generating electrical signals suitable for the transmission of a scene

noise anything that interferes with successful communication

nonlinear TV watching television on our own schedules, not the programmer's

normative ethics generalized theories, rules, and principles of ethical or moral behavior

normative theory an idea that explains how media should ideally operate in a given system of social values

O&O a broadcasting station that is owned and operated by a network

obscenity unprotected expression determined by (1) whether the average person, applying contemporary community standards, would find that the work, taken as a whole, appeals to the prurient interest, (2) whether the work depicts or describes, in a patently offensive way, sexual conduct specifically defined by the applicable state law, and (3) whether the work, taken as a whole, lacks serious literary, artistic, political, or scientific value

observational learning in social cognitive theory, observers can acquire (learn) new behaviors simply by seeing those behaviors performed

off-network broadcast industry term for syndicated content that originally aired on a network

offset lithography late 19th-century advance making possible printing from photographic plates rather than from metal casts

oligopoly a media system whose operation is dominated by a few large companies

ombudsman internal arbiter of performance for media organizations

open source software freely downloaded software

operating policy spells out standards for everyday operations for newspapers and magazines

operating system the software that tells the computer how to work

opinion followers people who receive opinion leaders' interpretations of media content; from **two-step flow theory**

opinion leaders people who initially consume media content, interpret it in light of their own values and beliefs, and then pass it on to opinion followers; from **two-step flow theory**

opt-in/opt-out consumers giving permission to companies to sell personal data, or consumers requesting that companies do not sell personal data

oral (or **preliterate**) **culture** a culture without a written language

P2P peer-to-peer software that permits direct Internet-based communication or collaboration between two or more personal computers while bypassing centralized servers

papyrus early form of paper composed of pressed strips of sliced reed

paradigm a theory that summarizes and is consistent with all known facts

paradigm shift fundamental, even radical, rethinking of what people believe to be true for a given body of knowledge

parchment writing material made from prepared animal skins

parity products products generally perceived as alike by consumers no matter who makes them

pass-along readership measurement of publication readers who neither subscribe nor buy single copies but who borrow a copy or read one in a doctor's office or library

pay cable cable television channels delivered to those viewers who pay a fee over and above their basic service charge

payola payment made by recording companies to DJs to air their records

pay-per-view cable television viewers pay a set fee for delivery of a specific piece of content

penny press newspapers in the 1830s selling for one penny

peoplemeter remote control keypad device for recording television viewing for taking ratings

performance-based advertising Web advertising where the site is paid only when the consumer takes some specific action

persistence of vision images our eyes gather are retained by our brains for about 1/24 of a second, producing the appearance of constant motion

personal computer (PC) see **microcomputer**

personal peoplemeter ratings technology; a special remote control with personalized buttons for each viewer in the household

pilot a sample episode of a proposed television program

piracy the illegal recording and sale of copyrighted material

pirate broadcasters unlicensed or otherwise illegally operated broadcast stations

pixel the smallest picture element in an electronic imaging system such as a television or computer screen

platform the means of delivering a specific piece of media content

platform rollout opening a movie on only a few screens in the hope that favorable reviews and word-of-mouth publicity will boost interest

playlist predetermined sequence of selected records to be played by a disc jockey

podcasting recording and downloading of audio files stored on servers

policy book delineates standards of operation for local broadcasters

pornography expression calculated solely to supply sexual excitement

preliterate culture   see **oral culture**

premium cable   cable television channels offered to viewers for a fee above the cost of their basic subscription

print on demand   publishing method whereby publishers store books digitally for instant printing, binding, and delivery once ordered

prior restraint   power of the government to *prevent* publication or broadcast of expression

product placement   the integration, for a fee, of specific branded products into media content

product positioning   the practice in advertising of assigning meaning to a product based on who buys the product rather than on the product itself

production values   media content's internal language and grammar; its style and quality

prosumer   a proactive consumer

protocols   common communication rules and languages for computers linked to the Internet

pseudo-event   event that has no real informational or issue meaning; it exists merely to attract media attention

psychographic segmentation   advertisers' appeal to consumer groups of varying lifestyles, attitudes, values, and behavior patterns

public   in PR, any group of people with a stake in an organization, issue, or idea

public domain   in copyright law, the use of material without permission once the copyright expires

public service remit   limits on advertising and other public service requirements imposed on Britain's commercial broadcasters in exchange for the right to broadcast

puffery   the little lie or exaggeration that makes advertising more entertaining than it might otherwise be

pulp novels   see **dime novels**

put   agreement between a television producer and network that guarantees that the network will order at least a pilot or pay a penalty

radio frequency identification chip (RFIC)   grain-of-sand–sized microchip and antenna embedded in consumer products that transmit a radio signal

rating   percentage of a market's total population that is reached by a piece of broadcast programming

recall testing   ad research technique in which consumers are asked to identify which ads are most easily remembered

recent catalogue albums   in record retailing, albums out for 15 months to 3 years

recognition tests   ad research technique in which people who have seen a given publication are asked whether they remember seeing a given ad

reinforcement theory   Joseph Klapper's idea that if media have any impact at all, it is in the direction of reinforcement

remainders   unsold copies of books returned to the publisher by bookstores to be sold at great discount

retainer   in advertising, an agreed-upon amount of money a client pays an ad agency for a specific series of services

revolutionary concept   normative theory describing a system where media are used in the service of revolution

ritual perspective   the view of media as central to the representation of shared beliefs and culture

ROI (return on investment)   an accountability-based measure of advertising success

safe harbor   times of the broadcast day (typically 10:00 p.m. to 6:00 a.m.) when children are not likely to be in the listening or viewing audience

satellite-delivered media tour   spokespeople can be simultaneously interviewed by a worldwide audience hooked to the interviewee by telephone

search engines   (sometimes called **spiders,** or **Web crawlers**) Web- or Net-search software providing on-screen menus

secondary service   a radio station's second, or nonprimary, format

selective attention   see **selective exposure**

selective exposure   the idea that people expose themselves or attend to those messages that are consistent with their preexisting attitudes and beliefs

selective perception   the idea that people interpret messages in a manner consistent with their preexisting attitudes and beliefs

selective processes   people expose themselves to, remember best and longest, and reinterpret messages that are consistent with their preexisting attitudes and beliefs

selective retention   assumes that people remember best and longest those messages that are consistent with their existing attitudes and beliefs

self-righting principle   John Milton's articulation of libertarianism

sender pays   charging "postage" for e-mail

share   the percentage of people listening to radio or of homes using television tuned in to a given piece of programming

shield laws   legislation that expressly protects reporters' rights to maintain sources' confidentiality in courts of law

shopbills   attractive, artful business cards used by early British tradespeople to promote themselves

short ordering   network practice of ordering only one or two episodes of a new television series

shortwave radio   radio signals transmitted at high frequencies that can travel great distances by skipping off the ionosphere

signs   in social construction of reality, things that have subjective meaning

siquis   pinup want ads common in Europe before and in early days of newspapers

skip   ability of radio waves to reflect off the ionosphere

skyscrapers   online billboards placed down the side of a Web page

sky waves   radio waves that are skipped off the ionosphere

slander   oral or spoken defamation of a person's character (typically applied to broadcasting)

smart mobs see **flash mobs**

social cognitive theory idea that people learn through observation

social construction of reality theory for explaining how cultures construct and maintain their realities using signs and symbols; argues that people learn to behave in their social world through interaction with it

social responsibility theory (or **model**) normative theory or model asserting that media must remain free of government control but, in exchange, must serve the public

soft news sensational stories that do not serve the democratic function of journalism

spam unsolicited commercial e-mail

spectrum scarcity broadcast spectrum space is limited, so not everyone who wants to broadcast can; those who are granted licenses must accept regulation

spiders see **search engines**

spin in PR, outright lying to hide what really happened

split runs special versions of a given issue of a magazine in which editorial content and ads vary according to some specific demographic or regional grouping

spot commercial sales in broadcasting, selling individual advertising spots on a given program to a wide variety of advertisers

spyware identifying code placed on a computer by a Web site without permission or notification

Standards and Practices Department the internal content review operation of a television network

stereotyping application of a standardized image or conception applied to members of certain groups, usually based on limited information

sticky an attribute of a Web site; indicates its ability to hold the attention of a user

stimulation model of media violence; viewing mediated violence can increase the likelihood of subsequent aggressive behavior

streaming the simultaneous downloading and accessing (playing) of digital audio or video data

stringers freelance reporters

stripping broadcasting a syndicated television show at the same time 5 nights a week

subscription TV early experiments with over-the-air pay television

subsidiary rights the sale of a book, its contents, even its characters to outside interests, such as filmmakers

surrogate service in international broadcasting, an operation established by one country to substitute for another's own domestic service

sweeps periods special television ratings times in February, May, July, and November in which diaries are distributed to thousands of sample households in selected markets

syllable alphabet a phonetically based alphabet employing sequences of vowels and consonants, that is, words

symbolic interaction the idea that people give meaning to symbols and then those symbols control people's behavior in their presence

symbols in social construction of reality, things that have objective meaning

syndication sale of radio or television content to stations on a market-by-market basis

synergy the use by media conglomerates of as many channels of delivery as possible for similar content

targeting aiming media content or consumer products at smaller, more specific audiences

taste publics groups of people or audiences bound by little more than their interest in a given form of media content

technological determinism the idea that machines and their development drive economic and cultural change

technology gap the widening disparity between communication technology haves and have-nots

telecommunications service legal designation rendering a telecommunication service provider a common carrier, required to carry the messages of others and with no power to restrict them

tentpole an expensive blockbuster around which a studio plans its other releases

terminals user workstations that are connected to larger centralized computers

terrestrial digital radio land-based digital radio relying on digital compression technology to simultaneously transmit analog and one or more digital signals using existing spectrum space

theatrical films movies produced primarily for initial exhibition on theater screens

third-party publishers companies that create video games for existing systems

third person effect the common attitude that others are influenced by media messages, but we are not

tier groupings of channels made available by a cable or satellite provider to subscribers at varying prices

time-shifting taping a show on a VCR for later viewing

trade books hard- or softcover books including fiction and most nonfiction and cookbooks, biographies, art books, coffee-table books, and how-to books

traffic cop analogy in broadcast regulation, the idea that the FCC, as a traffic cop, has the right to control not only the flow of broadcast traffic but its composition

transmissional perspective the view of media as senders of information for the purpose of control

trustee model in broadcast regulation, the idea that broadcasters serve as the public's trustees or fiduciaries

two-step flow theory the idea that media's influence on people's behavior is limited by opinion leaders—people who initially consume media content, interpret it in light of their own values and beliefs, and then pass it on to opinion followers, who have less frequent contact with media

typification schemes in social construction of reality, collections of meanings people have assigned to some phenomenon or situation

unique selling proposition (USP) the aspect of an advertised product that sets it apart from other brands in the same product category

URL (uniform resource locator) the designation of each file or directory on the host computer connected to the Internet

Usenet also known as network news, an internationally distributed Internet bulletin board system

uses and gratifications approach the idea that media don't do things *to* people; people do things *with* media

VALS advertisers' psychographic segmentation strategy that classifies consumers according to values and lifestyles

vast wasteland expression coined by FCC chair Newton Minow in 1961 to describe television content

vertical integration a system in which studios produced their own films, distributed them through their own outlets, and exhibited them in their own theaters

vicarious reinforcement in social cognitive theory, the observation of reinforcement operates in the same manner as actual reinforcement

video game a game involving action taking place interactively on-screen

video news release preproduced report about a client or its product that is distributed on videocassette free of charge to television stations

video-on-demand (VOD) service allowing television viewers to access pay-per-view movies and other content that can be watched whenever they want

viral marketing PR strategy that relies on targeting specific Internet users with a given communication and relying on them to spread the word

virtual worlds games see **massively multiplayer online role-playing games**

Voice over Internet Protocol (VoIP) phone calls transferred in digital packets over the Internet rather than on circuit-switched telephone wires

WAN (wide area network) network that connects several LANs in different locations

Web crawlers see **search engines**

Web radio the delivery of "radio" over the Internet directly to individual listeners

Webzines online magazines

Western concept of media systems; normative theory that combines libertarianism's freedom with social responsibility's demand for public service and, where necessary, regulation

Wi-Fi wireless Internet

willing suspension of disbelief audience practice of willingly accepting the content before them as real

wire services news-gathering organizations that provide content to members

wired radio employed in remote areas of many developing countries; centrally located loudspeakers that deliver radio broadcasts

World Wide Web a tool that serves as a means of accessing files on computers connected via the Internet

yellow journalism early-20th-century journalism emphasizing sensational sex, crime, and disaster news

zipping fast-forwarding through taped commercials on a VCR

zoned editions suburban or regional versions of metropolitan newspapers

zoopraxiscope early machine for projecting slides onto a distant surface

References

A candid conversation with the high priest of popcult and metaphysician of media. (1969, March). *Playboy*, pp. 53–74, 158.

Ad Age special report: Top 25 U.S. agency brands. (2006, May 1). *Advertising Age*, p. S-2.

Ad Age special report: World's top 25 marketing organizations (2004, April 19). *Advertising Age*, p. S-2.

Ad, subtract. (2001, January/February). *Adbusters*, p. 18.

Adams, M. (1996). The race for radiotelephone: 1900–1920. *AWA Review*, *10*, 78–119.

The advertising landscape. (2004, June). AdAge.com. Online: www.adage.com/images/random/tns_061604.pdf.

AFRTS. (2005). Mission statement. Online: www.eucom.mil/programs/afrts/index.htm.

Ahrens, F. (2005, February 20). Hard news; daily papers face unprecedented competition. *Washington Post*, p. F1.

Albiniak, P. (1999, May 3). Media: Littleton's latest suspect. *Broadcasting & Cable*, pp. 6–15.

Albiniak, P. (2002, April 29). Railing—but no derailing. *Broadcasting & Cable*, p. 7.

Albiniak, P. (2004, January 19). Quit crying, *Friends*. *Broadcasting & Cable*, pp. 1, 48.

Allen, T. B. (2001, December). The future is calling. *National Geographic*, pp. 76–83.

Allport, G. W., & Postman, L. J. (1945). The basic psychology of rumor. *Transactions of the New York Academy of Sciences, 8,* 61–81.

Alterman, E. (2002, May 20). Bad work. *The Nation*, p. 10.

Alterman, E. (2003, November 3). Abrams and Novak and Rove? Oh my! *The Nation*, p. 10.

Alterman, E. (2004, May 24). Is Koppel a Commie? *The Nation*, p. 10.

Alterman, E. (2005a, March 14). The pajama game. *The Nation*, p. 10.

Alterman, E. (2005b, January 31). Pundit limbo: How low can they go? *The Nation*, p. 10.

Andersen, R. (2003, May/June). That's militainment! *Extra!*, pp. 6–9.

Anderson, C. A., Berkowitz, L., Donnerstein, E., Huesmann, L. R., Johnson, J. D., Linz, D., Malamuth, N. M., & Wartella, E. (2003). The influence of media violence on youth. *Psychological Science in the Public Interest, 4,* 81–110.

Anderson, M. K. (2000, May/June). When copyright goes wrong. *Extra!*, p. 25.

Angell, R. (2002, March 11). Read all about it. *The New Yorker*, pp. 27–28.

Arato, A., & Gebhardt, E. (1978). *The essential Frankfurt School reader*. New York: Urizen Books.

Arbitron. (2002, June 18). Radio listening highest among well-educated, upper-income consumers. Online: www.arbitron.com/newsroom/archive/06_18_02.htm.

Arndorfer, J. B. (2005, October 18). $161 billion spent in direct marketing in 2005. *AdAge.com*. Online: http://www.adage.com/news.cms?newsId=46436.

Associated Press et al. v. United States 326 U.S. 1, 89 L. Ed. 2013, 65 S. Ct. 1416 (1945).

Atkinson, C. (2004, September 27). Press group attacks magazine product placement. *AdAge.com*. Online: www.adage.com/news.cms?newsId=41597.

Atkinson, C. (2005, October 24). VOD numbers small, interest high. *Advertising Age*, p. S-2, S-8.

Auletta, K. (2001, December 10). Battle stations. *The New Yorker*, pp. 60–67.

Auletta, K. (2005a, March 7). Sign-off. *The New Yorker*, pp. 48–61.

Auletta, K. (2005b, March 28). The new pitch. *The New Yorker*, pp. 34–39.

Auletta, K. (2005c, December 19). The inheritance. *The New Yorker*, pp. 66–77.

Ault, A. (2005, October 4). Turn on, tune out, get well? *Washington Post*, p. HE1.

Aumente, J. (1999, January/February). Cracking down: Yugoslavia's campaign against an independent media harkens back to the Cold War era. *American Journalism Review*, pp. 40–43.

Bacon, J. (2005, November/December). Saying what they've been thinking. *Extra!*, pp. 13–15.

Baer A. (2004, April 15). Call me e-mail: The novel unfolds digitally. *New York Times*. Online: nytimes.com/2004/04/15/technology/circuits/15nove.html.

Bagdikian, B. (2004, March). Print will survive. *Editor & Publisher*, p. 70.

Baker, R. (2003, June 23). "Scoops" and truth at the *Times*. *The Nation*, pp. 18–21.

Bal, S. (2004, July 9). India ink. *Entertainment Weekly*, p. 19.

Ball, S., & Bogatz, G. A. (1970). *The first year of* Sesame Street: *An evaluation*. Princeton, NJ: Educational Testing Service.

Bamford, J. (2005, November 23). James Bamford replies. *Rolling Stone*. Online: http://www.rollingstone.com/politics/story/_id/8868453.

Bandura, A. (1965). Influence of model's reinforcement contingencies on the acquisition of imitative responses. *Journal of Personality and Social Psychology, 1,* 589–595.

Banfield, A. (2003, April 29). MSNBC's Banfield slams war coverage. *AlterNet*. Online: www.alternet.org/print.html?storyid=15778.

Banning bad news in Iraq. (2004, August 10). *New York Times*, p. A20.

Baran, S. J., Chase, L. J., & Courtright, J. A. (1979). *The Waltons*: Television as a facilitator of prosocial behavior. *Journal of Broadcasting, 23* (3), 277–284.

Baran, S. J., & Davis, D. K. (2006). *Mass communication theory: Foundations, ferment and future* (4th ed.). Belmont, CA: Wadsworth.

Barlow, J. P. (1996). Selling wine without bottles: The economy of mind on the global Net. In L. H. Leeson (Ed.), *Clicking in: Hot links to a digital culture*. Seattle, WA: Bay Press.

Barmann, T. C. (2002, January 7). The information highway is getting more crowded. *Providence Journal*, pp. E1, E3.

Barnouw, E. (1966). *A tower in Babel: A history of broadcasting in the United States to 1933*. New York: Oxford University Press.

Barnouw, E. (1990). *Tube of plenty: The evolution of American television*. New York: Oxford University Press.

Barstow, D. (2006, April 6). Report faults video reports shown as news. *New York Times*, p. A17.

Barstow, D., & Stein, R. (2005, March 13). Under Bush, a new age of prepackaged television news. *New York Times*, p. 1.1.

Bart, P. (2000, January 3–9). The big media blur. *Variety*, pp. 4, 95.

Bart, P. (2006, December 26–January 1). Creative engines turn creaky in '05. *Variety*, p. 2.

Barton, L. (2002, July 30). Cereal offenders. *Guardian Education*, pp. 2–3.

The battle for our ears. (2006, March 24). *The Week*, p. 13.

Beck, D. (2000, July 2). Top U.S. book release ever is a thriller. *San Jose Mercury News*, pp. 1A, 17A.

Becker, A. (2005, December 5). TV braces for DVR ratings. *Broadcasting & Cable*. Online: http://www.broadcastingcable .com/index.asp?articleID=CA6288758.

Beech, H. (2002, July 22). Living it up in the illicit Internet underground. *Time*, p. 4.

Bennett, D. (2004, February). Our mongrel planet. *American Prospect*, pp. 62–63.

Bennett, W. L. (1988). *News: The politics of illusion*. New York: Longman.

Berelson, B. (1949). What "missing the newspaper" means. In P. F. Lazarsfeld & F. N. Stanton (Eds.), *Communication research, 1948–1949*. New York: Harper.

Berger, P. L., & Luckmann, T. (1966). *The social construction of reality: A treatise in the sociology of knowledge*. Garden City, NY: Doubleday.

Berkman, H. W., & Gilson, C. (1987). *Advertising: Concepts and strategies*. New York: Random House.

Bernays, E. L. (1986). *The later years: Public relations insights, 1956–1988*. Rhinebeck, NY: H & M.

Berners-Lee, T., & Fischetti, M. (1999). *Weaving the Web: The original design and ultimate destiny of the World Wide Web by its inventor*. New York: HarperCollins.

Big Battle Over Ad Budgets. (2005, September 15). Online: *eMarketer*. http://www.emarketer.com/Article.aspx?1003581.

Bing, J. (2006, January 2–8). Auds: A many-splintered thing. *Variety*, pp. 1, 38–39.

BISG. (2004, May 19). BISG's *Trends* predicts $44 billion book market in 2008. *Bookselling This Week*. Online: www.news .bookweb.org/m-bin?article_id=2548.

Bittner, J. R. (1994). *Law and regulation of electronic media*. Englewood Cliffs, NJ: Prentice-Hall.

Black and white and read by fewer. (2005, October 23). *Providence Journal*, p. E5.

Black, J. (2001). Hardening of the articles: An ethicist looks at propaganda in today's news. *Ethics in Journalism, 4*, 15–36.

Black, J., & Barney, R. D. (1985/86). The case against mass media codes of ethics. *Journal of Mass Media Ethics, 1*, 27–36.

Black, J., & Whitney, F. C. (1983). *Introduction to mass communications*. Dubuque, IA: William C. Brown.

Blais, J. (2003, July 23). Harry Potter casts a record-breaking spell. *USA Today*, p. 1D.

Bogle, D. (1989). *Toms, coons, mulattos, mammies, & bucks: An interpretive history of Blacks in American films*. New York: Continuum.

The bottom line. (2006, March 3). *The Week*, p. 34.

Bowles, S. (2006, January 22). Hollywood needs a good run. *USA Today*. Online: http://www.usatoday.com/life/movies/news/2006-01-22-2006-box-office-outlook_x.htm.

Boyd, A. (2003, August 4/11). The Web rewires the movement. *The Nation*, pp. 13–18.

Boyd, B. (2006, February 13–19). Clout and about. *Variety*, pp. B1, B6.

Bradbury, R. (1981). *Fahrenheit 451*. New York: Ballantine. (Originally published in 1956.)

Bragg, B. (2004, March/April). Interview. *Mother Jones*, pp. 82–83.

Bray, H. (2006, January 28). Google China censorship fuels calls for US boycott. *Boston Globe*, p. A10.

Breaking . . . (2004, June 28). *Broadcasting & Cable*, p. 3.

Bridges v. California 314 U.S. 252 (1941).

Brill, S. (2000, April). The mega threats. *Brill's Content*, pp. 23–27.

Brown, M. (2005, October 3). Media engagement study. *Advertising Age*, p. 59.

Burnham, V. (2001). *Supercade: A visual history of the videogame age 1971–1984*. Cambridge: MIT Press.

Burns, E. (2005, October 14). *Clickz.com*. Online: www.clickz .com/news/article.php/3556236.

Burstyn v. Wilson 343 U.S. 495 (1952).

Burton, B. (2005, November 15). Fake news: It's the PR industry against the rest of us. Online: http://www.prwatch.org/node/4174/print.

Bush's Baghdad bird a decoration. (2003, December 4). *CBSNews.com*. Online: www.cbsnews.com/stories/2003/12/04/politics/printable586761.shtml.

Canned news. (2003, November/December). *Columbia Journalism Review*, p. 9.

The Can-Spam Act. (2004, January 5). *Providence Journal*, p. A8.

Cappella, J. N., & Jamieson, K. H. (1997). *Spiral of cynicism: The press and the public good*. New York: Oxford University Press.

Carey, J. W. (1975). A cultural approach to communication. *Communication, 2*, 1–22.

Carnevale, D. (2005, December 9). Books when you want them. *Chronicle of Higher Education*, p. A27.

Carr, D. (2004, August 2). Publish till you drop. *New York Times*, p. C1.

Carter, B. (2003, November 11). NBC faults Nielsen for reduction in viewers. *New York Times*, pp. C1, C4.

Case, T. (2001, April 30). The last mass medium? *Editor & Publisher*, pp. SR16–SR18.

CBS News. (2005, April 26). Alabama bill targets gay authors. Online: http://www.truthout.org/docs_2005/042705N.shtml.

CBS v. Democratic National Committee 412 U.S. 94 (1973).

Center for Science in the Public Interest. (2002). Booze news. Online: www.cspinet.org/booze/alcad.htm.

Century, D. (2001, March). Black publishing's new colors. *Brill's Content*, pp. 84–87, 141.

Cha, A. E. (2005, July 3). The Internet is broken; can it be repaired? *Providence Journal*, pp. D1, D2.

Chandler v. Florida 449 U.S. 560 (1981).

Chester, J., and Hazen, D. (2003, May 1). Showdown at the FCC. *AlterNet*. Online: www.alternet.org/print.html?storyid=15796.

Chin, F. (1978). *Cable television: A comprehensive bibliography*. New York: IFI/Plenum.

China adopts new Net curbs. (1997, December 31). *San Jose Mercury News*, pp. C1, C4.

Chmielewski, D. C. (2003, January 9). Videogame industry has a blind spot to females. *Pittsburgh Post-Gazette*, p. C3.

Churnin, N. (2005, July 18). Harry mellows critics. *Providence Journal*, p. E1.

Circulation down, worldwide. (2004, June 1). *Editor & Publisher*. Online: www.editorandpublisher.com/eandp/news/article_display.jsp?vnu_content_id=10005.

Civil unions for gays favored, poll shows. (2004, March 12). MSNBC. Online: http://www.msnbc.com/id/4496265.

CJR Comment. (2003, September/October). 9/11/03. *Columbia Journalism Review*, p. 7.

Coates, T. (2005, July 10). The color of money: No longer Black and White. *New York Times*, p. 2.1.

Coen, R., & Hart, P. (2002, April). Last media ownership limits threatened by judicial action. *Extra! Update*, p. 4.

Cohn, D. (2005, December 12). TV writers must sell, sell, sell. *Wired*. Online: http://www.wired.com/news/0,1294,69775,00.html.

Cole, J. (2005, October 14). Judy Miller and the neocons. *Salon*. Online: http://www.truthout.org/docs_2005/101450L.shtml.

Cohen, W. (2002, June 20). CD burning. *Rolling Stone*, pp. 43–44.

Colorado Indy Media. (2005, May 17). Colorado passes anti-Patriot Act resolution. Online: http://colorado.indymedia.org/newswire/display/11125/index.php.

Compaine, B. M., & Gomery, D. (2000). *Who owns the media? Competition and concentration in the mass media industry*. Mahwah, NJ: Erlbaum.

Consoli, J. (2005, December 5). CBS: Mobile "attractive" but not TV threat. *Mediaweek.com*. Online: http://mediaweek.com/cpt&title=CBS%3A+Mobile+%.htm.

Cook, S. A. (2004, July 6). Hearts, minds, and hearings. *New York Times*, p. A19.

Cook, T. D., Appleton, H., Conner, R. F., Shaffer, A., Tamkin, G., & Weber, S. J. (1975). *Sesame Street revisited*. New York: Russell Sage Foundation.

The cookies in your computer. (2006, March 10). *The Week*, p. 11.

Cox, A. M. (2005, March). Howard Stern and the satellite wars. *Wired*, pp. 99–101, 135.

Cox, C. (1999, September/October). Prime-time activism. *Utne Reader*, pp. 20–22.

Cox, C. (2000, July/August). Plugged into protest? *Utne Reader*, pp. 14–15.

Creamer, M. (2005, July 21). Ad groups back switch from 'frequency' to 'engagement'. Online: http://www.adage.com/news.cms?newsID=45606.

The crisis in publishing. (2003, February 21). *The Week*, p. 22.

Cuneo, A. Z. (2005, October 24). Scramble for content drives mobile. *Advertising Age*, p. S-6.

Dargis, M. (2006, March 5). Hollywood's crowd control problem. *New York Times*, pp. 2.1, 2.21.

Davis, D. K. (1990). News and politics. In D. L. Swanson & D. Nimmo (Eds.), *New directions in political communication*. Newbury Park, CA: Sage.

Davis, R. E. (1976). *Response to innovation: A study of popular argument about new mass media*. New York: Arno Press.

Day, L. A. (2006). *Ethics in media communications: Cases and controversies* (6th ed.). Belmont, CA: Wadsworth.

DeFleur, M. L., & Ball-Rokeach, S. (1975). *Theories of mass communication* (3rd ed.). New York: David McKay.

deGraf, B. (2004, May 5). "Smart mobs vs. Amway." *AlterNet*. Online: www.alternet.org/print.html?storyid=18605.

DeMaria, R., and Wilson, J. L. (2004). *High score: The illustrated history of electronic games*. New York: McGraw-Hill.

Dempsey, J. (2005, September 26–October 2). Plugs spring a leak. *Variety*, pp. 20, 23.

Dennis, E. E. (1992). *Of media and people*. Newbury Park, CA: Sage.

Densmore, J. (2003, January 9). Should the Doors sell out? *Rolling Stone*, pp. 44–45.

Dickson, G. (2006, July 10). Satellite colossus emerges from deal. *Broadcasting & Cable*, p. 16.

DiOrio, C. (2002a, March 11–17). High price of peddling pix. *Variety*, p. 11.

DiOrio, C. (2002b, June 10–16). Promo blitz fuels booming biz. *Variety*, p. 9.

Dobbs, L. (2005, October 5). *Lou Dobbs Tonight*. CNN newscast.

Dobson, W. J. (1998, July 6). Protest.org. *New Republic*, pp. 18–21.

Donaton, S. (2006, January 23). Creating third-screen content? TV should not be your template. *Advertising Age*, p. 18.

Do we have a story for you! (2006, January 19). *The Economist*. Online: http://www.economist.com/business/story_id=5418124.

Dowd, M. (2005, January 27). Love for sale. *New York Times*, p. A25.

Drucker, P. E. (1999, October). Beyond the information revolution. *Atlantic Monthly*, pp. 47–57.

Drug war facts. (2004, April 13). Online: www.drugwarfacts.org/racepris.htm.

Drutman, L. (2005, June 24). Congress must battle spyware and adware. *Providence Journal*, p. B4.

Drutman, L. (2006, February 16). Google may be the least of three evils. *Providence Journal*, p. B4.

Dumenco, S. (2006, January 16). Oh please, a blogger is just a writer with a cooler name. *Advertising Age*, p. 18.

DVD sales likely nearing global peak. (2005, December 7). *News.com*. Online: http://news.com.com/2102-1026_3-5986016.html.

Elber, L. (2002, July 25). TV parents: Two's a crowd. *Providence Journal*, pp. G1, G8.

Elias, P. (2004, July 5). Videogame helps children cope with cancer. *Providence Journal*, p. E2.

Endicott, R. C. (2005, September 26). Magazine 300. *Advertising Age*, pp. S-1–S-6.

Entertainment Software Association. (2005). *2005 essential facts about the computer and video game industry*. Online: www.theESA.com.

Epstein, J. (1999, June 26). Sex and sleaze put Brazil's television viewers in a tizzy. *San Francisco Chronicle*, pp. A10, A12.

Erard, M. (2004, July 1). In these games, the points are all political. *New York Times*, p. G1.

Estes v. State of Texas 381 U.S. 532 (1965).

Ewen, S. (2000). Memoirs of a commodity fetishist. *Mass Communication & Society*, 3, 439–452.

FAIR. (2000, August 30). NAB 2000: Speak out for media democracy. Online: FAIRL@FAIR.org.

Falk, W. (2005, November 29). The trouble with newspapers. *Providence Journal*, p. B7.

Farhi, P. (2001, March). Can *Salon* make it? *American Journalism Review*, pp. 36–41.

Farhi, P. (2005, June/July). Under siege. *American Journalism Review*, pp. 26–31.

Farhi, P. (2006, February/March). A bright future for newspapers. *American Journalism Review*, pp. 54–59.

Faules, D. F., & Alexander, D. C. (1978). *Communication and social behavior: A symbolic interaction perspective.* Reading, MA: Addison-Wesley.

Feldman, G. (2001, February 12). Publishers caught in a Web. *The Nation*, pp. 35–36.

File-sharing software takes off. (2004, December 11). *Providence Journal*, p. A2.

Filler, L. (1968). *The muckrakers: Crusaders for American liberalism.* Chicago: Henry Regnery.

Finally, 21st century phone service. (2004, January 6). *Business Week*. Online: www.businessweek.com/technology/content/jan2004/tc2004016.

Fine, J. (2005, April 20). Analysts: Newspapers could lose $4 billion to Internet. *AdAge.com*. Online: http://adage.com/news.cms?newsId=44826.

Finke, N. (2004, October 1–7). When might turns right. *LA Weekly*. Online: http://www.laweekly.com/ink/printme.php?eid=57197.

Fisher, M. (2005, October/November). Essential again. *American Journalism Review*, pp. 18–23.

Fitzgerald, M. (1999, October 30). Robert Sengstake Abbott. *Editor & Publisher*, p. 18.

Fitzgerald, M. (2004a, March). Newspapers rock en Español. *Editor & Publisher*, pp. 26–31.

Fitzgerald, M. (2004b, November). Black is back. *Editor & Publisher*, pp. 43–46.

Fitzgerald, T. (2003, April 29). Growing army of folks kicking the Internet habit. *Media Life*. Online: www.medialifemagazine.com/pages/templates/scripts/prfr.asp.

Flanders, L. (2002, August 5/12). Librarians under siege. *The Nation*, pp. 42–43.

Fleishman, G. (2005, July 28). Revolution on the radio. *New York Times*, p. C11.

Fleming, M. (2005, June 6–12). H'wood's new book club. *Variety*, p. 3.

Fogarty, J. R., & Spielholz, M. (1985). FCC cable jurisdiction: From zero to plenary in twenty-five years. *Federal Communications Law Journal, 37*, 113.

Fonda, D. (2003, March 24). National Prosperous Radio. *Time*, pp. 49–51.

Fonda, D. (2004, June 28). Pitching it to kids. *Time*, pp. 52–53.

Franklin, B. A. (2003, July 1). Stay tuned? You won't have much of a choice from now on. *Washington Spectator*, pp. 1–3.

Fraser, R. (2003, March 17). DVD players: Cheaper and getting cheaper. *TV Guide*, pp. 42–43.

Free Press. (2005, August 5). Reclaim radio: The battle over low-power FM. Online: www.freepress.net/lpfm.

Friend, T. (2000, April 24). Mickey Mouse Club. *The New Yorker*, pp. 212–214.

Fritts, E. O. (2002, May 15). Broadcasters moving forward on DTV. Online: www.nab.org/newsroom/pressrel/speeches/051502.htm.

Fritz, B. (2005, April/May). Movies non-demand. *VLife*, p. 26.

Fritz, B. (2006, January 2–8). Videogames try to unstick the joystick. *Variety*, p. 39.

Fritz, B., & Graser, M. (2004, May 10–16). Is the game getting lame? *Variety*, pp. 1, 69.

Garchik, L. (2000, July 25). Death and hobbies. *San Francisco Chronicle*, p. D10.

Garfield, B. (2005, April 4). The chaos scenario. *Advertising Age*, pp. 1, 57–59.

Garland, E. (2002, April). Can this man save advertising? *Wired*, pp. 65–70.

Gerbner, G., Gross, L., Jackson-Beeck, M., Jeffries-Fox, S., & Signorielli, N. (1978). Cultural indicators: Violence profile no. 9. *Journal of Communication, 28*, 176–206.

Gerbner, G., Gross, L., Morgan, M., & Signorielli, N. (1980). The "mainstreaming" of America: Violence profile no. 11. *Journal of Communication, 30*, 10–29.

Germain, D. (2005a, June 17). Movie fans would rather stay home, poll finds. *Providence Journal*, p. A3.

Germain, D. (2005b, July 1). Summer flicks unlikely to halt box-office slide. *Providence Journal*, p. E5.

Germain, D. (2005c, December 14). Hollywood sees biggest box office decline in 20 years. *AOL News*. Online: http://aolsvc.news.aol.com/movies/article.adp?id=20051214130609990010.

Gertner, J. (2005, April 10). Our ratings, ourselves. *New York Times Magazine*, pp. 34–46.

Getting the news. (2003, March 24). *Broadcasting & Cable*, p. 58.

Gibbs, M. (2005, July 18). A new theory with consequences. *Network World*, p. 50.

Gilbert, A. (2004, December 22). Growth in U.S. net population levels off. *News.com*. Online: news.com.com/2102-1026_3-5131783.html.

Gillespie, E. M. (2005, August 20). Small publishers, big sales. *Providence Journal*, pp. B1–B2.

Gillies, J. S. (2004, April 3). Sesame Street at 35. *Providence Journal*, pp. D1, D4.

Gillmor, D. (2000, August 18). Digital Copyright Act comes back to haunt consumers. *San Jose Mercury News*, pp. 1C, 6C.

Gillmor, D. (2002, July 21). Hollywood, tech make suspicious pairing. *San Jose Mercury News*, pp. 1F, 7F.

Gillmor, D. M., & Barron, J. A. (1974). *Mass communication law: Cases and comments.* St. Paul, MN: West.

Ginsberg, T. (2002, January/February). Rediscovering the world. *American Journalism Review*, pp. 48–53.

Ginzburg v. United States 383 U.S. 463 (1966).

Gitlin, T. (1997, March 17). The dumb-down. *The Nation*, 28.

Gitlin, T. (2004a, July). It was a very bad year. *American Prospect*, pp. 31–34.

Gitlin, T. (2004b, November/December). The great media breakdown. *Mother Jones*, pp. 57–100.

Gitlow v. New York 268 U.S. 652 (1925).

Glasser, I. (2006, July 10). Drug busts=Jim Crow. *The Nation*, pp. 24–26.

Gnatek, T. (2006, February 23). Just for fun, casual games thrive online. *New York Times*, p. C9.

Goldsmith, J. (2002, June 10). With billions in play, studios keep toying with pic wares. *Variety*, p. 7.

Goldstein, P. (2002, March 14). Health group campaigns for a smoke-free screen. *Providence Journal*, pp. G1, G3.

Google sells out on way to China. (2006, February 20). *Advertising Age*, p. 11.

Graser, M. (2001, October 8). Digital pics flying with Boeing. *Variety*, pp. 7, 72.

Graves, L. (2004, June). You'll never get cable à la carte. *Wired*, p. 88.

Graves, L. (2006, February). The ad scientists. *Wired*, pp. 144–147.

Greenhouse, L. (2004, June 30). Court blocks law regulating Internet access to pornography. *New York Times*, p. A1.

Greider, W. (2005, November 21). All the king's media. *The Nation*, pp. 30–32.

Greppi, M. (2003, November 17). Nielsen: Finding lost boys. *Television Week*. Online: www.tvweek.com/topstorys/111703nielsen.html.

Gross, D. (2005, July 25). Innovation: The future of advertising. *Fortune*. Online: http://www.fortune.com/fortune/0,15935,1085988,00.html.

Gross, M. (2003, June 2). The crack epidemic. *Editor & Publisher*, p. 30.

Grossman, L. K. (1999, July/August). From Marconi to Murrow to—Drudge? *Columbia Journalism Review*, pp. 17–18.

Grusin, K., & Edmondson, A. (2003, Summer). Taking it to the Web: Youth news moves online. *Newspaper Research Journal*, 24, 91–96.

Guider, E. (2001, June 4). Global B.O. projection: $24 bil by '10. *Variety*, p. 10.

Guider, E. (2003, November 17–23). Can film biz curb squanderlust? *Variety*, pp. 6, 103.

Guider, E. (2004, March 29–April 4). Sudsers bubbling with relevance. *Variety*, pp. 7, 60.

Guider, E., & James, A. (2005, October 24–30). Buyers bank on Yanks. *Variety*, p. 18.

Hachten, W. A. (1992). *The world news prism* (3rd ed.). Ames: Iowa State University Press.

Hafner, K., & Lyon, M. (1996). *Where wizards stay up late: The origins of the Internet.* New York: Simon & Schuster.

Hall, E. T. (1976). *Beyond culture.* New York: Doubleday.

Hall, S. (1980). Cultural studies: Two paradigms. *Media, Culture and Society, 2,* 57–72.

Hamilton, A. (2000, August 21). Meet the new surfer girls. *Time*, p. 67.

Hamilton, A. (2005, January 10). Video vigilantes. *Time*, pp. 60–63.

Hansell, S. (2005, June 28). Cable wins Internet-access ruling. *New York Times*, p. C1.

Hansell, S. (2006, February 5). Postage due, with special delivery, for companies sending e-mail to AOL and Yahoo. *New York Times*, p. 19.

Hard lessons. (2003, September 5). *The Week*, p. 25.

Harris, M. (1983). *Cultural anthropology.* New York: Harper & Row.

Harrop, F. (2003, November 26). What God has joined, let no man . . . *Providence Journal*, p. B5.

Harwood, J., & Anderson, K. (2002). The presence and portrayal of social groups on prime-time television. *Communication Reports, 15,* pp. 81–91.

Hayes, D. (2003, September 15–21). H'wood grapples with third-act problems. *Variety*, pp. 1, 53.

Haynes, C. (2004, May 16). The price of a free student press. *Providence Journal*, p. 12.

Healey, J. (1999, May 4). Demand for data: More, more, faster, faster. *San Jose Mercury News*, pp. 1F, 4F.

Hellmich, N. (2004, March 10). Obesity on track as no. 1 killer. *USA Today*, p. 1A.

Helm, J. (2002, March/April). When history looks back. *Adbusters*.

Hettrick, S. (2004, January 12–18). Tube series boost bottom lines. *Variety*, p. A10.

Hewitt, D. (2004, May 12). Americans playing more games, watching less movies and television. Entertainment Software Association. Online: www.theesa.com/5_12_2004.html.

Hickey, N. (2002, May/June). Media monopoly Q&A. *Columbia Journalism Review*, pp. 30–33.

Higgins, J. M. (2003a, November 10). A pause in consolidation. *Broadcasting & Cable*, p. 32.

Higgins, J. M. (2003b, December 22). Fast forward. *Broadcasting & Cable*, pp. 1, 22.

Higgins, J. M. (2006, January 9). CBS: In the money. *Broadcasting & Cable*, pp. 16–17.

Hightower, J. (2002, July 22/29). POP-ing the bankers. *The Nation*, p. 8.

Hightower, J. (2004a, May). The people's media reaches more people than Fox does. *Hightower Lowdown*, pp. 1–4.

Hightower, J. (2004b, May 15). Grand larceny of pin-striped thieves. *Progressive Populist*, p. 3.

Hilliard, R. L., & Keith, M. C. (1996). *Global broadcasting systems.* Boston: Focal Press.

Hinchey, M. (2006, February 6). More media owners. *The Nation*, p. 15.

Ho, R. (2005, July 19). With 'podcasting' anyone's a DJ. *Providence Journal*, pp. G1–G2.

Holloway, D. (2005, October 12). It's not your imagination—shows are shorter, ads are longer. *Providence Journal*, p. G9.

Holson, L.M. (2005, May 27). With popcorn, DVD's and TiVo, moviegoers are staying home. *New York Times*, p. A1.

Hovland, C. I., Lumsdaine, A. A., & Sheffield, F. D. (1949). *Experiments on mass communication.* Princeton, NJ: Princeton University Press.

Howard, T. (2005, June 20). Advertisers forced to think way outside the box. *USA Today*, p. B5.

How do you measure a smile? (2005, September 26). *Advertising Age*, p. M6.

Howe, J. (2001, October). Licensed to bill. *Wired*, pp. 140–149.

Howe, J. (2005a, November). The hit factory. *Wired*, pp. 200–205, 218.

Howe, J. (2005b, August). The uproar over downloads. *Wired*, p. 40.

How they see us. (2005, November 4). *The Week*, p. 19.

Hu, J., & Reardon, M. (2005, May 2). Cities brace for broadband war. Online: http://news.com.com/Cities+brace+for+broad-band+war/2009-1034_3-5680305.html.

Huang, E. S. (2001). Readers' perception of digital alteration in photojournalism. *Journalism Monographs*, pp. 148–182.

Huffington, A. (2005, September 15). Howell Raines redux. *Progressive Populist*, p. 11.

Hustler Magazine v. Big Jerry Falwell 485 U.S. 46 (1988).

In fact. (2006, March 20). *The Nation*, p. 8.

International Marketing Data and Statistics. (2002). London: EUROMONITOR.

Internet Movie Database. (2006). Top grossing movies of all time at the USA box office. Online: www.imdb.com/ boxoffice/all-timegross.

Internet World Stats. (2005). Internet usage statistics—the big picture. Online: http://www.Internetworldstats.com/stats.htm.

Irvin v. Dowd 366 U.S. 717 (1961).

Irving, L. M. (2001). Media exposure and disordered eating: Introduction to the special section. *Journal of Social and Clinical Psychology, 20,* 259–265.

isc.org. (2005, July). Internet domain survey, July 2005. Online: http://www.isc.org/ops/ds/reports/2005-07.

Italie, H. (2003, July 26). Whirlwind, record sales of Harry Potter. *Providence Journal*, p. G3.

Italie, H. (2005a, July 19). *Harry Potter* sells 9 million copies in 24 hours. *Providence Journal*, p. G1.

Italie, H. (2005b, June 16). Kids may be tech savvy, but Potter and other bestsellers aren't online. *Providence Journal*, p. G3.

Ives, N. (2006, February 13). Print buyers search for real-time ad metrics. *Advertising Age*, p. S-2.

Ivins, M. (2006, February 1). Bush keeps getting it wrong. *Progressive Populist*, p. 22.

Iyengar, S., & Kinder, D. R. (1987). *News that matters: Television and American opinion.* Chicago: University of Chicago Press.

Jackson, J. (2001, September/October). Their man in Washington. *Extra!*, pp. 6–9.

Jackson, J., & Hart, P. (2002, March/April). Fear and favor 2001. *Extra!*, pp. 20–27.

Jamieson, K. H., & Campbell, K. K. (1997). *The interplay of influence: News, advertising, politics, and the mass media.* Belmont, CA: Wadsworth.

Jardin, X. (2004, January). Why your next phone call may be online. *Wired*, p. 32.

Jardin, X. (2005a, April). The Cuban revolution. *Wired*, pp. 119–121.

Jardin, X. (2005b, December). Thinking outside the box office. *Wired*, pp. 256–257.

John Paul II. (2005, April 11). Two cents: Letter to commemorate the Feast of Saint Francis DeSales. *Broadcasting & Cable*, p. 54.

Jones, A. (2002, April 15–21). China hits $8 billion in ads. *Variety*, p. A12.

Jones, J. M. (2004, April 20). Americans' trust in the mass media. *Gallup Reports*. Online: www.gallup.com.

Justices scrap Internet child porn law. (2002, April 17). *Providence Journal*, p. A3.

Kalet, H. (2004, May 15). PATRIOT games. *Progressive Populist*, p. 10

Kanter, R. M. (2006, January 29). Newspapers, reinvent thyselves. *Providence Journal*, p. D7.

Karr, T. (2005, April 18). Is low-cost Wi-Fi un-American? Online: http://www.inthesetimes.com/site/main/print/2071/.

Katz, E., & Lazarsfeld, P. F. (1955). *Personal influence: The part played by people in the flow of communications.* New York: Free Press.

Kaufman, G. (2003, June 6). Push the Courvoisier: Are rappers getting paid for product placement? *VH1.com*. Online: www.vh1.com/artist/news/1472393/06062003/nelly.jthml.

Kava, B. (2003, September 4). With goal of $10 CDs, record giant cuts price. *San Jose Mercury News*. Online: bayarea.com/mld/mercurynews/business/6688650.htm?template=contentmodule.

Kaye, K. (2004, June 10). Games for good: Conference promotes videogames as agents of change. *Media Post*. Online: www.mediapost.com/printfriend.cfm?articleid=254728.

Kennedy, D. (2004, June 9). Mad as hell at the FCC. *Boston Phoenix*. Online: www.alternet.org/print.html?storyid=16116.

Kennedy, L. (2002, June). Spielberg in the Twilight Zone. *Wired*, pp. 106–113, 146.

Kent, S. L. (2001). *The ultimate history of video games.* New York: Three Rivers Press.

Kern, T. (2005, December 5). Convergence makes a comeback. *Broadcasting & Cable*, p. 32.

Kids are getting lost in the tobacco deal shuffle. (1998, January 16). *USA Today*, p. 10A.

Kiley. D. (2005, July 4). Cable's big bet on hyper-targeting. *BusinessWeek*, p. 58.

Kim, B. H., Pasadeos, Y., & Barban, A. (2001). On the deceptive effectiveness of labeled and unlabeled advertorial forms. *Mass Communication and Society, 4,* 265–281.

Kim, G. (2004, March 18). Three out of four Americans have access to the Internet. *Nielsen/Netratings*. Online: www.nielsennetratings.com.

Kim, M. H. (2002, January 28–February 3). Filmmakers won't budge an iota on screen quotas. *Variety*, p. 16.

Kirk, L. M. (2003, February 16). Smaller and smaller. *Providence Journal Lifestyles*, pp. 8–10.

Klaassen, A. (2005a, February 15). Radio gets low ratings from marketers, agency planners. *AdAge.com*. Online: http://adage.com/news.cms?newsID=44322.

Klaassen, A. (2005b, December 5). Local TV nets try pay to play. *Advertising Age*, pp. 1, 82.

Klaassen, A. (2005c, December 5). Want a gold record? Forget radio, go online. *Advertising Age*, p. 12.

Klaassen, A. (2006, February 20). At the push of a button. *Advertising Age*, p. 3.

Klapper, J. T. (1960). *The effects of mass communication.* New York: Free Press.

Klein, J. M. (2004, July/August) Whose news? Whose propaganda? *Columbia Journalism Review*, pp. 54–55.

Klein, N. (1999). *No logo: Taking aim at the brand bullies.* New York: Picador.

Klosterman, C. (2005, August). What we have here is a failure to communicate. *Esquire*, pp. 62–64.

Kirsner, S. (2005, April). Hayden's planetarium. *CMO Magazine*. Online: http://www.cmomagazine.com/read/040105/planetarium.html.

Kohut, A. (2000, May/June). Self-censorship: Counting the ways. *Columbia Journalism Review*, pp. 42–43.

Konner, J. (1999, March/April). Of Clinton, the Constitution & the press. *Columbia Journalism Review*, p. 6.

Kristof, N. D. (2005, May 24). Death by a thousand blogs. *New York Times*, p. A21.

Kristof, N. D. (2006, February 19). China's cyberdissidents and the yahoos at Yahoo. *New York Times*, p. 4.13.

Kristula, D. (1997, March). *The history of the Internet.* Online: www.davesite.com/webstation/net-history.shtml.

Kuhn, T. (1970). *The structure of scientific revolutions* (2nd ed.). Chicago: University of Chicago Press.

Kunkel, D., Wilcox, B. L., Cantor, J., Palmer, E., Linn, S., & Dowrick, P. (2004). *Report of the APA Task Force on Advertising and Children.* Washington, DC: American Psychological Association.

Kunkel, T. (2005, June/July). As the world churns. *American Journalism Review*, p. 4.

Kuralt, C. (1977). *When television was young* (videotape). New York: CBS News.

Kurtz, H. (2000, January 17). When the news is all in the family. *Washington Post National Weekly Edition*, p. 7.

Kurtz, H. (2003, September 29). Media review conduct after leak. *Washington Post*, p. A4.

Kurtz, H. (2004, August 12). The *Post* on WMD: An inside story. *Washington Post*, p. A1.

Kurtz, H. (2005, October 17). The Judy chronicles. *Washington Post*. Online: http://www.washingtonpost.com/wp-dyn/content/blog/2005/10/17.

Kushner, D. (2004, June). The wrinkled future of online gaming. *Wired*, pp. 98–101.

Lamb, G. M. (2005, September 28). We swim in an ocean of media. *Christian Science Monitor*, p. 13.

L.A. Times takes itself to task over arena deal. (1999, December 21). *San Francisco Chronicle*, pp. A1, A7.

Lasswell, H. D. (1948). The structure and function of communication in society. In L. Bryson (Ed.), *The communication of ideas*. New York: Harper.

Lawson, T. (2002, April 29). Once reviled, geek becomes marketing force. *Providence Journal*, pp. D1, D4.

Layton, C. (2003, August/September). Miller brouhaha. *American Journalism Review*, pp. 30–35.

Lazarsfeld, P. F. (1941). Remarks on administrative and critical communications research. *Studies in Philosophy and Social Science, 9*, 2–16.

Learmonth, M. (2005, February 7–13). Can you read me now? *Variety*, pp. 1, 94.

Learmonth, M. (2006, January 9–15). A curious "state" of affairs. *Variety*, p. 8.

Leeper, J. (2004, January 8). A place for product placement. *GameSpy.com*. Online: archive.gamespy.com/ces2004/placement.

Lester, J. (2002, Spring). Carved runes in a clearing. *Umass*, pp. 24–29.

Levitas, D. (2002, July 22, 29). The radical right after 9/11. *The Nation*, pp. 19–23.

Levy, S. (2005, July 18). Pulling the plug on local Internet. *Newsweek*, p. 14.

Lewis, P. (2005, July 25). Invasion of the podcast people. *Fortune*, pp. 204–205.

Lieberman, D. (2005, November 29). TVs turning into vending machines for programs. *USA Today*. Online: http://www.usatoday.com/money/industries/technology/2005-11-29-tv-vod_x.htm.

Lienert, A. (2004, February 15). Video games open new paths to market cars. *Detroit News*. Online: www.detnews.com/2004/business/0402/15/b01-64356.htm.

Lindsay, G. (2006, January 2). One consumer at a time. *Advertising Age*, pp. 22–25.

Lovell, G. (1997, December 21). Branded. *San Jose Mercury News*, pp. 7G, 14G.

Lowenstein, D. (2005, May). 2005 state of the industry speech. Entertainment Software Association. Online: www.theesa.com/archives/2005/05/e3_state_0_1.php.

Lowery, S. A., & DeFleur, M. L. (1995). *Milestones in mass communication research*. White Plains, NY: Longman.

Lyman, R. (2002, August 25). How DVDs came to dominate home entertainment so quickly. *Providence Journal*, pp. A1, A5.

Lyons, D. (2005, November 14). Attack of the blogs. *Forbes*, pp. 128–138.

Lyons, G. (2004, October). Keep your eye on the big picture. *Progressive Populist*, p. 11.

MacArthur, K. (2003, November 18). KFC pulls controversial health-claim chicken ads. *AdAge.com*. Online: www.adage.com/news.cms?newsid=39220.

MacFarquhar, N. (2004, February 20). Washington's Arabic TV effort gets mixed reviews. *New York Times*, p. A3.

Magazine Publishers of America. (2005). Resources. Online: www.magazine.org/resources/fact_sheets/html.

Males, M. (2002, July/August). A cold shower for the "teen sex" beat. *Extra!*, p. 30.

Malveaux, J. (2000, August 27). Looking at the digital divide from the global perspective. *San Francisco Examiner*, p. B2.

Mandese, J. (2004, May 17). Study: Media overload on the rise. *Television Week*. Online: www.tvweek.com/planning/051704study.html.

Mandese, J. (2005, March 28). The art of manufactured news. *Broadcasting & Cable*, pp. 24–25.

Mangier, M., & Menn, J. (2005, June 19). In China, Microsoft blocks words of freedom. *Providence Journal*, pp. A1, A12.

Manly, L. (2005, April 5). Satellite radio takes off, altering the airwaves. *New York Times*, p. A1.

Markoff, J. (2006, January 18). Internet TV? Look out, cable. *Providence Journal*, pp. G5, G7.

Marlette, D. (2003, November/December). I was a tool of Satan. *Columbia Journalism Review*, pp. 52–55.

Marriage: The solution to urban poverty? (2004, January 30). *The Week*, p. 19.

Marriott, H. (2005, October 27). ICCO president Saunders calls for "ethical" approach. *PRWeek*. Online: http://www.prweek.com/uk/news/article/524519.

Marsh, A. (1998, June 15). Rewriting the book of journalism. *Forbes*, pp. 47–48.

Martinez, A. (2005, May 27). Coming soon—the Google Street Journal? *Providence Journal*, p. B5.

Mason, A. (2006, February 3). State of the news media. *CBS Evening News*.

Mast, G., & Kawin, B. F. (1996). *A short history of the movies*. Boston: Allyn & Bacon.

Mayer, C. E. (2003, September 25). Hold the phone: Judge puts do-not-call list in doubt. *Providence Journal*, pp. A1, A19.

McBride, S. (2006, January 30). Multimedia launch of *Bubble* gets mixed response. *Wall Street Journal*, p. B4.

McChesney, R. W. (1997). *Corporate media and the threat to democracy*. New York: Seven Stories Press.

McChesney, R. W. (1999). *Rich media poor democracy*. Urbana: University of Illinois Press.

McChesney, R. W. (2004, July). Waging the media battle. *American Prospect*, pp. 24–28.

McClellan, S. (2001, October 22). Eyes wide shut. *Broadcasting & Cable*, pp. 20–24.

McClellan, S. (2002, May 27). Winning, and losing too. *Broadcasting & Cable*, pp. 6–7.

McClellan, S. (2003, December 22). Ad clutter keeps climbing. *Broadcasting & Cable*, p. 13.

McClellan, S. (2004, June 21). An inside view. *Broadcasting & Cable*, p. 3.

McCombs, M. E., & Shaw, D. L. (1972). The agenda-setting function of mass media. *Public Opinion Quarterly, 36*, 176–187.

McConnell, B. (2002, April 8). Radio giants want more turf. *Broadcasting & Cable*, p. 34.

McConnell, B. (2004a, June 14). Bloated agenda. *Broadcasting & Cable*, p. 21.

McConnell, B. (2004b, March 8). One fat target. *Broadcasting & Cable*, pp. 1, 42.

McCowan, K. (2002, March 20). Films set off smoke alarms. Online: www.registerguard.com/news/20020320/1d.cr.mccowan.0320.html.

McCullagh, D. (2005, June 27). DSL providers hope to mimic cable's win. Online: http://news.com.com/2102-1034_3-5765085.html.

McHugh, J. (2004, July). Attention shoppers. *Wired*, pp. 44, 151–155.

McKelvey, T. (2004, August). Onward and forward. *American Prospect*, pp. 16–17.

McKenna, K. (2000, August). John Malkovich interview. *Playboy*, pp. 65–78.

McLean, T. J. (2005a, September 26–October 2). Future for 3G phones is now. *Variety*, pp. B1, B4.

McLean, T. J. (2005b, September 26–October 2). Pocket pics. *Variety*, p. B4.

McLean, T. J. (2006, February 13–19). Struggling labels find a hit. *Variety*, p. B4.

McLuhan, M. (1962). *The Gutenberg galaxy: The making of typographic man.* London: Routledge.

McLuhan, M., & Fiore, Q. (1967). *The medium is the massage.* New York: Random House.

McLuhan, M., & Stern, G. E. (1967). A dialogue: Q & A. In M. McLuhan & G. E. Stern (Eds.), *McLuhan: Hot and cool: A primer for the understanding of McLuhan and a critical symposium with a rebuttal by McLuhan.* New York: Dial Press.

McMasters, P. K. (2005, March 27). Censorship is alive and well, deadly to free expression. *Providence Journal*, p. I5.

McQuail, D. (1987). *Mass communication theory: An introduction.* Beverly Hills, CA: Sage.

Media Foundation. (2002). Campaigns. Online: adbusters.org/campaigns.

Meehan, M. (2004, January 20). The ratings game: System has its flaws, one of which is lax oversight. *Knight Ridder Tribune News Service*, p. 1.

Merton, R. K. (1967). *On theoretical sociology.* New York: Free Press.

Miller, M. (2005, May 23). Paper's aim: building blog for success. *Los Angeles Times*, p. E1.

Miller, M. C. (1997, March 17). The crushing power of big publishing. *The Nation*, 11–18.

Miller v. State of California 413 U.S. 463 (1966).

"Mission Accomplished" whodunit. (2003, October 29). *CBSNews.com*. Online: www.cbsnews.com/stories/2003/10/29/iraq/printable580661.shtml.

Moglen, E. (2003, October 27). Pay artists, not owners. *The Nation*, pp. 31–32.

Mohr, I. (2006, April 3–9). Exhibs fish for auds with lures. *Variety*, p. 9.

Moore, F. (1999, June 7). Free speech isn't free, reports PBS special. *Santa Cruz County Sentinel*, p. A11.

Morrissey, B. (2005, December 5). TiVo execs bet Google ad model will work on TV. *Adweek*, p. 12.

Morton, J. (2002, January/February). Why circulation keeps dropping. *American Journalism Review*, 64.

Morton, J. (2004, February/March). Nouveau niche. *American Journalism Review*, p. 64.

Morton, J. (2006, February/March). Keeping the faith. *American Journalism Review*, p. 68.

Moses, L. (2002, June 3). Youth must be served . . . but how? *Editor & Publisher*, pp. 12–14, 21.

Mossberg, W. S. (2002, March 17). It's time for consumers to stand up for technology rights. *Providence Journal*, p. D7.

MoveOn.org. (2004). Press coverage. Online: www.moveon.org.

Moyers, B. (2003, October 10). Big media gets bigger. *AlterNet*. Online: www.alternet.org/print.html?storyid=16941.

Moyers, B. (2004, September 11). Journalism under fire. *AlterNet*. Online: http://www.alternet.org/module/19918.

Musgrove, M. (2005, October 16). Videogame world gives peace a chance. *Washington Post*, p. F1.

Mutual Film Corp. v. Ohio Industrial Commission 236 U.S. 230 (1915).

Muwakkil, S. (2003, October 23). Racial bias still haunts media. *AlterNet*. Online: www.alternet.org/print.html?storyid=17027.

Nathaniel, M. (2001, November 10). You shouldn't print my name. *Providence Journal*, p. B7.

National Broadcasting Co. v. United States 319 U.S. 190 (1943).

National Cable and Telecommunications Association (NCTA). (2005). Industry Statistics. Online: www.ncta.com/docs/pagecontent.cfm?pageid=86.

National Commission Against Drunk Driving. (2002). Alcohol-related fatality rates. Online: www.ncadd.com/alcrate.htm.

National Institute on Media and the Family. (2002). Alcohol advertising and youth. Online: www.mediaandthefamily.org/research/fact/alcohol.shtml.

National Public Radio. (2004, February 7). Live from Virginia, it's Al-Hurra. Online: www.npr.org/features/feature.php? wfld=1658915.

NCTA name change. (2001, February 12). *Broadcasting & Cable*, p. 36.

Near v. Minnesota 283 U.S. 697 (1931).

Neumeister, L. (2005, September 20). Authors hit Google with copyright lawsuit. *Washington Post*. Online: http://www.washingtonpost.com/wpdyn/content/article/2005/09/20/AR2005092001328.

Newark pays paper to publish only good news on city. (2005, October 30). *Providence Journal*, p. D5.

New highs boost custom's profile. (2005, November 28). *Advertising Age*, pp. C1–C8.

The new imperative. (2005, September 26). *Advertising Age*, pp. M1–M24.

New York Times v. Sullivan 376 U.S. 254 (1964).

New York Times v. United States 403 U.S. 713 (1971).

Newspapers hold 8 slots on top 20 web list. (2004, May 19). *Editor & Publisher*. Online: www.editorandpublisher.com/eandp/departments/online/article_display.jsp?vnu.

Nielsen Media Research. (2006). *Inside TV ratings*. Online: www.nielsenmedia.com/nc/portal/site/Public.

Nichols, J. (2003, July 14). Moving on media reform. *The Nation*, p. 5.

Nichols, J., & McChesney, R. W. (2002, August). On the verge in Vermont. *Extra!*, pp. 26–27.

Ninety-Second Congress. (1972). *Hearings before the Subcommittee on Communications on the Surgeon General's Report by the Scientific Advisory Committee on Television and Social Behavior.* Washington, DC: U.S. Government Printing Office.

Norsigian, J., Diskin, V., Doress-Worters, P., Pincus, J., Sanford, W., & Swenson, N. (1999). The Boston Women's Health Book Collective and *Our bodies, ourselves:* A brief history and reflection. *Journal of the American Medical Women's Association.* Online: www.ourbodiesourselves.org.

Notebook. (2005, February 7). *Time*, p. 15.

Noted. (2004, April 2). *The Week*, p. 18.

Noted. (2005, June 17). *The Week*, p. 20.

Noted. (2006, January 27). *The Week*, p. 18.

N.Y. shock jocks canned over cathedral sex stunt. (2002, August 23). *Providence Journal*, p. A8.

O'Brien, T. L. (2005, February 13). Spinning frenzy: P.R.'s bad press. *New York Times*, p. 3.1.

O'Brien, T. L. (2006, February 12). Madison Avenue's 30-second spot remover. *New York Times*, pp. 3.1, 3.8.

Okrent, D. (2004, May 30). The public editor: Weapons of mass destruction? Or mass distraction? *New York Times*, Section 4, p. 2.

Oppelaar, J. (2003, May 12–18). Will Apple for pay keep doldrums away? *Variety*, p. 42.

Oser, K. (2004, June 16). Digital games luring away more TV viewers. *AdAge.com*. Online: www.adage.com/news.cms?newsld=40822.

Oser, K. (2005a, September 12). Online crisis looms as ad demand surges. *Advertising Age*, pp. 1, 51.

Oser, K. (2005b, September 12). Game enthusiasm rises up from the basement. *Advertising Age*, p. 51.

Oser, K. (2006, January 30). Dialing up content. *Advertising Age*, p. 26.

Outing, S. (2005, November 16). Investigative journalism: Will it survive? *Editor & Publisher*. Online: http://www.editorandpublisher.com/eandp/columns/stopthepresses_display.jsp?vnu_content_id=1001523690.

Owen, D. (2004, August). Making copies. *The Smithsonian*, pp. 91–97.

Packard, V. O. (1957). *The hidden persuaders*. New York: David McKay.

Packer, G. (2004, May/June). The revolution will not be blogged. *Mother Jones*, pp. 28–33.

Palast, G. (2003, July 31). Silence of the media lambs. *AlterNet*. Online: www.alternet.org/print.html?storyid=16524.

Palmeri, C. (2001, December 3). Boffo at the box office, scarce on the shelves. *Business Week*, p. 53.

Pariser, E. (2004, January 30). Issues left untackled. *Los Angeles Times*. Online: www.alternet.org/print.html?storyid=17702.

Parks, M. (2002, January/February). Foreign news: What's next? *Columbia Journalism Review*, pp. 52–57.

PCI. (2004). Population Communications International home page. Online: www.population.org.

Pearlstein, S. (2005, November 9). Prime time gets redefined. *Washington Post*, p. D1.

Pegoraro, R. (2005, August 14). Broadband is too important to be left to cable-phone duopoly. *Washington Post*, p. F7.

Pein, C. (2005, May/June). The new wave. *Columbia Journalism Review*, pp. 28–30.

Pember, D. (1999). *Mass media law*. Boston: McGraw-Hill.

Peterson, I. (1997, November 17). At *Los Angeles Times*, a debate on news-ad interaction. *New York Times*, pp. C1, C11.

Peterson, L. C. (1998, November). The *Wired* world atlas. *Wired*, pp. 162–167.

Pielke, R. G. (1986). *You say you want a revolution: Rock music in American culture*. Chicago: Nelson-Hall.

Pincus, J. (1998). Introduction. In Boston Women's Health Book Collective (Eds.), *Our bodies, ourselves for the new century* (pp. 21–23). New York: Touchstone.

Pitt, W. R. (2004, April 1). A NOC at Bush's door. *Progressive Populist*, pp. 1, 8.

Plate, T. (2003, January 23). Media giantism and the IHT crisis. *Providence Journal*, p. B4.

Poll says Americans relax with lots of media at once. (2000, June 29). *San Jose Mercury News*, p. 11A.

Pollitt, K. (2004, July 5). Sex and the Stepford wife. *The Nation*, p. 13.

Poniewozik, J. (2001, Fall). Get up, stand up. *Time*, pp. 68–70.

Poniewozik, J. (2004, September 27). The age of iPod politics. *Time*, p. 84.

Potter, D. (2006, April/May). For sale. *American Journalism Review*, p. 72.

Project for Excellence in Journalism. (2004). *The state of the news media 2004*. Online: www.stateofthemedia.org./2004/.

Project for Excellence in Journalism. (2006). The state of the news media 2005. Online: http://www.stateofthenewsmedia.org/2005/.

PRSA. (2006). The public relations profession. Online: www.prsa.org/resources.

Publishers Information Bureau. (2004). Ad revenue up 12.6%, pages up 6.9%. Retrieved December 10, 2002, from www.magazine.org/news/press_releases/02_nov_pib.html.

Quindlen, A. (2000, July 17). Aha! Caught you reading. *Newsweek*, p. 64.

Quote of the day. (2006, March 3). *NATPE Daily Lead*. Online: natpr@dailylead.com.

Rampton, S., & Stauber, J. (2003, September/October). The "sheer genius" of embedded reporting. *Extra!*, pp. 20–21.

Rathbun, E. A. (2000, August 28). Clutter, clutter everywhere. *Broadcasting & Cable*, p. 58.

Red Lion Broadcasting v. United States 395 U.S. 367 (1969).

Ricchiardi, S. (2003, May). Close to the action. *American Journalism Review*, pp. 28–35.

Rich, F. (2004, March 28). Real journalism's in trouble, while fake stuff flourishes. *Providence Journal*, pp. E1, E2.

Rich, F. (2005, February 6). The year of living indecently. *New York Times*, p. 2.1.

Rideout, V., Roberts, D. F., & Foehr, U. G. (2005). *Generation M: Media in the lives of 8–18-year-olds*. Menlo Park, CA: Kaiser Family Foundation.

Rieder, R. (2005, October/November). Playing big. *American Journalism Review*. Online: http://www.ajr.org/article_printable.asp?id=3960.

Rintels, J., & Charren, P. (2004, November 22). "Private Ryan" and public censorship. *Broadcasting & Cable*, p. 38.

Risser, J. (2000, January/February). The wall is heading back. *Columbia Journalism Review*, pp. 26, 29.

Robertson, L. (2006, December–January). Adding a price tag. *American Journalism Review*, pp. 52–57.

Robins, W. (2001, July 16). Newspapers get real. *Editor & Publisher*, pp. 16–18.

Roman, J. W. (1983). *Cablemania: The cable television sourcebook*. Englewood Cliffs, NJ: Prentice-Hall.

Romano, A. (2003, December 15). It's not just fellows who are missing. *Broadcasting & Cable*, p. 6.

Rosaldo, R. (1989). *Culture and truth: The remaking of social analysis*. Boston: Beacon Press.

Rosen, J. (2002, April). Making some noise. *American Journalism Review*, pp. 12–13.

Rosenberg, R. S. (1992). *The social impact of computers*. Boston: Harcourt Brace Jovanovich.

Roth v. United States 354 U.S. 476 (1957).

Saba, J. (2004, June). Readership pounded by "Perfect Storm." *Editor & Publisher*, pp. 44–46.

Saba, J. (2005, November). Evening the score. *American Journalism Review*, pp. 38–46.

Saia v. New York 334 U.S. 558 (1948).

Sampson, H. T. (1977). *Blacks in black and white: A source book on Black films*. Metuchen, NJ: Scarecrow Press.

Sandage, C. H., Fryburger, V., & Rotzoll, K. (1989). *Advertising theory and practice*. New York: Longman.

Sanders, L., & Halliday, J. (2005, May 24). BP institutes "ad-pull" policy for print publications. *AdAge.com*. Online: www.adage.com/news.cms?newsId=45132.

Sarnoff, D. (1953, September 21). Address to NBC Radio Affiliates Committee in Chicago. *Broadcasting/Telecasting*, pp. 108–112.

Sauer, A. (2006, February 27). Brandchannel's 2005 Product Placement Awards. Online: http://brandchannel.com/ar_id=303&section=main.

Schechter, D. (2003a, October 29). The media war comes home. *AlterNet*. Online: www.alternet.org/print.html?storyid=17071.

Schechter, D. (2003b, April 28). War coverage rewrites history. *AlterNet*. Online: www.alternet.org/print.html?storyid=15717.

Scheer, R. (2003, November 19). The education of Jessica Lynch. *AlterNet*. Online: www.alternet.org/print.html?storyid=17229.

Schenck v. United States 249 U.S. 47 (1919).

Schiesel, S. (2004, May 27). Aiming for hit games, films come up short. *New York Times*, p. G1.

Schiffrin, A. (1996, June 3). The corporatization of publishing. *The Nation*, pp. 29–32.

Schiffrin, A. (1999, July 5). Random acts of consolidation. *The Nation*, p. 10.

Schmitt, E., & Shanker, T. (2005, July 26). New name for 'war on terror' reflects wider U.S. campaign. *New York Times*, p. A7.

Schramm, W. (1954). *The process and effects of mass communication*. Urbana: University of Illinois Press.

Schwartzman, A. J. (2004, December 3). Media Access Project issues statement on Supreme Court order granting certiorari in *Brand X v. FCC*. Online: http://www.mediaaccess.org.

Scott, D. K., & Gobetz, R. H. (1992). Hard news/soft news content of the national broadcast networks, 1972–1987. *Journalism and Mass Communication Quarterly, 69*, 406–412.

Scribner, S. (2001, February 7). Conspiracy to limit the films we see. *Hartford Courant*, pp. D1, D3.

Seabrook, J. (2003, July 7). The money note. *The New Yorker*, pp. 42–55.

Seipp, C. (2002, June). Online uprising. *American Journalism Review*, pp. 42–47.

Seitel, F. P. (2004). *The practice of public relations*. Upper Saddle River, NJ: Pearson.

Sellers, J. (2001). *Arcade fever*. Philadelphia: Running Press.

Seriously missing. (2005, May 23). *Broadcasting & Cable*, p. 50.

Serverwatch. (2004, July 6). June 2004 Netcraft survey highlights. Online: www.serverwatch.com.

Shame on BP and Morgan Stanley ad pull policies. (2005, May 24). *AdAge.com*. Online: www.adage.com/news.cms?newsId=45141.

Shenk, D. (1997). *Data smog: Surviving the information glut*. New York: Harper Edge.

Sherman, E. (2005, February 15). Why are teens getting botox and breast implants? The plastic surgery epidemic. *Family Circle*, pp. 144–148.

Sherman, S. (2004, March 15). Floating with the tide. *The Nation*, pp. 4–5.

Should Comcast buy Disney? (2004, February 27). *The Week*, p. 39.

Siebert, F. S., Peterson, T., & Schramm, W. (1956). *Four theories of the press*. Urbana: University of Illinois Press.

Siklos, R. (2005, November 13). It's like selling meals by the bite. And it may work. *New York Times*, p. 3.5.

Siklos, R. (2006, March 5). How much profit is lurking in that cellphone? *New York Times*, p. 3.1.

Silverblatt, A. (2001). *Media literacy* (2nd ed.). Westport, CT: Praeger.

Skow, J. (1999, April 26). Lost in cyberspace. *Time*, p. 61.

Slagle, M. (2004, May 16). Interactive entertainment trade event offers first look at games, gadgets. *Providence Journal*, p. 16.

Sloan, W., Stovall, J., & Startt, J. (1993). *Media in America: A history*. Scottsdale, AZ: Publishing Horizons.

Smiley, J. (1999, December 2). Everything I never really wanted. *San Jose Mercury News*, p. 10B.

Smoke Free Movies. (2006). Act now! Online: smokefreemovies.ucsf.edu.

Smolkin, R. (2004, April/May). The next generation. *American Journalism Review*, pp. 20–28.

Snyder, G. (2004, May 31–June 6). DVDs spawn a new star system. *Variety*, p. 9.

Snyder, G. (2005, October 31–November 6). Plexes vexed by falling teen spirit. *Variety*, p. 11.

Snyder, G. (2006, December 26–January 1). Who's on top? *Variety*, p. 7.

Soaps save lives in Third World, producers say. (2003, November 18). *Yahoo! TV*. Online: tv.yahoo.com/news/va/20031118/106917210000p.html.

Soley, L. C., & Nichols, J. S. (1987). *Clandestine radio broadcasting: A study of revolutionary and counterrevolutionary electronic communication*. New York: Praeger.

Solomon, J. (2005, October 29). Cheney aide indicted in CIA leak scandal. *Providence Journal*, pp. A1, A9.

Sony Corp. v. Universal City Studios 464 U.S. 417 (1984).

Soundbites. (2005a, May/June). The consumer is always right. *Extra!*, p. 5.

Soundbites. (2005b, December). A better mousetrap. *Extra! Update*, p. 2.

Spector, J. (2001, March 6). Cheap shot artists. *[Inside]*, pp. 56–58.

Sproule, J. M. (1997). *Propaganda and democracy: The American experience of media and mass persuasion*. New York: Cambridge University Press.

Stanley, T. L. (2004, March 22). Videogames: The new reality of youth marketing. *AdAge.com*. Online: www.adage.com/news.cms?news/d=40096.

Stanley, T. L. (2005, December 19). Reasons people skip movies. *Advertising Age*, p. 20.

Stanley, T. L. (2006, February 6). Advergames, content role juice up marketer's game. *Advertising Age*, p. S-3.

Staples, B. (2003, February 20). The trouble with corporate radio: The day the protest music died. *New York Times*, p. A30.

Stauber, J. C., & Rampton, S. (1995). *Toxic sludge is good for you: Lies, damn lies and the public relations industry*. Monroe, ME: Common Courage Press.

Stein, J. (1999, November 8). Babe tube. *Time*, pp. 133–135.

Steinberg, S. H. (1959). *Five hundred years of printing*. London: Faber & Faber.

Stepp, C. S. (2004, January). Why do people read newspapers? *American Journalism Review*, pp. 64–69.

Stepp, C. S. (2006, February/March). The blog revolution. *American Journalism Review*, p. 62.

Sterling, C. H., & Kitross, J. M. (1990). *Stay tuned: A concise history of American broadcasting*. Belmont, CA: Wadsworth.

Steuer, E. (2004, June). Phone fiction. *Wired,* p. 56.

Stevenson, R. L. (1994). *Global communication in the twenty-first century.* New York: Longman.

The story of the Ad Council. (2001, October 29). *Broadcasting & Cable,* pp. 4–11.

Strauss, N. (2000, August 6). Toeing a slim, shady line on explicit lyrics. *San Jose Mercury News,* p. 5G.

Streisand, B., & Newman, R. J. (2005, November 14). The new media elites. *U.S. News & World Report,* pp. 54–63.

Streitfeld, D., & Piller, C. (2002, March 3). Identity crisis: That's what happens when high tech meets Big Brother. *Providence Journal,* pp. D1, D6.

Strupp, J. (2002, April 15). Editors call for forum on profits/quality question. *Editor & Publisher,* p. 3.

Sullivan, A. (2002, May). The blogging revolution. *Wired,* pp. 43–44.

Surowiecki, J. (2004, May 31). Search and destroy. *The New Yorker,* p. 31.

Surowiecki, J. (2005, August 8 & 15). Disk averse. *The New Yorker,* p. 40.

Szatmary, D. P. (2000). *Rockin' in time: A social history of rock-and-roll* (4th ed.). Upper Saddle River, NJ: Prentice-Hall.

Taylor, C. (2003, March 10). Day of the smart mobs. *Time,* p. 53.

Taylor, D. (1991). Transculturating TRANSCULTURATION. *Performing Arts Journal, 13,* 90–104.

Taylor, K. (2005, April). The state of digital cinema. *Wired,* p. 121.

Taylor, L. (2006, March 14). Rise in broadband changes consumers' Internet habits. *AdAge.com.* Online: http://www.adage.com/news.cms?newsId=48279.

Teague, D. (2005, May 24). U.S. book production reaches new high of 195,000 titles in 2004; fiction soars. Online: http://www.bowker.com/press/bowker/2005_0524_bowker.htm.

Tebbel, J. (1987). *Between covers: The rise and transformation of American book publishing.* New York: Oxford University Press.

Tebbel, J., & Zuckerman, M. E. (1991). *The magazine in America 1741–1990.* New York: Oxford University Press.

Teens almost totally online, and 66% of adults use Internet. (2005, July 28). *Providence Journal,* p. A9.

Tienowitz, I. (2003, January 29). FCC Chairman ho-hums anti-war ad controversy. *AdAge.com.* Online: www.adage.com/news.cms?newsid-37016.

Television Bureau of Advertising. (2006). TV basics. Online: www.tvb.org/tvfacts/tvbasics.html.

Thevenot, B. (2005, October/November). Apocalypse in New Orleans. *American Journalism Review,* pp. 24–31.

Thompson, C. (2005, January). The BitTorrent effect. *Wired,* pp. 151–180.

Tillinghast, C. H. (2000). *American broadcast regulation and the First Amendment: Another look.* Ames: Iowa State University Press.

Time, Inc. v. Hill 385 U.S. 374 (1967).

Tobin, A. M. (2004, December 7). Videogames: Some young people have an "overfascination" with videogames that can cause problems at home and school. *Phoenix Star,* p. B8.

Top consumer complaints in 2003. (2004, February 2). *USA Today,* p. 1A.

Trench, M. (1990). *Cyberpunk.* Mystic Fire Videos. New York: Intercon Production.

Trigoboff, D. (2003, June 9). Copps: Dereg foes will be back. *Broadcasting & Cable,* p. 36.

Tugend, A. (2003, March). Reading between the lines. *American Journalism Review,* pp. 46–51.

Turner, C. (1998, July 1). 19 nations join to counter spread of U.S. culture. Madison (WI) *Capital Times,* p. 1A.

Two cents: William Safire on re-reg vote. (2003, July 21). *Broadcasting & Cable,* p. 46.

UNESCO. (2005, October 20). General Conference adopts Convention on the Protection and Promotion of the Diversity of Cultural Expressions. Online: http://portal.unesco.org.

U.S. adult literacy rate is stalled. (2005, December 16). *Providence Journal,* p. A11.

USA Today. (2000, July 9). The *Potter* phenomenon: It's just magic. *Honolulu Advertiser,* p. E4.

Valentine v. Christensen 316 U.S. 52 (1942).

Vane, S. (2002, March). Taking care of business. *American Journalism Review,* pp. 60–65.

Vargas, J. A. (2004, August 7). Girls got game. *Providence Journal,* pp. D1, D2.

Variety's Global 50. (2002, August 26). *Variety,* p. B12.

Verbatim. (2002, August 19). *Time,* p. 16.

Victory for privacy. (2002, June 29). *Providence Journal,* p. B6.

Virgin, B. (2004, March 18). We've become instant billboards. *Seattle Post-Intelligencer,* p. E1.

Vise, D. A. (2005, October 20). Publishers sue Google to stop scanning. *Washington Post,* p. D1.

Waas, M. (2004, February 14). High crimes of Bob Novak. *American Prospect.* Online: www.alternet.org/print.html?storyid=17857.

Waller, D. (2000, April 10–16). Epoch of the Rolling Clones. *Variety,* pp. 1, 78.

Ward, E., Stokes, G., & Tucker, K. (1986). *Rock of Ages: The* Rolling Stone *history of rock & roll.* New York: Rolling Stone Press.

Wartella, E. A. (1997). *The context of television violence.* Boston: Allyn & Bacon.

Weber, B. (2004, July 8). Fewer noses stuck in books in America, survey finds. *New York Times.* Online: nytimes.com/2004/07/08/books/08read.html.

Weenolsen, P. (2005, November 14). Slope too slippery. *USA Today,* p. 20A.

Wellstone, P. (2002, November/December). Media & democracy. *Extra!,* pp. 25–26.

Westcott, T. (2002, April 15). Brits step up for right fare. *Variety,* p. A9.

When Saddam fell. (2004, July 5). *Editor & Publisher.* Online: www.editorandpublisher.com/eandp/news/article_display.jsp?vnu_content_id=10005.

Whitcomb, I. (1972). *After the ball.* New York: Allen Lane.

Whitney, D. (2006, March 27). Why the sleepy field of syndication is ready for video. *AdAge.com.* Online: http://www.adage.com/news.cms?newsId=48449.

Whois. (2005, August 16). Detailed domain counts and Internet statistics. Online: http://www.whois.sc/internet-statistics.

Why Elvis still lives. (2002, August 9). *The Week,* p. 9.

Williams, T. (2002, January/February). Dream society. *Adbusters,* p. 17.

Winokur, S. (1999, November 28). News, ads: Do twain ever meet? *San Francisco Examiner,* p. D3.

Wolf, E. (2005, September 26–October 2). Stream catchers. *Variety,* pp. B1–B2.

Wolf, G. (2003, December). The great Library of Amazonia. *Wired,* pp. 215–221.

Wolf, M. J. P. (2001a). The videogame as a medium. In M. J. P. Wolf (Ed.), *The medium of the videogame.* Austin: University of Texas Press.

Wolf, M. J. P. (2001b). Genre and the videogame. In M. J. P. Wolf (Ed.), *The medium of the videogame*. Austin: University of Texas Press.

Woodbury, J. (2006, January 26). New study shows thirty-five percent of American parents play videogames. Online: http://www.theesa.com/archives/2006/01/new_study_shows.php.

The world at a glance. (2005, May 20). *The Week*, p. 10.

World's 10 biggest global advertisers. (2005, November 14). *Advertising Age*, p. 30.

Wronge, Y. S. (2000, August 17). New report fuels TV-violence debate. *San Jose Mercury News*, pp. 1E, 3E.

Wulfemeyer, K. T. (1982). A content analysis of local television newscasts: Answering the critics. *Journal of Broadcasting, 26*, 481–486.

Yahoo, Google rebuked over China. (2006, February 16). *Providence Journal*, p. A7.

Yang, C. (2005a, September 5). Wi-Fi with its own Zip Code. Online: http://www.businessweek.com/magazine/content/05_36/b3949053_mz011.htm.

Yang, C. (2005b, June 28). Good for cable, bad for America. Online: http://www.businessweek.com/technology/content/jun2005/tc20050628_9131_tc120.htm.

Yglesias, M. (2005, July). We're Number 13! *American Prospect*, pp. 20–22.

Zeller, T. (2006, January 15). China, still winning against the Web. *New York Times*, p. 4.4.

Zinn, H. (1995). *A people's history of the United States, 1492–present*. New York: HarperPerennial.

Acknowledgments

PHOTO CREDITS

Chapter 1 p. 2, Photo by Matthew Rolston from Rolling Stone, July 13-27, 2006. © Rolling Stone LLC 2006. All Rights Reserved. Reprinted by permission; p. 11TL, Photofest; p. 11TR, © Peter Kramer/Getty Images; p. 11MR, © AP/Wide World Photos; p. 11M, © Michael Newman/PhotoEdit; p. 11BL, © Reuters NewMedia, Inc./Corbis; p. 12L, © FX/Courtesy Everett Collection; p. 12R, © E! Network/Courtesy Everett Collection; p. 13TL, © MGM/Courtesy Everett Collection; p. 13TR, Photo by Dima Gavrysh/Everett Collection; p. 13B, © Reuters NewMedia, Inc./Corbis; p. 14T, Photofest; p. 14M, Photo Robert Voets/© UPN/ Courtesy Everett Collection; p. 14B, © Warner Brothers/Courtesy Everett Collection; p. 15, © Reuters NewMedia, Inc./Corbis; p. 17, Extra!, the magazine of Fairness & Accuracy In Reporting; p. 22, © The Granger Collection, New York; p. 24, © Bettmann/Corbis; p. 25, © The Granger Collection, New York; p. 28T, © 20th Century Fox/Courtesy Everett Collection; p. 28B, © Warner Brothers/courtesy Everett Collection; p. 32, © Big Feats! Entertainment/Courtesy Photofest; p. 33, © Peter Kramer/Getty Images

Chapter 2 p. 36, Photo Mario Perez/© ABC/Courtesy Everett Collection; p. 38, © Magnolia Pictures/Courtesy Everett Collection; p. 40, CBS; p. 44T, © Reuters/Corbis; p. 44B, © AP/Wide World Photos; p. 49, © The McGraw-Hill Companies, Inc./Lars A. Niki, photographer; p. 51, Photo TM and Copyright © 20th Century Fox Film Corp. All rights reserved, Courtesy Everett Collection; p. 52, © Kurt Rogers/San Francisco Chronicle/Corbis; p. 55, © Miramax Films/Courtesy Everett Collection; p. 57TL, Reprinted with permission from Broadcasting & Cable, Issue date Feb. 27, 2006; p. 57TR, Courtesy Editor & Publisher; p. 57BL, Used by permission of Variety; p. 57BR, Advertising Age

Chapter 3 p. 62, Used by permission of Bob Gulla and Greenwood Publishing; p. 66, © The Kobal Collection; p. 67, © The Granger Collection, New York; p. 68, © Culver Pictures, Inc.; p. 70, © Ancient Art & Architecture Collection; p. 71T, © The Granger Collection, New York; p. 71B, Courtesy Random House, Inc.; p. 72, Courtesy Boston Women's Health Book Collective; p. 80T, © Ian Mainsbridge/PPL Photo Agency. Courtesy Pocket Books; p. 80B, Random House, Inc.; p. 84T, Courtesy Ten Speed Press, Berkeley, CA; p. 84B, © Rose M. Prouser/CNN/Reuters/Corbis; p. 87, © Michael Newman/PhotoEdit; p. 91, Harry Potter, characters, names, and all related indicia are trademarks of Warner Brothers, © 2006

Chapter 4 p. 96, © Mug Shots/Corbis; p. 100, Courtesy John Frost Newspapers; p. 101, 102, 103, 105, © The Granger Collection, New York; p. 107, © Lynsey Addario/Corbis; p. 110, Providence Journal; p. 112L, Courtesy Providence Phoenix; p. 112ML, Courtesy The Philadelphia Independent; p. 112MR, Courtesy AM New York; p. 112R, Sing Tao Boston; p. 117,

Courtesy Susan Baran; p. 122, Marin Independent Journal; p. 125, Boston Sunday Globe; p. 126, Hartford Courant

Chapter 5 p. 130, © Kevin Fleming/Corbis; p. 135, © The Granger Collection, New York; p. 136, © 1923 Time, Inc./Time Life Pictures/Getty Images; p. 137, Theodore Roosevelt Collection, Harvard College Library; p. 138T, © The Granger Collection, New York; p. 138B, © Alán Gallegos/AG Photograph; p. 139, People Weekly © 2006 Time Inc. All rights reserved.; p. 139, © The Granger Collection, New York; p. 139, Nathaniel Goldberg/GQ. © 2006 Condé Nast Publications. Reprinted by permission. All rights reserved.; p. 145L, Courtesy of American Airlines; p. 145M, Courtesy of Voyageur, Carlson Hospitality Worldwide's In-room Magazine. Cover Photograph by Jonathan Orenstein; p. 145R, Courtesy of American Airlines; p. 147L, Sea Ray Living is produced for Sea Ray Boats by Dino Publishing, a custom magazine publisher based in Chicago (www.dinopublishing.com). Cover photo by John Bildahl (www.johnbildahlphotography.com).; p. 147R, Reprinted by permission of WebMD; p. 148, Courtesy Psychologie Heute; p. 150, This advertisement is reprinted by arrangement with Sears, Roebuck and Co. and is protected under copyright. No duplication is permitted; p. 152, Courtesy CosmoGirl; p. 152, Jason Bell © GQ/The Condé Nast Publications Ltd.

Chapter 6 p. 156, © Warner Brothers/Courtesy Everett Collection; p. 160, © The Kobal Collection; pp. 161, 162, © The Granger Collection, New York; p. 163, Photofest; p. 164, © Edison Co. 1903/MP & TV Photo Archive; pp. 165, 166, Everett Collection; p. 167, © 20th Century Fox Film Corp. All rights reserved/Courtesy Everett Collection; p. 169, © 1927 Warner Brothers/MP & TV Photo Archive; p. 171, 173, Photofest; p. 177L, © Justin Sullivan/Getty Images; p. 177R, © Adrian Weinbrecht/Getty Images/Stone; p. 178L, © 20th Century Fox Film Corp. All rights reserved. Courtesy Everett Collection; p. 178M, © Warner Brothers/courtesy Everett Collection; p. 178R, Everett Collection; p. 179L, © Focus Films/Everett Collection; p. 179R, © Paramount/Courtesy Everett Collection; p. 180, © Lions Gate/courtesy Everett Collection; pp. 181, 183L, Courtesy Everett Collection; p. 183R, © Buena Vista/Courtesy Everett Collection; p. 186, © DreamWorks/courtesy Everett Collection

Chapter 7 pp. 192, 196, © AP/Wide World Photos; p. 197, © The Granger Collection, New York; p. 198, © Culver Pictures, Inc.; p. 199, © The Granger Collection, New York; p. 202, © Bettmann/Corbis; pp. 205, 206, © AP/Wide World Photos; p. 207, From Broadcasting/Telecasting Aug. 17, 1953; pp. 211M, 211L, 211R, © Bettmann/Corbis; p. 212TL, © AP/Wide World Photos; p. 212TR, © Jamie Squire/Getty Images; p. 212MR, © AP/Wide World Photos; pp. 212M, 212ML© Frank Micelotta/Getty Images; p. 212BL, © Hulton Getty/Getty Images; pp. 212BR, 215, © AP/Wide World Photos; p. 221, © Thos Robinson/Getty Images; p. 223, © Reuters/Corbis

Chapter 8   p. 230, Photo: Craig Sjodin/© ABC/Courtesy Everett Collection; p. 232, © The McGraw-Hill Companies, Inc./Jill Braaten, photographer; p. 234, © Smithsonian Institution, Neg. #85-12139; p. 235L, © Culver Pictures, Inc.; p. 235R, © The Granger Collection, New York; p. 237, © The Kobal Collection; p. 238, Photofest; p. 239, © AP/Wide World Photos; p. 241, © MTV/Courtesy Everett Collection; p. 243, © The Barco Library of The Cable Center, Denver, CO; pp. 244, 248TL, Everett Collection; p. 248TR, © NBC/Courtesy Everett Collection; p. 248B, Courtesy Everett Collection; p. 249, Used by permission of Home Box Office; p. 250, © David Young-Wolff/PhotoEdit; p. 252, © FX/Courtesy Everett Collection; p. 253, © Al Bello/Getty Images; p. 254T, © HBO/Courtesy Everett Collection; p. 254ML, Photo: Randy Tepper/© Showtime/Courtesy Everett Collection; p. 254MR, Photo: Peter Lovino/© Showtime/Courtesy Everett Collection; p. 254BL, © HBO/Courtesy Everett Collection; p. 254BMR, Photo: Liane Hentscher/© Showtime/Courtesy Everett Collection; p. 254BR, © HBO/Courtesy Everett Collection; p. 262, © Dish Network; p. 264, © David Silverman/ Getty Images

Chapter 9   p. 268, © Joel Saget/AFP/Getty Images; p. 272, Wayne Namerow Collection, Photograph courtesy of Wayne Namerow; p. 273T, © Computer History Museum; p. 273B, © Roger Ressmeyer/Corbis; p. 274, © Ralph H. Baer; pp. 275T, 275BL, © AP/Wide World Photos; p. 275BR, Courtesy Nintendo; p. 276L, Courtesy John Padilla; p. 276R, Courtesy Ubi Soft; p. 277, Courtesy of the author; p. 279T, Courtesy Greater Bay Area Make-a-Wish Foundation; p. 279BL, Courtesy Nintendo; p. 279BM, Courtesy Microsoft; p. 279BR Courtesy © 2003 Sony Computer Entertainment America Inc. "PlayStation" and the "PS" Family logo are registered trademarks of Sony Computer Entertainment Inc. The "PSP" logo is a trademark of Sony Computer Entertainment Inc.; p. 280, Courtesy Nintendo; p. 281L, Courtesy John Padilla; p. 281R, Courtesy Eidos; p. 283L, Courtesy © 2003 Sony Computer Entertainment America Inc. "PlayStation" and the "PS" Family logo are registered trademarks of Sony Computer Entertainment Inc. The "PSP" logo is a trademark of Sony Computer Entertainment Inc.; p. 283M, Courtesy Nintendo; p. 283R, Courtesy SL Interphase; p. 285, Courtesy John Padilla; p. 286L, © Warner Brothers/ Courtesy Everett Collection; p. 286ML, Courtesy John Padilla; p. 286MR, © Paramount/Courtesy Everett Collection; p. 286R, Courtesy Eidos; p. 287T, Courtesy Chrysler; p. 287B, Courtesy Bold Games; p. 289, Courtesy John Padilla; p. 290, Courtesy The Berndt Group, Ltd.

Chapter 10   p. 296, © Catrina Genovese/Getty Images; p. 298, © Robbie McClaren/Corbis Saba; p. 300T, © Bernard Gutfryd/Woodfin Camp & Associates; p. 300B, From The MIT Museum, © Koby-Antupit Studio, Cambridge/Belmont, MA, (617) 489-8757; pp. 301, 302, © AP/Wide World Photos; p. 303, © Archive Photos/Getty Images; p. 304, Courtesy Intel; p. 305TL, © Doug Wilson/Corbis; p. 305TR, © AP/Wide World Photos; p. 305B, © Roger Ressmeyer/Corbis; p. 307, © Reuters/NASA/ Archive Photos/Getty Images; p. 314L, © 1962 University of Toronto Press. Reproduced by permission of the publisher. Photo by Alán Gallegos/AG Photograph; p. 314M, The Medium is the Massage, by Marshall McLuhan and Quentin Fiore, produced by Jerome Agel. For further information, Jerome Agel 2 Peter Cooper Road, New York City, NY 10010 USA; p. 314R, Understanding Media by Marshall McLuhan is published by MIT Press.; p. 317, Courtesy MoveOn.org/MoveOn PAC. www. moveonpac.org & www.bushin30seconds.org; p. 318, © Alex Wong/Getty Images; p. 319, © AFP/Getty Images; p. 327, © Bryan Bedder/Getty Images

Chapter 11   p. 338, © AP/Wide World Photos; p. 342, Courtesy Kellogg's and Susan G. Komen Breast Cancer Foundation; p. 343, Courtesy Odwalla, Half Moon Bay, CA; p. 344, © Tony Freeman/PhotoEdit; p. 345, © The Granger Collection, New York; p. 347, © 1978 GM Corp. All Rights Reserved; p. 348, © Culver Pictures, Inc.; pp. 349, 350, Everett Collection; p. 354L, Courtesy Textron; p. 354M, Courtesy Astro-med, Inc.; p. 354R, © 2006 Hasbro, Inc. Used with permission.; pp. 357L, 357TM, 357BM, © AP/Wide World Photos; p. 357R, © Reuters/Corbis; p. 358, Courtesy Ronald McDonald House, Palo Alto, CA; p. 359, Courtesy Cambridge Consulting Corporation/USDA; p. 362, ©UPI/Corbis; p. 363, © The Granger Collection, New York

Chapter 12   p. 370, © Jeff Greenberg/PhotoEdit; p. 373, Courtesy Susan Baran; p. 374T, © Adam Woolfitt/Woodfin Camp & Associates; p. 374B, © AP/Wide World Photos; p. 375, © The Granger Collection, New York; p. 376, Milton Bradley; p. 377, © The Granger Collection, New York; p. 378, © Brown Brothers; p. 379, © Culver Pictures, Inc.; p. 381L, Courtesy the Ad Council; p. 381TR, © Keep America Beautiful, Inc. All rights reserved.; p. 381BR, McGruff the Crime Dog appears courtesy of the National Crime Prevention Council—The nation's focal point for crime prevention; p. 382, ©Timex/Timexpo Museum; pp. 384, 385, © AP/Wide World Photos; p. 387, Courtesy Adbusters Magazine/www.adbusters.org; p. 391, Courtesy WWE, Inc.; p. 392, American Airlines reserves the right to change the AAdvantage program at any time without notice. American Airlines is not responsible for products or services offered by other participating companies; p. 393, Advico/Young & Rubicam; p. 397, © Diane Bondareff/Burger King/Getty Images; p. 399, © Bill Aron/PhotoEdit

Chapter 13   p. 406, © Edouard Berne/Getty Images/Stone; p. 410, Courtesy of the author; p. 412, © HBO/ Courtesy: Everett Collection; p. 413, Skyy Spirits; p. 416, © The Kobal Collection; p. 417, Photofest; pp. 421, 425, © AP/Wide World Photos; p. 432, © Reuters/Corbis; p. 433, Photofest; p. 434, Courtesy Professor Albert Bandura, Stanford University; p. 437, © Columbia TriStar Television/Courtesy Everett Collection; p. 438, Bacardi-Martini USA, Inc.; p. 439TL, Photo Liane Hentscher/© Showtime/ Courtesy Everett Collection; p. 439TR, © NBC/Courtesy Everett Collection; p. 439BL, Photo: Matthew Peyton/© Bravo/Courtesy: Everett Collection; p. 439BR, Photo: L. Pief Weyman/Showtime, © Showtime/Courtesy: Everett Collection; p. 441, © David Young-Wolff/PhotoEdit

Chapter 14   p. 446, © Gianni Giansanti/Corbis; p. 450, © Justin Sullivan/Getty Images; p. 453, © AP/Wide World Photos; p. 454, © Culver Pictures, Inc.; p. 457, Courtesy John Frost Newspapers. © 2003 by The New York Times Co. Reprinted by permission; p. 459, © Tim Mosenfelder/Getty Images; p. 460, © AP/Wide World Photos; p. 461, © Warner Bros./Courtesy Everett Collection; p. 469, © AP/Wide World Photos; p. 470TL, © AP/Wide World Photos; p. 470TR, © Deanne Fitzmaurice/San Francisco Chronicle/San Francisco Chronicle/Corbis; p. 470B, Photo by Rick McKay/Washington Bureau/Cox News Service; p. 473T, © AP/Wide World Photos; p. 473BL, 473BR, © Alex Wong/Getty Images; p. 476, © Paramount/Courtesy Everett Collection; p. 477, © 1991 Benetton Group SpA.Photo: O. Toscani; p. 479, © Chris Livingston/Getty Images; p. 480L, 480M, 480TR, © AP/Wide World Photos; p. 480BR, © Neal Preston/Corbis

Chapter 15   p. 484, © ChinaFotoPress/Getty Images; p. 490T, © Hulton-Deutsch Collection/Corbis; p. 490B, Courtesy VOA; p. 491, Courtesy Radio Marti/VOA; p. 493, © Judy G. Rolfe; p. 494, © Hulton Getty Picture Library/Getty Images; p. 495,

© Reuters NewMedia, Inc./Corbis; p. 497TL, Ron Tom/ © ABC/Courtesy Everett Collection; p. 497TR, Jaimie Trueblood/ © UPN/Courtesy Everett Collection; p. 497B, Photofest; p. 499, Courtesy of The Sun; p. 501, © Peter Turnley/Corbis; p. 502, © Dennis Cox/ChinaStock; p. 503, © AP/Wide World Photos; p. 505T, © AP/Wide World Photos; p. 505B, © José Fuste Raga/zefa/Corbis; p. 506L, Courtesy Gonafilm and Kevin Williams Associates; p. 506R, Courtesy LifeSize Entertainment & Estonian Film Foundation; p. 509L, Courtesy Soul City Institute for Health & Development Communication; p. 509TR, Courtesy Wencai Audio Video; p. 509BR, © Devendra Sharmap. 510T, © 1999, Map provided courtesy of CNN. CNN is a trademark of Cable News Network. A Time Warner Company. All rights reserved. p. 510BL, 510BR, Dennis Publishing Groupp. 511T, © Paramount/Courtesy Everett Collection; p. 511B, © 2004 Marvel Characters Inc. Courtesy Gotham Comics; p. 512, © AP/Wide World Photos

TEXT CREDITS

Chapter 2 p. 44, Quote from Burt Neuborne in J. Konner, *Columbia Journalism Review*, March/April 1999. Used by permission; p. 47, Quote from Todd Gitlin, "The Great Media Breakdown," *Mother Jones*, Nov./Dec. 2004. Copyright 2004, Foundation for National Progress. Used by permission; p. 42, Quote from Bill Moyers, Alternet, 2004. Used by permission; p. 47, Quote from Ken Auletta in *The New Yorker*. Reprinted by permission of International Creative Management, Inc. Copyright © 2005 by Rigatoni, Inc.; p. 52, Quote from Tony Kern, 2005. *Broadcasting & Cable*. Used by permission; p. 53, Adapted from the September 26, 1005 issue of *Advertising Age*. Copyright Crain Communications, Inc. 2005

Chapter 3 p. 74, Excerpt from "Carved Runes in a Clearing" by Julius Lester. Copyright © 2002 by Julius Lester. Reprinted by permission of the author; p. 72, Quote from Jane Pincus in Introduction to *Our Bodies, Ourselves for the New Century* by Boston Women's Health Book Collective. Copyright © 1984, 1992, 1998 by the Boston Women's Health Book Collective. Reprinted by permission of Simon and Schuster Adult Publishing Group

Chapter 4 p. 116, Quote from Steve Proctor, *American Journalism Review* March 2002. Used by permission; p. 117, Quote from Ben Bagdikian, *Editor and Publisher*, March 2004. Used by permission; p. 117, Quote from Tim McGuire, president of the American Society of Newspaper Editors in J. Strupp, *Editor and Publisher*, March 4/15/02. Used by permission; p. 119L, Screen shot from Boston.com used by permission; p. 119R, Screen shot from Atlanta Journal Constitution used by permission; p. 107, Quote from Marc Fisher, 2005, *American Journalism Review*. Used by permission; p. 107, Quote from Brian Thevenot, 2005, *American Journalism Review*. Used by permission.

Chapter 5 p. 140, Quote from Project for Excellence in Journalism, 2004. Used by permission; p. 141, Adapted from the September 26, 1005 issue of *Advertising Age*. Copyright, Crain Communications, Inc. 2005; p. 148, Quote from David Carr. Copyright © 2004 by the New York Times Company. Reprinted with permission.

Chapter 6 p. 177, Quote from Richard Roeper in David Germain, Associated Press, December 15, 2005. Used by permission.

Chapter 7 p. 207, Quote courtesy of David Sarnoff Library, Princeton, NJ; p. 214, Lyrics from *FOR WHAT IT'S WORTH*. Words and music by STEPHEN STILLS. © 1967 (Renewed) COTILLION MUSIC INC., TEN EAST MUSIC, SPRINGALO TOONES and RICHIE FURAY MUSIC. All rights administered by WARNER-TAMERLANE PUBLISHING CORP. All rights reserved. Used By permission; p. 214, Lyrics from *OHIO*. Words and music by NEIL YOUNG. © 1970 (Renewed) BROKEN ARROW MUSIC CORPORATION. All rights reserved. Used by permission; p. 214, Quote from Brent Staples. Copyright © 2003 by the New York Times Company. Reprinted with permission.

Chapter 9 p. 289, Quote from Douglas Lowenstein, ESA president, at the Electronic Entertainment Expo 2005. Used by permission.

Chapter 10 p. 302, Quote from Paul Baran, 1962, courtesy of the Rand Corporation; p. 316, Quote from B. DeGraf, Alternet, 2004. Used by permission; p. 317, Quote from Andrew Boyd, "The Web Rewires the Movement." Reprinted with permission from the April 11, 2003 issue of *The Nation*. For subscription information, call 1-800-333-8536. Portions of each week's Nation magazine can be accessed at www.thenation.com.

Chapter 11 p. 366, Screen capture from Diane Farsetta and Daniel Price, "Fake TV News: Widespread and Undisclosed," Center for Media and Democracy (prwatch.org), April 6, 2006. Used with permission.

Chapter 13 p. 423, Quote from Maxwell E. McCombs & Donald L. Shaw, 1972, The Agenda-Setting Function of Mass Media, *Public Opinion Quarterly*, Vol. 36. Used by permission of Oxford University Press; p. 429, Quote from George Gerbner et al. 1978, The "Mainstreaming" of America: Violence Profile no. 11, *Journal of Communication, 30*. Used by permission of Blackwell Publishing; p. 440, Quote from J. Harwood and K. Anderson, 2002. The Presence and Portrayal of Social Groups on Prime-time TV, *Communication Reports*, 15, p. 89. Copyrighted by the Western States Communication Association. Used by permission of the publisher.

Chapter 14 p. 464, Quote from Jeff Howe, *Licensed to Bill*. Originally published in *Wired*, October 2001. Used by permission; p. 464, Quote from Wall Street Journal by W. S. Mossberg. Copyright 2002 by Dow Jones & Company, Inc. Reproduced with permission of Dow Jones & Company via Copyright Clearance Center; p. 477, Quote from J. Black & R.D. Barney. *Journal of Mass Media Ethics*. Used by permission of the author; p. 473, Quote from Russ Baker, *The Nation*, 6/23/03 (www.russbaker.com) Used by permission; p. 473, Quote from Eric Alterman "Is Koppel a Commie?" Reprinted with permission from the May 24, 2004 issue of *The Nation*. For subscription information, call 1-800-333-8536. Portions of each week's Nation magazine can be accessed at www.thenation.com; p. 472, Quote from Judith Miller on *Lou Dobbs Tonight*, CNN, October 4, 2005. Used by permission; p. 480, Quote from Pope John Paul II. Used by permission of *Broadcasting & Cable*.

Chapter 15 p. 493, Quote from Neil MacFarquhar. Copyright © 2004 by the New York Times Company. Reprinted with permission; p. 504, Quote from Nicholas Kristof. Copyright © 2006 by the New York Times Company. Reprinted with permission; p. 508, Quote from Population Communications International. Reprinted by permission.

Index

Boldfaced locators signify definitions in the text of glossary terms. *Italic* locators signify illustrations.